M000274309

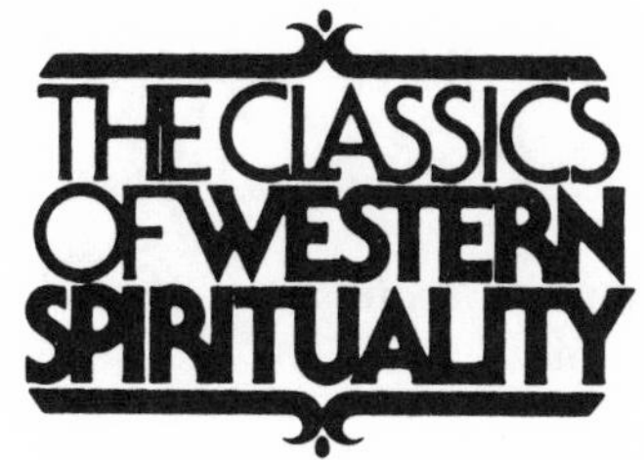
THE CLASSICS
OF WESTERN
SPIRITUALITY

THE CLASSICS OF WESTERN SPIRITUALITY
A Library of the Great Spiritual Masters

ISAIAH HOROWITZ

THE GENERATIONS OF ADAM

TRANSLATED, EDITED AND WITH AN INTRODUCTION BY
MILES KRASSEN

PREFACE BY
ELLIOT R. WOLFSON

PAULIST PRESS
NEW YORK • MAHWAH

Cover art: Cabbalistic Printing or Mizrach. Samuel Habib (maker), 1828. Jewish Museum, New York, U.S.A. Image used courtesy of Jewish Museum/Art Resource, NY.

Library of Congress Cataloging-in-Publication Data

Horowitz, Isaiah, ca. 1565–1630. [Toldot Adam. English]
The generations of Adam/Isaiah Horowitz; translated, edited, and with an introduction by Miles Krassen; preface by Elliot R. Wolfson.
p. cm.—(The classics of Western spirituality; #85)
Includes bibliographical references and index.
ISBN 0-8091-3590-6 (pbk.: alk. paper)—ISBN 0-8091-0474-1 (cloth: alk. paper).
1. Cabala—Early works to 1800. 2. Spiritual life—Judaism—Early works to 1800. 3. Judaism—Doctrines—Early works to 1800. 4. Ethics, Jewish—Early works to 1800. I. Krassen, Miles. II. Title. III. Series.
BM525.H57713 1995
296.1′6—dc20

95-42160
CIP

Published by Paulist Press
997 Macarthur Boulevard
Mahwah, New Jersey 07430

Printed and bound in the
United States of America

Contents

Editor and Translator of this Volume

MILES KRASSEN is Assistant Professor of Religion and Judaic and Near Eastern Studies at Oberlin College in Ohio. A specialist in hasidic and kabbalistic texts who received his Ph.D. in Religious Studies from the University of Pennsylvania, he is also well known for his work in the field of traditional Irish music. Dr. Krassen is currently engaged in a comparative study of meditative practice in Jewish and Buddhist tradition.

Author of the Preface

ELLIOT R. WOLFSON is Professor of Hebrew and Judaic Studies at New York University. He is also currently serving as Adjunct Professor of Jewish History at Columbia University. He is the author of *The Book of the Pomegranate: Moses de León's Sefer ha-Rimmon* (Brown Judaica Series, 1988), *Through A Speculum That Shines: Vision and Imagination in Medieval Jewish Mysticism* (Princeton University Press, 1994), *Along the Path: Studies in Kabbalistic Myth, Symbolism, and Hermeneutics* (State University of New York Press, 1995), and *Circle in the Square: Studies in the Use of Gender in Kabbalistic Symbolism* (State University of New York Press, 1995). He has also published widely in scholarly journals and anthologies in the area of Jewish mysticism and philosophy. He is currently working on a conceptual lexicon on Jewish mysticism (to be published by E. J. Brill) and on another volume tentatively entitled *Eclipse of the Moon: Imaginative Representations of the Feminine in Kabbalistic Myth and Ritual.* In addition to his own scholarly publications, Dr. Wolfson is the editor of *The Journal of Jewish Thought and Philosophy* and co-editor of the *Series in Judaica: Mysticism, Hermeneutics, and Religion* for the State University of New York Press as well as co-editor of *Études sur le judaisme medieval* for E. J. Brill. He is presently co-chair of the Study of Judaism in the American Academy of Religion.

Acknowledgments

The present work is truly the product of many people's cooperation and help. The original idea for a translation from Isaiah Horowitz's great text was the inspiration of my friend Hananya Goodman. His discussions with Professors Henri Atlan and Moshe Idel were instrumental in locating funding that would enable me to undertake this project. I am indebted to both Professor Atlan and Professor Idel for their advice and guidance throughout the entire project.

I would especially like to thank Mr. Igoin and the Yeshaya Horowitz Association of Jerusalem. Without the generous stipend provided by Mr. Igoin, a direct descendant of our author, this work would not have been possible.

The latter stages of my work were also supported by a research stipend from Oberlin College. I would particularly like to express my appreciation for the warm encouragement and supportive atmosphere provided by my colleagues in the Religion Department and Judaic and Near Eastern Studies Program at Oberlin. It is always a pleasure to have the opportunity to publicly acknowledge the kindness of one's friends.

My teacher, Professor Arthur Green, brought this work to the attention of Professor Bernard McGinn, editor of the series, The Classics of Western Spirituality. Art also generously allowed me to borrow his copy of a rare, early edition of our text. The conviction that sustained me through the many vicissitudes of completing this work was certainly strengthened by Art's confidence in me and interest in this project. Professor Elliot Wolfson was kind enough to share with me his own important research on Isaiah Horowitz. He also found the time to give special attention to the manuscript and graciously consented to write the preface. My friend Professor Elliot Ginsburg helped me decide some important issues concerning style and was particularly helpful in arriving at the meaning of especially obscure passages from kabbalistic sources. I also thank Rabbi Shimon Brand, who was an enthusiastic and helpful model reader of several particularly challenging sections of the manuscript.

My editor at Paulist, Maria L. Maggi, deserves mention for her tact and skill at relating to academic authors and her ability to transform their work into a book.

Finally, I would like to thank my partner, Kinerette Hasson, not only for her boundless emotional support, but also for sparing me the need to deal with numerous technical problems that she so generously and capably solved.

Preface

The *Sheney Luhot ha-Berit* of R. Isaiah ben Abraham Horowitz, known on the basis of this work as the Holy Shelah, is a classic work of East-European ethical literature of the seventeenth century. In spite of the fact that most of the composition of the book took place in the Land of Israel, the *Sheney Luhot ha-Berit* is a mirror that reflects the distinctive texture of rabbinic culture of Ashkenazi and Polish Jewry in the late-sixteenth and early-seventeenth centuries. The Shelah is a consummate scholar who demonstrates mastery in every aspect of rabbinic learning, to wit, halakhah and talmudic jurisprudence, homiletics and biblical exegesis, philosophy and ethics, and above all else the esoteric tradition known as the Kabbalah. Horowitz combines an extensive knowledge of talmudic-halakhic Judaism and kabbalistic lore and thereby forges a synthesis that he presents as the basic reality of Jewish religiosity.

Indeed, one of the most significant characteristics of the *Sheney Luhot ha-Berit* is the author's interweaving of the different threads of rabbinic learning to produce a seamless garment of mystical pietism. In the mind of a figure like the Shelah there is no discontinuity between the exoteric and the esoteric, no chasm separating normative halakhah and mystical rite. On the contrary, as Horowitz says quite explicitly in the *Sheney Luhot ha-Berit*, the revealed meaning (*nigleh*) is the hidden (*nistar*); that is, there is a complete overlapping of the exoteric and the esoteric dimensions of Judaism. This convergence is amply manifest not only in the Shelah's masterful ability to move effortlessly from one body of literature to another, but also in his application of talmudic modes of study (especially the dialectical approach known as *pilpul*) to the kabbalistic sources. In the Shelah's presentation of rabbinic Judaism there is perfect harmony between the outer and inner, legalism and mysticism. It is this feature that made the *Sheney Luhot ha-Berit* one of the most popular books among Ashkenazi Jews for generations.

(Even in our own day this continues to be the case as old editions of the work are often reprinted and new editions frequently appear to facilitate continued study of the Holy Shelah.) The Shelah was unquestionably one of the most important conduits for the transmission of esoteric motifs to a wider audience of literate Jews. Thus, as scholars have long noted, the Shelah was instrumental in the relative popularization of Kabbalah among the masses. In particular, the *Sheney Luhot ha-Berit* had a profound influence upon the pietistic movement known as Beshtian Hasidism, which emerged in eighteenth-century Poland and the Ukraine.

Miles Krassen has provided an exemplary translation of the introduction to the *Sheney Luhot ha-Berit* entitled *Toledot Adam*, literally *The Generations of Adam* (cf. Gen. 5:1). As Krassen points out, this introduction, correctly described as book-length in itself, presents the kabbalistic viewpoint on major theological and anthropological issues. A sustained reflection on an oft-cited passage in the *Zohar* that God, Torah, and Israel are one, the Shelah's introductory essay is an explication on how these three seemingly distinct entities are ontically identified. This ontic identification is rooted in the fact that the word *Adam* semantically refers to each of these three realities. Indeed, the anthropomorphization of God, Torah, and Israel as the Primal Adam is a hallmark of the kabbalistic worldview that is adroitly articulated by the Shelah's homiletical skills.

In addition to his annotated translation Krassen has provided a very thorough and eminently readable introduction to the intellectual biography of Isaiah Horowitz. Krassen has situated the *Sheney Luhot ha-Berit* in its proper cultural and religious setting. One has to be especially thankful to him for providing a careful account of the literary structure of the Shelah's magnum opus, a task that is by no means a small feat given the author's propensity for verbosity, long citations, and exegetical digressions. For the first time in English we have a reliable tool to assist in the study of this very rich but complicated work. In short, the scholarly efforts of Krassen will no doubt open this classic of Jewish literature to a wider audience. The translator is to be commended for transforming an archaic and arduous Hebrew text of the seventeenth century into a lively and engaging treatise that will be of interest to scholars of mystical pietism in the different religious traditions.

A Note on the Translation

This translation was made from several editions of Horowitz's work, *Sheney Luhot ha-Berit*. I had in my possession two recent offset editions, one published in Jerusalem and the other in New York. Both were made from nineteenth-century editions that proved to be highly flawed and unreliable, especially in distorting the texts that Horowitz so abundantly quotes. As a result, I made use of an early edition (Fuerst 1762), which was considerably better. I also had access to the Amsterdam 1648 edition at the University of Pennsylvania. In 1993 a new "complete" edition was published in Jerusalem by the kabbalists of Yeshivah Sha'ar ha-Shamayim. Based on the earliest editions, this work proved very helpful in checking difficult passages.

A work of this sort poses particular problems for the translator. Some of these stem from the obscurity of the subject matter. Some are due to the fact that the work anthologizes a virtual library of Jewish sources, written at different times by authors of varying skill in the art of writing Hebrew. In undertaking to make this work available to an intelligent, but not necessarily informed, English reader, I have made it my goal to make the text as readable as possible, striving for clarity and ease of comprehension rather than attempting to convey the particular stylistic qualities of Horowitz and the many individual writers that he quotes. The genre of classical rabbinic literature that this work represents does not easily lend itself to literal translation. Horowitz's style assumes a depth of knowledge that enables the reader to make appropriate associations to recognize allusions to earlier stages of rabbinic and mystical literature. This is a demand that would eliminate not only most native speakers of Hebrew in Israel, but a high percentage of the observant Jewish community as well. To remedy this difficulty, I have tried to complete references and to provide material alluded to wherever possible. I have also corrected grammatical inconsistencies in the hope of enhancing the non-specialist reader's ability to comprehend the text's meaning. The result, hopefully, is a text that is more readable in English than the author's sometimes clumsy Hebrew and Aramaic. Overcoming the problem of language, however, can only go so far toward eliminating the reader's difficulties. Another barrier to comprehension is the author's interest in kabbalistic concepts and terminology. Although I have tried to provide usable definitions and explanations wherever required, I have refrained from including a detailed, introductory exposition of the Kabbalah and its principles. The reader who feels a need for such background might begin with Daniel Matt's introduction to the *Zohar: Book of Enlightenment*.

Finally, the reader will soon discover that I have sometimes transliterated the original Hebrew or Aramaic. This has been done primarily to call attention to word plays that are essential to the text's meaning. Often, I have emphasized the word play by capitalizing those letters which enable the author to associate two words that are otherwise unrelated. One other matter that could cause some confusion has to do with the spelling of titles of works cited. In general, I have represented the title of a work as it is cited in the body of the text. For example, "the Maimuni," rather than "*Hagahot Maimuniyot*." However, in the footnotes I have tried to cite all titles accurately and consistently.

Introduction

The latter half of the sixteenth and beginning of the seventeenth centuries marked an important period for Hebrew religious literature in eastern Europe.[1] While virtually all genres of Jewish thought are represented in this period, it is especially noteworthy for the increased interest in Kabbalah that spread from Safed in the Land of Israel. Much of this interest was facilitated by the printing of the *Zohar*, the classic of Spanish Kabbalah, in Cremona and Mantua in the 1550s. Perhaps most important, however, were the writings and teachings of two kabbalists who flourished in Safed, R. Moses Cordovero (1522–1570) and his even more celebrated and charismatic disciple, R. Isaac Luria (1534–1572), "the Holy Lion." By the end of the sixteenth century several of Cordovero's major works were available and studied in Europe. In addition, *The Beginning of Wisdom*, by his student Elijah de Vidas, was printed several times and even appeared in a number of abridgements.[2]

Circulation of Luria's innovations was more problematic. The master himself wrote very little, and his foremost disciple, R. Ḥayyim Vital (1542–1620), was chary about sharing the Lurianic secrets. Nevertheless, by the 1590s manuscripts containing elements of Luria's teachings had made their way to Italy and from there to Poland. In addition, R. Israel Sarug, whose precise relationship to Isaac Luria is still a matter of controversy, had begun to teach Lurianic Kabbalah in Europe.

Although leading Polish halakhic authorities, such as R. Moses Isserles (1530–1572) and R. Solomon Luria (1510–1573), had already been concerned that the increasing interest in Kabbalah would undermine the study of the standard rabbinic curriculum, Talmud and Codes, few rabbis in this period remained unaffected by the Safed kabbalistic enterprise. Indeed, even where reservations remained concerning the appropriateness of widespread dissemination of the kabbalistic secrets, they were based more on respect and a sense of awe concerning this dimension of Torah than on skepticism regarding its importance or validity. The attitude that was emerging among many leading rabbis was that Kabbalah constituted the deepest truth of the Torah and that knowledge of its secrets, especially the theosophic meaning of the Jewish precepts and their theurgical effects, was essential for bringing about the two primary objectives of Jewish worship. These were the unification of the Divine Name, which is a precondition for the eschatological outcome, the ultimate spiritual condition of the World to Come, and the attainment of *devequt*, or mystical cleaving to God.

Among the most important rabbinic exponents of the Kabbalah in Europe at the turn of the seventeenth-century was R. Isaiah ben R. Abraham Ha-Levi Horowitz (c. 1570–1626), who served as rabbi in several of the most important European Jewish communities before becoming Chief Ashkenazic Rabbi of Jerusalem in 1621.[3] Horowitz was in many ways typical of the rabbinic class of his generation. His father, R. Abraham ben Shabbetai (c. 1545–1615), known as R. Abraham Sheftels, was a student of R. Moses Isserles, the leading Ashkenazic halakhic authority of his day and author of the authoritative Ashkenazic glosses on R. Joseph Karo's *Shulḥan Arukh* (*Set Table*). He served as judge on the rabbinic court in Lvov. Like his teacher, R. Abraham at first inclined toward philosophy and rational inquiry and was not known for expertise in Kabbalah. Nevertheless, when the influence of Kabbalah increased toward the end of the sixteenth century, R. Abraham Sheftels also seems to have come somewhat under its sway. In 1597 his book *Emeq Berakhah* (*Valley of Blessing*) was published in Cracow. Although the work is primarily concerned with halakhic issues pertaining to prayer and benedictions, it was accompanied by kabbalistic glosses that he instructed his son, Isaiah, to write in 1590. The book was later included almost in its entirety by R. Isaiah in his magnum opus, *Sheney Luhot ha-Berit* (*Two Tablets of the Covenant*). Another son, R. Jacob, wrote kabbalistic glosses to the father's ethical will in 1615. Thus one can find the increased importance of Kabbalah reflected in the writings of R. Abraham Sheftels and his sons as one approaches the turn of the seventeenth-century.

Isaiah Horowitz was in all probability born in Prague.[4] However, the precise date of his birth is unknown. Although some scholars have argued for an earlier date, it seems reasonable to assume that he was born about the year 1570.[5] For the most part R. Isaiah was educated in Poland, studying initially with his father. After his father, Horowitz's first teacher of Talmud and rabbinics seems to have been R. Meir ben Gedalia of Lublin (1558–1615), one of the leading Polish halakhic authorities and authors of the period. Somewhat later in the 1580s Horowitz studied with one of the most famous teachers in the Polish *yeshivot*, R. Solomon ben Judah (d. 1591). Although the latter wrote very little, he was instrumental in training several of the most important rabbis at a time when the Polish tradition of talmudics was at an especially high level. He is quoted frequently by Horowitz in *Sheney Luhot ha-Berit*. Since Horowitz was already capable of writing sophisticated kabbalistic glosses for his father's book, *Emeq Berakhah*, in 1590, it seems likely that his initial training in Kabbalah came under R. Solomon ben Judah. At some point during his studies with R. Solomon ben Judah, Horowitz married. His wife, Hayyah bat Abraham Maul (d. 1620), was famous for both her wealth and piety. From Horowitz's own accounts, Hayyah played an essential role in assuring the success of his career as a religious leader. She aided him not only by her personal spiritual qualities, but also by making her substantial dowry available in order to provide for the considerable needs of Isaiah Horowitz's many disciples and others who ate at his table wherever he served as rabbi. It is likely that Horowitz lived with his in-laws in Vienna for some time during the 1590s, either before or after completing his studies in Lvov with another major Polish rabbi, R. Joshua Falk (d. 1614).

Before settling in Jerusalem in 1621, Horowitz served as rabbi in four European communities. His career as rabbi seems to have begun in Dubnow, where he served from about 1600 to 1602. After Dubnow, Horowitz was appointed as rabbi in Ostraha, where he functioned as rabbi until 1606. During this period, his rabbinical reputation seems to have been established. He began writing approbations for rabbinical texts in which his name and approval appear alongside those written by older, more highly established rabbis. Although appointed as rabbi in two other important Polish communities, Posen and Cracow, Horowitz seems to have turned down these positions. From 1606 to 1614 he served as rabbi in Frankfurt-am-Main. An anti-Jewish uprising occurred there in 1612, and Horowitz was forced to flee the city in the summer of 1614, shortly before the Jewish quarter was plundered. From Frankfurt-am-Main, Horowitz was able to find refuge in his native city, Prague, where he was appointed to share the post of rabbi with R. Ephraim Solomon ben Aaron of Leczyca (1550–1619). R. Ephraim of Luntshits, as he was known, was one of the most famous preachers of the era. His sermons were collected in several well-known works that continued to influence Jews over the course of the following centuries. *Keli Yaqar* (*Precious Vessel*), a collection of his sermons on the weekly Torah readings, is included in a standard Hebrew edition of the Pentateuch. R. Ephraim was the successor of the even more famous Rabbi of Prague, R. Judah Loew ben Bezalel, the MaHaRaL of Prague (c. 1525–1609). The latter, a prolific author who had considerable influence on the development of Hasidic thought, was himself a student of Kabbalah, although his works do not tend to use explicitly kabbalistic terminology or concepts.[6] MaHaRaL was also a student of contemporary scientific and mathematical issues. Although Isaiah Horowitz must have been familiar with MaHaRaL's works and thought, he does not cite him in *Sheney Luhot ha-Berit*. Since R. Isaiah, while born in Prague, was primarily educated in Poland and only returned to Prague when he was at the height of his powers, it is possible that MaHaRaL's influence on him was limited.

Initially, Isaiah Horowitz apparently shared the rabbinical duties in Prague with R. Ephraim of Luntshits. It has been suggested that R. Isaiah acted as Head of the Rabbinical Court, while R. Ephraim continued to function as Preacher and Head of the *Yeshivah*.[7] However, following R. Ephraim's death in the spring of 1618, R. Isaiah assumed the post as sole Rabbi of Prague, a position of considerable prestige. He would retain this position for another three years, thus serving as rabbi during the outbreak of the Thirty Years War in 1618. Despite the political climate, Isaiah Horowitz's tenure in Prague was a successful one. For reasons that are not entirely clear, shortly after the death of his wife, Hayyah, in the spring of 1620, R. Isaiah began to think of resigning his position in Prague and settling in Jerusalem. It is reasonable to assume that Horowitz's motivation for living in the Holy Land was principally religious in nature. While the Land of Israel and particularly Jerusalem had retained an exalted status in Judaism from the origins of the rabbinic period, it was especially cherished by kabbalists. Thus R. Isaiah would have had good reason to have desired to spend his remaining years there. However, it is quite possible that in addition to the natural appeal that Jerusalem would have held for a kabbalist and pietist of Horowitz's stature, there may have been a more specific reason.[8]

Judging from R. Isaiah's glosses on *Emeq Berakhah*, which were written in 1590, he had at that time little or no familiarity with the Lurianic kabbalistic approach. It has been shown by Joseph Avivi that writings in the Lurianic mode began to be studied in Italy during the 1590s.[9] However, it is clear that by the first decade of the seventeenth-century, R. Isaiah had acquired some knowledge of Lurianic customs and praxis through the publication of such works as the *Tiqquney ha-Teshuvah*, which was printed at the back of Jacob Poyetto's condensation of *The Beginning of Wisdom* in 1600 in Venice.[10] The appearance of these Lurianic teachings had a considerable effect on kabbalists in Europe. Even where the theoretical, theological underpinnings were not understood, there was a sense that the Lurianic approach to practice was of great value. So influential a kabbalist as Menahem

Azariah da Fano (1548–1620), initially a proponent of the Kabbalah of Moses Cordovero, embraced and taught the Lurianic teachings when they arrived. It is clear that Isaiah Horowitz had knowledge of several of da Fano's works before he immigrated to the Land of Israel.[11] However, at the time that da Fano's work *Pelaḥ ha-Rimmon* (*Slice of Pomegranate*) was printed in 1600, a ban was pronounced against the dissemination of the Lurianic teachings, so that access to them in depth remained restricted.

Pelaḥ ha-Rimmon, although devoted to the explication of Cordovero's important kabbalistic compendium, *Pardes Rimmonim* (*Pomegranate Orchard*), contains an introduction which explains the Italian kabbalist's reasons for switching his allegiance from the system of Cordovero to that of Luria.[12] Isaiah Horowitz's kabbalistic writings remained heavily indebted to the works and thought of Cordovero. Nevertheless, it is clear from remarks made by Horowitz in his letters from the Holy Land and in his two principal works, *Sheney Luhot ha-Berit*, and his commentary on the Prayer Book, *Sha'ar ha-Shamayim* (*Gate of Heaven*), that his respect for the Lurianic Kabbalah exceeded even that of Cordovero. In one letter he mentions visiting Samuel Vital, son of Luria's chief disciple, in Damascus while enroute to Safed. Vital permitted R. Isaiah to read through his father's manuscript of the Lurianic teachings, *Eẓ Ḥayyim* (*Tree of Life*), and Horowitz describes the awe he felt while endeavoring to comprehend these teachings despite the difficulty he had in deciphering the Sefardi script in which they were written.[13] Occasionally R. Isaiah merely includes Isaac Luria in the already select company of R. Joseph Karo and R. Moses Cordovero, the three most illustrious kabbalists of Safed. For example, in his letter from Jerusalem he writes,

> These three supernal great ones lived at the same time, our Teacher and Rabbi Joseph Karo, our Teacher and Rabbi Moses Cordovero, and our Teacher and Rabbi Isaac Luria, of blessed memory. Angels of the Lord of Hosts actually appeared to them, along with *Maggidim*[14] from the *yeshivah* of the prophets and the *yeshivah* of the Tannaim, and even Elijah, may he be remembered for good. They are buried in the cemetery in the form of a *segol*. I kissed their graves.[15]

However, elsewhere he makes his view concerning Luria's status among these kabbalists more clear. In Horowitz's commentary on the Prayer Book, *Sha'ar ha-Shamayim*, which he wrote in the Land of Israel, he expresses his evaluation of Luria in the course of his comment on the recitation of the *Shema*, Deuteronomy 6:4, the declaration of divine unity which is central to the morning and evening services. After a lengthy explanation of the kabbalistic significance of this verse, according to the point of view of Cordovero, R. Isaiah permits himself to make a rare exception to his practice of not committing Lurianic teachings to writing.

> You have seen all that I have written concerning this verse of the unification, in accordance with what can be understood from the tradition of the kabbalists, in keeping with what is well known in their writings. However, there is an inner dimension to the inner [teachings], "*so deep, who can fathom it?*,"[16] "*but a wise man will draw it forth*."[17] He is the perfect sage and divine kabbalist, the great rabbi, the Lion, of blessed memory,[18] who enlightened the eyes of the wise with inner wisdom, "*the secrets of the Lord are to those who fear Him*,"[19] the purpose of the precepts and their reasons, and the unifications of prayers and praises. However, the secrets of recitation of the *Shema* exceed all of them. Fortunate is one who merits [knowing them]. Personally, I have always adhered to the principle, what is wondrous for you, do not reveal to the multitude. I have restrained myself from revealing his inner secrets to the unwise multitude, except for simple matters that can be understood from his words. For I thought, the masses are not worthy to make use of the concealed light. However, in the case of this verse, concerning accepting the yoke of the Kingdom of Heaven, my soul longed and desired to reveal some of his secrets, whose light I merited to enjoy here and there among the manuscripts of his holy disciples who are in the Land.[20]

Thus it is clear, from this passage and others that could be cited,[21] that R. Isaiah held the Lurianic teachings in the highest regard. They revealed a dimension of the inner teachings that was even more esoteric than that contained in the established kabbalistic traditions. He considered them to be so powerful and sacred as to require concealment and in general refrained from putting them into writing. Moreover, it is clear that he first gained access to these teachings before leaving Europe, although, as indicated, a ban was in effect that limited the availability of such teachings outside the Land of Israel. We may assume that, at the very least, Horowitz would have looked forward to the opportunity to gain further access to such teachings. When one further considers the extent to which his religious outlook was determined by Kabbalah, it becomes reasonable to posit that a primary motivation for Horowitz's decision to settle in the Land of Israel had to do with his desire to immerse himself in the Lurianic teachings and practices. Indeed that this is precisely what he did while he was in the Land of Israel is attested by the words of his son Sheftel. Concerning the circumstances that hastened R. Isaiah's departure from Prague, his son writes,

> It was from the Lord, so that he who was separated would merit seeing concealed treasuries, words of the mouth of grace, Kabbalah of the divine person, the perfect sage, the great rabbi, our teacher and rabbi, R. Isaac Luria, may the memory of the righteous be a blessing, his soul is bound in the Bundle of Life. These were not shown to anyone until my father and master, of blessed memory's [sic], arrival at his archives and house. For there, my father made his headquarters and his dwelling.[22] And he would study them from beginning to end.[23]

Even if we allow for the hyperbole of his son's account and the fact that there is some reason to doubt that Horowitz had access to writings that had not previously been made available to anyone else, the likelihood that R. Isaiah spent much of his time studying Lurianic Kabbalah rings true.

Sometime during the period between the death of his first wife in 1620 and his embarking for the Land of Israel in 1621, two important events occurred. Although Horowitz seems to have been devoted to his first wife, he began to seek a second wife about a year after her death, as is to be expected of a kabbalist who believed that his spiritual perfection was dependent on his marital relations.[24] According to family tradition, R. Isaiah at first wanted to marry a granddaughter of the MaHaRaL of Prague. However, she refused his offer. He then proposed to a woman named Havah bat Eliezer, who agreed to become his second wife. It was she who, shortly after their marriage, accompanied him to the Land of Israel.

The other important development in Horowitz's life, and one that would have far greater importance for posterity, was his decision to begin writing a work of ethical instruction for his descendents. These writings would become his magnum opus, a work of enormous proportions, which would be published posthumously by his son Sheftel under the title *Sheney Luhot ha-Berit* (*The Two Tablets of the Covenant*) and known by Jews as *Shelah ha-Qadosh* (the Holy *Shelah*.) We can learn something about the composition of this text from remarks made by Sheftel Horowitz in his introduction to the work, *Vavey 'Amudim*.

> Because of his great righteousness and piety, he abandoned his home and inheritance and ascended to the place concerning which the Lord said that He would cause His *Shekhinah* to rest there. However, before departing from his tent and native land, he began to compose this honorable and awesome work, in order to instruct his household . . . But due to the pressure to realize his wish to cause the light of his Torah to shine in the Land of Life, the work was not completed outside the Land of Israel, but rather in Jerusalem, two years after his arrival.[25]

Thus Horowitz began to write his masterwork before leaving Prague in 1621 and went on to complete it in Jerusalem in 1623. Although it is clear that the work was substantially affected by the access to kabbalistic writings that R. Isaiah had in the Land of Israel, it is not yet possible to determine precisely how much of the text was written before he left Prague.

Family tradition indicates that Horowitz kept his decision to settle in the Land of Israel secret until virtually the last moment. He took this step, presumably, to avoid the importuning of the Prague community, which would have wanted to prevent him from leaving. His son informs us that he only received knowledge of his father's imminent departure by accident. He was, it seems, quite affected by this news and attempted to prevail upon his father to change his mind. However, R. Isaiah, probably for the important spiritual motivations that have been suggested, was firm in his resolve. Clearly his commitment to strengthening the Jewish community in Jerusalem and to the Kabbalah, which was particularly associated with the Land of Israel, took precedence over his ties to family and the community in Prague. The fact that this decision was made only after the death of his first wife suggests that she may have been opposed to the idea, since it is unlikely that so strong a motivation would have materialized without prior development.[26]

At any rate, it is clear that R. Isaiah left behind two sons and a daughter. The older son, R. Sheftel, would later publish Horowitz's magnum opus. He was born in about 1590 in Lvov and later served as rabbi in Posen and Vienna before dying in 1660. Much less is known concerning his other son, Jacob, who died in Cracow in 1643, and his daughter, Nehama Mendelin, who was already married to a R. Phoebus.[27]

Isaiah Horowitz left Prague for the Land of Israel in 1621. He first travelled to his old community, Frankfurt, and then continued on from there to Venice, before embarking by boat from Italy. The voyage began sometime in late summer. In a letter written from Jerusalem Horowitz informs us that his ship reached Tripoli after a voyage of twenty-two days, on New Year's Day. However, a local war prevented his disembarking. Pursued by armed men, he managed to sail on to Syria, where he safely disembarked before *Yom Kippur*. On the way to the Land of Israel he made several stops, visiting such Jewish communities as Aleppo and Damascus. It seems that he was received with great honor wherever he arrived and delivered sermons in Hebrew in the local Sefardi synagogues. Out of modesty, he informs his family that the reception that he received was due to the honor and merit of his father. But there is little doubt that R. Isaiah had already far surpassed his father in prestige and owed his outstanding reception to his own reputation and position, however much his success may have been due to his father's influence. While he was in Damascus, he was approached by a delegation from Safed that wanted him to become rabbi of the small Ashkenazi community there. This would have been a very flattering offer to a person of Horowitz's kabbalistic propensities. Safed was, after all, the city of the kabbalists par excellence. Only fifty years before, Isaac Luria, Moses Cordovero, and Joseph Karo were all living there in the midst of a community of a number of other significant kabbalists. Moreover, the kabbalistic enterprise of the sixteenth-century had in large measure been located in Safed because of the sanctity of the graves that were believed to be located in the area, most notably the grave of R. Simeon bar Yohai, purported author of the kabbalistic classic, the *Zohar*. However, by the time of R. Isaiah's arrival, Safed was in decline. Moreover, Horowitz states directly in his letter from Jerusalem that Safed was at that time a rather dangerous place for Jews to live, due to the fact that it was not a walled city. On the other hand, while Safed somewhat recently had become a center for kabbalists, Jerusalem had always been the sacred city of Judaism and the kabbalists considered it the true *axis mundi*. At the time of Horowitz's arrival, Jerusalem was also a city of kabbalists, many of whom possessed their own copies of the Lurianic teachings. Moreover, both the Sefardi and Ashkenazi communities in Jerusalem were growing and felt protected by the city's walls. Thus it is not surprising that when a delegate from Jerusalem succeeded in contacting Isaiah Horowitz while he was enroute to Safed, he almost immediately made an agreement to become Head of the Rabbinical Court of Jerusalem.

Although R. Isaiah must have been anxious to reach Jerusalem, he first travelled to Safed. Given his position as a major rabbinic figure and kabbalist, whose arrival was clearly known and anticipated, he could have done nothing else. From his letter, it is clear that he was concerned not to offend the community in Safed. However, in the end he had to inform them that his heart was set on Jerusalem. Of course, he had his own personal spiritual reasons for visiting Safed as well. While he was there, he was privileged to hear some of the Lurianic teachings. In addition, R. Isaiah made it a point to visit many of the holy graves that are in the area in order to pray at them. The practice of praying and prostrating over graves of saints was a feature of Safed religiosity. It was especially emphasized by Isaac Luria as a means of enabling his disciples to form a spiritual bond with the soul of the deceased.[28] This could result in divine inspiration and the revelation of kabbalistic secrets. While it is not certain to what extent Isaiah Horowitz was involved in such mystical practices themselves, it is clear that his interest in these graves testifies to a deep piety that was typical of mystics of that period.

R. Isaiah finally arrived in Jerusalem on November 19, 1621, as he tells us in the preface to his commentary on the Prayer Book.[29] As it happened, his arrival coincided with the week during which the portion of the Torah was read that contains the verse ". . . *this is the Gate of Heaven*."[30] He commemorated the occasion by calling his commentary on the Prayer Book *Sha'ar ha-Shamayim* (*Gate of Heaven*). In Jerusalem, Isaiah Horowitz took on the leadership of a growing Ashkenazi community. Although he was officially Head of the Ashkenazi *Yeshivah* and Rabbinic Court, his stature in the community was more generally acknowledged. There is evidence that R. Isaiah was held in high esteem among the Sefardi community in Jerusalem as well.

In addition to undertaking his official duties and responsibilities as rabbi in Jerusalem, Isaiah Horowitz must have spent a considerable portion of his time in activities related to the study of Kabbalah. As has been indicated, Jerusalem was at that time a city of kabbalists and afforded Horowitz access to teachings that had not yet reached Europe. There can be no doubt that R. Isaiah was deeply involved in collecting and copying manuscripts containing these highly esoteric teachings. Among the works that made a deep impression on him was the mystical diary of R. Joseph Karo, *Maggid Mesharim*, which contains accounts of the teachings that Karo received over the course of forty years from his *Maggid*, the *Shekhinah*, or spirit of the Mishnah.[31] Excerpts from this book are included in *Sheney Luhot ha-Berit*. However, there is no doubt that the teachings of Isaac Luria, which he only now had the opportunity to study in detail, occupied most of Horowitz's interest. Although R. Isaiah felt that for the most part Lurianic teachings should only be disseminated through oral transmission, both of the major works that he completed in Jerusalem contain numerous examples of Luria's teachings.[32] In addition to the kabbalistic issues that R. Isaiah was able to study in the manuscripts, he was also in a position to observe customs that the kabbalists in Jerusalem and Safed had adopted. These customs, which were supported by kabbalistic arguments, particularly impressed him, which is evident from the fact that many were included in *Sheney Luhot ha-Berit.* When this work was later printed and became popular throughout eastern Europe, it became an important channel through which these often Lurianic customs reached large Jewish communities beyond the Land of Israel. As such, it was instrumental in spreading the Lurianic ethos that would prevail in many portions of the Jewish world during the seventeenth and eighteenth centuries. In addition to the opportunities they offered to pursue his kabbalistic interests, the initial years spent in Jerusalem also proved very productive in terms of Isaiah Horowitz's literary output. Although, it is clear, as he himself tells us in the introduction, that he began *Sheney Luhot ha-Berit* before leaving Prague, it is probable that a large portion of it was written in Jerusalem. In addition, *Sha'ar ha-Shamayim*, his commentary on the Prayer Book, was entirely composed in the Land of Israel.

Despite the many achievements that Isaiah Horowitz accomplished in Jerusalem, both through his leadership and efforts toward rebuilding the Jewish community there and his prodigious literary output, his tenure there was to be an abbreviated one. In 1625 an oppressive local Muslim ruler, Ibn Faruh, began extorting large sums of money from the Jews. During the summer of 1625 R. Isaiah was arrested along with fourteen other eminent rabbis and community leaders. He was released about two and a half weeks later, after the community had paid a huge ransom. As a result of these oppressive measures, which involved not only imprisonment but even torture, both the Ashkenazi and Sefardi communities quickly fell deeply into debt. After his release R. Isaiah at first tried to help the community raise the funds it needed from abroad. However, by winter it was clear that it would be impossible for him to remain safely in Jerusalem. Along with the other Ashkenazi leaders of the community, Horowitz was compelled to flee for his life to Safed. After a short stay there, he settled in Tiberias, where he died not long after in 1626.[33] There is reason to believe that R. Isaiah was buried in Tiberias, near the graves of Moses Maimonides and Yohanan ben Zakkai, although no inscription marked his tombstone.[34]

Sheney Luhot ha-Berit (Two Tablets of the Law)

Isaiah Horowitz's great work, *Sheney Luhot ha-Berit*, was first conceived in Prague, about the time that the author made his decision to settle in the Land of Israel. At least, so he tells us in his general introduction, which seems to have been written before he set out for the Land of Israel. This would suggest that he must have begun to compose the work sometime after his wife's death in 1620. His initial intention was to prepare a work of ethical rebuke for his descendents, as a kind of spiritual inheritance, just as Jewish masters from the time of Moses took leave of their followers amid words of ethical instruction. Originally, it seems that his intention was to call these ethical teachings *Derekh Ḥayyim* (*Way to Life*), after the verse from Proverbs, "*for the commandment is a lamp and the Torah is light and the way to life is the rebuke that disciplines.*"[35] His choice of these words from the verse, whose explication forms the unifying theme of his introduction, is due to the two meanings that can be associated with them. On the one hand, as the verse suggests, ethical instruction is in itself the "*way to life.*" But in selecting these words R. Isaiah was also intimating that they were written on the way to the Land of Israel, called the Land of Life because it is the locus of the Divine Presence. As he puts it,

> I am writing in great haste at the time of departure for the skilled way to the Holy Land in order to cleave to the Land of Life. Thus I am calling these writings "Way to Life," and also because of the [meaning of the] verse, "*the commandment is a lamp . . . and a way to life. . . .*" It is the way to eternal life.[36]

Although Isaiah Horowitz's original plan for the work was considerably more modest than the final result, he was not able to complete his task before undertaking the journey to the Land of Israel. While he was engaged in completing the work in Jerusalem, it seems to have occurred to him to call the work by another title, *Two Tablets of the Covenant*, under which it was published by R. Sheftel Horowitz in Amsterdam in 1649.[37] The new title alluded to the two additional sections that were added in Jerusalem. One section, entitled "The Written Torah," contains homilies on each of the Torah portions that are studied each week and read in the synagogues. The second new section deals with the methodology of the Talmud and is called "The Oral Torah." The general title, *Two Tablets of the Covenant*, alludes to the dual Torah, written and oral, which forms an inseparable unity.

Although the structure of the work was altered substantially and its scope considerably increased in Jerusalem, the original plan for the work is preserved in the general introduction, which refers to three parts, entitled "Ten Utterances," "Ten Words," and "Ten Praises." These titles correspond to three groups of ten expressions that have great significance in Jewish tradition: the "ten utterances," which according to rabbinic tradition were the means by which God created the world; the "ten *Diberot*" alludes to the ten commandments that were spoken at Sinai and ten words upon which the world is founded[38]; and the ten psalms of praise attributed to King David.

The first section, "Ten Utterances," consists of ten chapters devoted to general principles of mystical ethics.

1. God is one. This chapter discusses various implications of God's oneness, emphasizing the need not only to understand the theological concept, but also to have a personal realization of God's oneness in the heart that removes the distance between oneself and God. The need to understand kabbalistic conceptions of God is asserted. Basically, God is viewed as the only true existence, upon which everything else eternally depends, since God is constantly renewing the powers of creation.

2. Israel is one entity. This chapter focuses on the eternal divine basis of the souls of Israel. The focus is the interpretation of Moses' statement in Deuteronomy: "*The Lord our God made a covenant with us at Horeb. It was not with our fathers that the Lord made this covenant, but with us the living, every one of us who is here today.*"[39] Since Horowitz considers the Torah to be eternally true, these verses are interpreted as an eternally valid promise involving the souls of Israel in all generations. The chapter alludes to the secret of metempsychosis and stresses the exalted nature of Jewish souls, which have the ability to theurgically affect the upper worlds and are ontologically superior to angels.

3. Inner fear and love. This chapter distinguishes between external and inner expressions of fear and love as aspects of divine service. The basic distinction is that outer fear and love are self-centered, while inner fear and love mean fear and love of God, that is, they are theocentric in focus. These are, however, further subdivided into four categories. The most external level of divine worship, outermost fear and love, means that a person refrains from committing a transgression because of fear of punishment. Similarly, outermost love means fulfilling the precepts for the sake of a reward. The higher level of external love and fear is cited from a kabbalistic work *Eyn ha-Qore'*, by R. Shem Tov ben Shem Tov. This level of fear and love has a higher motivation but is still self-centered. It involves fulfilling the precepts in order to receive the supernal effluences that they cause to descend on the person who performs them. At this level the person also has the attainment of immortality as a motivation for serving God.

The truly inner levels of fear and love also have two degrees, one deeper than the other. The first level involves shamefulness, which results from a sense of the awesomeness of God. This sense of shamefulness and awe is fostered by contemplating the magnificent complexity of creation in detail, through all four worlds of the kabbalistic cosmology.[40] According to Horowitz, such contemplation and the state it produces lead directly to inner love, which is produced by contemplation of God's humility and generosity. This results in a state of joy and cleaving to God while fulfilling the precepts. However, an even higher level, innermost fear, is characterized by the desire to fulfill the precepts for the sake of "the need above," that is, specifically in order to perform the kabbalistic objectives of the precepts that unite and rectify aspects of the Divine Name, which remains impaired until the Messianic Age.[41] The ultimate level, called here "hidden love,"[42] is the quality of Moses' divine service and effects an even higher divine union that is beyond the power of all other people to accomplish.

4. Divine service for the need above. The concept which is the theme of this chapter is discussed in conjunction with the theme of the previous chapter, since it concerns the nature of worship at a very high level. Literally, the concept *Ẓorekh Gavoha* means to fulfill the need of the High One, that is, the divine need. This entails the cultivation of unceasing awareness of all that one does, in order to make sure that nothing occurs, even inadvertently, that will be a transgression. The purpose of this constant watchfulness is to ensure that none of one's actions is performed for personal benefit, but all is done for the sake of uniting aspects of the highest world, the "world of emanation," which is an extension of God.

5. Eternal service. The person who attains the highest level of serving God is absolutely constant in God's service. Even when he suffers afflictions, he remains undeterred from his worship of God. The chapter discusses various ways of understanding suffering and how it is viewed and handled by the righteous. Most of the material in this chapter, which deals with an early Jewish ethical value, is drawn from rabbinic rather than kabbalistic sources.

6. The essence of service in the heart. Since God is not a material object, divine worship has to occur within the heart, so that an intimacy between the worshipper and God, *devequt*, can occur. This chapter emphasizes the need for emotional arousal and especially joy as essential for divine service. The chapter contains one of Horowitz's more controversial teachings, the need to arouse and overcome the "evil urge" as an important part of serving God. He also advocates transformation of negative qualities through finding a positive expression for them rather than merely suppressing them. A discussion follows concerning the meaning of an ethical maxim from tractate *Avot*: "Whoever learns Torah for its own sake merits many things."

Two interpretations are offered. Although it is impossible for anyone to fulfill all of the 613 commandments in one lifetime, whoever fulfills those commandments that he is able to fulfill is considered to have fulfilled them all. The second explanation, which also follows a rabbinic precedent, is that when a person has in mind to fulfill a precept and is prevented from doing so, because of his good intention he is nevertheless credited with having fulfilled the precept.

7. Gate of the attributes. This chapter has two parts. The first discusses the attributes of God that are to be emulated. The second part discusses human attributes and is subdivided into two parts. The first deals with what is expected of human beings from the point of view of what the divine law requires and the category of saintly behavior that goes "beyond what the law requires." The second part deals with human virtues in general and how one should conduct himself in all aspects of life. However, the bulk of the chapter deals with how a person can emulate the inner attributes of God. In other words, ethical behavior is now modeled not on the explicit qualities associated with God in scripture, but with the attributes that the kabbalists associated with the ten *sefirot*, the hidden aspects of God that are manifest in the world of emanation.[43] In detailing a system of ethical behavior as imitation of God through relating ethical virtues to the *sefirot*, Horowitz follows in the steps of Moses Cordovero, whose ethical tract *Tomer Devorah* (*Palm Tree of Deborah*)[44] highly influenced R. Isaiah and is quoted elsewhere in his work. The entire discussion is focused on the verse, "*Be wholehearted with the Lord your God.*"[45]

8. *Devequt* (Cleaving) of the heart to God in all ways. The point of this brief chapter is that all of one's deeds should be for the sake of heaven. This means not only those acts which fall specifically in the category of divine service, but everything that a person does, whether nominally religious in nature or not. This quality is associated with the verse, "*in all of your ways know Him.*"[46]

9. Purity of thought in the heart. This quality follows from the previous chapter. The chapter emphasizes that divine service goes beyond dedication of actions and in actuality requires dedication of all of one's very thoughts to the divine purpose.

10. *Shekhinah* (Divine Presence) in the heart. Once one has attained the quality of purity of thought, there is an additional level to be attained. This involves constantly remembering God and is identified with the verse, "*I place the Lord constantly before me*,"[47] which is interpreted in a number of ways.

The first section, "Ten Utterances," is completed by an even lengthier discussion of kabbalistic ethics that treats many of the same themes, but expounds them in greater detail and depth. The subjects of this section are arranged in alphabetical order and are thus called "Gate of the Letters." They include the following:

Emunah and *Emet*: on faith and truth.

Briot: on the intrinsic connection between the commandment to love God and to love one's fellow as oneself.

Gerut: on the transitory nature of one's existence in this world. The soul's origin is really in the divine world.

Derekh Ereẓ: on perfection in regard to body, soul, and resources.

Hallel: on the need to praise God constantly for all that occurs.

Vatranut: on the proper way to practice liberality concerning one's possessions.

Zehirut and *zerizut*: on exercising caution before one acts and zeal when one acts.

Ḥaver Tov: on the importance of acquiring a good friend.

Tohorah: on purity in regard to spiritual and physical matters. The discussion deals with such matters as immersion in a ritual bath, defecation and urination, bodily cleanliness and clean clothing, and pure food.

Yeẓer Tov: Ostensibly on the "good urge," the discussion concerns various meanings of the word *tov* (good) in this world and the next.

Kaf Zekhut: on the need to judge others favorably.

Lev Tov: on the importance of keeping the heart pure.

Matun: on the importance of always acting deliberately and without haste.

Ne'eman Ruaḥ: on faithfulness of spirit, which here primarily means being able to keep one's own counsel and not to reveal all of one's thoughts unless and until it is necessary and proper.

Sippuq: on the importance of being satisfied with whatever one receives from God.

'Anavah: on the need for humility in thought, speech, and deed as a prerequisite for *devequt*.

Piryon: on the need to be well regarded by others as a result of one's actions and comportment.[48]

Ẓeni'ut: on the importance of modesty in regard to dress, food, and sexual relations. Also included in the category of modesty is the habit of secluding oneself so that a holy state can be maintained. One should only leave one's solitude in order to go to the synagogue or House of Study, or when it is necessary to perform some other precept in public.

Qedushah: on the inherent holiness of human beings that follows from the fact of their being created in the image of God. Every limb of the human body alludes to some supernal aspect in the upper worlds. The association of the limbs with the *sefirot* is explained in detail, drawing on kabbalistic texts such as the *Zohar* and Cordovero's *Pardes Rimmonim*. Horowitz also explains how such divine names as the YHVH and *SHa-DaY* (All Mighty) are contained in the human structure. He then goes on to explain at length how the holiness of each limb is bound up with the performance of particular precepts. This section contains a lengthy discussion of prohibited foods, including ninety-four halakhic principles, and a lengthy discussion on tithes and observance of precepts concerned with eating in the Land of Israel. This emphasis on clarifying precepts involving food is based on the view that the Temple altar has been replaced by one's dinner table. Thus, as R. Isaiah puts it, "the food is a sacrifice and the one who eats it is the priest who officiates." Because when the Temple stood, the Temple Service was invested with the highest degree of holiness, holiness is especially important in regard to food now that the Temple has been destroyed. Holiness here involves not only care in observing the laws regarding kosher foods, but also requires care in reciting the blessings before and after the meals and in appropriate behavior during the meal. One should have the holiness of the meal and its blessings in mind and should neither overeat nor drink excessively. The meal should be eaten in a joyful mood. To be complete, three things are required: food should be made available to the poor, words of Torah should be spoken at the table, and the blessing after the meal should be sung. The entire discussion is summarized under six categories:

1. The blessings over the table should be said in a loud voice with more *kavvanah* (concentration) than other blessings.
2. One should have in mind that he is eating in the presence of God. Therefore, he should make himself holy through not indulging his cravings, but rather eating for the glory of God.
3. One should avoid overeating and especially avoid intoxication.
4. Regardless of the quantity and quality of the food available, one should eat in gratitude and joy.
5. One should eat food that is healthy and conducive to healing and avoid what is only temporarily pleasing to the palate.
6. One should remain at the table long enough for it to become an altar of atonement. One should feed the poor there and teach them words of Torah. One should give them the best portions. Even if one is alone, a song or two should be recited.

Following this section R. Isaiah includes annotations that he had previously written for his father's book on blessings, *Emeq Berakhah*. The entire section on the holiness of the body is concluded by a very lengthy discussion of holiness in marital relations. The final section of the discussion of holiness centers on the holiness of the Land of Israel, where the highest degree of holiness can be attained by one who practices solitude in the Holy Land. The section concludes with the issue of holiness in dress, emphasizing the importance of observing the precept that prohibits garments made of mixed species (*shatnez*).

Raẓon: on the importance of maintaining a favorable state, which avoids anger and displeasure at others. Anger is considered the worst of vices. This follows from the kabbalistic view that the divine will is essentially characterized by favor. Divine anger and its consequences are only the result of human evil. It is anger that separates a person from the divine unity and causes divine anger to descend. However, one who possesses the attribute of *raẓon* (favor) cleaves to God. If he maintains a favorable state toward others, he will certainly not allow anything to come between himself and the Divine Presence.

Shetiqah: on the virtue of silence. Horowitz summarizes various rabbinic teachings concerning the importance of exercising care in one's speech. Idle talk is to be avoided. Cursing and profanity are absolutely prohibited.

Teshuqah: on the virtue of desire and love for God and the Torah and commandments. One should observe the precepts zealously as a result of joy. This attribute is combined with the previous two in order to attain the desired state of *devequt*, cleaving to God, which Horowitz here compares to the sexual union between a husband and wife. The three are now alluded to by the letters of the word *shevaḥ* (praise), whose letters are an acronym for *shetiqah* (silence), *bediqah* (examination), and *ḥashiqah* (desire). Silence is explained as incumbent on both the mouth and heart. One should not only avoid all kinds of negative speech, but also practice restraint in expressing one's thoughts where doing so would have negative consequences. *Bediqah* (examination) pertains to the attribute of *raẓon*. A person should check constantly to see whether he is in a state of favor. This is especially important before retiring. When these two are combined with desire for God and the Torah and commandments, *devequt* can be attained, as indicated by the verse, "*you who are cleaving to the Lord, your God, are all alive.*"[49]

Thus ends the discussion of *Teshuqah* (longing), which brings to a close not only the "Gate of the Letters," but the entire first section, "Ten Utterances." The second section, "Ten Words," owes its title to ten qualities that were emphasized by the rabbis as foundations of the world. These are Torah, divine service, acts of lovingkindness, judgment, truth, peace,[50] repentance, prayer, and almsgiving. The tenth quality is the one that includes all of the others, faith in God. However, the section is really organized around ten times of the year: weekdays, Sabbath, Passover, Shavuot, the 9th of Av, Rosh Hashanah, Yom Kippur, Sukkot, Hanukkah, and Purim. Each of these is associated with one of the ten qualities mentioned above, which befits this particular time. Each of these substantial sections is called, with little exaggeration, a tractate. The correlation between the times and the qualities is as follows:

Tractate *Ḥullin* (ordinary days of the week) is the Pillar of Truth, because the six days of the week testify to creation, which was accomplished in six days.

Tractate *Shabbat* (Sabbath) is the Pillar of Faith, because the Sabbath is the wonder of creation.

Tractate *Pesaḥim* (Passover) is the Pillar of Lovingkindness, because through this divine quality Israel was redeemed from Egypt.

Tractate *Shavuot* is the Pillar of Torah, since the Torah was given to Israel on this day at Sinai.

Tractate *Ta'anit* (Fast of the 9th of Av) is the Pillar of Divine Service, because the flesh and blood that is lost through fasting is in place of the sacrifices in the Temple, which was destroyed and will be rebuilt on this day.

Tractate *Rosh ha-Shanah* is the Pillar of Judgment, since it is the day of supernal judgment.

Tractate *Yoma* (Yom Kippur) is the Pillar of Repentance, because it is the day of repentance.

Tractate *Sukkah* (Sukkot) is the Pillar of Peace, because peace and joy are attained by merit of the afflictions undertaken during the days of repentance after the divine attribute of judgment is changed to the attribute of lovingkindness on Yom Kippur.

Tractate *Tamid* (Hanukkah) is the Pillar of Prayer, because prayer replaced the daily sacrifice (*Tamid*) and Hanukkah lights allude to the *ner tamid* (eternal light).

Tractate *Megillah* (Purim) is the Pillar of Almsgiving, since on that day alms are distributed.

Each of these substantial tractates is subdivided into three large sections. All three take their names from the verse that is cited in the general introduction as the focus of the work as a whole, "*for the commandment is a lamp, the Torah is light and the way to life is the rebuke that disciplines.*" The three parts are: "Commandment Is a Lamp," "Torah Is Light," and "Way to Life." In each tractate a broad spectrum of halakhic issues and matters pertaining to practice is discussed in detail in the section called "Commandment Is a Lamp." The section "Torah Is Light" deals with the kabbalistic reasons, intentions, and secrets that are related to the various aspects of observance that occur at the particular time. In the third section, "Way to Life," R. Isaiah discusses the spiritual and ethical qualities that are relevant to the particular section. In each of these three sections Isaiah Horowitz's general method is to state the issue that he wishes to discuss and to compare various points of view expressed in the wealth of rabbinic literature that he knew. After comparing various opinions, he often gives his own view concerning the correctness of a custom or practice or kabbalistic reason. While his general approach is typical of rabbinic style, the presentation and analysis of existing sources, R. Isaiah was not hesitant to include his own legal innovations. His son Sheftel tells us in his introduction that his father included more than four hundred *ḥiddushey Torah* (legal innovations) in the work.

The third section of the original plan, "Ten Praises," is preceded in the final edition by the two new sections that were conceived in Jerusalem, the collection of sermons on the weekly Torah portions, called "Written Torah" because it deals with the Pentateuch, and the analysis of talmudic method and rabbinic terminology, called "Oral Torah" because it deals with the oral tradition of the rabbis.[51] The final, uncharacteristically brief section, "Ten Praises," is a kind of recapitulation; it deals with the secret of the *Shema* and some of Horowitz's favorite moral issues.

In toto, *Sheney Luhot ha-Berit* is a massive work, more than ten times the length of the present volume. This considerable length is the result of a number of factors. On the one hand, it testifies to the vast expertise that Isaiah Horowitz had in several areas. Mastery is displayed in three distinct areas of rabbinic literature. Although not essentially a work of *halakhah*, R. Isaiah displays vast knowledge of the issues involved in the practical observance of Jewish law regarding both customs and *halakhah*. As his son asserts, he does indeed include numerous innovative legal decisions. In addition to the strictly rabbinic matters, which are treated in great detail, Horowitz demonstrates a comprehensive knowledge of Kabbalah and command of its sources. The work clearly benefited from R. Isaiah's study of Lurianic writings in the Land of Israel. This is most evident in the section "Ten Words," the ten tractates dealing with occasional observances and customs. Finally, Horowitz is without doubt a great moralist, deeply concerned with the spiritual dimensions of Judaism that determine the quality of divine service. Isaiah Horowitz could have established his reputation in any one of these three areas. What makes his masterpiece unique, however, is the fact that it delves so deeply into all three areas and combines them into a single unified work.

On the other hand, it must be said that much of the magnitude of *Sheney Luhot ha-Berit* is the result of Horowitz's style, which can be described fairly as tending toward prolixity. First of all, R. Isaiah rarely paraphrases the many sources that are cited in his writings.[52] His tendency is to cite these sources *in extenso*. This is in all probability a reflection of the fact that libraries were scarce at the time of his composition. Horowitz wanted to give his readers a fair opportunity to judge the texts for themselves. This intention was somewhat frustrated by the fact that the printed editions of his work are replete with errors in the texts cited. Further research would be required in order to determine whether these errors are the responsibility of copyists and printers or an indication that R. Isaiah may have been (at least in some cases) quoting from memory. Considering the considerable length of many of these citations, the first explanation presently seems more plausible. At any rate, it is clear that these sometimes excessive quotations greatly increased the work's length.

A second aspect of R. Isaiah's style also resulted in his work having a quality that would be considered unnecessary by modern standards. He has the tendency to repeat himself whenever an issue arises that is somewhat relevant to the matter being discussed. Horowitz characteristically will repeat almost verbatim the discussion of a subject where he deems it appropriate, even if he has already exhausted his thoughts on the issue previously. In other words, the work has a cumbersome quality, which modern editorial practices would eliminate. Here again it may be that R. Isaiah wrote this way because he did not have the means of indexing and cross-referencing that are now taken for granted. Notwithstanding these somewhat old-fashioned encumbrances, *Sheney Luhot ha-Berit* remains one of the great works of late rabbinic literature and certainly one of the most popular.[53]

Although originally intended as a spiritual legacy for his descendents, it is fortunate that his son Sheftel acted upon his father's instructions to allow not only relatives but students as well to benefit from this vast source of spiritual wisdom. As the result of printing the work, there were few students of Torah over the next several centuries who could not be counted among the disciples of Isaiah Horowitz. May their numbers continue to increase.

Toledot Adam (The Generations of Adam)

As is clear from the structure of the work as a whole, *Sheney Luhot ha-Berit* is essentially a comprehensive discussion of Judaism in many of its classical aspects. Ethical teachings, observance of precepts and customs coordinated with the sacred calendar, study of Torah as commentary on the Pentateuch, and analysis of the Talmud are all included. However, it is essential to note that Isaiah Horowitz's approach to these standard areas of Judaism is a very particular one. He is a committed student and exponent of the kabbalistic tradition. As such, his work is permeated by a kabbalistic point of view that shapes his approach to a number of issues, including especially the great emphasis he places on knowing the kabbalistic secrets concerning the meaning of the precepts and the ethical qualities that he values most highly. Horowitz studied Kabbalah from his student days in Poland during a century when the esoteric theurgic teaching was slowly gaining influence among the Ashkenazi and Polish rabbinic elite. By the time R. Isaiah had become the Rabbi of Prague, he was a confirmed kabbalist who considered the study of this esoteric tradition to be an essential and crowning dimension of the study of Torah in general. It is highly probable that his interest in Kabbalah, which was especially associated with mystical revelations and the Land of Israel, was a major factor in his decision to take up residence in Jerusalem. Thus it is not surprising that Isaiah Horowitz chose to begin his great work with an introduction entirely devoted to the basic principles of Kabbalah. That book-length introduction is entitled *Toledot Adam* (*The Generations of Adam*),[54] because, as he tells us, "all the causes and events of human life and its purpose have been mentioned within it."[55] In short, in this general introduction, Horowitz brought together his views concerning many of the most important issues addressed by kabbalists since the late twelfth century. These include basic theological questions concerning how God can be known, the true nature of the Torah, the divine origins of the human soul, the meaning and purpose of life in this world, the nature and theurgic efficacy of the precepts, and the ultimate reward of the Messianic Age and World to Come.

R. Isaiah's approach to these questions is similar to his approach to other issues that he considers in *Sheney Luhot ha-Berit*. He cites several authorities at length before revealing the full extent of his own view. Horowitz's position may be the result of harmonizing apparently conflicting points of view or, especially when philosophical and kabbalistic viewpoints are clearly at variance, R. Isaiah may put forth refutations of the philosophical point of view. Indeed, this ability to subject kabbalistic issues to an intellectual dialectic or *pilpul*, a process of argumentation and analysis that is more often associated with halakhic issues, is a characteristic that particularly distinguishes Horowitz as a kabbalistic writer.

It may well be that he considered this trait to be the defining feature that would enable him to contribute uniquely to the kabbalistic enterprise in the Land of Israel. At least, it has already been observed that R. Isaiah's interpretation of a curious rabbinic aggadah may have involved an allusion to himself. The aggadah claims that the sages in the Land of Israel are superior to the sages outside the Land of Israel, because they learn more *Ma'aseh Merkavah*[56] there, while outside the Land of Israel the sages are preoccupied with halakhic disputes. However, when one of the latter settles in the Land of Israel, he is superior to the sages there, because he brings his honed analytical skills with him and can apply the method of *pilpul* to the study of mysticism.[57]

Although the themes that Isaiah Horowitz treats in *Toledot Adam* are many and often complex, the entire introduction is presented as a commentary on a single teaching from the *Zohar*: "We have learned these three levels are interrelated: the Blessed Holy One, the Torah, and Israel."[58] Thus the entire work can be considered as a detailed explanation of the unique relationship that exists among God, the Torah, and Israel. The three are understood, from the kabbalistic point of view, to be interwoven to the extent of being inseparable. This association of Israel and its sacred scriptures with God obviously places Judaism at the center of existence. Jews and the Torah are both, in a sense, divine in origin and structurally related to the hidden nature of God, which is an essential component of kabbalistic studies. Indeed, the title, *The Generations of Adam*, refers to none other than the Jews, whose souls alone were contained in the primordial and originally entirely spiritual soul of Adam. Although their quality was reduced as a result of Adam's sin, the Jews still have enormous power to affect God by means of the Torah and ultimately will restore not only their souls to a more spiritual state but will actually attain a state that is superior to the one that Adam lost.

Briefly, then, *Toledot Adam* deals with the mysterious connection between Israel (the Jews) and God, the effects of Adam's sin, the means of rectifying it, and the ultimately superior end that will follow the Messianic Age. In order to make his major theme plausible, Horowitz is compelled to branch off into a number of interesting and related issues, some of which will be discussed below. For now, however, we turn to a summary of the general structure of *Toledot Adam*.

The basic structure of *Toledot Adam* consists of ten chapters or "houses" that are built within the "fortified city" of the *Zohar* teaching that serves as the underlying theme. The ten houses are called: "House of *YHVH*," "House of Wisdom," "House of Israel," "Faithful House," "The "Temple,"[59] "Ultimate House," "House of Choosing," "House of the Walled City," "House of David," and the "Great House." An additional section is called the "Great Gate." Each of the "houses" focuses on a specific theme.

"House of *YHVH*" treats basic theological issues concerning the nature of God. It is especially concerned with the mystery of the Tetragrammaton, *YHVH*, and other divine names and what in fact they name. This section deals with the ten *sefirot*, the secret of emanation and the four worlds that constitute the kabbalistic cosmology, and the concealed and unknowable aspect of God, referred to as *Eyn Sof*. In general, Horowitz attempts to explain the basic characteristics and structure of the manifest God, as associated with divine names, so that he can go on to demonstrate how these characteristics are also shared by the Torah and by the body and soul of Jews. One method, which Isaiah Horowitz uses repeatedly, is the technique of *gematria*. This involves converting letters into numerical values in order to draw attention to the otherwise concealed relatedness between entities. By demonstrating that the letters of the names of two distinct entities may be convertible to the same sum, a hidden relationship or identity is indicated.

"House of Wisdom" deals with the secret nature of the Torah. In essence, it entirely consists of divine names that are proclaiming God's existence. The written Torah originates in the divine world of emanation, from the *sefirah* of *Tif'eret*. The Torah is identified with the letter *yod*, which has three parts that can be compared to a point, a line, and a plane. Similarly, the Torah has three qualities, its attributes and commandments can be pursued in length and breadth, but its secrets or kabbalistic meaning are like a point, virtually invisible. The Torah text has special properties that distinguish it from all other texts. It can never become obsolete. Whereas other texts can be discarded once their content has been comprehended, involvement with Torah transcends intellect. It is unlimited and inexhaustible and is continually being revealed in all generations by its sages. Because of its divine nature, even a person who does not understand what he is reciting finds benefit in pronouncing the text of the Torah. Although the Torah's essence is purely spiritual, it has coarsened and taken on a material form as a result of Adam's sin.

The nature of the Jewish soul is the theme of "House of Israel." Adam was composed of all of the divine attributes, so that he could bear witness to the unity of God's Name. Adam was created in the image and likeness of God. "Image" refers to his divine soul and "likeness" refers to the human body, whose very structure corresponds to the structure of the world of emanation. Divine Names and their letters are also found to be concealed in the form of the human body. The limbs of the human body correspond to the letters of *YHVH* and to the ten *sefirot*. As a result of this divine likeness, the descendents of Adam have theurgic capabilities. The actions taken by their limbs and souls have an impact upon the divine world.

All of the souls of Jews were contained in the soul of Adam. When the nature of Adam's soul was altered as a result of his sin, the punishment was bequeathed to all the souls contained within his. Each of these souls consists of five potential degrees, all of which originate among the *sefirot* in the world of emanation. Although the three lower spiritual degrees of the divine soul can be attained during life in this world, the two highest degrees await the realization of the World to Come. As a result of the uniquely divine quality of Jewish souls, Jews should also have had a unique physical form that would have distinguished them from other human beings. However, since the souls of Jewish sinners can be compelled to transmigrate into the bodies of non-Jews, it was necessary for both Jews and non-Jews to share the same physical form.

Between the soul and body there is a third element, a spiritual body, that enables the two to be joined together.[60] The relationship between the soul and the body parallels the way that the Emanator and world of emanation are related. Finally, just as the Torah as well as God's Name were altered as a result of Adam's sin, the nature of Adam's descendents was changed. Their bodies and souls were coarsened and their intellects darkened and will essentially remain in this reduced condition until the Messianic Age.

"Faithful House" deals with the problem of God's attributes and anthropomorphism. Although it appears that language referring to human physical characteristics is used in scripture to allude to God, these usages are not mere metaphors. In fact the situation is entirely the reverse. It is rather divine aspects that are being used metaphorically to refer to human matters. However, this issue is explained more fully by R. Isaiah in conjunction with the discussion in the following section.

The apparently anthropomorphic nature of scriptural references to God is explained in "The Temple," which deals with the reason that the Hebrew of the Bible is called the Holy Language. One of the reasons that the Torah is unlike any other text is that it uses the Holy Language. This language is holy because of its origin and nature, which are not human. The meaning of its letters and words is not the result of custom and convention. Rather, the letters of the Holy Language are spiritual in nature and originate among the *sefirot*. Moreover, the holiness of this language consists in the fact that it names what really exists above in the divine realm. This language is used derivatively to apply to matters below, such as parts of the human body. The Hebrew names for these human organs are really names for entities in the divine realm whence they derive. These names are shared because, when a particular limb has been purified, its holy actions can have a direct effect on the divine entity by which it is called.

"Ultimate House" deals with the nature of rewards promised in the Torah. A central question treated here is why the language of the Torah seems to speak entirely of material rewards rather than those of a spiritual nature. After reviewing a number of approaches to this question in both philosophical and kabbalistic sources, R. Isaiah offers his solution. The answer to this question is linked to the discussion concerning Holy Language. It is only a misunderstanding of this concept that leads to the assumption that the Torah is only speaking of material rewards. In reality, all of the "material" language refers to the most spiritual matters, which are located in the world of emanation. From this point of view, the Torah does not speak of material rewards at all! Other related questions concern the way that the law of reward and punishment functions in regard to fulfilling or transgressing the precepts.

Although Isaiah Horowitz's initial statement concerning the ten houses suggests that the work will be divided into ten consecutive chapters, this is not the case. Since many of the issues require discussion in more than one house, the work frequently weaves back and forth among the various houses.[61] Even the static order of the chapters does not describe their actual order of initial appearance in our text. Thus the next chapter is "House of David," which is the seventh to be introduced, although it appeared ninth in the list of chapter headings.

"House of David" is essentially concerned with the Messianic Age. However, its true theme is spiritual transformation, the process by means of which the darkness that resulted from Adam's sin will be converted into a source of additional light. A second theme is immortality and its nature. Does it involve only survival of the soul or is the body also involved? Horowitz will argue that both body and soul will survive eternally in the World to Come, albeit in a spiritual state that is even finer than the one that Adam had originally. Nevertheless, all will not share equally in this state, which is dependent on one's deeds and the level of one's *devequt*, cleaving to God by means of the kabbalistic secrets in this world. A central issue here is the need to transform rather than suppress evil. In particular, R. Isaiah speaks in favor of involving the "evil urge" in the process of fulfilling the precepts. As a result, it too can contribute to the good by contributing additional light. Metaphysically, the *qelippot*, or shells that classical Kabbalah and the Lurianic teachings identify with evil, are transformed from intrusive forces that threaten the good into protective coverings that safeguard holiness.

The next chapter to be introduced is "House of the Walled City." Its theme is the mystery of the concealed divine will. The central issue is how to understand a series of paradoxes involving God's will. R. Isaiah wants to explain how prayer and repentance can be effective if, as he also maintains, God's will does not change. The answer, in part, depends on the fact that reward and punishment are not meted out in individual cases. Rather, they follow a process of natural law that can accommodate all possible cases.

The issue raised in the preceding chapter continues to be discussed in the following chapter, "House of Choosing." Here, however, the question is raised from a different angle. Before the question was how human action can be effective if the divine will is unchanging. Now the problem is how human beings can be free to choose, if God's knowledge is perfect.[62] Isaiah Horowitz's solution to this perennial theological problem is an interesting one. Borrowing to a certain extent from Maimonides's approach to the problem, R. Isaiah postulates that God's knowledge is equivalent to God's will. However, Horowitz departs from Maimonides's approach in interpreting the nature of the divine will from a kabbalistic perspective. This will is characterized by the *sefirot*, which contain all opposites. Thus all possibilities are always contained within the divine will and humans are free to make their own choices. When the future is revealed to a prophet, it is only conditional. Humans virtually always are free to choose, and the vision of the future revealed, however likely, is not binding until the choices are actually made.

The final chapter, dealing with the central theurgic kabbalistic assumption, is appropriately called, the "Great Gate." The theme of this chapter is, as it were, the entrance into the kabbalistic perspective. The discussion centers on the concept of *Ẓorekh Gavoha*, the divine need for human worship.

Basically, this chapter deals with how, by means of the Torah, Israel is capable of mending the damage that was caused in the world of emanation by Adam's sin. In addition, Horowitz explains the way in which supernal sources respond to Israel's worship and release *shefa'* (divine abundance) into the world below. Horowitz attempts to demonstrate that this kabbalistic principle was contained in scripture, rabbinic writings, and the *Zohar*. Also discussed are the various types of divine union that occur among the *sefirot*. R. Isaiah also takes up the question of how God can remain unchanging if such a divine need exists. Horowitz's solution is that while no true need actually exists, God does derive pleasure when God's will to bestow good is realized. At any rate, only the lower *sefirot* are affected by human worship. The first three, which are closer to the divine essence and beyond human contemplation, remain unaffected.

The final section is entitled the "Great House," because, as Isaiah Horowitz tells us in the introduction, it contains them all. In short, it is a summary of all the principal issues that have been discussed in the previous sections. These include the divine image and likeness of the human body, the change in Adam's nature from garments of light to garments of skin, the light that is concealed for the future, the restoration of God's Name from *YHVH* to *YHYH*, the effect of human free will on the *sefirot*, and the meaning and nature of the World to Come and eternity. All of these are summarized through an ingenious explication of a Talmudic passage involving the similarities of certain Hebrew letters.[63]

Although the themes treated in *Toledot Adam* are many and varied, it is possible to characterize the text as a whole as an attempt to present a kind of comprehensive spiritual history from the sin of Adam until the ultimate stages of the World to Come. Essential to this spiritual history are the centrality and instrumentality of human beings, the generations of Adam, although this concept is understood specifically as the history of the Jews. The kabbalistic cosmos adopted by Isaiah Horowitz emphasizes the continuity of the concealed spiritual and revealed material realms. Nevertheless, it is striking that so much depends on human action. While this emphasis may be said to be already typical of kabbalistic thought in its classical period in Provence and Spain from the turn of the twelfth and thirteenth century, R. Isaiah's essentially eschatological orientation certainly was strengthened by the more recent approaches of Safed in the sixteenth century.

The study and practice of Kabbalah, as presented in *Toledot Adam*, are primarily means for rectifying damage caused by Adam's sin. This damage occurred on all levels of existence, from the divine to the mundane, and, in a sense, altered nature. While the biblical account of the story of Adam seems to speak directly only of the changes that were wrought in human and earthly nature, in Horowitz's kabbalistic account divine nature itself was also impaired. Because of the continuum that connects the phenomenal and spiritual worlds, Adam's act also had ramifications that affected the hidden realm, where God in purest form is manifest as *sefirot* and Divine Names: the World of Emanation. In an important sense, it is this damage to manifest divinity, represented by the Name of God, that has to be repaired by kabbalistic worship. However, Isaiah Horowitz's interests are not so one-sided. The rectification that will occur as a result of the kabbalists' efforts also will result in a spiritualization of the mundane world, including the human body and soul.

However, these effects are not merely restorations of a pristine state. What is essential to Horowitz's Kabbalah is the ultimately superior spiritual state that finally will be achieved at the end of history, despite the progressive degeneration that followed upon Adam's sin. Isaiah Horowitz writes of a future state in which humanity not only will regain the purity that was lost, but indeed will attain a spiritual degree that transcends the original state. This is the inevitable result of the transformative nature of Horowitz's spiritual praxis, in which evil tendencies within the human heart are not merely suppressed but instead actively aroused so that they can be included and also play a part in the spiritual effort. Their energy, so to speak, can then be added to the light that is aroused by the holy motivation that carries out the performance of the divine precepts. The result is that darkness is itself transformed into light, which increases as a result. Consequently, Horowitz's outlook is essentially messianic-eschatological. He looks forward to a time when the ultimate perfection will finally be reached. Humans will attain a level that exceeds even the state of perfection in which they were created.

Some of the most interesting problems that R. Isaiah Horowitz takes up in *Toledot Adam* concern issues that arise from the fact that human action, more precisely the kabbalistic efforts of Jews, is given such emphasis. This is particularly apparent in Horowitz's approach to the problem of free will. His position, somewhat reminiscent of Gersonides, maximizes human freedom. Although there is considerable support for the notion of divine providence in ethical sources that Horowitz otherwise honors,[64] his efforts in providing an explanation that can account for both maximum human freedom and perfect divine knowledge tend to weaken the restrictive implications of the latter. God always knows what occurs, but divine knowledge of the future is only potential. This means two things. First, prophecy is only conditional. The anticipated future need not occur, because human freedom has the power to create an alternative future. Second, although this would seem to compromise the omniscience of God, Horowitz conceives of the potentiality of divine knowledge as inclusive of all possibilities. It is in this way that human beings are free to choose, since all of their possible choices are already potentially present within the divine will. This argument clearly intends to have it both ways. However, while it does preserve human freedom, divine knowledge clearly cannot know the future that human beings will select until they exercise their wills. To put it another way, while divine knowledge includes everything that may occur, it does not have foreknowledge of precisely what will occur.

Clearly, then, in Isaiah Horowitz's kabbalistic outlook the human being is the key player in the spiritual process that has as its goal the attainment of perfection. Although humans have much to benefit from in this achievement, it must be borne in mind that in some real sense the divine manifestation itself awaits this result of human effort and is itself perfected by it. Although the teachings of Isaac Luria are only mentioned a handful of times in *Toledot Adam*, this eschatological outlook suggests Lurianic influence. In Luria's great kabbalistic vision the kabbalist is called upon to restore the divine order to a state that it had yet to achieve, due to a cosmic catastrophe that was intrinsic to the process of emanation. Although Isaiah Horowitz seems to have deliberately refrained from including the mythic details of Luria's account in *Toledot Adam*, and stated elsewhere that he generally was opposed to transmitting such matters in writing, it may still be the case that the general outlook of Luria was nevertheless adopted and presented, shorn of its more controversial and restricted aspects.

Horowitz's great goal in *Toledot Adam* is to show how this awesome task can be humanly achieved. Among the focal points of his explanation are his theory of the Holy Language, the natural law of divine judgment as applied to reward and punishment, and his theory of *devequt*, or cleaving to God.

It has already been mentioned that Isaiah Horowitz views the language of the Torah (Hebrew), which tradition had already dubbed the Holy Language, as unlike all other languages. This means, of course, that whereas all other languages, as human constructs, are a matter of custom and convention, Hebrew, the Holy Language, is a divine creation. However, this distinction is not merely an expression of piety. R. Isaiah's theory has two principal aspects. First, it is meant to indicate that the real object that is communicated by this language is not to be found within the phenomenal world. Although there is an entity in our world of experience that corresponds to each term of the Holy Language, the objects in our world only borrow their names from corresponding entities in the divine world. Thus this theory of language not only is useful for answering the religio-philosophical issue of biblical anthropomorphism, but even more important, it supports the kabbalistic belief that a continuum exists that joins together the objects of our senses' experience and the transcendent entities that constitute the divine realm.

The second important consequence of Isaiah Horowitz's theory of Holy Language is that when it is utilized, whether orally or in writing, by a person in a state of holiness, the Holy Language has the capacity to convey a person's spiritual intention to the divine realm. Conversely, the language also functions as a medium for drawing down *shefa'*, the effluence which flows to the phenomenal world from the divine realm. Thus the theory of Holy Language is essential to Horowitz's argument concerning the special nature of kabbalistic worship.

Another interesting aspect of Isaiah Horowitz's Kabbalah is his theory of the "natural law" of reward and punishment. To a large extent Horowitz's understanding of God takes on a quasi-philosophical impersonal character. God is not emotionally affected by human behavior. Nevertheless, there are divinely determined consequences for human action that inevitably follow. The inevitability of this system of reward and punishment renders it a kind of natural law, a term that Horowitz in fact employs. God does not judge individual cases of human action. Rather, there is a kind of natural law, embedded in the creation itself, which guarantees that a particular action will have appropriate and preordained consequences. This natural law of divine judgment is, in a sense, a kind of kabbalistic version of the Asian theory of Karma. However, this idea of natural law also functions as an aspect of kabbalistic worship. It contributes to a kind of theory of miracles through explaining how performance of precepts with kabbalistic intent not only has consequences for the performer, but also inevitably affects the roots concealed above in the divine realm.

In order to accomplish the kabbalistic task a certain element must be present in the kabbalist which enables him to utilize the continuum joining the phenomenal world and the divine realm as a means for effecting its rectification. This conscious link is what R. Isaiah means by the classical mystical term *devequt*.[65] Specifically, Horowitz defines *devequt*, literally "cleaving (to God)," as knowledge of the kabbalistic secrets that direct acts of worship toward specific ends. Every aspect of worship has a precise purpose to accomplish regarding the particular aspects of the upper worlds and divine realm that are affected by the act in question. Through having this intention clearly in mind at the time of acting, the kabbalist establishes a conscious link between himself and the divine realm. As a result, the kabbalistic intention can be achieved.

All of the matters that we have been discussing are in essence only aspects of the central teaching that is contained in *Toledot Adam*. This is the kabbalistic teaching of *Ẓorekh Gavoha*: performing precepts, praying, and studying Torah in order to fulfill what is needed in the divine realm. In other words, the intention of every religious action is to perform it solely as a means of contributing to the rectification of the flaws in the world of emanation that are the result of Adam's sin. Since the kabbalistic endeavor as conceived by Isaiah Horowitz embraces all aspects of life, and there is an especially important moral and ethical dimension to this practice, it is no exaggeration to say that the teaching of *Ẓorekh Gavoha* can be understood as requiring a state in which one lives one's life exclusively for the sake of heaven. In R. Isaiah's moral-ethical teachings great emphasis is placed on understanding the consequences of each and every act, until the advanced kabbalist lives with a kind of permanent moral dread. This results in a constant awareness of the extent that one's actions affect the divine realm. In another sense the teaching of *Ẓorekh Gavoha* can be understood as a kabbalistic species of the classical spiritual directive to overcome self-centeredness. Just as the kabbalistic God takes on an impersonal character, the person of the kabbalist dissolves into an unself-centered and unceasing effort to advance the process that results in the perfection of God and Creation.

Although *Toledot Adam* is full of original positions concerning key kabbalistic issues, the extent to which Isaiah Horowitz depends on traditional sources cannot be exaggerated. As is typical of his writing throughout *Sheney Luhot ha-Berit*, Horowitz invariably approaches the issue at hand through selecting texts from classical sources and quoting them at great length. It is probably fair to say that considerably more than half of *Toledot Adam* consists of passages that have been cited from other works. These works include not only standard rabbinic works, but also medieval Jewish philosophical texts, ethical works, and, especially, the major kabbalistic sources. The latter include the early rabbinic mystical work *Sefer Yeẓirah*, the late twelfth-century Provencal *Sefer ha-Bahir*, the thirteenth-century kabbalistic classic *Sefer ha-Zohar*, and several other Spanish works by such major kabbalists as Joseph Gikatilla (1248–c.1325) and Menahem Recanati (fl. early fourteenth century). Occasionally Horowitz also cites two of the major kabbalists of sixteenth-century Safed, R. Joseph Karo, author of the halakhic standard *Shulḥan Arukh*, and the diary of teachings from his spirit mentor, *Maggid Mesharim*. However, there is no doubt that his two primary influences in *Toledot Adam* are the Spanish and

Turkish kabbalist Meir Ibn Gabbai (1480–after 1540),[66] and the great Safed master Moshe Cordovero.[67] The influence of these two is significant, since both represent what might be called the classical Kabbalah, before the advent of Isaac Luria's teachings.[68] In particular, R. Isaiah relies on Ibn Gabbai's *'Avodat ha-Qodesh* and Cordovero's *Pardes Rimmonim.*[69] Both are cited more than a dozen times, often at great length.

Finally, we should note that Isaiah Horowitz's great work, *Sheney Luhot ha-Berit*, was not only one of the most popular rabbinic works of the last three hundred years, but had considerable influence on the thought of the early Hasidic masters. Horowitz is cited frequently in Hasidic texts, including the important early anthology *Liqqutim Yeqarim* and in the vast literature of the HaBaD school.[70] Although Horowitz's influence is somewhat varied, it is worthwhile to specify some of the major ways that it was felt in early Hasidism. In general, Isaiah Horowitz can be viewed as one of the principal channels through which elements of Cordovero's Kabbalah were popularized in eastern Europe. Specifically, this influence involved several important aspects. One of the most significant lessons that the Hasidim derived from R. Isaiah's works, *Sheney Luhot ha-Berit* and his commentary on the Prayer Book, *Sha'ar ha-Shamayim*, is the concept of acosmism. The world as such has no independent existence. Rather, as Horowitz interpreted the verse, "*YHVH is God in heaven and on earth, there is nothing else.*"[71] A second major idea that is taken directly from Cordovero is Horowitz's discussion of the *ruḥaniyut*, or spiritual energy, that is contained in the letters of the Hebrew alphabet. This idea had a profound influence on the Hasidic approach to prayer.[72] A third way in which Horowitz certainly influenced early Hasidic thought was through his transformative approach to spirituality. His directive to include the "evil urge" in the spiritual path rather than to suppress it was a hallmark of early Hasidism, before its controversial implications led to its being restricted to the spiritual elite, once Hasidism succeeded as popular movement.[73] It is also possible that R. Isaiah's practice of *hitbonenut*, contemplation of the relationship of creation to the Creator, coupled with his acosmic principle, may have influenced R. Shneur Zalman of Lyadi, who made such contemplation a distinctive feature of HaBaD Hasidism.

In addition to these and other specific areas of influence on Hasidism, Horowitz's work exerted a general and far-reaching influence on eastern European spirituality in general. This was the result of the text's success in popularizing the practical and pietist-ethical aspects of the Kabbalah of Safed, while avoiding in large measure the more abstract and speculative dimensions of its theology.

Notes to the Introduction

[1] See Jacob Elbaum, *Openness and Insularity: Late Sixteenth Century Jewish Literature in Poland and Ashkenaz* (Hebrew) (Jerusalem, 1990).

[2] See Mordecai Pachter, "Elijah de Vidas' *Beginning of Wisdom* and Its Abbreviated Versions," *Qiryat Sefer* 47 (1972), pp. 686–710 (Hebrew). For a translation of part of Jacob Poyetto's condensation (first edition, Venice, 1601) see Lawrence Fine, *Safed Spirituality* (New York: Paulist, 1984).

[3] See Eugene Newman, *Life and Teachings of Isaiah Horowitz* (London, 1972), and H. H. Ben-Sasson, "Isaiah ben Abraham Ha-Levi Horowitz," in *Encyclopedia Judaica* (Jerusalem, 1972), vol. 8, 990–994.

[4] He refers to Prague as his *moledet* (place of birth) in his letters from Jerusalem. See Newman, p. 18.

[5] Ibid.

[6] See Byron Sherwin, *Mystical Theology and Social Dissent* (London, 1982), and Bezalel Safran, "MaHaRaL and Early Hasidism," in *Hasidism: Continuity or Innovation* (Cambridge, 1988).

[7] See Newman, pp. 44–45.

[8] See Elliot Wolfson, "The Influence of Luria on the Shelah" (Hebrew) in *Jerusalem Studies in Jewish Thought*, vol. 10, *Lurianic Kabbalah* (Jerusalem, 1992), p. 430.

[9] See Joseph Avivi, "Lurianic Manuscripts in Italy until the Year 1620," (Hebrew), in *Aley Sefer* 11 (1984), pp. 91–134.

[10] See Wolfson, pp. 428–429.

[11] Ibid.

[12] On the controversy concerning the status of Luria's teachings and the effect of Menahem Azariah's advocacy, see Isaiah Tishby, "*Ha-'Immut beyn*

Qabbalat ha-ARI le-Qabbalat ha-ReMaQ bi-Khetavav u-ve-Hayyav shel R. Aharon Berekhia mi-Modena," in *Studies in Kabbalah and its Branches* (Jerusalem, 1982), pp. 177–254.

[13] See Wolfson, p. 431.

[14] *Maggidim* (lit. speakers or preachers) were spirit mentors. These were often spirits of deceased saints who revealed secret teachings and spiritual instructions through the lips of especially favored mystics. Various meditative techniques were practiced in order to facilitate this experience. See Werblowsky, *Joseph Karo: Lawyer and Mystic* (Philadelphia, 1977), and Lawrence Fine, "Recitation of Mishnah as a Vehicle for Mystical Inspiration: A Contemplative Technique Taught by Ḥayyim Vital," *Revue des Etudes Juives* 141, no. 1–2 (1982): 183–199.

[15] Translated from the Hebrew text published in Newman, p. 204.

[16] Ecclesiastes 7:24.

[17] Proverbs 20:5.

[18] I.e., Isaac Luria, who is identified by the Hebrew letters *ARI* (Lion), an acronym for *Elohi Rabi Isaac* (Divine Rabbi Isaac).

[19] After Psalm 25:14.

[20] *Sha'ar ha-Shamayim* (Jerusalem, 1985), p. 170. Also see Wolfson, pp. 439–440.

[21] See Wolfson.

[22] Literally, "pitched his resting place and dwelling."

[23] *Vavey 'Amudim* (Jerusalem, 1975), introduction, columns 2–3.

[24] See Idel, "Sexual Metaphor and Praxis in the Kabbalah," in David Kraemer, ed., *The Jewish Family* (New York, 1989), pp. 197–224. Seymour J. Cohen, *The Holy Letter: A Study in Jewish Sexual Morality* (Northvale, N.J., 1993).

[25] *Vavey 'Amudim*, introduction, column 2.

[26] This remains for the present in the realm of speculation.

[27] See Newman.

[28] See Krassen, "Visiting Graves," *Kabbalah: A Newsletter of Current Research in Jewish Mysticism*, vol. 3, no. 1 (1988). On Safed spirituality, see Fine, *Safed Spirituality*, Werblowsky, *Joseph Karo: Lawyer and Mystic*, and Schecter, "Safed in the Sixteenth Century—A City of Legists and Mystics," in *Studies in Judaism*, Second Series, pp. 202–285.

[29] See Newman, p. 61.

[30] Genesis 28:17.

[31] See Werblowsky. Also see Louis Jacobs, "The Communications of the Heavenly Mentor to Rabbi Joseph Karo," in *Jewish Mystical Testimonies* (New York, 1977), pp. 98–122.

[32] For a detailed discussion of this issue, see Wolfson.

[33] This entire account follows the facts that have been sifted and recorded by Newman, based on an authentic document, *Ḥorbot Yerusahayim* (*The Destruction of Jerusalem*), published anonymously in Venice in 1627. See Newman, pp. 66–67.

[34] See Newman, p. 68.

[35] Proverbs 6:23.

[36] SheLaH, introduction, p. 20.

[37] See Newman, pp. 74–75.

[38] See below in our remarks on the content of this section.

[39] Deuteronomy 5:2–3.

[40] See the discussion below concerning the SheLaH's influence on Hasidism. Since it is known that R. Shneur Zalman of Lyadi, founder of HaBaD Hasidism, was deeply influenced by the SheLaH, it is highly probable that this section on *hitbonenut* (contemplation) of the various stages of creation, although not in itself representative of the Lurianic cosmology, may have contributed to the technique of contemplation that was developed in HaBaD.

[41] These concepts are explained below in the section on fundamental ideas in *Toledot Adam*.

[42] *Ahavah mesuteret.*

[43] For a discussion of the *sefirot*, see Daniel Matt, *The Zohar: Book of Enlightenment* (New York, 1983), pp. 33–37; Lawrence Fine, "Kabbalistic Texts," in Barry W. Holtz, ed., *Back to the Sources* (New York, 1984), pp. 318–326.

[44] For an English translation of this classic kabbalistic ethical work, see Louis Jacobs, *Palm Tree of Deborah* (New York, 1974).

[45] Deuteronomy 18:13.

[46] Proverbs 3:6.

[47] Psalm 16:8.

[48] Horowitz follows Rashi's definition of *ben Porat* in his commentary on Genesis 49:22, where the term is defined as *ḥen* (grace).

[49] Deuteronomy 4:4.

[50] These six are mentioned in the first chapter of *Avot*.

[51] Although no detailed study of these sections is yet available, a partial account can be found in Newman.

[52] A list of most of these sources appears in Newman, pp. 78–87.

[53] See Jacob Elbaum, *Repentance and Self-Flagellation in the Writings of the Sages of Germany and Poland 1348–1648* (Jerusalem, 1992) p. 179.

[54] Since in Hebrew *Adam* means "human," Newman refers to it as "The Generations of Man."

[55] *Toledot Adam*, "Great House," p. 352.

[56] Literally, the "Work of the Chariot," a reference to mysticism.

[57] The rabbinic text appears in B.T. *Ketubbot*, 75a. See "House of Wisdom," pp. 163 – 164, and see Wolfson's comments on this passage, p. 432.

[58] *Zohar*, v. 3, 73a, quoted at the end of the introduction, p. 58.

[59] Newman calls this chapter "House of Holiness."

[60] This "spiritual" body is discussed by Gershom Scḥolem in his article, "*Tselem*: The Concept of the Astral Body," which is included in his work, *On the Mystical Shape of the Godhead* (New York, 1991), pp. 251 – 273.

[61] Newman's distribution of the chapters on p. 76, footnotes 19 – 29, of his work is only partially complete. The order in which the chapters appear is considerably more complex.

[62] This classic medieval philosophical problem has a long history preceding Isaiah Horowitz's solution. See, for example, Alexander Altmann, "Free Will and Predestination in Saadia, Bahya, and Maimonides" in his *Essays in Jewish Intellectual History* (Hanover, 1981), pp. 35 – 64. For a late Polish Hasidic approach, see Morris Faierstein, *All Is in the Hands of Heaven: The Teachings of Rabbi Mordecai Joseph Leiner of Izbica* (New York, 1989).

[63] The passage is a *baraita* in B.T., *Shabbat*, 103b.

[64] For example, Bahya Ibn Paquda's *Book of the Direction to the Duties of the Heart* (*Ḥovot ha-Levavot*).

[65] The classical discussion of this concept is Scḥolem's article "*Devekut*, or Communion with God," in his *Messianic Idea in Judaism* (New York, 1971), pp. 203 – 227. Scḥolem's discussion has been broadened by Moshe Idel. See, e.g., *Kabbalah: New Perspectives* (New Haven, 1988), pp. 35 – 58. A brief history of the various uses of this term appears in my dissertation, *Devequt and Faith in Zaddiqim: The Religious Tracts of Meshullam Feibush Heller of Zbarazh* (University of Pennsylvania, 1990).

[66] See Elliot K. Ginsburg, *Sod ha-Shabbat (The Mystery of the Sabbath) from the Tola'at Ya'aqov of R. Meir ibn Gabbai* (Albany, 1989).

[67] Cordovero's influence on Isaiah Horowitz is discussed by Bracha Sack in "The Influence of Cordovero on Seventeenth-Century Jewish Thought," in Isadore Twersky and Bernard Septimus, eds., *Jewish Thought in the Seventeenth Century* (Cambridge, 1987), pp. 365 – 372.

[68] The question to what extent Isaac Luria deviated from the classical Kabbalah of *Sefer ha-Zohar* is an interesting one that has not yet been completely decided. Although Scḥolem and his student, Isaiah Tishby, tended to emphasize the innovative quality of Luria's teachings, more recent research,

especially by such scholars as Moshe Idel and Yehuda Liebes, has clarified the extent to which Luria must be regarded as a perceptive interpreter of the *Zohar*, many of whose "innovations" can be found in earlier kabbalistic sources. In addition, Bracha Sack's studies of Cordovero's writings have disclosed that many of the "classic Lurianic concepts" were already present in his teacher's thought. On the relationship of Luria to the *Zohar*, see Yehuda Liebes, "The Messiah of the Zohar: On R. Simeon bar Yohai as a Messianic Figure," in his *Studies in the Zohar* (Albany, 1993). On the notion of "the classical Kabbalah," see Elliot K. Ginsburg, *The Sabbath in the Classical Kabbalah* (Albany, 1989).

[69] Although Bracha Sack has demonstrated that Cordovero's oeuvre does contain concepts that previously had been considered Lurianic innovations, for the most part these are not to be found in Cordovero's early work *Pardes Rimmonim*. See the previous two footnotes.

[70] For a general discussion of Horowitz's influence on Hasidism, see Bracha Sack, "Cordovero's Influence on Hasidism (Hebrew)" in *Eshel Be'er Sheva* 3 (1986), pp. 229–246. On Horowitz's influence on the HaBaD school, see Roman A. Foxbrunner, *HaBaD: The Hasidism of R. Shneur Zalman of Lyady* (Tuscaloosa, 1992), pp. 45–46, 132, 133; and Naftali Loewenthal, *Communicating the Infinite: The Emergence of the Habad School* (Chicago, 1990), p. 146.

[71] Deuteronomy 4:39. The acosmic interpretation appears, among other places, in *Sheney Luhot ha-Berit*, *Asarah Ma'amarot*, first discourse, toward the beginning. For a discussion of acosmism and its theological and practical implications in the HaBaD school, see Rachel Elior, *The Paradoxical Ascent to God* (Albany, 1993).

[72] See Miles Krassen, *Devequt and Faith in Zaddiqim* (University of Pennsylvania dissertation, 1990), p. 268. Also see Moshe Idel, "Perceptions of Kabbalah in the Second Half of the Eighteenth Century," in *Jewish Thought in the Eighteenth Century*.

[73] This matter is discussed by Mendel Piekarz in *The Beginning of Hasidism: Ideological Trends in Derush and Musar Literature* (Hebrew) (Jerusalem, 1978), pp. 211, 389.

The Generations of Adam (Toledot Adam)

Introduction

For the sake of uniting the Holy One, blessed be He, and His *Shekhinah* by means of that hidden and concealed One: Blessed is *YHVH* forever.

"*For the commandment is a lamp and the Torah is light and the way to life is the rebuke that disciplines.*"[1]

The simple meaning of the verse is that the commandment is like a lamp that shines before you, as it is written, "*The commandment of YHVH is clear, enlightening the eyes.*"[2] And the Torah is as light for those that study it, "*whereas a fool walks in darkness.*"[3] Now "lamp" and "light" have two meanings. First, a single source of light[4] is called a lamp, while "light" refers to a great bonfire. This accords with the reckoning of our sages of blessed memory, "study is great[er] than action because it leads to action."[5] The commandment, which is action, is called a lamp; the Torah, which is study, is called light.

According to the second explanation, a lamp itself is directly connected to light. For it is the lamp that receives the light, for example, a candle or wick in oil placed in a vessel. The light takes hold of it and they cleave together.[6] Each requires the other, since the lamp's light can only take hold because of the lamp. For it is the nature of light to return to its source when it lacks something to take hold of. Also, a lamp can only cast light because of the light that takes hold of it. Similarly, in the case of the commandment, study is the cause of action. As we have learned, "Hillel says, an ignorant person does not fear sin."[7] However, study has nothing to take hold of without action. As we have learned, "R. Hanina ben Dosa says, whenever one's fear of sin precedes his wisdom, his wisdom endures."[8] These two teachings seem to contradict each other. But if you examine them well, you will see that both are true. A person is not able to reach the crown of Torah if he has not prepared himself in fear of sin, so that his soul and pure heart long for *devequt* with God, blessed be He. Otherwise, it is said concerning him, "*and God said to the wicked, who are you to recite My laws?*"[9] Consequently, one has to clothe himself so that fear of *YHVH* is evident.[10]

However, still concealed from him are the specifics of fear of sin, along with the principles and details of the commandments, laws, and statutes [that must be learned] before one merits the crown of Torah. For then one goes from study to action in the fullest possible sense.

There is still another matter to resolve and it is more internal. The Torah is both practical and theoretical, revealed and concealed.[11] The revealed aspect of Torah involves fulfilling its commandments, which are 248 positive commandments, and observing its cautions, which are 365 prohibitions. For both types of commandments there are concealed reasons, divine secrets. All of these are connected to His great Name.[12] Concerning those who know [these secrets], it is said, "*I shall uplift him because he knew My name.*"[13] And in them the verse is fulfilled, "*and you who cleave to YHVH, your God.*"[14]

Now the order of the levels is as follows. "An ignorant person does not fear sin."[15] So one must first learn the 613 commandments. Then study will lead to action and one will become a fearer of sin. Once one has attained this, every action becomes a ladder for ascending to the theoretical, which is the concealed part [of the Torah]. Then he will merit "*to gaze on the pleasantness of YHVH.*"[16] This is the true wisdom, knowing the secrets of the commandments which are divine secrets. But in order to obtain this wisdom, one must first acquire fear of sin. As it is written, "*Behold, fear of the Lord is wisdom.*"[17] Then "his wisdom endures."[18] Mysteries of the Torah will be revealed to him so that he will be "a sage who understands from his own mind."[19] We have seen for ourselves and [also] heard of many pious ones who, before concerning themselves with divine secrets, would examine their deeds, confess their sins, and clothe themselves in fear of God.

Afterward he said,[20] "*And the way of life is the rebuke that disciplines.*"[21] First, he spoke concerning one's own perfection. One should be complete in "*the commandment is a lamp and the Torah is light.*" Afterward, one should perfect others as well. This is the way to eternal life: to merit and cause others to merit "to study and teach, to observe [restrictions], and to do . . ."[22] and never to refrain from rebuking others and teaching them wisdom and discipline to grasp words of understanding. Thus he used the expression "way," just as Jethro said to our teacher, Moses, "*And you caution them concerning the laws and teachings and you let them know the way they should follow and the deed they shall do.*"[23]

He said, "*the rebuke that disciplines,*" which is redundant. The meaning is rebuke concerns the past, if they departed from the good and straight way. And discipline means instructing them in the way that they should follow hereafter. As it is written, "*Heed discipline and become wise, do not spurn it.*"[24]

Rebuke is a positive commandment, as it is written, "*You shall rebuke your fellow.*"[25] It is a very great commandment. In tractate *Shabbat*, chapter *kol kitvey*,[26] [is written],

> Rav Amram, the son of Rav Simeon bar Abba, said in the name of his father that Rabbi Hanina said that Jerusalem was only destroyed because they did not rebuke each other. As it is said, "*Her leaders were like stags that found no pasture.*"[27] Just as in the case of stags, one's head is next to the other's tail, so Israel in that period hid their faces in the earth [and did not rebuke each other].[28]

And in chapter *bameh behemah*[29] [is written],

> Whoever could have forewarned his household and did not do so is held responsible for [the wrongdoings of] his household, [if he failed to forewarn] the residents of his city, he is held responsible for [the wrongdoings of] the residents of his city, [if he failed to forewarn] the entire world,[30] he is held responsible for the [wrongdoings of] the entire world.[31]
>
> It is also written in that chapter,[32]
>
> Rav Aha bar Hanina said no good measure ever went out of the mouth of the Holy One, blessed be He, and was changed to evil except for this matter. As it is written, "*And YHVH said to him, pass into the midst of the city . . . and put a mark on the foreheads of the men who moan and groan because of the abominations that are done . . .* "[33] The Holy One, blessed be He, said to Gabriel, "Go and record a mark of ink on the foreheads of the righteous, so that the avenging angels will not have power over them and a mark of blood on the foreheads of the wicked, so that the avenging angels will have power over them." The attribute of judgment said before the Holy One, blessed be He, "How are these different from those?" He replied, "These are completely righteous and those are completely wicked." [The attribute of judgment then] said,

> "They could have forewarned them and did not." He replied, "It is clear to Me that if [the righteous] had forewarned them, [the wicked] would not have accepted it." [The attribute of judgment] answered, "Master of the Universe, it may be clear to You [that the rebuke would not be accepted], but is it clear to them?" That is why it is written, "*Kill the old ones, youth and maiden, infants and women. However, do not go near anyone who has a mark. Begin at My Sanctuary.*"[34]

And Rashi comments,

> At first He said, "do not go near," and finally He said, "Begin at My Sanctuary."[35] "And it is written, '*So they began with the elders who were before the House.*'[36] Rav Joseph taught, do not read '*at My Sanctuary,*' but '*with My sanctified.*'[37] These are people who fulfilled the entire Torah from A to Z."[38]

In the Maimuni glosses to the sixth chapter of the *Hilkhot De'ot*, it says:

> However, if it is clear to him that they will not accept [the forewarning], then it seems that he is exempt [from the commandment to rebuke]. For the attribute of judgment said before the Holy One, blessed be He, "It may be clear to You [that they would not accept the rebuke], but is it clear to them?" The meaning is that if it was clear to them [that the wicked would not accept their forewarning], they would not be punished [for failing to rebuke them]. And the same meaning appears in the *Tosefta* to chapter *ḥezqat ha-battim*. And so he wrote[39] in *Sefer ha-Mizvot*, "It is good for him to be silent. For it is preferable for Israel to be unknowing transgressors."[40] And RAM wrote that he is exempt from the punishment, but not from the act of "*and you shall rebuke.*"[41] But Rabbi Moses of Coucy wrote concerning one who performs the act of levirate marriage, just as one must say something which will be heeded, so it is a commandment not to say something that will not be heeded. As it is written, "*Do not rebuke a fool lest he hate you.*"[42,43]

It seems to me that evidence to support RAM's view, that one is not exempt from the act of "*you shall rebuke,*" can be brought from chapter *yesh be-'arakhin*. "To what point does the commandment to rebuke apply? Rav said until [one receives] blows and Samuel said until cursing and Rabbi Yohanan said until [one is] reproached."[44] Clearly [Rav] thought that even if the point of reproaching [the rebuker] and even cursing [him] had already been reached and one then knows for certain that his rebuke will not be accepted, nevertheless he is not exempt from the act of "*you shall rebuke*" until he receives blows. And the Maimuni to chapter six of the *Hilkhot De'ot* ruled according to Rav's view, even though the author of *Sefer Mizvot Gadol* is surprised at him and ruled according to the view of Rabbi Yohanan. For, [according to a halakhic rule], where Rav and Rabbi Yohanan disagree, the *halakhah* is according to Rabbi Yohanan's view, and even more so in regard to Samuel's view in cases of prohibition.

Nevertheless, the *Hagahot Maimuni* wrote,

> In the *Midrash Tanhuma, ki tis'a*, the interpretation agrees with the words of our teacher, the author who said, "The attribute of judgment said, 'Master of the Universe, how are these different from those?' " . . . "Nevertheless, they should have allowed themselves to be shamed for the sake of sanctifying Your name and have taken upon themselves to receive blows from Israel, just as the prophets suffered. For Jeremiah and Isaiah bore many afflictions from Israel. As it is written, '*I gave my back to floggers.*' "[45] Immediately, the Holy One, blessed be He, reversed Himself and said to the avenging angels, "[Kill] *the old and young, infants and women.*"[46]

Also, in answer to the *Sefer Mizvot Gadol*, which ruled according to Rabbi Yohanan's view—that [one must rebuke] until being reproached and no further—it is proven from the views of Rav and Samuel that even when one knows that his rebuke will not be accepted, there is an obligation to rebuke. For Samuel, who is more lenient than Rav, reasons that even after being reproached, when one knows for certain that [his rebuke] will not be accepted, one is obligated to rebuke. And Rabbi Yohanan does not differ with Rav and Samuel on this point. But he reasons that the rebuker does not have to suffer the maximum and to rebuke after being reproached. Nevertheless, he does not deny that he was obligated to rebuke before being reproached even though he had reason to believe that the rebuke would not be accepted. Furthermore, it is said that Rabbi Yohanan dissents and his reason for holding [that one must rebuke] until being reproached and no further is that then it is revealed to him that his rebuke that disciplines will not be accepted. Consequently, it is not proper to rule according to the view of

Rabbi Yohanan, who is alone in this reasoning against Rav and Samuel, who believe that the command of rebuking applies even after one has been reproached, at which point we [already] know for certain that the rebuke will not be accepted. Since the words of Rabbi Yohanan are cancelled by the weight of their two opinions, it is proper to rule according to Rav's view. For, [according to a halakhic rule], when Rav and Samuel disagree, the *halakhah* is according to Rav's view in cases of prohibitions. It is possible that this is the reason that the Maimuni ruled according to Rav.

Now for the issue raised in chapter *ha-ba 'al yevimeto*.[47]

> Rabbi Elai said in the name of Rabbi Eleazar ben Rabbi Simeon that just as it is a commandment to say something that will be heeded, so one is commanded not to say something that will not be heeded. Rabbi Abba says it is a duty, as it is said, "*Do not rebuke a fool, lest he hate you, rebuke a wise person and he will love you.*"[48, 49]

I say that this is a separate matter in its own right and concerns a case where the sinners do not know that what they are doing is forbidden. They mock the rebuker and will transgress in any case. Consequently, it is better for them to be inadvertent transgressors and not to be intentional violators. This is similar to the matter that is found in tractate *Shabbat*, chapter *shoel*, and in tractate *Beyẓah*, chapter *ha-mevi'*, concerning adding time to the Day of Atonement. Although we see that they are eating and drinking [on the eve of the Day of Atonement] until it becomes dark, we do not say anything to them for the reason that it is better that they transgress inadvertently rather than flagrantly.

The Maimuni writes as follows in the first chapter of *Hilkhot Shevitat Asor*:

> [In the case of] women who are eating and drinking [on the eve of the Day of Atonement] until it becomes dark and who do not know that it is a commandment to add from profane time to sacred time, one does not admonish them so that they will not become intentional transgressors. For it is impossible for there to be an enforcer in each and every house to caution them. And it is better for them to be inadvertent transgressors and not to be intentional. And so it is in similar matters.[50]

Here is what Rabbi Asher ben Yehiel[51] wrote on tractate *Beyẓah* at the beginning of chapter *ha-mevi'*:

> The author of the *Ittur*[52] wrote that this applies precisely to laws that are the result of interpretation, such as additional self-affliction on the Day of Atonement. However, for matters that are explicitly written in the Torah, we rebuke concerning such a matter and punish them until they desist.

Thus the reason is that since the prohibition is not completely clear, we are concerned lest they not believe us and be lead astray. Therefore, there is an obligation not to mention a matter that will not be heard, since it is better that they be inadvertent transgressors. But when a prohibition is well known and clear, "*you shall surely rebuke*,"[53] even a hundred times.

There is more to say concerning the statement of Rabbi Eleazar ben Simeon "not to say something which will not be heard," in other words, in the case of a person who mocks the words of the rebuker and laughs at him. For even when Israel were sinners and did not heed the voice of their prophets, it was not a matter of mockery. Rather, they were led astray by false prophets and thought that their words were true. Similarly, when one rebukes his fellow, he may respond by saying, "I did not do such a thing." Or, he may say, "Indeed, I did that." Thus it is necessary to rebuke in a manner that is appropriate to the response. However, if one laughs at the words of the rebuker and makes fun of him, it is incumbent on the rebuker not to speak. It is also possible to interpret the statement of Rabbi Eleazar ben Simeon as applying to one who wishes to assume a greater stringency and to rebuke beyond the measure that requires that the rebuke be appropriate to the response. Thus he said that it will do no good and that it is good not to say something that will not be heard, as implied by the verse, "*Do not rebuke a fool.*"[54]

In light of the Maimuni's ruling, it seems to me that his reasoning is as I have explained. One should rebuke like a pillar of iron, even where those of great stature are involved. In chapter *Ḥeleq* [of tractate *Sanhedrin*] is written, "Why did Jeroboam merit kingship? Because he rebuked Solomon."[55] In the last chapter of tractate *Ketubbot* is written, "That student of the rabbis was spared, not because he was more highly regarded (*ma'ale tafe*), but because he did not rebuke them."[56] Now our rabbis of blessed memory interpreted the verse, "*A person shall stumble over his brother*,"[57] as meaning "because of the transgression of his brother. [It teaches that] all Israel are responsible for each other."[58] But once he has fulfilled the commandment of rebuking, he is released from this responsibility.

Just as it is a great commandment for the rebuker to rebuke, it is a great commandment for the one rebuked to accept the rebuke. In the first chapter of tractate *Tamid* is written,

> It is taught in a *baraitha*, Rabbi says, what is the straight way that a person should choose? He should love rebuking. For whenever there is rebuking in the world, well being (*naḥat ruaḥ*) comes to the world. Good and blessing come to the world and evil leaves the world. As it is written, "*There will be comfort for the rebukers and the blessing of good will come upon them.*"[59,60]

And in chapter *Yesh be-Arakhin*:

> Rabbi Yohanan ben Nuri said, "I make heaven and earth my witnesses that many times Akiva was punished by lashes as a result of my complaining about him before Rabban Simeon the son of Gamaliel and all the more I increased his love, in keeping with the verse, '*Do not rebuke a fool lest he hate you; rebuke a sage and he will love you.*'"[61,62]

Thus the greatness of the commandment of rebuking has been explained. It is therefore worthwhile for each person to express words of rebuke according to his ability. It is true that everything mentioned above concerns the need to rebuke for a transgression that has already been committed. Nevertheless, we can also learn from this to take a stand and admonish concerning the future, to indicate the good and upright way. Those who fear heaven fulfill both of these obligations. For rebuking over the past and teaching ethical behavior for the future are both included in our rebuking. There is one reason in praise of both of them: "*So that they will hearken and learn . . . and take care to fulfill all the words of Torah.*"[63] Our Rabbi Moses, peace be upon him, did both after he had taught Torah and commandments to all of Israel. When the time came for him to travel the ways of eternal life, close to his death, he fulfilled the commandment of ethical rebuke. "*These are the words . . . ,*"[64] words of rebuke. He rebuked them for their past sins from the time that they departed from Egypt, and he taught them ethical behavior for the future. This involved both fulfilling the Torah and its commandments through learning and deeds and taking on such qualities as would lead to *devequt* with the Blessed One and to following His ways and attributes as is explained in many of the verses in Deuteronomy. And know, my sons, may God protect them, that all of the ethical teachings that are mentioned in the words of our rabbis, of blessed memory, in the

Talmud and Midrash, and what was later expounded by the authors of works of repentance and ethics, as well as by those who speak of the secret of *devequt*, such as the Holy Rabbi Simeon bar Yohai, peace be upon him, in the *Zohar* and *Tiqquney Zohar*, and those who followed after him, both early and later masters, all of these are alluded to in the ethical teachings of our Rabbi Moses, peace be upon him. A person of insight will see with the eye of the intellect that all is well explained. Fortunate is the eye that has seen all of these.

"*And these are the words which Moses said*"[65] when he was close to his death, while following the Way of Life. The way which the lord of prophets followed was also pursued by the prophets: rebuking Israel [for past sins] and cautioning them concerning the future. They did this most of all close to their departure from the world. Thus did Joshua, Moses' disciple. Similarly, concerning Samuel, is written, "*And it came to pass when Samuel grew old.*"[66] Also earlier in Israel our forefather Jacob summoned his sons before his death. Such is the way of all of the righteous; at the time of their departure they concern themselves most [with such instruction].

I know that my soul has not merited to be numbered among the righteous, nevertheless, it is written, "*Go forth after the sheep and shepherd your flocks.*"[67] Therefore, I will follow the footprints of the early masters to know wisdom and ethics in order to impart words of understanding for the Lord's blessed, my sons and daughters, my sons-in-law and daughters-in-law, my grandchildren, and their children, and the children of their children, forever. May they stand upon the blessing and may the Lord increase it a thousandfold. I shall compose a work of ethical rebuke for them, just as a person would instruct his son. For now is the time for me to speak, since I am taking leave of them in order to take repose, with God's help, in the Holy Land. In chapter *'Elu megalḥin* is written, "Resh Lakish said to Rabbi Yohanan, Elijah lives. He said to him, since it is written, '*and they did not see him again*,'[68] as far as he is concerned, he is like a dead person."[69] I apply to myself the verse with which I began, by way of allusion, "*and a way of life is the rebuke that disciplines.*"[70] It is the way to God's Presence, the Land of Life. For there the Lord commanded the blessing of eternal life.

"*Fortunate are they whose way is blameless, who follow the Torah of YHVH.*"[71] For I have meditated in order to find support for every ethical teaching in words of Torah, in length, breadth, and depth, so that they will more readily enter the heart. Thus our prayer will be fulfilled which says, "to learn and to teach, to guard and to do" and also a saying of our rabbis of blessed memory, "One who takes leave of his friend should only do so from the midst of words of Torah, for thus he will recall him."[72] By "words of

Torah" they meant pleasant basic teachings (*peshatim*), which are ethical insights that enter deep within the heart. Thus they specifically used the expression "from the midst of words of Torah." For I have already indicated the need for words of ethical instruction when one takes leave of his fellow. When such ethical instruction is adorned and beautified by words of Torah, it enters more deeply into the heart. Thus we say in the blessing, "great love," "allow our hearts to understand and know, to hear, and to learn and teach, to keep."[73] Then "*the Torah of his God is in his heart*"[74] and fulfilled is "your faith within his heart." Thus they said "from the midst of words of Torah."

These ethical words of Torah bear fruit and make an impression because they enter the heart. Such learning leads to action. Thus when the opportunity arises to act, one remembers the friend who taught him this matter. Therefore the saying ends, "thus he will recall him." So remembering and acting are connected. In other words, he saw the deed and recalled the *halakhah*: the simple words of Torah that were said concerning this, and he remembers who said them. Thus he brings redemption, as it is taught, "Whoever says a word in the name of the one who said it brings redemption to the world"[75] and if he is dead, "*the lips of the sleeping tremble.*"[76,77] Thus there are two aspects to the recalling: the deed causes him to remember the *halakhah*, that is, the words of Torah, and he remembers his friend. Both together are good. As the verse alludes, "*The commandment is a lamp.*"[78] This is the case in its fullness and goodness from all that we have said when it becomes a way of life. Then one will be sure to depart with "*a rebuke that disciplines*" and a rebuke that disciplines will be with "*Torah is light.*" Then he will merit "*the commandment is a lamp,*" for learning leads to action.

In order to fulfill this verse, "*for the commandment is a light,*" I considered the commandment of our rabbis of blessed memory who said, "Whoever begins a commandment is told, finish the matter, and not merely half of it."[79] For since I intended to be of benefit to you, my children, may God protect them, to make you worthy of the World to Come, I meditated that it is impossible to reach the purpose of *devequt* except through "*the commandment is a lamp and the Torah is light,*" I mean by arousing you concerning the act of the commandment and cautioning you about some matters concerning the prohibitions and positive commandments. For admonishment is not offered for many of them. This is for two reasons. First, sometimes it is a result of what our rabbis of blessed memory have said, "When a person has committed a transgression and repeated it, it appears to him as permitted."[80] Due to our many transgressions, there are many immured in them who walk in darkness. As our rabbis of blessed memory testified concerning robbery, sexual impropriety, and evil speech, "The majority are guilty of robbery, a minority is guilty of sexual impropriety, and all besmirch themselves in the dust of evil speech."[81] I will give you a sign concerning this. There is no command that does not have some relation to the sin of the *'egel* (golden calf). For the letters of "*'eGeL*" are the first letters of these three sins, *'arayot* (sexual impropriety), *Gazel* (robbery), and *Lashon Ha-ra'* (evil speech). That is why "we have robbed, we have slandered, we have acted perversely" are grouped together in the confession. For "acted perversely" alludes to sexual impropriety. As the author of the *Rokeaḥ* wrote in his secrets,[82] when *'AVoN* (iniquity) is spelled *'yn Vv Nun* it equals 248. For the only transgression that is felt by all 248 limbs is fornication. Thus our rabbis of blessed memory bore witness that these three are extremely serious transgressions and are commonplace.

But there is another cause as well. It is sometimes due to lack of knowledge. For this commandment and that issue are not known to the multitude and a matter of common parlance. Therefore I need to inform you concerning it. There are also a number of original insights, which I have arrived at with God's help, and which have not been mentioned by my predecessors. All of this comes under the heading, "*The commandment is a lamp.*"

"*The Torah is light*" will be realized through knowing the reasons for the commandments and their secrets, concerning which it is said, "*A person will do them and live in them.*"[83] As it is said, "*will do*" means the actual doing of the commandment and "*live in them*" means *devequt* through the implications of the commandment, which is the spiritual vitality of the commandment. As a result of this spirituality, which is contained in thought, one has *devequt* with His Blessed Name. For the *kavvanah* (intention)[84] of the commandment is the secret of His Blessed Name. Other than this, there is no *devequt* leading from the corporeal action to the spirituality which is the ultimate spirituality, His Blessed Name.

Also prayer, the service of our heart, which has replaced Temple offerings (*QuRBan*), which bring one close (*meQaReV*) and cause us to cleave to the Blessed One, must be a prayer with *kavvanah*. Then it is a body with a soul. The "body" of the prayer is the order that has been arranged for us by our sages of blessed memory in fear and trembling, while its "soul" is the *kavvanah*, the secrets of prayer. Our rabbis of blessed memory said, "Why is it that Israel prays and is not answered? Because they do not know how to pray with the Name. As it is written, '*for he knew My Name. He will call Me and I will answer him.*'[85]"[86] I have already mentioned at the beginning of the introduction that "learning leads to action" and action leads to insight (*'iyyuni*). Thus we may understand the order in the blessing, *'ahavah rabbah*, which says, "Allow our hearts to understand and know, to hear, to learn, and to teach, to keep, and to do, and to fulfill." We ask for learning that will bring us to action so that we may do and fulfill. Afterward we ask, "Enlighten our eyes in Your Torah and cause our hearts to cleave to Your commandments, and unite our hearts to love and fear Your Name." This means that the Blessed Holy One should enlighten us concerning the secrets of the commandments. Concerning this, King David also prayed, "*Roll my eyes that I may see wonders from Your Torah*."[87] Thus we can cleave to His Holy Name in love and fear. It is explained in the *Zohar* and in the writings of the kabbalists that from the corporeality of the commandment, Torah, and prayer, that is, action and speech, garments are made for the soul and the level of the lower Garden of Eden. But there is no contact or *devequt* with the supernal Garden of Eden, which involves very subtle spiritual levels, except through the *kavvanot*, which are the secret knowledge of the Divine Names. However, I will only speak of this fine subject later, in its place. For now I am only mentioning its main points as far as is necessary.

Know, my children, may God protect them, that you must not think that what I will mention of the secrets of the commandments and prayer in these pages means that I have reached the very depth of the matter, or even so much as a drop compared to the great sea. For there is no end to these secrets. If a person could live for a thousand years twice over, he would not reach the ultimate degree of a single commandment in its depth, root, and supreme root. The exception is Rabbi Simeon bar Yohai and his associates, whose dwelling place was not among ordinary mortals. His students also had a great knowledge, as well as their students, who had the merit to enjoy his great light. But not every mind is capable of this. As for me, I have only come to reveal very little of what I received from the mouth of writers and books that follow the *Zohar*, especially the great later masters, the holy books of the divine Rabbi Meir Ibn Gabbai of blessed memory,[88] and the divine Rabbi Moses Cordovero of blessed memory,[89] and the last great master, the divine one, the Holy Lion of blessed memory (Rabbi Isaac Luria).[90] I will add a bit of what I have arrived at with my own understanding in uniting the various matters in order to comprehend them. It is known that holiness is an endless spring. If a person sanctifies himself a bit below, he is sanctified a lot from above and the Holy One will grace him with wisdom, understanding, and knowledge. Then he will merit to enter the innermost chambers, through many myriad good levels to the Presence, blessed be He.

Thus these pamphlets I am bequeathing to you are the triple thread of the "*rebuke that disciplines*" and "*the commandment is a lamp*" and "*Torah is light*." They are indicated by "*MeNaT ḥelqi*" (my portion), which alludes to *musar* (ethics), *ner* (lamp), and Torah.

Since students are also called children,[91] and, thanks to God, I have managed to acquire many students, if any of the students should desire to copy the pamphlets, I order you not to withhold the good from those who have a right to it. As for you, my children, hearken to the ethical instruction of your father, let it be a memorial between your eyes. Bequeath the pamphlets to your children. For this is your life and the length of your days. Most of all, my children, may God preserve them, be careful concerning additional holiness and purity and *devequt*, for "*there are many aspects to wisdom*,"[92] infinitely more than I have recalled. This is all the more so since I write in great haste at the time of departure for the skilled way to the Holy Land in order to cleave to the Land of Life. Thus I am calling these pamphlets *Way to Life*, and also because of the verse "*the commandment is a lamp . . . and a way to life*."[93] It is the way to eternal life. Since "as much as the sole of the foot can tread on" has three sections, as mentioned in the laws pertaining to torn animals and *kashrut* of the leg, I will arrange three sections for the straight leg that would tread the path to the Tree of Life:

Section 1: Ten Utterances
Section 2: Ten Commandments
Section 3: Ten Praises

These three sections bring a human being, who is the purpose of creation, to his true end. Thus the Men of the Great Assembly established the prayer for New Year's Day which says, "This is the day on which the first human was created," for he is the purpose of creation. As we say in tractate *Rosh ha-Shanah*, "According to whose view do we now pray, 'This day is the beginning of Your deeds?' According to the view of Rabbi Eliezer, who holds that the world was created on the 25th of *Elul* and man, who is the principle of creation, was created on New Year's Day, the sixth day."[94] The Men of the Great Assembly established the saying of ten verses of sovereignty, memorial, and the ram's horn, corresponding to the three matters mentioned above. We read in tractate *Rosh ha-Shanah*,

> Those ten verses of sovereignty correspond to what? Rabbi says that they correspond to the ten praises that David said in the Book of Psalms. Rav Joseph says they correspond to the ten commandments that were spoken to Moses on Sinai. Rabbi Yohanan said they correspond to the ten utterances with which the world was created.[95]

Now there is a definite order to the saying of the sages. They place the words of Rav Joseph before those of Rabbi Yohanan, even though the latter preceded him by a long time. See *Pardes Rimmonim*, chapter eight of *Gate 2: Reason for the Emanation*, where Cordovero explained this according to the kabbalistic secret. However, according to the plain meaning, it seemed to him that we consider the order from above to below. In other words, the order should be ten utterances of the act of creation, ten commandments in the giving of the Torah, and the ten praises in the book of Psalms. However, due to Rabbi's honor, he was placed first and the order proceeds from below to above.

Nevertheless, one might still ask why [Rabbi] skipped [to ten praises] when he should have said that "the [ten verses of sovereignty] correspond to the ten utterances." The same question can be raised in regard to Rav Joseph's view. You may answer such a person that each one spoke according to his level of cleaving and attribute. This is similar to what is said in chapter *Ḥeleq*:

> What is the name of Messiah? Those of the school of Rabbi Shila said, "His name is Shiloh," as it is written, "*until Shiloh comes*."[96] Those of the school of Rabbi Yannai said, "His name is Yinnon," as it is written, "*May his name be forever before the sun, his name is Yinnon*."[97] Rabbi Hanina said, "Hanina is his name."[98]

Rashi commented that each one based his answer on his own name. Similarly, here each one spoke according to his attribute and *devequt*. Rabbi, who was descended from the House of David, said that they correspond to the ten praises which David said. Rav Joseph was Sinai, as is said, "Rav Joseph is Sinai, Rabbah is an uprooter of mountains."[99] Therefore Rav Joseph said that they correspond to the ten commandments that were spoken on Sinai. As for Rabbi Yohanan, "The beauty of Rabbi Yohanan was like the beauty of Adam,"[100] who was the praise of the work of creation. Thus he said that they correspond to the ten utterances. Concerning the "beauty of Rabbi Yohanan," a statement in chapter *ha-po'alim* in tractate *Baba Meẓi'a* goes too far and is refuted,

> Is he [so beautiful]? But Mar said, the beauty of Rav Kahana is like the beauty of Rabbi Abbahu and the beauty of Rabbi Abbahu is like the beauty of our forefather Jacob. The beauty of our forefather Jacob is like the beauty of Adam. But Rabbi Yohanan is not considered so. Rabbi Yohanan is different because he lacks a beard.[101]

The meaning is that the beauty of Rabbi Yohanan was also comparable to the beauty of Adam, whose heel outshone the sun. This is the reason for the order of these three. However, the basic order is ten utterances, ten commandments, ten praises. Thus I called the three sections by these names.

I considered it important to begin with an introduction that would reveal to you how awesome is man and to let you know the meaning of his formation, image, likeness, Torah, and end. For it all reaches the highest heights. His hand rules over everything, making an impression that ascends to the highest level above, to cleave to the Blessed One. If he acts negatively, the result is the opposite, an awesome descent, God forbid. In seeing this a wise person's heart will be aroused to be perfect with YHVH our God, to follow His words, and to cleave to Him with the levels of *deveqah*, *ḥasheqah*, and *ḥafeẓah*,[102] with great and eternal love.[103] He will take to heart all the words of "*ethical rebuke*," "*the commandment is a lamp*," and "*the Torah is light*." Even more, the sage will hearken and increase the lesson.

Thus I am giving this introduction the name *Toledot Adam* (*The Generations of Adam*), since in it will be revealed the events of human life in this world and the next. This is similar in meaning to the verse, "*These are the toledot of Jacob, Joseph*,"[104] where the meaning of "*toledot*" is "events." Discussed in this introduction is the level of the individual person, and afterward, the collective "Adam," the Israelite people, who are called "Adam," as they explained, "*for the portion of YHVH is His people*."[105] "*The righteous one will rejoice for he has seen . . .*"[106] and he will say this is our God. This I am beginning with the help of God, my Rock and Redeemer.

". . . *in the Name of YHVH. This is the book of the generations of Adam, in the day that God created the human, He made him in the image of God*."[107] "*Male and female He created them and He blessed them and called their name, Adam, in the day that they were created*."[108] Adam was created in the image of God to know that *YHVH* is God, and to be like God. These are the three roots of existence: the root of the existence of *YHVH*, the root of the Torah of *YHVH*, the root of *devequt* with the Name.

Adam was made and created in the image of God. He is a sign and indication of the divine existence. This is the secret of the verse "*and on the likeness of the throne a likeness like the appearance of Adam*."[109] It is also written, "*And from my flesh I see God*."[110] I will explain all of this at length, if God will be with me.

As for being created to know that *YHVH* is God, this is by means of God's Torah. As it is written concerning the giving of the Torah, "*You have been shown to know that YHVH is God, there is no other beside Him.*"[111] We will explain this at length and the meaning of this knowing.

Adam's ultimate purpose is to be like God through *devequt* with His Name. As it is written, "*You who are cleaving (ha-deveqim) to YHVH, your God, are all alive today.*"[112] This is the true reward to be eternal like God. This verse, "*and you who are cleaving . . .* " means while still living in this world and refers to the matter of "*today to do them,*"[113] to cleave to God by means of His commandments and attributes. Nevertheless, it is this very *devequt* of "*today to do them*" that is the essential cause of "tomorrow: to receive their reward,"[114] *devequt* in the life of the world to come. This is eternal spiritual life, which is the secret of "the reward of a commandment is a commandment and the reward of a transgression is a transgression."[115] For reward and punishment are not determined by convention, but are essential, the true vitality of the world to come, contained in their roots above. The same may be said regarding transgressions, God spare us. The punishment of the transgression is the transgression itself, that is, its evil root, "*poison weed and wormwood.*"[116] God willing, this matter will be explained at length. All depends on human choice. Indeed for this purpose God created Adam to choose the *devequt* of life. As it is written, "*I have placed life and death before you, the blessing and the curse, so choose life.*"[117] Rashi commented,

> I am instructing you so that you will choose the portion of life. It is like a person who tells his son, choose a fine portion of my inheritance. He positions him before the finest portion and tells him this is what you should select. Thus it is written, "*YHVH is my portion and cup, You support my lot.*"[118] You place my hand on the good lot, saying, take this one.[119]

All goods and evils come from God by design and not as Rabbi Levi ben Gershom and his party reasoned. They stated that the goods are sent from God in essence, but that evils are accidental, resulting from the necessity of matter. This is not so. Rather, everything comes from Him by intention. For the Blessed One "*makes peace and creates evil.*"[120] The reward for fulfilling a commandment is connected to the essence of the commandment, and the punishment for a transgression is essentially connected to the transgression. However, the goods are intended for their own sake, while evils serve another purpose. If we examine this carefully, we will find that the ultimate purpose of the evils is equivalent to the ultimate purpose of the goods. For everything that the Holy Blessed One created was only created for His glory. If not for the evils, one would not fear God. And "from action that is done for ulterior motives one comes to action that is done for its own sake."[121] Our rabbis of blessed memory already said, "The Holy Blessed One has no other interest than fear of heaven."[122] And it is written, "*I have known that all that God will do will be forever.*"[123] God made it so that they would fear Him. Thus this entire matter may be explained as follows: Just as God sanctifies Himself with the righteous, so He sanctifies Himself with the wicked. "*YHVH has made Himself known: He does justice.*"[124] The principle that emerges is that the goods are the essence of divine love, while evils are related to fear. However, God supports our lot, so that we will select life, which is the ultimate purpose. Evils do not come from the mouth of God, only good. In other words, God supports our lot, so that we choose good. These matters also will be explained at length.

Thus the three roots are three principles of faith that the author of the *Iqqarim*[125] established in his book: the existence of God, Torah from Sinai, and reward and punishment. The verse with which I began, " . . . *in the Name of YHVH. This is the book of the generations of Adam* . . . ,"[126] alludes to these three, even though the words "*in the Name of YHVH*" belong with the preceding verse. Nevertheless, the Torah is interpreted by allusions before and after, above and below. "*In the Name of YHVH*" refers to the existence of God. "This is the book" refers to this book of Torah, which is "Torah from Sinai." This language was specifically chosen, like one who points with a finger. It could easily have said "these are the generations of Adam" just as in all other cases where the word *generations* is used. But he wished to allude here to the fact that the Torah has a dual nature, a written Torah and an oral Torah, in the likeness of male and female. This is mentioned in the *Zohar* and also by the authors, both those who follow the way of truth[127] and those who explicate the plain meaning. Nevertheless, our rabbis of blessed memory said, "The entire Torah was spoken in masculine language because the female is included in the male and shines with his glory."[128] There is an allusion to this matter in the fact that *zeh* ("this," masculine) and *zo't* ("this," feminine) have the same value, when the value of each letter is reduced to a single integer.[129] This indicates their unity. It is also written, "*You will have one Torah.*"[130] Therefore, the verse said "*This is the book*" in the masculine. The meaning of "*generations of Adam*" is like "*these are the generations of Jacob.*"[131] As Rashi explained: These are their settlements and transformations until they fulfilled the settlement [of the Land of Israel.][132] Similarly, the "*generations of Adam*" are the events that occurred until they fulfilled the eternal settlement of the Land of Israel that is above.

The verse continued, "*on the day of God's creating . . .* "[133] My explanation relates this to these three roots. "*On the day of God's creating the Adam, He made him in the likeness of God.*" This is a commentary on "*in the Name of YHVH,*" as I have already said. God willing, we will explain at length the meaning of "*and from my flesh I see God*"[134]; from the image and likeness of a human being, the existence of God can be known and is revealed. "*Male and female He created them.*" This is explained in reference to the "*book.*" For the purpose of creating Adam with His Torah and his formation is the secret of the dual nature. "*And subdue her*" is written.[135] "*And He called their name 'Adam.'* "[136] This is explained in reference to the "*generations of Adam*" and his end, if he cleaves to what is above and becomes similar to the Blessed One, following in His ways. Then his name is essentially called "Adam" from the expression "*'eDaMeh (I will be like) the supernal*"[137] and as in the verse "*and on the likeness of the throne . . . the likeness of Adam.*"[138] But if he separates himself from *devequt*, he is called "Adam" after *'ADamaH* (earth), from which he was taken. For dust he is and to dust he will return.[139] However, the name Adam that comes from "*I will be like the supernal*" addresses the essential purpose. For evil was only created for the sake of the good, as has been explained. Thus this is the name of Adam in essence. For it has the same numerical value as the Great Name when spelled *Yvd Ha Vav Ha.*

These three roots require a broad explanation in order to reach the end of His knowledge, in order to show the nations the meaning of the awesome and great work of God as reflected in the essence and quality of Adam. We have already recalled how these three roots appear in the *Zohar*, where their manner of being interconnected and united is discussed. It is a wonderful passage, which we shall explain to the extent that God permits us. After explaining it, we will find the way opened to the three gates mentioned above. Through each gate, one enters many rooms, which will be filled with knowledge.[140]

Here is what is written in the *Zohar*, *'aḥarey mot*:

> We have learned these three levels are interrelated: the Blessed Holy One, the Torah, and Israel. Each one has two degrees, concealed and revealed. The Blessed Holy One is level upon level, concealed and revealed. The Torah is also concealed and revealed. Israel is also level upon level. Thus it is written, "*He tells His words to Jacob, His statutes and judgments to Israel.*"[141] These are two levels, Jacob and Israel, one revealed and one concealed.[142]

The passage is long and I have only copied what is necessary for our discussion. There are a number of observations to be made. First, it says that "there are three levels that are interrelated." This means that there are three distinct things that are related to each other. Whatever applies to one applies to the other two. Otherwise it would have said, "These are three levels: Israel is connected to the Torah and the Torah is connected to the Holy Blessed One," as the *Zohar* says in another place: "Fortunate are these righteous ones. Their *nefesh* cleaves to their *ruaḥ* and their *ruaḥ* to their *neshamah*."[143] Thus the meaning here is that the three are interrelated. What is said about the Holy Blessed One applies to the Torah and Israel. What is said about the Torah applies to the Holy Blessed One and Israel. What is said about Israel applies to the Holy Blessed One and the Torah. It requires deep thought to understand these matters.

Second, what new teaching has this passage taught us? Who does not know that God is revealed and concealed? His essence is concealed and His actions are revealed. And even the youngest student knows that the Torah is revealed and concealed.

Third, why did the passage repeat "level upon level, concealed and revealed"? It should have simply said "level upon level" and then mentioned at the end, "These two levels are Jacob and Israel, one is revealed and one is concealed." Certainly this double expression is no empty matter, but rather wondrous wisdom. We should also note that, concerning the Torah, it said concealed and revealed, while in connection to Jacob and Israel it said "one is concealed and one is revealed."

The House of *YHVH* [I]

Since this holy teaching[1] is a great and fortified City, containing much in each and every word, I will interpret it in length, breadth, and depth, proceeding from matter to matter, unto the Mountain of God, where light exists. In this City, with the help of the mighty and awesome God, I will build ten Houses and a Gate for the Houses, which is a Gate of Light. These are their names: the House of *YHVH*, the House of Wisdom, the House of Israel, the Temple, the Faithful House, the Ultimate House, the House of Choosing, the House of the Walled-City, the House of David, the Great House.

The House of *YHVH* speaks of God's existence; the House of Wisdom discusses Torah from Heaven; the House of Israel speaks of Israel's virtue, humanity (adam), because Israel is called "human"; the Faithful House speaks of the attributes of God, blessed be He, which are faithful; the Temple deals with the virtue of the holy tongue and the attributes; the Ultimate House speaks of the spiritual reward which ultimately comes; the House of Choosing is a homily concerning free will (*beḥirah*); the House of the Walled-City is a homily on the hidden and concealed divine will; the House of David deals with the Messiah; the Great House is the House that contains all of the Houses; the Great Gate is a homily on the divine need for human worship (*avodah ẓorekh gavoha*). This is the Gate for all of the Houses.

Having thus begun, we shall begin to speak of the House of *YHVH*, His existence, be He blessed and exalted.

The existence of the Name: It is well known that God's proper name is *YHVH*.
Torah: It is well known that its essence is 613 [commandments].

It is well known that the essence of human existence is [the power of] choosing, the will. As a result of this choosing, reward and punishment are earned. Due to the connection [between them] the matter of will applies to both the Torah and Israel. Now the connection involves three against three,[2] beginning, intermediate, and end. The beginning is the Holy One, blessed be He, the first with no beginning to His beginning. Intermediate is the Torah in the middle. Through fulfilling the Torah and commandments, His blessed divinity will be revealed to man, the end, or purpose (*takhlit*) of creation. "*The sum of the matter, when all has been heard: fear God . . . for this applies to every person.*"[3] God is the beginning, intermediate, and end. He was, is, and will be, omnipotent and containing all of these together.

Now, with God's help, I will explain each one separately. But before [beginning] my commentary, I will explicate the basic idea of the passage which states "concealed and revealed." The author of the passage informs us that what is revealed (*nigleh*) and what is concealed (*nistar*) are one and the same. In other words, the revelation of what is concealed and its manifestation (*hishtalshelut*) is called *nigleh*. Thus *nigleh* is *nistar*. The same applies to the Torah. The exoteric teachings (*nigleh*) are not a separate matter from the esoteric teachings. Although the masses believe that the esoteric teachings are one thing and the exoteric teachings another, this is not so. Rather, the esoteric teachings are made manifest and revealed. This is alluded to by the verse, "*Apples of gold in silver settings, each word according to its manner.*"[4] In other words, just as silver is very similar to gold, except that it is a lower level [on the scale of precious metals], so is the relationship between exoteric teachings and esoteric teachings. Something very similar to this is found in the *Guide of the Perplexed*:

> The sage said, "*Apples of gold in silver settings, each word according to its manners.*" Hear now an explanation of this matter which he mentioned. For "settings (*maSKiyyot*)" means filagree openings, i.e., hollowed out places whose openings are very fine like the work of silversmiths. They are so named because sight passes over them. Onkelos's Aramaic translation for "and he looked" is *va-iStaKe.*[5] For he said, just like an apple of gold in silver settings whose holes are very small, so is a word said according to its manners. See how wonderful is this analogy that is based in wisdom. For he is saying, concerning a matter that has two aspects, exoteric

> and esoteric, that the exoteric aspect must be fine like silver and the esoteric must be finer than the exoteric. So the inner aspect in comparison to the revealed will be like gold compared to silver. And the exoteric aspect must conceal what will be learned when one meditates on what is within, just as the golden apple covered by very fine filigree of silver will appear to be a silver apple when seen from afar or without contemplation. But when someone sharpsighted looks at it very intently, what is within will be clear to him. He will know that it is golden.[6]

Similarly, what is revealed in a person is based on what is concealed.

Now that God has granted some understanding of this, I will go on to explain what I started.

First, [I shall discuss] the principal Divine Name, *YHVH*. Afterward will be explained how the name *YHVH* is revealed in regard to the Torah and Israel. Here is what the divine Rabbi Moses Cordovero said in his work the *Pardes*, Gate of the Tetragrammaton, chapter one.

> The reader must not think that when we speak[7] of the proper Divine Name (*shem ha-'eẓem*), that it is the essence of the emanator, *Eyn Sof*, God forbid. For this is not correct, as I explained at length in the Gate "Is the *Eyn Sof Keter*," chapter one. For our intention in using the term proper Divine Name is [to refer to] the essence of the *sefirot*. [It is the] Name that contains all of the essence of the *sefirot*. And it is known that the divine emanation is the Name of the *Eyn Sof*, i.e., it teaches about (*moreh*) His essence. There is an analogy for this. For example, the name Isaac is a tool which one may verbally use to refer to a person. If this name were not attributed to him, we would not be able to speak of him, for we would not know him. Similarly, in regard to the *Eyn Sof*, the divine emanation is a tool and name for Him which teaches about His existence so that we will be capable of concerning ourselves with Him.[8] Therefore the Tetragrammaton is a name which refers to the entire divine emanation in its totality and in its details, both great and small. Thus we attribute it to Him and His Name means His emanation. But, neither the Tetragrammaton nor the other Divine Names are like the proper names of people. Their names are merely attributed. Our forefather Abraham decided to call his son Isaac for one reason or another, but the name Isaac was in no way given to him because of its quality or because it teaches about

> his essence.[9] But His names, blessed be He, are not so. For all of them teach about the nature of the matter that names him. That is why we said that the proper Divine Name does not teach about the essence of the emanator. For there is nothing that can limit His essence and unity,[10] God forbid. This being true the sages of Israel and their prophets decided to refer to Him by names that teach about what is concealed, as I explained in the aforementioned Gate. They teach about the concealment of His holiness from the reflection of the heart. And this is His Name by which all the heavenly host, camp after camp, call to Him in the heavens above: "where is the place of His Glory,"[11] to glorify Him. For they do not know His place and they do not understand His character. However, it is His emanations that reveal to us His divinity and a bit of His loftiness. According to the way of truth,[12] then, it is correct [to say] that His emanation is His Name which teaches some of the secrets and concealed matters.[13] And the proper Name, which is the Tetragrammaton, teaches about the essence of His emanations, in general and in detail, as revealed by His compassionate will for our merit to our teacher, Moses, of blessed memory. Many commentaries explain the existence of the various emanations, as will be explained, with God's help, in a separate chapter.[14]

The perfect sage, our teacher and master, Rabbi Menahem Azariah da Fano, wrote in *Pelaḥ ha-Rimmon*, page 24a:

> [The Tetragrammaton] is the Name for the essence of the divine emanation. Not, God forbid, for the essence of the emanator, but for the innermost part of the divine emanation, which is the soul within the *sefirot*. And in regard to it, they are like vessels for the actions which extend from it to the world of separation below. Since the sage, of blessed memory, in Gate 19, chapter 1, of his work[15] put off association of the Great Name even from the essence of the divine emanation, I must caution the reader that this is extremely proper, according to his approach.[16]

Nevertheless, both are words of the living God. *"For one watchman is higher than another, and there are higher ones over them."*[17] A broad explanation is required. As a result of our explanation, a teaching from the chapters of Rabbi Eliezer, which the kabbalists[18] referred to in their works, will be explained. Rabbi Judah Hayyat, in *Ma'arekhet ha-Shemot*, wrote:

> For the letters from which the Name was built did not [yet] exist. Thus they are called letters (*'otiot*) from the root *ata* (come). For they came after the divine emanation was revealed . . . And so it is clearly in the *Ra'aya Meheymena*, chapter *Bo*:[19] "*To whom can you liken Me and I will be comparable?*"[20] For before the Holy One, blessed be He, created a likeness in the world and constructed a form, He was alone without form and likeness. Just as it makes known that before creation, He was without likeness, so it is forbidden to make a form or likeness for Him in the world, neither from the letter *yod*, nor from the letter *heh*, and not even from the Tetragrammaton, nor from any letter or [vowel] point in the world. This is [the meaning of] "for you have not seen any likeness."[21] You did not see one among everything that has a likeness and image. But after He made that likeness of the Chariot, upon which the supernal man descended, he is called through that likeness, *YHVH*, so as to be knowable in each and every one of His attributes. And He is called *'El*, *'Elohim*, *Shadday*, *Ẓeva'ot*, *Ehyeh* in order to make Him known through all of His attributes, through which the world is conducted in loving kindness and judgment, depending on the deeds of man. For if His light did not extend over every creature, how would they know Him and how would the verse be fulfilled, "the whole world is full of His Glory?"[22,23]

If this is so, how could [Rabbi Eliezer] say "before the world was created, He and His Name alone [existed]"?[24] Now there have been many commentaries and commentators on the words of *Pirqey de-Rabbi Eliezer*, which we have mentioned. Nevertheless, I will reveal to you some of what has been made clear to me, concerning this passage, based on foundations that I acquired from authors and books, with the aid of the One who grants knowledge to man.*

* Note. And you, my descendants, may their Rock and Redeemer protect them, my intention in this work, *Derekh Ḥayyim*, is to teach you understanding, to instruct you in the way that leads to *devequt*. As it is written, "*you who are cleaving to YHVH, your God, are all alive today. . . .*"[25] In other words, first to fulfill, "*turn from evil,*"[26] so that no division and separation will come between you and God, as indicated in the verse, "*except that your*

iniquities separated between you and Me";[27] and afterward fulfill "*and do good.*"[28] Then, "whoever comes for the purpose of purification, receives aid."[29] Holiness is increased at every moment. Then one cleaves to his Master, on condition that he knows His Name in regard to the [kabbalistic] intention of the practical commandment and the secret of prayer. Everything depends on the secret of His Name. Thus I was moved to reveal some of the basic ideas of the Kabbalah[30] [and] to make them understandable. This will be of value, for then you will understand why I began with an explanation of the passage from the *Zohar* with which I am concerned. Also, from what is said concerning the secrets of the Name in this work, there will be value in the future.

In this saying of Rabbi Eliezer, it is necessary to look very closely at the language he used. For he said: "before the world was created." Already protest has been raised by those who have examined carefully the wording of the prayer, "You [were] Our God, before the world was created,"[31] which is printed in all of the Ashkenazi prayer books. And they emended the text to read: "You [were] Our God, before You created the world." For "was created" implies, God forbid, that it was created by another and not by Him. And so it is in the Sefardi prayer books. However, similarly to emend the text of *Pirqey de-Rabbi Eliezer* I cannot allow. Indeed the author of *'Avodat ha-Qodesh* and *Tola'at Ya'aqov*[32] wrote in both of these works that there are versions of *Pirqey de-Rabbi Eliezer* that read "before it was created" and others which say "before He created." However, in almost all of the kabbalistic works, the version is "before the world was created, He and His Name alone [existed]." Therefore, I say that this is the correct wording and one should not emend and change the earlier version in the Ashkenazi prayer books. Moreover, the reading, "You existed, before the world was created," appears in the *Tosafot* to chapter 3, *she-akhlu*, and in the *Tosafot* to chapter *Arvey Pesaḥim*, and also in the *Tur*, *'Oraḥ Ḥayyim*, section 46.

Now God has graced me with two ways of explaining the words of Rabbi Eliezer. But all lead to one place, the secret of His unity. According to one way, the word "existed (*hayah*)" will be closely considered. For he said, "*He and His Name existed.*" According to the other way, the word "*He*" will be closely examined. For he said, "*He and His Name existed.*" Both will be correct. We shall begin with the latter.

All interpreters of our Torah, whether kabbalists, explicators of the simple meaning, or philosophical commentators on our holy Torah, unanimously agree that *YHVH* is the proper Divine Name and the root for all the names. They are emanated from It and It contains them all. We shall explain them to those who are privy to the secret of *YHVH*. For there are three levels through which the proper Name is distinguished.

There are ten Divine Names written in the Torah which it is forbidden to erase: *'EHYeH*, *Yah*, *YHVH* with the vocalization of *Elohim*, *El*, *Elohim*, *YHVH* with the vocalization of *Ẓevaot*, *YHVH Ẓeva'ot*, *Elohim Ẓeva'ot*, *Shadday*, *Adonay*. And these ten Divine Names are the emanation of ten *sefirot*: *Keter*, *Ḥokhmah*, *Binah*, and so on. The *sefirot* are the Divine Names and the Divine Names are the *sefirot*. For the *ruḥaniyut*[33] of the *sefirot* breathes and shines over the Divine Names through the intention of the one who writes them or who utters them in holiness and purity. Just as the Temple is a chamber and resting place for the *Shekhinah*,[34] since the divine light is concentrated between the two boards of the ark [of the covenant],[35] so these ten Divine Names are chambers for the *ruḥaniyut* of the *sefirot*, which are alluded to in the Name *YHVH*. For *yod* alludes to *Ḥokhmah* and the tip [of the *yod*] alludes to *Keter*. The first *heh* alludes to *Binah*. *Vav* alludes to *Tif'eret* with the six extremities.[36] The final *heh* alludes to *Malkhut*. This matter will be explained in detail, below.

The *ruḥaniyut* of the *sefirot* are garments for the inner *ruḥaniyut*, which is represented by the Tetragrammaton that is in each *sefirah*, as discussed in the *Tiqqunim*.[37] They are distinguished by their vocalization, as follows. *Keter Elyon*: *YHVH* with a *qamaẓ* under each letter. The vowel point indicates *Keter* and the four letters represent the ten *sefirot* within [*Keter*], so there will be no separation between them, God forbid. The Divine Name for *Ḥokhmah* is *YHVH* with a *pataḥ* under each letter. This is the Name with which *Ḥokhmah* will be revealed. *Binah* also has a Name, *YHVH* with a *ẓere* under each letter. This is the Name with which *Binah* will be revealed. Also *Ḥesed* has a Name, *YHVH* with a *segol* under each letter. Through this Name, *Ḥesed* will be revealed. The Name for *Gevurah* is *YHVH* with a *sheva* under each letter. Through this Name, *Gevurah* will be revealed. *Tif'eret* also has a Name, *YHVH* with a *ḥolem*. The Name for *Neẓaḥ* is *YHVH* with a *ḥiriq* under each letter. This is the Name through which *Neẓaḥ* will be revealed. Also *Hod* has a Name, *YHVH* with *qibbuẓ sefatayim* under each letter. The Name for *Yesod* is *YHVH* with a *shuruq* under each letter. For *Malkhut*, the Name is *YHVH* without any vowels at all.

There is, however, another simple[38] *YHVH* which represents the entirety of the divine emanation in its concealed state. But these ten forms of *YHVH*, each with its specific vowel indicating one of the *sefirot*, are branches of the simple *YHVH*. This is what is meant by the emanated divine essence, which is mentioned in kabbalistic writings. For the root and basis of the unity of the divine emanations in their source are contemplated when the intellect focuses on the Name *YHVH* without any vowel. For this is the root of the Name *YHVH,* which is revealed through the manifestation of the ten Divine Names that are not erased, in the places where the Name *YHVH* contains them, as we will explain. The stages of emanation of this essence through the ten Divine Names, with their various ascendencies, levels, degrees of refinement, and closeness to the emanator, are alluded to when we say that *Keter* has a *qamaẓ* under each letter and that *Ḥokhmah* has a *pataḥ* [under each letter, etc.].

Thus there are three degrees, one above another. First, the emanation of the Divine Names which are the *sefirot* and their unity by virtue of the relationship of cause to effect. *YHVH* is the basis of [the totality] of this divine emanation. This is what is discussed in *Pardes*, Gate of the Tetragrammaton.[39] Second, the secret of the simple Name *YHVH* without any vowels. [Its] branches, the ten vocalized forms of *YHVH*, are clothed by the *sefirot*. This simple *YHVH* is the basis of the inner aspect of the divine emanation which is [like] a soul within the *sefirot*, as Rabbi Menahem Azariah da Fano wrote in *Pelaḥ ha-Rimmon.*[40] Now concerning the Name *YHVH*, which refers to the totality of the divine emanation, the verse said, "*This is My Name le-'oLaM.*"[41] [It is spelled] *le-'LM* [and thus can be read *le-'AleM* (to conceal)]. My Name is not pronounced as it is written. It is not pronounced but it is written and most sublime. In other words, *YHVH*, the soul of the divine emanation, the simple *YHVH* with its branches, is neither pronounced nor written, but only conceived through understanding the secret of Oneness in the heart. These two stages, the ten vocalized forms of *YHVH* and the [ten] names [of the *sefirot*], are what is referred to by "He and His Name." "He" is the secret of the ten vocalized forms of *YHVH* which represent the soul [of the divine emanation] and "His Name" refers to the manifestation of the Divine Names [as] in *Sefer ha-Zohar.*

> "*For I invoke the Name YHVH, render greatness to our God.*"[42] Why does it say, "for I invoke the Name *YHVH*"? Rabbi Simeon said, for it is written, "render greatness to our God." Rabbi Abba said, "give greatness," this is *Gedulah* (greatness).[43] "*The Rock, His deeds are perfect,*"[44] this is *Gevurah*. "*For all of His ways are just,*"[45] this is *Tif'eret*. "*A God of faith,*"[46] this is *Neẓaḥ*. "*And never false,*"[47] this is *Hod*. "*Righteous,*"[48] this is *Yesod*. "*And Upright,*"[49] this is *Ẓedeq* (Righteousness).[50] All of this is the holy Name of the Holy One, blessed be He. That is why the verse says, "For I invoke the Name *YHVH*." . . . Rabbi Hiyya said, we have learned

> high wisdom from this verse. And so it is. But [it is] the end of the verse that binds the knot of faith, through the addition, "is He," as it is written, "*Righteous and Upright is He.*"[51] In other words, it is all He. He is one without any separation. For if you say that all of these are many [individuals], the verse goes back and says, "is He." Everything ascends, is connected and united as One. It is all [summed up by] He is, He was, and He will be. And He is One. Blessed is His Name for ever and ever.[52]

The word "He," moreover, is the third person personal pronoun called "*nistar* (concealed)." For it is the secret of the soul which unites and binds them together.

Thus He and His Name have been distinguished as two aspects. However, above in the uppermost regions, in the root of all roots, before the divine emanation was made manifest, He and His Name were a single essence. There, the Great Name is only attributed to the divine will, in its desire to do good through making the vocalized forms of *YHVH* and the names [of the *sefirot*] knowable. This Will is the source of the vocalized forms of *YHVH* and the names [of the *sefirot*]. But, He and His Name are one, for there, He is His Name and His Name is He. [This] is alluded to by the word *hu'* (He). For *hu'* is an acronymn for "He and His Name are One."[53] And there, no Name applies. [At that level] *YHVH* is neither pronounced, nor written, nor held in thought, not even by the Archangel Michael. There, in the uppermost regions, when we speak of His essence, we mean to say "He," the secret of the divine will. This is the concealment of the Name *YHVH*, as mentioned. And this will, at the level of utmost concealment, is called His Name. For *shemo* (His Name) has the same numerical value as *razon* (will).[54] This indicates the power of the concealment of *YHVH* which [also] numerically equals the value of His Name and Will. How so? YH multiplied by YH and VH multiplied by VH equals *shemo* (His Name, 346).

We also find in *Zohar*, *Piqudey*, when referring to the concealment of the Cause of Causes, he said, "*Eyn Sof*, for it is not knowable. . .*Eyn Sof*, there are no wills [there]."[55] And he[56] wrote in *Pardes*, Gate of *Ẓaḥẓaḥot*, chapter 5:

> "*Eyn Sof*, there are no wills [there] . . ." The meaning is that will is not attributable to the Creator, i.e., *Eyn Sof*. For if we would say that He wills, it would imply that He changes from one will to another. But this is ruled out by definition of *Eyn Sof*, the neces-

> sary existent which is not subject to change. However, the divine will refers to the first emanation which emerged from Him. Through this will, He accomplishes His will according to the model[57] of the inner essence and vessels. For the vessels are subject to change and the inner essence effects the changes [in them]. Thus the beginning of emanation is the will to manifest emanation. However, this will is concealed, for it is not a truly revealed emanation. Nevertheless, it is indeed a will through which He determines to bring about the emanation. This will is not the One who wills; the essence of the *Eyn Sof* is the One who wills. He is called "Willer" by virtue of the will, as we explained regarding judgment and limitation in the Gate of *'Aẓmut ve-khelim*, chapter 4. Accordingly, since the will is so close to the emanator, it is not really [part of] the divine emanation; it is essence, yet not truly essence.[58] It exists as the arising of His will to manifest the emanations. Thus the will is the emanations themselves. For they came to be as a result of its existence as the arising of His will to manifest the emanations, as explained in chapter 3. According to [what is written there], there would already have been a will to produce a will [latent in *Eyn Sof*]. As a result of this will to produce a will, there is a common point between the emanator [and the will to manifest emanation]. And these wills, through the secret of their essential union in the essence of the emanator, are the wills [referred to in the *Zohar* passage, above]. Because of the concealment of the *Eyn Sof*, in which the wills are contained, it said, "*Eyn Sof*, there are no wills [there]."[59]

He continues according to his method in the Gate of *'Aẓmut ve-Khelim*, chapter 9.

> For they attributed knowing to the Creator and said that He knows, wills, and is capable of acting. For although the other [positive] attributes must not be attributed to Him, these we must [attribute]. And so wrote some of the kabbalists. But I say, it has already been stated above that the Creator is wise because of [His] attribute wisdom and not as a result of some wisdom that exists outside of Him, as we have explained in breadth in the previous chapters. Similarly, we may say that *Keter* is called will and that the Creator wills with it. With God's help, we shall discuss this at length in *Sha'ar ha-Ẓaḥẓaḥot*, chapter 6. Similarly, the Creator is

> capable of acting through *Binah*, which is called *koaḥ* (power), as is known. And He knows through [the *sefirah* called] *Da'at* (knowledge). For the attribute of *Da'at* is the Creator's knowledge. In other words, He knows by means of it and from within it, in the way that we explained above. And it is also proven that this *Da'at* is His knowledge and His knowing. For so the verse said: "*Through His Da'at the depths were pierced.*"[60] And we will find no difficulty, then, in concluding that He and His knowledge are not one, just as we are not bothered by the assertion that He and His wisdom are not one, as was explained above.[61]

Now this refers to our understanding [of *Eyn Sof*] before the will to be revealed arises. Then *Eyn Sof* is not knowable, and He is without beginning or end. For He is absolutely primordial. At that point it is not even proper to speak of Him as essence or root of roots. For this only applies when the will to be revealed arises. And it[62] is the root of roots. Then, He and His Name are one entity, as explained. Then one may speak of *Eyn Sof* that is ready to make itself manifest. This is the basis for His Name [*Eyn Sof*]. When one wishes to allude to His concealment, say *Eyn Sof.* For even though, from the point of view of the emanations, divine revelation has begun, it has no end. But, it is obvious that the aspect [of *Eyn Sof*] that is not knowable has no end, for it clearly does not have a beginning.

Now our master and teacher, Rabbi Menahem Azariah da Fano, wrote as follows in *Pelaḥ ha-Rimmon*:

> *Shemo* (His Name) has the same numerical value as *raẓon* (will). . . . And it is known that He and His Name are one; He and His will are one. And this Name of His, which is His will, is united to His thought, blessed be He. There is no question that it is unvocalized. For we cannot know how the divine thought is extended by it. But even its letters are not letters, God forbid. Rather, it is the root and beginning for all the various vocalized forms of *YHVH,* which are branches of the absolute will to be called by name for the benefit of others. And it is [this Name] that is truly called *Eyn Sof.* For the One beyond the name clearly has no end since it has no beginning. Consequently, the *RaMBaM*[63] did not mention the eternity of God, blessed be He, in the principles of religion. For it is obvious that He is eternal, since He is primordial. And it is known that anything primordial must be eternal. For through the divine will, many created things will be eter-

> nal. These things are clear in themselves and proven by their sources, although the critics of *RaMBaM* failed to fully comprehend the issues and [did not argue] with wisdom. So here, we have to assert that His Name and His will, which is a beginning for them,[64] have, in regard to Him, a beginning in the divine will that is not temporal, but no end at all.[65]

The point that emerges from our discussion is that before the world was created through the arising of His will for it to be, He [existed as] the root of the roots of roots and He and His Name alone [existed]. In other words, He was One and His Name One.

The vocalized forms of *YHVH* and the names (of the *sefirot*), which are the two aspects joined together, were revealed in their places. But it is not proper to speak of essence and root when referring to the aspect of *Eyn Sof* that is not knowable, before the will [to manifest emanation] arises. Rather, He is His Name and His Name is He. Then His will, His knowing, and His capability are [indistinguishable from] His nature. Although we speak of His will, His knowing, and His capability, it is not proper to distinguish them by name. Only, we are unable to restrain ourselves from attempting to explain His absolutely primordial nature.

As for the aspect [of *Eyn Sof*], when His will arises, then He and His Name alone [exist] in the secret of He and His Name are One. An allusion to the meaning of this is found in the verse, "*One* [*watchman*] *is higher than another, and there are higher ones over them.*"[66] "One is higher than another." In the aspect following revelation, the secret of He is higher than the secret of His Name. That is the meaning of "*One is higher than another.*" But in His concealment, before the world was created, the secret of He and His Name is not distinguished in terms of "*one is higher than another.*" For [at that point] everything is an absolutely complete unity. Therefore, the verse said, "*And there are higher ones over them.*" Understand that this is the secret of the verse, "*He spoke and it came to be, He commanded and they were created.*"[67] The *RaMBaN*,[68] in his commentary on Genesis, explains every case where it says "*and He spoke*" as indicating divine will and desire. Thus "*He spoke*" means the will for revelation arose. Then, "*and they came to be*" alludes to the secret of the vocalized forms of *YHVH*.[69] "*He commanded and they were created*" alludes to the secret of the revelation of the names [of the *sefirot*]. And do not be surprised by the use of the expression "*they were created*" [in this context]. For we find this usage in the verse "*in the beginning He created, . . .* " which the kabbalists have interpreted as referring to the secret of divine emanation.

Now the reason why [the passage in *Pirqey de-Rabbi Eliezer*] used the expression "*before it was created*" and not "*before He created*" will be explained. We shall begin, by way of a brief introduction, with what is written in *Pardes*, *Sha'ar ha-Meẓi'ut*, chapter 1.

> Holy matters, divine emanation, and subtle *ruḥaniyut* are not like matters in this lowly material world. For corporeal matters involve material of little value. When a person wishes to have an effect on something material, apart from himself, the person is not able to bring about the desired effect, unless the entire original physical state of the material things [to be effected] will first be cancelled, so that they may be transformed into the thing that is desired. For example, when a person desires to create a garment for himself to wear, he will shear the wool or hair from a certain animal. Now, in truth, the wool has acquired a different function from that which it had and the animal is left lacking, naked, without anything. Thus the former state has been cancelled through being transformed into another state. Afterward, he will bleach that wool. So after its bleaching, the previous state which it had when it was sheared will no longer remain. For the former material condition has gone and [the wool] has taken on a lovely state which is better than its former one, the state of pure, bleached wool. Now when they spin that wool, its former state will no longer remain. For it has already become something finer, spun wool. Now when they weave the garment, its state of being spun wool will not remain. For as a result of the work, it has shed its prior form and taken on a more developed form. In this way, as the labors increase, forms will be discarded, cancelled, and will pass away, as if they had never existed. Its prior forms will be forgotten. This applies to material things. However, holy matters, and *ruḥaniyut*, and divine emanation, are different from this. For they do not undergo these stages. And although various divine emanations and spiritual entities become manifest[70] and take on a more revealed form than they had before manifestation, this does not cause their prior state to be cancelled, God forbid. On the contrary, the holy things will increase infinitely, ascending endlessly. Even if a subtle spiritual entity is transformed into a more revealed state, nevertheless, its prior state does not move from its place and its station is not lacking. Spiritual entities differ from corporeal ones in this matter

> in another way. For material things ascend as their states are transformed, especially through the actions performed on them by human beings. For in being affected it comes closer to the desired end and this is its praise. But spiritual things are not like this. On the contrary, as long as it is revealed, the prior state [remains] the basis and root for all of its transformed, emanated states. And each root draws from a higher root, according to the multiplicity of states, so that one depends on another, up to the one that precedes them all. As they ascend, they are praised [for being] closer to the source and the true root which is the root of roots, and source of all states, the King of the kings of kings.[71]

Later in the same chapter he also writes as follows:

> For when the will to cause them to emanate arose before Him, the very subtle and concealed *ẓaḥẓaḥot* were formed, as we explained at length in *Sha'ar ha-Ẓaḥẓaḥot*. And from that subtle state [of manifestation], degrees were emanated until the revelation of thought. There also, a second state [of manifestation] is formed. We said second, because one must not inquire at all concerning what is between *Eyn Sof* and *Keter*. Only, [one may say] that they are subtle [entities] within *Eyn Sof* and they are emanated into *Keter*, which we called the state of the revelation of thought. The subtle entities within *Eyn Sof* extend *shefa'* to the subtle roots that are in *Keter*. Similarly, various states [of manifestation] are emanated, from level to level. As long as they approach the emanator, they are called faces and as long as as they remove themselves, they are called backs. Consequently, there are many faces to the awesome faces and many backs to the backs which are seen.[72]

Thus matters in their roots are incomparably higher and infinite. If we would say "before He created the world," it would imply that the world was created, God forbid, even in its very root. But this is not so. For there is no change or renewal regarding it,[73] but only regarding the created things which come to be and are now revealed.

The holy man of God, the ARI of blessed memory,[74] brought [teachings involving] four ways of completing the spelling of the Name *YHVH*:

yod vav dalet hey yod vav yod vav hey yod[75]
yod vav dalet hey yod vav alef vav hey yod[76]
yod vav dalet hey alef vav alef vav hey alef[77]
yod vav dalet heh hey vav vav hey hey.[78]

The ARI revealed this mystery in the verse, "[*And God said,*] *let there be light and there was light.*"[79] [The verse] speaks of things in the lower worlds and alludes to matters in the higher realms. He mentioned a great allusion. *'Or* (light) has the same numerical value as *Eyn Sof,* which is a great light without beginning or end. *Yehi 'or* (let there be light) has the numerical value of 232, which is also the sum of the four ways of completing the spelling of *YHVH.*[80] This is the secret of the saying of our rabbis,[81] of blessed memory, "*and there was light,*" which means that there already was. For they were concealed in the absolute light.

We shall also explain the words of Rabbi Eliezer the Great in another way, concerning the implications of the word *hayah* (he was).[82] For he [literally] said, "*hayah He and his Name alone.*" We shall begin with the words of *Sefer Ginat Egoz* concerning the Name *YHVH.* It is the United Name which refers to the absolutely primordial being, the necessary existent.[83]

> For this Name verifies that something exists. It is the beginning of all beginnings and the basis of all beginning, the cause of existence. He, be He blessed, must be called by the Name of Being (*shem HaVaYaH*),[84] since He is the cause of all existence. Thus because His being is verified, everything else may exist. For if they were to lack a foundation of being, namely He, be He blessed, they would have no possibility of existing. Thus there is testimony that from the certainty of the existence of all other things, we can attest to the truth of His existence, blessed be He. For if one thinks that He exists, it follows that everything else must exist as a result of the certainty of His being and existence, be He blessed. And if one denies that He exists, nothing else can possibly be and exist, without Him, blessed be He. For since He is the truth of all being, all existences depend on Him, and all existences would be cancelled were His existence cancelled, since He is the foundation of the truth of their being and existence. However, His existence would not be cancelled, [even] if the existence of everything other than Himself were cancelled. For He is Himself the truth of being and existence, which is not dependent [for its existence] on any

> other thing. Therefore, you have the secret of the Name that is unique to Him,[85] blessed be He, which is the Name of Being before anything else came into existence. By virtue of His existence, they exist. Were it not for the Name of Being, nothing that exists would have come to be. But, in our referring to His Name, [we do not mean] the form of the letters, but rather the true essence of Being. Thus it is clear that when He, blessed be He, is called by the Name of Being, it indicates that all beings exist as a result of the truth of the existence of His being. Because of His existence, blessed be He, they came to exist. If you would think that He does not exist, all beings would be cancelled. For He is the cause of the truth of all beings. If they were all cancelled, He would not be cancelled. For there is no other Name of Being that would be the cause of His being.[86]

Rabbi Eliezer the Great was alluding to this matter [when he said] that He and His Name [alone] *hayah* (existed). As was explained, *Hayah* means the necessary existent. That is what is implied by "*hayah* He and His Name." But this does not mean that the form of the letters of the Name *YHVH* [are themselves the necessary existent], God forbid. Rather, the truth of His being [is the necessary existent]. However, when the world came to be and the forms of the letters were generated, being rested on the forms of the letters. For the forms of the letters cannot exist without being. When the forms of the letters were generated, all the other Names were generated. For from within the letters, being enters into the rest of the Names, since they are extensions of being, but not from within being itself. For it only rests upon something that truly has being like His, blessed be He. Therefore, when the forms of the letters were generated and the world came to be, all of His other Names, blessed be He, which are extensions of being, were generated. All of the preceding is from the words of *Ginat Egoz.* Thus the words of Rabbi Eliezer the Great regarding the Name *YHVH* and its concealment are correct and upright. Therefore, it should not be emended. The two ways [of explaining the matter], which we mentioned, are ultimately one way, which teaches about the necessary existent: He was, is, and will be.

Also explained, is the evidence of the *Zohar*, "level upon level, concealed and revealed." For they are the three degrees that we explained above[87]: the secret of divine emanation in its place and the uniting of [the two aspects alluded to in the verse,] "*one is higher than another* [*and higher ones above them*]."[88] The process of emanation is contained in the Name

YHVH. It is the essence of divine emanation, as written in the *Pardes*. In this case the Name is written, but not pronounced. And this condition of emanation comes from the inner condition, the unvocalized Name *YHVH*, which is the secret of the manifestation of the essence that is the soul of divine emanation. It is the secret of the unvocalized *YHVH* that is neither written nor pronounced, but only held in thought. But the essence in the root of all roots is entirely concealed, according to the secret of "He and His Name are One," as has been explained. These matters will be properly explained through an explanation of the *Zohar* passage. I have already explained its general intent, that the exoteric is similar to the concealed. They are one level above another, three degrees *in toto*.

Now we come to the explanation of how the Name *YHVH* contains all of the divine emanation. Concerning this, all the kabbalists have said that the letter *yod* alludes to *Ḥokhmah* and its tip alludes to *Keter*. The first *heh* alludes to *Binah*, *vav* to *Tif'eret* with the extremities, that is, *Ḥesed*, *Gevurah*, *Tif'eret*, *Neẓaḥ*, *Hod*, *Yesod*. The final *heh* alludes to *Malkhut*. God is concealed from me, for there are many wondrous and exalted matters concerning this. Nevertheless, I will reveal one way that God has permitted me to understand, through the words of scholars and books. In the *Zohar*, *Tazri'a*, page 43, [the following is written:]

> Rabbi Abba said, "*How manifold are Your deeds, YHVH,* [*You did all of them with Ḥokhmah, the earth is full of your possessions*]."[89] How many are the acts of the Holy King and all of them are concealed in *Ḥokhmah*. That is why it is written, "*You did all of them with wisdom (be-Ḥokhmah)*."[90] All are contained in *Ḥokhmah* and only emerge from it by means of known paths that reach *Binah*. From there all are made and established. Thus it is written, "*And with understanding, it is established*."[91] Therefore "*You made all of them in Ḥokhmah*" by means of *Binah*.[92] "*The earth is full*." The earth is *Keneset Israel*,[93] for there it is filled by everything. As it is written, "*All rivers lead to the sea*."[94] "*Your possessions*." For [the earth] later sent them forth. Thus it is written, "*These are the generations of heaven and earth be-HiBaR'Am*."[95,96] With [the letter] *heh*,[97] He created them *(BeRa'Am)*. Accordingly, "*The earth is full of Your possessions*."[98]

Know that the divine emanation was only manifested in order to reveal His divinity as expressed in His governing of the world with lovingkindness *(Ḥesed)*, judgment *(din)*, and compassion *(raḥamim)*. And [the modes] of this governance, lovingkindness, judgment, and compassion, are effected by the seven *sefirot, Ḥesed, Gevurah, Tif'eret, Neẓaḥ, Hod, Yesod,* and *Malkhut,* through the secret of male and female. Six extremities, in the secret of the male that bestows; six extremities in the secret of the female, which receives the bestowal in order to regulate the worlds. This is what the *Pardes* says in chapter 5 of *Seder ha-'Aẓilut*:

> The basis of the governance of the lower worlds is only by means of the six extremities which are *Gedulah,*[99] *Gevurah, Tif'eret, Neẓaḥ, Hod, Yesod.* They are the streams which judge the world for good or evil, according to the will of their Master. Now these six extremities may be likened to a tree that requires planting and seeding. The meaning is that what is required first is a hidden stage through which this tree will be watered. [This refers to] its roots, which are inserted and planted within *Binah.* From there, the stream that goes out of Eden waters the garden[100] of delights so that it will be "*producing fruit after its kind, containing its seed, on the* [*lower*] *earth,*"[101] which is *Malkhut.* Consequently, these extremities, which we referred to in the previous chapter as *havayot* and as the root of judgment, have three necessary stages. These are the stage of planting, or the roots; the stage of seeding, or the branches of the tree; and the stage of the fruit, which is below in the place where the effects of the divine bestowal [are manifest]. Now since the divine emanation requires [all] three of these matters, when the will arose to plant them in *Keter,* they were not viable. The same occurred in *Ḥokhmah,* due to the closeness [of these two *sefirot*] to their source, as I explained. [For there], the *havayot* had the quality of pure compassion, and judgment, which the divine governance requires, was not discernible in them, as I have explained. Consequently, the extremities were first planted in *Binah.* There, their root is located, so that [the extremities] can obtain the *shefa'* that is bestowed upon them from the root which is concealed in *Binah.* And their root in *Binah* comes from their root in *Ḥokhmah* and their root in *Ḥokhmah* from their root in *Keter.* But, there, in *Binah,* is the first stage in which the extremities are revealed with the qualities of both judgment and compassion. For they do exist at the stage of *Ḥokhmah* as well, as [the *Zohar*] attested in saying, "He inscribed . . ." He inscribed it in the curtain. This refers to their existence in *Ḥokhmah,* as we shall explain. But in *Binah* the stage in which the qualities of both

> judgment and compassion are manifest was revealed. This is related to the [aspect of *Binah* as the source in compassion] from which judgment is aroused, as we shall explain in *Sha'ar Mahut ve-Hanhagah*. After this, the extremities were manifested in a second stage. From *Binah* they were seeded in their own place, as the six extremities, all shining and performing their functions. They are like the main part of a tree, which draws from its roots. So the *sefirot* draw from their concealed root in *Binah*. This is a second stage of manifestation for the extremities as a whole. Afterward, the tree produces its fruit, which are the functions of the *sefirot* that are carried out by *Malkhut* as is known. But these six extremities are double, six for judgment and six for compassion. These are the twelve *havayot* that are in *Tif'eret*, which are the twelve boundaries.[102]

From this, the passage concerning the verse, "*How manifold are Your deeds* . . . ,"[103] may be explained.[104] In other words, "*How great are Your deeds,*" for the totality of Your deeds is concealed in *Ḥokhmah*, which, except for its existence, is beyond comprehension. Despite the fact that only its existence can be comprehended, nevertheless "*all of them*," that is, the totality of the ten *sefirot*, are contained within it, in concealment. Thus "*all of them* [*are*] *in Ḥokhmah*." "*All of them*" means the totality, and the preposition that precedes *Ḥokhmah* [in the Hebrew verse] indicates place, just as in the [examples], "*a garden in Eden*,"[105] in the house, in the field. The use of the preposition is the same here. For all of them were placed in the inner aspect of *Ḥokhmah* and all are concealed in its inner aspect. Afterward, the verse says, "*You made*," to indicate the stage that is in *Binah*. For there the *sefirot* are established. This refers to the stage of the extremities' roots, which are rooted there in the secret of planting. Afterward, the verse said, "*full of*" to allude to the stage of *Tif'eret* filled by the six extremities that become manifest from the concealed roots in the secret of seeding, until as a result of its magnitude and the measure of its filling, it appears revealed and filled by its six extremities over all of its banks, until every one of its extremities contains [all] six extremities. And every extremity contains all ten *sefirot*, full of *shefa'* and the will to bestow to *Malkhut*. After this, [the verse continues], "*the earth is* [*full of*] *Your possessions*." This alludes to the stage of *Malkhut* which receives and is filled by her six extremities. [This is] the secret of her being the earth and the place of fruit from the six extremities of *Tif'eret*, her husband, which are full of *shefa'* to bestow. She merits that *shefa'* like a person who merits his property.

In order to understand this matter well, you must know that, although the ten utterances[106] are the secret of the emanation of the *sefirot*, nevertheless the root of the building of the world depends on two *parzufim*,[107] *Tif'eret* and *Malkhut*. "*For YHVH made six days*."[108] These are the six supernal days, the six extremities, *Tif'eret*, which contains six *sefirot* that are its pride. "*From my flesh, I can see God*."[109] It is like the [male] body which has its two arms and two legs and penis, which bestows [*shefa'*] to the *sefirah*, *Malkhut*. [This is] "*YHVH in His holy chamber*."[110] This is the chamber of *YHVH* which receives the *shefa'*[111] and later empties it out below, bringing into existence the worlds *Beri'ah*, *Yeẓirah*, and *'Assiyah*. For the first three *sefirot*, *Keter*, *Ḥokhmah*, and *Binah*, are concealed being so close to their source that they are unable to conduct the administration of the world with lovingkindness, judgment, compassion, and their offshoots. They are absolutely beyond comprehension. But they are the secret of His thought, His wisdom (*Hokhmato*), and His understanding (*Binato*), which is the Knowledge, the Knower, and the Known. From their concealment, two *parzufim* are revealed which are emanated in their place. And this may be compared to one who thinks, plans, understands, and designs how he will construct a building. The building is [first] concealed in thought and later revealed. The same is true of the pure and holy divine emanation. Thus it was said, concerning the first three *sefirot*, that it is beyond a person's ability to comprehend or contemplate them. For they are beyond his understanding and world. For a person is only permitted to contemplate his world and its structure. [This means] from the divine structure, that is, the "seven days of creation," and below. From there and above, the gate is closed. The kabbalists received [a tradition] that this is what [the sages] were referring to in *Hagigah*, chapter *Eyn dorshin*.

> The sages taught, you might think a person can inquire concerning what was before the world was created. Thus the Torah teaches, "*from the day that God created a person on the earth*."[112] You might think a person cannot ask about the six days of creation. Thus the Torah teaches, "[*Ask concerning*] *the first days which were before you*." You might think a person can ask concerning what is above, what is below, what is before, what is after. Thus the Torah teaches, "*from one end of the heaven to the other*." You may inquire concerning what is between one end of heaven and the other. But you do not inquire concerning what is above, what is below, what is before, what is after.[113]

Thus they, of blessed memory, explained that a person is only permitted to inquire and contemplate from the divine structure and below, which is from one end of the heavens to the other. [This] is [called] his world. But do not touch from there and above.

However, what is first in thought is last in deed. Now the root of the six extremities and the administration of the world by means of *Malkhut* is called in the Midrash the architect who carries out the work of the six supernal days. Above, among the first three [*sefirot*], this root is called *Da'at*, which is the concealed portion of *Tif'eret*. For when it arises in the absolutely primordial will to create all being, it is called *Eyn Sof*, ready to become manifest by making known its absolute existence through its emanations. In the first three [*sefirot*], which are considered as one, this act of making itself known occurred through the secret of He is the knowledge (*Da'at*), He is the Knower, He is the Known. Later, two *parzufim* were revealed and made known in their place [and] called times. For they are the six supernal days. And *Tif'eret* and *Malkhut* are the attributes of day and night. Time is derived from them, as is the governing of the world, at one time with judgment and at another with compassion, depending on the matter. The sages, of blessed memory, alluded to the concealed aspect [of the *parzufim*] in a midrash. "*And there was light*" teaches that there was a prior temporal order, that is, the concealed aspect of the times above, in the secret of Knowledge (*Da'at*), Knower, and Known. Even though everything [at that level] is one unity and everything is concealed, nevertheless there are various degrees of concealment. For *Keter* with its powers is completely concealed and called "Nothing" (*Ayin*) and *Ḥokhmah* is called "Something from Nothing." Although it is concealed, it is called "Something" in order to distinguish the aspect of existence within it. This existence is revealed in a subtle state by means of *Binah*. This was alluded to when the kabbalists gave *Ḥokhmah* and *Binah* the names Father and Mother, and *Tif'eret* and *Malkhut* [the names] Son and Daughter. "*And from my flesh I can see God.*"[114] The existence of the son comes from father and mother. Before the son was revealed, he existed as part of the father in great concealment, that is, as the seed which is sent from the brain, through the spinal cord, and later [becomes] most discernible as the embryo within the mother. Afterward, when he emerges from his mother's womb, he is revealed to all.

However, there is an even greater degree of concealment than this one, in the will, the thought to arouse the coupling. We may say that the potential [existence] of the son was inherent in this will, in great concealment. Later, it was drawn from the brain, through the father's power, and bestowed upon the mother. Similarly the two *parzufim* first existed in the secret of the will, the thought, [i.e.,] in the secret of *Keter*, which is called will. As explained in *Pardes*, *Sha'ar ha-Ẓaḥẓaḥot*, [*Keter*] is absolutely concealed and *Ḥokhmah* is the beginning of revelation, in comparison to the deep concealment. This beginning of revelation is revealed by *Binah*. Then *Binah* is *BeN YaH*, *Tif'eret* in its place.[115] And its place of reception is *Malkhut*, along with him. For the emanation of the six extremities into their place occurred by means of bestower and the receiver, *Ḥokhmah* and *Binah*. In the same way, when the extension of the six extremities which are above produce the worlds *Beri'ah*, *Yeẓirah*, and *'Assiyah*, *Tif'eret* bestows and *Malkhut* receives this bestowal and actualizes it. Son and Daughter are comparable to Father and Mother, except Father and Mother are responsible for revealing the emanation of the six extremities and the effect [of what is enacted by the *sefirot*] is revealed by Son and Daughter.

Now that this fundamental matter has been explained, you can understand how *YHVH* includes all of the divine emanation. But another fundamental matter still needs [to be understood]. The kabbalists, especially in *Sefer ha-Pardes*, have already discussed at length the linkage of the worlds. For the upper and the lower cleave together. The upper bestows upon the lower, and the lower is a shadow of the upper. What is in one is in the other—even if the one below is material and the one above spiritual. It is always a case of one being parallel to the other. The entire *Ma'aseh Bereishit*[116] speaks of [matters in] the lower worlds and alludes to the higher worlds. For He, blessed be He, brought all the worlds into existence and all the worlds depend on His great light. Althought the light is revealed in a much more refined way in a certain world than in another, this is due to the process of extension. However, everything is from His great light. I will give you an example. The light of the sun casts its light on the moon. Afterward the moon shines in the atmosphere of the world. From there, the light proceeds from the atmosphere of the world into a single room. The light progressively becomes coarsened because of the process of extension, but it is all one light. So it is with the extension of the worlds, *'Aẓilut*, *Beri'ah*, *Yeẓirah*, *'Assiyah*.

The secret of the world of *'Aẓilut* is that it is like a flame attached to a coal. It is not something separate from it. For [the source of] the flame is in the coal and in hovering over the coal, the flame is revealed and it is tightly bound to it. Similarly, [the world of] emanation (*'Aẓilut*) consists of rays of light from the coal, which were concealed [within it] in perfect unity. The light of emanation consists of supernal lights, beyond comprehension. These lights were revealed in the secret of the verses, "*and God said let there be light and there was light*"[117] [and] "*and the spirit of God hovered.*"[118] The secret alluded to by the hovering is the arising of the will to contract His light so that it could emanate. This involves no change in either the emanator or the emanation, according to the secret meaning of "*and there was light*," which our sages, of blessed memory, said means that there already was light. Only, [the light] was completely concealed in its root and supernal source, as was said above. That is the secret of His divinity. For the *Eyn Sof* is a soul to the soul of the *sefirot*. They are the souls of everything that would later be brought into existence. And the Cause of Causes is a soul to them, according to the secret of emanated divine essence. Afterward, the world of *'Aẓilut* was extended by means of *Malkhut*, through the contraction of its light, and the world [of *Beri'ah*] came into existence. The world of *'Aẓilut* is a soul to the world of *Beri'ah*, just as *Eyn Sof* is a soul to the world of *'Aẓilut*. Afterward, the world of *Beri'ah* was extended through the contraction of its light and the world of *Yeẓirah* came onto existence. The world of *Beri'ah* is a soul to the world of *Yeẓirah*. Afterward the world of *Yeẓirah* was extended through the contraction of its light and the world of *'Assiyah* came into existence. All of this occurs through the power of the Cause of Causes, *Eyn Sof*, which is the power of the world of *'Aẓilut*. And the power of the world of *Beri'ah* depends on the power of *'Aẓilut*. So the power of *Beri'ah* depends on the power of *'Aẓilut*, whose power depends on *Eyn Sof*. This world of *Beri'ah* is the power of the world of *Yeẓirah*. So *Yeẓirah* is in the power of *Beri'ah* which is in the power of *'Azilu*t which is in the power of *Eyn Sof*. This world of *Yeẓirah* is the power of the world of *'Assiyah*, only the light has become concealed and coarsened, according to the nature of the receivers.

Thus the world of emanation can be compared to a flame in a coal. The flame is revealed through the will, which hovers above and is tightly bound to the coal. The world of *Beri'ah* is like one who lights a torch from a flame. The light of the torch does not remain connected in perfect unity to the light of the flame from which the torch was lit. Nevertheless its level is great. The torch contains a great light in which the light of the flame inheres. The world of *Yeẓirah* is comparable to lighting a candle from a flame, and this candle illuminates a dark room.

"*And there was light*." All stages of the extension of the worlds are parallel. Only, one is secret, the next more revealed, and the next even more revealed. So it is explained in the *Zohar* and brought in the *Pardes*, *Sha'ar Mahut ve-Hanhagah*, chapter eleven: "There are four elements in all the worlds." Only, they are material in the world of *'Assiyah* and at a higher level they are spiritual in the world of *Yeẓirah*. In other words, Michael is water, Gabriel is fire, Uriel is ether, and Raphael is earth.[119] Above, in the world of *Beri'ah*, they are [still] more spiritual, the four *ḥayyot* that bear the Throne [of Glory].[120] Later, above they become the four legs of the Throne. Ultimately, in the world of *'Aẓilut*, they are most spiritual. *Ḥesed* is water. *Gevurah* is fire. *Tif'eret* is ether. *Malkhut* is supernal earth. Each level contains the roots for the level below. Thus everything that exists in the lower worlds alludes to the upper worlds, and from the revealed we reach the concealed.

Every material entity has length, breadth, and depth. There is no material thing in the world that lacks these three dimensions. For they are the boundaries of the solid. If only two dimensions were formed, namely length and breadth without depth, [what is created] would be called a plane (*SHeTaḤ*). The reason is that it is like a color that is spread (*SHaTuaḤ*) over a sheet of paper. Length and breadth may be attributed to it, but not depth. Thus it is called a plane (*SHeTaḤ*). When we draw a figure of only one dimension, namely length without breadth, it is called a line. The meaning is a line of [a certain] length, lacking breadth and certainly without depth. When we conceive of negating all three dimensions of the body, [the result] is called a point. It is so termed because it has neither length, breadth, nor depth, but not because it can actually exist. Rather it is called a formal point, that is, the entity formed through the negation of the [three] dimensions of a body, which is not to imply that it can actually exist.

Now the ten *sefirot* are represented by [the letter] *yod*.[121] And the letter *yod* is spelled *yod vav dalet*. These three letters allude to point, line and plane within *yod*. *Yod* is a point [י], *vav* is a line [ו], and *dalet*, which contains length and breadth, is a plane [ד]. All are included in the point of *yod* itself. How so? The letter *yod* has a middle part, a foot, and a tip. Through the extension of the foot, *vav* is formed. Through the extension of the middle part, *dalet* is formed. The tip alludes to *Keter*, where the concealed aspects are located. As I have already mentioned, *Keter* is called *Ayin* (Nothing) and cannot be comprehended at all, not even formally as a point. Rather, *Ḥokhmah*, which is the beginning of a slight degree of revelation, is alluded to by *yod* and *Keter* by the tip of the *yod*. For in *Keter* everything is in such a state of concealment that it is called *Ayin*. But [the verse says], "*Ḥokhmah* comes into existence from *Ayin*."[122] In other words, its existence is from *Keter* and it is called "Something from Nothing (me'*Ayin*)." Thus how the *yod* of the Divine Name *YHVH* alludes to *Ḥokhmah* has been explained.

Now there is a concealed part of *yod* within *Ḥokhmah*. This is alluded to by the letters that complete the spelling of *yod*: *vav* and *dalet*. For there, in a concealed way, the secret of the two *parzufim*[123] began to be revealed. Like the example of the son, which exists by virtue of the power of the father's brain, *vav* is the secret of the line. This is *Tif'eret*. For it is known that the three lines are the line of lovingkindness, the line of judgment, and the line of compassion. The line of compassion is *Tif'eret*, and it blends together and contains all of the lines. Thus *Tif'eret* contains six extremities and bestows *shefa'* to *Malkhut*. This is alluded to by the verse, "and a line will be inclined toward Jerusalem."[124] "Jerusalem" alludes to *Malkhut*, as is known. For the Temple is there which contains *YHVH*, that is, *Tif'eret*, which is called *YHVH*. Consequently, [the Tetragrammaton] was pronounced in the Temple. For *Malkhut* is a chamber for *YHVH*. Thus *vav*, which is a line, represents *Tif'eret*. It is the great line that extends above as the secret of *Da'at* (knowledge) up to *Keter*, which is the uppermost heights. This is the secret of "the portion of Jacob is a portion without constrictions." As is known, Jacob is a chariot for *Tif'eret*. However, the line of lovingkindness (*Ḥesed*) only extends to *Ḥokhmah*, and the line of judgment only reaches *Binah*.

The letter *dalet*, which is an expansion in length and breadth, represents *Malkhut*. For all the bestowal of the divine emanation reaches there. And she is also *dalet*, because she is the fourth leg of the Chariot.[125] Also *dalet* equals ten when it is added to the sum of the numbers that precede it, that is, 1+2+3+4=10. For it is the tenth *sefirah*. Moreover, *dalet* is related to the word for door (*delet*), for it is "*the gate to YHVH, the righteous enter by it*."[126]

Line, plane, and point are alluded to in the letter *yod*. Now among material things, all have line, plane, and height or depth. So here, the height and depth are alluded to by the tip of the *yod*, which is the high point. Similarly, its depth is "so very deep, who can discover it?"[127] From this depth, the depths mentioned in *Sefer Yeẓirah* were extended.

> The depth of beginning and the depth of end, the depth of goodness and the depth of evil, the depth above and the depth below, the depth of east and the depth of west, the depth of north and the depth of south. And One Lord, God, Faithful King, rules over all of them in His Holy Dwelling, forever and ever.[128]

The reason the word *depth* is used in each case is to indicate that although beginning and end and east and the rest imply limitation, they are nevertheless [immeasurable] depths, "*so very deep, who can discover it?*" They cannot be comprehended because they are without limit. An explanation of this *mishnah* may be found in *Pardes*, *Sha'ar 'Im ha- 'Eyn Sof Hu' Keter*, chapter 4.

The letters [*vav* and *dalet*] which complete the spelling of *yod* are extended into *Binah*, as the bestowal from the father to the son. There, it is most discernable as her embryo. In *Binah*, *vav dalet* becomes *dalet vav*, in the secret of the two (*d"u*) *parzufim*. The two *parzufim* were joined together as one, just like Adam, below, in the beginning of creation.[129] Through inserting a *vav* [ו] into *dalet* [ד], a *heh* [ה] is produced. This is the secret of the first *heh* from the Name [*YHVH*] which alludes to *Binah*. And *heh* has three legs which are the expansion of the emanated six extremities.[130] In *Binah* they acquire their root, somewhat revealed, like a son in his mother's womb. And the kabbalists said that *heh* is open at the bottom in order to bestow *shefa'* to the divine emanation and slightly open above, in order to receive from *Keter*. It is wide open at the bottom, in order to bestow *shefa'* upon the entire expansion [of *sefirot*]. For *Binah* is called "Supernal Mother." From there the entire structure is emanated.

Afterward, *Binah* caused these two *parzufim* to be emanated to their place. The *vav* within the *heh* was emanated as *Tif'eret* in its place. It contains six extremities and is the line that contains all the lines. Thus the secret of the letter *vav* in the Name [*YHVH*] alludes to *Tif'eret*. Afterward, *Malkhut*, the *dalet* that remained from *Binah*, was emanated in its place. And the *vav* also entered this *dalet*. For *Malkhut* is the receptacle for the six extremities and a chamber for them. And six are clothed in six. *Tif'eret*, within the six extremities, is clothed by *Malkhut*, which is its chamber. For she has six rooms for receiving the six. And this *vav*, which has been inserted in *dalet*, becomes a *heh*. Thus *Malkhut* is the final *heh* from the Name [*YHVH*]. The kabbalists said that this *heh* is open and wide below, in order to bestow *shefa'* upon the worlds, *Beri'ah*, *Yeẓirah*, and *'Assiyah*, and narrowly open at the top, in order to receive the subtle supernal [effluence]. It is also wide at the bottom, in order to receive all of the prayers and services[131] and to raise them up in a very refined form through the fine opening above.

Also through the secret of the concealed coupling, a *heh* is produced which indicates the female. And it says in the *Zohar*, concerning the verse, "*That was a night (leyl) of watching for YHVH . . . that very night (laylah)*,"[132] "*before she received the male, she was called leyl, after she received the male, she was called laylah*."[133] Also see the wonders in *Pardes*, *Sha'ar Seder ha-'Aẓilut*, chapter 2.

Also, the final *heh* is similar to the first *heh* in respect to the three lines. Only, the first *heh* deals with the secret of the emanation of the three lines and the final *heh* deals with their actual functioning.[134]

Thus the Name *YHVH* includes all of the divine emanation and the basis of the emanation is *Tif'eret*, the structure of the world. [This occurs] by means of *Malkhut*, which is part of himself,[135] in the secret of "his wife is like himself."[136] For *Tif'eret* consists of six extremities and these six extremities are double, containing six for judgment and six for compassion. These are the twelve diagonal boundaries, in the secret of the twelve permutations of *YHVH*. Above, [*Tif'eret*] is concealed in the secret of *Da'at*. All of this is *Tif'eret*, except *Da'at* is the concealed part of *Tif'eret*. However, it is all *Tif'eret*. Thus *Tif'eret* is called *YHVH*, for every Name *YHVH* in the Torah is vocalized with *ḥolem*, *sheva*, and *qamaẓ*. This is indicated by "*YHVH* desired me."[137] Such is *Tif'eret*, since the Name *YHVH* includes all of the divine emanation, as I explained, and the basis of the divine emanation is *Tif'eret*.

The whole emanation is represented by the Name *YHVH*, for it is the proper Divine Name. Consequently, it is called the United Name (*shem ha-meyuḥad*), because it unites together all of the divine emanation. It is also called the Explicit Name (*shem ha-meforash*). The following is written in *Sefer 'Avodat ha-Qodesh*, *Ḥeleq ha-Yiḥud*, chapter 15.

> The sacred Name which is written *yod ha vav ha* is called the Explicit Name and the United Name. This appears in the teachings of our Rabbis, of blessed memory. They said in *Sifre* and in *Sotah*, chapter *'Elu Ne'emarin*, " '*So you shall bless* [*the Children of Israel*].'[138] [Bless them] with the Explicit Name. You think it has to be with the Explicit Name? Perhaps the divine epithets [may be invoked for them]. Thus the Torah says, '*And you shall place My Name* [*upon the Children of Israel* . . .]'[139] [to specify] My Name which is unique to Me."[140] And the *RASH*[141] wrote in *Sefer ha-Yiḥud*, "These four letters, *YHVH*, are called the Explicit Name. It explains (*ha-meFaReSh*) all of the *sefirot* that indicate what the Creator manifested through revealing His powers in them along with all beings that ever were or will be."[142]

And the Sage, Rabbi Todros ha-Levi, said in his commentary to the *Aggadot* in tractate *Pesaḥim*, chapter *'Elu 'Ovrim*:

> Know that all the true principles of Kabbalah and all of its cornerstones are based on this great, holy Name, with which the complete union is made clear (*mitPaReSH*). Thus it is called the Explicit Name. That is to say it makes the divine essence clear, expressing through His concealed and united inner powers, the essence of His holy and pure unity.[143]

It has already been explained in the preceding discussion that the emanation is contained within the Emanator in a complete unity and concealed within it. The Tetragrammaton is attributed to the unique Lord. Or it is His Name and He and His Name are united and not separated. It has also been explained that the divine emanation must of necessity attest to and declare the existence and unity of the Root of all Roots. It is this Explicit Name that contains and unites all of the emanations. It is so termed, because it explains and reveals the existence and unity of the unique Lord, blessed be He. It explains and clarifies because this Name unites His powers with Him. This is the reason why this great Name is called "Explicit" (*meforash*) and not "Explicating" (*mefaresh*).[144] This indicates that the Name and essence are one. This Name, particularly indicates *Tif'eret* Israel, the Torah, which owes its name to the fact that it teaches and reveals that which was concealed.[145] It is written in the Midrash of *RASHBY*,[146] of blessed memory, " 'the Tree of Life,' this is the Torah. For it is a great and mighty supernal tree. Why is it called Torah? Because it teaches and reveals that which was concealed and unknown." However, this Name is called the United Name, because through the structure of its letters, it unites the entire divine emanation to Him. [The emanation] is His divinity. Thus [the sages] said, "*my Name which is united to Me*."

> All the interpreters of our holy Torah, kabbalists, exotericists, and philosophers, have unanimously agreed that this Name and no other is the proper Divine Name. They included it among the other holy Names that may not be effaced. Ultimately, they said that even the Name *'EHYeH*, as awesome as it is, may not be compared to this Name. There are a great many reasons for this, but the decisive one is that all of the other Divine Names that may not be effaced [have a form] for which some linguistic rationale may be deduced. Only the letters of the Tetragrammaton do not allow for any linguistic explanation. This is because Names like *'Elohim, 'Eloha, 'El,* are derived from a root implying greatness, power, and might. So [we find in the verse], "*He carried away the nobles ('eyley) of the land*."[147] Also, [in the verse], "*Your beneficence is like the high ('el) mountains*."[148] These are cases where the root implies greatness and might. The Name *Shadday* (Almighty) declares that He can overturn (*SHoDeD*) the laws of nature. The word *Shadday* and the word overturn (*SHoDeD*) have the same implication. The Name *Ẓeva'ot* (of Hosts) indicates that He is master of supernal hosts. It is derived from the root *ẓb'* (assemble). The Name *Adonay*

expresses the concept of lordship (*'ADNut*), since He is the Lord of the entire earth. It is derived from the plural for Lord. The Name *'EHYeH* indicates the future tense of the verb "to be" in the light conjugation. Thus our Rabbis, of blessed memory, explained the meaning of this Name, "I was with them in the redemption from Egypt and I will be with them in other redemptions . . ."[149] However, the Tetragrammaton is very awesome. What explanation can contain it? For it has no linguistic explanation whatsoever.

A second reason [why this Name is incomparable] is that all the other Names may be used in regard to matters other than God, if desired. But this is not true for the Tetragrammaton. How so? Scripture uses the word *'el* to indicate something other than God, [as in] "*another god.*" Similarly, [in the verse], "*like the high ('el) mountains.*"[150] There are many other examples. Similarly, [in the case of] *'Elohim*, [we find the verse], "*See I have made you 'Elohim to Pharaoh.*"[151] Also, "*Do not curse judges ('elohim).*"[152] And there are many other examples. [Concerning the] Name *Shadday*, [we find], "*The creatures of the field (SaDaY) are with Me.*"[153] "*He shall lie between my breasts (ShaDaY).*"[154] The letters are those of the [Divine Name *Shadday*], but they are used to indicate something other than God. [Concerning the] Name *Ẓeva'ot*, [we find], "*All the hosts (ẓeva'ot) of YHVH went out* [*of the Land of Egypt*]."[155] And there are other cases. [Concerning the Name] *Adonay*, [we find], "*And he said, my Lords, . . . do not pass beyond* [*your servant*]."[156] Some of our rabbis say that [Abraham] was speaking to the greatest of [the three messengers]. But even though there are differences of opinion concerning [the interpretation of this verse] and some say that the one addressed was holy, nevertheless, it is clear that all agree that if one wishes to address his master as *'Adonay*, literally, "my Lord," he is permitted to use the name without referring to God. [Concerning the Name] *'EHYeH*, [we find], "*Why should I be ('ehyeh) like one who strays?*"[157] and "*I will not be (lo' 'ehyeh) a binder of wounds.*"[158] And there are many more examples like these. But this is not so in the case of these four holy letters, *YHVH*. For although three of them may be found in reference to something other than God, [all] four cannot be found [in such a context.] For example, it is written, "*Wherever a tree falls, there it will (yehu')* [*remain*]."[159] But the entire Tetragrammaton is not found. This reason is somewhat similar to the first one.

> There is a third reason. All the Divine Names are pronounced as they are written, except for this holy Name. For this Name was only pronounced according to its letters in the Temple, during the priestly blessing and by the High Priest on the Day of Atonement. The reason is that the other Names directly govern the world, as is proven from their meaning. But the Tetragrammaton has no explanation or direct functioning manifested in this world, except through being clothed by the other Names, as we will explain. Therefore, it is permitted to pronounce the other Names. For when those letters [are pronounced], they become spiritual entities (*ruḥaniyut*), like a person's soul, and they clothe themselves in the air of this world, in order to perform their activity. But, due to its great holiness, the Tetragrammaton does not clothe itself in the air of this world, except in the Temple, particularly during the Priestly Blessing. Concerning this, is written, "*I will come to you in every place where I cause My Name to be mentioned, and I will bless you.*"[160] It can be clothed in pure and clear air, for the *Shekhinah*, the Name ADoNaY, clothes itself in the air of the Temple. [That is why we say], "*YHVH* in His Holy Chamber."[161]

The author of *Sha'arey 'Orah*[162] wrote as follows, in his introduction.

> Know that all the holy Names that are mentioned in the Torah, depend on the Tetragrammaton, *YHVH*. If you say, but is not the Name *'EHYeH* the root and source, know that the Tetragrammaton is like the trunk of the Tree and the Name *'EHYeH* is this Tree's root. There, everything is rooted, and [from it] branches extend to every side. The rest of the holy Names are all like branches and stems that extend from the trunk of the Tree. Each of the branches produces fruit, after its kind.[163]

He explained that all of the Names that may not be effaced depend on the Tetragrammaton. They extend out from it and are nourished by it. The question he raises is, Why should they not depend on the Name *'EHYeH*, which is *Keter* and the root [of the supernal Tree], just as they depend on the Tetragrammaton, which is not [*Keter*], but *Tif'eret*? And he answered his question well. For the Name *'EHYeH* is the essence of the Tree and its root, while the Name *YHVH* is the trunk of the Tree. Thus the branches extend from the trunk and not from the root, as is known. For *Keter* is the essence and due to its great concealment, the branches do not extend from it. But *Tif'eret* is the trunk from which the branches emerge. Also, the word *Tif'eret* is [derived] from *po'rot*, which means branches, as is known. Moreover, the six extremities branch out from it. Thus [Gikatilla's] words are true words of the living God.

Nevertheless, the problem remains, for we may raise the question in another manner. Even according to his words, it is not denied that the Name *'EHYeH* is greater and more highly regarded than the Tetragrammaton, except that the branches do not emerge from it. And the Tetragrammaton is related to *Tif'eret*, which is highly regarded, but not as much as the Name *'EHYeH*, which is the essence of the Tree. If so, why is it that the Tetragrammaton, which is associated with *Tif'eret*, is not pronounced according to its letters? God forbid that we say that *Keter* is a branch of *Tif'eret*. For this is in our view one of the most serious heresies, touching the very essence of divine emanation, upsetting everything, and cutting the shoots. But, if we recall what we already introduced from *Sha'ar shem ben dalet*, in the beginning of this chapter, the matter will be well resolved. For the Tetragrammaton is also concealed in *Keter* in utmost concealment. As for these Names, although their holiness is great and they may not be effaced, nevertheless they are chambers for the vocalized forms of *YHVH*, as we have explained. Because of *Keter*'s concealment, no Name is revealed in it that would, by virtue of its implications, limit and define its *ruḥaniyut*, as would the Tetragrammaton and the other Names. But the meaning of the Name *'EHYeH* implies concealment. For it means "I am about to be." In other words, although one may speak of the *sefirah*, *Keter*, it is not because it may be in any way comprehended, but because it will be made manifest in *Ḥokhmah* and *Binah*. And so the great masters have explained. For the meaning of *Keter* is to wait, as in the verse, *"wait (KaTaR) for me a while, and I will expound . . ."*[164] In other words, do not go deeply into it, for it cannot be comprehended. Its comprehension is through the rest of the *sefirot*. Thus the meaning implied by its Name is the cause of its loftiness and concealment, as we have explained. But if the Tetragrammaton were pronounced according to its letters, it would imply that the divine emanation could be comprehended. And this is ruled out by its great concealment. Thus we pronounce it in its chamber, because *Tif'eret* can be comprehended in *Malkhut*, as implied by "and *YHVH* is in His Holy Chamber." This is the secret implied by the fact that *heykhal* (chamber) and *Adonay* have the same numerical value.[165] The meaning is that the Name *YHVH* which is concealed in *Keter*, i.e., *YHVH* vocalized with a *qamaẓ* under each letter, is more distinguished for the loftiness of its manifestation of the divine essence than the

Name *YHVH* vocalized with a *ḥolem* above each letter, which is concealed in *Tif'eret*.

Evidence that all the other Names are united to the United Name may be found in the secret that it is alluded to by the numerical value of all ten Names. The Name of *Keter* is *'EHYeH*. It is also derived from the notion of being. And *'EHYeH* has the numerical value of [the letters] *yod heh vav*,[166] which are the letters of the Name *YHVH*, since the letter *heh* appears twice. This is the secret of the verse, "*And I was (ve-'EHYeH) with Him as a confidant*."[167] The verse says "*ve-'EHYeH*," with an additional *vav*, and did not merely say " *'EHYeH*." For in the Name *YHVH*, *yod* precedes *heh*. But according to alphabetical order, *heh* comes before *yod*. Nevertheless, the letters of *YHVH* can be found in the sum of the numerical value of the letters *alef, bet, gimmel, dalet, heh, vav*. For *alef* plus *bet* plus *gimmel* plus *dalet* equals *yod*.[168] And after [these letters] comes *heh* and *vav*. Thus [we have] *YHV*, which is the numerical value of *'EHYeH*. In other words, if you consider the letters from *alef* to *vav*, which are the letters of *YHVH*, the sum also will equal the numerical value of *'EHYeH*.[169] The Name for *Ḥokhmah* is *YaH*, which is half of the Name *YHVH*. Its other half may be completed by spelling it thus: *yod vav dalet heh alef*, which equals 26. The Name for *Binah* is *YHVH*, vocalized like *'Elohim*. The Name for *Ḥesed* is *'El*, which has the same numerical value as *YHVH* plus its four letters and one for the word itself.[170] *'El* is also the secret of the letters that complete the spelling of the Name of 63 (*shem s'g*), that is, *yod vav dalet heh yod vav alef vav heh yod*.[171] It contains three *yod*s and one *alef*.[172] But the Name of 45 (*MaH*), that is, *yod vav dalet heh alef vav alef vav heh alef*, is the opposite. It contains three *alef*s and one *yod*. These spellings of *YHVH* are indicated by "one God" (*'El 'eḥad*). In other words, three *yod*s and one *alef* equal *'El* (God) and three *alef*s and one *yod* equal *'eḥad* (one). Thus the Name *'El* is alluded to by the Name *YHVH*. The Name for *Gevurah* is *'Elohim* and it is included in *YHVH*. This is already indicated by the verses, "*YHVH is God (ha-'Elohim) ... YHVH is God (ha-'Elohim)*."[173] Even though the Name *YHVH* denotes compassion and the Name *'Elohim* denotes judgment, they are united together in one union. The words are repeated twice to reveal to us twice how His Name alludes to the secret of this union. *YHVH* equals 26, which is represented by the letters *kaf* and *vav*. When these letters are spelled *kaf peh vav vav*, their first letters are *kaf vav*, 26, the value of *YHVH*, and their last letters are *peh vav*, 86, the value of *'Elohim*. This is the secret of "*I am the first and I am the last*."[174] Concerning this, the verse said, "*YHVH is God*." And he said, "*YHVH is God*" a second time, because there is a second allusion to this. When the Name *YHVH* is spelled *yod vav dalet heh alef vav alef vav heh alef*, it equals 45, represented by *mem* and *heh*. When these letters are spelled *mem mem heh alef*, they equal 86, the sum of *'Elohim*. These two matters are alluded to in the Priestly Blessing, *"May YHVH bless you and keep you (YevarekheKHa YHVH Ve-yishmereKHa)."* The first letters, two *yod*s and a *vav*, equal 26 and the final letters, *kaf heh kaf*, equal 45. The Name for *Tif'eret* is *YHVH*. The Names for *Neẓaḥ* and *Hod* are *YHVH Ẓeva'ot* and *'Elohim Ẓeva'ot*, and we have already explained *"YHVH is God (ha-'Elohim)."* The Name for *Yesod* is *Shadday*. We have already mentioned that the proper Divine Name is *YHVH*, as it is written, *"This is My Name forever."*[175] This is in essence the Divine Name and the rest of the Names are derived from it. It is written, *"I appeared to Abraham, Isaac, and Jacob* [*as 'El Shadday*], *but I did not make Myself known to them by My Name YHVH."*[176] However, when *YHVH* is added to *Shadday*, the sum is the same as *shem* (name).[177] He is called *Shadday*, because He said to His world, "That is far enough (*day*)."[178] The Name for *Malkhut* is *Adonay*, which is alluded to by *YHVH*.[179] Moreover, it is the chamber for the Name *YHVH*. Indeed they cleave together in the secret of "his wife is like himself." That is why we pronounce the Name *YHVH* as *Adonay*. For there is no apparent reason why this Name in particular should be used to pronounce it. However, the reason is because it is the chamber for *YHVH*, as it is written, *"And YHVH is in His Holy Chamber, be silent before Him."*[180] The Name *Adonay* has the same numerical value as *has* (be silent) and *heykhal* (chamber). For it is the chamber for *YHVH*. And this is the allusion, "Be silent," for [the Name] is not to be uttered. In other words, because the verse says, *"This is My Name . . . and this is My memorial,"*[181] it is not pronounced as it is written. So how is it pronounced? The verse said, "*has* (be silent)." In other words, it is pronounced as the Name *Adonay* which has the same numerical value as "*has*." And why "*has* (be silent)," because it is not to be pronounced as it is written. Thus *Adonay* is the chamber of *YHVH*.

Nevertheless, there are even more indications of the [relationship between] *Adonay* and *YHVH*. This is because both *YHVH* and the letters it becomes, according to the various systems for exchanging letters of the alphabet, are holy. According to one system, it becomes the Name *KIZI*,[182] which consists of the letters that follow *YHVH*. [This Name] is alluded to in the verse, *"Surely it was this (zo) YHVH against whom we sinned."*[183] *"YHVH zo"* is the secret of *KIZI*; through it, *YHVH* alludes to the number of *KIZI*. Calculate the Name and its substitute. In other words *YHVH* and *KIZI* equal Adonay.[184]

There is also an allusion in *"for My Name is in him."*[185] For when *YHVH* is spelled with *yod*s, as follows, *yod vav dalet heh yod vav yod vav* *heh yod*, it equals 72. This sum may be found within Adonay. That is, when Adonay is spelled *alef lamed peh dalet lamed tav nun vav nun yod vav dalet*, the middle letters also equal 72.

Thus *YHVH* is the United Name that unites all of the Names. All of them emerge from it, are alluded to in it, and form a complete unity with it. And [*YHVH*] includes all of the divine emanation in the secret of *yod*, which has been explained as point, line, and plane.[186] The whole is one perfect unity, for the secret of *yod* is the secret of *alef*, which indicates unity. The kabbalists said that the letter *alef* alludes to the United Name. For *alef* [א] is formed by a *yod* above, a *yod* below, and a *vav* in the middle, which equals 26. However, I received [a tradition] that the lower *yod* is a bit larger than the higher one, compared to which it is like a small *dalet*. Thus [*alef*] is composed of a *yod* above, a *vav* in the middle, and a *dalet* below. These are the letters that spell *yod*, which alludes to [the secret that] the *yod* is *alef*. It is all a true unity "and both ways are words of the living God," indeed. Below, also, *yod* appears as a small *dalet* to allude to this.

I will also mention a great allusion regarding the secret of how the *alef* indicates the oneness of the United Name. When you say that it equals 26, it has the same numerical value as *YHVH*.[187] When you say that the *alef* contains the letters that spell *yod*, it also alludes to *YHVH*. In addition to what we have explained above, concerning the secret of *yod*, there is another known allusion. For the form of the letter *heh* is explained in two ways, and both are true. Sometimes the form of *heh* [ה] is interpreted as *dalet vav* [דו], as we explained above, and sometimes the form of *heh* is interpreted as *dalet yod* [די]. And the kabbalists found an indication of this in the word "*DODiY* (my beloved)," which is found in the verse, "*I am my beloved's* . . . "[188] In other words, "*my beloved*" alludes to the two forms of *heh*, *dalet vav* and *dalet yod*. Now another insight is presented which differs from what I wrote above. Although we said that the first *heh* [in the Name *YHVH*], which alludes to *Binah*, involves the secret of *dalet vav*, nevertheless, this *vav* is small and may be compared to a *yod*. Thus the final *heh*, [of the Name *YHVH*], which represents *Malkhut*, is really *dalet vav*. The reason is that divine emanation from *Ḥesed* and below is arranged according to three lines, the line of lovingkindness, the line of judgment, and the line of compassion. These three lines are concealed in their roots above. *Keter*, *Ḥokhmah*, and *Binah* are the roots of these three lines. *Keter* is the root of the line of compassion. *Ḥokhmah* is the root of the line of lovingkindness, and *Binah* is the root of the line of judgment. Because of their great concealment, they are called three *yod*s. For the top of a *vav* is a *yod* and when the *yod* is expanded, it becomes a *vav*, which is a line, as is explained at length in *Sefer Pardes*.

I also say that although the first *heh*, which is *Binah*, alludes to the secret of *dalet vav*, nevertheless, the small *vav* is somewhat similar to a *yod*. The final *heh*, which represents *Malkhut*, the secret of receiving the three lines. It is entirely *yod*.[189] Thus [the secret of the two *hehs*] is represented by *DODiY* (my beloved). After God showed us this, He further enlightened us. For the writing of *yod* alludes to *YHVH*. How so? *yod* and *vav* as they are written. Then *dalet* remains. Consider that when *yod* and *vav* are added to *dalet*, in the secret of *DODiY*, two *hehs* are formed. Thus [the letter *yod* alludes to] *YHVH*. Through this, God, blessed be He, enlightened us to reveal another allusion concerning *"YHVH is God (ha-'Elohim)*."[190] Consider that the sum of the integers for each of the letters of *yod* (which is *YHVH*) equals the numerical value of *'Elohim*. For the sum of the letters from *alef* to *yod* equals 55. Then reckon from *alef* to *vav*. The sum is 21. Then reckon the letters from *alef* to *dalet*. The sum is 10. The total is 86, like the numerical value of the Name *'Elohim*.

Thus this union [of the divine emanation] involves the three Names, *'EHYeH*, *YHVH*, *Adonay*, which are the beginning, middle, and end of the divine emanation. How so? Take the first two letters of each of these three Names, namely, *'AH YH 'AD*. The sum is 26, the same number as *YHVH*. Now take the final two letters, *YH VH NY*. The sum is 86, like the number of *'Elohim*. The total is included in the Name *YHVH*. [The latter equals 26, which may be spelled] *kaf peh vav vav*, which equals 112. This is the Name *YBQ*, which emerges from the first letters of "He shall answer us *(ya'anenu)* in the day *(be-yom)* we call *(qore'nu)*." It equals the sum of *YHVH 'Elohim*. *'Elohim* equals the sum of *'EHYeH YHVH*. And it is all a single unity, founded in *YHVH*, the proper Divine Name. Also, *'Elohim* is composed of the letters *y h m l '*. When you complete the spelling of (*Male'*) *yod heh* as *yod vav dalet heh alef*, the sum is 26, as we explained above. Also *y h m l '* alludes to all the ways of completing the spelling of *YHVH*. This is indicated by "*May (YeHe') His Great Name* [*be blessed*]."[191] In other words, [His Great Name is blessed] through completing its spelling with *yod*, *heh*, and *alef*. [The letters *y h m l '*] directly mention *yod* and *heh*, which allude to the spellings completed by *yod* and *heh*. Then [the letters] *m l '* allude to *YHVH*, when its spelling is completed by the letter *alef*. How so? The letters of *YHVH* equal 26. When their spelling is completed with the letter *alef*, they equal 45.[192] When 26 is added to 45, the total is 71, the value of the letters *y h m l '*.

THE HOUSE OF *YHVH* [I]

We now return to the explanation of the passage [from the *Zohar*]. The meaning of "*YHVH*: level upon level, concealed and revealed" has been explained. The *YHVH* that includes the [entire] divine manifestation is written, but not pronounced. The *YHVH* that contains the inner part of the divine emanation is neither pronounced nor written. It is the secret of the extension of the divine essence, which is represented by the forms of *YHVH* that are vocalized by *qamaẓ*, *pataḥ*, and so on. And the *YHVH*, which is indicated in "He and His Name alone [existed]," is neither written nor pronounced, but only held in thought. And the passage said, "Three are bound together." For the Torah is also bound to the Name *YHVH* and so is a human being, as we shall explain.

The House of Wisdom [I]

The Torah

"*The Torah of YHVH is complete (temimah).*"[1] The Torah is complete. It was woven in completeness out of *YHVH*. For the entire Torah consists of God's Names. And it is given through the Name *YHVH*, the secret of *Tif'eret*. As it is written, "*From heaven, He let you hear His voice and on the earth, He showed you His great fire.*"[2] It is well known that heaven and earth are the secret of the two *parzufim*. They are the written Torah and the oral Torah. The entire Torah was spoken in male language. This is the secret of *Tif'eret*, the Name *YHVH*. The oral Torah is its explanation. Just as the Name *YHVH*, *Tif'eret*, contains ten *sefirot* within *Tif'eret*, which is revealed along with its concealed part, the secret of *Da'at*, so the Torah is contained in the secret of the Ten Commandments, which correspond to the ten *sefirot*. The kabbalists said that the Torah is given through the Name *YHVH*. This is because *YHVH* equals 26. The sum of the letters that spell 26 (*'esrim ve-shishah*) equals Ten Commandments (*'aseret ha-dibrot*) and also *Keter Torah* (Crown of Torah).[3] "Moses received the Torah at Sinai and transmitted it."[4] It is known that Moses' prophecy came from *Tif'eret*, which is called the clear lens. That is why the [Sabbath] liturgy says, "You placed a crown of *Tif'eret* on his head when he stood before You at Sinai."[5] It is significant that the liturgy says "a crown of *Tif'eret*," for it might have said, "You placed *Tif'eret* on his head." This is a fine allusion to something that is found in the *Tiqqunim* and brought in *Pardes*, chapter two of the first Gate.[6]

> Jacob is surely the likeness of the central pillar, but Moses was also there. However, the latter was from the inner part and the former from the outer part. Jacob was from the body [of *Tif'eret*] and Moses was from its soul.[7]

The meaning is that Jacob was a chariot for *Tif'eret* in its place and our teacher, Moses, was a chariot for its concealed portion, the secret of *Da'at*. This is the "crown of *Tif'eret* (*kelil Tif'eret*)." For *Da'at* is a crown for *Tif'eret* in its place, the secret of the Name *YHVH*.

It is also explained that the Torah is the secret of the four letters of His Name. For the written Torah and the oral Torah were given to us in the secret of [the letters] *vav heh*, as was explained. But their root is in the secret of the holy Torah, which is concealed in its place, that is, the secret of [the letters] *yod heh* from His Name. The root of the written Torah, which is [the letter] *vav* from His Name, is primordial *Ḥokhmah*, the secret of *yod*. Our rabbis, of blessed memory, alluded to this when they said, "*The Torah is unripe fruit which has fallen from Ḥokhmah above*."[8] And they also alluded to this in saying, "The Torah preceded the world by two thousand years." For every *sefirah* is called a thousand. [This is] according to the secret that each *sefirah* consists of ten. Each of these contains ten, for a total of a hundred. Then each one has a hundred, making a thousand, which returns to one through the secret that a thousand indicates oneness. This process extends infinitely: a thousand from a thousand, and so on. The secret of "two thousand years" is the secret of two *sefirot* that precede the building of the world [which begins with] *Ḥesed*, as it is written, "*A world of Ḥesed will be built*."[9] These two are *Ḥokhmah* and *Binah*, where the roots of the written Torah and the oral Torah are found. As they said, "Torah is the unripe fruit fallen from *Ḥokhmah* above." This thought is deep and [only] somewhat revealed through the secret of the fifty gates of Understanding (*Binah*). There are forty-nine pure aspects and forty-nine impure aspects, which were grasped by our teacher, Moses, of blessed memory. But he did not attain the fiftieth Gate. The oral Torah, which is the final *heh* of the Tetragrammaton, was revealed from the first *heh* and given to Israel by Moses.[10] [This is] the secret of "*and YHVH let you hear His voice from heaven, and on earth He let you see His fire*." Thus "*the Torah of YHVH is complete*." For it is completely the Name *YHVH*. Accordingly, the Torah begins with the letter *bet* and ends with the letter *lamed*, which are the thirty-two[11] paths of *Ḥokhmah*. A wonderful allusion to the thirty-two paths is found in the fact that there are no other letters besides *lamed* and *bet* to which all of the letters of Divine Name, *yod*, *vav*, and *heh*, can be joined as in saying *li lo lah*, *bi bo bah*.[12] Thus the

Torah is connected to the Name *YHVH*. As I wrote above, the Name *YHVH* is alluded to by *yod*. And *yod* is an *alef*.[13] Similarly, 613 [commandments] are alluded to in the *yod* (Ten) Commandments, as has been written.[14] And *yod* is *alef*, because the Ten Commandments were said in one utterance. Thus He began [the Ten Commandments by saying] "*'anokhi (I am [YHVH your God])*,"[15] with an *alef*. Just as [the letter] *yod* represents point, line, and plane, which is length and breadth, so concerning the Torah, [the verse may be applied], "*longer than the earth is its quality (middah) and wider than the sea*."[16] And it is written, "*Your commandment is very wide*."[17] The meaning is that we are able to proceed at length in its qualities (*middot*) and in breadth, when it comes to fulfilling its commandments. But, in its secrets, it is like a point. For we cannot reach its depth, as it is written, "*so very deep, who can find it?*"[18] I have written similarly above concerning the secret of *yod* which contains *YHVH*. Then from the *yod*, an *alef* is formed: *yod* above, *vav* in the middle, a small *yod* below.

The House of Israel [I]

The soul of a human being derives from the extension of the Name *YHVH*. Even the appearance of one's body is inscribed and indicated by the Name *YHVH*. Thus one may explain the divine image (*ẓelem*) and likeness (*demut*) in which the human being was created and fashioned. This matter requires an extensive explanation. As a result, a person's heart will be aroused to "*turn from evil and do good*"[1] and to sanctify himself. For this is the reason that he was created and creation was for the sake of the human being, just as we say [in the liturgy] on Rosh Hashanah, "*This day is the beginning of Your deeds.*" And we say in tractate *Rosh ha-Shanah* that we pray according to the opinion of Rabbi Eliezer, who held that the world was created in the month of *Tishrei*. But an objection may be raised. Do we not hold that the world was created on the twenty-fifth of *Elul*? [The answer is] that his expression, "the beginning of Your deeds," refers to the creation of the human being, which is the ultimate purpose of the creation, and he was created on Rosh Hashanah.[2] Similarly, the verse says, "*How awesome are Your deeds.*"[3] The verse uses the singular form for awesome, when it should have used the plural. But all of the divine acts have one ultimate end, the human being. The kabbalists already explained this at length and chastised the philosophers who walk in darkness without any light. We shall explain this at length, below.

The will and simple desire arose in the Unique Lord, Root of Roots, *Eyn Sof*, to manifest a holy emanation from His concealed light, which would testify to the necessity of His absolute and concealed existence. Similarly, the will arose to create one perfected and complete creature, fashioned in the divine image and likeness, according to the pattern of the sacred, supernal sanctuary, the divine emanation which is called Supernal Person, as we shall explain. Concerning this creature, it was said, "*Let us make a human being in Our image.*"[4] This is what is written in *'Avodat ha-Qodesh.*

> In *Bereishit Rabbah* they asked concerning this expression, "With whom did He consult? Rabbi Joshua said in the name of Rabbi Levi, He consulted with the work of heaven and earth, like a common person who had two counselors and would do nothing without their opinion. Rabbi Samuel bar Nahman said, He consulted with the work of each day, like a king with a counsel who would do nothing without consulting it. Rabbi Ami said, He consulted with His heart, like a king who had a palace built by an architect. He saw it and it did not please him. With whom can he be angry? Not with the architect! He could only grieve with his own heart."[5] And [it says] in *Pirqey de-Rabbi Eliezer*, "The Holy One, blessed be He, immediately said to the Torah, "*let us make a human being . . .* " All of the explanations have the same intention; the kabbalists indicated to us that He did not consult with something ouside of Himself. For the one who said "with the work of heaven and earth," alluded to two known divine functions.[6] And the one who said "with the work of each day," alluded to the six supernal days of creation.[7] And they said in the Midrash of Rabbi Simeon bar Yohai, of blessed memory,[8] "the world was created with two colors, with right and left [and] with six supernal days, six supernal days were made to shine, as it is said, '*for YHVH made six days.*'[9]"[10] The one who said "with His heart" meant the Bride which contains thirty-two wondrous paths of wisdom. It is the Torah. The secret of the matter is that the human being is composed of all of them, fashioned after the entire pattern, as we shall explain with God's help. The concealed reason is so that [the human being] may also attest to the Oneness of the United Name and to its manifestation as divine emanation, in which it is contained. Thus a human being has been made in the divine image, as a likeness and sign which attests and proclaims divinity. In order to reveal and make this known, he was created in the image of God. They said in chapter eleven of *Pirqey de-Rabbi Eliezer*, "he stood on his feet and was formed in the likeness of God. The [other] creatures saw him and were afraid. For they thought that he was their creator . . . " Because of this secret, the form of a human being is

> called an image (*deyoqan*) and all forms are thus designated, because of the form of the human being. As they said in *Baba Qama*, chapter *Ha-Gozel 'Eẓim*, "One does not send money with a figure (*be-deyoqeni*)."[11] For the form of a human being is second to its Master (*Qoneh*) and no other form may be compared to it. This is similar to the verse, "*For He made the human being in the image of God.*"[12] And [the letters] *DYO* [from the word *deyoqan*] are like the two (*d"u*) *parzufim* [and the letters] *QNY* are like *QoNeh* (his Master). For he is in the likeness of his Master. [His form] bears this name in order to be composed of the supernal powers which are contained in the secret of the Great Name. And in chapter *Ḥezqat ha-Batim*, they said, "You have seen the likeness of My *deyoqan*, do not look at the *deyoqan*, itself."[13] And in chapter, *'Elu Megalḥin*, [it says], "I gave them a likeness of My image,"[14] even the divine image which is translated *deyoqeni*. Thus as a result of his containing the supernal degrees and being fashioned according to the pattern of the sanctuary, he has the power and means to unite and establish the *Kavod* (Glory), for that was the purpose of [his being created].[15]

I shall add my own insight, in order to explain the passage from *Midrash Rabbah*, which is cited above. The nature of the soul's relationship to *YHVH* will be explained.

Before I begin my discussion, I will raise a great question. Why do our rabbis, of blessed memory, the kabbalists, always speak of [only] three levels of soul in a person: *nefesh*, *ruaḥ*, and *neshamah?* For example, in the *Zohar* we read, "Fortunate are these righteous ones that cleave *nefesh* with *ruaḥ* and *ruaḥ* with *neshamah* and *neshamah* with the Holy One, blessed be He."[16] Are there not five levels: *nefesh*, *ruaḥ*, *neshamah*, *ḥayah*, and *yeḥidah*? Do not say that the three levels *nefesh*, *ruaḥ*, and *neshamah* always cleave together and that one cannot have one without the others, whereas *ḥayah* and *yeḥidah* are aspects of the additional soul [which is obtained on Sabbaths]. This is not so. For it is clearly explained in *Zohar*, *va-Yiqra'*, "There is one who has merited a *neshamah*, and one who has merited an arousal of the *ruaḥ*, and there is one who has only merited a *nefesh*."[17] Also consider what is written in *Pardes*, *Sha'ar ha-neshamah*.

> There are those who do not even merit a *nefesh*. They have only a vital, natural soul, which is a chariot to the divine soul. When one so merits, he attains a divine *nefesh*. If he further merits, they be-

> stow upon him a *ruaḥ*. If he further merits, they bestow upon him a *neshamah*.[18]

Therefore, the problem remains unresolved.

Now listen, my sons, and enliven your souls. The *neshamah* is emanated from the shining splendor of His Glory, composed of the supernal lights. Just as we explained regarding the secret of the Name *YHVH*, that there are four *sefirot* corresponding to the four letters: *Ḥokhmah*, *Binah*, *Tif'eret*, and *Malkhut*, and a fifth *sefirah*, concealed, in the secret of *Keter*, which is alluded to by the tip of the *yod*, so it is with the aspects of the human soul. This is what Nahmanides wrote in his commentary to Genesis.

> "*And He blew into his nostrils a neshamah of life.*"[19] This verse alludes to us concerning the level of the soul, its foundation, and secret. For the full Divine Name is mentioned in the verse. And it said, "*For He blew into his nostrils a neshamah of life*" to let us know that it did not come from the elements, as alluded concerning the soul of moving creatures, nor by way of extension from the separate intellects.[20] But it is a spirit from the Great Name, "*from His mouth are knowledge and understanding.*"[21] For whoever blows into another's nostrils, fills him from his soul.[22] Thus it is written, "*The soul of Shadday shall cause them to understand.*"[23] For [the *neshamah*] is from the foundation of *Binah* (understanding), by way of truth and faith.[24] This is what they mentioned in *Sifre* "[concerning] vows, when one swears an oath on the life of the king, it is like swearing on the king himself." Although there is no proof for this, it is indicated by "*ḥay YHVH ve-ḥey nafshekha* (by the life of *YHVH* and by your life)."[25,26] And in the *Midrash* of Rabbi Nehuniah ben ha-Qanah,[27] is written, "What is the meaning of '[*on the seventh day He rested*] *ve-yinafash?*'[28] It teaches that the Sabbath day sustains all of the souls (*NeFaSHot*), as it is written, '*ve-yiNaFaSH.*' "[29] From here, you can understand [what is meant by] "*speaking an oath of God.*"[30] And the enlightened will understand.[31]

The words of Nahmanides are obscure. Nevertheless, they are explained by the passages from the *Zohar* which are brought by the divine author of the *Pardes* in *Sha'ar Mahut ve-Hanhagah*, chapter twenty-two. [This] concerns the essence of the union of *Tif'eret* and *Malkhut*, which I call the secret of the coupling. [From this coupling] the souls were constituted.

It is written in the *Zohar, va-Yiqra'*, " '*and the daughter of a priest.*'"[32] This is the holy soul, which is called the daughter of the king. For it has been explained [that] the holy soul emerges from the coupling of the King and the Lady (*Matronita*). Consequently, just as below the body comes from the [union] of male and female, so it is concerning the soul above."[33] Thus [the *Zohar*] teaches that the coupling is in order to receive the souls. Similarly, it is explained in section *Lekh lekha*, " '*and its fruit is sweet to my palate.*'[34] These are the souls of the righteous, all of which are the fruit of the actions of the Holy Blessed One and exist with Him above. Come and see. All the souls of the world, which are the fruit of the actions of the Holy Blessed One, are one in one secret. When they descend to this world, they separate in the colors of male and female. And these male and female [souls] join together as one. Come and see. The desire of a female toward a male makes a *nefesh* and the desire of a male toward a female makes a *nefesh*. From the will of the male's desire toward the female and his cleaving to her, a *nefesh* is released. It contains the desire of the female and takes it. The lower desire is contained in the upper desire, and they become one will with no separation [between them]. Then the female contains all and she becomes pregnant from the male. The desires of both of them cleave as one. Thus all are included together. When souls emerge, male and female are included in them as one. Afterward, when they descend, they separate, one to this side and one to the other. The Holy Blessed One brings about their coupling later. And the right of bringing couples together is given to no other than the Holy Blessed One. For He alone knows their mates, to join them together as they should be. Fortunate is the person who succeeds in his actions and follows the path of truth in order to be joined *nefesh* with *nefesh* as they were originally. For one who succeeds in his deeds is a complete person, as he should be. Thus it is written, '*and its fruit is sweet to my palate.*' For such a person is blessed with *tiqqun*,[35] so that the world may be blessed by him, since everything depends on the actions of humans, whether they succeed or not. Rabbi Hezekiah said, thus I have heard, for it is written, '*your fruit is provided by Me.*'[36] The Holy Blessed One said to *Keneset Israel*, your fruit is indeed provided by Me.[37] '*My fruit*' is not written, but '*your fruit.*' [It refers to] that desire of the female which makes a *nefesh* and is included in the power of the male. It is contained as *nefesh* with *nefesh*. They

> become one, contained together, as we have said. Afterward, both of them are found in the world. Certainly, the fruit of the female is produced with the power of the male. Another explanation. Through the desire of the female, the fruit of the male is produced. For were it not for the desire of the female toward the male, fruit would not be produced in the world. Thus it is written, '*your fruit is provided by Me.*' "[38] In general, the passage explains that souls are the result of the coupling of *Tif'eret* and *Malkhut*. When we understand it in depth, we learn from it that the soul of the male and the soul of the female are joined together in one *'ibbur*.[39] It is impossible to imagine the soul of the female without the male or the soul of the male without the female. The reason is that they are two powers from two *sefirot* that are united together. From the power of the female, a female *nefesh* is produced and from the power of the male, a male *nefesh* is produced. We have found that the souls, whether male or female, are constituted from the union of *Tif'eret* and *Malkhut*.[40]

The rabbi who wrote the *Pardes* raised the objection that in many passages in the *Zohar* it is explained that the soul comes from [the *sefirah*] *Binah*. And thus it is explained in the *Tiqqunim*:

> "*The lamp of YHVH is the human soul.*"[41] "*Lamp* (*NeR*)" is *nefesh ruaḥ*.[42] These are the emanations of the *Shekhinah* and the Central Pillar which contains six *sefirot*.[43] "*The human soul* " is the emanation of the Supernal Mother.[44]

The *Pardes* discusses the matter at length; however, here is the issue in brief. The *neshamah* is bestowed from *Binah* in concealment and in a subtle state to *Tif'eret* and *Malkhut*. Later, *Tif'eret* and *Malkhut* unite and then the *neshamah* enters a state of existence. See there at length.[45] The principle that emerges is that the *nefesh* comes from *Malkhut*, the *ruaḥ* comes from *Tif'eret* and the *neshamah* from *Binah*. And [the soul] is produced by the uniting of *Tif'eret* and *Malkhut*. This is the "full Divine Name" mentioned by Nahmanides, as it is written, "*And YHVH 'Elohim formed the human being.*"[46] *YHVH 'Elohim is Tif'eret and Malkhut*. Afterward, the verse continues, "*and He blew into his nostrils the soul of life.*" It is from *Binah*. "*And the soul of Shadday will cause them to understand (taViNem).*"[47]

Tif'eret, which includes six extremities, along with *Malkhut* is the secret of the oath (*shavu'a*), which is related to the word seven (*shiv'ah*). From there the negative and positive precepts are drawn. For *Tif'eret*, which inclines to the right is *Ḥesed*, the secret of the positive precepts. *Malkhut* inclines to *Gevurah*, which is the left, the secret of the negative precepts. Thus if a person swore to abrogate the precept, it has no significance. For what strength does an oath, whose source is seven, have to abrogate the precept, whose source is also from seven? And the precept was already received at Mount Sinai through an oath. However, the place of a vow (*neder*) is in *Binah*, which is the tower that flies in the air of *Tif'eret*. For [the oath] is called *Tif'eret* and [the vow] is above *Tif'eret*. *NeDeR* (vow) alludes to *N DaR*, which are the fifty Gates of *Binah*.[48] Therefore, a vow applies to the precept and the oath is sworn on the king himself, in his being united with the queen and their becoming one. One who makes a vow on the life of the king is even more important. Even if they are different categories, the "life of the king" and the king are united. Thus the verse says, "*the soul of life*,"[49] which refers to the "life of the king," or *Binah*. It is similarly explained in Nahmanides's commentary.

Now I have come to the explanation of the end of the verse, which says, "*and the person became a living soul (nefesh)*." Before I explain this verse, I shall present a brief introduction. Thus the passage from *Midrash Rabbah*, mentioned above, will also be understood in length, breadth, and depth. I have already mentioned that the souls are produced through the coupling of *Tif'eret* and *Malkhut*. In other words, the *nefesh* comes from *Malkhut* and the *ruaḥ* from *Tif'eret*. Even the *neshamah*, which is from *Binah*, reaches *Tif'eret* and *Malkhut* in a subtle and concealed state. And through the coupling of *Tif'eret* and *Malkhut*, the *neshamah* comes into actual existence. You need to know that in speaking of the coupling of *Tif'eret* with *Malkhut*, we mean all six extremities. These are the arms, thighs, and genitals which pertain to the act of coupling, in the secret of the embrace (*ḥibbuq*), as explained in *Pardes*, *Sha'ar Mahut ve-Hanhagah*, chapter twenty-one. Thus the *nefesh*, *ruaḥ*, and *neshamah* are from the union of *Tif'eret* and *Malkhut*, involving all six extremities, in their place, which is the secret of the structure.[50] However, we have already mentioned above that the root of the six extremities and *Malkhut* is in *Binah*, which is the place of seeding.[51] They acquired a revealed state, to a certain degree, in this root. But they were united together there in the secret of *d"u parzufim* which is the secret of the *heh* that is in *Binah*, as explained above at length.

You also need to know that the soul of Adam and Eve was emanated from *Tif'eret* and *Malkhut*, in this secret of *d"u parzufim*. This means [that they were] not [emanated] from *Tif'eret* and *Malkhut* in their places, but from their root. Just as the *d"u parzufim* in *Binah* are the root of the six extremities in their place, so the soul of Adam is the root of all the souls. For from the soul of Adam, 600,000 souls were extended in every generation. And it is the soul of our teacher, Moses, of blessed memory, concerning which our sages said, "one woman in Egypt gave birth to 600,000 in one belly: this is Moses."[52] An allusion to this is "*six hundred thousand . . . in whose midst I am.*"[53] For they were really with him and emerged from him. Since Adam's soul is the root of all the souls and all the souls are derived from it, when it was fined by God because of him, all the souls which come from him were fined. For all of them potentially existed within him.[54] And the following is written in *Midrash Rabbah, parashat Ki Tisa'*:

> While Adam was still a soulless lump (*golem*), the Holy Blessed One showed him every righteous person who would ever derive from him. There were those who derive from the hair of his head, and those who derive from his forehead, those who derive from his eyes, and those from his nose, those who derive from his mouth, and those from his ears, those who derive from his ear lobes (where earrings are placed). You should know that when Job wanted to argue with the Holy Blessed One he said, "*if only I knew how to find Him . . . I would set my case before Him.*"[55] And the Holy Blessed One answered, "*you wish to argue with Me? 'Where were you when I formed the earth?'* "[56] What is the meaning of "*where*"? Rabbi Simeon ben Lakish said, "The Holy Blessed One said to Job, 'In what place did your "*where*" derive? From the head, or the forehead, or from one of his limbs? If you know in what place your "*where*" was, you may argue with Me.' That is what is meant by '*where were you.*'" [57]

Through our explanation, the meaning will be entirely clear. [The *Midrash*] said, "While Adam was still a soulless lump," because after the Holy One, blessed be He, established him in his place, the plantings were manifested into the Garden of Eden, until they had bodies in which to clothe themselves. Concerning this soul, which contained all of the souls, our rabbis said that the souls existed before the world was created. The meaning is that the building (*binyan*), which begins from *Ḥesed*, is called world, as it is written, "*a world of Ḥesed will be built.*"[58] But the *nefesh*, *ruaḥ*, and *neshamah* that are produced by the coupling of *Tif'eret* and *Malkhut* in their place are the secret of the new souls, which are prepared for the time when the Holy One, blessed be He, will cause his world to be created anew. This is explained in *Pardes*, *Sha'ar Mahut ve-Hanhagah*, chapter twenty-three. Thus it has been explained that the soul of Adam and Eve is the secret of the *d"u parzufim* in *Binah*. This is the meaning of the verse, "*and He blew into his nostrils the soul of life.*"[59] It refers to the "life of the king," which is in *Binah*. Thus the reason why the verse says "*into his nostrils*" may be appreciated. For it might have said "*into his nostril.*" However, Adam existed in the secret of the *d"u parzufim*. Thus the verse said "*into his nostrils*," because they are also two, which may be easily understood.

Next, the subtle meaning of the passage from *Midrash Rabbah*, quoted above, may be understood. "Rabbi Joshua said in the name of Rabbi Levi, 'He consulted with the work of heaven and earth.' " It is known that "heaven and earth" in union are *Tif'eret* and *Malkhut*. He alluded to the soul of Adam and Eve in the secret of the *d"u* [*parzufim*] in *Binah*. "Rabbi Samuel bar Nahman said, 'He consulted with the work of each day.' " They are *Tif'eret* and *Malkhut* in their place, in the secret of the six extremities. They are [also] all of the renewed souls which are produced from them. In either case, the souls come from *Tif'eret* and *Malkhut*, whether in their place, which is the six extremities, or whether in their root, *Binah*, the secret of *d"u*, which is the root of the building, the secret of *heh* as *Binah*.[60]

It is also known that the six extremities are the cause of this world. Our rabbis, of blessed memory, said this world was created with [the letter] *heh*.[61] Even though the *heh* alludes to *Malkhut* and is the small *heh* in [the word] "*be-hibar'am* (*in their being created*),"[62] nevertheless this final *heh*, which brings into actuality the bestowing of the six extremities, is from the first *heh*. In other words, [it derives] from *Binah* which is the root of the extremities. However, the cause of the World to Come, which was created with [the letter] *yod*, is beyond this. It is higher than the aspect of the three lines, which are [the extensions of] the three *yods*: *Ḥokhmah* is the body of the *yod*, *Binah* in its higher aspect is the foot of the *yod*, and *Keter* is the tip of the *yod*. Therefore, there is a soul of souls, a root higher than the roots of the building. Thus the additional soul is from [*Ḥokhmah*], as indicated in the verse, "*and Ḥokhmah will enliven (teḤaYeH) its possessor.*"[63] This level [of the soul] is called *ḥayyah*. It is the fourth aspect to the secret of the soul: *nefesh*, *ruaḥ*, and *neshamah* [correspond to] *Malkhut*, *Tif'eret*, and *Binah*. And the *ḥayyah* comes from *Ḥokhmah*. There is another extremely concealed [aspect of the soul], the secret of *Keter*, which is called *yeḥidah*. However, the two levels *ḥayyah* and *yeḥidah* are the secret of the additional soul for the World to Come. [This is alluded to in the verse,] "*No eye has seen* [*them*] *God, besides You.*"[64] They come from *yod*. However, the levels *nefesh*, *ruaḥ*, and *neshamah*, for those who attain them in this world, are from the letter *heh*.

Thus in a general way the question has been answered, why, for the most part, only the three levels, *nefesh*, *ruaḥ*, *nesḥamah*, are mentioned. Are there not two additional levels, *ḥayyah* and *yeḥidah*? The *ḥayyah* and *yeḥidah* are the secret of the additional soul in the World to Come and the *nefesh*, *ruaḥ*, and *nesḥamah* the secret [of the soul] in this world. Do not object on the basis of what is found in the later kabbalists concerning the secret of these five [aspects of the soul]. [They say that the parts of the soul] are divided according to the times: *nefesh* during the intermediate days of a Festival and during the additional prayer on the New Moon, *ruaḥ* during Holy Days, *neshamah* on the Day of Atonement, *ḥayyah* on the Sabbath, *yeḥidah* in the World to Come. As an indication of this, they interpret the five words "*olah hu' 'isheh reaḥ niḥoaḥ* (*it is a burnt offering, by fire, of pleasing fragrance*)."[65] The level of *reaḥ* (fragrance) stands for the Sabbath. Thus we smell spices at the end of the Sabbath. This [teaching] is a very subtle spark from [the kabbalists]. It is consistent with a saying of our rabbis, of blessed memory, "Sabbath is one-sixtieth of the World to Come."[66] However, essentially, *ḥayyah* and *yeḥidah* pertain to the World to Come, which is the letter *yod* of the Divine Name with its tip. They said in the *Tiqquney Zohar* and it is quoted in *Pardes*, *Sha'ar Mahut ve-Hanhagah*, that Adam and Eve are *Ḥokhmah* and *Binah*. For although they were considered together as *d"u parzufim* (in *Binah*), nevertheless the level of Adam is superior. This is in accord with what is written in [the *Gemara*], chapter *Ha-Roeh*, concerning *d"u parzufim:* "Which of them goes in front? Rav Nahman bar Isaac said, 'It is evident that the male goes in front.' "[67] The soul of Adam was from *Ḥokhmah*, which is the soul level called *ḥayyah*. Thus the verse says, "*And Adam became a living (ḥayyah) soul.*"[68] It alludes to the secret of the *ḥayyah*. This is despite the fact that the verse said earlier, "*and He blew in his nostrils the soul of life.*" And we explained "*nostrils*" as referring to Adam and Eve and "soul of life" as *Binah*.

It has already been explained that the higher aspect of *Binah* is also *yod*. And Eve also approached him, as indicated in the secret [of the verse], "*for she is the mother of all life (ḥay).*"[69] She should have been called *ḥayyah*, but was called *Ḥavvah* (Eve), because she inclines toward *Binah*, in the secret of the root of the six extremities. Thus *yod* became a *vav* and the name *ḥayyah* became *Ḥavvah*. Nevertheless, Rashi explained *Ḥavvah* as being the same as *ḥayyah*, just as these words have the same meaning. Understand this. This *ḥayyah* was the source of "life of the king," from which comes "*soul of life.*"[70] The verse said, "*and Adam became a nefesh ḥayyah (living soul).*" In other words, he contained the soul levels from *nefesh* to *ḥayyah*, including *ḥayyah*: *nefesh*, *ruaḥ*, *neshamah*, *ḥayyah*.

Now a problem can be resolved which troubled me for many years. The verse says, "*YHVH 'Elohim took Adam and placed him in the Garden of Eden.*"[71] Rashi explains, "He took him with pleasant words and enticed him to enter." This is difficult to understand. Is it not our entire intention to go to the Garden of Eden and fortunate is he who succeeds? Yet Adam did not want to enter until the Holy Blessed One enticed him? However, the explanation is that there is a lower Garden of Eden and a higher Garden of Eden. These have their root even higher in the building,[72] from whose root this world is projected, where the lower Garden of Eden is located. The root of the higher Garden of Eden is located above the building. Thus Adam, who now had attained the level of *ḥayyah* which emanates from the root of the upper Garden of Eden, thought he would enter the upper Garden of Eden and had to be enticed [to enter the lower Garden of Eden]. This is alluded to in the verse, "*and YHVH 'Elohim said, lest Adam be like one of us.*"[73] "He is unique (*yaḥid*) in the lower world, just as I am unique above . . ."[74] The meaning is that he had reached the level of *ḥayyah* and would also want to ascend above in order to make use of *Keter*, *yeḥidah*, the fifth soul level which is called *yeḥidah*. The Holy One, blessed be He, said I will prevent him and drive him out. Concerning the Tree of Life, I have already written that [the *Ma'aseh Bereishit*] speaks about matters below and alludes to what is above. The Tree of Life is a unique (*yeḥidi*) tree that is the source of *Ḥokhmah* which bestows life[75] and the "life of the king" is from *Ḥokhmah*. Understand this.

Now Rabbi Eliezer the Great said in his chapters that the Holy Blessed One consulted with the Torah when He said, "*Let Us make a human being.*"[76] And Rabbi Ami said in the Midrash, quoted above, that He consulted with His heart. They both have the same meaning and allude to Adam's soul level, *ḥayyah*, which comes from *Ḥokhmah*. We have already mentioned above that the primordial Torah is the secret of *Ḥokhmah*. Thus it begins with the letter *bet* and ends with the letter *lamed*, the secret of heart (*lev*),[77] which is the secret of the thirty-two (*l"b*) paths of *Ḥokhmah*.[78] The kabbalists have already written that *Malkhut* is called *Kavod* (Glory)[79] and the heart[80] of heaven. *Kavod* has the numerical value of 32. *Malkhut* is called [*kavod* or heart] when She contains the *shefa'* that descends from the thirty-two paths of *Ḥokhmah*. Thus both of them[81] said the same thing.

The will is like the stages of the human soul. The secret of *ḥayyah* is from *Ḥokhmah*, and *Binah* is emanated in the secret of *d"u* (*parẓufim*) when *Tif'eret* and *Malkhut* are above. They become actualized by means of *Malkhut*. Thus *Malkhut* is the fourth stage, corresponding to the four letters of the Divine Name: *nefesh* is from the final *heh*, *ruaḥ* from the *vav*, *neshamah* from the first *heh*, *ḥayyah* from the *yod*, *yeḥidah* from the tip of the *yod*, the secret of *Keter*.

Now we return to our subject. Just as the [letters of the] Name *YHVH* [correspond to] four stages in the divine emanation along with its tip, so it is with the human soul. And just as each individual contains ten *sefirot*, so it is with the souls, as indicated in the *Ra'aya Meheymna*. "[There are others], masters of the secrets of the Torah, the masters of the qualities (*middot*), who inherit souls from the side of the holy *Malkhut* which contains ten *sefirot*. For whoever inherits it and merits it, merits ten *sefirot* without separation."[82] The passage is quoted at length in *Pardes*, in the fifth chapter of the first Gate, and is well explained there. And the following is written in *Midrash Ruth* from the *Zohar*.

> The Holy One, blessed be He, created in a person *YHVH*, which is His Holy Name, a soul to the soul, and this is called Adam. And its lights are expanded into nine lights, which manifest from the *yod* and it is one light without separation. Because of this, the human body is called the garment of Adam. *Heh* is called *neshamah* and couples with *Yod*, and extends to many lights. It is one, *Yod Heh* without separation. Concerning this is written, "*And God created Adam in His image in the image of God He created him, male and female He created them.*"[83] "*And He called their name, Adam.*" [The letter] *vav* is called *ruaḥ* and it is called the son of *yod heh*. [The letter] *heh* is called *nefesh* and it is called daughter. Thus [the letters of the Divine Name are] father and mother, son and daughter. The secret of the matter is that *yod vav dalet heh alef vav alef vav heh alef* is called *adam* (human being). Its lights expand into forty-five lights, which is the numerical value of *adam* and equals *yod vav dalet heh alef vav alef vav heh alef*.[84] And the Name, *Y"H V"H*, "*He created them male and female.*"[85] He called them Adam. After this He formed the body, as it is said, "*and YHVH 'Elohim formed Adam, dust from the earth. And He blew into his nostrils the soul of life.*"[86] What is the difference between *Adam* and Adam? *YHVH* is called Adam[87] and the body is called Adam. How is one distinguished from the other? Wherever the verse, "*God created adam in His image*," applies, [Adam] is *YHVH*. Wherever it is not said to be "*in His image*," [Adam] refers to the body.[88]

What I have written is explained in this passage. Now *adam* equals 9, according to the unitary system.[89] For *adam* is not included in the secret of the *yeḥidah*, or *Keter*, the tent and supreme level. This is the meaning of the verse, "*I found one man me-'LF.*"[90] Do not read "from a thousand (*me-'elef*), vocalized with a *segol*, but rather *me-'alef*, lacking one [*'alef*].

Nevertheless, *adam* is the seal of truth. For truth (*'emet*) also equals 9, according to the unitary system.[91] The human being was made with the seal, as was explained concerning the verse, "*and God created the adam in His image.*"[92] Also the final letters of the verse, "*and He blew into his nostrils the breath of life (va-yipaḤ be-'apaV nishmaT ḥayyiM),*"[93] spell seal (*ḤOTaM*). At the end of the *Ma'aseh Bereishit*, you find the seal of *adam* and the seal of truth. *Adam*: "*God saw* [*all that He had made*] *and, behold, it was very good (tov Me'oD).*"[94] [This refers to the human being (*adam*)], for "*very (Me'oD)*" has the same letters as *adam*, the basis of creation. "[*He rested from all the work of*] *creation which He had done (asher bara' 'ElohiM la-'asoT).*"[95] The final letters spell truth (*'emet*). Concerning this, it is said, "*You give truth to Jacob.*"[96] [He is] a chariot for *Tif 'eret* [and] father of the emanantion of souls with *Malkhut*, his wife. This is alluded to by the verse, "*for the portion of YHVH is 'mo Jacob, the ḥevel of His inheritance.*"[97] Do not read "*His people,*" (*'amo*) with a *pataḥ*, but "*with Him,*" (*'imo*) with a *ḥiriq*. For the Torah is not vocalized, so that it may be interpreted in many ways. [Thus the meaning is] that they are really "*with Him,*" with the Name *YHVH*. And "*ḥevel*" means extension,[98] by means of Jacob, as explained above.

Thus the human being is connected to *YHVH*, through his soul, just as the Torah is connected with *YHVH*. This is the secret of "*Let Us make the human being in Our image.*"[99] It is alluded to in the word *ẓelem* (image). The kabbalists refer to the extension of the worlds as a tree. And this tree of the Holy One, blessed be He, is the true Tree of Life, the soul of all life. The Name *YHVH* is alluded to in the word *'eẓ* (tree), when certain mathematical functions are performed on the first two and last two letters. How so? *yod-heh*: *yod* multiplied by *heh* and *heh* multiplied by *yod* equals 100.[100] Then, *vav heh*: *vav* multiplied by *heh* and *heh* multiplied by *vav* equals 60.[101] Thus the total is equal to the numerical value of *'eẓ*.[102] Concerning this, there is an allusion in the verse, "*Is there a tree ('eẓ) in it or not.*"[103] In other words, determine whether God's providence is in it and if "*it is a land which YHVH watches over*"[104] or not. It is as if the verse had said, "Is *YHVH* in its midst, or not?" And Caleb said, "*Their shadow (ẒiLaM) has turned away from them and YHVH is with us.*"[105] *ẒLM* has the same numerical value as *'eẓ*.[106] For we are sitting in His secret place. This is the meaning of "*and YHVH is with us.*" Now the Torah is also called *'eẓ*, as in "*she is a tree ('eẓ) of life, for those who hold on to her.*"[107] And beloved is the human being who was created *be-ẒeLeM*, which also has the same numerical value. They are [both] connected with the Name *YHVH*. Thus the verse said, "*Let Us make man in Our ẓelem.*"[108]

As for the expression, "*in Our likeness* (*ki-demutenu*)," this refers to the likeness of the human body. For although the term *adam* (human being) specifically applies to his inner part, the soul, [nevertheless] the body is called the flesh of *adam*, as explained in the *Zohar:* "The human body is called the garment of man."[109] Similarly, even with the forces of impurity, "pig flesh" refers to their garment which is called "flesh" and the form, which comes from the impure spirit, is called "pig." And so the verse said, concerning the clothing of the soul within the limbs of the body, "*You clothed me of skin and flesh and wove me of bones and sinews.*"[110] If the skin and flesh is a garment for the human being, we must say that the inner spirit is what is [properly] called *adam* (human being), and not the skin and flesh. It says in *Sefer ha-Zohar*:

> Every form that is contained within this extension is called *adam*, "you are *adam*."[111] You are called *adam* and not the rest of the nations, the idol worshippers. And every spirit (*ruḥa'*) is called *adam*. The spirit of the holy concealment. Its body is a garment. Concerning this, is written, "*You clothed me of skin and flesh.*"[112] The flesh of *adam* is a garment. Wherever, "flesh of *adam*" is written, *adam* is within, flesh is the garment of *adam*.[113]

Thus it is clear that the term *adam* applies to the form and not to the matter. Consequently, the nations of the world are not called *adam*, for their soul derives from the impure spirit. However, the soul of Israel is from its Holy Spirit, as it is said, "*Your fruit is provided by Me*"[114] "*and his fruit is sweet to my palate.*"[115] This alludes to the tree which is called "all." For the souls, which are called *adam*, fly forth from there. They are in the image of God. Our sages, of blessed memory, explained the verse, "*Its inner part was covered with love by the daughters of Jerusalem.*"[116] The souls of Israel are separate from the souls of the nations. For the souls of the righteous are not mixed together with the souls of the wicked.

Nevertheless, there is a certain relevance to the likeness of the body, since it is harnessed to the soul, as we have learned, "One saves the book chest (from a fire), along with the book."[117] And you, my sons, may their Rock guard them and grant them life, pay careful attention to what I will show you concerning what a human being is in his inner aspect and what is alluded to by his likeness. Then who would not be moved to sanctify himself in speech, thought, and deed? The following is written in the *Zohar*, concerning the body of Adam.

> Rabbi Simeon got up and said, "I saw[118] that when the Holy Blessed One wanted to create Adam, the upper and lower forces were shocked. And the sixth day ascended its levels until it reached the supernal will. It caused the beginning of all lights to shine and the gate of the east opened. For light goes forth from there. And the south showed the might of the light, which it took from the head and it became stronger in the east. The east strengthened the north and the north was aroused, expanded, and called out with great force to the west to approach and to join with it. Then, the west ascended to the north and joined together with it. Afterward, the south went and took hold of the west and north and south surrounded it. This is the secret of the borders of the garden. Then east came close to west and the west rested in joy and asked of all of them, saying, '*Let us make adam in our image, in our likeness*.'[119] He should be like this, with four sides, above, and below. And the east cleaved to the west and produced him. We learn concerning this, that *adam* emerged from the place of the Temple."[120]

The wise person, upon whom the spirit rests, will meditate on this wondrous secret and will understand the secret of "*Let Us make adam in Our image, in Our likeness*." It is not proper to explain more than this.

However, just as the true being within [the human being] comes from four supernal extremities, so this being is linked to four lower extremities. This is what was written in chapter eleven of the chapters of Rabbi Eliezer the Great. "He began to gather together the dust of *adam* from the four corners of the earth: red, white, black, and green."[121] [In the *Zohar* text], above, it says that the lower *adam* emerged from the place of the Temple. This corresponds to what was written in *Bereishit Rabbah*:

> "[*And YHVH 'Elohim formed the adam dust*] *from the earth*."[122] Rabbi Berakhiah and Rabbi Helbo said in the name of Rabbi Samuel bar Nahman, "He was created from the place of his atonement. How so? As it is written, '*Make me an altar of earth*.'[123] The Holy One, blessed be He, said, 'I will create him from the place of his atonement and, hopefully, he will be able to survive.' "[124]

And it says in the Midrash of Rabbi Simeon bar Yohai, of blessed memory:

> Rabbi Simeon said that Rabbi Hezekiah said that when the Holy Blessed One created Adam, he was created from the dust of the lower Temple and his soul was given to him from the dust of the upper Temple. Just as when he was created from the dust below, three sides, the elements of the earth, were joined to him, so too, when he was created from the dust above, three supernal sides were joined to him and he became a complete *adam.*[125]

Thus the body is a lower Temple and the soul a higher Temple. And the Temple below corresponds to the Temple above. For the human being, who is called a little world, is patterned after the great Adam, the secret of divine emanation.

There is also [a correspondence] in the likeness of the body. For just as *Ḥokhmah*, *Binah*, and *Da'at*, the first three [*sefirot*], are considered as one, so the human head includes the brain, the skull, and the tongue, which correspond to these three. *Gedulah* (greatness)[126] and *Gevurah* correspond to the arms. In the Midrash of Rabbi Nehuniah ben ha-Qanah, of blessed memory, they said the following:

> The Holy One, blessed be He, has seven holy forms and all of them are paralleled in the human being, as it is written, "*For He made the human being in the image of God,*" [127] "*male and female, He created them.*"[128] These are [the seven forms]: the right and left thigh, right and left hand, the torso with [the mark of] its covenant and the head. That makes six. But seven was said. You must include his wife, for it is written, "*they become one flesh.*"[129,130]

Also the Name *YHVH* is alluded to in the structure of a human being, from top to bottom and from bottom to top. How so? The head is like a *yod.* The torso is like a *vav.* The ten fingers, five on each hand, are the two *heh*s. Also, the ten toes, five on each foot, are the two *heh*s. The length of the penis is a *vav.* Its tip is a *yod.* In the beginning of *Pardes*, it is written that toes are like shadows to the fingers. This alludes to the world of *Beri'ah* (Creation), which is a shadow to the world of *'Aẓilut* (Emanation). Now I am going to help you understand his words. For he does not mean *Beri'ah* in its place. Rather, [he is referring to] the sources of *Beri'ah,* which sparkle in *Malkhut.* They are still in the stage of *'Aẓilut.* By means of them, the shadow will return ten levels. However, the sources are in *'Aẓilut.* Therefore, it is well that they are part of the *tiqqun* of the human being, who is made in the image of God.

Also, in the likeness of the face, there are two eyes and a nose. This is like two *yod*s and a *vav*, which add up to 26, the numerical value of the Name *YHVH*. The great level in a human being is when he lowers his eyes. Then they all remain in [a contemplative] union. But, when he raises his eyes, then the eyes look out from the nose and *YHVH* does not rest on the Throne of Compassion. Only the nose remains. Then there is divine anger in the world.[131] When he lowers his eyes, then the attribute of compassion, *YHVH* [is present].[132] Under the nose are two nostrils which form a *shin*. So, the Name *YHVH* in the alphabet of *a"t b"sh*, becomes *mzpz*, which equals 300, the value of [the letter]*shin*.[133]

There is also an allusion to *YHVH* in the ten fingers of the hands, which are the number of the ten *sefirot*. How so? In each finger there are three segments, except for the thumb which has two segments. And the One "*who formed the human being with wisdom (Ḥokhmah)*,"[134] formed him thus with a wondrous intent. The right hand alludes to the letters *yod heh* and the left hand alludes to the letters *vav heh*. Spell out the letters *yod heh* as follows: *yod vav dalet heh alef*. They are five letters, corresponding to five fingers of the hand. Take these letters and spell them out fully a second time as follows: *yod vav dalet vav alef vav dalet lamed tav heh alef alef lamed peh*. Now in four of the letters there are three segments and in the letter *heh* there are only two segments.[135] Similarly, each of the four fingers has three segments, while the thumb has only two. Therefore hand is called *yad*, because it has fourteen segments.[136]

The left hand corresponds to the letters *vav heh*. When they are spelled as *vav alef vav heh alef*, they equal five. Then complete their spelling as follows: *vav alef vav alef lamed peh vav alef vav heh alef alef lamed peh*. Thus for four letters there are three segments, and for one letter, two segments. There are fourteen segments among the five fingers. This is the left hand. This is the meaning of the verse, "*They walk before the pursuer without strength (koaḥ)*."[137] For these two [hands of fourteen segments] are the strength [twenty-eight] and when Israel are righteous they add to the power that is above.

There is also an allusion to *Shadday* in the hand. How so? Take the last three fingers and spread them like a *shin* and then bend the index finger like a *dalet*. Afterward, bend the thumb, which is shorter, like a *yod*. This is what is meant by the Holy One, blessed be He, appeared to Abraham as *'El Shadday* and not with a truly strong hand, which is the form of *YHVH*. Also, the Name *Shadday* is alluded to in the form of the body, as follows. The person's head and two arms, straightened above, appear in the form of a *shin*. When the left arm is extended and the right one rests [at the side], it is like the shape of *dalet*. And the crown of the sign of the covenant is like a *yod*.[138] But the uncircumcised nations are indicated by [the letters] *SHeD* (demon),[139] God spare us. When a person is circumcised and keeps the holy covenant, he cleaves to *YHVH*. Then the form of the covenant is a *vav* and the two testicles are in the form of two *yod*s. This equals 26.[140] There is an allusion concerning this in the verse, "*who will ascend to heaven for us (MI Ya'aleH LanU Ha-shamaymaH)*."[141] The first letters of each word spell *MILaH* (circumcision) and the last letters spell *YHVH*.

Also see the wonders concerning the form of the human body in *Pardes, Sha'ar ha-neshamah*. You will find that due to the body's mobility, it is worthy of being a dwelling-place for the soul. And the levels of *nefesh*, *ruaḥ*, and *neshamah* have as dwelling-places in the body, the brain, heart, and liver,[142] which are indicated by *MeLeKH* (king).[143]

The portion of the *nefesh* is in the liver which is the vital, or natural, force. It contains the power which nourishes, the power that draws nourishment to all the limbs, the power that holds food for the appropriate amount of time, and the power that governs growth, the power that gives birth to a similar offspring, and the power of the senses—hearing, seeing, smelling, tasting, and touching. All of these powers are in the natural soul.

The portion of the *ruaḥ* is in the heart, which is the [seat of the] will. It governs the powers according to its will, like a king who leads his people according to his will. [It is] also like a king who sees to the needs of his ministers, servants, and slaves, providing each with his needs, sustenance, and allotted bread, as is appropriate to each one, according to his level. Similarly, the living *ruaḥ* that is in the heart provides for all of the powers and nourishes and supplies each of the limbs, according to what is appropriate for it.

The portion of the *neshamah* is in the brain. It is the intellect that reigns over all of [the parts of the soul]. To comprehend this, know that before the will, which is in the heart, is moved to do something which it wishes to do, it arises in thought, within the brain, which considers what to do. After there is agreement concerning what to do, within the mind that is in the brain, then the thought is clothed in the will that is in the heart. Thus the thought is completed by the will in the heart, which is the *ruaḥ*. For this reason the power in the heart is called *ruaḥ*. For *ruaḥ* means will, as indicated in the verse, "*They went wherever the ruaḥ impelled them to go*."[144] The *ruaḥ* that is in the heart is clothed in its forces, which extend from the *nefesh*, which is in the liver, and acts through them. Thus it completes the activity that was thought in the brain, according to the will, which is in agreement with the thought. Therefore, all of [the parts of the soul] are united in a complete unity. The *nefesh* receives from the *ruaḥ* in the heart, which is the will. The will only acts in agreement with the brain's thought. They only act in accord with the brain's decision.

In order to indicate to you how holy the body is, I will copy what is written in *Sefer 'Avodat ha-Qodesh, ḥeleq ha-Yiḥud*, chapter eighteen.

> I saw wondrous things concerning the formation [of the body] in the treasuries of those who delve deeply in wisdom. I bring them now to be of use to those who pursue the word of *YHVH*. From what has been written, it has been explained that the human being is [created] in the image of God. [Also explained] is who is among the inner powers and the perfection he merited and who is among the outer powers. For each one is given a place, according to his honor, as ordained by the wisdom of the only Lord. [This is] in order to bestow upon and connect each of the forms to the place that is right for it, by means of Sandalfon. The secret of his name is matter and form. For the form is given according to the matter, as ordained by the supreme wisdom. There are cases where a *nefesh* is emanated from the inner aspect of the *sefirot*. And there are those that are emanated from the outer part. There are those that come from the wings. There are those who are essentially from the side of good and others from the side of evil. Now the *nefesh* of the holy nation that was chosen to be the special one of the Holy Blessed One, is from the side of holiness and purity. However, there are distinctions among them. For the *nefesh* of a righteous person is not like the *nefesh* of a wicked person. Also among these [two types], there are distinctions in regard to the levels of the *nefesh*. However, the *nefesh* of the idol worshippers is from the side of impurity and they are impure. I saw in *Sefer ha-Yiḥud*, which was written by the author of *ha-Temunah*, something wonderful concerning this matter. He said there, "the [physical] forms of Israel should have been different and separate from the type of Adam, just like their powers and *nefesh*. But [this could not be], because of the law of *shemitah* and its difficulties. For the powers are intermixed and reincarnated in various physical bodies and all return to their places by means of the sacrifices which are offered for favor on the altar, from the cows." The meaning is that the form of Israel should have been different from the rest of the crea-

tures. Just as their *nefesh* and powers are separate and different, so their bodies should have been different. But the order of *shemitah* and its difficulties does not permit this. For the powers and souls are mixed together and reincarnated with the sins of the bodies. In other words, the *nefesh* of an Israelite is mixed together with the bodies of idol worshippers. Those that are mixed with the body of cows are redeemed through the sacrifice that is offered for favor, from among the cows. However, the *nefesh* cannot be redeemed from the body of an idol worshipper, until he converts. So much for this concealed matter. However the holy author of *ha-Qanah*, may his memory be a blessing for the life of the World to Come, gave another answer to his holy son, Nahum, may his memory be a blessing for the life of the World to Come. You will find it in his *Sefer ha-Peli'ah*. Now I am returning to my discussion of the matter of formation. I will say that the *sefirah*, *Malkhut*, contains all of the forms. Within it are ordered [everything from] the innermost to the outermost, as ordained by the supernal wisdom. The forms are given by Sandalfon and the roots of the higher powers are preserved to give to each and every spiritual body that is joined with the [physical] body, the form which is appropriate for it. The secret of the matter is that the United Name contains ten *sefirot* that are ten holy Names. They are vessels for the Separate Intellects which are not grasped by thought. For they are the secret of the concealed Name. And these are a soul to those. There are epithets for each of these Names. The wings are attached to the epithets and the Heavenly Ministers are attached to the wings. Each of the Heavenly Ministers has chariots and forces. Thus everything depends on the United Name. He directs His world with lovingkindness, the secret of the Explicit Name in which the United Name is clothed. And it is inscribed on the staff which is directed toward *Ḥesed*, in the secret of the palaces of *Malkhut*. They are like a spiritual body to receive the inner intellects which are like forms for them. The *qelippot* are harnessed to them and are like forms for them. Accordingly, [the verse says], "*Let Us make the human being in Our image*."[145] For they are the basis of his matter. And the division of his limbs are [according to] the Explicit Name which is inscribed on the staff, the secret of a staff directed toward *Ḥesed*. Also his form consists of three levels, one within the other, *nefesh*, *ruaḥ*, *neshamah*. They are [connected] in one strong bond and one is a throne to the next. They draw from their roots. The *nefesh* [draws] from the bride,[146] in the secret of "*I desired You, with my nefesh, at night.*"[147] And the *ruaḥ* [draws] from the bridegroom,[148] in the secret of, "*I even seek You with the ruaḥ within me.*"[149] And the *neshamah* [draws] from the wedding canopy,[150] in the secret of "*all of the neshamah will praise Yah.*"[151] These forms also have a spiritual body, which is mentioned above. It joins together the form and the body which is patterned like the *qelippah*, which is mentioned in the teaching of the Great Light, Rabbi Simeon bar Yohai, of blessed memory. "I found in the book of King Solomon, when coupling occurs below, the Holy Blessed One dispatches one likeness of the human face, inscribed in an image. If the eye were permitted to see, a person would see above his head, an image inscribed with a human face. In that image, a human being is created. Until that image exists, which his Master placed over his head, and is found there, a human being is not created. As it is written, '*and God created the human being in His image.*'[152] That image is prepared for him until he goes out to the world. When he goes out, he is grown in that image. In that image, he walks about. As it is written, '*A person only walks about in an image.*'[153] This image comes from above. At the time that these spirits leave their places, each and every spirit is prepared before the Holy King in precious preparations, with the countenance that exists in this world. From that precious, prepared countenance, that image emerges."[154] It is this spiritual body which sustains the [physical] body, even though it joins with [both] the body and the form. For two opposites can only be joined together by means of an intermediary and this is the spiritual body. It is connected with the body, even though the latter is formed from the dust of the Temple which is in Jerusalem, where one of the entrances to Gehinnom is found. In *Bereishit Rabbah*, they said, " '[*and YHVH 'Elohim made the human being dust*] *from the earth.*'[155] Rabbi Berakhiah and Rabbi Helbo said in the name of Rabbi Samuel bar Nahman, he was created from the place of his atonement. How so? As it is written, '*Make Me an altar of earth.*'[156] The Holy one, blessed be He, said I will create him from the place of his atonement and, hopefully, he will be able to survive."[157] And the human being contains two hundred and forty-eight limbs which are vessels for the two hundred and forty-eight powers and branches of the soul. [These] are patterned after the Explicit Name, in conjunction with the thirty-two wondrous paths of *Ḥokhmah*,

> through which all that exists was actualized. For the Explicit Name is seventy-two Names, built from the verses which begin, "*va-yis'a (and [the angel of YHVH] travelled),*" "*va-yavo' (and [the pillar of cloud] came),*" "*va-yet (and [Moses] streched out [his hand]).*"[158] Each of the seventy-two Names is formed from three letters, containing the right, left, and center. Separately, they are two hundred and sixteen letters.[159] These letters allude to the wisdom (*Ḥokhmah*) of the inner elements that are contained in the secret of the concealed God, which contain all being. When the thirty-two wondrous paths of *Ḥokhmah* are joined with the two hundred and sixteen letters of the Explicit Name, the power of the south is in the east and the son emerges from the father. [Together,] they total two hundred and forty-eight. When the pure will arose to create the human being, He created and established him with two hundred and forty-eight limbs which are two hundred and forty-eight thrones to the powers of the soul, which branch out from it.[160]

I have more to say concerning the spiritual body that acts as an intermediary between the soul and the body. For the form, if one might say so, is similar to the One who fashioned it. For the kabbalists have already said, by way of example, that *Eyn Sof* is a soul to the souls. For we call the divine emanations souls for all that exists, and *Eyn Sof* is a soul for those souls.[161] For, in comparison to Him, those souls are like a body to a soul. The divine emanation is called the Great Adam, as it is written, "*And on the [likeness of the] Throne, the likeness of [the appearance of] a human being.*"[162] We will explain this thoroughly below. And the human being, who is called the Small Adam, was created in the image and likeness. The soul in the body is, *mutatis mutandis*, like *Eyn Sof* in regard to the divine emanation. As we explained above, there is a concealed aspect between the essence of *Eyn Sof* and the unity of the divine emanation. This refers to the extension of the essence indicated by *YHVH*, vocalized with a *qamaẓ*, in *Keter* and *YHVH*, vocalized with a *pataḥ*, in *Ḥokhmah*, and so on. This is called the manifested essence. This manifestation is the unity and connection of the flame to the coal. Similarly, in the case of the human being, the spiritual body is the connection of the soul and the body.

I will also copy the words of the *Rav*, our teacher and master, Rabbi Mattathias Delacrut, concerning the unity of the divine emanation with *Eyn Sof* and the connection of soul and body.

The beginning of every thing is God, blessed be He. He is the first of all, precedes all, and is exalted above all. He is called the Cause of all Causes. Before the world was created, all things were concealed and hidden with Him. What existed in potential was not known. As our sages of blessed memory said, "Before the world was created, only He and His Name existed." For they attributed all of the ten *sefirot* to the proper Divine Name, as will be further explained. And it was said that only He and His Name were known, in its basic sense, but not in terms of its implications. For the attributes were entirely concealed in *Eyn Sof* in its simple unity, until the thought arose to create a world with creatures that would recognize and know His ways and actions. Then He was revealed to each and every one, according to his power to grasp and to see the manifestion of His truth. This was revealed by means of the *sefirot*, which are the essence of His Glory and attributes, with which He acts and creates. For God, blessed be He, is known by means of His attributes, just as, by way of example, the truth of the soul is known through its powers and actions with the limbs of the body. But do not think that this involved something created anew within Him, or a change of will and division in regard to Him. For these *sefirot* are His powers. They always existed within Him in actuality, only they were concealed and joined to Him as one. They are the titles of His actions and attributes, which were later revealed. They were not a new creation, but the revelation of the truth of what was concealed, which was revealed to the creatures by way of many levels. For He, be He blessed, was revealed through His actions. They were designated through the titles of these intermediaries and numbered as ten, even though they are all one. They came from His unique power and return to Him. One may reflect on something similar, regarding human actions. They emerge from the source of the soul, which rules over him by means of the limbs of the body. Actually, there is no intermediary that initiates the revelation of its powers. The beginning of the manifestation of the power of the soul is in thought. Through the power of thought it becomes wise. Afterward it understands the dwellings without dwellings.[163] These things are attributed to the brain and, taken together, are called the *neshamah*. Also the power of sensing emanates from the soul and causes all of the limbs to move and act with a living spirit. Afterward, it arouses toward good, evil, and neutral [actions]. Sometimes, it will arouse a person to be gracious and kind. Other times, when it sees an evil deed, it will arouse [a person] toward retribution and will raise smoke from his nose to take cruel vengeance. And when it sees a good deed, it draws favor and pleasure from the brain, by way of the spinal cord, to be merciful and beneficent in judgment and charity. These powers, taken together, are called *ruaḥ*. Also, the power which nourishes and grows and the power which desires emerge from the liver. This power is called the *nefesh* and it inclines toward material things and sustains the body as long as is possible. We shall also consider the power that binds all of these things together and directs them properly. This is the disposition and nature that is in every person, according to his composition. It is known that all of these activities are only from the *neshamah* and cleave to it. They are its powers, which are nourished and revealed by it. Although one part is called *ruaḥ* and another *nefesh*, this applies to [the soul's] proximity to corporeality. However, the *neshamah* is always undivided and inseparable, a single, concealed element. We cannot know its essence, but may only say that it is the spiritual element over all of these activities. For it is proper that the nature of the source be found in what is derived from it and vice versa. As the activities are revealed by the means which have been mentioned, so we can imagine, by way of example, divine emanation, its expansion, splendor, or spark, call it what you will. [It] was revealed to His creatures from His very essence, through the divine power which is attributed to and described by means of *YHVH*. [The components of divine emanation] were actualized as creatures, by degrees, from emanation to emanation, even though it was entirely atemporal and indivisible. Consequently, the kabbalists sustained, received, and arranged for us the order of divine emanation. They called it *sefirot*, because of the connotation of clarity and brightness, from the expression "*livnat ha-SaPiR*."[164] Just as forms are reflected within a mirror,[165] the *sefirot* are the template and form for everything that exists. But they are not additions to [the *Eyn Sof*], just as what is seen in a mirror does not add to it. The sage Rabbi Azriel said that the *sefirot* are a power which applies equally to a thing and its opposite, just as opposites appear equally in a mirror. Similarly, the beings concealed within the depths of *Eyn Sof*[166] are revealed by them and activated by the [*sefirot*]. But they are not, like our attributes, additions or implications of multiplicity within the

Cause [of Causes], just as all the things and actions that one can see in a mirror are not additions and imply no multiplicity within it. Consequently, one is permitted to know God by these attributes. They said that when God, blessed be He, wanted to make His truth known and to create a world, a shining force sparkled from Him over creation. They compared it to thought, as when a builder, for example, thinks about his building, wisely contemplating it at the outset. They called it *Keter 'Elyon* (supreme crown), because it crowns everything. Then the point of the *yod* was revealed from the proper Divine Name. That light became six hundred and twenty sparks, like the sum of *Keter.*[167] And [the shining power] was not satisfied until the spark of *Ḥokhmah* gradually sparkled from *Keter*, and the thick part of the *yod* was revealed. And it sparkled into thirty-two sparks which are called the thirty-two paths of *Ḥokhmah.* But the power of this shining spark was not satisfied until a spark called *Binah* sparkled and was also emanated from *Ḥokhmah* by degrees. It burst into fifty sparks, called the fifty gates of *Binah*, and the letter *heh* was revealed. Similarly, a power sparkled and was emanated from *Binah*, called *Ḥesed.* It burst into seventy-two sparks, seventy-two bridges, which they called the seventy-two Holy Names. As is known, they are formed from the letters of the three verses that begin, "*va-yis'a (and [the angel of YHVH] travelled),*" "*va-yavo' (and [the pillar of cloud] came),*" "*va-yet (and [Moses] streched out [his hand]).*"[168] Similarly, from *Ḥesed, Paḥad*[169] [sparkled and was emanated] in forty-two sparks, called the Name of forty-two. As is known, this Name is formed by the first forty-two letters in Genesis, until the *bet* in *va-Vohu.*[170] From [*Paḥad*], *Tif'eret* sparkled into seventy sparks, called the seventy branches of the tree. These include the two colors, white and red, the *d"u parzufim*, which makes seventy-two.[171] And it includes twelve forms of *YHVH*. For the letters of *YHVH* can be ordered in twelve ways and these produce seventy-two permutations. For each of twelve branches can have no less than six extremities: above, below, right, left, front, back, totalling seventy-two. Corresponding to this is the Name of twelve, which emerges from the verse, "*YHVH is King, YHVH was King, YHVH will be King forever and ever,*"[172] through exchanging their vowels. There are those who say that it is produced by permuting the twelve letters of *'EHYeH*, *YHVH*, and *'ADNY* and then multiplying by the *vav* of the Name. And *Neẓaḥ* emerged from *Tif'eret*,

> and from *Neẓaḥ*, *Hod* emerged, and from *Hod*, *Yesod*. Afterward, the power that binds together and directs all of the powers emerged. It was called *Malkhut*, and the final *heh* of the Name was revealed.[173]

These are the words of Rabbi Mattathias, who discussed the matter at great length. The upshot of this entire discussion is that there is a certain similarity between the way that the soul is in the body and the secret of how divine emanation is present within the emanator.

My sons, may their Rock guard and protect them, now that God has made this matter known, let us go on to the depth of the matter. [Let us] understand what is meant by referring to God, blessed be He, as the Great Adam, as in the verse, "*and on the likeness of the throne, the likeness of the appearance of a human being*."[174] Then you will understand the meaning of "*Let Us make a human being in Our image*."[175] And your hearts will be enthused with love for God, to cleave to Him and to be a branch of the Patriarchs, concerning whom the rabbis, of blessed memory, said, "They are the Chariot."[176]

The Faithful House [I]

Among the most perplexing things that are found written in our Torah are [such expressions as] "*under His feet . . .* ," "*written with the finger of God . . .* ," "*the hand of YHVH*," "*the eyes of YHVH*," "*the ears of YHVH*," and the like. These expressions refer to parts of the body. Yet such a thing cannot be attributed to God, for He is neither a body, nor a power in a body. Therefore, these matters also cannot be attributed to His *sefirot*. For they are remote from all characteristics of the body. For otherwise, since it is known that He is a soul to the *sefirot* and the power within them, therefore, God forbid, it would imply that He is a power within a body. Therefore, it is proper to exclude characteristics of the body from the *sefirot*. And we are obligated in this, just as we are so obligated to exclude [physical characteristics] from the essence of *Eyn Sof*.[1]

And not only are characteristics of the body rejected, even characteristics of angels may not be attributed, just as the author of the poem *Yigdal* established. "He has no likeness of a body and no body."[2] According to the order of the words, [the addition of "and no body"] did not have to be said. However, the meaning is that He has no likeness of a body and not even a likeness from something that is not a body, as for example, an angel. This is easy to understand.

Thus we have to reflect on what is meant by the attributes that are attributed to Him, blessed be He. The simple meaning of some of the attributes can be explained according to what is written in *Sefer 'Arugat ha-Bosem.*

> I found a division of the verb into four categories, namely an active verb, and a verb that is used metaphorically, and a verb that is meant to make a matter known, and a passive verb that does not involve an action that someone does, but only reveals a matter that occurs by means of something [else]. Examples of the first type are, "*they left the city*"[3] [and] "*and every wise hearted person did* [*the work*]"[4] and the like. The verb is directed away from the one who performs it. An example of the second type is "*He conceives mischief and gives birth to fraud.*"[5] Here conception is compared to thought and birth to the deed. Another example is "*Bring them and plant them* [*in the mountain of Your inheritance*]."[6] Planting is compared to establishing in a designated place. Similarly, "*For then the anger of YHVH will smoke.*"[7] and "*My nose will burn.*"[8] This alludes to the arousal of divine judgment, according to the kabbalists. Also divine speech and saying and the "*voice of YHVH*" are used metaphorically to refer to prophetic experiences. For they descend by stages from their concealed sources until they reach the ear of prophets. Expressions involving saying (*'aMiRah*) and speech (*dibbur*) are also metaphors for will and thought. For example, "*Whatever you wish (mah t'OMaR nafshekha)* [*I will do for you*]."[9] Further examples are, "*And God said, 'Let there be light,'*"[10] "*who thinks to herself (ha-'OMeRah be-levavah)* [*I am, and there is no other*],"[11] "*and she shall be a wife to the son of your lord, as YHVH said,*"[12] "*I thought to myself (DiBBaRti 'ani 'im libi).*"[13] Also calling (*qeri'ah*) is a metaphor for influencing (*hashpa'ah*). For example, "*Deep calls to deep,*"[14] "*and one calls to the other.*"[15] The Aramaic translation says: "and one receives from the other." And [there are other examples of metaphor among the] teachings of our rabbis, of blessed memory. "How do we know that the Holy One, blessed be He, puts on *tefillin*?"[16] As the kabbalists know, putting on *tefillin* is a metaphor for God's being united to His attributes, so as to bestow in accordance with the arousal below, when people put on their *tefillin*. There are many examples of this type among the teachings of our rabbis, involving metaphor and analogy. For example, the rabbis, of blessed memory, said, concerning the verse, "*May he kiss me with the kisses of his mouth . . .*"[17] "may he arm me, purify me, and cause me to cleave [to Him]."[18] For "*may he kiss*

me (yiShaQeni)" means "may He arm me against the evil urge."[19] As the our rabbis, of blessed memory, said, "If that ugly one meets you, [drag him to the House of Study]."[20] [This interpretation of *Yishaqeni*] is from the expression, "*he flees from iron arrows (NeSHeQ).*"[21] And it also means "May He purify me from the sickness of harmful traits,[22] as a person levels two ponds and they are pure."[23] "May he cause me to cleave" refers to the success of the soul, as in the verse, "*you who are cleaving to YHVH, your God,* [*are all alive today*]."[24]

An example of the third type is, "*King Ahasuerus made* [*Haman*] *great (giddel).*"[25] He made his greatness known. Similarly, "*until* [*Isaac*] *was very great.*"[26] In other words, his greatness was made known by his deeds. As our rabbis, of blessed memory said, "[People] were speaking about the manure of Isaac's mules and not about the silver and gold of Abimelech."[27] This is because it was already written, "*The man became greater and greater until he was very great.*"[28] In my opinion the following examples can also be added: "*he will fear* [*something*] *other than me.*"[29] In other words, he will see and find something other than Me that makes fear known. Then he explains how. But what is the conclusion? "*No vessel formed against you will succeed.*"[30] Also, "*and God tried Abraham.*"[31] He made Abraham well-known for his trial, until everybody knew about his being tested. Similarly, "*Now I know that you are God-fearing.*"[32] [It means] I made it known in the world and placed it within the realm of knowing, so that everybody would know that you are God-fearing. Another example is "*Exalt YHVH with me.*"[33] They make God's greatness known. Similarly, "*and we shall raise up His Name,*"[34] "*you did not sanctify Me* . . . ,"[35] "*and you shall be full and bless* . . . ,"[36] "*honor YHVH with lights*"[37] "*to know that I YHVH sanctify you.*"[38] And in the liturgy, "And You glorify and exalt the spirit of all flesh." In all of these cases the meaning of the verb involves making the matter known. This is also found in the teachings of our rabbis, of blessed memory. "My sons *niẓẓeḥuni.*"[39] They made known My being eternal and unchanging.[40] And so may the word that comes from my mouth be, *turn aside many.*[41] Also, "*My soul will weep in secret places.*"[42] Its meaning is the making known of weeping in the place of secrets, as the kabbalists called it.[43]

> An example of the fourth type is "*from the break of day until the stars appeared.*"[44] For the stars cast their light both day and night. But the light of the sun prevents the eye from seeing the gleam of the stars during the day. As a result of the sun's setting, the light of the stars is revealed, and it seems as if they are performing the act of emerging. This is the meaning of "*I will go out in the midst of Egypt.*"[45] In other words, as a result of the plague of the first-born, which involved distinguishing who was a firstborn child and who was not, it seemed as if God went out in the midst of Egypt. Another example is "*YHVH descended . . . on Mt. Sinai,*"[46] even though "*the whole earth is full of His Glory.*"[47] The meaning is that because of the great lights which were at that chosen location, it seemed that something divine descended there. Similar to this is "*I will descend and see . . .*"[48] "*And YHVH left . . .*"[49] "*And behold, YHVH was standing before him.*"[50] "*And God departed from him.*"[51] "*Now I will rise, says YHVH,*"[52] and the like. Their meaning is not that God is transported from place to place, but rather that His light is revealed by a certain matter in one place rather than in another. For it was concealed in that place. Another example of this is found in the teachings of our rabbis, of blessed memory. "The Holy One, blessed be He, does not act until He looks at the heavenly retinue." They also said, "until He consults with the heavenly household."[53] The meaning is that just as we see reward and punishment blended together, according to various levels, the heavenly household are like a musical instrument which is perfectly arranged, so that they appear within. It seems as if He looks within it and consults with them. And so it is with all God's actions.[54]

"*The wise person will hear and increase his lesson.*"[55]

Maimonides explained all of the divine attributes in the first part of the *Moreh Nevukhim*. He said that they are metaphorical terms for God. He explained each and every attribute, indicating its metaphor applies to God. He explained them carefully and reasonably, according to their simple meaning. But the kabbalist rabbi [Meir Ibn Gabbai] who wrote *'Avodat ha-Qodesh* took issue with him in section *ha-Takhlit* and explained their metaphors according to the secret meaning. This is what is written in *Sefer Sha'arey 'Orah*.

> Know that the very essence of the Creator is not comprehended by other than He. There is nothing among the supernal multitudes

that knows His place, let alone His very essence. Do you not see that the supernal angels say, "Blessed be the Glory of *YHVH* from His place."[56] [Meaning,] wherever He may be. If the supernal ones [do not know His place], the lower creatures certainly cannot know. Therefore, know and believe that all of these things that we read in the Torah such as hand, foot, ear, eye, and others of this sort, although they declare and attest to God's truth and greatness, no creature is able to know and contemplate the essence of what is referred to by [such anthropomorphic terms]. Even if we are made in the image and likeness [of God], do not think that the eye or hand referred to has the form of an eye or hand. But they are most inner aspects of the truth of God's existence, blessed be He. From them is the source for all of the *shefa'* that goes out to all that exists. But the essence of "hand" is not like the essence of a hand. And their structures are not equivalent. As it is written, "*To whom will you compare Me and I will be equal?*"[57] Know and understand that there is no similarity between us and Him from the standpoint of essence and structure, but the forms of our limbs, which are made like indicators, allude to concealed, supernal matters that the mind can only know as a kind of mnemonic. It is like writing [the name] Reuben ben Jacob. For these letters are not the very form of Reuben ben Jacob, his form, structure, and being. They are only a mnemonic. This Reuben ben Jacob, which is written, is a sign which corresponds to that known essence and structure which is called Reuben ben Jacob. Since God, blessed be He, wished to favor us, He created many limbs in the human body, concealed and revealed, in the likeness of a sign for the Work of the Chariot.[58] If a person succeeds in purifying a certain limb, that limb becomes like a throne for the inner, supernal matter that is called by that name. If the eye [is purified], then [it becomes a chariot for the supernal] eye; if the hand [is purified], then [it becomes a chariot for the supernal] hand; and so on. How so? For example, a certain person may be very careful concerning what he permits his eyes to see. He does not look or gaze at any unseemly thing or anything else that is worthy of contempt, but only turns his eyes toward everything that involves God's holiness and service. Then his eye becomes like a throne for that supernal matter that is called "eye." And the same applies to the hand and foot and the rest of the limbs. Concerning this, our sages, of blessed memory, said: "The patriarchs are the chariot."[59] They did not say that each one of the

> patriarchs is the chariot. How so? Our Father, Abraham, peace be upon him, took the right side in purity and inherited the supernal right side, which is the attribute of *Ḥesed.* Concerning this, the verse says, "*Abram journeyed by stages toward the south.*"[60] Isaac took the left side in purity, which is *Paḥad.* Concerning this, the verse says, "*Jacob swore by the Paḥad of his father Isaac.*"[61] Jacob took the middle line in purity.[62] Concerning this, the verse says, "*Jacob was a mild person who dwelled in tents.*"[63] [He dwelled] between the tent of Abraham and the tent of Isaac. Therefore, the three patriarchs are a throne to the Chariot.[64]

The same appears in the Recanati commentary on *va-yehi,* and it is also quoted in *Sefer 'Avodat ha-Qodesh.*

However, we still need to be informed by the *Zohar* and other kabbalistic writings concerning the use of such surprising terms as father, mother, son, and daughter, and the like, to describe divine emanation. And they use the expression "coupling" in regard to *Tif'eret* and *Malkhut*, like a man with his wife. And *Yesod* is the sign of the covenant, the sexual organ which effects a complete union, through which a man cleaves to his wife. "*And I am establishing My covenant.*"[65] This is *Yesod*, the covenant of circumcision. The verse said, "*I am establishing (haQi-Moti),*" which is related to the expression for rising up (*qimah*). This is as if to say, "*from my flesh, I see God.*"[66] The matter of embracing and kissing is also mentioned and alluded to in the verse, "*His left hand is under my head and his right hand embraces me.*"[67] And it is written, "*Let him kiss me with the kisses of his mouth.*"[68] We need to know and understand [the meaning] of such things. So I will copy what the *Pardes* wrote concerning this in the *Sha'ar 'Erkhey ha-Kinnuyim.* He said that such things are

> descriptive terms (*To'ar*) for concealed matters, not really seeing, hearing, and speech. There is no doubt that eye, ear, and mouth are not called *'eyin*, *'ozen*, and *peh* in the Holy Language,[69] by accident, or by convention, as in other languages. The proof for our language being the Holy Language lies in its being a divine creation, not like other languages. There is no doubt that it is the language that the Holy One, blessed be He, used when He created the world. Therefore, clearly, this language preceded the world.[70]

He also said:

> When the light of our Father Abraham, peace be upon him, shined forth, the Holy One, blessed be He, divided the seventy nations according to seventy supernal princes and seventy languages. He chose for us as our portion, divine speech, which is our destiny, the Holy Destiny and Holy Language, a divine agreement that the ear be called *'ozen* and that the mouth be called *peh*. This is to make known that the supernal powers are a shadow over a person's head. The limb is emanated from the supernal power which causes it to emanate and bestows *shefa'* upon it. Now, in truth, *'ozen* does not mean the physical ear, but the activity which is performed by the ear through the power that is bestowed upon it. Concerning this, the verse said, "*Shall He who implants the ear not hear, He who forms the eye not see?*"[71] The meaning is as follows. The human limbs are created through permutations of holy alphabets which draw *shefa'* from the supernal powers, the roots which are united in the Root of Roots. Therefore, the letter must contain that power of action which is performed by the created limb and it is also in the root which bestows *shefa'* on the letter. And so it is from cause to effect until [the *shefa'*] arrives below. For through the actions, the powers are made known. The power of hearing and seeing is necessitated because that root contains those powers. But this is not physical hearing and seeing, but rather a spiritual matter. For example, when people hear the sound of speech in their ears, they distinguish the matter that is heard. Similarly, the supernal power that receives the voice examines it to see whether it is worthwhile to receive it or not. This is called *'ozen*. Concerning this, the verse says, "*for 'ozen examines words*."[72] And it is similar, regarding the angels who have no physical power of speech, like our mouth, with which they could produce speech which is corporeal. However, when one angel looks at another, the angels understand each other. For the *shefa'* of the Name *YHVH* is in the spiritual essence of the letters which are transmitted for the chosen matter. By means of this, the angel understands the matter that is transmitted to him. This is their "speech," and they [also] have no eyes, like those with which humans see. However, they have a spiritual function which performs sight. With it they can discern and see at a distance. And it is superior to our way of seeing, just as the intellect's manner of seeing is superior to that of the eye.

For the eye can only see what is before it, and not even everything that is before it, but only something so limited that the physical eye is capable of grasping it. But the intellect can see even that which is not before the eye, just as a person can now see with his intellect many things which he has not seen for many years and even things that he has never seen. He can cause his mind to look at a certain matter, until the intellect's manner of seeing becomes so subtle that it perceives subtle matters that the eye is not able to see. Greater than this is the sight of the prophets. For the prophet grasps the spiritual matters with his intellect. The breadth of the prophetic attainment depends on the breadth of the intellect. So said King Solomon, peace be upon him, "*Like one face looking at itself in water, so one person's heart is reflected in another.*"[73] For one human heart understands another through understanding itself. It is a physical organ and contains this power because of the influence of the *nefesh* and the intellect which dwells in it. Nevertheless, since it is something limited, its attainment is limited. According to the measure of the prophet, so is the level of his prophecy. From this matter we can proceed to the way that angels understand each other and from there we will grasp many levels toward knowing the nature of sight and physical activity among the spiritual entities. As the prophet said, "*I see a golden candelabra.*"[74] Similarly, "*What is now called a prophet, used to be called a seer.*"[75] The meaning is not seeing with the eyes, nor is the use of the word for seeing meant allegorically, but it refers to the actual seeing of comprehension. Similarly, in the case of angelic sight, it is the power of comprehension through which matters are grasped. This is what was involved in the story of Rabbi Eleazar, the son of Rabbi Simeon, who went to visit his father-in-law, Rabbi Yose ben Lequnia.[76] On the way, they saw a snake, and Rabbi Eleazar said certain things that amazed his companions. He told them that he did not comprehend that matter through *Ḥokhmah*, but through a vision that he had. Can one imagine that Rabbi Eleazar saw such things with his physical eyes? Surely it was meditative seeing, through which a person comprehends future and past matters. Through the subtle power of the intellect he can hear the matters. In this way, one may see higher and higher matters until "*One watchman is higher than another.*"[77]

This is not surprising, for even in regard to our physical vessels, the eye is not called eye because of the eye itself, but because of the power of sight, which [designates] what is truly called an eye. Similarly, the hand is not called a hand because of the hand itself, but [due to] the action which is derived from the hand, it is truly called a hand. A proof for this is what our rabbis, of blessed memory, said in *Gittin*, concerning whether allusions (*yadayim*) that are not beyond doubt are or are not binding. In other words, [indications are called *yadayim* (hands) because] they provide something to be taken hold of.[78] So Rashi, of blessed memory, explained. *Yadayim* means a handle, something to grasp and to say [this writing proves that he divorced her.][79] Similarly in cases of marriage and divorce. "Does a female minor have a '*hand*' or not?" And the meaning of "she has no hand" is not that it is amputated. It refers to her capacity to receive the [status of] marriage or divorce. Similarly, it is typical of rabbinic language to describe something as having or lacking feet. This expression is not meant to be taken literally, but is a metaphor. Just as feet [provide a] person with the means of standing and support him, so when something has a condition of stability in the intellect, it is said to have feet. But when the matter is not settled, it is said to lack feet. Similarly, the Torah states, "*an eye for an eye, [a tooth for a tooth], a hand for a hand, a foot for a foot.*"[80] We interpret this verse by comparing it to another verse which deals with the act of striking, "*Whoever strikes dead a beast, shall make restitution for its life for life.*"[81] According to tradition, the meaning is not that if someone cut off another's hand, his hand should be cut off, and similarly in the case of other limbs. Rather, he should make monetary restitution for the full value of the hand, and similarly in the case of other limbs. What is meant by "eye, hand, foot" [in the verse] is a sum equal to the value of the capacity of the eye, hand, and foot. It is similar in regard to the spiritual entities. The power of the *Eyn Sof*, which is extended from the *sefirot* in order to watch over the world, is called "eyes." Thus the verse says, "*These seven are the eyes of YHVH wandering over all of the earth.*"[82] The kabbalists explained that they are seven powers called, "*'ORPeNeY'eL, TaGRY'eL, DeNeR'eL, PaLMY'eL, ASYMON, SaFY'eL, BO'eL.*" They oversee the matters of human beings. Since they have the power of providence, they are called "eyes." Not that they are eyes, but they are responsible for spiritual providence, as explained above. All deeds are recorded in them, both good and evil. Through their agency, the two Lights testify before the seventy judges concerning human actions, thoughts, machinations, and impulses, as was explained in *Sha'ar Heykhalot*, *Heykhal Zekhut*, chapter four. And there are other eyes above these eyes. "*For one watchman is higher than another and there are others over them.*"[83] The same is indicated in the verse, "*Hear, O mountains, the case of YHVH.*"[84] The mountains hold the world [in place] and position it on the scale, as our rabbis, of blessed memory, explained. And they are high in the upper regions of the world. Similarly, the patriarchs strengthen us with their merit and cause the world to stand. They also stand in the upper regions of the world. Similarly, our teacher, Moses, said to Jethro, "*and you will be our eyes.*"[85] Rashi, of blessed memory, explained, "You will enlighten us concerning every matter that is hidden from our eyes." For just as the eyes let the body know where the straight path lies, so the teacher of righteousness is called "eyes." By analogy, we can understand all of the other things that are used as designations for the *sefirot*, such as father and mother. The meaning is not that a father and mother are there. For this would be heresy, God forbid, but the meaning is that bearing a child involves the joining of male and female, and through that joining, the embryo is produced. What occurs among the *sefirot*, through the joining of *Ḥokhmah* and *Binah*, is analogous. The bestowing of *shefa'* from *Ḥokhmah* to *Binah* is the cause of all of the divine emanation. For *Ḥokhmah* contains all of the subtle essences, just as the son is concealed within the brain of the father. After they are extended to *Binah*, they become more substantial and take on a more revealed form. Accordingly, *Ḥokhmah* is called Father. For a father's offspring are contained in a most subtle form, like a drop, within his essence and brain. Through the joining together of male and female, that drop is aroused and becomes sperm. It is bestowed upon the female and as a result, the embryo is formed within the female. Thus *Ḥokhmah* is the father and *Binah* the female which receives all of the forms bestowed by *Ḥokhmah*. A more revealed form is produced within her and she makes manifest the divine emanation. Thus she is called female and the mother to the divine emanation. The divine emanations are called their children, for the reason mentioned. It is all by way of analogy from the physical to the spiritual. This also applies to *Tif'eret* and *Malkhut*, who are called Bridegroom and Bride, and *Binah*, which is called Mother or Mother-in-law, and *Ḥokhmah*, which is called Father or Father-in-law. Sometimes, the two are called Bridegroom and Bride, and *Ḥokhmah* and *Binah* are called Father and Mother. Sometimes [*Tif'eret* and *Malkhut*] are called Son and Daughter. Sometimes, *Malkhut* is [called] the Daughter of *Ḥokhmah* and the Daughter-in-law of *Binah*. At other times, she is [called] Daughter-in-law of *Ḥokhmah* and Daughter of *Binah*, and so on. It is worthwhile to expand the explanation of these matters. *Tif'eret* and *Malkhut* are emanated from *Ḥokhmah* and *Binah*. In their simple state of emanation, they are not joined together as a couple, as we have explained above in *Sha'ar ha-Mi'ut*. Their uniting only occurs after they are rectified, armed, and adorned. Therefore, in [their simple state], *Tif'eret* and *Malkhut* are called Son and Daughter, and *Hokmah* and *Binah* [are called] Father and Mother. *Ḥokhmah* is called Father to *Tif'eret* because of the concealed *Da'at*. *Binah* is called Mother to *Tif'eret* because she prepares him. For this is an additional state to that which was emanated from *Ḥokhmah*, as was explained above. For they receive a very subtle state from *Ḥokhmah*, and *Binah* adds a more revealed state. So they are called Children of *Ḥokhmah*, because of their subtle state, which is *yod* for *Malkhut* and the firmament for *Tif'eret*. This is explained in chapter two of the first gate and in *Sha'ar ha-Meẓi'ut*, chapter four. And due to the revealed state that they receive from *Binah*, they are called Children of *Binah*. They are later called Bridegroom and Bride, Husband and Wife, when they are united in the secret of the crowns that they put on, as indicated in the verse, "*Daughters of Zion, go out and see King Solomon* [*in the crown with which his mother crowned him on the day of his wedding and on the day of the rejoicing of his heart*]."[86] And there is a distinction between these two designations. For before their union, when they are being made ready for the uniting, they are called Bridegroom and Bride. They have adornments like a bridegroom and bride. After they have been in union they are called Husband and Wife. There are many differences and aspects of union which will be explained, with God's help, in their respective places in *Sefer 'Or Yaqar*. When the revealed state of one is united with the revealed state of the other or when they are united in their concealed states, they are merely [called] Children of *Ḥokhmah* and *Binah*. They are joined together in a complete union. They are a son and daughter, brother and sister, who are permitted to each other. However, they are not designated as Bridegoom and Bride and Son and Daughter to

> *Ḥokhmah* and *Binah*. For if *Tif'eret* is a son to *Ḥokhmah*, he is a son-in-law to *Binah*. Then *Binah* is called his mother-in law or *Ḥokhmah* is called his father-in-law when he is a son to *Binah*. Similarly, if the revealed aspect of *Tif'eret* is united with the concealed aspect of *Malkhut*, then *Ḥokhmah* is the father of *Malkhut* and *Binah* is the mother of *Tif'eret*. And *Malkhut* is a daughter-in-law to *Binah* and *Binah* is a mother-in-law to *Malkhut*, while *Tif'eret* is a son-in-law to *Ḥokhmah* and *Ḥokhmah* is his father-in-law. But if the concealed state of *Tif'eret* couples with the revealed state of *Malkhut*, then he is a son to *Ḥokhmah* and she is a daughter to *Binah*. *Malkhut* is then the daughter-in-law of *Ḥokhmah* and *Ḥokhmah* is her father-in-law. *Tif'eret* is the son-in-law to *Binah* and *Binah* is his mother-in-law. By way of analogy, one can generate all of the categories. In this way, all of the other surprising things written in the works of the kabbalists may be understood. For it is permissible to make use of analogies as much as is necessary so that a person may understand, comprehend, and deal with them. Concerning this, the verse says, "*And from my flesh, I can see God*."[87] "*And blessed be the Name of the Glory of His Kingdom forever and ever*."[88]

I copied his words in their entirety, so that his view concerning the divine attributes and other strange expressions would be understood and [we might appreciate] how this divine sage interpreted things. However, his discussion does not explain the essence of the matter mentioned above, regarding the eye, ear, hand, and so forth. He only refers to a concealed matter. With the aid of the One who grants knowledge to human beings, I will add my own views. I shall make use of certain principles from the *Pardes* and the matter will be explained in essence. However, before I enter into the explanation of this matter, I will examine another issue, concerning why our language is called the Holy Language.

The Temple

This is what Nahmanides wrote in the Torah section *ki tiss'a*.

I know the reason why our rabbis call the language of the Torah the Holy Language.[1] It is because the words of the Torah and the prophecies, and all words of holiness were said in this language. This is the language which the Holy One, blessed be He, may His Name be exalted, speaks to His prophets and with His community. [For example,] "*I am [YHVH] your God*"[2] and "*You shall have no other God before Me*"[3] and the rest of the sayings of the Torah and the Prophets. With this language, He is called by His holy Names, *'El*, *'Elohim*, *Ẓeva'ot*, and *Shadday*, and *YaH*, and the Great United Name. With it, He created His world and gave names to heaven and earth and all that is in them, including His angels and all of His hosts. "*He called each by name*"[4] in this language, such as Mikhael and Gavriel. He used it to name "*the holy ones in the Land*,"[5] Abraham, Isaac, and Jacob and Solomon and the rest. The Rabbi[6] said in the *Moreh Nevukhim*, "Do not think that our language is called the Holy Language because of our conceit or by mistake, for it is rightly so. For this language is holy. It contains no words for the male and female genitals and none for sperm, urine, and excrement, except indirectly. But do not be misled by the word *shegal*, for it is the term for a woman who is destined for sex. The verse says, '*yishgalenah*,'[7] concerning what is written about it. The meaning is he will take a woman as a concubine. But there is no need for this reason. For it is clear that the language is the Holy of Holys, just as I have explained. The reason that he mentioned is, in my opinion, not correct. For the fact that *yishgalenah* is read as

> '*yishkavenah*' (he will lie with her) indicates that *mishgal* is the noun for sexual intercourse. They also specified '*to eat their excrement*,'[8] which is an improper term. If the reason given by the Rabbi were correct, they would have used a euphemism,[9] as we learn in the *mishnah*, '[He is not considered a rebellious son] until he grows a beard. This means hair of the genitals and not the face, except the sages expressed themselves euphemistically.' "[10] They also said [in the Midrash], "*except the bread which he eats*"[11] is a euphemism.[12] And there are many similar examples.[13]

I do not understand Nahmanides's words. For he only explained why we call our language the Holy Language. He said it is because all holy things were said in this language. But the problem still remains unanswered. Why, in fact, did God choose this language and sanctify it?

The Ultimate House

There is a third matter to be considered that has been investigated by the early and later sages. Then "*the threefold cord will not be broken*."[1] After an introductory discussion, with God's help, I will deal with the three of them and they will be well explained. The third topic of investigation is discussed in *Sefer 'Avodat ha-Qodesh*, chapter seventeen of the section on *'Avodah*. I will copy his discussion.

> I wish to clarify the discussion of material promises which are explained in the Torah and spiritual promises which constitute the ultimate purpose and happiness acquired by the soul. According to the opinion of all the sages, this is not explained in the Torah. However, they constantly referred to them explicitly, in saying, "The commandments lead one to acquire true life, the life of the world to come." Many of our sages, of blessed memory, already discussed this in order to explain why this life was not explained in the Torah. So I decided to add my own view. However, I wish to begin with their words. What has become well known is contained in three views. The first view is that of Maimonides, of blessed memory. He gave the following reason. Since the whole Torah was given to a vast and diverse people who do not comprehend the essence and truth of its contents, the divine Torah exchanged the concealed matters for revealed ones, so that it could be comprehended and received, as it did with the attributes of God, blessed be He. Since they only know of corporeal success, due to their inability to imagine the sweetness of the intellect and

its success, the Torah concealed this from them and revealed to them what they would long for from among those imaginary acquisitions. That is [Maimonides's] view. The later sages, of blessed memory, have already enumerated the refutations that would follow from his argument. They include the following. [Maimonides] would say that when [the people] see the material promises fulfilled, they will believe in the spiritual promise that they learn of through some allusion in the Torah. This is no proof. For how can you draw evidence from what is mentioned explicitly in the Torah and apply it with certainty to what is not mentioned at all? They will not comprehend it. Moreover, the Torah did explain to the masses deep principles concerning the unity of God and His existence. For these are things that the masses cannot easily understand, since they do not understand something that is not material. But by virtue of understanding this, they would be able to understand other things that are not material. This is indisputable. Thus they would be able to comprehend the spiritual reward, just as they were able to understand the existence of a spiritual being.

[Maimonides] wrote the reason for the material promises in chapter nine of the Laws of Repentance. "For He promised them to us in the Torah to say that if we practice it in joy and with goodwill and constantly meditate on its wisdom, he will remove from us all of the things that prevent us from practicing it, such as sickness, war, and famine, and the like. And He will bestow upon us all of the good things that strengthen our hands to practice the Torah, such as abundance and peace and much silver and gold, so that we will not have to work all of our days for things that the body requires. But we will be free to learn wisdom and to do the commandments, in order to merit the life of the world to come."[2] Consequently, we would learn according to this line of thought that when He promised us those good things it was, actually, to let us know that we will become perfect through the freedom that we will have in order to perfect ourselves. But this is not sufficient. For while He promised to us the way that leads to the ultimate, He did not explicitly promise the ultimate itself. So we are still not certain of it. However, it would have been otherwise had He promised the ultimate. For we would be certain of a way that leads to it, since there is no doubt that He would create a way for us to attain it. For otherwise it would be impossible to reach the ultimate. Therefore, He should have explained the spiritual reward to us and we would have understood by ourselves that He would supply us with the means to attain it and would not discuss its promise at length. For example, a king called to one of his servants, sitting before him, who was one of the king's intimates. He commanded him to go to one of the islands of the sea in order to do the king's work and to perform the king's service there. The king assured him that while he was doing his work he would eat the best of that island ['s food] and he would enjoy its delights. He is still not certain that the king will restore him to his palace and original level, when he has completed his work. But once he has assured him that he will return to it, he is certain that the king will see to his needs, so that he will be free to do his work, even if he did not promise this explicitly. For otherwise, it would be impossible to do his service.

There is another problem with [Maimonides's] view. For when it is examined closely, it implies that the goodness and success are not an extension of the Torah and commandments and necessitated by their nature. This places a defect in the sacred. This is a general account of the view of the Rabbi, of blessed memory, concerning the two rewards and what may reasonably be objected to it.

The second view is that of Nahmanides. It is found in [his commentary] on the Torah section, *va-'era'*. There, he said the following. "A person does not receive goodness as the reward of a commandment or evil as a punishment for a transgression except by a miraculous act. If it were left to a person's own nature and fortune, his actions would neither add nor subtract anything from him. But the reward of the Torah and its punishments in this world are all miracles which are concealed. Whoever sees them thinks that they are the custom of the world, but they are truly a person's reward and punishment. For this reason, the Torah deals at length with the promises of this world and does not explain the promises of the soul in the world of *neshamot*. For these are wonders corresponding to the effects[3] and existence of the soul and its cleaving to God. It is proper that, in its outcome, the soul should return to God which gave it. And I shall explain this further, if God permits me."[4] This refers to what he wrote in the Torah section, *'aḥarey mot*, concerning the punishment of cutting off of the soul that is mentioned [there]. For he said that [these punishments] are a great assurance regarding the existence of the souls after death and the granting of a reward in the world of the *neshamot*. What emerges from his discussion there is that immortality is necessarily extended to the soul, since it lacks any basis for dissolution and will not die of its own. Consequently, there was no reason at all to promise all of the rewards of its existence. For this is necessitated by its outcome. Therefore, its promise is not found in the Torah. But the Master of Reward had to promise us these good things which do not at all come to us by way of nature, to let us know that these promises are realized for us by way of miracle. Thus the Rabbi ruled that the reward of the entire Torah consists of miracles that are concealed.

And the Rabbi had more [to say] about these promises in section *'im be-ḥuqotay*. There, he said the following: "We have already explained that all of these blessings are miracles. It is not by way of nature that, through our practicing the laws and commandments, the rains come and that we should have peace from our enemies, and that the fear of you should enter their hearts so that a hundred flee from fifty. Neither [is it natural] that the opposite should occur, because we planted during the seventh year."[5] All of this is the opinion of the Rabbi, of blessed memory, concerning the two rewards.

It is already quite well known that the Rabbi is one of the great believers in and an outstanding authority on the Kabbalah, the true wisdom. And his belief that the promises of the Torah are miracles surprises me, considering that he is great in wisdom. For the sages have said that a miracle is something that occurs independent of its essential causes. Yet, in his opinion, the good things and successes that are promised in the Torah are not the result of the commandments and are not necessitated by them at all. There is no connection between performing the commandments and the ascent of vapors or the falling of rain, whether the earth is thirsty and dry has no connection whatsoever. And there is no connection between a fast and the purification of moldy, unhealthy air. But, the Rabbi considers it miraculous when all of these things follow the [performance] of the commandments. The commandments are in no way their cause. Yet, we find the opposite view among his allusions to the secrets of the Torah, according to the Kabbalah. Thus the students who learned Kabbalah from him interpreted many of his secrets. And this view is the true one. For the supernal entities are blessed by the arousal of the beings below, through their worship. From there, the blessing goes on to the causes. Those that understand the truth would not say that this is miraculous. The nature of the worship requires this, as was explained and will be explained further.

Perhaps the Rabbi intended to answer the old question, according to the exoteric Torah, to provide the multitude of sages with a way of responding to the disputants, and it is enough to be satisfied with what he alluded to in his secrets for the elite who stand in the counsel of our God. Thus the heart would be settled and the mind would be at rest.

However, the Rabbi's statement that immortality of the soul is natural to its outcome has already been disputed by some of the later sages. Among them is Rabbi Joseph Albo in his *Sefer ha-'Iqqarim*, essay four, chapter thirty-nine. He wrote as follows. "This is also a weak argument. For immortality is no more natural to the soul than free will is to a human being. Yet the Torah said, '*See I have placed before you today, life and good* [*and death and evil*] *... choose life*.'[6] Since immortality is not something well known, why didn't the Torah inform us about it, as it informed us about free will and the creation of the world and similar true opinions and beliefs that are presented in the Torah? Moreover, according to some views, the spiritual reward applies equally to the body and soul. But it is not natural for the body to exist forever. Therefore, the Torah should have told us this explicitly."[7] But the Rabbi may be saved from his net by the answer that we will suggest for him. For free will is natural to a human being as long as he bears this name and is alive. The material promises are also natural to a person because of the Torah and the commandments, for they shall be attracted to them and necessitated by them, by nature. For so the nature of worship requires, as has been explained in the preceding chapter and as will be explained with God's help. The Rabbi would accept this view, as I wrote above. And there is no doubt that the pure soul is the cause of these good things which are of benefit to the body, as a result of its adhesion to the source, its good deeds, and its worshipping of its God, which is the union [of the *sefirot*]. These good things are the result of practicing the Torah and the commandments and are necessitated by them. Since the soul is their cause, how much more should [practicing Torah and the commandments] lead to the soul's remaining permanently in the pleasantness of that place to which it was turned while still connected to the body? For immortality and delight are also the natural result of practicing the Torah and its commandments. And this follows *qal va-ḥomer*.[8] If the Master of Reward, blessed be He, had explicitly promised the spiritual reward, it would have been redundant and completely unnecessary, since we can deduce it *qal va-ḥomer* from the material reward. For both are the result of the commandments and necessitated by them, by nature. Now one cannot object to the Rabbi's view on the basis of free will. For it was necessary to mention it, since we have nothing from which to derive it. But we can infer the spiritual reward from the material [because their causes are the same]. Thus mentioning it would be redundant and completely unnecessary. For by mentioning the material reward, the spiritual is also included. Thus the other objection which [Albo] raised there can also be answered. He said: "The greatest problem with all of this is that if [the Torah] did not mention the spiritual promises which are the essence of the reward, why should it mention the material promises which are not the essence of the reward?"

He also said: "Some are of the opinion that the spiritual reward applies equally to the body and the soul. But it is not natural for the body to exist forever." This is the opinion of the Rabbi and it is the truth. Such was the intention in creating Adam, except that he sinned and sin caused death. When the world is renewed, it will return to its original nature. Therefore both will exist as one, for the intention will return to its place.[9] Therefore, there was no need to mention it. I will have more to say concerning this, with God's help. But [Albo] did not believe this because philosophy separated him from it and compelled him to believe the opposite, according to its custom of withholding the truth and righteousness from its lovers who pursue the reasonings of their own minds and abandon supernal knowledge.

Among [such philosophers] is the sage Rabbi Joseph ben Shem Tov, of blessed memory, who said the following in his *Sefer 'Eyn ha-Qore'*, second essay. "Even if we agree with Nahmanides in all that he has left and that has been proposed in support of his view, how does he know that that state of eternal success is the result of the guiding commandments? For we may agree with him that the soul by nature is immortal and is not subject to destruction with the loss of the body, since it is not intermixed with it, but only bound to it by the bond of existence. However, we cannot agree with him that it remains in pleasantness and in joy in the Garden of Eden. He also would not assent to this. But, according to his view, the [soul's] survival in delight is the result of the commandments. Although it is true in itself, this state of success after [fulfilling] the commandments is not natural according to the human intellect. This has been much explained."[10] I already wrote above that the Rabbi knows the secret of worship. For it is its nature to bring success to the body, and even much more so to the soul. For that is the essence of worship. Thus his position is explained. He knew in truth that the state of eternal success is the result of the guiding commandments, by nature. If this is not natural according to the human intellect, it is natural according to the divine intellect. Thus the doubt is removed. This is a general account of the view of [Nahmanides], of blessed memory, along with supporting arguments that counter objections.

The third view is the view of Rabbenu Nissim Gerondi, of blessed memory,[11] who wrote the following in *Derashat Bereishit*. "There is no doubt that the beliefs in those days concerned the same matters that we are concerned with. In other words, they were all promises concerning the soul's future reward, after its separation from the body. But their testimonies were obscure. They were not able to give a close and concrete sign.[12] When our Torah appeared among those beliefs, it was distinguished by its evidences, just as it was distinguished in quality. For [the Torah] verified [our beliefs], while they were not able to do so. The basis of the Torah is the Exodus from Egypt, through which it became evident that divinity adhered to us. The magicians were not able to match this, but failed in most of their advice. Similarly, the Torah continued its promises in such a way as to make perfectly clear that no other Torah could promise this matter. Had it promised the soul's reward after death, it would have appeared that it and the other Torahs were equal and its superiority over them, in regard to its promises, would not have been known. For since all of them promised the same abstract thing, each could claim that the truth was with it. Therefore, the Torah did not have to make promises concerning matters in the world to come, but it produced stories about things that would verify it without doubt."[13]

Rabbi Joseph criticized his argument in the second essay, in *Sefer 'Eyn ha-Qore'*. "For the argument which he cited provides a sufficient reason for the promises concerning material goods, but it provides no reason at all for omitting mention of the true goal. For both should properly have been mentioned."[14] I am amazed. For it seems that he only cited that part of Rabbenu Nissim's argument which would enable him to doubt it, but what would have spared him this doubt, he omitted. For Rabbenu Nissim already avoided this problem in what he said at the outset. "Thus it is clear that the body and its powers do not sustain the soul, but weaken its powers, so that if this impediment were removed the soul would be more perfect. All the promises of the Torah concerning corporeal matters are meant to indicate that if it is clear that a person can cleave to God when he is subject to something that prevents him from attaining it, namely the body, there is no doubt that he will be assured a perfect *devequt*, to the extent that this is possible, when the troubling impediment has been removed [from the soul]. . . . For there is no doubt that the beliefs in those days, etc. . . . " Therefore divinity can cleave and rest upon him even though he is subject to the troublesome impediment. This is the great proof and wonder concerning his cleaving to [God] when he is subject to the oppressor. Since the *devequt* in this life is a strong indication of the spiritual reward, the Torah had no need of mentioning it. For it would be redundant and superfluous.

The sage Rabbi Abraham ben Bibago, of blessed memory, also wrote concerning this in his *Sefer Derekh 'Emunah*, second essay, Gate five. "This answer is also insufficient. For if immortality of the soul was well known, then it must have been well known to our forefather Abraham, along with God's existence and Unity. Therefore, just as the divine Torah brought us [evidence] of God's existence, in saying '*I am YHVH, your God . . .*,'[15] which certainly had to have been well known, it should have also brought [evidence] for the immortality of the soul."[16] But this has no weight. For if God's existence and His Unity were well known in the time of Abraham, it was not well known at the time that the Torah was given. Thus Israel, which became great among the Egyptians, had to hear this from God, because the Egyptians denied both of these. It was already said in *Midrash Rabbah*, *Shemot*, "[Pharaoh] told them at first, you have told me lies. For I am lord of the world and I created myself and the Nile, for it is said, '*My Nile is mine. I made it for myself.*'[17]"[18] However, they never lost their belief in the immortality of the soul. I also have to say that

> immortality of the soul would have been explicitly mentioned in the Torah, except that it more wisely decided to bring it as a wonder which follows from the sense's testimony that a person may cleave to God while still linked to the impediment.[19] Consequently, we can infer immortality of the soul by *qal va-ḥomer*, which cannot be challenged. And divine wisdom found it preferable that [immortality] be derived from this, just as Rabbenu Nissim, of blessed memory, wrote. But there was nothing from which God's existence and unity could be derived. Thus the Torah brought them. This follows if we concede that the verses "*I am YHVH, your God* . . . " and "*There shall be no other gods* . . . "[20] came to certify God's existence and unity. But if this was not the reason, but the verses were meant to instill in us faith in the principle that there is a Torah from heaven and that we should not worship any other god, as Rabbenu Nissim wrote in his *derashah on ve-'ethanan*, then there is no basis for [Abraham ben Bibago's] objection on the basis of God's existence and unity. The truth is that Torah did not need to bring this explicitly, for [God's existence] would have been verified for them beyond any doubt from what they saw in Egypt and at the Reed Sea, as well as from what they knew through the patriarchs. This is an account of what I thought necessary to bring concerning this matter, according to the ways that these sages, of blessed memory, formulated and commented upon it in their views. After introducing their words, I wanted to clarify the truth for myself regarding these two rewards, according to the opinion of the Torah and as established by supernal wisdom which enlightens the path of truth before those who seek it.[21]

This is the account of the author of *'Avodat ha-Qodesh*, who copied the opinions on these sages in this inquiry. And [Ibn Gabbai's] own view concerning why the spiritual promises are not mentioned in the Torah, I will transcribe later. Now the time has come to let you know what God has graced me with and the three investigations that I mentioned will be linked together. "*And the threefold thread will not be broken*."[22]

The Faithful House [II]

Know that the holy letters and holy words are entirely spiritual in their root. The kabbalists said that the letters are from *Binah*, the vowel points from *Ḥokhmah*, and the cantillation signs from *Keter*. To explain this, I will copy a passage from *Pardes Rimmonim*, *Sha'ar ha-'Otiot*, chapter one.

> Many thought that these letters are a matter of convention. In other words, the sages made indicators for the orifices of speech. How so? They agreed that the labials, which are b,w,m,p should be represented by the form of *bet*, the form of *vav*,[1] the form of *mem*, and the form of *peh*. And similarly [for the forms of the letters] agreed upon for the other consonants. Thus all the other languages of the nations have [written] indicators for all that they need, just as the mathematicians invented ten indicators through which all numbers may be represented, depending on the various levels and multiplicities, as is well known to mathematicians. Therefore, according to this, there would be no difference between these letters and the other indicators of the nations with their [various] languages, lands, and peoples. Only these are conventional for the Israelite people, as advised by Moses, through prophetic inspiration. They are a product of intellectual agreement which invented them thus. It follows from this conventional [nature of the letters] that there is no basis for some inscribed writing other than to reveal the intention of the one who communicates. When a physician writes his wisdom in a book of medicine, the intention is not at all that the book be medicine.

His intention in writing the book was to reveal his knowledge or whatever he desires concerning the matter of healing. When a person has understood the essence of the wisdom that is written in the book, no usefulness will remain in the book itself at all. Similarly, the philosopher told his students, "Do not trust the skins of dead carcasses."[2] It follows, then, that if a person studies that book for countless years, if he does not understand the subject, it will not be of use and he will not perfect his soul at all, through his studies. For he does not understand the discourses of wisdom. On the contrary, he wastes his time with what will harm him and be of no benefit. For he will harm himself through wasting his time and depleting his powers. It will not benefit him because he learned nothing at all from it. They have the same opinion concerning Torah studies. [They think] that the intention is to reveal the [Torah's] inner aspects and guidance toward perfection of the soul. Whoever does not know the subjects of its discourses will derive no benefit from his studies, God forbid. But this is impossible. For certainly words of Torah restore the soul. A proof for this [is the fact] that we are obligated to complete the reading of the Torah by reading it twice in Hebrew and once in the Aramaic translation,[3] including "*Atarot and Divon.*"[4] This indicates the perfection of the Torah and that it contains an inner, concealed aspect, spirituality, and divine energy. So Rabbi Simeon explained in [the *Zohar*],[5] *be-ha'alotekha.*[6]

See the *Zohar*, where this is discussed at length. He also wrote there that studying works of Torah in order to know [what is written in them] is like studying books of history. This certainly will not be of use and no benefit will come from such study. Hopefully, he will not lose [through this approach]. But when a person approaches the study of Torah, he must have in mind that what he is learning are words of God, whose essential inner aspect is concealed from him. In this way, all the Torah that emerges from his mouth "*will be more pleasing before the Holy One, blessed be He, than oxen,*"[7] even if he understands nothing in it but the basic story. And there is no need to say that even someone who does not understand at all [what he is learning in the Torah], because he is not proficient in the meaning of the language, but is merely occupied in reading [aloud], also has a good reward for his effort. Concerning these and similar cases, it is written, "*and he studies his Torah day and night.*"[8] The [rabbis] taught, the verse does not say "he studies Torah" but "he studies his Torah," meaning according to the measure of his knowledge. For even a person who does not know how to combine the words will also receive a reward if he concerns himself with it day and night. His labor is before him, as long as he constantly progresses. For you must [add this condition], since the *mishnah* says, "Whoever does not increase will be cut off."[9] See there at length. He also wrote as follows in the second chapter of the *Sha'ar ha-'Otiot*:

> The letters of the Torah are not [formed by] convention. They are rather *ruḥaniyut*, whose form is related to the inner aspect of their soul. Thus our rabbis, of blessed memory, were careful in their explanation of the form of the letters and their tips, crowns, and their tails. For they allude to *ruḥaniyut* that applies to the supernal *sefirot*. Each and every letter has a spiritual form. A fine light, emanated from the *sefirot*, is extended level after level, according to the extension of the *sefirot*. The letter is a palace and dwelling place for that *ruḥaniyut*. When a person utters and sets in motion one of the letters, he necessarily arouses that *ruḥaniyut*, and the holy forms [of the letters] are produced by the breath of his mouth and ascend and are bound to their root which is the root of divine emanation. Moreover, even in their existent state, that is, when they are written down, *ruḥaniyut* rests on those letters. This is the reason that a Torah scroll is holy. And this is the reason that [the letters] *mem* and *samekh* that were on the Tablets [of the Covenant] miraculously stood. It was because the *ruḥaniyut* caused that pure matter to stand. This also explains why in explaining the shattering of the Tablets, [the rabbis] said that the letters flew away. The *Midrash* says, "He looked at the Tablets and saw that what was written on them had flown away. The [Tablets] became heavy in Moses' hands and they fell from them and were broken."[10] Also in the Palestinian Talmud, the matter is explained. "Rabbi Azaryah said in the name of Rabbi Yehuda, the Tablets weighed forty *seah* and the writing bore their weight. When the writing flew away, the Tablets grew heavy in Moses' hands and they fell and were broken. Thus every place where the Holy One, blessed be He, removes His *Shekhinah*, can no longer exist."[11] And it says in the *Midrash*: " '*And his flag over me is love*.'[12] At first whoever pointed to the statues of the king with his finger was killed. Children going to school pointed their fingers at the warning. The Holy One, blessed be He, said, '*ve-diglo (over me is love)*,' do not read '*ve-diglo* (and his flag),' but '*ve-godlo* (and his

> greatness).' "[13] All of this concerns the *ruḥaniyut* of the letters. This is also the reason for what our rabbis, of blessed memory, said concerning a Torah scroll that is burned, God forbid, "[Whoever sees a Torah scroll that is mutilated is obligated to] make two cuts [in his garment]" and they proved it from the verse, "*after the king burned the scroll and the words.*"[14] "One makes one cut for the scroll and one for the writing."[15] In other words, for the *ruḥaniyut* of the letters. There are many examples like these concerning the *ruḥaniyut* of the letters, [which is present] even when they are only written, how much more so when they are uttered, and even more when they are properly intended.[16] The written letters serve as a body and place for the letters which are formed by the mouth. By analogy, the written letters can be compared to corporeality and the spoken ones to *ruḥaniyut*. This is the reason for the written Torah and the oral Torah. For the written Torah is *ruḥaniyut* in a lofty place and a sheath is required to clothe its light in material letters. But the oral Torah is itself a sheath and requires no garment of sheathing at all. So the written letters are a body and palace for those uttered by the mouth. The [letters] that are within the heart are the divine emanation known in the heart of the enlightened ones of Israel.[17]

The letters have *ruḥaniyut*, both because of their image and their number. The image of the letters and what they allude to is explained in *Sefer ha-Temunah* and in *Pardes*, *Sha'ar ha-'Otiot*. [After learning these sources], you will know that most of all, when the holy letters are combined and words are made from them, the *ruḥaniyut* of this word is a great matter above. And just as the vocalized forms of *YHVH* and the Divine Names are the secret of divine emanation, except that the Divine Names are an extension of the vocalized forms of *YHVH*, so the epithets are an extension of the divine names and there are epithets to the epithets. Similar are all the words of our Holy Language. All the words are above. Everything that exists below in corporeality is a manifestation and extension of *shefa'* from above that was extended level after level, through thousands upon thousands of stages, until it took on a material form in this material world.

Now the name for a certain thing is really the name for what is above in its root. For the root is where these letters are joined together, except that every stage of the chain of manifestation is called by this name, as a metaphor for its root. Therefore our language is called a Holy Language because all of the names and words exist above in their root, in the supernal place of holiness. Later, when something descends and is extended from this holy place, this manifestation is called by that [supernal] name, as a metaphor. As the author of *Pardes* wrote, the "handles" of a vessel are metaphors for human hands. Similarly, [one speaks of] the foot of the throne. Thus I say that this *ruḥaniyut*, the power of the human hand, which is called "hand," is not properly so called, but is metaphorical. The same applies to "eye," which refers to the eye's power of sight, and "ear," which refers to the ear's power of hearing. All the names are metaphorical, for a hand for a hand, an eye for an eye, a foot for a foot, and all of the rest.[18]

In saying that this language is holy, I mean that what is [really] called "hand" exists above in the place of holiness. Later, during the process of its manifestation through all of the worlds, from one stage to another, through myriad levels, the manifestation is called "hand" at every level, as a metaphor. This "hand" is [a metaphor] for that "hand" and that "hand" is [a metaphor] for the "hand" [on the level above it] all the way back to the source of holiness that is the hand, in essence. Therefore, our language is a Holy Language; that is, each thing that we call by a certain name only bears that name as a metaphor. That which properly bears the name is actually located above. It is similar to the four elements, fire, water, air, and earth. Concerning them, the *Zohar* wrote at length that they are extentions of the supernal Chariot. *Ḥesed* is water, *Gevurah* is fire, *Tif'eret* is air, and *Malkhut* is earth. These words, *water*, *fire*, *air*, and *earth*, essentially refer to something located in holiness. We call, metaphorically, what is later manifested from them, "fire," "water," "air," and "earth,"in the secret of the four animals [that bear the Chariot]. In the next stage, the manifestation of bands of angels, Michael is the element of water, Gabriel is the element of fire, Uriel is the element of air, and Raphael is the element of earth. This process continues through the manifestation of the orbs, until the elements are in their places. In each one of the stages of manifestation, mentioned above, there are myriad upon myriad levels. "Water" for "water" and "water" for "water," countless times. Similarly, "Fire" for "fire," and all of the rest, until [the manifestation] of these material elements. The burning, hot, and dry element is called metaphorically, fire. The cool, moist element is called water. The hot and moist element is called air. And the cool and dry element is called earth. However, the essence of the names *water*, *fire*, *air*, and *earth* is holy language, meaning that their source is in holiness. For *Ḥesed*, *Gevurah*, *Tif'eret*, and *Malkhut* are called in essence, water, fire, air, and earth. By way of example, people in every generation are called Abraham, Isaac, Jacob, Reuben, Simeon, and so on. The person now called Abraham is named after his grandfather or uncle, or some other relative, who was also named after his grandfather or uncle. And this process extends back to our forefather Abraham, whose name was truly Abraham because he was *Av Aram* (the father of Aram) and *Av Hamon* (the father of a multitude). Everyone who is called Abraham is named metaphorically and all names are like this.

Therefore, all of the divine attributes, "eye," "ear," "foot," "hand," etc. and also such matters as "coupling," "embracing," "kissing," "father" and "mother," "son" and "daughter," "father-in-law" and "mother-in-law," and so on, are all Holy Language. They refer essentially to something located in the realm of holiness, which is subsequently manifested and called metaphorically [by the same name]. So, finally, even material things are called by these names, metaphorically. Thus it is understood that, on the contrary, all of the parts of the Chariot essentially refer to God, blessed be He, and He is the supernal Adam. But our limbs are named metaphorically and are so called because they are a sign for what is above, just as [the name] Reuben ben Jacob is a sign [for the person so named], as the author of *Sha'arey 'Orah* wrote. The Holy One, blessed be He, created the lower Adam containing signs for the supernal Adam, so that he could be a chariot for the true existence. There are subtle inner matters which are absolutely spiritual. They are the segments of the Chariot from which light and *shefa'* are extended to those manifestations which function in its image. These are called hands, feet, eyes, ears. Not that the essence or structure of our hand is like the essence or structure of the hand above, God forbid. For, it is written, "*To whom will you compare God?*"[19] There is no similarity between us and God, in essence and structure. However, a person is established and made in this likeness to indicate that if he succeeds in purifying one of his limbs and to perfect it through those commandments that depend upon it, that limb will become like a chariot and throne of glory for that supernal, inner matter that is called by the [same] name, whether eye or hand or foot, etc. The kabbalists have an indicator for this. They say, "One limb holds another." For the whole person who has perfected himself like his master, who is established in his deeds, in Torah, and in purity of his limbs, perfects and establishes all of his limbs in the likeness of the structure of the Great Adam, in whose image he was made. For he perfected every one of his limbs through the commandments that are connected to it. Thus he is like that limb in whose likeness he was made.

This is the wisdom that Adam used when he indicated the names by which everything would be known. Thus it was said that his level in this [wisdom] was greater than the ministering angels. For through the Holy Spirit that [rested] upon him, he built letters and words connected to the inner speech,[20] so that those names would indicate the root of that particular thing. It is practically said that through knowing the things below, he knew the secret of the supernal Chariots. For every creature below has a root above. For otherwise, how could the parts of this world be interconnected if there is no root above for the elements? If the creatures have no root above, how can *shefa'* and providence reach them from the Lord of all? This was a wondrous wisdom. For he grasped the source and root of everything and called it by that name, which is its name indeed.

As a result of this, one may truly object to the apparent meaning of the saying of our rabbis, of blessed memory, "The Torah used human language"[21] in order to make obscure matters comprehensible. According to my view it is the opposite. For, when applied to God, blessed be He, these names are true, and words which human language [applies to things] are metaphors. However, the meaning [of this saying] is as follows. The Torah speaks of these attributes in man as if human language dealt with essentials and not metaphors. In reality, human language is only a Holy Language. So the Torah had to mention them regarding man in another context. Thus they answered, "to make obscure matters comprehensible." I still have to explain their speaking of "another context." There is a wonderful allusion which is explained in the *Zohar.* The *Pardes* discussed at length the divine emanation produced by the *Eyn Sof.* (As I explained, divine emanation is called the Great Adam). [The purpose] was to make His divinity known. For it would have been absolutely impossible to know Him, because of His great concealment, which is total, except by means of this emanation which takes the form of "a human being who is his own relative."[22] As for their saying, "The Torah spoke in human language . . . ," the Torah's speech refers to this stage of revelation which was meant to make things comprehensible in human terms so that they would understand and know His divinity. Therefore, emanation was manifested which is truly [in the form of] the human being, as has been explained. Then the secret of His divinity is revealed to some degree through His governance and providence, through the power of the Reason of all Reasons, and Cause of all Causes, and He is made known to human beings. The enlightened will understand.

Thus the reason [our language] is called a Holy Language has been explained. And the supernal Adam, the Great Adam, has been explained, "*Great is YHVH and much praised.*"[23] It is the extension of divine emanation which is united to the essence of *Eyn Sof* and it is a soul within them.[24] A great sign and allusion to the secret of unity is found in the saying which is characteristic of our rabbis, of blessed memory, "A person is close to himself."[25] Thus there are two aspects, when He is close to Himself and when He is one. Thus, in actuality, the supernal Adam is close to His concealed essence. But everything is united as a unity, like a flame attached to a coal.

Thus an explanation has also been given for why the spiritual promises are not mentioned in the Torah. For they are mentioned repeatedly, in essence and not metaphorically. It is like this. I will bring you an example of the first promise, in the section *be-ḥuqotay* [it says,] "And I shall bestow your rains . . . "[26] The word *rain* is holy language. For those watery drops that fall are not what the name rain refers to in essence. Rather, the power of bestowal which is high above in its root is called rain. It later descends and penetrates and is called rain in all of the worlds, metaphorically. But [it continues] level after level, until the verse is fulfilled, "*saith YHVH, I will respond to the sky and the earth shall respond.*"[27] Then these drops which water the earth are formed and cause birth and blooming and life for the world. But the level which is above this is also called rain. It [bestows] a more spiritual form of life, until in the very highest level, rain in essence is the eternal spiritual energy which is the secret of eternal delight of the world to come. Similar are all of the promises in *be-ḥuqotay*. Thus it has been explained that, indeed, the spiritual reward is mentioned in essence. As long as we are material, the words are explained for us in reference to material things, according to our present interest. Thus everything has been well explained. I trusted in the One who graces me with knowledge, that He would lead me in the path of truth. Blessed is the One who bestows knowledge.

We shall return to our subject, an explanation of the nature of man.

The House of Israel [II]

The nature of a human being has been explained, both from the standpoint of the soul and the form of the body. Concerning this, it has been written, "*Let Us make a human being in Our image and according to Our likeness.*"[1] The image [has been explained] as the secret of the soul and the likeness as the secret of the body. The likeness, which is revealed, is referred to by the verse, "*and from my flesh, I can see God.*"[2] The image, which is the secret of the soul, is concealed. Similarly, concerning the Great Man who sits on the Throne, it is said, "*likeness of man.*"[3] For one [level] is higher than another.[4] The secret of *Adam Qadmon*[5] is *Ḥokhmah*, where the limbs of man are concealed. Later, concerning *Tif'eret*, it is written, "*like the Tif'eret of man, to dwell in a house.*"[6] For there, He is revealed with His six extremities, which is His likeness, united in a complete unity.[7] He is only the revelation of what was concealed. This man, which is male and female, is called Adam, meaning *Tif'eret* and *Malkhut*. This is alluded to in the secret of the name *YHVH,* which when spelled *yvd ha vav ha* equals the numerical value of Adam. Adam's wife is [alluded to] by the letters that complete the spelling [of *YHVH*]. For she was filled[8] by him, the secret of impregnation. When *vd a av a*[9] are added up, their sum equals Eve.[10] What is below alludes to what is above. Thus the image and likeness of Adam [was so similar to God] that the ministering angels erred and wished to bow down before it. Adam said to them, "Come, let's bow down, surrender, and offer blessing to *YHVH*, our Maker," as mentioned in the *Midrash*.[11] It also says in the *Midrash*, " '*and YHVH 'Elohim caused a deep sleep to descend over Adam.*'[12] When the Holy One, blessed be He, created Adam, the ministering angels erred and wished to say 'Holy!' before him. This may be compared to a king and his viceroy [who were riding in a travelling carriage. The subjects wished to sing praises to the king, but did not know which one he was. What did the king do? He pushed the viceroy out of the carriage. Then everyone knew that he was the viceroy].[13] And concerning the time that is coming, when the intention of creation will be fulfilled and human beings will be like Adam before he sinned and even higher in level, the sages said, in chapter 'the one who sells the boat,' 'Rabbi Eleazar said, in the future they will say before the righteous, "Holy!" just as one says it [now] before the Holy One, Blessed be He.' As it is written, '*and it shall be that those who remain in Zion and who are left in Jerusalem will be called Holy. . . .*'[14]"[15] The meaning of all this is that when a person is complete, he cleaves to the name *YHVH*.

As I wrote above, the name *YHVH* is included in the letter *yod* and the *yod* is an *alef*. Just as I explained this concerning the cleaving of the Torah, so it is with the human being. As for his *neshamah*, it comes from the secret of the *d"u parẓufim*, as I explained.[16] The secret of the *neshamah* of the *neshamah* comes from the secret of the *yod* and its tip. It is referred to as *ḥaY*, *ḥayyah* and *yeḥidah* from *Ḥokhmah* and *Keter*, as I explained. In actuality, it is all one *alef*, since the light of the *neshamah* is only divided according to the level of its receiver. For it is comparable to light. There is one who may enjoy light and yet be incapable of gazing at the light in its strength, and there are other [higher levels]. It all depends on the degree to which the recipient has been prepared.

It is similar in regard to the likeness of the body. The body has the form of *yod vav dalet*.[17] For the human body has a front and back, a left side and a right side. This is *dalet*, which corresponds to the four directions of the world. The head, which is above the body, has the form of a *yod* and it is above. The legs are below the body and extend like a *vav*. Thus [the human body has the form of] *yod vav dalet*. And they are six extremities, above and below and the four directions.[18] Yet they are all one body. Thus the Torah is interpreted by the human being who cleaves to the name *YHVH*.

The Torah is interpreted in general and in particular. I mean that we have been speaking about the secret of the individual person. However, the Israelite nation as a whole is called human being[19] and the generality does not differ from the individual. For the generality involves a great cleaving to *YHVH*. As it is written, "*You who are cleaving to YHVH your God are all alive today*."[20]

Now it is known that the four ways of completing the spelling of *YHVH* are the Names of 72, 63, 45, and 52. The Name of 72 is formed through completing the spelling with *yods*: *Yod Hy Vyv Hy*. The Name of

63 uses three *yods* and one *alef* [to complete the spelling]: *Yod Hy Vav Hy*. The Name of 45 has three *alefs* and one *yod*: *Yod Ha Vav Ha*. This way of completing the spelling has the same numerical value as Adam. The Name of 52 is spelled with *hehs*: *Yod Hh Vv Hh*.

Blessed is He in whose great Name we are called. This may be interpreted in regard to the Name of 72, the root of Israel. They are the seventy elders, as it is written, "*Gather me seventy men from the elders of Israel.*"[21] And Moses and Aaron are over them. And similarly, there were always a president and chief justice of the court [over the Sanhedrin], thus making seventy-two. This is indicated by the verse, "*And they shall place My Name over the Children of Israel.*"[22] *A"B* is an acronym for *'al beney* (over the children). There is another great allusion. When the Name of 72 is combined with Israel, the sum is 613, like the 613 commandments.[23]

[It can also be said] concerning the Name of 63. The letters that complete the spelling are the secret of *'El.*[24] It is the seal of *Yisrael*: *Ysr 'el*. For Your Name *YHVH* is in our midst, as we explained above. His Name is in His midst, which alludes to the middle of the Name *Adonay*. When it is spelled *Alf Dlt Nvn Yvd*, the middle letters equal 72,[25] which eludes to the Name that completes the spelling of *YHVH*. Similarly, the number of *YHVH* [26]is in the midst of Yisrael. How so? *'El* is the seal, as has been explained. What remains? *YSR*. Write it *Yvd Syn Rysh*. What is in the midst of *YSR*? The middle letters *vyy*, which equal *YHVH*.

Next, the Name of 45 equals *adam*, and Israel is called *adam*. Also the letters that complete the spelling of the Name of 45 equal *'eḥad* (one).[27] Israel is called one, as we say in the liturgy of the Sabbath afternoon standing prayer, "You are one and Your Name is one and who is like Your people Israel, one nation." This is the meaning of the verse, "*for YHVH will not abandon His people, for the sake of His Great Name . . .* "[28] For when *Keneset Yisrael* is joined to the Holy One, blessed be He, *'eḥad* to *'eḥad*, they become *'aḥadim.*[29] This equals 26 like the value of the Great Name, which indeed equals two times *'eḥad*. For the Blessed One chooses His people Israel in love. Love (*'ahavah*) equals *'eḥad.*[30] And love of Israel for the Holy One, blessed be He, begins when one reaches the age of *'eḥad*. A person enters the covenant of fulfilling the commandments when he is thirteen years old. Corresponding to this, the Holy One, blessed be He, is aroused with thirteen measures of compassion.

As for the Name of 52 (*B"N*), beloved is Israel for its people are called Children (*BaNim*) of God. There is another secret regarding this. The Holy One, blessed be He, said to Ezekiel, the prophet, "*And you, human being (ben adam) . . .* "[31] He always called him *ben adam* and not just *adam*, because the level of the prophets depends on the ascension of Israel. When Israel descends, God forbid, the prophets descend from their level. As the sages, of blessed memory, said, concerning the verse, *"Go, descend [for your people have acted wickedly . . .]"*[32] "Descend from your greatness. Did I give you greatness for any other reason than because of Israel? . . . "[33] Now Israel is essentially called *adam*, "you are adam," because of the secret of the image and supernal likeness of the Great Adam. However, the offspring, the branch which is extended [from Adam], is called *ben Adam* (son of Adam).

And this is the meaning of [the name] Ben He He, the secret of converts.[34] They are called children of Abraham, as it is written, *"father of a multitude."*[35] But we, the seed of Israel, are called Abraham. Thus it is written, *"that YHVH might bring about for Abraham [what He has promised him]"*[36] It is not written "for the House of Abraham," but "for Abraham." This teaches, according to Rashi, "If one produces a righteous son (*ben ẓaddiq*), it is as if he has not died."[37] For Abraham is called the Great Adam and Israel are called *adam*. The secret of *adam* is the Name of 45. The secret of son (*ben*) is the Name of 52 (*Shem B"N*).[38] It is called *"ben Adam."* The spelling of this Name is only completed by its own letters themselves: *hh vv hh*. (For the letter *yod* is spelled the same way in all of these Names. Also *yod* completes itself, since *vd* equals *y*).[39] This is the secret of why [the Tanna] was called Ben He He. For the Name of 52 is [the one spelled] *heh heh*. And [the name of the Tanna] Ben Bag Bag[40] also alludes to this name, except Ben He He is the aspect of *heh* and Ben Bag Bag is the aspect of *vav*.[41] How so? Twice *gimmel* equals *vav*. This is *B"G*, the aspect of twice *gimmel*.[42] For the aspect of *vav* in this Name contains two groups of three (*sefirot*), *Ḥesed*, *Gevurah*, and *Tif'eret* and then *Neẓaḥ*, *Hod*, and *Yesod*.

We shall return to our original discussion. Israel is called according to the designation of *Yisrael Sabba*,[43] *"like the tif'eret of adam."*[44] This involves the secret that *adam* is the name of male and female. For *"YHVH is in the chamber (heykhal) of His holiness."*[45] [*Hekhal*] is 65. Before it is the Name *ADoNaY* in which *YHVH* dwells.[46] And the Name *ADoNaY*, the source of Israel, is a receptacle for the souls of Israel, which are bestowed from *Tif'eret* to *Malkhut*. Just as the Name *ADoNaY* equals 65, so it is for the House of Israel. It is said concerning them, *"For you are the least (ha-me'at) of all the nations."*[47] As Rashi states in his commentary, [This may be read as] "five less than all the nations."[48] For Israel consists of sixty-five families and they are five less than the seventy nations.

There is another secret to this *heh* [in the word *ha-me'at*]. It [can be understood as] *heh me'utah*. In other words, a small *heh*. This is the small *heh* in the word *be-hibbar'am* (*"in their being created"*).[49] With it, the world was created for Israel, which is *Keneset Yisrael*, just as the small *heh* takes in (*maKeNeSet*) all the *shefa'* which comes to it from *Yisrael Sabba*. Blessed is *YHVH*, *'Elohay Yisrael*. *'Elohay* equals 10, according to *mispar qatan*.[50] Similarly, *Yisrael* equals 10, in *mispar qatan*.[51] And the *Shekhinah* does not rest on fewer than ten Israelites.[52] And all involves the secret of *yod* (ten).

There is a wonderful allusion [to Israel] in the acronym formed by the first letters of the names of the *sefirot*: *Keter*, *Ḥokhmah*, *Binah*, *Gedulah*, *Gevurah*, *Tif'eret*, *Neẓaḥ*, *Hod*, *Yesod*, *Malkhut*: *KḤ"B, GG"T, NHY"M* equals *Yisrael*.[53] This is the meaning of "[*Their king marches before them*] *and YHVH at their head (be-r'osham).*"[54] "*Their head* (*r'osham*)" has the same numerical value as *Yisrael*.[55]

Here is what Rabbi Menahem Azariah da Fano says in *Pelaḥ ha-Rimmon*.

> The thought of Israel precedes everything. This is the meaning of "*You have done much, YHVH, my God, Your wonders and thoughts* [*were*] *for us.*"[56] And Rabbi Simeon taught, three crowns are assigned: to the *Nasi'*, the High Priest, and the King. Due to the extreme level of their awesomeness, in governing the chosen people, we had need of the chief of the priests, the viceroy, and the Head of the Rabbinical Court. Under them were three flocks of sheep, the hosts of Israel. They are the divisions of priests, the lovers and pursuers of peace, the officers of the soldiers who subdue the people, and the Sanhedrin, occupiers of seats for justice. The eyes and hearts of all of them are turned to *Keter Shem Tov*,[57] the community of Jacob, the mother of all of them.[58]

The secret of the *Nasi'* is *Keter*. The High Priest is *Ḥokhmah*, which is the secret of "*terumah* is great. It has no measure [from the Torah]. Even one bunch of wheat discharges [the duty of *terumah* for the entire store]."[59] This is because of the limited extent to which it is comprehensible. The King of the World is *Binah*. For the world consists of six extensions.[60] The chief of priests, viceroy, and Head of the Rabbinical Court correspond to *Ḥesed*, *Gevurah*, and *Tif'eret*. This is the secret of the Patriarchs, who are an extension of the roots. And the divisions of the priests, the officers of the soldiers, and Sanhedrin are branches of the Patriarchs. They are the offspring (*banim*), the secret of *Neẓaḥ*, *Hod*, *Yesod*. And *Keter Shem Tov*, Community of Jacob is *Keneset Yisrael*.[61]

Thus is the secret of *adam* and the secret of Israel which is called *adam*. Both the generality and the individual are included in the secret of *YHVH*.

The ultimate purpose of creation came from God as a gift, in His great goodness to benefit others, so that they would recognize His blessed divinity. As a result they would cleave to Him, eternally. For this is the ultimate reward that is hoped for. As for the punishment that God created, its intention was not, essentially, for the sake of punishment, but for the reward. For God acted so that they would fear Him. Then "the reward is according to the trouble taken," just as I wrote above.[62]

This is also alluded to in the Name, *YHVH*, just as Rashi wrote at the beginning of section *va-'era'*.

> " '*And He said to him, I am YHVH.*'[63] Faithful to pay a good reward to those who walk before Me. Not for nothing did I send you, but to fulfill My word which I said to the first Patriarchs." And we found that this expression is interpreted in a number of places. "I am *YHVH* . . . " faithful to punish, when it is said concerning a punishment. For example, "[*Do not swear falsely on My Name*] *and profane the Name of YHVH, your God. I am YHVH.*"[64] And when it is said in regard to fulfilling a commandment, such as "*You shall keep My commandments and do them. I am YHVH,*"[65] [means] faithful to pay a good reward.[66]

And so Rashi wrote afterward:

> I heard something similar to this matter, concerning this section, from Rabbi Barukh the son of Rabbi Eliezer. He brought me evidence from this verse: "*This time I shall make My might and power known to them and they shall know that I am YHVH.*"[67] It teaches us that when the Holy One, blessed be He, guarantees his words, even for chastisements, He makes known His Name *YHVH*, and all the more so when the assurance is for good.[68]

Now, at first glance, one might object that it is well known that the Name *YHVH* indicates the attribute of mercy and the Name *'Elohim*, the attribute of judgment. So how can it be said that the Name *YHVH* is faithful to pay a reward and to chastise? However, the meaning is as I have explained. The punishment is for the sake of the reward. For evil is a cause for good. This is the meaning of "*YHVH is the 'Elohim.*"[69] This is also alluded to in the beginning of section *va-'era'*: "then *'Elohim spoke* [*to Moses*] *and said to him, I am YHVH* . . . "[70] In other words, you complain that "[*since I came to Pharaoh to speak in Your Name*], *he has done evil to this people.*"[71] God spoke to him with the Name 'Elohim; "You should know that I am *YHVH*. For 'Elohim is *YHVH*. The attribute of justice is for the sake of compassion. "*For as a man chastises his son, so YHVH, your God, chastises you.*"[72]

Know that there are two kinds of chastisements. Chastisements of love are those which the Holy One, blessed be He, exacts upon a person. Chastisements which are not of love are those which remove the wicked from the world. Similarly, regarding the war of Gog and Magog, it is written, "*I will manifest My greatness and holiness and be made known to many nations. And they shall know that I am YHVH.*"[73] Even here, the Name *YHVH* applies. For evil destroys itself and as a result good is drawn to those who cleave to *YHVH*. For they are the purpose of creation.

I will bring forward what Rabbenu Tam wrote in the first Gate of *Sefer ha-Yashar*.

> We should know and understand that the Creator did not create the world for the wicked and those who anger Him. For this would not obligate that Intellect. On the contrary, He created it for the *ḥasidim* who know His divinity and serve Him properly. His only intention was to create the *hasidim*, but the wicked were created through the power of the nature of creation. Just as a fruit has a shell and the select portion is within the shell, so the *hasidim* are the fruit if the creation of the world and the wicked are like shells. And as we see the intention of the sower is to cause wheat alone to grow, but the power of growth brings forth weeds with the wheat, and thorns along with roses, so the Creator's intention was to create *hasidim*, but the power of creation brought forth the wicked with the *hasidim*.[74]

Thus when the wicked fall, the inner part is eaten and the shell is discarded, which is the purpose of creation. Then the inner portion remains, clean without any dross and admixture of the shell. It is entirely Holy to *YHVH*. Then the truth of the Name *YHVH* is known and *YHVH* alone is exalted. For the meaning of *YHVH* is faithful, as Rashi explained. And the meaning of faithful is eternal, for everlastingness which will never fail is its true nature. And *YHVH* is known through the cleaving to Him of those who are worthy of eternity.

Now we shall return to our subject. It has been explained that the Torah and Israel are connected to the Holy One, blessed be He, through the Name *YHVH*. For the three essentials are the existence of God, Torah from heaven, and reward and punishment. Now we shall go on to the completion of the explanation of the passage from the *Zohar*. To this point, we have been explaining the first matter, the existence of God that is made known by the Name *YHVH*, to which the Torah and Israel also cleave. As was stated above, "three upon three." In other words, the Torah and Israel are bound to the Name that is made known through the existence of God. And God, so to speak, and Israel are bound to the Name that is made known as Torah. And God, so to speak, and the Torah are bound to the Name that is made known as Israel. Now we shall explain the Name that is made known as Torah.

The House of Wisdom [II]

This is the meaning of 613, as explained at the end of tractate *Makkot*.

> Rabbi Simlai explained that 613 commandments were said to Moses: 365 negative commandments, like the number of the days of the solar year, and 248 positive commandments, corresponding to the limbs of a human being. Rav Hamnuna said, what is the meaning of the verse, "*Moses commanded us a Torah, the heritage* [*of the community of Jacob*]?"[1] Torah has the numerical value of 611. Therefore, they heard, "*I am YHVH your God*. . ." and "*you shall have* [*no other God before Me*]"[2] directly from God.[3]

It says in the *Zohar* passage mentioned above that "the Torah is also concealed and revealed." This was not stated to inform us that the Torah has an exoteric and esoteric aspect. For this is known even to the masses. Surely this holy passage, which contains many matters, is meant to teach us something new.

My sons, may God protect and keep them, listen to me. Know, my sons, we were commanded to observe these 613 commandments in this world.[4] [As the sages said,] "Do them today and tomorrow, receive their reward."[5] Reward and punishment is not [merely] conventional, it is a natural spiritual consequence. As we have learned, "The reward of a commandment is a commandment, the reward of a transgression is a transgression."[6] For the reward of a corporeal commandment that one does is the commandment itself. In other words, the *ruḥaniyut* of this commandment [is its reward], as I wrote above. For the root and essence of all words and attributes that are mentioned in the Torah are the Holy Language. That is, the name as it [applies to an entity] in the uppermost regions truly is holy, but when [that entity] has extended below, a material entity is called by that name, by way of metaphor. It is similar in regard to carrying out the commandments. Even the most minor commandment has a great root above. This root is itself the reward. For the soul [of the person who carries out the commandment] cleaves there. And the opposite occurs in the case of a transgression, God spare us, as the sages of the *Mishnah* hinted. "[Reflect on three things] and you will not fall into a transgression."[7] For one who commits a transgression falls into the hands of the transgression, which is the *qelippah*, the root of the transgression, God spare us.

Here is what the Recanati wrote at the beginning of section *be-ḥuqotay*:

> "*If you follow My statutes . . . and I shall grant you your rains in their seasons.*"[8] Know that the blessings and curses that are written in the Torah are not merely a matter of reward and punishment, but are truly a part of nature, like the sower who reaps. As it is written, "*Whoever works his land will have plenty of food . . .* "[9] and vice versa. For the honored Name of God, may He be blessed and exalted, which is called "Well" will receive all kinds of *shefa'* and emanations from the upper levels, by way of the Great Name, may He be exalted. In it the streams will be joined together that are extended from the thirteen levels of *Keter*, from the thirty-two paths of *Ḥokhmah*, and from the fifty Gates of *Binah*, from the seventy-two bridges that are in the supernal waters which are called the waters of *Ḥesed*, from the forty-two kinds of fire that flame from *Gevurah*, and from the seventy branches of the middle pillar. All of them pass through *Neẓaḥ* and *Hod* and are joined together in *Yesod*. And from there, they reach the Well, which is *Keneset Yisrael*. Since all of these are drawn there, *YHVH* is One and His Name is One, a complete union. The entire world is blessed from there and all the various kinds of creatures are filled with goodness. For the channels of judgment are reduced and the channels of mercy enlarged, due to the *ḥasidim* and *ẓaddiqim* of Israel. They sustain the Heart and the Heart sustains them, according to the meaning of the verse, "*She bestows good and not evil on him all the days of her life.*"[10] In other words, as long as she sucks from the World of Life. Thus all the blessings in the Torah are part of the natural order. However, when human beings sin, the channels of mercy are reduced and the channels of judgment are

> enlarged. Then the world is completely in suffering and lack. Worst of all is when the supernal channels are completely closed and [energy] is drawn from the external channels, the forces of evil and evil waters. Then lands are destroyed, [nations] are uprooted and exiled. This is the meaning of the rebukes that are written in the Torah.[11]

In section *teẓaveh*, he discussed this at length:

> Do not think that the punishments that are written in the Torah are like punishing a person for transgressing the command of a king. They are not so, but are in reality a natural consequence. For whoever annuls the goodness of a commandment of the Torah, which would have been bestowed had he carried out the commandment, is prevented [from receiving that goodness]. It is like someone who does not sow his field and thus cannot reap it, or if one does not dress, his body will be cold. Just as it is the nature of fire to heat, and the nature of water to dampen, and the nature of bread to satisfy, so it is the nature of each and every commandment to bring about those benefits that are said concerning it or those punishments that are said concerning its neglect. But not all of the transgressions are equal. There are transgressions that afflict the Inner Chamber, such as idol worship, incest, murder, and the like. And there are transgressions whose affliction lies outside the Chamber, such as eating impure things. Thus people are called *ẓaddiqim* because they set things up properly.[12]
>
> *Sefer ha-Zohar*: "Rabbi Simeon opened the verse, '*It is time to act for YHVH, they have violated Your Torah.*'[13] Why is it '*time to act for YHVH?*' Because '*they violated Your Torah.*' What is the meaning of '*they violated Your Torah?*' The Torah which is above which is cancelled if it is not served according to the *tiqqunim* of this Name. Rabbi Judah said, '*it is time to act for YHVH,*' in order to prepare and perfect everything. This is as our rabbis, of blessed memory, said, 'Whoever fulfills My commandments is considered by Me as if he had made Me, as it is written, "*It is time to make YHVH.*" '[14] To literally make (*la-'ASot*) [*YHVH*]. That is why the *ḥasidim* were called men of deed (*anshey ma'ASeH*). And the opposite is '*for he made the Temple of YHVH impure.*'[15] This is the meaning of their saying, 'you should aid me.' And they also said, 'nevertheless, I live.' Rava said, 'You give me life with your

words.' This is the secret of 'Ishmael, my son, bless me.'[16] And the secret of 'He nodded his head to me.'[17] He made it known that through the blessing of Rabbi Ishmael, the good oil was drawn from the *'Ayin*. This is the meaning of 'Do not underestimate the blessing of an ordinary person.'[18] For a covenant is made by the lips."

Once we know that we have the power to rectify the upper and lower matters and to sanctify the name of Heaven above or to cast a flaw in the sanctities of heaven, and how far our purity and impurity reaches, we have to clarify the way that one cleaves to the united Name, as it is written, "*and you shall cleave to it*."[19] For when a person purifies his limbs and establishes them according to the intention of creation, he adds the likeness of that limb above and it cleaves to God, as it is said, "*the likeness of a man upon it from above*."[20] Thus a limb strengthens a limb.[21] Since we have these powers to strengthen the *sefirot* through the measure of pure thought, according to the majority of our action, out of His great love for His beloved children, people of faith, God gave us the secret of the form of the ten *sefirot*, in His Torah. And He added an explanation. For every *sefirah* has a *tiqqun* of its form and a way of joining and kissing the *sefirah* that is next to it, until they are all joined as one, making one form. In accord with the depth of this attainment, the entire Torah was given to us, complete, from "*In the beginning . . .* "[22] until "*in the eyes of all Israel*."[23] Now all the letters of the Torah in their forms, combinations, separations, and the letters which are not written straight, or are extra or lacking, big or small, open and closed, [allude to] the form of the ten *sefirot*. And the pauses and divisions are in the likeness of the structure, just as a human body contains connections between the hands, feet, and [their] sections. I already alluded to this. Thus it is known that whoever fulfills a commandment bestows, so to speak, power upon it from above, in the supernal form, by way of the channels of thought which reach that part. Those above are blessed as a result of those below. The Great Name is blessed and there is *shefa'* from the depths of the earth[24] until it is crowned and ascends because of those who are serving with love. Concerning them, it is said, "*And He said to me, you are My servant Israel, in you I am glorified*."[25] In other words, because of you, I receive an abundance of *shefa'* from the source. In the *Midrash Yelamdenu*, our Rabbis said that the Holy one, blessed be He, said, I am sanctified through you, as it is said, "*For when his children see* [*the work of My hands in his midst, they will sanctify My Name.*]"[26] And He also says, "*Israel in whom I am glorified.*" And you are sanctified through Me, as it is written, "*Be holy* [*because I, YHVH, your God, am holy*]."[27,28]

To complete the explanation of this wonderful matter, I will copy from *Sefer 'Avodat ha-Qodesh*, section *'Avodah*, chapter 18.

We have already explained above the truth that it is the nature of worship, which is the union [of the *sefirot*] to open the source and to draw forth blessing from the beginning of thought and to its end. From there it extends to those below, who are the cause of this, through their uniting. And in the *Midrash* of Rabbi Simeon bar Yohai, peace be upon him, they said, " '*and I will exalt Him*'[29] with all, to include whoever knows how to unite the Great Holy Name. For that is the worship of the Holy One, blessed be He."[30] It is also said there, " '*YHVH is close to all who call upon Him in truth.*'[31] What is the meaning of '*in truth?*' As we have explained, '*You grant truth to Jacob . . .*'[32] because he knew how to unite the Holy Name properly and this is the worship of the Holy Name. Whoever knows how to unite the Holy Name, establishes the unique people in the world. As it is written, '*And who is like Your people Israel, one nation in the world.*'[33] Concerning this, they have explained that the worship of any priest who does not know how to unite the Holy Name properly is not [true] worship. For everything depends on this, both supernal and lower worship. He must purify[34] the heart and will in order that the supernal and lower ones will be blessed."[35]

This matter is repeated in many places in the *Midrash* of Rabbi Simeon bar Yohai, peace be upon him. The intention of all this is to impress in us what we have frequently repeated. Study of Torah and keeping its commandments draw light and an abundance of blessing from the source of being to the supernal and lower ones. This is the cause of all the benefits in this life. For their nature necessitates this, since the Torah is truly the Great Name. And in the *Midrash* of Rabbi Simeon bar Yohai "we learned that the Holy One, blessed be He, is called Torah. There is no water, except Torah and no Torah, except the Holy One, blessed be He."[36] The Great Name is the source of all benefits and successes, because He is in Himself, the Completely Good. Thus it is fitting that all of that good be drawn to the Torah which is inscribed from Him. In that way it attests to its source. King David alluded to this when he said, "*The testimony of YHVH is faithful.*"[37] Whoever merits this receives all of its wealth and happiness, through the Great Name indeed, as I wrote in chapter twenty-three of this work. See there, for it is astounding. Since this is the case, all of the benefits and successes are drawn to [the Torah] and necessitated by it. For the King so founded its nature that it be necessitated according to the source from which it is hewn. For it is proper that the nature of the source be present in what is hewn from it, as I wrote in that chapter, with God's help. Thus we can easily understand the blessings that come from the Torah for those who follow the Torah of God. The secret concealed in this is that these benefits are not like the designations of a king who stipulates a certain salary to pay his servants in exchange for their work. For the benefit that follows from such stipulations is not drawn to the service itself or necessitated by its nature. This is a great defect in the law of service which is not the case when the benefit is drawn to the service and obligated by its nature. For the latter indicates the praise and honor of the level of the service that is performed. Now since our Torah is infinitely superior to all [other] teachings and religion, and hence is called the Torah of *YHVH*, our service to our God is true service, preferred over all [other] service.[38] Thus the Supreme Wisdom saw fit to form it in a manner that all benefits and successes would be drawn to it and necessitated by it as a complete necessity. The sign and wonder concerning this is that "*great voice which will not cease.*"[39] Included in it is everything that will occur in the future in every generation, as will be explained in chapter twenty-three of the third part, with God's help. Through it came the reward and punishment for every matter. But they only came in this section of the Torah to make known that that reward is drawn from and necessitated by that commandment.

In the *Midrash* of Rabbi Simeon bar Yohai, peace be upon him, it says, "And indeed each and every word was full of all of these reasons. And all of these words enact rewards and punishments, secrets and mysteries, like that threshold."[40] Therefore, all of the benefits and successes that come to those who keep the Torah are only simply stated, that is, through keeping this Torah and fulfilling its commandments, all of those benefits will necessarily be drawn forth. For they are the true and proper key for opening the source of all benefits and happiness, since they have been hewn from that source and this has been placed in their nature. Thus through opening that source, an abundance of light and blessing will necessarily be drawn from the beginning of thought, which is the source, until its end. Upon reaching there, it will of necessity extend to those below who are worshipping. For the nature of the worship requires this. I already wrote that the holy emanation is the vessel for pouring out the *shefa'* and blessing to the world. Otherwise, it is in no way possible. Only according to it and its will the worlds will be blessed, and proper worship necessitates this. For when it ascends with the proper intention, the *shefa'* is aroused toward it and descends below.

In the *Midrash* of Rabbi Simeon bar Yohai, they said the following." '*It is like fine oil on the head* . . . '[41] What is '*fine oil*?' It is the holy anointing oil that emerges and descends from the Holy Ancient One, which is found in that supernal stream that nurses the children in order to kindle sparks. That oil descends upon the head of the king and from the king to the glory of his holy beard. From there it descends to all those precious garments that the king wears. As it is written, '*that descends according to his attributes* . . . '[42] Literally, according to His attributes. These are the king's crowns. His Name is found in them.

"Come and see. No extension or joy of the world descends in order to bless, except by means of these holy crowns which are the Name of the Holy King. Thus it is written, '*that descends according to his attributes*.' According to his attributes, indeed. Just as it is written, '*They shall be according to Aaron and his sons* . . . ,'[43] so '*according to his attributes*,' [it] descends and extends to all the worlds, that blessings may be found for all.

"Come and see. That '*fine oil*' is not summoned until that hour when the worship below has ascended and they delight in each other. As it is written, '*Oil and incense gladden the heart* . . .'[44] '*Oil*' above and '*incense*' below. Then is the joy of all."[45]

Thus they explained all that we required and said "*Oil and incense delight the heart*." This is the heart of heaven. Concerning it is written, "*And YHVH said to His heart* . . ."[46] The oil which descends from the source onto the head and the incense are the secret of worship which rises from below. They are called and gathered there and gladden that heart. From there the joy and light are extended to all of those below. Were it not that they reached there first, those below would not be able to eat well. For from there, livelihood is arranged for all of the worlds, according to the secret of [the verse], "*The eyes of all are turned in hope toward You and You give them their food in its time*."[47] And they said in the *Midrash* of Rabbi Simeon bar Yohai, peace be upon him, "What is '*its time*'? The time of the *Ẓaddiq*. This is the Lady[48] who is called the 'time of the *Ẓaddiq*.' Consequently, all wait for that time. All that are nourished below are nourished from that place. We have explained this secret. '*The eyes of all are turned toward You in hope and You give them their food in its time*,' as we explained.

"Come and see. At that hour, all perfume '*its time*' and join themselves to it. All worlds [do so] with joy; all worlds [are joined] with blessings. Then peace is found above and below."[49]

And in the *Midrash* of Rabbi Nehuniah ben ha-Qanah is written: "Rabbi Raḥumai said, were it not for the righteous and pious of Israel, who, through their merits, raise Me over all of the world. The Heart is sustained by them and the Heart sustains them."[50] I already wrote this. The great cause for this is learning Torah and fulfilling its commandments. Since this is so, all of the blessings and benefits in the Torah come by way of statement, and they are not promises at all, as we wrote. It is a kind of revelation that through our keeping the Torah and the commandments, this goodness necessarily will be drawn from them. For this is the nature of worship. Since this is undoubtedly so, there is no reason to ask why, having designated the material benefit, [the Torah] did not designate the spiritual benefit; or, why, having neglected to mention the spiritual promise, which is the essence of the reward, [the Torah] mentioned the material promise, which is not the essence of the reward. For it is not meant to promise at all, but to reveal what necessarily follows from the nature of worship. All benefits and successes follow from the commandments because of the divine nature that is implanted in them. [The Torah] made use of this manner of revelation in stating, "*if you follow My statutes and keep My commandments, and do them*."[51] "*If you follow My statutes*" refers to learning Torah and "*and keep My commandments*" refers to fulfilling its commandments. "*And do them*" refers to the supernal *tiqqun*, the *tiqqun* of the Glory, which is effected through learning Torah and fulfilling the commandments, which is the way to effect that *tiqqun*. Afterward, [the Torah] explained what necessarily follows from this and said, "*I will grant your rains in their season*"[52] and the rest of the benefits such as peace and victory over enemies and our fruitfulness and increase.

They said in the *Midrash* of Rabbi Simeon bar Yohai, " '*and do them*' is written. If you labor to do them in order to properly effect a *tiqqun* of the Holy Name, all of these blessings that are above will be found among you, through their proper *tiqqun*. '*And I will grant your rains in their season . . .* ' Each one will place its power over you. What are these? The *tiqqun* of that Holy Name that you effected. Similarly, it is written, '*They shall keep the way of YHVH by doing what is just and right.*'[53] Since it is written, '*They shall keep the way of YHVH,*' what is the meaning of '*by doing what is just and right*'? Whoever guards the ways of Torah, '*makes,*' so to speak,[54] what is just and right. What is 'just and right?' The Holy One, blessed be He."[55]

The Rabbi and kabbalist Rabbi Joseph Gikatilla, of blessed memory, wrote in *Sefer Sha'arey 'Orah*, in [the chapter on] the *sefirah Binah*, "Know and believe that the *sefirah Binah* and the *sefirah Malkhut* are turned toward each other. When *Malkhut* is set in order by the *tiqqun* of Israel through fulfilling the Torah and commandments, *Binah* appears and pours out all kinds of *shefa'* and blessings through the channels until *Malkhut* is blessed and filled. Then all the creatures of the world exist in peace and quiet. The blessing is sent with all manner of food and the blessing cleaves to the earth. This is the secret of the order of the blessings, '*If you follow My statutes . . . I will grant your rains in their season and the earth will yield its produce . . .*' and the whole Torah section."[56]

This is as we have said, the *tiqqun* of the Glory depends on fulfilling the Torah and commandments and all of those benefits will be drawn to them as a result of this *tiqqun*. This benefit does not come by way of [arbitrary] stipulation. For something whose nature it is to be produced from something else on which it depends, does not have to be stipulated. It needs only to be revealed in a statement that this necessarily follows from that matter by nature, just as in the case of fulfilling the Torah and commandments which are the essential key to the source of all the benefits. For they depend on them and necessarily will result from that opening which is the fulfilling [of the commandments]. Were it not for this wonder in the nature of fulfilling the commandments, we would have to say that there is no connection between fulfilling the commandments and those benefits, which do not result from them by nature. Yet, since we see that those benefits do occur for the keepers of the Torah, we would have to say that this is because [God] promised them and He is faithful with His covenant and keeps His word, but not that the nature of fulfilling the Torah and commandments necessitates this. But because we know well that it is from the nature of fulfilling the Torah and the commandments that all of those benefits are drawn to them, we can say that what is said concerning them in the Torah is a statement and revelation of the matter. For it would be superfluous to promise what necessarily results by nature.

From this we can learn how much good is caused by those who perfect their ways and how much evil by those who spoil them. King Solomon alluded to all that we have spoken about in saying, "*He who works his land will have plenty of bread, but he who pursues vanities will have plenty of poverty.*"[57] For the owner of a field fertilizes it, hoes it, and sows it and rain causes it to grow and sprout. The earth, through its nature, brings forth its produce. So the one who labors "*will have plenty of bread.*" For this necessarily results from the nature of his work. But he who leaves it wild and does not work it will certainly have plenty of poverty. For what will he eat, since he did not prepare his land or set it in order? Thus they said, "*He who pursues vanities will have plenty of poverty.*" There is a secret of the verse in what is alluded to. In his wisdom, he let us know about one who serves the supernal earth (*'adamah*), the final *heh*, which is so called because it was emanated from the supernal Adam. [It refers] to the *tiqqun* through learning Torah and [keeping] the commandments, which are compared to sowing the field after fertilizing and hoeing, a metaphor for the proper intention in worship.

In the *Midrash* of Rabbi Simeon bar Yohai, peace be upon him, is written, "Rabbi Yosi opened the verse, '*A locked garden is my sister, bride, a locked fountain, a sealed spring.*'[58] '*A locked garden*': this is the *Keneset Israel*, which is a locked garden. For Rabbi Eleazar said, just as this garden requires guarding, hoeing, watering, and pruning, so *Keneset Israel* requires hoeing, watching, watering, and pruning and is called a garden and a vineyard. Just as this vineyard requires hoeing, watering, pruning, and digging, so does Israel, as it is written, '*For the vineyard of the Lord of Hosts is the House of Israel.*'[59] And it is written, '*He hoed it and removed the stones from it.*'[60]"[61]

When it is properly prepared in this way, the supernal light takes note and sends down rain of light and blessing over this earth. It yields its produce and the worker eats well. For all of that goodness will necessarily be drawn by nature through his work. This is the secret of "*If you follow My statutes . . . and do them. I will grant your rains in their season . . . ,*"[62] as I wrote above. "*But he who pursues vanities*" did not complete the supernal *tiqqun*. "*The pit is empty, it has no water in it.*"[63] Surely, "*he will have planty of poverty.*" For the *tiqqun* of the Glory, which is study of Torah and fulfilling the commandments, is the cause of all the benefits and blessings. Without it, no benefit or blessing comes to the world. For this depends on that.

The prophet Isaiah alluded to this in his prophecy, "*Let the skies pour down from above and the heavens rain down righteousness and let the earth open and salvation sprout and fairness spring up together: I YHVH have created it.*"[64] The secret of "*Let the skies pour down*" is this: act in such a way that, in accord with the secret of "*You may hear in the skies,*"[65] the supernal heavens will receive *shefa'* of light and blessing from the supernal source above and the heavens will receive from the skies and "rain down righteousness." In *Hagigah*, chapter *'eyn dorshin*, it is written, "heavens in which mills stand that grind manna for the righteous (*ẓaddiqim*)."[66] These are the righteous one (*ẓaddiq*) and righteousness (*ẓedeq*)[67] which are called "the righteous" (*ẓaddiqim*). This is the secret of the heavens. They are the "*disciples of YHVH,*"[68] Jachin and Boaz,[69] "*his thighs are pillars of marble.*"[70] They bestow the light that they receive from "the skies" to *ẓaddiq*, the life of the worlds, and *ẓedeq*, the secret of the kingdom (*Malkhut*) of the House of David. Once it reaches there, it is extended to those below. Thus the verse says, "*Let the earth open*" and may the world "*sprout salvation.*" When it says, "*and fairness spring forth together,*" it alluded to the cause for all of this benefit that comes from above to below. It said that it is because of the *tiqqun* that the servants of *YHVH* enact through studying the Torah and fulfilling the commandments, through the secret of "*it will be fairness for us* [*that we observe faithfully all of this commandment. . . .*]"[71] It said that because of the fairness, which is the merit of this *tiqqun*, [they] "*will sprout together,*" [meaning] light and *shefa'* above and

> goodness and salvation below. Thus it said, "*together: I YHVH have created it.*" In other words, I established and arranged that *tiqqun*. And it has been set up in such a manner that all of this will necessarily result from it by nature. The lord of the prophets, of blessed memory,[72] alluded to this in saying, "*There is none like God, Jeshurun, riding through the skies to help you, and* [*through*] *the heavens in His pride.*"[73] In chapter seventy-five of *Bereishit Rabbah* it says, " '*And there is none like God . . .*' and who is like God? Jeshurun, the pleasant and praiseworthy among you." In other words, those who through their worship, complete the intention of the supernal *tiqqun*, which is the uniting, are like God, in accord with the secret of "*and the God of Israel called him 'El.*'"[74] This was explained when the verse said, "*riding through the skies to help you.*" This is the secret of the uniting which they cause through their worship. It is the aid which is alluded to when it says "*to help you.*" This is the supernal *tiqqun* which is the *tiqqun* of the Glory. It is the pride which is caused by them, in accord with the secret of "*Render power to God, His pride is because of Israel.*"[75] Through what Israel does below, He takes pride above. When the verse said "*the heavens,*" it alluded to what necessarily follows from the "*help*" and "*pride*" which is caused by the worshippers. The supernal source is opened for them and releases *shefa*' to "*the skies.*" "*The heavens,*" which grind manna for the righteous, receive from them. In other words, Jachin and Boaz, the secret of "*the heavens,*" are prepared for them. From them all of the benefits and blessings are bestowed which are received from above. For this is required from the nature of the worship, which is what we desired to prove in this chapter.[76]

I copied the entire chapter because of its great importance for the matter that I am dealing with. It also contains many exceptional teachings that are relevant to other issues that will be treated below, with God's help.

Now we return to our subject. It has been explained that the Torah, in its root, is entirely Names of God, blessed be He, according to the secret of Holy Language that we explained above. It has been extended [from this root] in stage after stage until it took on material form. It is similar in regard to the actions of the commandments which a person does. Through them, he lives the life of the souls, the 600,000 souls of Israel, from the 600,000 letters of the Torah. For there is one judgment for the Torah and the person who fulfills it. For the Torah has taken on a material form, and in ascending the stages, one after another, the words [begin to] shine. The same is true for Adam. Had he not sinned, his matter would only have been spiritual[77] and "*the earth [would be] filled with knowledge*,"[78] even the earthiness that is in him.[79] Now, no part of his body remains that knows except the heart. This is like the allusion that has been explained elsewhere, "*A person sees what appears to the eyes, but God looks into the heart*."[80] For Adam followed what appeared to his eyes, as it is written, "[*YHVH God caused every tree*] *of pleasant appearance* [*and good to eat to spring forth* [*including*] *the tree of life and the tree of the knowledge of good and evil*]."[81] "*But YHVH only looks into the heart*." If Adam had not sinned, he would have remained in the Garden of Eden, "*to work it and guard it*."[82] Our rabbis explained this as alluding to the positive and negative commandments.[83] He would have fulfilled the commandments in a different way which is more spiritual,[84] as is written in the *Pardes*, Gate of the Soul.

A human being and the Torah are comparable. (This is indicated by "*This is the Torah of Man*").[85] Two hundred and forty-eight limbs and 365 sinews correspond to the 613 commandments. Six hundred thousand souls correspond to 600,000 letters of the Torah. The aspect of "*to work it and guard it*" has become corporeal. Nevertheless, they emerge from the source of holiness and [the two levels] correspond. For the reward of [fulfilling] a corporeal commandment is the spirituality of that commandment. This is the meaning of the saying of the rabbis, "If a person sanctifies himself a little below, he is sanctified a lot from above."[86]

Take, for example, *ẓiẓit*. Now that we are corporeal, they are these threads, material things. Nevertheless, according to the ladder of [spiritual] levels, they ascend far above, all the way to the ultimate degree, where *ẓiẓit* are supernal things. "*No eye has seen them, O God, but You*."[87] And so it is with all of the commandments. This is the meaning of "the reward of a commandment is the commandment" itself; in other words, the root. For the reward is not conventional, but by nature, as was explained at length above. This is the meaning of "a commandment leads to a commandment." Similarly, in regard to a transgression, its punishment is the transgression itself; in other words its root in the *qelippah*, God spare us. For the revealed and concealed in study and in deed are all one, united according to the secret of the Holy Language. And even profane materiality is constructed according to the purity of the sacred.

From this the matter of revealed and concealed in the entire Torah can be explained. The world thinks that the concealed is something separate from the revealed. This is not so. Only the concealed has coarsened and taken on a material form, which reveals it. It is like the verse, "*apples of gold in settings of silver, each matter according to its manner.*"[88] In other words, just as silver is similar to gold, but is a lower level than it, so is the revealed in comparison to the concealed. From this, a saying of our rabbis, of blessed memory, in tractate *Sukkah*, can be understood. "They said concerning Rabbi Yohanan ben Zakkai that he never neglected [the study] of scripture, *mishnah* . . . [including even] a great matter and a small matter. A great matter is *Ma'aseh Merkavah* and a small matter is the disputes of Abbaye and Rava."[89] This is perplexing. For [such discussions] are our life and the foundation upon which everything depends. How could he have called it "a small matter?" The author of the *'Eyn Ya'aqov* brought the opinions of Rabbi Yom Tov ben Abraham Ashvili and Rabbi Solomon ben Abraham Aderet [in order to explain this].[90] However, according to my method, the matter can be explained well. For the disputes and arguments establish the laws of the Talmud, which is the complete explication of the written Torah, so that we can understand the actions of the commandments "*which a person must do and live by*."[91] The meaning of this verse is that the spiritual vitality is actually within [the commandments]. This is as I have said, the reward of a material commandment is spiritual and eternal. This is the meaning of [the talmudic saying], "Do them today and receive their reward tomorrow"[92] indeed. For the reward is not mere convention, but is [inherent in] the commandment itself, as has been explained, "If a person sanctifies himself a little below he is sanctified a lot from above."[93] Just as a star appears to be very small from below, so the aspect of performing the commandments which is called "do them today" is "a small matter." But their root above in the Chariot is a great and eternal matter. The "small matter" is actually "a great matter," just like a grain of wheat from which a stalk grows. Thus it can be explained that the oral Torah, which is the revealed aspect that a person must do, is itself the concealed aspect, the secret of the written Torah, which is entirely Names of God, the *Ma'aseh Merkavah*.

This is also what is meant by the "*two great lights, the great light* [*to rule by day*] *and the small light* [*to rule the night and the stars*]."[94] The kabbalists already wrote that the secret of the sun and the moon is the secret of the written Torah and the oral Torah. Now, in a time of materiality, they are a great light and a small light, as mentioned above, "a great matter and a small matter." However, in the spiritual aspect of their root, they are two great lights which make use of one crown of Torah. This is what is meant by "all of the oral Torah is alluded to in the written Torah," like "from where [do we know this" means] from [what verse] are these matters [derived]. Thus we can understand " '*and the Torah is light*'[95] is written, because it shines from His Glory." And in *Midrash Rabbah*, *Bereishit*, it is written, "Rabbi

Simon said, light is written here five times, corresponding to the five books of the Torah."[96] And in tractate *Sanhedrin*, the verse is explained, " '*He made me dwell in darkness like the long dead.*'[97] Rabbi Jeremiah said this [refers to] the Babylonian Talmud."[98] At first glance, this is very perplexing. For it is light and enlightens us. The Torah is our life and the length of our days. Yet he calls it "long dead." Also [perplexing] is the *Midrash* of Rabbi Simon, which explained the light that is mentioned at the beginning of the Torah as referring to the five books of the Torah. It is also written there, [concerning the verse], "*and God separated between the light and the darkness*,"[99] that the Holy One, blessed be He, concealed it.[100] How does concealing apply? However, it all has a single explanation, which is the cause of concealing the light of Adam, the garments of light,[101] which I explained at length elsewhere. This is the concealing of the light of the Torah. The plain meaning and Rabbi Simon's explanation are in accord.

From the previous discussion, it has been explained that the Torah is in itself Holy Language, the secret of "it is all Names of God." And the fulfillment of the Torah, "*to work it and to guard it*,"[102] is entirely *Ma'aseh Merkavah*. Thus the Torah is entirely clear light. However, Adam took on a material form and the light departed, the secret of the garments of light replaced by garments of skin (*'oR*), which blinded (*'iVeR*) him.[103] The tree of life departed and caused death. Thus the Torah took on a material form "*to work it and to guard it*," the act of fulfilling the material commandments.

Nevertheless, [the Torah is compared to] "*golden apples in settings of silver*."[104] Thus one finds in the Torah secrets and allusions, which the scholars have designated "*PaRDeS*,"[105] which is an acronym for [the four levels of scriptural interpretation], *peshat* (plain meaning), *remez* (allusion), *derash* (homiletical meaning), and *sod* (mystical meaning). *Sod* is the hidden light, which is presently concealed from us due to the departure of the light of the garments of light. It is the essence of the Holy Language. *Remez* refers to the actions of fulfilling the material commandments, because it is their name, as I explained.[106] The oral Torah is alluded to in the written Torah, for example, "every time [it says] from where do we [know this], it means from what [verse] are these matters [derived]." There is nothing that is not clearly alluded to in the Torah, except that the intellect has darkened from what it should have been. And "*the earth is full of knowledge*"[107] is now limited to the heart's knowing. The written Torah is only understood after great effort. As the rabbis, of blessed memory, said, "Words of Torah are only fulfilled by one who kills himself for it, as it is written, '*This is the Torah of a man when he dies in a tent*.'[108]"[109] Therefore the written Torah requires an explanation and commentary, namely the Talmud. For otherwise, it would have been self-explanatory, as we see in another age, the age of the earliest authorities. They possessed a clear intellect and thus understood a deep matter without a commentary. Later, they did not understand without a commentary. And then there were commentaries on the commentaries, as a result of the darkening of the intellect. Therefore, if Adam had not sinned and had [retained] a clear intellect, he would have understood the written Torah. From this understanding, he would have known everything and there would have been no need for an oral Torah. But, since he sinned, the light departed, and he brought death to the world. Therefore he had to make a great effort and an oral Torah was required. This is the commentary and he has to "kill himself over it." Finally, the oral Torah had to be written.

Now we can explain " '*He sat me down in the dark like the long dead*'[110]; this [refers to] the Babylonian Talmud."[111] In other words, the darkness and death that he brought to the world caused this. If the Temple had remained in existence, the light would have continued to increase into the future. Then [the verse], "*and the Torah is light*"[112] [would have applied] and it would have delighted the heart. [The intellect would not] have darkened and [there would be no need] to kill oneself over it.

This is the secret of "*the two lights (me'orot)*."[113] It has already been written in *Sefer Qol Bokhim* that the letters of *me'orot* spell *'or* (light) *mavet* (death). This is the meaning of "*He sat me down in the dark like the long dead*."[114] The *me'orot* (lights) became *mavet* (death) and the letters, *'or* (light) from *me'orot*, darkened and do not shine.

Also, [according to the verse], "*and the Torah is light*," there should have been one Torah and now there are two. This is the meaning of [the talmudic saying], "Matters that were transmitted to you in writing, you are not permitted to transmit orally, and matters that were transmitted to you orally, you are not permitted to transmit in writing."[115] The meaning is in accord with what is found in chapter *ha-Boneh*, with those fine sayings that the young students expounded with the alphabet. They said, he made indications. Rashi explained, "in the order of teachings, so that it would not be forgotten . . ."[116] Now who can remember the oral Torah, since "*its measure exceeds the earth*"?[117] However, all of the allusions are in the written Torah, and whoever understands it thoroughly, remembers everything, because everything has an indication in it. But the written Torah may not be transmitted orally, because many of the allusions depend on the spelling. And the oral Torah may not be transmitted in writing, because the main thing is to remember everything. The statement "he made indications" refers to the written Torah. Because of our sins, [our intellect] has darkened until the Temple was destroyed, and darkness increased to such an extent that finally the Babylonian Talmud had to be written down. This is the meaning of the light concealed in the five books of the Torah, which is the *sod*, as I explained above. So one makes use of *remez*, but also here, only with great difficulty, each according to his level, and only after he kills himself over it.

A great allusion is mentioned concerning our teacher Moses. "*And YHVH saw that he turned aside to see.*"[118] Our teacher Moses, saw well. This is the secret of the shining lens. "*For the light of his face shined.*"[119] "The face of Moses is like the face of the sun,"[120] which is "*and the Torah is light.*"[121] When God gave him the written Torah, there was no darkness in his countenance, only a clear intellect, full of knowledge. So he understood, on his own, the oral Torah. This is the meaning of "*He turned aside (SaR) to see.*" "*SaR*" is an acronym for *Sod Remez.* This is the meaning of the rabbis' *midrash*, " '*and He gave to Moses ke-khalloto . . . two tablets of testimony . . .*'[122] He transmitted the principles (*kelalim*) to him."[123] So he understood, on his own, the oral Torah, as I explained at length in another place, concerning Moses and the Ethiopian woman whom he took [for a wife].[124] [This] is the secret of the oral Torah, which is the secret of the wife (*kalat*) of Moses, which is also alluded to in the word "*ke-khalloto.*" [Thus the verse may be read, "*He gave to Moses*] *as his bride,*" which, with God's help, will be explained at greater length.

In *Midrash Rabbah*, at the end of section *ki tisa'*, it says, " '*Write for yourself* [*these words*]'[125] The ministering angels began to speak before the Holy One, blessed be He. Master of the Universe, you are giving permission to Moses to write what he wishes, so that he can tell Israel, I gave you the Torah. I am the one that wrote and gave it to you. The Holy One, blessed be He, replied to them, God forbid that Moses would do such a thing. And even if he does, he is faithful, as it is written, '*Not so is My servant Moses, he is trusted throughout My household.*'[126]"[127]

Therefore the Torah is called the "*Torah of God*" and "*the Torah of Moses.*" For Moses understood and attained the oral Torah, on his own. Thus it is called by his name.

(But do not err in thinking that I am denying that the Holy One, blessed be He, explicitly transmitted the oral Torah to Moses, God forbid. But Moses grasped the allusions of the written Torah and the Holy One, blessed be He, said, "You have done well, for such is the oral Torah." And the Holy One, blessed be He, told it to him. He thoroughly explained it to him in word and in meaning and with explanations, indicating exactly how it should be explained to Israel. However, see chapter *Torah 'Or* of tractate *Shavu'ot.* There I explained this matter and these sayings very clearly.)

This is the meaning of "*This is the Torah of a man when he dies in a tent*."[128] It is written, "*and this is the Torah that Moses placed* [*before the Children of Israel*]."[129] For the Torah of Moses, which is the Talmud that he grasped and applied as *halakhah*, is the Torah over which a person kills himself because of the complicated argumentation of the issues. Moses understood the entire written Torah because there was no darkness in his countenance, because light shone from his face, which is the shining lens. And the rabbis, of blessed memory, said that he is worth 600,000. For there are 600,000 souls [of Israel] and 600,000 letters of the Torah.

Now we will return to the meaning of [our saying that] the written Torah is *sod* and *remez*. *Sod* is a "great matter," the *Ma'aseh Merkavah*, and *remez* is "a small matter," the disputes of Abbayye and Rava. The oral Torah is the Talmud and the disputes of Abbayye and Rava. The written Torah is Holy Language, as we explained, while the oral Torah is in [Aramaic] translation which is close to Holy Language. This is the secret of "[One must read the] Torah portion twice [in Hebrew] and once in [Aramaic] translation."[130] The Hebrew scripture, which is the written Torah, contains two and the [Aramaic] translation, one. "*He sat me down in darkness*"[131] refers to the Babylonian Talmud, which is in [Aramaic] translation.

But the Land of Israel is on a higher level, according to the secret of the Holy Language and the world which was created with Holy Language. This is alluded to by the foundation stone of the Temple from which the world's basis [is derived]. In the Palestinian Talmud, in the first chapter of tractate *Shabbat*, "It is taught in the name of Rabbi Meir, whoever is permanently located in the Land of Israel, and eats his ordinary meals with the purity [required for sacred food], and speaks the Holy Language, and recites the *shema'* in the morning and evening, is assured of life in the world to come." Such is the level of the Holy Language in the Land of Israel. For light emerges from there, "*and the Torah is light*."

This is the meaning of the passage in chapter *ha-madir*, "Abbayye said one of them [in the Land of Israel] is better than two of us [here in Babylon]. Rava said, one of us who went there is better than two of them. For when Rabbi Jeremiah was here he did not know what our rabbis were saying. When he went there, he called them 'foolish Babylonians.' "[132]

There is a passage in tractate *Ḥulin*, chapter *gid ha-nasheh*, concerning this matter. " '*And on the vine were three branches*.'[133] Rabbi Hiyya bar Abba said in the name of Rav, these are the three ministers of the proud that emerge from Israel in each and every generation. Sometimes two are here and one is in the Land of Israel. Sometimes two are in the Land of Israel and one is here."[134] Again, the meaning is that one in the Land of Israel is equal to two that are here. Later, the opposite is the case. One from here is worth two that are there. This is in accord with our explanation of "Hebrew scripture twice, [Aramaic] translation once." The Land of Israel is [equated with] the Holy Language. There is *sod* and *remez*, as has been explained.

Remez refers to matters of oral Torah, but they are pleasant to learn, because they are closer to the root, which is Holy Language. It is like *halakhot* that have been decided. It is otherwise in the Babylonian diaspora. For distance becomes a factor as well as the secret of the [Aramaic] translation and the matter of "*darkness*."[135] Because of this, [the verse] "*a man that dies . . .*"[136] [applies to one that learns Torah there], due to the multiplicity of variants. These are sometimes distorted so that it is necessary to produce light from darkness. Consequently, disagreement has increased. It is explained in the following passage.

> Rabbi Oshayah said, why is it written, "*I got two staffs. One, I called pleasantness and the other, I called unity (ḥovelim).*"[137] "*Pleasantness*" refers to the sages in the Land of Israel who treat each other pleasantly in their learning of *halakhah*. "Unity" refers to the sages in Babylon who damage (*meḥabbelim*) each other in their learning of *halakhah*. "And he said, these are the two anointed dignitaries who stand [by the Lord of all the earth]."[138] Rabbi Isaac said, these are the sages of the Land of Israel who are easy with each other in their learning of *halakhah*. And the two olive trees, mentioned above it,[139] are the scholars of Babylon who embitter each other in their learning of *halakhah* like olives.[140]

Thus the sages of the Land of Israel are called "*yizhar*," which is oil that illuminates. "*And the Torah is light*," light and joy. They are like the allusion to the oral Torah and do not become so heated in their argumentation as in Babylonia. Therefore, they concern themselves much more with secrets of the *Ma'aseh Merkavah*, which is "a great matter." But the sages of Babylonia are the opposite. Their learning is almost completely restricted to "a small matter," the disputations of Abbayye and Rava. They hardly concern themselves with "a great matter" at all. Therefore, the Land of Israel is "Hebrew scriptures, twice" and Babylonia is "[Aramaic] translation, once." However, when one of us, who has already learned the methods of disputation, goes to the Land of Israel to learn the secrets of the Chariot, he is equivalent to two of them. For the secrets of the Chariot also require deep and sweet disputation, such as is found in *Pirqey ha-Merkavah*. "They would ask a person, 'Did you view my Chariot? Did you dispute with *Ḥokhmah*?' "[141] According to the *Zohar*, "There is a place for questioning and answers, and one for questioning, but not for answers. And there is a place where questions may not even be asked."[142] When an exceptional person settles in the Land of Israel, he is on a higher level for fulfilling "did you dispute with *Ḥokhmah*?" The discussion turns from one matter to another.

The conclusion that follows from all of the above discussion is that the material entity cleaves to its spiritual essence and is it. "Fulfill them today" and tomorrow, cleave to the reward for the deed. For "the reward for a commandment is the commandment" itself. There is a great allusion [to this matter] in the words of the Tanna in the *Mishnah*, *Pesaḥim*. "As a person acts during the week, so is his action on the Sabbath."[143] For the very deed that a person does during the "six days of action," that is, the period of six thousand years during which this world will exist, will be his deed during the Sabbath, in the world that is entirely Sabbath. Only, during the week his deed is material, while on the Sabbath it is spiritual.

This is the secret of [the passage from], "*And He completed the heavens and the earth . . .* "[144] until "*which God created to do.*"[145] Nahmanides already wrote in his commentary on the Torah that the six days of creation allude to the six thousand years that this world will exist and the seventh day corresponds to the world that is entirely Sabbath. It seems that an allusion concerning this comes in the verse, "*Work will be done six days and on the seventh day, it will be sacred for you, a Sabbath of Sabbaths.*"[146] A question arises, What need is there to say "*work will be done*"? Is it obligatory to do work? There is another problem. The verse says, "*and on the seventh day*," when it should have said "and the seventh day." However, this peculiarity is a great allusion concerning the work of keeping the commandments, "fulfill them today." "*And on the seventh day*" refers to those actions which were mentioned as "fulfill them today." The verse said, "*and on the seventh day*," which is the world to come, the work will be "*sacred*," in other words, spiritual. This is the work that was done on the seventh day, as it is written, "*and God finished the work that He had done on the seventh day.*"[147] [This verse is understood], according to the secret of this allusion. For God created free will in man and the bestowing of a reward [for choosing good]. Thus the verse ends, "*which God created to do.*" "Fulfill them today."

This is the secret of Rashi's commentary on the verse which follows a saying of the rabbis, of blessed memory. "What did the world lack? Rest. When the Sabbath came, rest came to the world."[148] The question arises, How does creation apply to rest? For rest is the opposite of activity. But the "rest" is the world to come. But the rabbis, of blessed memory, said, "Scholars have no rest either in this world or in the world to come, as it is written, '*They go from strength to strength.*'[149]"[150] Know that the reward of the commandment, which is "rest," is beyond measure and infinite. Even if a person merits a portion of it, as the sages said, "all of Israel has a portion of the world to come,"[151] that portion is not the whole. Moreover, the portions are not equal. Thus if a person desires to merit to progress from one degree of "rest" to another, his deeds are examined. For there are those who are worthy of the lower Garden of Eden and those who are worthy of the upper Garden of Eden. The possible degrees are innumerable, as indicated in the *Mishnah, Hagigah.*

> The clothes of an *'am ha-'arez* [152]can take on uncleanness of the first degree (*midras*) for *perushin*,[153] the clothes of *perushin* can take on uncleanness of the first degree for those who eat the heave-offering,[154] the clothes of those who eat the heave-offering can take on uncleanness of the first degree for those who eat Holy Things, the clothes of those who eat Holy Things can take on the first degree of uncleanness for those occupied with the sin offering . . .[155]

So when a righteous person wishes to merit additional "rest" beyond that which he has attained, an inquiry is made concerning the judgments of that righteous person. Even if his judgments had been examined at first, when "*he goes from strength to strength*,"[156] the judgments are examined again. It depends entirely on the majority of his deeds. If he never rested in this world, but constantly increased holiness to holiness, then he will also go "*from strength to strength*" in the world to come, and be innocent in his judgments. And "they have no rest" means that there is no end to rest.

Now we shall return to our original discussion, the meaning of the language used in the *Zohar* passage that we originally cited. "The Torah is sealed and revealed" because the revealed is what is sealed, "as one acts during the days of the week, so is his deed during the Sabbath." "His deed during the Sabbath" refers to the level upon level of cleaving to *YHVH*. However, [the *Zohar* passage] says "sealed and revealed" and does not mention "level upon level." For this is in itself "level upon level," like the aspect of *YHVH* that was mentioned in the beginning [of the passage]. "The Holy One, blessed be He, is level upon level." This "level upon level" in itself is the secret of the *devequt* of the eternal reward, the sealed portion of the Torah, which is entirely Names of God. We can be satisfied with the general statement the author of the passage made at the beginning. "There are three levels connected together, the Holy One, blessed be He, the Torah, and Israel. Each one is level upon level, sealed and revealed." Afterward, when he went into specifics, he said, "The Holy One, blessed be He, is level upon level, sealed and revealed." Concerning the Torah, he only said, "sealed and revealed," because the revealed portion, which is the sealed portion of the Torah, and entirely Names of God, is included in the "level upon level" that he mentioned in regard to the Holy One, blessed be He.

Now, the three of them, the Holy One, blessed be He, Israel, [and the Torah] are also connected in regard to the aspect of 613. Concerning the Holy One, blessed be He, in the *Zohar* and *tiqqunim* it is said concerning the name *YHVH*, " '*This is My Name ... and this is My memorial ...*'[157] '*My Name (shemy)*' plus *YH* equals 365. *VH* plus '*My Memorial* (*zikhry*)' equals 248. Total: 613."

Here is what is written in the *Pardes*, chapter one of the Gate of Names.

> Rabbi Simeon Bar Yohai explained in another place, in the *tiqqunim*, the meaning of [the rabbinic saying], "He whose fear of sin precedes his wisdom, [his wisdom endures]."[158] He said "Even so, I will place a *sheva*, which [represents] fear, in the name *YHVH*, before love which is represented by a *qamaẓ*, love. *Sheva* is from the side of *Gevurah*, '*For he is judged with the fire of YHVH.*'[159] *Qamaẓ* is on the right '*and the priest shall take a handful (ve-qamaẓ).*'[160] 'For one is elevated in holiness and not made to descend.'[161] Thus they placed 365 negative commandments, which are fear, before the 248 positive commandments, which are love. Thus it is written, '*This is My Name forever ...*'[162] '*My Name* (*shemy*)' plus *YH* equals 365. '*My memorial* (*zikhry*)' plus *VH* equals 248."[163]
>
> The meaning is that judgment always receives *shefa'* from compassion. For the female is judgment and the male is compassion, as explained in the Gate "From Below to Above." Consequently, it is necessary to place fear which is from the female side, judgment, before love, which is compassion. Thus the *yod* from *'ADoNaY* comes before the *yod* of *YHVH*. Because the former is at the end of the word below, in the beginning of the entrance [into holiness] and the latter is above, at the end of the ascent. The reason is that "one is elevated in holiness and not made to descend." Consequently, it is necessary that fear, which is [the basis] of the negative precepts, come before the positive commandments. [As the verse implies,] "*Turn away from evil and do good.*"[164] For the 365 negative precepts are from the side of the female and the 248 positive commandments are from the side of

> the male. Thus the Torah said, "*This is My Name forever . . .*"[165] There it speaks of the United Name. And " 'My Name (*shemy*)' plus the letters of the male, which are *YH*, equals 365." "My Name" is in *Malkhut*. In order to express the attribute of day with night, it is necessary to mix *YH* with it. "*And My memorial* (*zikhry*)," which is the male (*zakhar*) plus *VH*, which are the letters of the female, equals 248. We unite "*My memorial* (*zikhry*)" with *VH* in order to express the the attribute of night with day. The Tetragrammaton is divided into two parts, *YH VH*, male and female. Rabbi Simeon bar Yohai, of blessed memory, explained in the *tiqqunim*, "Everything is created and established with the Name *YHVH*, which is [the meaning of] '*et ha-shamayim (the heavens)*.'[166] And the secret of the matter is *YH* is in the heavens, as it is written, '*Let the heavens rejoice . . .* '[167] and *VH* is in the earth, '*and may the earth exult.*'[168]"[169] The meaning is, "The heavens" are *Tif'eret*, which is called "heavens" and *Malkhut* is called "*et*."[170]

It seems to me that the meaning of [expressing] "the attribute of day with night" and "night with day" is as follows. The written Torah is [called] "*heh* (five) books of the Torah" and the oral Torah is [called] "*vav* (six) orders of the *Mishnah*." It should have been the opposite. For it is known that the written Torah is *Tif'eret*, which is the *vav* of the Tetragrammaton, and *Malkhut* (the oral Torah), is the final *heh* of the Tetragrammaton.[171]

These are the basic principles.

Now I shall explain the meaning of the 248 limbs, according to the secret of divine emanation, which is the secret of the supernal world. They are the 216 letters of the Name of 72: VHV YLY SYT and so on.[172] The source of this name is in the *sefirah Ḥesed*, as the kabbalists explained. It is also known that the root of the *sefirah Ḥesed* is in *Ḥokhmah*, where the secret of the "thirty-two paths of wisdom" is found.[173] That makes 248.[174] Moreover, it is known that the 248 positive commandments are from the side of *Tif'eret*, which inclines toward *Ḥesed*. And the 365 negative precepts are from the side of *Malkhut*, which inclines toward *Gevurah*. Thus 248 (*RMḤ*) is equivalent to the root *RḤM* (love), while 365 (*SHeSaH*) is related to incitement (*SHiSuy*) since judgment incites [the forces of chastisement]. Corresponding to this in a person, there are 248 white limbs and 365 red sinews, as will be explained below.[175] Thus the Name *YHVH 'Elohim*, which is *Tif'eret* and *Malkhut*, is the secret of the 613 commandments. It is known that *Malkhut* is called *'Elohim*, [which is] from the side of *Gevurah*, because it is the aspect of mild judgment which emanates from the aspect of severe judgment. Through this, I discovered another aspect of the number 365. For the aspect of severe judgment is the aspect of judgment, in its full spelling. I mean *'Elohim*, spelled as follows. *ALP LMD HY YVD MM* equals three hundred.[176] Next add the aspect of mild judgment. But do not use its full spelling, because it is not as full of judgment as the aspect of severe judgment. Just take it as it is. In other words [add] the Name *'ADoNaY* which equals 65. Together, the total is 365.

This is despite the fact that it has already been made known that this spelling of *'Elohim*, that I wrote, which equals 300, inclines toward compassion. For 300 equals *MZPZ*, which is a permutation of the Name *YHVH* which equals "with compassion."[177] This results in the positive commandments containing the negative and the negative containing the positive.

Similarly, the Name *YHVH 'Elohim* is united above in its root, which is in *Binah*. This is the secret of the *d"u parzufim*, which we explained earlier. From there, the secret of 365 is extended, as the *Pardes* wrote in the Gate of Gates.[178] For the year (*shanah*) is in *Binah*. Even though the [days of the] year are calculated by the sun, which is associated with *Tif'eret*, nevertheless, its root is in *Binah*, which is the root of the six extremities that are composed of compassion and judgment, which is the secret of the twelve months. We find that New Year's Day is associated with New Year's Day itself and also with the Day of Atonement. For it is written in Ezekiel, "*on New Year's Day, on the tenth of the month . . .*"[179] This is cited in the *Tur*, *Oraḥ Ḥayyim*, Laws of the Day of Atonement. The meaning is as follows. It is known that the secret of repentance is *Binah*. Whatever a person, through sinning, has spoiled, effected the governance of the six days of action, which is the secret of the [six] extremities. From there, all life will return to its root and there find its *tiqqun*. Now, from the Day of Atonement, which is [called] New Year's Day, until New Year's Day [itself] is 355 (*SHaNaH*) [days]. The year is called "*shanah*" because of the 355 days. Although some years have 353, 354, or 355 days, depending on the yearly cycles, it does not matter. For [it is only a question of] differences in the calendars which are made up. Nevertheless, the solar year is always 365 days, and the allusion is to *Binah*.

On the revealed level, the calculation is determined by the intercalations that we make in order to equalize the lunar and solar years. According to the concealed level, *Binah* is the root and source for all. The number of the days of the year are 355, like the value of year (*shanah*). There are ten additional days, since the solar year has 365 days, ten more than the lunar year which has 355. The latter plus the ten days of repentance form the correct total. All of the 355 days [return] to their root and source, the place from which they emerged. In other words, "repentance," which restores things to their root and source, alludes to the *sefirah Binah*, which is called "repentance." It contains the ten *sefirot* that are called the "ten days of repentance." They are the root and source, since the year emanates from them, as has been explained. Every year, the year with all of its 355 days returns to their root and source, according to the secret of *Binah*, which is the secret of repentance. As we explained, [this means] the return of things to their root and source in which they rest in peace and quiet. Following these ten days of repentance in *Binah*, that is after all the days of the year return to their source and rest there, a new and different year is emanated from its source, the secret of *Binah*. [This new year] is created after the Day of Atonement. Therefore, during these ten days between New Year's Day and the Day of Atonement, a person can correct what he spoiled during the entire year.

The end of the ten days of repentance, the tenth day [itself], is the day that gathers together all of the [355 days of the] year along with the nine days of repentance that belong to it. This is the Day of Atonement, which is *Binah* itself along with the nine *sefirot* of repentance that are contained within it. This is alluded to by the Day of Atonement, which is the seal and source for every year. It is a particular day of rest in which all of the worlds that have emanated from it, through the secret of "world, year, and soul" (as explained in *Sefer Yeẓirah*), are at rest. Therefore, before coming before the Great Source, to see the face of the Lord, God of Hosts, every person should correct, during the ten days of repentance, what he has spoiled. If he has not corrected [his sins during the nine days], he should, at least, correct them during the Day of Atonement. For it is the seal for all and the source for all. For each of these ten days of repentance is a source for the one that came before it. The closer a day is to the Day of Atonement, the more inclusive a source it is, until the Day of Atonement [itself] is the source of all sources, according to the secret of *Binah*, which contains nine *sefirot* that are called repentance. She, herself, is the tenth, the source of all. If a person has even failed to correct [his sins] on the Day of Atonement, God forbid, there is no possibility for rectification. For now, after the Day of Atonement, another year is emanated. The year is a branch that has emerged from its source. How can one rectify on the branch what has [already] been revealed before the source, the Lord, God of Hosts, on the Day of Atonement? Therefore, it is necessary to make the rectification in *Binah*, which is the Day of Atonement. Thus the secret of the year with the 365 days of the solar year emanates from *Binah*, from which forces of judgment are aroused. For it is the root of the side of judgment. They are united, according to the secret of *Tif'eret,* which is called the sun. It inclines toward mercy (*Ḥesed*). All of this is in accord with the secret of the unity of the *d"u parzufim.*

We have found that the positive commandments are included in the negative commandments and the negative commandments are included in the positive commandments. Rashi explained that the positive commandments are included in the negative commandments in his commentary to section *Mishpatim* on the verse, "*Be on guard concerning all that I have told you.*"[180] [He commented,] "to fulfill every commandment with a caution. For whenever the Torah speaks of 'guarding,' it is a warning instead of a negative commandment."[181] And the negative commandments are included in the positive, as it is written, "*to guard [and] to do all of the words of this Torah.*"[182] The guarding is included in the doing.

Here is what is written in *'Avodat ha-Qodesh*, chapter twenty-five of section *ha-Yiḥud*:

> Positive commandments and negative commandments are one Torah. The positive commandments are derived from the attribute of "*remember [the Sabbath day . . .]*"[183] and ascend to it. The negative commandments are from the attribute of "*guard [the Sabbath day] . . . ,*"[184] which is the secret of fear. They declare this through the secret of the punishments. The Torah contains both of them in the attribute of fear in the verse, "*fear YHVH your God.*"[185] It is a positive commandment which contains all of the negative commandments. For whoever refrains from committing a transgression is a God-fearer. Similarly, the Torah contained the positive commandments in the negative, when it said, "*Do not add to it and do not subtract from it.*"[186] Whoever annuls a positive commandment, diminishes. Thus a person who remains idle from fulfilling the commandments is worthy of punishment. For he diminishes [the Torah]. But whoever refrained from committing a transgression deserves a reward; as they said in the first chapter of *Kiddushin*, "Whoever refrains from committing a transgression is given a reward like one who fulfills a commandment. . . . This refers to a case where an opportunity to transgress arose, and he was saved from it."[187] As it is written, "*They have done no wrong, but have followed His ways.*"[188] King Solomon explained this secret when he said, "*The sum of the matter, when all is said and done: fear God and guard His commandments. This is all of a person.*"[189] For when he said, "*fear God,*" he hinted that the positive commandments

include the negative. And when he said, "*guard His commandments*," he hinted that the negative commandments included the positive. He said, "*this is all of a person*," because a person contains all of them. For his 248 limbs correspond to the 248 positive commandments and his 365 sinews [correspond to the] 365 negative commandments. He is composed of matter and form. Therefore, the negative commandments are fulfilled by the intellect alone and the positive commandments are also fulfilled materially. He said that these two portions of the commandments are the whole of a person. If a portion is lacking, he is not a [whole] person.[190]

Now I shall explain the secret of the inclusion of the negative commandments in the positive commandments and the positive commandments in the negative commandments. How do the positive commandments contain the negative? Every commandment that a person fulfills has to involve an arousal of the heart. It must not be done by rote, but like a newlywed. It should be done for the sake of heaven. Even though [physical] matter objects and [fulfilling the commandment] is contrary to the desire of the body, a person should break his desire and fulfill the commandment with caution and zeal. When the opportunity to fulfill a commandment arises, one should reflect, if it were up to my [physical] matter and its desire, I would not do this thing. However, I am doing it because God commanded me. Thus through thinking that he would not do this thing on his own, but [only] acts because of God's command, the action is preceded by a negative. This is the meaning of [the rabbinic interpretation of the verse,] " '*with all of your heart*,'[191] with your two urges, the evil urge and the good urge."[192] In other words, he should reflect from the point of view of the evil urge, which [creates an opportunity to observe] a negative[193]; however, I will do it because my Father in Heaven decreed it for me. This is similar to the opposite that we find regarding negative commandments. "It is taught [in a *baraita*], Rabban Simeon ben Gamaliel said, a person should not say I do not desire pork, but should say, I do desire it, but what can I do? My Father in Heaven decreed [that I may not eat it]."[194] Thus in both cases, positive commandments and negative commandments, the positive contains the negative and the negative contains the positive. For in both cases, one serves God with the evil urge and the good urge. In [fulfilling] a positive commandment, [there is an opportunity to fulfill] a negative commandment, because of the evil urge. He overcomes it and fulfills the positive commandment with the negative commandment of the evil urge [included] within the positive commandment. Since he overcomes the negative, the negative is also [included] in the [fulfillment of the] positive commandment. In other words, the secret of this overcoming [of the evil urge] is the arousal of the heart.

Concerning this, it is taught at the end of *Makkot*, "Whoever refrains from committing a transgression is rewarded like one who fulfills a commandment."[195] This is because of the thought, since the thought is added to the deed. Thus it is written, "*They have done no evil, but followed His ways.*"[196] In other words, even when he did no evil, that is, when fulfilling the negative commandment, he followed His ways. He fulfilled the commandment through overcoming the evil urge, when he thought, "I want to, but what can I do?"

Now we are able to resolve a contradiction. [It is] well known in the *Zohar*, in all of the kabbalistic works, and in other [religious] books that the 248 positive commandments correspond to 248 limbs [of the body] and the 365 negative commandments correspond to the 365 sinews. Yet in the words of Rabbi Simlai at the end of tractate *Makkot* of the Babylonian Talmud, which I quoted above, he said, "The 365 correspond to the days of the solar year." This may be explained, according to the *sod*, as I indicated above. The 365 days of the solar year come from *Binah*, from which the red judgments are aroused. Nevertheless, it can also be rationally interpreted in a way that is close to the plain meaning.

I learned this from the words of the kabbalist Rabbi Menahem Azariah da Fano in *Sefer 'Asarah Ma'amarot*, in the name of Rabbi Abraham ibn Ezra, that a human body contains 365 throbbing sinews and 365 motionless ones. The throbbing ones correspond to the days and the motionless ones correspond to the nights in which they rest. Similarly, in regard to the days of a solar year, a day includes both a day and a night. Nevertheless, in actuality, there are 365 days and 365 nights. Now one who fulfills the 365 negative commandments without the arousal, mentioned above, that is [one who] merely refrains from committing a transgression, corresponds to the 365 nights. However, the 365 days correspond to a person who fulfills the negative commandments while including the positive within them,[197] through the arousal of "I do want to do it, but what can I do?" Then the lamp of the commandment shines for him. Therefore, the words of our rabbis, of blessed memory, in the *Gemara* and the words of the *Zohar* are completely in accord. Indeed, the *Gemara* is most explicit. It is always the case that all 613 correspond to the human structure: 248 limbs and 365 sinews. However, the *Gemara* specifies that the 365 [negative commandments] should not be equated with the 365 sinews, which are called nights, that is, with merely refraining from committing transgressions, but should be equated with the days of the solar year, the 365 throbbing (*dofeqim*) sinews. This corresponds to [the verse], "*The voice of my beloved knocks (dofeq), open to me.*"[198] All the words of our sages, of blessed memory, are true. Their Torah is true and everything leads to one place for one who understands their words.

Now we return to the meaning of the secret of the name *YHVH 'Elohim*, which is the secret of " 'remember' and 'guard' [contained] in one utterance."[199] The positive and negative commandments are united. This matter of the unification of the positive and negative commandments also has the same meaning. For "*God made this corresponding to that.*"[200] The positive aspect is the secret of the strengthening of holiness and the negative commandments correspond to the *qelippot*, so that impurity may not enter the Temple. This is the secret of "these declare fit and those declare unfit, these say pure and those say impure, these acquit and those condemn. Both these and those are words of the Living God."[201] For these incline toward mercy (*Ḥesed*) and those incline toward judgment (*Gevurah*), but it is all in complete accord. Here is what is written in *Pardes*, *Sha'ar ha-Makhri'im*, chapter two:

> The rabbis, of blessed memory, said, "Both these and those are words of the Living God (*'Elohim Ḥayyim*). . . ." The meaning is that *'Elohim Ḥayyim* is *Binah*, from which the entire structure receives *shefa'*. They said that there are those who declare impure, unfit, and who convict. For they incline toward *Gevurah*, toward the stringent view, in order to show that there is the domain of the *qelippot*. Thus [they declare] guilty, unfit, impure. And there are those who declare pure, fit, and who acquit. For they incline toward *Ḥesed*, to show the reader that there is no authority and rule of the *qelippot* [there]. Thus they declare innocent, fit, and pure. But both are from *Binah*, from which both extremes receive their *shefa'*. Whenever the power and *shefa'* of one of these sides increases, then the *halakhah* is in accord with it, to forbid or to permit, etc. Thus the one who declares pure and the one who declares impure are both correct. Accordingly, the *halakhah* occasionally follows the view of the school of Shammai, with difficulty, since it mostly inclines toward the side of *Ḥesed*. To make us aware of this, our rabbis, of blessed memory, said, "The school of Hillel inclines toward the lenient view and the school of Shammai inclines toward the stringent view." One inclines toward *Ḥesed* and the other toward *Gevurah*, according to their disposition, except for the matter of their number, as is known. The reason for the

change is in keeping with the meaning of the verse, "*Here I am, my son.*"[202] For sometimes *Ḥesed* is on the side of *Gevurah* and *Gevurah* on the side of *Ḥesed*, for the fire contains water and the water contains fire.[203]

It has been said that the positive and negative commandments are alluded to in the verse, "*God made these corresponding to these.*"[204] Yet, one might object that they are not equal in their number. For these are 248 and these are 365. My sons, may their Rock protect them, I will make known to you what God has graciously [revealed to] me. Know that the 248 positive commandments along with their root are 365. We have explained that the 248 limbs of the supernal Adam are 216 letters of the Name of 72 and the 32 paths of *Ḥokhmah*, making a total of 248. Know that the root of the totality of the 216 letters is the 72 Names, *vav heh vav*, *yod lamed yod*, *samekh yod tet*, etc. There are two aspects. When you count the words, there are 72 and when you count the letters, there are 216. This is the secret of the verse, "*and YHVH passed by (ve-ya'avor) his face and he cried out.*"[205] The kabbalists have explained that the secret of *ve-ya'avor* is the letters, *'ayin bet resh yod vav*, the totality and individual elements of the Name of 72.[206] The totality is 72 and the individual elements are 216. The root of the individual elements is the totality, the secret of *Ḥesed*, which equals 72.

Next, the totality of the 248 limbs is the secret of Adam, whose lights extend into 45 lights. This is the secret of *yod vav dalet heh alef vav alef vav heh alef*, which equals 45, the value of Adam. I already mentioned above, that the secret of the positive commandments is *Tif'eret Adam*, which inclines toward *Ḥesed*. Therefore, add those two sources, which are 72 and 45 and combine them with 248. The total is 365. There is an allusion to this in the public sacrifices, "*perfect, two per day . . . forever.*"[207] And the *Ba'al ha-Turim* wrote, "The first letters of '*temimim shenayim la-yom* (perfect, two per day)' is *tshl* (730)," because 730 is twice 365. Each day they were offering a sacrifice in the morning and in the evening. Thus the total [of sacrifices] was 730. It has already been made known that the positive and negative commandments are the attributes of night and day. There is an allusion here that the positive commandments also partake of the secret of the number 365.

The principle that emerges is that the aspect of 613 applies to the supernal Adam and is the secret of the verse, "*my love is clear-skinned and ruddy.*"[208] The positive commandments derive from the whiteness of compassion and the negative commandments derive from the redness of judgment. The 613 lights that are within God are spiritual lights that are concealed beyond the intellect's capacity to know their essence. Thus the soul is contained within the extension of the 613 commandments of the Torah. For the soul is a "*portion of God from above*,"[209] and the likeness of whatever is in the whole is found in the part. This is alluded to in the levels of the soul: *nefesh*, *ruaḥ*, *neshamah*, whose first and last letters equal 613. The middle letters equal *YHVH*, *Shadday*, *'Elohim*. We have already explained above that the secret of the coupling of *YHVH* and *'Elohim*, which is *Tif'eret* and *Malkhut*, takes place by means of *Yesod*, which is called *Shadday*. The secret of the coupling of male and female is the written Torah and the oral Torah, as is known.

You have to know that because the soul is composed of 248 white limbs and 365 red sinews which are spiritual, it clothes itself in the human body. This is in accord with Job's statement, "*You clothed me in skin and flesh and wove me of bones and sinews*,"[210] in [the soul's] image and pattern. [That is,] in the pattern that was made for it, in the garment of the 248 white, physical limbs, which are the white bones of the human body, and the 365 red, physical sinews, which are the red sinews of the human body that are full of blood. For the garment has to be made in the pattern and likeness of the one who wears it.

Now you already know that the soul is a "*portion of God from above*."[211] Therefore, it must resemble God as well, just as the Holy One, blessed be He, is called a person. As it is written, "*and on the likeness of the Throne, a likeness resembling the appearance of a person*."[212] This is the secret of *YHVH* which, when spelled in full, equals Adam.[213] This is the supernal, spiritual Adam, blessed be He, which is composed of 248 limbs and 365 spiritual sinews of the concealed lights. Similarly, the soul, which is called the lower spiritual man, is composed of 248 limbs and 365 sinews which are concealed and spiritual. Just as the image of God, which is called Adam, contains 248 limbs and 365 sinews, which are concealed and spiritual, the lower Adam is made in the same image, containing 248 limbs and 365 sinews that are concealed and spiritual.

The reason that the soul clothes itself in the body of flesh, skin, sinews, and bones is so that it can be extended and revealed through the power of its 248 limbs and 365 sinews, which are concealed and spiritual, within the 248 limbs and 365 sinews that are physical and revealed. This is so that its concealed powers can be revealed in this material world and to demonstrate its power and ability to act with all of its 248 limbs and 365 sinews, through the Torah and its commandments which are also 613 limbs and sinews. [These are] the 613 commandments which are hewn from the 613 limbs and sinews of the supernal lights of the supernal Adam. [Thus] the 613 limbs and sinews [of the soul], by means of the 613 commandments which are the limbs and sinews of the Torah, can be connected and cleave to the the 613 spiritual limbs of the supernal lights of the supernal Adam, blessed be He, in the divine emanation, where [the soul's] root is located. For through the connection and cleaving [of the soul's] 613 limbs and sinews with the 613 commandments of the Torah, which is hewn from the 613 supernal lights, it can merit to increase the light in its 613 spiritual limbs and sinews. [As a result, through] the supernal lights of the supernal Adam, blessed be He, *shefa'* and beneficent favor full of the blessing of God are released to all of the lower worlds. For every commandment that a righteous person fulfills shines and increases the light in its root, in the place from which his soul was hewn, in the spiritual light above that corresponds to that very commandment. And the light of the supernal commandment is aroused to bestow *shefa'* from its light to all of the lower worlds, as is explained in the *Zohar:* "Through the arousal from below the action of the supernal forces is aroused."[214] For since a person's soul is a "*portion of God from above*,"[215] his likeness and image are in the image of God, the 613 of the lower Adam correspond to the 613 of the supernal Adam, blessed be He. Therefore when [the lower Adam] arouses from below, through the good deeds of the righteous who properly fulfill [one of] the 613 commandments, there is a corresponding arousal above, in its root, the place from which it was hewn, which illuminates the supernal lights in the roots of the commandments and causes light of beneficent *shefa'* to be bestowed from the supernal lights to all of the lower worlds, just as "the reward of a commandment is a commandment." For we explained above that it is the [spiritual] commandment [above] which corresponds to the [physical] commandment that a righteous person fulfills below, in other words, the secret of the supernal lights, that grants the righteous person his reward and bestows its light upon the worlds below, because of the righteous person who increased [the commandment's] light above in its concealed source, which is beyond comprehension. It is the righteous person who causes this. Thus after his death, when his soul ascends above, it clothes itself in the place of the light that it opened. This will be explained in detail below, with God's help.

Thus the root of the 613 commandments of the Torah is the secret of the supernal Adam, and the manifestation of the Torah is the secret of the lower Adam which is [also] 613. We have received [a tradition] that the 600,000 letters of the Torah correspond to the 600,000 souls of Israel, all of which are contained in the soul of our teacher, Moses, of blessed memory, as it is said, "Moses is equal to all of Israel."[216] Our rabbis, of blessed memory, alluded to this in saying, "One woman gave birth to 600,000 in one belly."

Consequently, "Our teacher, Moses" equals 613,[217] and he is a man of God. For *YHVH 'Elohey Yisrael* (*YHVH* the God of Israel) also equals 613.[218] All of Israel and Moses are equal. Similarly, Israel can be added to the 70 elders with Moses and Aaron above them, since there are always a President and Head of the Rabbinic Court, making a total of 72. Add 72 to Israel and the result is also 613, as indicated above.[219] Thus all three are connected through the aspect of 613.

The House of Israel [III]

The author of the saying continued, "Israel is level upon level." It is well known that the quality by which a person is tested is the will, the freedom to choose. For a person's actions are not determined. "And everything is in the hands of heaven, except for the fear of heaven."[1] A human being is given the ability to choose and everything is according to his will. The *nefesh* functions in a number of ways that are virtual opposites, such as love and hate, anger and levity, and other such opposite functions. This will emanates from a person's *neshamah*, which is part of the divine emanation. Most of the kabbalists have agreed that the *sefirot* contain many oppositions, such as judgment and compassion. Sometimes [a *sefirah*] clothes itself in judgment and sometimes in compassion. Also, [the *sefirot*] can be compared to a person who may either receive or bestow. Each of these two modes may be subdivided into two, depending on whether the bestowal is good or evil and whether the reception is good or evil.

Just as a tiny human limb, with its various modes, behaves according to the will of the *nefesh*, so it is among the *sefirot*. Each and every *sefirah* has the capacity to act according to myriad changing functions, each depending on its matter [of concern], power, apprehension, knowledge, and the nature imparted to it by the emanator.

I have already explained at length above that the secret of the *nefesh*, *ruaḥ*, and *neshamah* comes from the coupling of *Tif'eret* and *Malkhut*, in the aspect of the six extremities that are composed of judgment and compassion. Above this is the secret of the *d"u parzufim* in *Binah*. Above, I also explained at length that the soul of Adam and Eve derived from the *d"u parzufim* in *Binah*, but that now the souls derive from the coupling of *Tif'eret* and *Mal-*

khut in their [proper] place, which is the secret of the six extremities.[2] This is the secret of the freedom to choose, "*to know good and evil.*" As the verse says, "*Behold the person has become like one of us, to know good and evil.*"[3] For the six extremities, which are composed of judgment and compassion, are the root of good and evil. But the purpose of creating Adam was above [the six extremities]. It was not made known within the range of good and evil, for [Adam's] soul [originated] above the extremities. Hence he was like a holy angel. This does not mean that he had no freedom to choose at all, for this is not so. If he had been absolutely compelled in his action, he could not have sinned. However, the ability to choose was not so revealed, but was concealed like the *d"u parzufim*. They are the root of the extremities, concealed within *Binah*. Nevertheless, judgments are aroused from the side of *Binah*, even though, in essence, judgment is not revealed there. So Adam aroused this [latent quality] and brought it into actuality. He entered the knowledge of good and evil, and the ability to choose was made known.

Do not be surprised by my words, for we also find a certain aspect of the ability to choose among the supernal angels. For the angels of Sodom sinned in attributing greatness to themselves, when they said, "*We are going to destroy* [*this place*]."[4] They were punished by being removed from their place for 138 years, as mentioned in *Midrash Rabbah*.

> "*For we are going to destroy* [*this place*]." Rabbi Levi said in the name of Rabbi Samuel bar Nahman, because the ministering angels revealed secrets of the Holy One, blessed be He, they were removed from their place for 138 years. Rabbi Hama bar Hanina said, because they took pride and said, "*For we are about to destroy this place.*"[5]

The secret is that every creature is deficient. Even if he is complete, there is a slight deficiency due to the deficiency that preceded existence. I will now copy what the kabbalist, Judah Hayyat wrote in the Gate of Destruction. Even though only a portion of it is required here, we will have need of it further on in this work, with God's help.

> I learned from my teacher, the Rav, Rabbi Samuel Ibn Shraga, of blessed memory, that the reason for the snake's seduction of Adam was because he and his party were jealous of divinity. "*They are rebels against the light*,"[6] because they are the *qelippot* and had need of the body of Adam, who was created of the *qelippah* and *nefesh*. These *qelippot* are alluded to in the verses, "*These were the potters*

who dwelt at Netaim [and Gederah]. They dwelt there in the king's service."[7] " . . . *And the records were ancient.*"[8] "*These are the kings who ruled in the Land of Edom before a king ruled in Israel.*"[9] For in all matters, lack precedes existence. And it is written in the *Tiqqunim*, " '*And the earth was waste and void [and darkness covered the face of the abyss]*.'[10] Now '*the earth*' is one, '*tohu*' is two, '*bohu*' is three, '*darkness*' is four, and '*the abyss*' is five. These four are contained in the body and are the four elements, which are the *qelippot* of the walnut.[11] Thus the verse says, '*and the earth was waste*.' This has been explained: '*was*' means 'previously.' Such is the way of the *qelippot* to precede the inner portion."[12]

Thus with the manifestation of the point of divine emanation, the *qelippot* were first emanated and existence proceeded from deficiency which cleaves to the created thing when it is subsequently created and revealed. [The created thing] is dependent on its cause. Thus [the *qelippot*] came first, since they derive from deficiency and deficiency preceded existence. This matter is also alluded to in a saying of our sages, of blessed memory, "He was building worlds and destroying them."[13] These are the worlds which are the source of destruction and desolation. In the future, they will be swallowed up, as it is written, "*He will destroy death forever, the Lord, God will wipe away the tears [from all faces]*."[14] And all the chariots that are within are [also] without. If they had not changed their places, they would have been good. For "*He did not create [the world] to be waste, but formed it to be settled.*"[15] And it is known that [destruction] is the result of desire. Just as in the human body, the *qelippah* surrounds the *nefesh*, as it is written in [the book of] Job, "*You clothed me in skin and flesh*,"[16] so above, "*on every side the wicked roam*."[17] For the fruit is guarded and concealed within its *qelippah*, and the four *qelippot* of the walnut allude to them, as I wrote at greater length in explaining the Recanati commentary.

Thus they were jealous of divinity. For "*the snake was naked*."[18] In other words, it was on the outside like a garment which surrounds the one who wears it. Thus it was "*naked and bare*"[19] without a garment, for it was itself the garment that stands on the outside. Thus it wanted to revolt. But this was prevented except in regard to human beings, who are composed of *qelippah* and *nefesh*. The [*qelippot*] thoroughly penetrate within [the human being], in no other manner. Thus they caused him to eat the fruit which is assigned to desire. And the proof is that they were ashamed because they ate of it, just as a person is embarrassed by the sight of something that is a disgrace for him. Then they felt that that sense was a disgrace for them, because it derived from the animal power, and when this one rises the opposite [power] falls. Thus when the animal power becomes strong, which is desire that derives from the snake, that effect arouses its like above, and [the *qelippot*] also become strong. Then there is a revolt and the slave rules, just as is the case now, due to our sins, in addition to the great evil that resulted from cutting the fruit from the tree. And there is a saying of our rabbis, of blessed memory, that [the fruit] was an *etrog*, as it is written [concerning the tree], '*and that it was a desire to the eyes*.'[20] The [Aramaic] translation says, '*desirable to the eyes*.' Thus they said, concerning the *etrog*, that if the upper stem has been removed, it is not acceptable. For part of the tree from which it is nourished has to remain with it and not to be cut off. Therefore, [Adam's] sin caused two evils. He was also commanded [not to eat from] the Tree of the Knowledge of Good and Evil in order to distance him from the changes which derive from that tree. For it is a tree that indicates both good and evil. The intention of the Holy One, blessed be He, was that Adam should be like an angel of God on the earth, who in his choosing does not incline toward evil. Rather, he should be one with his parts, inclining toward the united One. Thus He told him that he should eat from the Tree of Life, instructing him thus in order to keep him away from evil and death. As long as he would act in this way below, he would also arouse unity above. The *qelippot* would be subjugated and each would find peace in his place. But [Adam] did not do so. In his choosing, he sinned in thought and in deed, inclining in his choosing toward the tree of the female "*whose feet descend to death*."[21] He bowed down to it and immediately became inconstant. His choices became inconstant and brought about death which is the evil and bitter change, the opposite of life.

In the *Zohar* it is written, " '*The woman saw that the tree was good to eat and that it was a desire for the eyes and that the tree was pleasant as a source of wisdom, so she took its fruit and ate*.' "[22] Come and see. For human beings do not know, heed, or see. When the Holy One, blessed be He, created Adam and honored him with His Glory, He wanted him to cleave to Him so that he would be united with a united heart, in the place of united cleaving, that never changes or is transformed, with the connection and faith with which everything is connected. Thus it is written, '*and the Tree of Life in the midst of the garden*.'[23] Afterward, they turned from the tree of faith and abandoned the unique supernal tree that is beyond all trees and went to cleave to the place that changes from color to color and from good to evil and from evil to good. They descended from above to below and cleaved below with great changes. They abandoned the most supernal tree which is one and never changes, as it is written, '*God made men upright, but they sought many reckonings*.'[24] '*They sought many reckonings*,' indeed. Then their hearts changed in that very side: sometimes toward good, sometimes toward evil, sometimes toward compassion, sometimes toward judgment, like that thing to which they really cleaved. '*They sought many reckonings*' and cleaved to it. The Holy One, blessed be He, said to Adam, you have abandoned life and cleave to death. '*Life*', as it is written, '*a Tree of Life in the midst of the garden*.'[25] [It is] a tree which is called '*life*', for whoever holds it never tastes the taste of death. And you cleave to another tree which is certainly death for you, as it is written, '*her feet descend to death*.'[26] And it is written, '*I find woman more bitter than death*.'[27] Indeed in the place where he cleaved to death and abandoned the place of life. Therefore, death was decreed for him and all of the world. If he sinned, how did all of the world sin? If you say that every creature came and ate of this tree and it resulted from all of them, this is not so. But from the moment that Adam stood on his feet, all of the creatures saw and feared him. They emulated him like slaves before a king. He told them, let's go and bow down, and surrender to, and bless our Creator. They all followed him. When they saw that Adam bowed down and cleaved to that place, they were all drawn after him and caused death for him and for all of the world. Then Adam was changed to many colors, sometimes good and sometimes evil, sometimes angry and sometimes pleasant, sometimes judgmental and sometimes compassionate, sometimes [toward] life and sometimes [toward] death. He never remained permanently in one of these, as a result of that place. Thus it is called, '*the fiery sword which turns*'[28] from this side to that side, from good to evil, from compassion to judgment, from peace to war. It changes to everything and is called '*good and evil*,' as it is written, '*Do not eat from the Tree of the Knowledge of Good and Evil*.'[29] The supernal king, who loves the work of His hands, rebuked him and told him, '*Do not eat from the Tree of the Knowledge of Good and Evil.*' But he did not accept [the rebuke] from Him. He was drawn after his wife and banished forever. For the woman ascends to that place and no further and the woman caused death to all. Come and see.

Concerning the world to come, it is written, '*For the days of My people are like the days of a tree.*'[30] Like the days of that tree which is known.[31] [Concerning] that time is written, '*Death will be destroyed forever, and God will wipe away the tears from every face.*' "[32,33]

Thus this passage explains what I said [above]. The intention of the Holy One, blessed be He, was to cause [Adam] to cleave to Him, since He is the true unity, and to distance him from the changes. This may have been the meaning of the verse, "*now Adam has become like one* . . . "[34] In other words, at first, the Holy One, blessed be He, had in mind to make him "*like one*," like that tree that indicates oneness. From it, he was to know good and evil, that is to say, through his choosing, he tended to be drawn after the Tree of the Knowledge of Good and Evil.[35]

We may now return to the discussion of the passage, "level upon level." One level of the soul is derived from the coupling of *Tif'eret* and *Malkhut*, which is the secret of the six extremities. But "level upon level" derives from *Binah* and above, according to the secret of *ḥ*"y, the *ḥayyah* and *yeḥidah*. It was explained above that this is the secret of the World to Come, when Adam will be on the first level. From beyond these is the world that is completely good. Evil will vanish and become completely good. The enlightened one will understand. Thus the secret of Adam and "level upon level" have been explained.

Now in regard to the will, all three are connected. Thus it applies [not only to Adam], but also to the Holy One, blessed be He, so to speak, and to the Torah. It applies to the Holy One, blessed be He, as we explained, the divine emanation contains oppositions in the will of the *nefesh*. Moreover, at a higher level than this, in concealment, is the issue of the impulse in the divine will to bring all of the Divine Names into existence. This will is concealed and secret. However, we know that it was all an expression of good will. [God] was not obligated, but acted out of generosity. Thus the inquiries of the philosophers deviated in raising such questions as how multiplicity arose from unity, how complexity emerged from simplicity, how the limited emerged from the unlimited, and the like. Even some of our sages pursued these issues, rationalized a good deal, and said various things. But their words are worthless, because all of their rational inquiry assumes the necessity of nature. But in actuality, the Creator, blessed be His Name, created His world with His good will. The [divine] will operates entirely according to its own desires without any compulsion.

Nahmanides wrote an example of this in his commentary on Genesis.

> Know that composition does not imply loss, except according to the opinion of those of little faith who think that creation [was conditioned] by necessity. However, according to the view of the faithful who hold that the world was created because of God's desire, it is also clear that existence will continue as long as this [divine] desire. This is patently true.[36]

The verse alludes to this, "*And He is one* (*be-'eḥad*), *who can dissuade Him? His nefesh desires and He acts.*"[37] The verse says that "*He is be-'eḥad.*"[38] [He is] in His [state of] simple oneness, even after He brought the world into existence. "*And who can dissuade Him?*" In other words, there is no one who can refute this and dispute how oneness can give rise to multiplicity, complexity, and materiality. "*For His nefesh desires and He acts.*" This is to say, such was His will. He was not compelled. His *nefesh* desired to manifest existence, according to His will. Later, it says, at the end of the next verse, "*There are many more such with Him.*"[39] In other words, even though I told you that everything is done by will, do not think that they are separate from Me and are created by will for no reason. Do not think in this way. Rather these "many more" are "with Him." He formed them with wisdom. For all of existence is like a candelabra composed of interconnected parts, beginning with the first point and until the last [stage] of emanation, in accord with the secret of cause and effect. [This continues] from [the world of] emanation to the [world of] creation, and from [the world of] creation to the [world of] formation, and from [the world of] formation to the [world of] making; then to the world of the spheres, and to the elements, until the foundation of the earth, which is the lowest point of materiality. All of this is the result of divine will, not by compulsion, but as a free gift.

How wonderful that the first point of the divine emanation is the secret of the will. *Keter* is the will, as explained above. The final point, the earth, is called earth (*'ereẓ*) because of the will (*raẓon*), as explained in the *Zohar*, *Bereishit*, on the verse, "*God called the dry land earth.*"[40]

> What was dry land became earth, for producing fruit and planting trees. Thus it is written, "*God called the dry land earth.*" That lower union of earth and will was complete as it should be. Thus it says, "*for it was good,*" "*for it was good,*" twice. Once for the upper union and once for the lower union. Once it was united on two sides, from then on, "*Let the earth bring forth vegetation.*"[41] It was prepared to produce fruit, as it should be.[42]

In the liturgy it says, "We were exiled from our *'ereẓ* (country) because of our sins and distanced from our *'adamah* (land)." Rabbi Moses Cordovero, of blessed memory, wrote, "*Malkhut* is called *'ereẓ* (earth) because of its association with *raẓon* (will), when [providing] an abundance of *shefa'* and favor (*raẓon*). And it is called *'adamah* because of its association with red (*'adumah*), when it receives judgment. We have even been distanced from this."[43] Thus *'ereẓ* is related to *raẓon*.

Although all of the above alludes to the supernal *'ereẓ*, also in the lower realm, this material earth is called *'ereẓ* because of the association with will (*raẓon*). Thus is the secret of the seal of the will from the first point to the last. Thus will is associated with the Holy One, blessed be He. There is another great matter concerning the will to be explained below in a discussion concerning the Torah.

The Torah is connected with the will, because "a person who sinned under compulsion is exempted from punishment by God."[44]

There is also the matter of the will of the Torah, the secret of "and it is this." For the Torah is not determined by one point of view, but includes many points of view, like the matter discussed in the first chapter of [tractate] *Eruvin*.

> Rabbi Abba said in the name of Samuel, the school of Shammai and the school of Hillel were divided for three years. One said the *halakhah* is according to our opinion and the other said the *halakhah* is according to our opinion. A heavenly voice went out and said to them, both of these views are words of the Living God, but the *halakhah* is according to the words of the school of Hillel.[45]

And in the first chapter of [tractate] *Ḥagigah*, it says:

> The Masters of the Councils (*ba'aley 'asufot*) are the sages who sit together in groups (*'asufot 'asufot*) and concern themselves with the Torah. These declare unclean and those declare clean, these

> prohibit and those permit, these declare unfit and those declare fit. Then how can I learn Torah? The Torah says, "*They were all given by one Shepherd.*"[46] They were given by one God and one leader said them, from the mouth of the Lord of all creation, blessed be He, as it is said, "*God said all of these things.*"[47] So make your ears like a grain hopper and acquire for yourself an understanding heart to hear words which declare unclean and words which declare clean, words which forbid and words which permit, words which declare fit and words which declare unfit.[48]

This is not the place to explain these passages. We shall do so later, if the Creator permits. Nevertheless, we see that the Torah is not absolutely determined by one view but by the wills of those who comprehend and cleave to it.

Thus the three are connected to the matter of the will.

The author of the passage next wrote, "The two levels are Jacob and Israel. One is concealed and one is revealed." "Level upon level," which was written at the beginning of the passage, concerns the *neshamah*, as has been explained. What is said here, "One is concealed and one is revealed," concerns the body. It is possible to explain the statement, "One is concealed and one is revealed" rather than saying "concealed and revealed." For, concerning the body, there are two aspects which are completely different, as I shall explain. Our rabbis, of blessed memory, said in their *Midrash*, "In the Torah of Rabbi Meir, it was written, 'God made for Adam and his wife garments of light and clothed them.' " 'Light' with an *alef*.[49] Here is what the *Zohar* says in section *Piqudey*.

> Come and see. The soul does not ascend to appear before the Holy King until it merits to be clothed in the supernal garment, to be seen there. Similarly, it does not descend below until it is clothed in the garment of this world. The same is true for the supernal, holy angels. For, concerning them, it is written, "*He makes the winds His angels, fiery flames His servants.*"[50] When they act as emissaries in this world, they do not descend below until they are clothed in the garment of this world. It entirely depends on the place to which it goes. And so we have explained it. The soul only ascends in that garment which shines.
>
> Come and see. When Adam was in the Garden of Eden, he was clothed in a garment like the one above. It is the supernal garment that shines. When he was expelled from the Garden and

> had need of the colors of this world, what is written? "*The Lord God made for Adam and his wife garments of skin.*"[51] Previously, they were garments of light, light of that supernal light that he used in the Garden of Eden. For in the Garden of Eden he made use of the supernal light that shines. Thus when primordial Adam entered the Garden, the Holy One, blessed be He, clothed him in a garment of that light and brought him in there. Had he not first been clothed in that light, he would not have entered there. When he was expelled from there, he needed another garment. Then, "*The Lord God made for Adam and his wife garments of skin.*" It was all as required. Similarly, here, "*They made service garments for serving in the sanctuary,*"[52] in order to enter into holiness.
>
> And it has been explained that a person's good deeds that are performed in this world draw light from the supernal splendor, the garment that has been prepared for that world, in order to appear before the Holy One, blessed be He. And in that garment that he wears, he enjoys and sees the shining mirror, as it is written, "*to view the pleasantness of YHVH and to visit His chamber.*"[53] Therefore, the soul is clothed in two worlds, so that it will be complete in everything, in this world below and the one above. Concerning this, it is written, "*The righteous shall praise Your Name, the upright will dwell in Your Presence.*"[54] "*The righteous will praise Your Name*" in this world, "*the upright will dwell in Your Presence*" in that world.[55]

The implications of this homily are lengthy and will be explained in their place.

It is explained here that the garment of Adam's soul that he had before he sinned was a pure, clean, holy body which inclined toward spirituality. And so it will be in the future, concerning which, it is written, "*and the earth will be full of knowledge.*"[56] In other words, even the earthiness of the body will be entirely intellect and knowledge, as it was for Adam before he sinned.[57] When he sinned, the garment of the soul [became] "*You clothed me in skin and flesh,*"[58] which is the murky body. Thus the allusion is fulfilled, "*Man sees what is before the eyes, but YHVH looks into the heart.*"[59] In other words, when Adam followed what appeared to his eyes, as it is written, "*for it was a desire for the eyes,*"[60] he was clothed in materiality. Spirituality only remained in his heart, for the heart still understands. This is the meaning of "*YHVH looks into the heart,*" for He sees no knowledge [of God] in a person's body, except in his heart. This is the meaning of the verse, "*and God was saddened in his heart,*"[61] in the human heart. For the only [part of the body] left to him that understands is the heart.

Now the subtle, pure body, which is the garment of light, is called concealed. And the murky body, which is presently material, is called revealed. Therefore, the *Zohar* text says, "One is concealed and one is revealed." When this one rises, that one falls. And they are Jacob and Israel. Concerning Jacob is written, "*His hand gripped the heel of Esau.*"[62] For [Esau] is the primordial snake, as shall be explained in its place. And Israel is power, freedom from subjugation, and the angel of death.

This completes the explanation of the *Zohar* passage concerning the three that are interconnected: the Holy One, blessed be He, the Torah, and Israel. On the basis of this, the level of a human being will be explained, how he is in the image and likeness [of God].

In order to complete my intention in this introduction, which is called *The Generations of Adam*, I have to inform you about the human being of free will, who includes both the upper and the lower realms. When he ascends, he reaches the heights, and when he descends, he hits the very bottom. This is exemplified by a saying in tractate *Megillah*, "This people is compared to stars and compared to dust. When they ascend, they ascend."[63]

The explanation is as follows. Know that "*God made this, corresponding to this.*"[64] A holy emanation was manifested which is the secret of unity, called supernal Adam, as it is written, "*and on the throne, the likeness of a human being.*"[65] Similarly, He made a worthless Adam, who is like a monkey in comparison to Adam, called the world of the *qelippot*. It contains ten *sefirot* and seven palaces. Just as the holy emanation contains the *d"u parzufim* in *Tif'eret* and *Malkhut*, so the world of the *qelippot* contains Samael and Lilith, God spare us. Their names and aspects are discussed at length in *Pardes*, *Sha'ar ha-Temorot*. If you ask, What was the source of the *qelippot* and "*who made a pure thing from an unclean one?*"[66] the *Pardes* has already provided the answer. The truth is that above, in the divine emanation, no evil thing descends from heaven. For above, matters are extremely subtle. However, when they coarsen and descend the secret emanated levels, the matter is compelled to separate, just as [in the course of digestion], food [is separated] from food, until residue is produced.

There is another fine example. It is very analogous to human sperm, which is the finest product of the human body. It emerges from the brain, by way of the blood stream, to the penis. From that drop, in the fullness of the womb, an embryo is formed as well as other polluted things. Could one have imagined that a polluted entity would be created from human seed which is the finest product of the body? Certainly not. For if so, it would immediately come to an end.[67] But this polluted matter is produced through drawing the spermal drop from place to place and from level to level. The polluted matter comes to be through separating out the select elements, from which the embryo is created. The polluted matter is constituted from the rest. Similarly, in the divine emanation above, in its place, there is nothing evil. However, when extended below, as the pure and holy is separated out, something impure is produced, which is the residue, [like] sediments of gold. See the full discussion in *Pardes*.[68]

He also wrote, "And so is the law concerning spilling seed. Even though it has been removed from its place, in order to emerge, as long as it does not emerge, it is not subject to any impurity and its producer is still considered clean. It does not confer uncleanness until it emerges from the penis."[69]

Know that although a person has been created in the supernal image and likeness, since he has become clothed in the impurity of the snake, knowing good and evil, if he chooses evil, he changes his countenance and is compared to an animal, appearing like a monkey. Our rabbis, of blessed memory, said, "A beast does not rule over a person until he appears to it like an animal."[70] The evil beast that gathers prey is the *qelippah*. Thus within the level and exaltation of the human being, the opposite is alluded to. For every matter that has pure aspects, there are evil aspects in its opposite side. It is written, "*and the person became a living soul*."[71] This refers to his exalted level, as I discussed at length above. However, upon changing his quality, then [the verse reads] "*and the person became the soul of a beast*."[72] For the evil beast rules over him, God spare us.

This is the meaning of the two urges, the good urge and the evil urge, that have been in a person since he has had knowledge of good and evil. Consequently, the evil urge is present in a person before the good urge, for the *qelippah* is formed before the fruit grows. Here is what is written in the *'Avodat ha-Qodesh*, *Ḥeleq ha-Yiḥud*, chapter 18:

> I have already written in *Sefer Tola'at Ya'aqov* that there were ten fingers on Adam's hands, corresponding to the supernal wisdoms. For the hands and the fingers are instruments for serving the soul. Similarly, the ten utterances are tools for the only Lord. And the ten toes are the foundations of the body, corresponding to the ten final levels. He is also composed of the lower Chariots which are close to holiness. The bones divided off from them. This is the finest *tiqqun* in the body. Concerning them, it is written, "*He will give strength to your bones*."[73] He is also composed of good and

> evil. Consequently, a way of life and death was given to him, in other words, the good urge and the evil urge, corresponding to good and evil from which he is composed. Choice was given to him, corresponding to the point. However, his evil portion is the flesh which comes to an end and perishes. Thus it is called "*the end of all flesh . . .*"[74] for it only has governance over its portion. Also, those that are subject to it, its forces, over whom it is minister, provide their portion. These are the sinews and veins. [The flesh] is also composed of heaven and earth. However, its heavenly portion is the covering of skin, which covers over everything. The earthly portion derives from the four elements. Such is the totality of the lower Adam, whom the sages call "a small world."[75]

Now, in rabbinic language, the *qelippah* is called "guard." This is a great matter. I have already written that the *qelippot* derive from the residue of holiness. Had Adam not sinned, the *qelippah* would not oppose, but rather guard the fruit, like a king who sits within and is guarded by his slaves. However, due to the sin, rebellion was aroused in them and they became rebels. In tractate *Sanhedrin*, chapter *'Arb'a Mitot*, the following is written.

> For it is taught that Rabbi Simeon ben Menasya said, alas for a great servant that was lost to the world. For had the snake not fouled up, every Jew would have been served by two good snakes. He would have sent one to the north and one to the south, to bring him precious jewels.[76] Moreover, a strap would have been fastened under its tail. With it, it would bring dust for his garden and ruin.[77]

This passage alludes to what we have said, and so it will be in the future. The *qelippot*, which are evil, will return to being good, according to the secret of "an evil angel [has to] answer amen."[78] The prophets alluded to this in many verses. Isaiah said,

> *And a wolf will dwell with a lamb, the leopard will lie down with the goat, the calf and the beast of prey will feed together, with a little boy to herd them. The cow and the bear shall graze, their young shall lie down together; and the lion will eat straw, like the ox. A baby will play over a viper's hole, an infant will pass its hand over an adder's den. In all of My sacred mountain, nothing evil or vile will be done.*[79]

All of this alludes to the powers above. For "every knee will bend." Then the *qelippot* are called a guard, for they guard the fruit. Cain alluded to this when, in trying to confuse the supernal mind, he said, "*Am I the guard of my brother*?"[80] It is known that Cain was acquired from the side of impurity, from the pollution which Eve received from the snake. Abel is from the side of holiness, and Cain is the *qelippah*. Abel is the fruit of the holy Tree of Life. And [Cain] said, "*Am I the guard of my brother?*" This is strange, but the [verse] is fulfilled according to the teaching that I revealed. In other words, he is a guard and not a *qelippah*. For the *qelippah* is what is discarded, like the matter that is discussed in [tractate] *Hagigah*. "Rabbi Meir ate the inner portion and discarded the *qelippah* (shell)."[81] For the *qelippah* opposes and accuses. But [Cain] wanted to fool the supernal mind. So he said that he is the guard of the fruit, a faithful servant to his Maker. And so he shall be in the future.

Now I shall explain this passage from [chapter] *'Arb'a Mitot*, to the extent that God permits. For a number of important insights emerge from it, in *The Generations of Adam*, that a person should contemplate in order to cleave to holiness. First, however, I will provide an introduction.

It is written in the Recanati commentary on Genesis and also found in *Sefer 'Avodat ha-Qodesh*, concerning the Tree of Life and the Tree of Knowledge, that they had a single root below, despite the fact that they are two [distinct trees] in their branches. Thus Onkelos translated, concerning both of them, "*in the middle of the Garden*."[82] But it is impossible for two trees to be both in the center, unless they are connected and joined in a single root. Here one speaks of lower matters and alludes to what is above. The secret of this matter is in accord with the secret of the divine emanation, the supernal tree which is not cut. Now many commentaries exist which explain the Tree of Life and the Tree of Knowledge and the fruit of the Tree of Knowledge above. However, the clearest is that *Tif'eret* is the Tree of Life. In other words, [*Tif'eret*] is the tree of *Binah*, which is called "Living God." And the root of *Binah* is in *Ḥokhmah*, which "*enlivens its possessor*."[83] For there the root of *Tif'eret* is concealed. In its place, it is a tree that has been planted, as I explained at length above.

The Tree of Knowledge is *Yesod*, from the verse "*and Adam knew his wife*."[84] For it is the covenant of the genitals which joins the *d"u parzufim*. And the fruit of the Tree of Knowledge is *Malkhut*, which leads the world with supernal power for good and for evil, depending on the arousal caused by the world's deeds. Our rabbis, of blessed memory, said, "The world stands on one pillar and *ẓaddiq* is his name."[85] It is known that "*The ẓaddiq is the Yesod of the world*,"[86] for all of the streams go to *Yesod* and all of the channels go to *Yesod*. *Malkhut* has one channel, the channel that runs from *Yesod* to *Malkhut*, and *Malkhut* is called world. For *Malkhut* leads all of the worlds, of creation, formation, and making. This single channel is the one pillar. The *shefa'* of the six extremities consists of judgment and compassion. All of them go to *Yesod* and from *Yesod* to *Malkhut*. This is the secret of the two channels. Here is what the *Pardes* writes in chapter four of *Sha'ar ha-Ẓinnorot*.

> Another channel extends from *Yesod* to *Malkhut*, for it is the prolongation of the great stream that emerges from the delights of *Binah* to water the Garden. By means of this channel, it holds *Malkhut*, so that [she can] couple with her husband above. And through this channel she is disturbed by transgressions. We have seen something about this channel in Ben Farhi's *Ta'amey Miẓvot*, concerning the negative commandment not to drink wine of idolators. He writes, "There are two orifices in the supernal covenant. One bestows to the *Shekhinah*. That *shefa'* which emerges is called sweet water. This is the origin of many reasons for the Torah that are called water, as it is written, '*all who are thirsty, come to water*,' "[87] and water can only mean Torah.'[88] The second orifice carries *shefa'* to the evil forces which are called *wine of idolators*."[89] From his language it is clear that his words are words of Kabbalah, which amply prove that "*from my flesh, I see God*."[90] For in a man there are two orifices, one to bestow [seed] to his female, in order to give birth to his likeness, and the other to discard the superfluous and loathsome.
>
> We also find a similar view in a work of unknown authorship that is a commentary on the Song of Songs and the [Torah] section *Terumah*, partially written in Aramaic. "Now we have to tell the secret of *ayin*, their source. What was its image? Thus concealed secrets were engraved. Under the chariot of the Holy King is the secret of the Holy Covenant of the Holy One, blessed be He, which is called '*Ẓaddiq*, the *Yesod* of the world.' It is a spring that draws water to the Holy Well, which is the Lady. The two heads [of the letter] *ayin* are the secret of those two orifices within the penis. These are two springs. The Holy Spring on the right nourishes the Lady. From there are nourished the prophets, pious, pure-hearted, and righteous who are pampered in the Garden of Eden. The second spring provides sustenance for the impure bands and the angels who accuse the world. From there, they nour-

> ish evil Balaam and from there benefit comes to the wicked who succeed in this world. Thus it is written, 'and shakes the wicked out of it.'[91] [The word wicked *(risha'Im)* is written] with a large *ayin*, for they are nourished from the second head of the *ayin*." His words may be understood as an aid to the Kabbalah of Ibn Farhi, quoted above, which says that there are two channels in *Yesod*, one holy and the other for the dross.[92] He also wrote the following in explaining the letter *Ẓaddi*. "The letter *Ẓaddi* has two heads which allude to the *Ẓaddiq*.[93] These are two Holy Springs. One flows and draws water to the Lady. From there, those above and below are blessed. '*For there YHVH ordained blessing*.'[94] From this spring holy angels and many holy souls are created. The second spring flows to the left side [of the Holy One]. From there the '*forbidden woman*'[95] and the adulteress are nourished. If Israel are meritorious, that stream is sealed and the Holy Spring of the right side is opened. If not [meritorious], [the other] stream is opened, which draws for the '*forbidden woman*' the unclean forces that dwell beyond the supernal [holy] dwelling. [These unclean forces] are called *others*.[96] From this second spring, demons, evil spirits, succubi, and the evil of the left side, emanate."[97,98]

This good and evil is revealed by *Malkhut*, below. Not, God forbid, that a revelation of evil is there. For it is written "*No evil can dwell with You*."[99] However, "*her legs descend to death*."[100] The legs of *Malkhut* are the extension of the worlds of creation, formation, and making, which reach the evil *qelippot*. They are in the world of making, surrounding the world of formation, which is called Metatron. Concerning him, it is written, "*The wicked walk on every side*."[101]

Whenever the kabbalists speak of the entrance of the *qelippah* into holiness, it is necessary to understand the matter. For when there are righteous and pious in this world, *Malkhut* raises up the aroma of the deeds of the righteous. This is what the *Zohar* calls "female waters that are poured toward her." Then the channel of *shefa'* and blessing is opened. But, if the opposite occurs, God forbid, then the power of judgment is aroused through the entrance of the accusations of the *qelippot*. In other words, the *qelippot* cry out and charge, "These people are idol worshippers. These people are idol worshippers," and the like. This is called the entrance of the *qelippah* into holiness. Then the divine bestowal flows through the channel of dross and the bestowal that should flow from the right side to those who go to the right in the Torah, is channeled from the left side to those who go to the left. For the Holy One, blessed be He, is a true judge.

All of the teachings allude to this. The snake violated Eve and implanted pollution within her, the matter of menstruation, God forbid. These things are not to be taken literally. The meaning is the entrance of the voice of accusation of the *qelippot* above. The bestowal of dross is released, that is the powers of judgment, and the pride of Israel is taken and given to the nations of the world. For they settle in the best parts of the earth,[102] while we are in exile. This is the secret of the *Shekhinah* in exile.

Although the verse "*I YHVH do not change*"[103] is true, the Holy One, blessed be He, desires lovingkindness and for everything to be from the side of absolute goodness, that Goodness may come and be received. I abridged the discussion of the entrance of the *qelippot*, God forbid, and [Eve's] menstruation, but they are thoroughly explained in *Pardes*, chapter six of *Sha'ar ha-Temorot*. This has to be carefully studied, for who can handle such matters and remain unscathed?

Here is what is written in *Sefer Qol Bokhim*, concerning the verse, "*He has handed over to the enemy the walls of its citadels.*"[104]

> These are the walls of the upper Jerusalem. Despite the guards, as it is written, "*I assigned guards on your walls, Jerusalem*,"[105] so that the external forces would not be able to enter them, during the destruction, he "*handed over the walls to the enemy.*" And the *qelippah* ruled over them. This is what is written in section *Bereishit* [of the *Zohar*] in the homily on the departments. In the first commentary on these departments, it says, "The third department is a place of flames and smoke, there the flow of the river Dinur springs up and emerges. . . . There slanderers of Israel are sometimes found . . . and wicked Samael is there."[106] My teacher, of blessed memory, explained that [Samael] is only there when he ascends from the female of the Great Abyss to this department, in order to accuse Israel. From there, he and his party cry out in the voice of accusation and say "*Will the Judge of the entire world not do justice?*"[107] From there the voice of their accusation ascends above and the King of Justice necessarily has to incline His ear to the voice of their accusation. This is the meaning of "*They raised a voice in the House of YHVH* [*like the day of assembly*]."[108] It is the voice of accusation, like that day when the golden calf was made, for then [these voices] were produced. *Malkhut* is called "the Tent of Assembly (*Mo'ed*)." It is designated (*meyu'ad*) for the uniting at

designated times. This is the meaning of "*like the day of Assembly*," like the day that is called "*Mo'ed*." There is a time for uniting; uniting is not constant. The voice that was produced on the days of destruction was like the day that the Tent of Assembly was made. For there, without doubt, the accusation became very strong. Therefore, *House of YHVH* refers to the departments which are a house and department for *Malkhut* that nests[109] in them in a manner that they are departments, as explained in the *Tiqqunim*. The author of Lamentations, incidentally, hinted at an important principle. The *qelippot* do not, God forbid, enter into [the worlds of] emanation, creation, and formation. But the secret of the entrance of the external powers into holiness, which we are discussing, is that there is a female in the departments, which is called the female of the Great Abyss. From there, many torturers of the law emanate. When the innocent multiply in the world, that female is sealed and the [torturers] do not come out. But when the guilty multiply, that female opens and many torturers of the law emerge and warders are unleashed in those departments. They ascend until the department that is next to the palace of *Gevurah*, the *heykhal Zekhut* (Merit), where Isaac's son Esau is connected, and [until they reach] the department that is next to the palace of *Ḥesed*, the *heykhal ahavah* (Love), where Ishmael, the son of Abraham, is connected. There they cry out with the voice of accusation and it enters further above until it comes before the upright King. Then the decree is issued, depending on the time and the transgression. Thus no external power [actually] enters any of the places of holiness. This is alluded to here by the author of Lamentations when he says, "*He handed over to the enemy, the walls of its citadels*."[110] This is in accord with the first explanation. And there, "*in the House of YHVH*," that is, in the departments, as has been said, "*they raised a voice*" of accusation, "*like the day of assembly*," as has been explained.[111]

Now God warned not to eat the fruit of the Tree of the Knowledge of Good and Evil. For then the root of evil would be aroused and would become evil in essence. For as long as it was in its root, it was the root of the excesses, and functioned as a guard and not as a *qelippah*. However, if he would eat the fruit from the tree, he would cause a rent [in the cosmic order] and arouse two authorities. For the guard would become a *qelippah*, peeled from the food, and would be called, "impure impure," because the *qelippah* is discarded outside the camp of settlement. Adam and his wife caused this through following the advice of the snake. For the snake's root is from the essence of the Tree of External Forces, Samael and his consort. They incited the couple, Adam and Eve.

It is written in *Sefer ha-Bahir*:

> His disciples asked him, tell us how this occurred. He told them, the wicked Samael made a bond with all of the supernal forces against his Master, because the Holy One, blessed be He, said, "*Let him rule over the fish of the sea and those that fly in the heavens.*"[112] He thought, how can I cause him to sin and drive him out from before me? He descended with all of his forces and looked for a friend for him on the earth and found the snake. It looked like a camel and he rode upon it. He went to the woman and said to her, "*Did God say that you should not eat from any tree of the Garden?*"[113] He thought, I'll seek more and add [to what God commanded] and let her subtract. She said, "He only restricted us *from [the fruit of] the Tree of Knowledge that is in the midst of the Garden, God said do not eat of it and do not touch it, lest you die.*"[114] She added two things. She said "*from the fruit of the tree*" and He only said "*from the Tree.*" And she said, "*do not touch it, lest you die.*" What did wicked Samael do? He went and touched the tree. The tree cried out, "*Let not the foot of the arrogant come upon me or the hand of the wicked drive me away.*[115] Wicked one, do not touch me!" He then said to the woman, "There, I touched the tree and did not die. You touch it too, and you will not die." The woman touched the tree. She saw the Angel of Death appear before her and thought, perhaps I will die now and the Holy One, blessed be He, will make him another woman and give her to Adam. So, I will cause him to eat with me. If we die, both of us will die, and if we live, both of us will live. She took some of the fruit of the tree and gave it to her husband. "*And the eyes of both of them were opened*"[116] and his teeth were set on edge. He said, "What is this that you gave me to eat?" For just as his teeth were set on edge, the teeth of all creatures will be set on edge.[117]

It is called snake (*naḥash*) because all of the impure forces of divination (*niḥushim*) and sorcery originate there. Also, the word *naḥash* plus one for the word itself equals *Satan*. There is a great allusion in the fact that one has to be added for the word. For "with the word," the snake brought about

Satan. I mean that this was caused by the utterance of his lips, the expression of slander against his Creator.

The likeness of Adam changed. "*For man does not rest in honor*."[118] He caused death and his countenance was changed. For Adam was created for eternal life, as I shall explain. "*The end of the matter, when all is said and done: fear God and guard His commandments, for this is all of a person*."[119] "*The end of the matter*" is Adam, who was created last. And the first in thought is the last in deed. He was created at the end so that he could include everything in his image and likeness. He was created with 613—248 limbs and 365 sinews, corresponding to the positive and negative commandments. "*Fear God*" refers to the negative commandments "*and guard His commandments*" refers to the positive commandments. Thus it is written, "*for this is all of a person*." For a person is constructed from limbs and sinews. In the first chapter of [tractate] *Berakhot*, it is written:

> What is the meaning of "*for this is all of a person*"? Rabbi Eleazar said, the Holy One, blessed be He, said the whole world in its entirety was only created for this one. Rabbi Abba bar Kahana said, this one is equal to the entire world. Rabbi Simeon be Azzai said, and some say it was R. Simeon be Zoma, the entire world in its totality was only created to join to this one.[120]

These sages are alluding to the creation of the *qelippot*. Rabbi Eleazar spoke in the manner that Rabbenu Tam wrote in *Sefer ha-Yashar*, in the first Gate:

> The world was only created for the pious and the servants of God and not for the wicked. The intention of creation was for [the former], but the wicked were created in the nature of creation, as it is the nature of a fruit to have a *qelippah*. Just as it is the intention of the sower that only wheat should grow, but through the power of vegetation, weeds are produced with the wheat and thorns with the lilies, so it was the Creator's intention to create [only] the pious, but the power of creation brought forth the wicked with the pious.[121]

Rabbi Abba bar Kahana adds that there is even a benefit in their creation. For, as the *Zohar* explains the benefit of creating the evil urge, it is to bring a person to his true purpose. If he overcomes his [evil] urge, the reward is commensurate with the effort. This is explained at length in *Pardes*, *Sha'ar ha-Temorot*. Then, "even an evil angel answers 'amen.' " For the evil urge also does so to honor its Creator, so that a person will be tested and withstand the test. When he does so, "the person is equal to the entire world" and decides for everything.

"Rabbi Simeon says, it was only created to join to this one." This is what I said above. They serve and submit to him. This explains the *baraita* of Rabbi Simeon ben Menasya, "Alas for the great servant who perished . . . "[122] And there is a great allusion concerning Sandalfon. For the sanctuary of the *qelippot* surrounds the world of Metatron, "*the wicked surround all sides*."[123] This refers to [the world of] Making, whose root is Sandalfon, as is known. For *YHVH* is the world of Emanation, Abatryel is the world of Creation, Metatron is the world of Formation, and Sandalfon is the world of Making. He is holy, but the sanctuary of the *qelippot* is located there as well. These were the *qelippot*, according to the secret of the guard, just as they will be in the future, when they are purified.

The House of David [I]

As our sages, of blessed memory wrote, "In the future pig will become pure."[1] This also refers to Sandalfon. Now that they are *qelippot*, there is a distancing. For the side of holiness is called the right side and the side of impurity is called the left side. "*For evil will break forth from the north*."[2] But if they are sanctified, everything will be [part of] holiness. This is the secret of the two Sandalfons, one toward the south and one toward the north. For there will also be great good from the north, because everything will be returned to the right [side].

Their expression "good stones"[3] also contains a great allusion. The author of *Sefer Yeẓirah* calls the letters "stones." It is taught there, "Two stones build two houses, three stones build six houses, four stones build twenty-four houses. . . . "[4] In other words, a word of two letters has two permutations. For example, *b'a* (he came) and *'av* (father). A word of three letters, such as *abg*, has six permutations, and so on. All of the permutations refer to matters and their opposites. As written in *Sefer Yeẓirah*, the transposition of *'oneg* (delight) is *nega'* (plague).[5] Thus a transposition is a matter and its opposite. "For there is nothing [in good] that is higher than *'oneg* (delight) and nothing [in evil] that is lower than *nega'* (plague)."[6] In the future they will all be "good stones." There will be no evil transposition.

There is also a secret in their saying, "A strap would be fastened under its tail."[7] *Malkhut* is the final level in [the world of] emanation. But it is also the first, the head of all those that are created, formed, and made.[8] Through it, everything is bestowed to the worlds, whether judgment or compassion. Thus this *sefirah* is "a tail for lions and a head for foxes." Insofar as this *sefirah* is a tail, it is the final *sefirah*; it also bestows to the *qelippot*, "*for her feet descend to death*,"[9] as was explained above. The *qelippot* are called the "primordial snake." This is the secret of Moses' staff changing into a snake. The Holy One, blessed be He, said, "*Grab its tail* [*and he put out his hand and held it*,] *and it became a staff* [*in his palm*]."[10] As we have said, the *qelippot* are sweetened through their drawing near to the root from which they are nourished. For above in their root, everything is holiness. Then the snake is a staff of God. This is the meaning of grabbing its tail, the secret of a "tail for lions." There [in *Malkhut*] is the root of their bestowal. But through becoming impure, as a result of Adam's sin, the staff is a snake, because of their accusation. The enlightened will understand. When they are made pure, the strap is under their tail in order to bring dust to the garden.[11] For had Adam not sinned, his dwelling place would be in the Garden of Eden. The secret of the dust is the holy earth, corresponding to the supernal dust, the supernal land. "*And Your people are all righteous, they will forever inherit the land*."[12] It also says that [the snake would bring dust] "to his ruin." For what is now destroyed, because of our sins, was whole. Ruin and the breach are because "*whoever breaches a fence will be bitten by a snake*."[13] And in the future, I will fill up the ruin through the Holy Building. Ezekiel the prophet said, "*And the desolate land will be tilled, after having been lying waste* [*in the sight of every passerby*]. *And they will say, that once desolate land has become like the Garden of Eden; and the cities, once ruined, desolate, and destroyed, are now populated and fortified*."[14]

Here is what Rabbi Galante wrote concerning the verse, "*Rejoice and be happy, daughter of Edom*."[15]

> Here is an excellent principle that I received from my teacher, of blessed memory. All of the *qelippot* will not be entirely annulled, but the Holy One, blessed be He, will root out that bitter and hard side from the world. The good and sweet part will remain. The meaning is that the Holy One, blessed be He, will sweeten the external forces from their bitterness, until they enter within the [realm of] holiness. This is the secret of "*a nurseling will play over a serpent's pit and one who has been weaned will pass his hand over an adder's den*."[16] For you already know that the secret of the union and coupling is called "playing." The joy of this playing will descend to the nurseling, who is Metatron, an infant sucking on his mother's breasts. Through him, the union is made during the six days of the week. This playing descends until the "*serpent's pit*," that pit which is the female of the Great Abyss, the dwelling place of the impure.

"*Over an adder's den*" refers to the female of this serpent, sorcerer, and adder who is cursed, as indicated by the spelling.[17] "*One who has been weaned*" is Sandalfon who has been weaned of his mother's milk. His hand and place are extended. All of this refers to the sweetening of the external forces. Their bitterness will pass from the world and they will remain without pollution. This is the secret of the name *ḥazir* (pig). For it will return (*leḥahzir*) [to its root] in the future. Now it is forbidden to make use of the evil urge without a divine command, for its nature applies to all of it. Therefore, it is now forbidden to approach this pig. Do not approach the opening of its house. But when it is sweetened in the future, it will be permitted. This is the meaning [of its name] *ḥazir*. For in the future they will return to their root, which is the place of holy powers (*gevurot*). This is the meaning of "*I will remove the heart of stone from your flesh*."[18] For what is characteristic of part of a stone is characteristic of the whole. This evil urge is similar. I will remove it from your midst "*and I will give you a heart of flesh*."[19] The side that is on the fire is roasted while the other side is cold. This is the heart of flesh. As explained in the *Zohar*, a heart of flesh is a heart for making flesh. In other words, the evil urge only extends beyond its boundary at the time of coupling between a man and his wife. The man heats up only in order to make flesh and not for any other reason. This is the secret of what is written in the *Zohar*, *parashat Pinḥas*, "In the future, the Holy One, blessed be He, will break the leg of the letter *qof* of [the word] *qnh* and it will remain *hnh* . . . "[20] The meaning is the side of the letter *qof* which extends beyond its measure. It is like that external force which mimics a human being like a monkey (*qof*). Just as the side of holiness consists of ten levels and seven palaces, so it is with the [other side]. There are a number of [other aspects in common as indicated by the verse], "*God also made this corresponding to that*."[21] Also, as indicated in *parashat Piqudey* concerning the secret of the ten levels that are in [the other side] and the secret of the connections of the two arms and two thighs, [there is] a likeness of the supernal limbs. And there are many similarities like them. Consequently, it is called a monkey (*qof*). In the future, the Holy One, blessed be He, will break that leg of the monkey and *hnh* will be left from *qnh*. This is the meaning of "*the first to Zion, heneh, here they are*."[22] It is also the secret of "*death will be destroyed forever*."[23] The verse does not say that the angel of death

> will be destroyed, but death. Death will be destroyed and a holy angel will remain. Similarly, in the case of Samael, the aspect of *sam* (drug) will be annulled and removed from it, and it will remain *'el*, which is holy. That is it will be divine and spiritual. And this is the secret of the snakes that were found in the cave of the *ẓaddiqim*. As they wrote in the *Gemara*, "Snake, snake, open your mouth and let the son enter to his father."[24] For they extinguished their evil urge. It was sweetened until it became a guard and servant for them. Similarly, our rabbis, of blessed memory, said, "Alas for the great servant who perished from the world. For had he not sinned, Adam would have attached a strap under the snake's tail."[25] And he would have carried away garbage and brought him jewels from distant lands. This illustrates what we have said: Had not Samael rebelled and become bitter, the world would have been served by him. They would have acquired their world through him. For he would have aided in the removal of the filthy refuse of the transgressions and in keeping [Adam] away from doing evil. And he would have had the benefit of bringing jewels and doing *miẓvot*. As it is written, "*And YHVH 'Elohim . . . placed him in the Garden of Eden to till it and guard it*."[26] "*To till it*" is a positive commandment and "*to guard it*" is a negative commandment. However, its basic inclination took it over, and it rebelled and went out and sinned and caused Adam to sin. This is also what was said in *Pirqey Rabbi Ishmael*, "until all of his ministers were destroyed and thrown above like goats and lambs of the Day of Atonement. In saying "the Day of Atonement," they alluded to the secret of the sweetening. They will be sweetened and left above and they will enter within to the Holy. This is the secret of menstrual blood which is sweetened, [until] impure menstrual blood becomes pure milk. This is an indication of what will occur in the future.[27]

Thus, when sweetened, the *qelippot* draw near to their root and are purified. But now, due to Adam's sin, they are aroused in bitterness until the end time.

You might then ask, How did they become bitter before Adam's sin? For "Samael formed an alliance against his Maker," as stated in the passage from *Sefer ha-Bahir* that I cited above.[28] Know that at first he sinned for the sake of a *miẓvah*. Afterward, he did not do it for its own sake, and as a result, he came to transgress for its own sake. In other words, Samael was a pure angel. The kabbalists said that he was one of the *serafim*. It seems that there is an allusion to this in the fact that the snake is called "*saruf* (burned) and clothed in envy." This is the "envy of scribes." He was envious of the level of Adam, for he wanted to approach within to holiness. "The envy of scribes increases wisdom"[29] for those who act for its own sake. Nevertheless, he contained a bit of the power of the excess, as I alluded above. For every creature has some deficiency, even if it is not material, and thus is capable of sin. This is proven by the angels of Sodom who took credit for the greatness, although this is only a remote possibility.

Nevertheless, it is possible that there was more of the transposition concealed in Samael. Through his envy of Adam, Adam was aroused against him. This was an aid to transgression, until he became an accuser and evil urge. Adam was ready to sin, because he inclined away from the side of pure good and clothed himself in the knowledge of good and evil. Then Adam had two likenesses: the likeness of holiness, [which is] the likeness of the supernal Adam, and the likeness of the worthless (*beliya'al*) Adam, which is like a monkey compared to a man. Thus choice was given to him, as it is written, "[*See, I have placed before you this day,*] *life and good, death and evil.*"[30] When he follows the good way, he cleaves to life, the secret of the Tree of Life. When he follows the evil way, he cleaves to death and his likeness changes. How so? When he follows the good way, then his likeness (*demut*) is in accord with the secret of *MiDOT* (attributes) cleaving to *YHVH*. As our rabbis, of blessed memory, said concerning the verse, "*you who are cleaving to YHVH* . . . ,"[31] "cleave to His attributes."[32] Then he is called "Adam," from the expression, "I will be like (*'ADaMeh*) what is above." When he follows the opposite path, his likeness (*demut*) changes and becomes the blood of death (*DaM MaVeT*). Then he is called "Adam," from the word *'adamah* (earth). "*For you are dust and to dust you shall return.*"[33] Blood from Adam and death from Eve caused death for the world. How so? For the act of creation is sealed with *'emet* (truth). "*And God saw all that He had done and it was very good.*"[34] The final letters of "*ve-yare' 'ElohiM eT* (and God saw)" spell *'emet* (truth). And there is an allusion to Adam. "And it was very good," *me'od* (very) is the same letters as Adam, for he is the ultimate purpose of the entire act of creation. He was created in order to be *'emet* (truth), in other words, eternal. For the meaning of truth is true, eternal existence which will not be false. Rather, it is a peg that will not slip. The ultimate purpose of creation was for him. He was to live forever as eternal vitality. This requires a broad explanation.

Know that those who study nature have said that death is natural for a human being because every being perishes. Man is a being composed of four elements. Thus, he necessarily must perish. All of our sages who are enamored with Greek wisdom have been drawn to this opinion. They render the judgment and intention of our Torah bitterness. But the true sages of the Torah who possess true faith, our rabbis, of blessed memory, believe that death is not natural. They said, "Had he not sinned, he would never have died." The sage of truth and true believer, our rabbi, Moses Nahmanides, of blessed memory, wrote as follows in [his commentary on] *parashat Bereishit*:

> Know that composition does not imply decomposition except according to the opinion of those of little faith who think that creation was necessary. But according to the opinion of the men of faith who say that the world was created by divine desire, it is clear that its existence also depends on [God] forever, as long as this desire exists. This is patently true.[35]

Certainly the students of nature walk in darkness, for *devequt* with God is above nature. It is God's will that man's *devequt* will be eternal. For necessity applies to nature, and this inclines the believers in eternal existence to hold that everything is the result of necessity. But we true believers hold that everything is the result of divine will, and it is God's will that man be eternal if he remains in *devequt*.

And in *Ba-Midbar Rabbah*, *parashat Naso*, and in *Midrash Hazit*, it is written, concerning the verse, "*you are beautiful, my darling, as Tirzah*,"[36]

> Rabbi Meir says, until now [the calves and cows continue to] exist. They were not confounded, were free from disease, and did not grow old, but continue to live and exist. From this we can learn, by way of *qal ve-ḥomer*, if the cows, who man caused to cleave [to God] through the work of the Tabernacle, were granted life, and live and exist forever, how much more so, Israel, who cleave to eternal life, As it is written, "*And you who are cleaving to YHVH your God are all alive today*."[37,38]

And it is written in *Shoḥer Tov*,

> "*A psalm. I will sing of faithfulness and justice*."[39] Rabbi Ibo said in the name of Rabbi Meir, until the time that is coming, they are prepared to exact retribution from the wicked, as it is written, "*each morning I will destroy all of the wicked of the land*."[40] It refers

> to those ignorant people. Those cattle convict the wicked, since sin causes death. Since they distanced themselves from God through their transgressions, they die. Thus in the future they will have to face judgment for having killed themselves. For those cattle, who were not commanded by a *mizvah,* but were made to cleave to God by man, in the work of the Tabernacle, merited existence. Thus they convict the wicked in the time that is coming.[41]

And in *Yoma*, chapter *B'a lo*, [they explained the verse,] " '[*You shall make the planks of the Tabernacle of*] *standing Acacia wood.*'[42] They stand forever and ever."[43]

In *Pesiqta* is written:

> Our rabbis taught [in the *Mishnah*], "In the case of a fire, one saves the book chest along with the book."[44] Are words of Torah written in it? Since it cleaved to the book, it merits to be saved along with it. Similarly, King Solomon said, "*One who walks with the sages will become wise.*"[45] The Holy One, blessed be He, said, Adam listened to his wife and was banished [from Eden]. If he had cleaved and listened to Me, he would be like Me. Just as I live and exist [forever], so he would live and exist [forever].[46]

They compared the body to the book chest and the soul to the book. One saves the body from death, which is the fire, along with [the soul]. Since [the body] cleaves to it and hearkens to it and does not betray it at all, it deserves not to be subject to death, just as [the soul] is not subject to death. Both of them will exist together. Just as we found that the enemy does not prevail against the deeds of the righteous, certainly it is fitting that he not prevail over them, except for the sin. As they said, in the first chapter of [tractate] *Sotah*,

> Rabbi Hanina bar Papa explained the meaning of [the verse], "*Rejoice, righteous ones, in YHVH, it is fit that the upright praise* [*Him*]."[47] Do not read *na'avah tehillah* (fit is praise), but *navveh tehillah* (dwelling-place) [of glory is that of the upright]. This refers to Moses and David, for the enemies could not prevail against the work of their hands. David, for it is written, "*Her gates sank in the earth.*"[48] Moses, for Mar said, "Since the first Temple was built, the boards, bolts, pillars, and sockets of the Tent of Assem-

> bly were hidden. Where? Rav Hisda said that Abbimi said, beneath the underground passages of the *Hekhal*."[49]

How much more fitting is it that the enemy that is death and destruction not prevail over the handiwork of the Holy One, blessed be He.

This is also connected to the "garments of light," for even the book chest, that is, the body, was pure and subtle. The following is found in *Pesiqta*, *parashat ba-Ḥodesh ha-Shelishi*, and in *va-Yiqra Rabbah*, *parashat 'Aḥarey Mot*, and in *Midrash Mishley:*

> Rabbi Levi said in the name of Rabbi Simeon bar Menasya that the ball of Adam's heel made the orb of the sun [seem] dark. Do not wonder at this. According to convention, a person makes two saucers, one for himself and one for his household. Whose does he make well? Is it not his? So Adam was created to serve the Holy One, blessed be He, the orb of the sun [was created] to serve the creatures. Is it not fitting that the ball of Adam's heel should make the orb of the sun [seem] dark? And *qal ve-ḥomer*, if the ball of his heel made the orb of the sun [seem] dark, how much more so, his face?[50]

In addition, my sons, may their Rock protect them, I will help you understand the meaning of the "garments of light." What is the light? Light continues to increase immeasurably from lamp to lamp and from lamp to lamp. Take a candle and light a piece of wood with it and another piece of wood with the first piece and continue infinitely. The light will increase beyond limit. Similarly, the creation of Adam immediately reached its ultimate stage. Now that he has sinned, the opposite is the case, for it is said, "*Better . . . is the day of death than the day of birth*."[51] For as long as he lives [his life is] the life of vanity, that is, the life of this world. So he walks in darkness until the day of his death, when the impurity of matter that comes from the snake departs from him. Then he merits the supernal light that is called "the world that is coming," for it comes to man after death.

When he was without sin, this light reached him at the time of his formation so that he could cleave to the supernal light eternally. For, indeed, his soul was from the *d"u parẓufim* in *Binah*, the secret of the world that is coming, which is the root of the supernal Garden of Eden, the secret of the Holy of Holies. Afterward, his body was taken from the place of holiness, the site of the altar below, which is opposite the one above. His place, in body and soul, was in the Garden of Eden below, which branches out from the root of the structure above, which is the manifestation of the *d"u parẓufim*. This is the structure in its [proper] place, which became Adam and is sealed with these seals. Together, the body and soul would be whole, and he would proceed from *devequt* to *devequt* and from enlightenment to enlightenment, until he would reach the stage of being taken, like Enoch and Elijah, and a thousand levels beyond this, in such a way that he would be constantly an eternal vitality, shining from light to light. For this world for him is an imprint of the world to come. The structure emanated in its place is in complete unity with its concealed root in *Binah*. When it ascends, [this structure] ascends from its place to *Binah*. Similarly, the departure of Adam [from this world] would not have been [through] death, but through ascending and being taken above in body and soul. For all [of him] would have been eternal.

As long as he was in the Garden of Eden, his work was done by itself. There was no need for plowing and planting or for any other work. Everything was from the side of holiness, and there was no deficiency in all of creation. For such is required by the nature of *ruḥaniyut*, since it is in a state of total perfection, *shefa*ʿ comes and penetrates all of the worlds. Just as [the verse says], "*I will answer the heavens, says YHVH, and they will answer the earth*."[52] There is blessing everywhere and peace is the seal of all the blessings. For everything was in a state of perfection. There was no Satan or devil. Everything was constantly in a state of eternity. The meaning of eternity is that there was no pause between one enlightenment and another, for there is no limit to the degrees of enlightenment concerning God. This is the meaning of the teaching concerning the World to Come, "In the future one will proceed from strength to strength."[53] Thus anyone of intelligence can see that Adam reached his ultimate state at the time of his creation. If he had maintained this level, he would have immediately seen his [place in the] World [to Come]. For the lower Garden of Eden is an imprint of the upper Garden of Eden. The Torah was at that time also spiritual in nature (*ruḥaniyut*), and he would study it and fulfill its commandments entirely in a spiritual manner. See the discussion at length in *Pardes*, *Shaʿar ha-Nishamah*, chapter six. Thus his Torah exists forever and his work was done by itself.

We have already written above that reward and punishment are not a matter of convention but follow the requirements of nature. For it is the nature of *devequt* above to open the source and to draw blessing from the beginning of [divine] thought to its end. From there it is extended to the lower worlds. This goodness would have been unceasing and eternal. Adam would have proceeded from eternity to eternity. For he would have continued to increase in wisdom without limit. This is in itself the good that was bestowed upon him. For this goodness would have increased from [one level of] goodness to [another]. That is in itself [the goodness], as I explained above, "the reward of a commandment is the commandment itself." This was the intention of creating Adam, who was made in the image and likeness. The Holy One, blessed be He, commanded him not to eat of the Tree of the Knowledge of Good and Evil. The meaning is that the emanation of the structure was composed of judgment and compassion. They are the "depth of good" and the "depth of evil" that are mentioned in *Sefer Yeẓirah.*[54] In other words, these are the roots from which good and evil are drawn. Not, God forbid, that there is [actual] evil there, "*for evil will not reside with You,*"[55] but [only], the excesses[56] of holiness. As was explained above, through human arousal they become evil, which is the bitterness of the *qelippot* that was explained above. Then evil destroys itself.

Adam was created from the Temple below and the Temple above, in such a way that he would be completely good. Then he would live forever and his world would be a world that was entirely good without pause, as has been explained. These extremes were guards for the fruit [whose powers were] subdued and annulled. Thus he was commanded not to arouse their power. Then, just as his soul was supremely high, as was explained, so the soul's container, which is the garment of the body was light. This is the meaning of "garments of light."

However, "*Man does not remain in honor,*"[57] because of the snake, "*and a grumbler alienates his friend ('alufo).*"[58] In *Bereishit Rabbah* is written, " '*A shifty person causes strife.*'[59] This is the snake who shifted the words of his Creator and who spoke rebelliously against his Creator. For he said, '*You will not die.*' "[60,61] There is an allusion here that he separated out the *'alef.* In other words, there should have been "garments of light" (*kutenot 'or*) spelled with an *'alef.* And now, "[*He made me dwell*] *in darkness like those long dead.*"[62] For there is darkness and no light. The garments are only of skin, *'or* spelled with an *ayin*, and he is blind (*'iver*), for he did not see. In other words, he became material, [a creature of] skin and bones. Then he had a material nature, concerning which the philosophers said that everything that is composite will ultimately decompose. This is death.

But the punishment of death was not by convention, but by nature. For the punishment of a transgression is the transgression itself, since it withheld itself from the source of life. Afterward, [Adam] sired offspring and the offspring produced offspring. It all derived from a putrid drop. For the drop became putrid as a result of the contamination of the snake. Were it not for this contamination, the drop would be holy, like a plastered cistern that does not lose a drop.

Now the snake gave false testimony. For he testified that its Creator ate from this tree and created the world. [The snake] separated the *'alef* from Adam and from *'emet* (truth). How so? I hinted above, concerning the verse, "*God saw all that He had done and, behold, it was very good.*"[63] The seal *'emet* (truth) and *me'od* (very) refer to Adam.[64] All was good and not evil, except that the power of the snake and Samael seduced Adam and Eve and they brought out evil from potentiality to actuality. Where Adam had been worthy of being true, that is to say, eternal, he now was bound up with lack. The *'alef* was separated from Adam and he remained *dam* (blood), which indicates redness, the power of judgment. And the *'alef* was separated from *'emet* (truth), and it remained *met* (dead). *Demut* (likeness) became *dam mavet* (blood of death), *dam* from Adam and *mavet* from Eve, who was the cause of death in the world.

In *Zohar*, *'Eykhah*, is written:

> Rabbi Haninai said that the Holy One, blessed be He, taught the Torah to Adam. As it is written, "*Then He saw it and gauged it; He measured it and probed it. And He said to Adam* ..."[65] And the ministering angels were offering praises before him. Finally, Samael saw in heaven and was jealous of him. He came down from heaven in the form of a shadow over the snake. The snake appeared with the shadow over him, which is his power and might. That snake approached the woman, for her mind was easier [to seduce] than the man's. From here we learn that a woman is only seduced by another woman. "*And he said to the woman, Did God really ('af) say* [*you shall not eat from any tree of the Garden*]*?*"[66] He began immediately with [the word] *'af* (anger). From here we learn that from the way a person begins to speak, we can recognize who he is. Thus [the snake] began with *'af* to make known who he is. He took this sign to see if she would be receptive or not and continued speaking to her until she began with the letter *mem* and said, "We may eat from every tree of the garden." The snake immediately took the letter [*mem*] and placed it on his left arm, and he waited till the letters, *vav* and *tav*, would come from her mouth, so that *mavet* (death) would be established before them. He began to seduce her, until it is written, "*And the woman saw* [*that the tree was good to eat*] ..."[67] with a great and strong taste. This teaches that the letters *vav* and *tav* flew and went off to join together with the letter *mem*. The letter *mem* was ascending and descending and not joining with them until she was seduced. *Vav*

and *tav* flew four times and surrounded the letter *mem* on four sides. As it is written, "*And she took (Va-Tiqaḥ) some of its fruit and she ate (Va-To'khal) and she gave (Va-Titen) also to her husband with her and he ate. And the eyes of both of them were opened (Va-Tipaqaḥenah).*"[68] Thus the letters *vav tav* are repeated four times. This teaches that they surrounded the letter *mem* on four sides. *Mem* was in the center, death on every side. As it is written, "*For death ascended in our windows.*"[69] This is Samael, who is one of the windows of heaven. Thus it is written, "*What man can live and not see death?*"[70] Immediately, he ruled over her and placed the contamination in her. The Holy One, blessed be He, descended to see, and Adam and his wife hid. Come and see. Before they sinned, the *Shekhinah* was a crown above their heads, so that She could rest in the world for them. Since they sinned, Her power, so to speak, weakened, went off, and did not rule [over the world].[71]

The explanation of "*death ascended in our windows*"[72] is that the final letters of "*and she took some of its fruit and ate, and gave*"[73] spell *ḥalon* (window). The meaning of the window is that light cannot now enter it, except as a result of death. Thus the verse says, "*Death ascended in our windows.*" For now a person can only merit this light through stripping off the garments of skin and flesh that are from the putrid drop, which is the result of the snake's contamination, and by girding his loins in the clothes of honor that are made of the Torah and commandments. With God's help, we will explain this below. And the [meaning of the] verse, "*Behold, it was very good,*"[74] was inverted, according to what was said in the *Midrash*. " '*And behold, it was very good,*' this is [the angel of] death"[75] And some places say, "this is the evil urge."[76] All have the same wondrous meaning, as I shall explain.

First, I shall explore one matter. The Holy One, blessed be He, created the world for the human being. He made the human being upright. Nevertheless, He gave him the power to turn aside from the good way and to arouse evil. Indeed, that is the way it turned out. If so, how could [God] have created the world for him? Since he would not be absolutely good, the ultimate purpose would be annulled. However, all of this will be explained.

I will begin with a citation from tractate *Eruvin*:

The rabbis taught, for two and a half years, the School of Shammai and the School of Hillel were divided. One school said that it is better for a person not to have been born than to be born and the

> other school said that it is better to be born than not to be born. They were polled and concluded that it is better for a person not to have been born than to be born and now that he has been born, he should investigate what he has done (*yepashpesh be-ma'asav*). And some said, he should examine what he is doing (*yemashmesh be-ma'asav*).[77]

One may object to those who argued that it is better for a person to have been born. Does not a verse in Ecclesiastes explicitly contradict their words? For it is written, "*And I praised the dead who have already departed more than the living who are still alive. And better than both is he who has not yet come into being.*"[78] This [verse] indeed inclines toward the view of those who said, "It is better not to have been born than to be born." And so the translator translated, "And better than both is he who has not yet come into existence and was not created."

Since this verse has come to our attention, I will ask concerning it, What is the relevance of saying, "*better than both is he who has not yet come into being*"?[79] For a person who has not come into existence is nothing, absent, and nonexistent. How can one apply the term *good* to something that does not exist?

Rabbi Abraham Ibn Ezra wrote:

> Many wondered at their saying that it is better for one who has not been born. And so our sages, of blessed memory said, "Fortunate is he who has not been created and does not exist."[80] And it is surprising, because of brevity, to only speak by way of analogy. So the sages of balanced mind said, every matter either exists or does not exist. If it is something that exists, how can it not exist?[81]

And Rashi wrote, " '*He who has not yet come into existence, who has not seen the evil deed* . . .'[82] I saw in *Midrash Kohelet*, 'These are the 974 generations that rushed forward to be created and were not created.'[83]"[84] According to this, [the question] may be answered. For they rushed forward to be created but were not created. Nevertheless, in my mind it is very perplexing that [the verse] would say that the 974 generations are better than the living and the dead. Did our rabbis, of blessed memory, not say in tractate *Hagigah*,

> From where does the river Dinur emerge? From the sweat of the [holy] animals. To where does it flow? Rav Zutra bar Tuvyah said in the name of Rav, onto the heads of the wicked in Gehinnom.

> As it is written, "*Behold, the storm of YHVH goes forth in fury, a whirling storm, it whirls down on the heads of the wicked.*"[85] And Rabbi Aha bar Jacob said, onto those who rushed forward [to be created]. As it is written, "*They were shriveled up before their time and their foundation poured out like a river.*"[86] It is taught, Rabbi Simeon the Pious said, these are the 974 generations that rushed forward[87] to be created before the world was created and were not created. The Holy One, blessed be He, went and planted them in each and every generation, and they are the brazen ones of each generation.[88]

Here is another problem. How could they say that they rushed forward to be created and were not created, when in fact they were created in each and every generation? There is a further problem regarding the opinion of those who said that it is better not to have been born than to be born. They are, in a manner of speaking, pretending to be wiser than the Holy One, blessed be He. For if the Holy One, blessed be He, created a person, it is self-evident that it is good that he was created. And so the verse testifies, concerning all of creation, that it is "*very good.*"[89]

Now I will explain the matter. Know that the Holy One, blessed be He, created the world for the ultimate purpose of the human being. God made man upright in order to be entirely good and light. In this sense, if Adam had not aroused evil and had been completely good, everyone would agree that it was good for him to have been created. The disagreement concerning whether it would have been better for him not to have been created or to have been created, arises after Adam misused his free will and the intention of creation was annulled.

I will advance another principle concerning the damage caused by Adam. The world has not yet realized the intention of creation, as long as the damage has not been rectified.[90] You have to know that when the human being will be rectified, the garments of skin that are now blindness and darkness and not light will become light again. And they will be more light than they were before he sinned. This is the meaning of "*light is superior to darkness.*"[91] For light has a superiority over the power of darkness. Our rabbis, of blessed memory, said, "Eve strained a bunch of grapes."[92] There is a great allusion in this. As long as they are grapes, one can speak of the residue, but it is mixed together. The [residue] is not discernible until a person squeezes the grapes and makes wine. Then the residue is distinguishable from the wine. The residue, which was previously in a state of potential rather than actual existence, now emerges. In this there is a diminution in quality for the dregs. For at first they were indistinguishable and united [with the rest of the grapes]. Now they have become dregs and are bad. But the wine now undergoes the greatest increase in quality, for it becomes clear, without any sediment. It is entirely clean, so that the wine remains *meshumar*,[93] that is, rid of residue (*shemarim*), as if [it had been dispersed] by a guard (*mishmeret*). It is purer and clearer than it was before the straining. Similarly, in the case of man, when he was in garments of light and entirely good, he still contained a potential arousal of the *qelippah* in concealment. But now, in causing it to emerge [from concealment], it truly becomes an evil *qelippah*. It is Satan, the evil urge. But when someone overcomes, subdues, and annuls it completely, it swiftly departs. [Then] the good of the soul is a clear and pure goodness without any residue.

This is the "whole person" who conquers his evil urge and overcomes it.[94] It is said, "who conquers [it]" and not "who kills [it]." This indicates that he does not kill it but holds it in submission, so that it will be good, the opposite of what it was. This is a great matter. For he overcomes [his evil urge] and purifies it, until an evil angel is transformed to good.

Take, for example, evil attributes, such as jealousy, lust, and hate, and so on. He does not eliminate them but gains control over them, in order to purify them. That is, jealousy is transformed to the rivalry of scholars, lust becomes concealed passion [for God], and hate becomes the hatred of the wicked, as David wrote, "*I hate them with perfect hatred*."[95] There are a thousand matters like these.

This is the meaning of "*very good*."[96] As the rabbis explained, " '*Good*' refers to the good urge, '*very*' refers to the evil urge." For then evil is the cause of great good. For evil is not merely eliminated but transformed to good. This will occur in the future, after the purification through destructions and sorrows that will be endured. Repentance will be aroused and the *qelippot* will rest. In the future, the angel of death will be destroyed and evil will be sweetened through the merit of the righteous who subdued their evil urge, as explained above, and brought it over to the service of the Holy. Then the garments of *'or* (skin), spelled with an *ayin*, which represents blindness (*'iver*), will be transformed into a seeing *ayin* (eye). For [with the addition of] the power of the blind eye, sight will be increased and there will be a superiority to light over darkness, [because of the addition] of the power of darkness. This, however, will not merely restore the world to the intention of creation, so that there will be garments of light, but there will even be an addition of light, according to the secret of the verse, "*For an eye with an eye will behold YHVH's return to Zion*."[97] For the evil eye, which is the garments of skin, will be restored to a good eye, seeing good. There will be such a great light that was not attained by the prophets. As it is written, "*No eye has seen* [*it*], *O God, but You.*"[98] Our rabbis, of blessed memory, said, "This is wine preserved in its grapes from the six days of creation."[99] This refers to the "preserved wine" that I mentioned, from which the residue has been removed. Then, in the future, the garments of light will be of greater light, for that goodness will not contain any residue mixed in, not even in concealment.

The reference to the six days of creation also alludes to a wondrous matter. Our rabbis, of blessed memory, said, "Until the time of redemption, neither the Name of God nor the Throne is complete. For the letters *vav* and *heh* are missing. As it is written, '*for hand upon the throne (kes) of Yah.*' "[100] And the *'alef* is missing from *kise'* (throne). The meaning is that [the *qelippot* have no contact] with the root of the emanated structure, that is, the six extremities within *Binah*, and certainly not with *Binah* and above, which is included in the letters *yod heh*,[101] as is known. This wine is untouched by idol worshippers, for there is no basis there for the root of the princes of the nations, except from *Binah* and below, which is contained in the letters *vav heh*. This is *Tif'eret* and the six extremities along with *Malkhut*. As was explained at length above, [among these seven *sefirot*], there is a basis for the princes above. In other words, Ishmael emerged from the side of *Ḥesed*, for which Abraham was a chariot. And Esau emerged from *Gevurah*, for which Isaac was a chariot. Thus there are seventy princes. Thirty-five go to the right and thirty-five go to the left. Everything related to the *qelippot* in this world is drawn from them. It is drawn from the basis of their root in the structure of the six extremities, which are the secret of the six days of creation, as is known and as I explained at length above. However, *Binah*, which is "the great Shabbat," is the secret of the World to Come, which is completely Shabbat. There, in the root of the structure, the idol worshippers have no contact. For they have no basis there. It is only prepared for Israel, who is called "Adam (human being)" because of the secret of his soul, which originates in the *d"u parzufim* in *Binah*, as I explained at length above. In the future, all of the souls will be renewed and they will ascend very high.

This is the secret of the verse, "*Ve-Ha-naḥash (and the snake) was crafty.*"[102] The secret is "*vav heh naḥash.*" The snake found a basis for his root in the secret of this world, [represented by the letters] *vav heh*. He caused a separation of the letters *vav* and *heh* in the coupling of *vav* and *heh*, that is, *Tif'eret* and *Malkhut*. The snake's intention was to cause a separation between Adam and Eve below, so that Adam would die and [the snake] could marry Eve. And it caused a separation between [the *sefirot*] cleaving above.

In the future the garments of light will be restored. For the snake and his soldiers will be annulled and the wine, which alludes to supernal bestowal, which is "wine that rejoices," will be "preserved wine." And it [is preserved] from the six days of creation. In other words, it is above the place of the six days of creation, that is, in their root above in *Binah*. Thus "wine that is preserved" means that no gentile comes in contact with it. The divine bestowal extends so that the Name of God will be complete. "On that day, *YHVH* will be One and His Name One."

The secret of the Throne is the human being who will be a chariot for the *Shekhinah*, bearing the *Shekhinah*. For the human being [is created] in the supernal image and likeness. Thus he will be a Throne. And the *'alef*, which was lacking because "*a grumbler alienates his friend ('alufo)*,"[103] will return. Then the Throne will be complete. All of it will return to *'alef*, light. It will be light in essence, lacking any residue of darkness, entirely clear light.

We shall now return to an explanation of the passage [from *Eruvin*], in *Sefer 'Avodat ha-Qodesh*, in which the following is written.

> "They said that it is better for a person not to have been born," because, due to his matter and the Satan that stands at his right side, he is prepared to incline toward the opposite of what was meant for him and is good for him.[104]

It is also written there:

> He should not have been created to increase sin and guilt. It is not enough that he will not complete the union that he was created to unite, but he will cut off and separate what was joined. This is the opposite of what was intended in creating him. And there are those who say that it is better for him to have been created. For if [God] created an evil urge and matter that would cause him to turn aside from the way, He created a Torah and remedy for him. And it will advise him to preserve his creation and not to become ill. It will guide him along the straight way, to find desirable things in order to complete the purpose that was intended for him, which is the uniting and completion of the Glory. "They took a poll and concluded that it would have been better for him not to have been created." Because the possibility of his deviating from the way is very likely, due to his matter and the evil urge. "And now that he has been born, he should investigate what he has done" and check

> himself for transgressions that he has already committed and extirpate them. In other words, he should confess and turn in repentance. Thus he will be rectified and the Torah and commandments will restore him to health which has left him, so that he became ill. "And some say, he should examine what he is doing." He should look at his ways and not let his mind wander at all. He should be careful in his actions and remember and take to heart the intention for which he was created, namely, the uniting and service, and he should complete it. For this reason, they said, "a person is obligated to examine his *tefillin* at every hour."[105] The reason that he should not let his mind wander from them at all is so that he will take to heart that he is a Throne of Glory and dwelling place for the *Shekhinah*. He will sanctify his deeds and purify his thoughts. Thus they said, "He should examine what he is doing." Through examining what he is doing, he will justify [their saying] that "it is better for him to have been created."[106]

However, I say that there is a further allusion in "he should investigate [what he has done]" and "he should examine [what he is doing]." For it alludes to what we have explained. It is not enough that a person eliminate evil, but he should conquer it, holding it under his control, and thus purify it. "And he should investigate" means that he should turn from evil and "he should examine" means he should hold it [under his control]. For the righteous person should take hold of the way of the evil urge in order to purify it, as has been explained. For then he becomes a greater light than the garments of light that existed before he sinned. Because of this [superiority of light], at first, the position of those who said that it is better for a person to have been created was expressed. And the position of those who said, "They took a poll and concluded that it would have been better for a person not to have been born," is [in accordance with the saying of Rabbi Simeon bar Yohai], that "I saw the sons of heaven and they are few."[107] And the sinners who do not overcome their evil urge and follow its ways are great in number.

Yet, the intention of the Holy One, blessed be He, was to create the world for the sake of man, since God created him upright, [with] garments of light. Then the entire world would be entirely light. Even though He created the power of transposition in [man] as well, nevertheless, this was [an expression of] the Creator's wisdom. For there are two ways to goodness. In other words, if he will remain "garments of light," everything will be filled with light. And if he becomes "garments of skin," nevertheless, the select and refined, even though they are few in number, will have additional light. For there will also be a sect of righteous ones (*ẓaddiqim*) that will strengthen the light from the darkness.[108] But the intention of "they were polled and concluded that it would have been better for him not to have been born," is as follows. If this aspect of garments of light did not exist from the beginning and there was no other way to create him except [as a creature] knowing good and evil, then he should not be created. But those who said that it is better for man to have been created were holding that even if this were the only way to create him, God would create man, because "[*the paths of YHVH are smooth*] *the righteous will walk on them*,"[109] and what do we care about the sinners?

The verse, "*and better than both of them is he who has not yet been created*,"[110] may be well explained on the basis of both of these views. At first, a verse speaks about the present time, when we are all "*garments of skin*." It says, "*For I praise the dead who have already departed more than those who are still alive*,"[111] [referring to] the life of vanity. "*For precious in the eyes of YHVH is the death of his pious ones*,"[112] since " '*very good*' refers to [the angel of] death," as I explained above. However, there are holy souls who are concealed above and who are ready to be created, but have not yet been created. That is, they are ready for the Messianic Age when the world will be restored to garments of light and [there will be] a great light. Thus they are superior to the living and the dead that have departed, because their lives will be eternal and spiritual. In this, everyone agrees that they are more fortunate than all that has passed, including even the garments of light, for this [future] light will be free of residue, as has been explained. The disagreement concerns only the beginning of creation. If there had been no other way to create [man], should God have created him or not? Study this well.

The future light will be free of residue, because the *qelippah* will return [to holiness]. This matter shall be explained along with an explanation of the passage in *Midrash Qohelet* that explains the verse concerning 974 generations. Rashi explained, in [his commentary on] *Hagigah*,

> It was decreed that 974 generations would be created before the giving of the Torah, in order to fulfill the verse, "*He commanded a word for a thousand generations*."[113] "The Torah should have been given at the end of a thousand generations. But when He saw that the world could not exist without the Torah, He stood and banished them and gave the Torah at the end of twenty-six generations, from Adam until Moses."[114]

I found written in a kabbalistic work:

> "*He commanded a word for a thousand generations.*"[115] The supernal Adam extended for a thousand generations. For he is the secret of the ten [divine] utterances and each utterance contains all ten. Thus the total is a hundred. Then each one contained all of them, for a total of a thousand (*'elef*) (and *'elef* returns to *'alef*, as is known). Also the wicked man (*adam beliya'al*) (who is like a monkey compared to man) [extended for a thousand generations]. "*For God also made this one opposite that one.*"[116] Now as soon as that muddy spring was opened into existence, Cain, the artist (*qeynay*) of impurity, was worthy of being extended in this world for a thousand generations. And the extension of the Tree of Life would be concealed all of that time. However, God's compassion increased after the reincarnation of Adam in the Patriarchs. So the Tree of Life only remained concealed for twenty-six generations. And 974 generations preceded the world, just as the *qelippah* precedes the fruit. They were later planted in every generation. It is self-evident to every wise person that the intention of the Holy One, blessed be He, was to annul the *qelippah* and to extirpate the 974 generations that He planted in every generation, [that is,] the brazen ones.[117]

This planting was not a creation that was meant to exist [permanently]. It was placed in the brazen, who will perish. Gehennom hovers over their heads, so that their existence will be blotted out and annulled. Both the 974 generations and the brazen will perish. As a result, there will be garments of great light in the future, which will be increasingly revealed as the time draws near, because God has annulled the existence of the 974 generations of the *qelippot*.

And in *Midrash Qohelet*, the verse is also explained as I did. "And thus it said, '*and better than both of them*'[118] will be the new creations"[119] whose holiness is drawn from the annulling of the *qelippot*, which was a great cause of this. These are the 974 generations who were to be created and were not created. He uprooted them in every generation, by means of the brazen who will all perish. Then the deeds of the righteous who conquer their evil urge will also draw this near and the world will be restored to light, speedily in our days, and the light will be greater [than at first].

Then, "*YHVH will rejoice in His deeds.*"[120] For then the intention of creation will be complete. Man will be in garments of light. Knowledge [of

God] will increase and their work will be done by itself. "*And the trees of the field will yield their fruit.*"[121] Even barren trees will be full of fruit. And [the verse] says "*trees of the field*" because the taste of the tree will be like the taste of the fruit, as was the case in the beginning of creation. There are many examples like this. For our rabbis, of blessed memory, said, "In the future the Land of Israel will bring forth cakes and garments of fine wool."[122] And all of the good promises, stated in *be-ḥuqqotay*, that have not been fulfilled, will be fulfilled.[123] "*For the earth will be full of knowledge.*"[124] Immediately, those good promises will be drawn through the nature of the matter. For the blessings and curses in the Torah are not at all the result of promises. Rather, the Torah tells a story in which, through our observing the Torah and the commandments, this goodness will necessarily have to result. For it is the nature of divine service that all of the benefits and successes will result from [fulfilling] the commandments, through the divine nature that has been embedded in them. This has already been explained at length above.

In explaining this matter, *'Avodat ha-Qodesh*, *ḥeleq ha-'avodah*, contains a response to a prior problem, which I discussed at length above. Why are the material promises mentioned in the Torah, while the spiritual promises are not mentioned? Either both should be mentioned or neither should be mentioned. But the [*'Avodat ha-Qodesh*] responded that the material promises are also not mentioned. For [the language in the Torah] is not meant to promise at all, but to reveal and tell what necessarily must result from the nature of divine worship, and that all of the benefits and successes are caused by the commandments through the divine nature that is embedded in them. This goodness does not come merely because it was promised. For something which results from something else, whose nature it is to produce it, is dependent on that cause. Thus there is no basis or need to promise it, but only to reveal it through a declaration or account that one thing necessarily must result from the other by nature. This is the case regarding the Torah and commandments, which are the essential key for the source of all of the benefits. For the latter depend on them and must necessarily follow from that opening which is the fulfilling [of the commandments]. One should not object that the [basis for] producing spiritual benefits should also be made known by way of declaration and account. For this follows, *qal va-ḥomer*, if even the material benefits are the result of acts of divine service.

What is the cause of this *devequt* and acts of divine worship? It is due to the *devequt* of the pure soul. It benefits the body as a result of cleaving to its source and good deeds, and its divine service of God, which is the uniting [of the *sefirot*]. Since these benefits are the necessary result of keeping the

Torah and commandments, and [such divine service] is caused by the soul, they will certainly be of benefit for remaining constantly [in *devequt*] with the Pleasantness, in that place to which the soul was turned while it was still joined to the body. For immortality and that delight are also dependent on the Torah and its commandments by nature. It follows, *qal va-ḥomer*. If the Bestower had explicitly promised spiritual recompense, it would have been completely redundant and superfluous, since we derive it, *qal va-ḥomer* from the material promises, which necessarily must follow from [fulfilling] the commandments by nature. All of the above is the position of the *'Avodat ha-Qodesh* in resolving this problem. The Hasid Rabbi Joseph Yaabetz wrote in a similar fashion in his work *Yesod ha-'Emunah*. I revealed my own view in the exploration above. "Words of Torah are '*like a hammer that shatters a rock*.'[125]"[126] "Both these and those are words of the Living God." In particular, a sage who understands independently will recognize that his words and mine approach one root. The enlightened will understand.

These benefits, mentioned in section *ḥuqqotay*,[127] which will not be fulfilled until the future, [may it be] speedily in our days, are arranged in an ascending order, according to the increase of the benefits. It begins with plenty, followed by peace, followed by the greatest of all promises, "*I will place My Tabernacle in your midst*."[128] This is the secret of the *Shekhinah* in the lower world, as the Holy One, blessed be He, desired at the beginning of creation, "*and a man does not remain in honor*."[129] But in the future, he will be eternal and the [scriptural promise], "*and live forever*,"[130] will be fulfilled. For *devequt* will be with the Tree of Life and [the verse], "*and I will walk in your midst and be a God for you*,"[131] will be fulfilled. For we will be the chariot in essence, above the level of the angels, "*and now it will be told to Jacob and Israel, what God has planned*."[132] For there will be perfection in body and soul, which is Jacob and Israel.

A great argument has already arisen concerning whether the ultimate eternal perfection will involve only the soul or the body and the soul. Maimonides and his party hold that it is only for the soul. But the kabbalists follow Nahmanides's view that eternity is for the body and the soul. For just as it was during the [period of] divine service, so it shall be at [the time of] receiving the reward. Divine service involved the body and the soul in this world and so the reception of the reward will involve body and soul. Thus there will be a great resurrection of the dead, so that they will exist eternally in body and soul. In the words of our rabbis, of blessed memory, this is called the World to Come, a world that only contains life, a world that is totally good. Concerning it, is written, "[*You shall keep My laws and My rules*] *by pursuit of which a person shall live*,"[133] which Onkelos translated,

"You shall live through them eternal life." This World to Come is [the same] as this world. In other words, it involves eternal life in body and soul and a person's eternal and unceasing ascension by degrees. These matters are discussed in detail by various authors, and especially in *Sefer 'Avodat ha-Qodesh*. For the sake of brevity, I will transcribe [only] some of their words.

> Here is what Maimonides wrote in chapter eight of *Hilkhot Teshuvah*. "The World to Come contains no bodies, but only the souls of the righteous, without bodies, like the ministering angels. Since there is no body in it, there is neither eating or drinking in it, nor any of the things that human bodies require in this world. And nothing occurs there that applies to bodies in this world, for example, sitting and standing, sleep and death, sadness and mirth, etc. So the early sages said, 'The world to come has neither eating, nor drinking, nor sex in it, but the righteous sit with their crowns on their heads and enjoy the splendor of the *Shekhinah*.'[134] Thus it has been made clear that there is no body there, since there is neither eating nor drinking. As for the expression 'the righteous sit,' this is a metaphor. In other words, the souls of the righteous exist there without labor and toil. The same holds for their saying, 'Their crowns are on their heads.' [The crowns alluded to] knowledge. The knowledge that they acquired is present with them; because of it they merited the life of the world to come. It is their crown, as was mentioned in regard to Solomon, '*in the crown with which his mother crowned him*.'[135] Indeed the verse says, '*and eternal joy on their head*.'[136] Joy is not a body that will rest on a head. Such is the crown that the sages mentioned here; it is knowledge. And what is the meaning of their saying, 'and enjoy the splendor of the *Shekhinah*'? They know and grasp the truth of the Holy One, blessed be He, which they did not know when they were with a dark and lowly body."[137]
>
> Although he would believe that the main part of this reward is for the soul alone, there is still another reward for the body in this world in the Messianic Age. This is the resurrection of the dead, when the completely righteous will live. There are a number of reasons for Maimonides's view [concerning the resurrection of the dead]: It may be so that the miracles and faithfulness of the Holy One, blessed be He, will be made known in the world. Or, it may be so that [the righteous] will then obtain some of the corpo-

real pleasure, in proportion to the days they were afflicted, or more, according to what the supernal wisdom will decree. Or it may be so that they can attain more of the perfection than they attained at first, when they were not able to attain, during their lives, the level that they deserved, according to the uprightness of their heart, because of the afflictions and yoke of exile. Nevertheless, according to what he wrote in his Commentary to the *Mishnah*, *pereq ḥeleq*, and in his "Epistle on the Resurrection of the Dead," Maimonides's view is as follows. They will die after having lived and will return to their dust. Then these souls will merit a greater level in the World to Come than they had attained before the resurrection, according to the truth of the Holy One, blessed be He, that they attain during their second life. According to [Maimonides's] view, [the sages] also said concerning this, "The World to Come has neither eating nor drinking. . . . " For there is no body there. If there were a body there, the limbs would be wasted, since there would be no corporeal activities, such as eating, drinking, and sex, to make use of them. In the "Epistle on the Resurrection of the Dead," he said that one should not bring as evidence, the wonder of Moses and Elijah. [One might argue] that Moses and Elijah existed a long time without eating and drinking while they had bodies. So will be the wonder of the World to Come: there will be bodies that will exist, just as Moses and Elijah existed. [Maimonides] rejected this argument and explained that if, [in the cases of Moses and Elijah], the corporeal powers were annulled, this was only a temporary condition. This is not a case of "wasted limbs," since they used them before and after the wonder. But, in the case of the inhabitants of the World to Come, which lacks eating, drinking, and the other corporeal functions, it is written that God will create a new [earth].[138] That they will exist there in body and that their limbs would return empty is impossible. For it is not the way for the Wise Worker to activate His Hand in vain, God forbid. Thus every enlightened person should believe that the inhabitants of the world to come have no bodies, but only souls. This is the basis of Maimonides's view and what emerges from his words.

Rabbi Abraham ben David of Posquieres, of blessed memory, has already criticized him for this and wrote as follows:

> The man's words seem to me to come very close to saying that there is no resurrection of the dead for the body, but only for the souls. On my life, this was not the view of the sages of the Talmud. For they said, "In the future the righteous will stand in their garments. [This follows] *qal va-ḥomer*, from the case of wheat. [Just as wheat, which is buried naked, emerges in many garments, how much more so the righteous, who are buried in garments?]"[139] Thus they would command their sons, "Do not bury me in white garments or in black ones, [white,] lest I [do not merit the resurrection and will appear like a bridegroom among mourners; black, lest I] merit [the resurrection and will appear like a mourner among bridegrooms.]"[140] They also said "The righteous will not return to the dust, but will stand with their bodies,"[141] and "They stand with their defects and are healed."[142] All of these prove that they will stand alive with their bodies. However, it is possible that the Creator will make their bodies stronger and healthier, like the bodies of angels and Elijah, may he be remembered for good, and the crowns will be meant literally, and not metaphorically."[143,144]

Clearly, Maimonides holds that perfection is for the soul, whether now, in the death of the righteous, whose souls merit the Garden of Eden, or after the resurrection of the dead, which will take place so that they can acquire additional perfection and die and their souls will reach a greater level in eternity. The followers of Maimonides wished to find support for him from the liturgy of the Sabbath prayer, *Yoẓer*.

> Four different expressions are used [in reference to] receiving the reward. It seems that they are four kinds of reward, as we explained. For [the liturgy] says, "None compares to You and there is none besides You, there is nothing but You and who is like You." They immediately explained these four expressions as referring to the four separate times for the four kinds of reward. [The liturgy continues], "None compares to You, *YHVH*, in this world, there is none beside You, our King, for the life of the world to come." These are the two basic times for receiving the reward. Next is explained the select portion of the reward in this world that was mentioned at first. It says, "There is nothing beside You, our Redeemer, for the Messianic Age." Next comes the select portion of the reward in the World to Come, after death, which is the resurrection of the dead. And it mentioned the World to Come

after this world, because it comes immediately after death for everyone, before the Messianic Age and the resurrection of the dead. This agrees more with the view of Maimonides. For if it were in agreement with Nahmanides's view, it would have had to mention the Garden of Eden after this world, for it is the level that follows this world, and not the life of the World to Come which is the final level, according to Nahmanides. But since the Garden of Eden is not mentioned at all, it seems the term *World to Come* includes all of the levels that come to a person after death, and it mentioned the "life of the World to Come," which is the choicest of all of them.[145]

Nahmanides's position, in accord with the kabbalists, is that the world which now comes to a person after death is, in fact, the world of souls. For the body, which comes from a putrid drop of the contamination of the snake, is murky, and this World to Come, which now follows death, is called the "world of souls." However, the resurrection of the dead will involve the body and the soul. [During it], the body will be purified and will become completely light. After this, the resurrection will be eternal in body and soul. In order to strengthen Nahmanides's words and to contradict the evidence of Maimonides, I will transcribe from *'Avodat ha-Qodesh*, chapter forty-two of *Ḥeleq ha-'avodah*.

> The Mishnah teaches us that "all of Israel has a portion in the World to Come, as it is written, '*All of your people are righteous, they will inherit the land forever, they are the shoot that I planted, My handiwork in which I glory.*'[146]"[147] The World to Come that they mentioned here is the one that comes after the resurrection of the dead and is not the one that comes to a person immediately after his death. The proof of this is the verse that they brought, "*They will inherit the land forever.*" In other words, "*forever*," without any end, for there is no measure to the length of days and the goodness in that world. In the first chapter of *Kiddushin* and in chapter *Shiluaḥ ha-Qen*, is written, "It is taught, Rabbi Jacob says, there is no commandment written in the Torah, whose reward is mentioned along with it, that does not involve the resurrection of the dead. Concerning honoring a father and a mother, it is written, '*so that you will lengthen your days and so that it will be well for you.*'[148] Concerning [the commandment] to drive away the mother bird from the nest, it is written, '*so that it will be well for you and*

you will lengthen days.'[149] His father said to him, go up to the Temple mount and bring me young birds. He went up to the Temple mount and drove away the mother and took the children. While returning he fell and died. Where is the goodness of this person's days? Where is his length of days? But, '*so that it will be well for you*' [means] in the world that is entirely good and '*so that you will lengthen your days*' [means] in the world whose days have no end."[150] If this is said about the World to Come, then immediately after death it is not [immeasurably] good and long. For there is a further end and measure to its length and goodness. In the future, one must arise and return in the resurrection of the dead. But, that world is not considered long and since there is an end to it, it is not absolutely good. It still remains to ask, where is the length and betterment of that person's days? Therefore, it is certain that [the verse] can only refer to the World to Come which is after the resurrection of the dead. For it has no end and there is no measure to its length and goodness. This [explanation] is required from the context which says "that does not involve the resurrection of the dead." And they said, "in the world whose days have no end" and "in the world that is completely good" to indicate that this world comes after the resurrection of the dead and is dependent on it, because it comes after it. It is the final stage of bestowing the reward of the commandments for the body and soul together. They said in the *Midrash*, "The bestowal of the reward for the commandments is only in the World to Come, as it is written, '*and she will laugh on the last day.*'[151]"[152] The world that comes to a person immediately after death is not worthy of being called "the last day." For it is followed by the World to Come that is after the resurrection.

According to the view of Maimonides and his followers, those who are resurrected will die. They concede that the world that immediately follows their death is worthy of being called by the name "*last day*" and not the one that immediately comes to a person after his death in this world. Therefore, the verse, "*They shall inherit the land forever,*"[153] means, without end, they will inherit the land of life, which is the World to Come. In it they will merit the reward of the Torah and commandments in body and soul. In saying, "*They are the shoot that I planted,*" the verse explained the reason that eternal existence will be given to the body and soul together in that world. It said that the reason why eternal existence is decreed for [the shoot] is because it is a shoot from the supernal planting, the secret of divine emanation, according to the secret of the verse, "*The trees of YHVH drank their fill, the cedars of Lebanon, which He planted.*"[154] The human being is made in its likeness and image, as has been explained in the first part of this work. The shoot will be fruitful and multiply and will exist in its root. From it, eternity will be drawn and will emanate upon it. Consequently, there is no basis for arguing that since the World to Come does not involve corporeal functions, and you are attributing eternal existence to [the body], therefore its limbs would serve no purpose, and God's actions are never without purpose. For these limbs are fashioned according to the pattern of the limbs of the chariot, the chariot of the One who rides in the primordial heavens, the secret of the divine emanation, as we have explained. Thus it is necessary that these limbs have an eternal existence, since they draw existence from their source and root. Their existence does not depend on eating and drinking, but on their cleaving to their root. They are essentially prepared for this, during this period when the evil urge is annulled, for it prevents the cleaving (*devequt*) that causes eternal existence. Since the lower likeness is like the supernal one, existence has to be ordained for it, so that it can testify to the [supernal likeness] and its unity. Its loss would imply a denial and limitation of the [divine] likeness, God forbid. To make note of this and to impress it upon the hearts of the believers, the upright said in chapter, *hayah qore'*: "Rav was in the habit of saying, this world is not like the World to Come. The World to Come lacks eating, drinking, sex, business, jealousy, hate, and competition. The righteous sit with their crowns on their heads and enjoy the splendor of the *Shekhinah*, as it is written, '*They saw God and ate and drank.*'[155]"[156]

I call to you people, look and see that the World to Come does not lack a body. How could Rav mislead us with idle words, saying that this world is not like [the World to Come]? The World to Come lacks eating, and so forth. Everyone knows that, according to Rav's view, all of these functions are corporeal, and if there is no body there, then [obviously] these functions would be annulled. Did he intend to tell us matters of no consequence? Why was he in the habit of saying this? However, if we accept that there is a body there, then the marvel that Rav intended to make us aware of is very great. Even though there is a body [in the

World to Come], no use is made of its functions [there], since its existence does not require eating and drinking, but only *devequt* with its root. Then the supernal light shines on it and sustains it, according to the secret of the verse, "*In the light of the king's countenance is life*."[157] Thus [Rav] said, "but the righteous sit," and this "sitting" is the existence that is decreed for them. "And their crowns are on their heads" refers to the crown of beauty that sustains them, which is joy, as it is written "*and eternal joy is over their head*."[158] For they become a dwelling place for it and a throne of glory, since the lower structure is like the supernal one, which is [the source of] its existence.

In chapter, *ha-mokher et ha-sefinah*, is written: "Rabbah said in the name of Rabbi Yohanan, in the future, the righteous will be called by the Name of the Holy One, blessed be He, as it is written, '*all who are called by My Name and for My Glory, I have created, formed, and even made*.'[159]"[160] The "*righteous one, foundation of the world*"[161] is called "*all*," according to the secret of the verse, "*for all that is in heaven and earth*."[162] It is [*Yesod*] that connects heaven with earth. Those who cleave to it are called "righteous," according to its name, for they connect and unite heaven with earth. And it is said that they are made in the likeness of the supernal Glory, for just as the supernal Glory contains Creation, Formation, and Making, so the righteous below contain all of these, in order to rectify the Glory below, as was thoroughly explained in the first part of this work, as well as in the second part. They are fashioned according to the pattern of the lights that are contained in the Name *YHVH*, as the kabbalists know, and as I have already explained. In the future, that Name will be revealed over them and will rest upon them to grant them eternal existence. Then they will truly be called by the Name *YHVH*, for their name will be *YHVH*. Since eternal existence is necessarily attributed to the Name *YHVH*, so it will be for the righteous. For they attest to [*YHVH*] and He is made known through them, as I wrote above.

It is also written there: "Rabbi Eleazar said, in the future 'holy' will be declared before the righteous in the same way that it is [now] declared before the Holy One, blessed be He, as it is written, '*And it shall be, that those who are left in Zion and who remain in Jerusalem will be called holy*.'[163]"[164] This refers to the existence that is decreed for them, as I have written, The ministering angels will declare before them, "holy," for they will exist through them.

This is also mentioned in chapter *Ḥeleq*: "It is taught, according to the School of Elijah, the righteous whom the Holy One, blessed be He, will restore to life, will not return to their dust, as it is written, '*And it shall be that those who are left in Zion . . . will be called holy.*'[165] Just as holiness exists forever, so they will exist forever. If you object that during those [thousand] years, the Holy One, blessed be He, will recreate His world, as it is written, '*YHVH alone will be exalted on that day.*'[166] So what are the righteous doing?[167] The Holy One, blessed be He, will make them wings like eagles, and they will fly over the face of the waters, as it is written, '*Therefore we will not be afraid, though the earth reels and mountains topple into the heart of the sea.*'[168] And lest you say that they suffer, scripture says, '*But they who trust in YHVH will renew their strength as eagles grow new plumes.*'[169]"[170]

Thus they explained that in the World to Come that follows the resurrection, the world will return to its original state. The righteous shall exist in body and soul and will never again return to dust. For they will enjoy the supernal splendor and that clear light sustains [them]. Thus they said, "And they enjoy the splendor of the *Shekhinah*, which is the true eating and food, upon which eternal existence depends." We have already seen that pure souls sustain their bodies with very subtle things. And the most pure and spiritual are nourished by even more subtle things than they. For the generation of the wilderness was sustained by manna, which was swallowed by the body (*'eyvarim*). It was a generation of the supernal light and splendor, which would descend and materialize for their needs, in order to elevate their souls. From the time that their souls were elevated through the [enlightenment] that they attained at the [Reed] sea, they merited [the manna]. And the lord of the prophets, who was more elevated than they and was united with the knowledge of his Creator, did not require a ray of the light, but was sustained by the light itself, which is the splendor of the *Shekhinah*. We also believe with perfect faith that the inhabitants of the World to Come will be sustained in eternal existence by that light. It is the presence (*qiyyum*) of the supernal will and [God's] spirit in them. That is their existence. Thus our teacher, Moses, of blessed memory, alluded to them, when he said, "*He subjected you to the hardship of hunger and then gave you manna to eat . . . in order to teach you that man does not live on bread alone, but that man may live on what issues from the mouth of YHVH.*"[171] The meaning is that the manna was not suited and intended for their nature and constitution, so that they would be sustained by it all of that long time. Rather, that food was decreed so that they would know that even if bread is suited to their nature and constitution, it is not [the bread itself], that is the source of [their] sustenance and existence, but rather the will of God, which cleaves to it and sustains it. To establish this faith in them, He gave them the manna as food, which "*issues from the mouth of YHVH,*" according to the secret of the verse, "*I hereby cause bread to rain down to you from heaven.*"[172] It became corporeal and they were nourished by it, as if they were nourished by "*what issues from the mouth of YHVH,*" and from His spirit, and were sustained by it. If they were nourished by the light itself, and not by the manna, which is a generation of it, their soul would merit an elevation to *devequt* with that light, until their bodies and souls would be sustained in eternal existence. The inhabitants of the World to Come will merit to live and be nourished by that light. They will acquire eternal [life] and will merit [such] existence in body and soul. Thus they said, "They will not return to their dust."[173] For then, the verse will be justified which says, "*My handiwork in which I glory,*"[174] because of the existence that is decreed for them. For it is the true glory, since His handiwork neither perishes nor is destroyed, for they are "*a shoot of My planting,*"[175] as I explained above. And our great rabbi[176] explained that the wings[177] refer to the clothing of the soul in works, and the body is clothed along with it. It will not be annulled in the cancelling of the elements. Thus it has been explained that when our rabbis, of blessed memory, stated that "All Israel has a portion in the World to Come," they were referring to the World to Come after the resurrection.[178]

As for the four times mentioned in the *Yoẓer* prayer of the Sabbath liturgy, which was brought as evidence, Maimonides wrote as I cited above. The author of *Sefer 'Avodat ha-Qodesh* answered this in *Ḥeleq ha-'Avodah*, chapter forty-one.

This *tiqqun* does not contradict Nahmanides's view, but is in accord with it and against the position of Maimonides. I have reasons for [maintaining] this. One of them is [based on the fact] that the World to Come is the ultimate hope of everyone who has hope in his worship and ability in his activities and study of Torah in this world. Thus the World to Come was placed after the resurrection in this world, since it is its ultimate end. Another reason is to allude that the [conditions for] receiving the reward will be just like [the conditions under which] the worship [was done]. Just as the worship was done in this world in body and soul, so the receiving of the reward will be with body and soul. This cannot be in the world of souls, but may occur in the World to Come, which is after the resurrection. Thus the [World to Come] was placed next to [this world], and there is no reason to mention the Garden of Eden here. Another reason is that the intention of those who perform *tiqqunim* is to include the times in which everyone will be able to see the wonders of the Holy One, blessed be He. The wonder will be great and well known among the inhabitants of the World to Come that is after the resurrection. For they will have eternal existence in body and soul. This was also the intention of this world, were it not for the sin [of Adam], and in the future, the crown will be restored to its former [glory]. Therefore the two worlds were placed together, to indicate that what was lacking in this world will be completed in that one.[179]

I must also explain a related matter. Although we said that when our righteous Messiah will come, the world will be restored to its proper condition (*tiqqun*) and will be eternal, there will be degrees [in attaining] this eternity. [These involve] elevation after elevation, according to the secret of "the world exists for six thousand years and for one thousand years is destroyed."[180] Our rabbis, of blessed memory, said in chapter *Ḥeleq*, "Just as during the sabbatical year, the land is left fallow, once in seven years, so the world is left fallow for one thousand years in seven thousand years."[181] It is also known how the kabbalists explained the secret of the sabbatical years, and the Jubilee is seven sabbatical years. Then the Jubilee is the secret of *Binah*. The *Zohar* alluded to this by saying "Fifty years of the Jubilee are fifty thousand generations that the Holy One, blessed be He, prepared for returning the spirit to Him."[182] Thus in each of the sabbatical years there is an addition of goodness, beyond what existed before it.

Our rabbis, of blessed memory, addressed this in chapter *'Eyn 'Omdim*:

> Rabbi Hiyya bar Abba said in the name of Rabbi Yohannon, all of the prophets only prophesied concerning the Messianic Age. As for the World to Come, "*No eye has seen it, but You, O God.*"[183] He diverged from the opinion of Samuel, who said, there is no difference between this world and the Messianic Age except sovereignty, as it is written, "*There will never cease to be needy ones in your land.*"[184,185]

Thus in the World to Come, which is the great resurrection of the dead that occurs during this year of the Jubilee, a person will be restored to his position with an additional degree of spirituality and eternity greater than in the Messianic Age. Nevertheless, both periods involve body and soul.

It seems that, according to the view of Samuel, nothing will be added during the days of King Messiah to the way that the world operates today. Maimonides inclined toward this view in chapter twelve of *Hilkhot Melakhim u-Milḥamotehem*. He wrote there as follows:

> Do not imagine that during the Messianic Age, any aspect of the conduct of the world will be annulled or that there will be any innovation in the Work of Creation. On the contrary, the world continues after its custom.[186]

However, I say, in fear and trembling, that it is possible that Samuel intended [his position to refer only] to the end of these six thousand years. However, afterward, Samuel would concede to all that we have said. And it is possible, that even during the sixth thousandth year, Samuel would agree that all that we have said applies to those who are born from the coming of Messiah and afterward. They will merit new souls. He only spoke in regard to those souls who are born from the polluted drop, before the coming of Messiah. They will be subject to death. Afterward, they will [return to] life in the great resurrection of the dead. However, death will never again prevail over those who are born in holiness. This [applies to] the dead who will live at the time of the coming of Messiah. Their bodies, which are murky from the pollution [of the snake], will perish, and they will remain alive and existing. As for the statements of Samuel and Rabbi Hiyya bar Abba, they addressed different matters and there is no disagreement.

Even though [the *Gemara*] says "and he diverged from the opinion of Samuel," "diverged (*pleyg'a*)" means division, for each is speaking about a different matter.

The author of the *'Avodat ha-Qodesh* explained Samuel's words in connection with another matter. Here is what he wrote in chapter thirty-eight of *Ḥeleq ha-'Avodah*:

> It is possible to establish what has been said. For Samuel meant that the Holy One, blessed be He, will not initiate anything beyond nature. Things will be according to their nature and root, as they were when they were created and first came into existence. It is known that in the beginning of creation, the nature of the world was already for the benefit of Adam and his enjoyment of the perfection and inner good that was possible for him. It was also intended for him to live an eternal life, as I have already written. But because of his sin, the nature of the world was changed toward him and all that came after him. Adam's end was death, as the verse attests, "*and now lest he reach out his hand and take also from the Tree of Life and eat and live forever.*"[187]
>
> Our rabbis, of blessed memory, said in chapter *'eyn dorshin*, "Since he stank, the Holy One, blessed be He, placed His hand on him and reduced him."[188] From all of this, it seems that all of the perfection that was possible for Adam was in his power, had [God] not reduced him because of his sin and punished him, as is apparent from Adam and his wife's punishment. And the earth was also punished, as it is written, "*Cursed is the earth because of you, by toil you shall eat all the days of your life, it shall sprout thorns and thistles for you.*"[189] Thus [the earth] was also punished so that it would not continue to yield its power, according to its nature at the beginning of creation. Thus may be established the writings that attest that in the future the features (*ma'alot*) and benefits will return to the nature and perfection that they had in the beginning of creation, [before] they were reduced because of the sin. Thus the verse was precise in saying, "*the vine shall produce its fruit . . .*"[190] In other words, the fruit that it was meant to yield, as it was in the beginning of creation. Similarly, [the verse continues], "*the ground shall produce its yield, and the skies shall provide their moisture*," which was withheld because of Adam's sin. Everything will be restored to its former condition, as I explained at the beginning of this chapter. The prophet alluded to the secret of the restoration of all things to their former condition and rectification, and to their emergence from diminution and the curse that resulted from the sin, and their return to fullness and perfection, as was intended

for them in creation. "*Shout, O heavens, for YHVH has acted.*"[191] This refers to the diminishing of the lights, which were afflicted and reduced because of the sin. For this reason, "*lights*" is spelled defectively,[192] because of their deficiency. [The verse continues], "*shout aloud, O depths of the earth.*"[193] This refers to the fruit of the earth and fruit of the tree, and the curse of the earth, which resulted from the sin. Thus [the verse] continued, "*shout for joy, O mountains, O forests with all of your trees.*" The [prophet] explained the reason for this in saying, "*for YHVH has redeemed Jacob and has glorified Himself through Israel.*"[194] For then, everything will return to its rectification and all of the deficiencies will be filled. This will occur when the sin that caused all of this will be wiped out. Thus [the prophet] began by saying, "*I wipe away your sins like a cloud . . .*"[195] "*Shout, O heavens . . .*" For the primordial sin caused the diminution and curse, both above and below. When they return to their former condition, as the supernal wisdom intended for them, that perfection to which they return is [the basis of] their exultation and rejoicing in the fulfillment of the intention of their creation. All that is written in the words of the prophets and [by] those who speak with the holy spirit, have this explanation as their meaning. There is no doubt that Samuel would agree that the world does not operate after the sin the way that it did before the sin. For the sin caused and death, disruption of the worlds and the loss of the orders of creation, and a change in the world's nature. Thus he must believe that the supernal intention of creation has not yet arrived and reached its completion. Nevertheless, it is necessary that it will arrive and be completed. Yet, this has not occurred until the present day, and it will not come until it will be revealed that judgment is His. Then the original sovereignty of the supernal will and desire will be restored to its former condition.

The resolution of the [apparent disagreement in] the passage [from *Berakhot*][196] is as follows. The opinion of Rabbi Yohanan is that the benefits and consolations that were prophesied by the prophets refer to things that will be introduced during the days of King Messiah, which did not exist at the time of creation or before Adam's sin. And the opinion of Samuel is that the matters that the prophets spoke of only refer to the restoration of the world to its original nature and custom, which applied at the beginning of creation and before the sin. But when Adam sinned, [the world's]

> nature was changed, and it will be restored to its former character in the days of King Messiah. For then the supernal intention will be completed.[197]

However, the way that I explained it above seems more correct. "They addressed different matters and there is no disagreement [between them]." For it may be that Samuel is referring to the sixth thousandth year and Rabbi Yohannon is referring to afterward. Thus a problem may be resolved which has always troubled me. In *parashat Shoftim*, it is written, "*And when YHVH your God enlarges your territory . . . then you shall add three more towns.*"[198] Rashi explained, "There are nine [cities of refuge], three are across the Jordan River, three are in the Land of Canaan, and three will be in the future." This is perplexing, for when this perfection arrives, it is certain that no evil will occur. For evil will perish from the world and there will only be absolute good. Evidence for this can be brought from *Midrash Tehillim*. "*Mizmor le-Todah.*"

> Rabbi Yohannon says in the name of Rabbi Menahem of Galatia, all of the prayers will be annulled in the future, but the [prayers of] thanksgiving will not be annulled. All of the offerings will be annulled in the future, but the Thanksgiving offering will not be annulled.[199]

Here is what [Ibn Gabbai] wrote in *Sefer Tola'at Ya'aqov*, in the secrets of *Shavuot*:

> You already know that sin causes the earth to be distanced [from its source]. Therefore, the offerings[200] are necessary to perfume the world and to open the source, so that *shefa'* will be bestowed, to draw the attributes near and to distance everything evil. In the future, when the evil urge will be annulled and sins will vanish from the earth, there will be no need for offerings, for the attribute of judgment will be elevated with compassion. "On that day, *YHVH* will be One and His Name One." But the Thanksgiving offering will not be annulled, for it does not serve any [theurgic] purpose, nor is it meant to arouse divine favor, but is an example for the attribute of judgment and compassion. However, it will be complete, because there will no longer be a Canaanite in the House of *YHVH Ẓeva'ot*. And "the Kingdom will be *YHVH*'s" and "*YHVH* will be king over all the earth." Those that delve

> deeply into the wisdom [of the Kabbalah] said that, consequently, the Thanksgiving offering will not be annulled. For it is necessary for the thanksgiving of the souls, when each one emerges from its exile, as is known. They are raised to *Tif'eret*, the place of the uniting and the place of thanksgiving, like the four who are required to give thanks upon reaching their home in peace. [They are] required to say, "*Let them praise YHVH for His mercy, His wondrous deeds are for mankind.*"[201] For they have arrived in peace at the world of souls, the tree from which they fly and the site of their lofty return.[202]

[Ibn Gabbai] wrote in a similar vein in *Sefer 'Avodat ha-Qodesh*, *Ḥeleq ha-'Avodah*, chapter forty-three:

> In the World to Come after the resurrection there is neither sin nor death. Thus there are no sin or guilt offerings or any other offering in the future, except the daily burnt offering and the additional [holy day] offerings, and the thanksgiving offering, which will never be annulled. For sin and guilt offerings come because of sin and in a time where there is no sin, they are superfluous. In *Midrash Shoher Tov*, is written:
>
> " '*Come to His gates in thanksgiving, to His courtyards in praise, give thanks to Him, bless His Name.*'[203] Rabbi Pinhas said in the name of Rabbi Levi, all of the offerings will be annulled, but the thanksgiving offering will never be annulled, as it is written, '*I will render thanksgiving offerings to You.*'[204] There are two. One is prayer and the other is the offering. And so scripture says, '*The voice of gladness, the voice of joy . . . the voice of those saying give thanks to YHVH. . . .*'[205] This refers to the prayers of thanksgiving. '*As they bring thanksgiving offerings to the House of YHVH.*'[206] Here we have the offering of thanksgiving."[207]
>
> The secret of the matter is that sin causes the distancing of the supernal land and cutting off and separation from the unity. Therefore, offerings are required to perfume the world and to open the source and spread its light, to draw near the distant and to keep away every evil and impure thing from the Temple. In the future, when the evil urge, which causes sin, will be eliminated and sins will perish from the earth, there will no longer be a need for the offering, for the attribute of judgment will be elevated with

compassion. "And *YHVH* will be King over all of the earth. On that day, *YHVH* will be One and His Name, One."[208,209]

I have another problem with the verse mentioned above, "*then you shall add another three towns . . .* "[210] Our rabbis, of blessed memory, explained, "[This refers to] '*the Kenites, the Kenizzites, the Kadmonites . . .* '[211] which is Ammon, Moab, and Edom. For the Holy One, blessed be He, promised Abraham ten nations and only seven were given. In the future, there will be another three."[212] There is a problem here: will there be a limit [to divine sovereignty] in the future? Is it not written, "*and let him rule from sea to sea*?"[213] Surely, Messiah will reign from one end of the world to the other. It does not make sense to say that all of the nations of the world are included in these three. Concerning this, it is possible to say that Messiah will rule from sea to sea. In other words, all of the nations will be subject to him and will pay him a tax. However, the ten nations[214] will be entirely his. However, it is also unlikely that any sovereignty and rule will remain among the nations. Therefore, it seems that all of the great successes will not take place immediately upon the coming of the redemption, but over the course of time, as knowledge [of God] will increase in Israel and they reach the level of "garments of light." Then the *qelippah* will be entirely annulled and the verse, "*and let him reign from sea to sea*," will be fulfilled. Then all of the offerings, except the thanksgiving offering, will be annulled and there will be no need for cities of refuge.

I found the following in the Palestinian Talmud, tractate *Ma'aser Sheniy*, concerning the *mishnah*,

> And it was made a condition that when the Temple will be rebuilt, the matter will return to its former quantity.[215]

"Rabbi Aha said that this means that the Temple will be rebuilt before the restoration of the sovereignty of the House of David. Thus is explained why they had to make it a condition that the rabbinic court should issue a decree, according to their will, when the Temple is rebuilt. They were concerned that the rabbinic court might not be greater than they in wisdom and number, and thus be able to annul their words."[216] There is a difficulty here. Can it be that the rabbinic court of Messiah will not be greater than they? Therefore, they had to say that the Temple will be rebuilt before the arrival of the son of David. And it may be that this will be in the time of Messiah, the son of Joseph.

Now we can say that those words and their like were said concerning the time prior to the coming of Messiah, the son of David, and blessed is the One who knows. As a result, we can resolve another great difficulty. Ezekiel's Temple is the Temple of the future. Yet, he mentions sin and guilt offerings. This is a problem, because of what is said in the *Midrash*, mentioned above. Will not all of the offerings, except the daily burnt offering, be annulled in the future? There is a further difficulty there. Ezekiel mentions that [the priest] will take on impurity for the death of his father or mother.[217] But, is it not written, "*Death will vanish forever*"?[218] Therefore, it seems best to explain that all of this refers to the time of Messiah, the son of Joseph, while the great promises are fulfilled in the time of Messiah, the son of David. And blessed is the One who knows.

A long time after I wrote the above, I found among the argumentation in the holy writings of Rabbi Isaac Luria, of blessed memory, that he was also moved to explain the three cities of refuge [that will be added] in the future. He wrote a solution, with God's help, which I shall transcribe.

> *And when YHVH your God enlarges your territory . . . then you shall add three more towns.*[219] It is a problem to say that three cities of refuge will be added to the former [six], after the arrival of our Messiah. For then, there should not be murderers, as it is written, "*Nation shall not raise a sword against nation.*"[220] However, know that all of Abel's seed were condemned to death. Thus Cain killed him. Indeed, Moses killed the Egyptian before his time, in order to elevate him by means of the Name of 72. Thus he sinned and was condemned to exile. This is the meaning of the verse, "*I set aside a place for you, that he may flee to there (SHaMaH).*"[221] The letters *SHaMaH* (to there) are the same as the letters of *MoSHeH*. Now Abel sinned with the thought of *'Imma'*, with the [letters] *'alef yod* from the Name *ADoNaY*, which is the secret of [the Name *'EHYeH*, according to the secret of [the verse], "*'EY (where is) Abel, your brother?*"[222] Therefore, he and all of his offspring were condemned to death. This is the secret of the verse, "*the voice of the bloods of your brother,*"[223] his blood and the blood of his offspring. Abel's *tiqqun* is through being killed; he ascends to the fifty gates of *Binah*. Thus the secret of the *qelippah* of Abel is Balaam, who was separated from Moses, as has been explained.[224] When he was killed, that holy spark within him had the merit to ascend to *Binah*. Accordingly, Abel and Nabal contain equivalent letters, except that the *heh* of Abel is exchanged for the *nun* of Nabal. This alludes to the fact that he began to be rectified, according to the

secret of *Binah*, with which he had sinned. This is the secret of the verse, "*Should Abner die the death of Nabal?*"[225] For Abner also derived from the secret of Abel, and he was killed in order to be elevated to *Binah*, like Nabal. This is sufficient for those who understand. The same is true for the rest of the [offspring] of Abel who were killed. Now [the *tiqqun* of Abel] is effected by the two [possible] ends [alluded to in the rabbinic commentary on Isaiah 60:22], "if [Israel] merits, '*I will hasten* [*the end*],' if they do not merit, '[*it will occur*] *in its time*].' "[226] If the end comes "*in its time*," then the *tiqqun* of all of Abel's offspring will be complete. However, if [Israel] merits and the time of the end is advanced, the *tiqqun* of Abel will not yet have been completed. Thus [the verse says], "*When YHVH your God enlarges your territory . . . if you faithfully observe all of this commandment . . .* "[227] In other words, if, as a result of your merit, [the time of the end] is advanced, "*then you shall add three more towns,*"[228] in order to complete the *tiqqun* of the offspring of Abel. However, they will not die as the result of deliberate acts, but only through inadvertent actions. For in that period, "*I will remove the spirit of impurity from the earth.*"[229] However, they will be killed as a result of an unavoidable accident. The killers will then be condemned to exile. Accordingly, there will be need for an additional three cities [of refuge], in order to complete [the *tiqqun*] of [Abel's] seed with great haste.[230]

The principle that emerges from all of our discussion is that once death is eliminated, there will be no dying, but all will live an eternal existence. The verse will be fulfilled which says, "*I will place My Tabernacle in your midst.*"[231] The *Shekhinah* will be among us, in body and soul, eternally. As long as people increase in age, their wisdom will increase. They shall progress from strength to strength, infinitely. The beginning[232] will involve complete abundance without effort, for their work will be done by itself. "The Land of Israel will bring forth cakes and garments of fine wool."[233] Afterward there will be peace in the land. "*I will give the land respite from evil beasts.*"[234] This refers to the secret of the *qelippah*. Its bitterness will be removed and it will be subdued as a guard to the fruit, as was explained above. "*I will make you fertile and multiply you*"[235] with an upright posture,[236] just as Adam had before he sinned. "*And I shall place My Tabernacle in your midst . . . and be present among you.*"[237] All of this, in itself, refers to the [period of] eternity. For as soon as these blessings occur, eternity begins.

The only objection to the mention of eternity [here] is in the view of Maimonides. He holds that this goodness comes to an end and that they will return and die after the resurrection of the dead. Then there will be eternity for the souls alone. Thus the question remains, Why did the Torah not mention this? However, the kabbalists agree that eternity involves both the body and soul and will not come to an end. Rather, it will constantly increase in quality, infinitely. Then everything comes out properly. Thus I realized through understanding the opinion of the author of *Sefer 'Avodat ha-Qodesh*, who discussed this in great detail in his book. Several aspects of his discussion were transcribed, in order to explain matters well. Also [it has been particularly helpful] for treating the problem of why [spiritual] goals are not [explicitly] mentioned in the Torah. For those [apparently material] goals are the spiritual goals. A person will live eternally in body and soul. There will no longer be death, but only eternal *devequt*. However, he shall ascend by degrees in this eternal *devequt*, until he reaches the level of being taken, like Enoch and Elijah, and even a level, one thousand times higher than theirs, which is without measure. I have already written that, even though I have offered my explanations with God's help, all of [the sages' explanations] are true. Everything returns to one place, for those who understand.

Thus the meaning of the "garments of light" has been explained. "*And man does not remain in honor.*"[238] [Accordingly,] they became "*garments of skin*" and in the future they will be restored as "garments of light." "*YHVH will rejoice in His deeds.*"[239] It does not say "rejoiced," because the world has yet to realize its [full] goodness. It says, "*will rejoice*," which refers to the future coming of our righteous Messiah. There is a [hidden] allusion to this in the fact that the letters *YiSMaḤ* (will rejoice) are the same as the letters *MaShiYaḤ* (Messiah). Then [the verse that says] "*light is increased by darkness*"[240] will be fulfilled. For through the removal of the contamination of the "*garments of skin*," light will be increased. Then the verse will be fulfilled that says, "*now it will be said to Jacob and to Israel, what God has planned.*"[241] They are the two aspects mentioned in the *Zohar* passage that we are concerned with, which says, "Jacob and Israel, one is concealed and one is revealed." Then the Holy One, blessed be He, the Torah, and Israel, which are mentioned in that *Zohar* passage, will be joined and cleave together in one strong bond.

As a result of our understanding of the meaning of the increase of light, the wording at the end of [the following] three blessings can be explained: "the One who forms the lights," "the One who gives the Torah," "the One that chooses His people Israel with love." All of these use the present tense, when the past should have been used: "formed the lights," "chose His people Israel." In tractate *Berakhot*, chapter *'Elu Devarim*,[242] there is a conclusion concerning whether [the blessing] "the One who creates lights of fire" means creates or created. All agree that the meaning is "created." This is proven from the verses, "*I form light and create darkness . . .* ,"[243] "*who formed the mountains and created the winds*,"[244] "*who created the heavens and stretched them out*."[245] Nevertheless, in every case where one word may have two senses, one must assume that there is some allusion involved. Otherwise, the sages would have chosen as proof a verse in which the verb is clearly in the past tense.

The House of *YHVH* [II]

Since I have learned the reason, I will tell you why we bless "the One who creates lights of fire" and not "the One who created," which would be clearer. The *Tosafot* wrote, [concerning the passage] in *Berakhot*, 52b: "[Even though everyone agrees that the meaning is 'who created [the fire, during the six days of creation],' the language of scripture takes precedence." However, I say that there is a secret in the matter. Now the passage says, "The School of Shammai and the School of Hillel disagreed as to whether [the blessing should say] 'light' or 'lights.' The School of Shammai held that there was one [shade of] light in the fire, and the School of Hillel believed that there were several [shades of] light in the fire."[1] Rashi explained, "There was a flame of red, white, and green." However, this is a problem. Did the School of Shammai not see that there are a number of shades in the fire's light? There is another great matter. "As to whether the meaning is 'who created [during the six days of creation]' or 'who [continues to] create,' there is no disagreement."[2] Nevertheless, we see that the blessing, according to the School of Shammai, was "who created the light of the fire" and, according to the School of Hillel, was "who creates lights of fire." However, both are words of the Living God.

It is known that the divine emanation is like a flame that is connected to a coal. This is all in accordance with the secret of complete unity. Even [the colors] white, red, and green, which [represent] the lines of mercy, judgment, and compassion, form a complete union, when they are in their place [in the world of emanation]. However, in the manifestation that results from actions performed in this world, which is an extension of [the world of] emanation, mercy, judgment, or compassion is activated below. Thus, in the [world of] emanation, the [blessing], "who created the light of fire," applies. For [there], everything is one united light that has already been created. I mean to say "emanated." The School of Shammai alluded to this aspect in saying, "who created the light of fire." However, the School of Hillel alluded to the actions which are initiated and extended from [the qualities in the world of emanation]. These are many and initiated at every moment. This is the meaning of "who creates lights of fire." The secret behind why the School of Shammai speaks of one aspect and the School of Hillel of the other has already been explained in the *Zohar*. Shammai was from the side of *Gevurah* and Hillel was from the side of *Ḥesed*. Therefore, Shammai always had to elevate his attribute, *Gevurah*, and to place it within its root and source. Thus it would be sweetened and not destroy the world. However, Hillel was from the side of *Ḥesed*, and through the manifestation of *Ḥesed* the world is built.

For the sake of completeness of the explanation of the "lights of fire," I will transcribe what the *Zohar* writes in sections *Bereishit* and *Terumah*:

> Come and see. "*For YHVH your God is a consuming fire*."[3] It has already been said among the fellowship that there is a fire that consumes fire. It eats and destroys it. For there is a fire that is stronger than fire. They have explained this.[4] But, come and see. Whoever wishes to know the wisdom of holy union should gaze at the flame that rises from the coal, or from a candle that is lit. For the flame only ascends when it is united to a coarse matter. Come and see. In an ascending flame, there are two shades of light. One is white and shines, and there is another, joined to it, which is black or blue. That white light is above, and shoots straight up. Below it is the blue or black light that is a throne for the white one. That white one rests upon it and they are joined together, so that all is one. The black, or blue-shaded one, which is below, is a throne of glory for the white one. Thus it reveals the secret of the blue [light]. But that blue-black throne is joined to something else below, so that it may be lit. That other matter arouses it to be joined with the white light. That blue-black light sometimes turns red. But the white light that is above it never changes, for it is always white. But that blue one changes color. Sometimes it is blue or black, and sometimes it is red. It is joined to two sides. It is joined above to the white light and it is joined below to the other matter that is prepared for it, so that it may shine and cleave to it. This [blue light] constantly consumes and destroys the matter, that

other matter that is prepared for it. For as long as it is joined to it below, and rests upon it, the blue light consumes and destroys it. For it is its way to destroy. The death and destruction of everything depends on it. Thus it consumes everything that cleaves to it below. But it never consumes or destroys that white light that rests upon it. Its light never changes. Thus Moses said, "*For YHVH your God is a consuming fire.*"[5] "*Consuming*" indeed. It consumes and destroys everything that rests below it. Thus it is written, "*YHVH your God,*" and not [merely], "*your God.*" For Moses was [connected to] that white light above, which does not destroy or consume. Come and see. There is no arousal to cause that blue light to shine and be joined with the white light, except through Israel. For they are joined to it from below. Come and see. Even though it is the way of that blue-black light to destroy everything that cleaves to it from below, Israel cleaves to it from below and continues to exist. As it is written, "*And you who cleave to YHVH your God are all alive today.*"[6] "*To YHVH your God,*" [is written], and not "our God." [In other words], to that blue-black light that consumes and destroys everything that cleaves to it from below. Yet, you cleave to it and exist, as it is written, "*you are all alive today.*" Above that white light rests a concealed light that encompasses it. There is a supernal secret here. It is all to be found in an ascending flame, which alludes to high wisdom. Rabbi Pinhas came and kissed [Rabbi Simeon bar Yohai]. Blessed is the compassionate One, that we happened upon you here. They walked with Rabbi Pinhas for three miles. Rabbi Simeon and the fellowship returned. Rabbi Simeon said, that which we spoke about is a secret of [high] wisdom, concerning the holy union. For the final letter *heh* of the Holy Name is the blue-black light that is joined with *YHVH*, which is the white light that shines.[7]

Thus the secret of the union is like the colors of a flame. The white flame is above. It never changes, nor does it burn [what is connected to it]. The same is true of the attribute of compassion. It is above and never changes or burns [what is below it]. It never exacts judgment. The white fire alludes to *Tif'eret* Israel and the black fire alludes to *Keneset* Israel. When Israel unites the Holy Name and cleaves to the *Shekhinah*, there is a complete union, *heh* with *heh*, with the *Shekhinah* of His power, just as the white and black of the flame form one blade [of fire]. This is the secret of "like a flame connected to a coal." When the flame is connected to the coal, the white and black lights are united in a single blade and single flame. Understand this. Were it not for the wick or coal, the flame would not appear and the white and black lights would not be united. Similarly, were it not for Israel, who are the wick, the *Shekhinah* would not cleave to the Holy One, blessed be He, and would not receive supernal *shefa'*. Thus the meaning of the "lights of fire" is explained.

We must also find [kabbalistic] allusions in the wording of the three blessings that were mentioned above. I found the following in a note to *Tefillat Haderat Qodesh*:

> I raised the objection that [the blessing] should conclude "who gave the Torah," just as the blessing began with "who chose us and gave us [His Torah]," which uses the past tense. However, it seems to me that the blessing concludes with "who gives the Torah," which is in the present tense, because *shefa'* constantly descends every day. This is alluded to in the verse, "*like the dew of Hermon that descends on the mountains of Zion. For there YHVH ordained the blessing, eternal life.*"[8] This is the secret of the four fathoms of the *halakhah* that the Holy One, blessed be He, has in His world.[9] The conclusion of the blessing for the Torah is like the conclusion for the lights: "For in His goodness, He renews each morning, every day, constantly, the Work of Creation." This also concludes the blessing, "who forms the lights." The end of the blessing, "who chooses His people Israel in love," is also in accord with this secret. For every day, He chooses among the elite remnant that *YHVH* calls.[10]

I will expand the discussion, to the extent that God enables me, and explain these three blessings, according to the matters that I have discussed at length above. The general principle is that "forms," "gives," and "chooses," [in the present tense], allude to the increase in holiness that flows from the source as a result of the arousal which increases power above.

The House of David [II]

The meaning of "who chooses Israel" is that He chooses [Israel to attain a higher level] than He chose for them [before]. I mean that if humankind had remained in "garments of light," as was chosen for them at the beginning of creation, they would not shine with so great a light as will be the case when the garments of skin are annulled and they are restored to light. Then, the verse may be applied, which says, "*No eye has seen, O God, but You*,"[1] as I explained at length above. For "*light is increased by darkness*."[2] As a result of the increasing [quality] of darkness in its generations and purifications, the clear light will be increased in the future. In this sense, [God] is constantly choosing Israel [to reach higher levels of spiritual development].

The House of Wisdom [III]

The meaning of [the blessing], "who gives the Torah," is as follows. In truth, God has already given the Torah. However, He continues to give it and will not cease [doing so]. This requires a broad explanation. The verse says, "*YHVH said these words to your entire community on the mountain, from the midst of the fire, the cloud, and the darkness,* [*in*] *a great voice, ve-lo' yasaf.*"[1] Rashi explained, "We translate '*ve-lo' yasaf,*' 'and it did not cease,' because His voice is strong and continues forever. Another possibility is that '*ve-lo' yasaf*' means that 'He did not add to' what appeared in that display."[2] There is a secret concealed here and both of the interpretations are entirely true. When "*lo' yasaf*" is understood as "He did not add to," it indicates that the commandments of the rabbis, with their stringencies and precautionary measures, were not yet commanded from the mouth of the Almighty. And the meaning of "it did not cease" is that [God's commandments] did not cease with what was explicitly stated by that voice, for [the rabbinic commandments] were contained in that voice, potentially. However, the proper time had not arrived for each to emerge from potential to actuality. For this requires the arousal below, depending on their being, quality, and the level of their souls, in each and every generation. Then the sages went on to arouse additional supernal power, and it was actualized in their time and knowledge. This is not to say, God forbid, that the sages introduced anything from their own minds. Rather, they focused on the supernal mind (*da'at 'elyon*) and their souls which had stood on Mount Sinai. For all of the souls received [the Torah] there. So, on the basis of their souls and [the merits of] their generation, it was fitting [for them to bring into actuality what was concealed in God's voice]. [Thus their commandments] are from the mouth of the Almighty. There is an allusion to this: *mi-de-rabbanon* (commandments of the rabbis) has the same numerical value as *mi-pi Gevurah* (from the mouth of the Almighty). In *Shemot Rabbah* and in *Midrash Yelamdenu*, is written:

> "*And God said all of these things, saying . . .*"[3] Rabbi Isaac said, what the prophets would prophesy in the future, in every generation, they received from Mount Sinai. For Moses said to Israel, "*but with those who are standing with us today [before YHVH our God] and those who are not here with us today.*"[4] "*Not standing with us today*" is not written, but "*not with us today.*" These are the souls that would be created in the future and are not yet actualized. Thus "standing" is not said concerning them. Although they were not [physically] present at that hour, each one received his own [portion]. Similarly, the verse says, "*a pronouncement: the word of YHVH to Israel in the possession of Malachi.*"[5] It does not say, "*in the days of Malachi,*" but "*in the possession of Malachi.*" For he already possessed the prophesy from Mount Sinai and until that hour, he had not been granted permission to prophesy. Similarly, Isaiah said, "*From the time anything existed, I was there.*"[6] Isaiah said that from the day that the Torah was given on Sinai, I was there and received this prophesy. But "*Now the Lord YHVH has sent me and His spirit.*"[7] Till now, permission had not been granted to me to prophesy. And not only the prophets received their prophesy from Sinai, but also the sages who exist in every generation. Each received [his portion in Torah] from Sinai. Thus the verse says, "*YHVH said these things to your entire community . . . in a great voice, ve-lo' yasaf.*"[8,9]

Thus they explained that everything that the sages introduced in all of the generations, they had received on Sinai from that voice. It was not according to their intellect and reasonings. Since this is true, He commanded us in His Torah, through His prophet, the faithful one of His House, "*Act according to the Torah that they will teach you and according to the statute that they will say to you. Do not turn aside to the left or the right from the word they will say to you.*"[10] Whoever will not hearken to them deserves death, since their voice is that great voice "that did not cease." The verse says, "*The person who will deliberately act without listening to the Priest . . . or to the judge, that person shall die.*"[11] In the Palestinian Talmud, *Peah*, they said, "Even what a faithful student will teach in the future before his teacher was said to Moses on Sinai."[12] Thus it has been explained that all of the words of the sages in every generation that they initiate and all of their argumentation (*pilpulam*) is from Sinai. It is not [the product of the] human intellect, but from the divine intellect. They have only brought it from potential to actuality.

Here is what is written [on the matter] in *Sefer 'Avodat ha-Qodesh, Ḥeleq ha-Takhlit*, chapter twenty:

> It has been explained that the source of external wisdom is the evil that is in the Tree of Knowledge. We have been far removed from that side and separated in order to be a people of [divine] inheritance. As it is written, "*I will separate you from the nations to be Mine.*"[13] From this, it will also be explained that it is forbidden for us to weigh any of the Torah's words in our minds and to be drawn after intellectual inquiry in order to investigate its secrets and reasons. The holy kabbalists explained this and enlightened us concerning it in the *Midrash* of Rabbi Simeon bar Yohai. They said there:
>
> " '*Do not make a graven image for yourself.*'[14] Rabbi Isaac opened with the verse, '*Do not let your mouth cause your flesh to sin.*'[15] How much reason is there for a person to be careful with the teachings of the Torah! How much reason is there for him to be careful not to go astray in them and not to derive from the Torah something that he did not know or receive! It is written, '*Do not make a graven image for yourself or any representation.*' The Holy One, blessed be He, will call him to account in the World to Come. At the time that his soul wishes to enter to its place, it is driven out. It is separated from that place in which the rest of the souls are bound up in the bundle of life. Rabbi Judah said, as we have learned, '*Why should God be angered by your voice?*'[16] This refers to a person's soul. Rabbi Hiyya said, it is written, '*For I YHVH your God am a jealous God.*'[17] What is the reason? Because He is jealous for His Name in everything. In the case of idolatrous forms (*parẓufin*), He is jealous for His Name because they lie in His Name. In the case of Torah, it is taught, the Torah is entirely the Holy Name.[18] For there is no word in the Torah that does not contain the Holy Name. Consequently, it is necessary to be careful, so as not to err with the Holy Name, and not to lie [in Its Name]. Whoever lies [in the Name of] the supernal King is not permitted to enter the King's palace, and he is separated from the World to Come?

"Rabbi Abba said, here it is written, '*Do not make a graven image for yourself, or any representation.*'[19] There it is written, '*Carve for yourself two tablets of stone.*'[20] In other words, '*Do not make a graven image*' [means] do not make for yourself another Torah that you did not know, which your teacher did not say to you. What is the reason? '*For I YHVH your God am a jealous God.*'[21] I am the One who will call you to account in the world to come, when the soul wishes to enter before Me. How many are they who will use it to lie and to cause it to enter Gehinnom?"[22]

The kabbalist, Rabbi Shem Tov ben Shem Tov, wrote concerning this as follows:

"Cast your eyes on the words of the most holy patriarchs of the world, who have seen the Countenance of the King. See how they compared the way of error and reasoning to the graven images and representations. The one reason for this is that the intention of the artists is to make those representations in order to receive from those powers and so that [the representations] will be turned toward them as a sign and memorial. There is no permission to make these representations, except according to the way in which Bezalel and Solomon made them. For they knew how to permute the letters with which heaven and earth were created. They made them according to the [Holy] Name. Thus these forms were sanctified and prepared and meant for the Glory of the God of Israel. And each of them [was constructed] in the proportions allotted to them, according to the vision that *YHVH* showed Moses, for the plan of the holy, concealed Chariot, the Chariot of the One who rides in the primordial heavens. But, if someone else would consider making the likeness of these forms, they would not be sanctified or prepared at all for the Glory [to rest upon it], just as a soul cannot rest on a representation crafted by an artist. The distance between them is like the distance between the Creator and something created. But, according to the concealed wisdom (*'eẓah*), it is prepared for the external power, which is called the power of impurity. For the *Shekhinah* is held captive, outside the camp. [The external powers] open and approach whoever intends to become impure and they fill him with the fruit of his deeds. Thus he goes astray with [the unsanctified image] and is uprooted from the world. For he exchanges the King for a slave and good for evil, and falsifies the Lord of all. And so it is with the letters of the Torah. Although they are material, they allude to

> divine Names and wisdom that emanates from the Lord of all. One must set up their form (*gufan*) and meaning in a way that conforms with what is concealed within them and alluded to by them. Thus matter is related to the form. But when another way is followed in regard to them, that form will not be prepared to rest upon the matter. Such a person's wisdom and Torah is without God and his wisdom is flawed and nullified."[23]

This is related to the saying, "The Holy One, blessed be He, says Torah from the mouth of all of the rabbis." Some use [this saying] to explain the meaning of our request [in the Sabbath prayer], "Grant us a portion in Your Torah." In other words, let our portion be in the Torah that the Holy One, blessed be He, teaches. May we merit that the teaching be said in our name. The meaning is that the sages say new things or [they emerge] from their argumentations. However, it is all from the power of the voice that was mentioned, and the time has arrived for them to bring it from potential into actuality through their meditation. Surely, "*our Lord is great and full of power, there is no limit to His understanding.*"[24] For this power did not cease [at Sinai]. It is limitless and infinite in regard to the innovation and source of souls in every generation, and in regard to the power of the people below who arouse the supernal power. Therefore, the Holy One, blessed be He, gave the Torah and He [continues to] give the Torah at every moment. The flowing source does not cease. What He [continues to] give was contained in the potential of what He gave [at Sinai].

I will further explain the matter in essence. We see that stringencies increase in every generation. In the days of our teacher Moses, of blessed memory, only what was clearly received at Sinai was forbidden. However, he added whatever decrees he saw as necessary. This was also the case for the prophets, *tannaim*, and sages of every period. The reason is that the more the pollution of the snake is manifest, the greater the need for fences [against transgression]. "*And whoever breaches a fence will be bitten by a snake.*"[25] The Holy One, blessed be He, commanded 365 prohibitions, so that the pollution of the snake would not be aroused. But, as the pollution of the generation becomes manifest, it is necessary to add more prohibitions. If this had been true at the time that the Torah was given, it would have been written in the Torah. However, [the additional prohibitions] are included in what the Torah forbade. For it is all the same principle. Therefore, God commanded, "*Make a guard for My guard.*"[26] In other words, all are related in principle. It necessarily follows that in every generation, whenever it is proper to add stringencies, everything follows from the Torah. Since the pollution of the snake becomes more manifest, [the prohibitions of the Torah] emerge from potential to actuality. "The Holy One, blessed be He, created the evil urge, and He created [the Torah] in order to season it."[27] For then we have need of a supernal arousal in order to draw the prohibitions from potential to actuality, until in the future we can cleave to the supernal source. This is sufficient for the enlightened.

I must also reveal secrets that are related to this matter, in order to understand that all the words of the sages are words of the Living God. To understand this, one should meditate on what is written in *Eruvin*, chapter one:

> Rabbi Abba said in the name of Rabbi Samuel, for three years the School of Shammai and the School of Hillel disagreed. One said, the *halakhah* is according to our opinion, and the other said, the *halakhah* is according to our opinion. A voice from heaven emerged and said, both opinions are words of the Living God, and the *halakhah* is according to the School of Hillel.[28]

Rabbi Yom Tov ben Abraham Ashvili wrote in his novella:

> The rabbis of France were asked, how is it possible that both can be words of the Living God, when one forbids and the other permits? They answered, that when Moses ascended on high in order to receive the Torah, he was shown forty-nine ways to decide each case as a prohibition and forty-nine ways to decide each case as permitted. So he asked the Holy One, blessed be He, about this. He said that [the power to decide] is entrusted to the true sages of Israel in every generation. This is correct, according to homiletic interpretation, and there is also a kabbalistic reason.[29]

However, I say that if it were possible to maintain both positions, their declaration that both are words of the Living God, would be justified. Indeed, this is justified in the case of the concubine in Gibeah, which is discussed in the first chapter of *Gittin*. "My son Avitar said [a fly found her]. My son Yonaton said [an ant found her]. He said to him, God forbid, is there a doubt before heaven? He answered, both of these are words of the Living God."[30] [In this case], it is possible to maintain both of their views.[31] However, [in the case of the School of Shammai and the School of Hillel], one forbids and the other permits. It is impossible to maintain both positions. For the determination can only be to one side and we do not fulfill the other position. If they are, nevertheless, "words of the Living God," how can we throw one [expression] of His words to the earth? Therefore, the mind will not be satisfied with the words of the rabbis of France. For they are not sufficient. However, it will be eased by the secret and [kabbalistic] reasons that are in it, as alluded to by the rabbi.

In the first chapter of tractate *Hagigah*, the following is written:

> "*Those that are arranged in groups*,"[32] these are the scholars who sit in groups and study Torah. Some declare impure, others declare pure, some forbid, others permit, some disqualify, others declare fit. This being so, how can I learn Torah? Thus scripture says, "*They were given by one shepherd*."[33] One God gave all of them. One leader said all of them, from the mouth of the Lord of all creation, blessed be He. As it is written, "*and God spoke all of these words, saying* . . ."[34] Thus you should make your ear like a grain hopper and acquire a heart to hear the words of those who declare impure and those who declare pure, those who forbid and those who permit, those who disqualify and those who declare fit.[35]

Thus they testified that all of the disagreements and contradictions [of the sages] were given by one God and said by one leader. This matter is very far from human understanding. It can only be grasped when accompanied by the paved way of God, the way in which the light of truth resides.

In *Sefer 'Avodat ha-Qodesh, Ḥeleq ha-Takhlit*, chapter twenty-three, the following is written:

> For that source, which constantly flows, has a front and back. It is the origin of the changes and opposites, the alternating faces that change from impure to pure, from forbidden to permitted, from disqualified to fit, as is known to the wise of heart. The "*great voice that did not cease*" extends from the source and includes all of the changing faces, for nothing is lacking in it at all. Due to the magnitude and strength of that voice, things were changing on every side, from one to another. Each of the prophets and sages received his portion. One received [the principle] of the impure and another [the principle] of the pure, depending on the place where he received [his portion]. But everything comes from one place and returns to one place. In the *Midrash* of Rabbi Simeon bar Yohai, the following is written: "Come and see. Of all the conflicting

words of the rabbis concerning the Torah, every one goes to one place and enters one source. Thus it is written, '*goes*,' as the verse says, '*All of the streams go to the sea.*'[36] And it is written, '*Everything goes to one place.*'[37]"[38]

The meaning is that all the words [of the sages] emerge from the source, the beginning of supernal thought, and continue on to its end, which is the ultimate sea. That is one place where everything is united. There the union is complete. Thus the verse says, "*They were given by one shepherd.*"[39] And they said, "One God gave them all,"[40] in order to state that the oppositions and changes did not come from different authorities, but all came from one united place, which contains no change or permutation. In order to demonstrate this wondrous secret, each of the sages supports his opinion and brings evidence from the Torah for his view. The union is not complete without all of this. Just as everything was established above, so one must establish and act for God below. Thus they said, "Make your ear like a grain hopper and acquire a heart to hear the words of those who declare impure, etc,"[41] since the *tiqqun* and perfection require acting for God. Thus they said, "Both are words of the Living God," since "[the secret of] *what occurs is elusive and very deep; who can discover it?*"[42] For this matter depends on [divine] thought that is impossible to comprehend and the fiftieth Gate remained concealed from even the faithful Moses, of blessed memory. All of these words appear to contradict each other and be opposites. But this is [only] from our point of view. For we lack authority and sufficient power to comprehend them. Therefore, it is impossible to fulfill two contradictory opinions and the *halakhah* is determined according to one of the views. Thus they said, "Both are words of the Living God." It is all one, from the point of view of the Bestower, blessed be He. But, from our point of view, they are different matters and the *halakhah* is according to [the view of] the School of Hillel alone.[43]

Similar to the position of the author of *Sefer 'Avodat ha-Qodesh* are the words written in *Pardes, Sha'ar ha-Makhri'im*, at the end of the second chapter:

[It is otherwise][44] in a disagreement that is for the sake of heaven, like the dispute between Hillel and Shammai. For Hillel was the president [of the Sanhedrin] and a man of *Ḥesed*, and Shammai was the Head of the Rabbinical Court and was characterized by *Gevurah*. Their characters are well known. Hillel never grew angry, and avoided flawing his attribute. Shammai was irascible, as a result of his attribute. The essence of their dispute was for the sake of heaven, to receive the decision. Accordingly, their dispute has endured. Thus one may understand what our sages, of blessed memory, said in *Eruvin*, "Why did the School of Hillel merit that the *halakhah* would be determined according to their view? Because of their humility."[45] The meaning is that they were cleaving to the side of *Ḥesed* in humility and submission and were at ease. Thus the *halakhah*, which is the *Shekhinah*, is like them. It inclines toward the side of *Ḥesed*, as [the sages] said, "Esther was of a greenish complexion, but a thread of *Ḥesed* was drawn over her."[46] Thus one may understand the saying of the sages, "Both are words of the Living God." "The Living God" is *Binah*, from which the entire structure receives *shefa'*. Those who declare impure, who disqualify, and convict, incline toward *Gevurah* and stringency, in order to show that the *qelippot* have jurisdiction there. Thus [they declare] guilty, disqualified, impure. Those who declare pure, fit, and who acquit, incline to the side of *Ḥesed* and leniency, in order to show that there is no jurisdiction and rule of the *qelippot* there. Consequently, [they declare] innocent, fit, and pure. Nevertheless, everything comes from *Binah*, from which both sides are empowered. When one of the sides becomes stronger and has more *shefa'*, the *halakhah* is in accord with it, either to forbid or to permit. Consequently, both the words of the one who declares pure and the one who declares impure are justified. Accordingly, occasionally, the *halakhah* is also according to [the view of] the School of Shammai, with difficulty. For most of the inclination is toward *Ḥesed*. To alert us to this matter, our rabbis, of blessed memory, said, "The School of Hillel [inclines] toward the lenient view; the School of Shammai [inclines] toward the stringent view." The one inclines toward *Ḥesed*, and the other toward *Gevurah*, according to their attributes, except for a number of cases, as is known. The reason for the occasional switch is in accordance with the [secret of] the verse, "*Here I am, my son.*"[47] For sometimes *Ḥesed* is on the side of *Gevurah* and *Gevurah* is on the side of *Ḥesed*. For fire is contained in water and water is contained in fire, as I explained in chapter sixteen of *Sha'ar Mahut ve-Hanhagah*. This is the reason for the binding of Isaac, as explained in the *Zohar*, in *parashat ha-'Aqedah*.[48]

I added a touch of my own, in explaining the passage in *Yalqut*, *parashat Yitro*:

> Rabbi Aha said in the name of Rabbi Yosi bar Hanina, when Moses ascended on high, he heard the voice of the Holy One, blessed be He, who was sitting and studying *Parashat Parah*. He said, My son Eliezer says, heifer means a two-year-old cow and calf means a one-year-old cow.[49] Moses said before the Holy One, blessed be He, Master of the Universe, the upper and lower orders are under Your authority, and You sit and say the *halakhah* in the name of a creature of flesh and blood! The Holy One, blessed be He, answered Moses, in the future, one righteous person will stand in My world. He will open with *Parashat Parah* first: Rabbi Eliezer says, a heifer is two years old. . . . Moses said before Him, Master of the Universe, may it be Your will that [this righteous person] will issue from my loins. The Holy One, blessed be He, answered him, on your life, he will issue from your loins, as it is written, "*one was named Eliezer*."[50] The name of that special one is Eliezer.[51]

There is a problem here. For the *halakhah* is not according to Rabbi Eliezer, who said a heifer is two years old, but according to the opinions of our sages, who said a heifer of three or more years of age. Another question is what is the relevance of saying "The upper and lower orders are in Your power"? Also, what is the meaning of the response of the Holy One, blessed be He? And what is the significance of the fact that the tractate on the heifer will begin with "both are words of the Living God"?

It seems to me that the matter may be clarified by what is written in chapter *ha-Zahav*, concerning the disagreement between Rabbi Eliezer and Rabbi Joshua. "*It is not in heaven* . . ."[52,53] I have already explained above, at length, that every commandment has a series of roots above, extending to the root of roots. According to the *devequt* above, so is the material commandment below. One can be certain of the *devequt* above from how the commandment is performed below. However, there are levels upon levels and one enters and cleaves above more than another. Therefore, one says the judgment concerning the commandment is such, depending on his *devequt* above, and another says it is so, depending on his *devequt*. The *halakhah* is decided according to the majority. For if the majority holds [that such is the *halakhah*], it means that its *devequt* is [in accord with this]. The bestowal of *shefa'* in *Malkhut* is according to the majority. For the inclination [to one side or another is decided in *Malkhut*]. Although the words of the individual may be extremely high, it is certain that if the majority is in agreement with him, so would be the *halakhah*, for such would be the bestowal of *shefa'* in *Malkhut*, on a high and lofty level. However, the *halakhah* is in accordance with the arousal below and "both are words of the Living God."

I will bring an example from the disagreement between Rashi and Rabbenu Tam, concerning the [scriptural verses to be contained in] *tefillin*. The *tefillin* approved by one are considered unfit according to the view of the other. Is it possible to imagine that either of these did not fulfill the commandment of *tefillin*, all the days of his life? However, the explanation is that each view has its own *devequt* above and the *halakhah* which is *Malkhut* follows the majority in inclining to [one side or the other]. Accordingly, the passage in *Parashat Parah*, in which the Holy One, blessed be He, spoke in the name of Rabbi Eliezer, may be explained. Our teacher Moses, of blessed memory, understood that in the future Rabbi Eliezer would stand and introduce a new teaching, which would not be, God forbid, to make a new source. Moses said the upper and lower orders are entirely Yours, so how can a creature of flesh and blood come and introduce something that did not exist? The Holy One, blessed be He, answered that it is not the case that he would make new things, but that Rabbi Eliezer's level would be so high and his *devequt* so high that he would cleave to the root of the commandment of the red heifer, which is very deep. He would enter into its root of roots, which is the secret of the beginning. For the beginning is the root of all roots, and afterward its roots and branches are extended. Thus it said, "with it he will begin the tractate of the heifer." However, the majority are not on this level, but have another [level of] *devequt*. Thus the *halakhah* is according to their view. If they were all on [Rabbi Eliezer's] level, so would be the *halakhah*. However, Rabbi Eliezer is one extremely high, special individual, just as our teacher Moses, of blessed memory, was distinguished above from all the enlightenments (*hasagot*) of the sages of Israel. Therefore, "like father, like son."[54] Rabbi Eliezer had to be a descendant of our teacher Moses, of blessed memory.

The number of degrees of enlightenment and levels above are infinite. Therefore, [the verse], "*a great voice that lo' yasaf*,"[55] means "it does not cease." It [also means] "it does not add." For everything is included in the secret of unity and the particular expression is contained in the principle. Thus [the meaning] of "who gave the Torah" and "giver of the Torah" has been explained.

The House of *YHVH* [III] The House of David [III]

The Blessing: "Former of the Lights"

It is the clear custom of the Ashkenazim to conclude [the section of the blessing that begins] "As it is said, '[*Give thanks*] *to the Maker of great lights, for His loving-kindness is forever.*' "[1] "Cause a new light to shine upon Zion and let us all swiftly merit its light. Blessed are You, *YHVH*, Former of the lights."[2] This has been explained by the *Tur, 'Oraḥ Ḥayyim*, *siman* 51. There, he wrote,

> The RASH, of blessed memory, wrote in a responsum that [this wording] serves well as an ending and beginning. "Former of light" refers to the light that the Holy One, blessed be He, created during the six days of creation. The world was not worthy of using it, so He concealed it for the righteous in the future. Concerning this light, it is said, "*And nations shall walk by your light.*"[3] In other words, this refers to the "new light," which was created during the six days of creation, and which the Holy One, blessed be He, will renew for us in the future.[4]

The secret of the concealed light is alluded to in the verse, "*to the Maker of great lights.*" It goes on to speak of "*the sun*" and "*the moon.*"[5] Therefore the "great lights" refer to the concealed spirituality of the sun and the moon. It is concealed within the "hidden treasures," which is the secret of "the great lights," *Tif'eret* and *Malkhut*. Originally, the intention was [for these lights] to shine upon Adam. Had he not sinned, he would have been in "garments of light." Indeed, the purpose of emanating the structure [of the *sefirot*] into its place, was for the human being, as I have explained at length. [*Tif'eret* and *Malkhut*] are the secret of the root of the lower Garden of Eden, which is the "finest portion" of this world. It is the secret of the letters, *vav heh*, of the Name *YHVH*, as I explained above. The letters, *yod heh*, of the Name *YHVH*, are alluded to in the verse "for in *YaH YHVH* is a *Ẓur 'Olamim.*"[6] In other words, the circumference of the world (*'Olam*), which is the "structure of the seven days of creation,"[7] was formed (*niẒtaYeR*) by the letters *yod heh*, which are *Ḥokhmah* and *Binah*. Thus the verse says that with the letters *yod heh*, *YHVH* formed the *'Olamim*,[8] those circumferences. For every *sefirah* presides over a forty-nine year cycle[9] and the secret of the circumference is the seven *shemitot* and the Jubilee.[10] The letters *yod heh* are roots from the root of the Upper Garden of Eden. The ultimate purpose of "*Ẓur ha-'Olamim*" was the human being, "*to serve it and preserve it.*"[11] However, when he went astray and brought the corruption [of the snake] upon himself, he damaged the letters *vav heh*. He drew down the corruption in such a manner that he brought about actual non-Jewish contact with that circumference. This is not the case from *Binah* and above. [It is called] "protected wine" and is not subject to non-Jewish contact, as I explained above. After the flaw, the human being was clothed in garments of skin and the Divine Name was no longer complete. For the letters *vav heh* took hold of the flaw, so to speak, as we shall explain below. Then, as it were, the letters *vav heh* did not ascend to *yod heh*. But when the world will return to its original state of garments of light, the Name will be complete. I already explained at length how light is increased through the power of darkness and that in the future goodness will be absolute. The worlds will no longer be damaged, for the cloud will already have been destroyed and will depart. The letters *vav heh* will be like the letters *yod heh*. They will not be subject to any damage, for they will always ascend to their root in *Ḥokhmah* and *Binah*. The son will ascend to the father, in other words, *vav* will ascend to *yod*. And the daughter will ascend to the mother, the final *heh* will ascend to the first *heh*. When the letters *vav heh* have ascended to their root, they will also be *yod heh*. Then the secret of the Name *YHVH* will become

YHYH. For *vav heh* will also be *yod heh*. I came to understand this from the Kabbalah of the divine Rabbi Isaac Luria, of blessed memory.

The order of the levels will be as follows. First, the Name will be complete, that is *YHVH*. His great Name will be sanctified and magnified through the revelation of the "hidden treasures." And "*YHVH will be (YiHYeH)*"[12] is the secret of *YHYH*. This is alluded to in the verse, "*and YHVH will be king over all of the earth. On that day, YHVH will be One and His Name One*."[13] At first the Name will be sanctified and magnified. This is the letters of "and . . . will be (*Ve-HaYaH*)." These are the letters of *YHVH*, for the Name will be complete. The Throne will also be complete. These are the letters, *hu'*.[14] This is indicated by "*He has desired ('iVaH) it for His seat*."[15] This is the meaning of "*and YHVH will be king on that (hu') day*," "*He has desired ('iVaH) it for His seat*." Afterward [the verse deals with] His great Name from ascension to ascension [and says,] *yihyeh YHVH*. The meaning is that the letters *YHVH* will return to being the letters *YHYH*. Then "He is One and His Name is One." This is the secret of two kings who make use of one crown in their root above in *Binah*. Now *YHVH* and His Name are One and "*YHVH is in His Holy Chamber*." This is the secret of the great light and the small light. But when they ascend high above, the two lights are great, according to the secret of "crown of beauty (*'ateret Tif'eret*)."

In order to understand this properly, I will indicate that the subject involves three matters. First of all, the true light is God. "*YHVH is my light*."[16] "*Arise and shine, for your light has come and the Glory of YHVH has shone upon you*."[17] This involves three matters, as I shall explain.

First, I will begin with the verse that says, "*Let there be (yehiy) light and there was light*."[18] We have also found the three letters of the Name together [in the verse], "*In the place that the tree falls, there it will remain (yehu')*."[19] These are the letters of *YHVH*, because the final *heh* is a duplicate. Now the light concealed in the "hidden treasures" is the letters *yhy* instead of *YHV*. For then, the Name *YHYH* replaces *YHVH*. This is alluded to in the verse "*YeHiY (Let there be) light*." It was concealed and became "*Va-YeHiy (and there was)*." In other words, the first three letters of *va-yehiy* are the letters *YHV*. *YHY* became *YHV*. When the letter *vav* is removed from *va-yehiy*, it will return to being *yhy*. In other words, after six thousand years,[20] it will return to being light. Thus when the sages, of blessed memory, said, " '*and there was light*,' it already existed."[21] This is the secret of the verse, "*Let there be light, and there was light*."

Now the Name will be explained that is interpreted as meaning, "He was, He is, and He will be (*yihyeh*)." The question is, How are the letters

YHYH alluded to in the Name *YHVH*? However, according to what I have written above, it works out well. Thus the verse says, "*That which was (she-hayah) is what will be (she-yihyeh)*."[22] For He and His Name existed and were concealed. But in the future, the Name will return to being *YHYH*. Now, even when the Name is spelled in full, it is in accordance with the secret of *YHV*. This is alluded to in the verse, "*meh hoveh la'-adam*."[23] For the Name *YHVH*, when fully spelled out as *yod vav dalet heh alef heh vav alef vav heh alef heh*, equals *meh*, which is equal to *adam* (man).[24] From the time that Adam caused harm, there have been several *tiqqunim*, such as the reception of the Torah and the construction of the Temple, which was the moon in its fullness. Nevertheless, the Name still did not return to the aspect of "*hayah (what was)*," but only to "*hoveh (what is)*." For the *tiqqun* of the world has not yet been completed. Only with the coming of Messiah will the *tiqqun* be complete and the concealed light revealed. This is the allusion in the verse, "*In the place that a tree falls* . . . ," which is the tree from which Adam ate, "*there it will remain (yehu')*."[25] Even after this *tiqqun*, [the letters of the Name] will not yet have returned to *yhy*, but will remain *YHV* until the future. Then "*That which was is what will be*."[26] But now, "What is (*hoveh*)" is still in effect. That is the meaning of "*hayah hoveh yihyeh*."[27]

At the time of the damaging, that is to say, when the Temple was destroyed, the Name is not entirely complete. The letters *vav heh* are lacking. This is the secret of the verse, "*Hovah 'al-hovah (calamity upon calamity)* [*will come*]."[28] Not only are the letters *hvh* lacking, but there is an additional *hvh*, because of our sins. For also with these letters, the Name remains incomplete.

Thus there are three stages. One is *hayah yihyeh* (was will be), which is the secret of the concealed light. Two is the aspect, *YHVH*, the *tiqqun* of the Name at the time of the Temple. Three is at the time of the destruction [of the Temple]. Then the Name is not totally complete, until a spirit from on high will be stirred and "*YHVH will be king over all of the earth, on that day, YHVH will be (yihyeh)* . . . "[29]

This is the secret of "*the mother of all life*,"[30] who was called Ḥavvah. It would have been more proper to call her Ḥayyah. Rashi, of blessed memory, wrote that Havvah is like Hayyah, just as *meh hoveh* is like *meh hayah*. Whoever is intellectually alert will discern the secret that I wrote. For now, even at the time of the *tiqqun*, the concealed *yod heh* has become *vav heh*. This is itself the allusion in the verse, "*meh hoveh* . . . ,"[31] as I have explained. In the future the letters will return to their root, which is the secret of "*mother of all life*." For *Binah* will couple with *Ḥokhmah*, which gives life,[32] as was explained above. Then the letters *vav heh* will be restored to *yod heh*.

This is the secret of the teaching of our sages, of blessed memory, " 'a new song' is in the female gender, but in the future, it will be male."[33] For even at the time of the song, namely, when the Temple was built, it [was sung] according to the secret of the verse, "*Let the heavens rejoice and the earth be glad.*"[34] The first letters of each word spell *YHVH*.[35] The *Zohar*'s "*Let the heavens rejoice*" is in the male gender. Thus *yod heh* is male. "*And the earth be glad*" is in the female gender. Thus *vav heh* is female. However, in the future the letters *vav heh* will also be *yod heh*. Everything will be male (*zakhar*), which has the same numerical value as blessing (*berakhah*), adding one for the word itself.

According to what I have written, the following passage in *Midrash Rabbah*, *va-yera'*, can be explained.

> Abraham called it "*Yir'eh*," as it is written, "*Abraham called the name of that place, YHVH yir'eh (will see).*"[36] Shem called it "*Shalem*," as it is written, "*and Melchizedek, the King of Shalem.*"[37] The Holy One, blessed be He, said, if I call it "*Yir'eh*," as Abraham called it, Shem, a righteous man, will be angry. If I call it "*Shalem*," Abraham, a righteous man, will be angry. Therefore, I am calling it "Jerusalem (*Yerushalayim*)," as both of them called it, *Yir'eh Shalem, Yerushalayim*. Rabbi Berekhiah said in the name of Rabbi Helbo, before it was complete (*shalem*), the Holy One, blessed be He, made a booth for Himself and would pray within it. As it is written, "*Shalem became His abode, Zion, His den.*"[38] What would He say? "May I see the building of My House?" Another interpretation. It teaches that the Holy One, blessed be He, showed him the Temple, destroyed and built, destroyed and built. As it is written, "[*Abraham called*] *the name of that place, YHVH will see.*"[39] Thus it was built. How so? As the verse says, "*Three times a year* [*all of your males*] *will appear (yera'eh) ...* "[40] "*Whence the present saying, on the Mountain of YHVH ...* "[41] Thus it was destroyed, as it is written, "*because of Mount Zion that was made desolate.*"[42] "*Yera'eh (there is vision),*"[43] it will be built and perfected in the future, as indicated in the verse, "*For YHVH built Zion, He has appeared in all His Glory.*"[44,45]

One question that arises from this *Midrash* is why Abraham is twice mentioned before Shem. First, it says, "Abraham called it '*Yir'eh*' ... Shem called it ['*Shalem*.']" Then, in the saying of the Holy One, blessed be He, "If I call it '*Yir'eh*' ... " it also places Abraham before Shem. Then a third time, in choosing the name, Jerusalem, *Yeru*, which comes from the name *Yir'eh*, is placed before the name *Shalem*. This may be explained in terms of the plain meaning; it is for the same reason that the Holy One, blessed be He, did not say the same thing regarding Shem that He said regarding Abraham. In the case of Abraham, He said, "If I call it '*Yir'eh*', as Abraham called it." But, in the case of Shem, He said, "if I call it '*Shalem*,' " and did not say, "as Shem called it." The reason is that Shem never gave the city the name. It was always called "*Shalem*," and Shem also called it so. But Shem did not coin the name *Shalem*. However, Abraham coined the name *Yir'eh*. Therefore, since Abraham played a more essential role in bestowing names, he was given precedence. However, having said this, it is necessary to look more deeply. How does Shem derive honor from the fact that [a portion of] the name remained "*Shalem*," when he did not invent it? It is because he is called "*Melchizedek, the King of Shalem*." If the name of *Shalem* had been changed, we would not know the greatness of Shem. For who would have known that he ruled over the Holy Land, the "*land that YHVH Your God looks after*"?[46] For the later generations would have forgotten what Shalem was. They might have thought that a foreign land bore this name. This is indeed the explanation of the passage.

Nevertheless, it is necessary to look still more deeply into this *Midrash* and to broaden its meaning. It may still be asked, When the Holy One, blessed be He, made a compromise, calling it Jerusalem, why didn't he call it "*Yir'eh Shalem*," since Abraham called it "*Yir'eh*" and not "*Yeru*"? In Rabbi Berekhiah's words, an explanation is also required for the meaning of [God's] prayer and its essence. Indeed, we can find many similar cases in the Talmud and *Midrash* and many commentators dived into the powerful waters and came up empty. As for us, we have only words of the Living God, and what we can join together from the teachings of the kabbalists, who are true and their words are "*the secret of YHVH is for those who fear Him*."[47] Also, what is the meaning of "destroyed and built, destroyed and built?" In fact, I have seen texts in which the first "destroyed" has been excised. However, how wonderful it is when it is possible to resolve an apparent textual difficulty. I also want to give the reason why Jerusalem is spelled deficiently, yet we pronounce it "*Yerushalayim*."

First, our sages, of blessed memory, said, "Jerusalem is its name, after the name of '*El*, its King. The city, in which *YHVH* is present (*shamah*). Do not read "*shamah*," but "*shemah (its name)*."[48] They also said, " '*The Holy One in your midst*.'[49] I will not come to the upper Jerusalem until I come to the lower Jerusalem."[50] The plain meaning is that the "lower Jerusalem" is that Jerusalem that is located in the Holy Land and for whose swift rebuilding we are hoping. It is turned toward the upper Jerusalem, which is the secret of the supernal Land, the desired Land, the Palace of *YHVH*. Concerning it is said, "*And YHVH is in His Holy Palace, be silent before Him all the earth.*"[51] However, there is level upon level. For according to the inner meaning of the secret of coming to the lower Jerusalem, "*YHVH is in His Holy Palace*," the joining together of *YHVH* and *ADoNaY*. This is the secret of the lower coupling, *vav* with *heh*. [Coming to] the upper Jerusalem is the union of *Ḥokhmah* and *Binah*, the secret of the upper coupling, *yod* with *heh*. This is explained in the *Zohar* and *tiqqunim* and is brought in *Pardes*, *Sha'ar Mahut ve-Hanhagah*, chapter thirteen. And so taught Elijah in *Zohar*, *Shir ha-Shirim*:

> Just as a joyous arousal is necessary in order to raise something from this world above, so a joyous arousal is necessary from the world of the moon [in order to ascend] to the higher world. Consequently, worlds exist according to one pattern, and no arousal ascends, except from below to above.[52]

Thus the *'El* of the supernal union, that is, the *'El* of *Binah*, requires an arousal from *Malkhut*. See *Pardes*, *Sha'ar ha-Mahut ve-Hanhagah*, chapter twenty and chapter six, concerning the arousal for the coupling of *Tif'eret* and *Malkhut*, the lower Jerusalem, which arouses the coupling of *Ḥokhmah* and *Binah*, the upper Jerusalem. The Jerusalem that is built at the lowest level below is turned toward the levels that are above.

Now Shem, the son of Noah, was the first to go and conquer and merit Jerusalem. "First is thought, last is the deed." In other words, his name alludes to that aspect of the Divine Name that will be complete, uniting the letters *vav heh* as *yod heh*, according to the secret of the Name *YHYH*, as has been explained. This is "first is thought," which is the secret of "Let there be light," and it was concealed and not actualized. Nevertheless, the first to hold this lower Jerusalem was Shem and his name alludes to this. He was the king of *Shalem*. For *Shalem* is the secret of the complete Name (*shem shalem*), the Jerusalem that is high above, according to the secret of *YHYH*. Afterward, the Land of Israel was given as a promise to our Father Abraham. "*And YHVH said* [*to Abram*], *go forth from your Land* [*and birthplace and the house of your father*] *to the Land that I will show you.*"[53] There is a well-known *midrash* of our sages, "*These are the generations of heaven and earth be-hibar'am (in their being created).*"[54] *Be-hibar'am* is the same letters as "*be-Avraham.*"[55] It was all for Abraham. For he is the structure of the world: "*Ḥesed to Abraham*"[56] [is written] and it is also written, "A world of *Ḥesed* will be built."[57] Thus the secret of the letters *YHVH* was alluded to in the verses, "*Go forth . . . and be a blessing.*"[58] For then, the [concealed] light was not actualized. Even when the *tiqqun* of the Land of Israel was effected, only the Name *YHVH*, in accordance with the secret of *YHV*, [was operative]. It will only become *YHYH* in the future. This is the secret of the verse, "*And Abraham hayo yihyeh (is to become)* [*a great and populous nation.*]."[59] Now the aspect of *hayo*, which is *YHV*, exists. This is the secret of the verse, "*In the place that the tree falls, there it will remain (yehu).*"[60] "*And Abraham said, rest under the tree.*"[61] The *Zohar* has already explained that this tree was the *tiqqun* for what Adam spoiled with the Tree of Knowledge. Therefore, the verse said, "*and Abraham hayo*" [referring to the present] and in the future "*yihyeh.*"

Here there is an allusion to the thought that is concealed for the future. Abraham, who is *Ḥesed*, the building of the world, is the cause of the *tiqqun* of the Name *YHVH*. In one of its spellings, it is also an allusion to *Ḥesed*, through the secret of the 72 bridges that are in *Ḥesed*.[62] For when the Name is spelled with *yods*, *yod vav dalet heh yod vav yod vav heh yod*, it equals 72. Thus he called [Jerusalem] "*Yir'eh*," which equals 216 (*RYO*). There is no distinction between *Yir'eh* and *RYO*, because the Name of 72 has 216 letters.[63] This is alluded to in "*va-ya'avor (and he passed)*, it is made up of the letters *'aB RYO*. Thus it is written concerning Abraham, "*And Abram passed through the Land.*"[64] Also *Yir'eh* contains the same letters as *'Aryeh* (lion), which is an extension of *Ḥesed*.[65] This is the secret of "*Three times a year* [*all your males*] *yera'eh (will appear)* . . . "[66] It equals 72. How is it figured? Three times "*be-shanah* (in a year)" equals 1071. If the zeroes are disregarded, one thousand becomes one. Therefore, the total is 72.

Thus what is alluded to by Abraham preceded the allusion of Shem, which refers to the "beginning of thought," which will be manifest when the deed is complete in the future, in the secret of *YHYH*. But Abraham preceded in actuality, for the Name *YHVH* was revealed in the Temple. This Name equals 216, as has been explained.[67] Thus in the passage from *Midrash Rabbah*, Abraham preceded Shem. Similarly, when the name Jerusalem was chosen, *Yeru*, which is the secret of *YHVH*, preceded *Shalem*, which is the secret of *YHYH*. We call it *Yerushalayim*, with an extra *yod*. This alludes to the *yod* that will ascend when the Name *YHVH* becomes *YHYH*. Since the allusion of *Shalem* is so great and Shem alluded to this when he conquered the Land and was called "*king of Shalem*," it is certainly a great honor for him. He would have had a great grievance if this name had been taken from him.

We can now also explain why the *Midrash* said "destroyed and built, destroyed and built." For the first "destroyed" alludes to the first light that was concealed. "*God said, Let there be light* . . . " and it was concealed. Thus it was built and destroyed. In other words the "building" of revelation was destroyed, because the light was concealed. The first "built" alludes to the Name *YHVH* in the building of the Temple. "Destroyed" alludes to the present time, when, due to our great sins, the Name is not complete. The second "built" alludes to the final building, the secret of *YHYH*.

The saying of Rabbi Berekhiah can also be explained. "Until it is complete, the Holy One, blessed be He, made Himself a *sukkah* (booth)." It is known that *sukkah* is the secret of *KV HS*, the union of *YHVH* and *'ADoNaY*. *YHVH* equals 26 (*kv*) and *'ADoNaY* equals 65 (*hs*). Specifically, this refers to *vav heh*, the coupling of *Tif'eret* and *Malkhut*, which we merited in the Temple. It is explained in the *Zohar* and brought in *Pardes*, *Sha'ar Mahut ve-Hanhagah*, chapters six and twenty, that *Malkhut* sings in order to arouse the supernal union of *Ḥokhmah* and *Binah*. For just as through the power of our arousal below, we arouse the union of *Tif'eret* and *Malkhut*, so the arousal above comes from *Malkhut*. This is the secret of the prayer that Rabbi Berekhiah mentioned. The Holy One, blessed be He, prays in the *sukkah*, "May I see the building of My House?" In other words, the arousal ascends from the secret of *sukkah*. *Malkhut* sings to that Jerusalem that is above it. This is the building of the House, "*a house is built with Ḥokhmah*,"[68] according to the secret of *Shalem* (complete). Then the verse will be fulfilled that says, "*And His sukkah will be in Shalem*,"[69] alluding to the secret of *YHYH*.

We now return to our subject. As a result of the daily process of annulling (*hashbatat*) and purifying the *qelippot*, "a new light will shine on Zion." This is the secret of "Former of the lights," rather than "who formed." For [the light] was concealed. However, each and every day, what was said in the verse, "*with YaH YHVH formed the worlds*,"[70] becomes more true, so that the lights also become formers. In other words, *vav heh* also becomes *yod heh*. Then the secret of *YHYH* [will be realized]. In the word *Yoẓer* (Former), it is also alluded that it will form a form within a form. The *yod* is the former of the *vav*. This is the meaning of "Former." The *vav* will also become a *yod*. May God forgive me for having revealed these allusions at such length.

Thus the text of the blessings, "Former of the lights," "Giver of the Torah," and "Chooser of His people Israel with love," has been explained. These are three that are interconnected, the Holy One, blessed be He, the Torah, and Israel. "*The portion of YHVH is His people, Jacob is the portion of His inheritance*."[71] It is like a rope that is connected above.[72] When someone grabs it from below and shakes it, he is lifted above. If one connects himself to the right side of holiness, he draws down holiness and good *shefa'*. But, if he connects himself to the left side of impurity, he draws down impurity and brings evil upon himself. Then "a *hevel* (portion) of His inheritance" becomes "*haval* (too bad) for what was lost." This is from the *Midrash*, "*haval* for the great sun . . . ," which I cited above. For a person created in the supernal image and likeness also contains the side of evil. This is the secret of "*God also made this in contrast to that*."[73] This is the side of impurity, which is like a monkey before a person, who is aroused by the person's sin. A person has the free will to decide toward which side he wishes to incline. "Whoever comes to purify is aided, if one comes to make impure, it is made possible for him."[74] Reward and punishment are entirely in accord with the nature of the deed that one does. They are not arbitrarily decided, as in the case of a mortal king who dispenses rewards to those who do his will and punishes those who transgress his will, however he decides, and could have rewarded or punished in another manner. However, the admonitions and commands of God are all essential, for the "reward of a commandment is the commandment itself" and there [in its root] a person cleaves. And the reward of a transgression is the transgression itself, for it brings the transgressor to the root of the transgression, which is the *qelippah*, God spare us. There is his portion. I already discussed this at length above.

As a result, we can well understand what eluded the philosophers who attempted to explain rationally the meaning of changing of the divine will.

The House of the Walled City

[One should not think], God forbid, that the Holy One, blessed be He, issues a decree and that afterward, as the result of repentance, prayer, and charity, it is changed for the good, or that occasionally it changes from favor to ill. Those [who hold this view] walk in darkness, for there is no change [in God's will], God forbid. There is only unity, a matter of one will. For if reward and punishment were a matter of agreement that was decided conventionally, it would appear, God forbid, as if one will changes to another. Now God agrees that it should be thus and another time He agrees that it should be so. However, the divine will involves the secret of the revelation of the divine emanation, which contains all opposites. According to the nature of the arousal, one draws forth a result, according to the essence and nature of the matter. If one sanctifies himself from below, he is sanctified from above, according to the nature of the matter that was aroused. If he makes himself impure from below, he is made impure from above, according to the nature of the matter that was aroused. If subsequently he is aroused, and rids himself of his idols and cleaves to holiness, he is sanctified by nature. The will of heaven has not changed. On the contrary, thus the will was manifested. "Everything is foreseen, yet freedom is granted." This matter is involved in the rabbinic saying, "the Holy One, blessed be He, arises from the Throne of Judgment and sits on the Throne of Compassion." This is according to the way that human beings speak, but in essence, the meaning is that as a person chooses, so is the arousal [above]. This is also true in regard to a number of biblical verses that speak of judgment and "*the anger of YHVH will flare up against you.*"[1] There are many like this. The meaning is not, God forbid, [that God experiences] an emotional arousal, like a person who was feeling pleased and then became angry because of those who rebelled against him. Rather, the person, through [the action that he] chose, brought upon himself an arousal of anger and its root, which is contained in the will.[2]

This is also illustrated by a saying of our rabbis, of blessed memory, "When a sage becomes angry, it is the Torah that makes him angry."[3] In other words, if a sage becomes angry, God forbid that he become angry through clothing himself in anger. Rather, it is the Torah [that is angry]. In other words, he carries out the judgment of the Torah. For example, if a rabbinical court issues a judgment of the four deaths, do they act out of hatred and anger? God forbid! Rather, they carry out the judgment of the Torah.[4]

The same is true for blessings. There is no change [in the will], but only an arousal of beneficial *shefa'*, through this good act. For the primordial will contains opposites. There is also "*the great voice that does not cease*"[5] in the giving of the Torah, which is the revelation of the divine emanation. This voice also consisted of forty-nine aspects of impurity and purity, of the forbidden and the permitted, of guilty and innocent, as I explained at length above.

As a result of what I have written, I now enter in awe, fear, and trembling, the Gate of the "House of Choosing."

The House of Choosing

I mean to speak of the issue of divine knowledge and human will,[1] which has been addressed by earlier and later authorities. Maimonides was impelled to write of this in *Sefer ha-Mada, Hilkhot Teshuvah*, and in the eighth chapter of the *Shemonah Peraqim*, which he wrote as an introduction to tractate *Avot*.

> Perhaps you will say, but did not the Holy One, blessed be He, know all that would occur before it occurs? Did He know that a certain person would be righteous or wicked, or did He not know? If He knew that the person would be righteous, then it is impossible that he would not be righteous. For if you say that He knew that he will be righteous and it is possible for him to be wicked, He did not know the matter completely.[2]

The upshot of his words is that God's knowledge and essence are a unity, since His knowledge is not like ours. Just as we cannot comprehend His essence, so we cannot comprehend His knowledge. See what Maimonides has written there.[3] Rabbi Abraham ben David of Posquieres commented on this, as did many of the great early and later authorities. I also wish to take a stand and to contemplate this matter, for "*nothing prevents YHVH from offering salvation by many or by few.*"[4] I mean to say that He grants knowledge to a person. Not that He only grants wisdom to the wise, who are already full of knowledge, understanding, and insight, but even to those of little knowledge, such as myself. This is the case whether one does much or little, as long as what he does is for the sake of heaven. May God, be He blessed, grant me knowledge, understanding, and insight, that I may not stumble, God forbid, and "*my mouth will express truth.*"[5]

> First of all, I want to explain Maimonides's words, "He is the Mind and He is the Knower."[6] The explanation of this matter is that the manner of knowing of the Creator is not like the manner of knowing of other entities. For in the case of other entities, they and their manner of knowing are not a unity. Rather, they know things in a manner of knowing that is external to them. For example, a person knows a certain form or matter that is inscribed within his mind. Thus there will be at least three things: the knowledge of that form which was lacking before his knowing of it, the act of knowing with which he knew and recognized that form, and the known form which is inscribed in his mind. These are three: the knowledge, the knower, and the known. Some have called these intellect, intelligence, and object of intelligence (*sekhel, maskil, muskal*). But, the manner of knowing and what is known are not the same for the Holy One, blessed be He. Rather, He is the Knowledge, the Knower, and the Known.
>
> The meaning is that His manner of knowing is not a matter of His watching over them thus after they have been separated from Him. Rather, through the comprehension and knowing of His essence, He knows and watches over every matter in the world. Everything that exists is united to Him in His essence; He is the template of every single thing that exists. Each is present within Him in a subtle and most highly refined state, so that nothing is complete, except by virtue of that most highly refined state in which it is united to its Creator. To the extent that they descend from before Him, they descend from their completeness and exaltation. Now everything that exists is inscribed in the *sefirot* and the *sefirot* are inscribed in their Emanator.

"See *Pardes, Sha'ar Mahut ve-Hanhagah*, chapter thirteen."

It is also written in the *Tola'at Ya'aqov*, in the *Secrets of Rosh Ha-Shanah*, "You remember the creation of the world."

> Now the recollections begin, which is the secret of the "Book of Recollection," in which all the acts of creation are recorded. This is the secret of recollecting "and He counts (*u-foqed*) all of the early creations," according to the secret of the counting. For all

> secrets are revealed before Him and there are many concealed matters from the beginning. For everything is before Him and through knowing what is before Him, He knows everything. Thus He remembers every activity and no creation is denied to Him. For since the root of every creation is before Him, nothing that has ever existed or will ever exist can possibly be concealed from Him. Thus He looks and gazes upon the end of all generations. As a result, a person cannot stir below without leaving an imprint above. Everything is revealed before Him, for everything reaches Him. This is a great secret.[7]

Now we should carefully consider Maimonides's assumption that if we say that God does not know completely, a defect in God's knowledge is implied, God forbid. For, according to what we have written, His mode of knowing involves knowing Himself and not the knowing of something other than Himself. The opposite is the case. For how can we say that He knows what a person will choose when this choice is not determined by Heaven but is allotted to man? It is he who determines it. God's knowing only concerns His essence. Thus one must say that His knowing is only in force after the choice has taken effect and made an impression above within Him. Then He knows, because the knowing is knowledge of Himself.

Therefore, Maimonides's question is no question. Nevertheless, the question can still be raised in regard to another issue. For true and absolute faith states that "*in heaven above and on the earth below, there is no other.*"[8] The meaning of the verse is not as some have said, "*there is no other*" [means] that there is no other god but He. For this we already knew [from the verse], "*YHVH is God, YHVH is One.*"[9] Rather, the meaning is that there is nothing else in the world besides His divinity. I mean that there is no thing in the world of any kind, possessing vitality, power, and movement, and including inorganic matter, that has not been emanated from Him, in accord with the verse, "*You enliven all of them.*"[10] God brings them into existence and enlivens them. Otherwise, they would not exist. Before He brought them into existence, He knew them. For He brings them into existence and His knowing is His decree. He decreed, spoke, and commanded, "Let there be." Whoever does not believe this and separates out and attributes to something power of its own, God forbid, would seem to affirm two authorities. However, with proper inspection, it will come out all right, with God's help. [The following is written] in chapter *ba-meh madliqin*, page 32a.

> The school of Rabbi Ishmael taught, "*When you build a new house, make a parapet for your roof, so you do not bring bloodguilt upon your house, if the one who falls should fall from it.*"[11] That person deserved to fall from the six days of creation, for he did not fall and scripture already calls him "*the one who falls.*" Rather, merit is carried forward by means of the innocent and guilt by means of the guilty.[12]

Here is Rashi's comment:

> "From the six days of creation," for it is written, "*He who announced the generations from the start.*"[13] For the generations and their deeds and the fine of their chastisement rose up before Him. For when the Torah was given, that person had not yet fallen. Yet, scripture calls him "*one who falls.*"[14]

Thus he clearly states that everything was already known before the person acted, even his reward and punishment.

Here is what Rashi wrote in his commentary on *parashat zo't haberakhah*, based on the teachings of our rabbis, of blessed memory:

> "*And YHVH showed him all of the Land. . . .* "[15] He showed him all of the Land of Israel in its time of peace and the enemies who would assail it in the future. "*Until Dan.*"[16] He showed him the descendants of Dan worshipping idols. As it is written, "*and the descendants of Dan set up the idol for themselves.*"[17] And He showed him Samson who, in the future, would emerge from [the tribe of Dan] as a savior. "*And all of Naftali.*"[18] He showed him his land in peace and in destruction. And He showed him Deborah and Barak from Kedesh in Naftali, battling with Sisera and his troops. "*And the land of Efraim and Menashe.*"[19] He showed him their land in peace and in destruction. And He showed him Joshua, who came from Efraim, battling with the kings of Canaan, and Gideon, who came from Menashe, battling with Midian and Amalek. "*And all of the land of Judah.*"[20] In peace and in destruction. And He showed him the Kingdom of the House of David and their victory. "*Until the final sea.*"[21] The land of the west in peace and in destruction. Do not read "*the final sea (yam),*" but "*the final day (yom).*" The Holy One, blessed be He, showed him all of the events that would occur to Israel, before the resurrection of the

> dead. "*And the plain.*"[22] He showed him Solomon casting the vessels for the Temple, as it is written, "*In the Jordan plain, the king had them cast in the thick of the earth.*"[23]

According to what is said, this knowing was absolute, a knowing that decreed [what would occur]. Therefore, what later occurred was entirely of necessity and not by choice.

Similarly, our rabbis, of blessed memory, said that the Holy One, blessed be He, showed Adam each and every generation with its expounders, sages, and leaders. Therefore, these expounders, sages, and leaders already were decreed and fulfilled these roles of necessity. Similarly, the Holy One, blessed be He, showed them to Moses, our rabbi, of blessed memory, until He revealed to him the level of Rabbi Eliezer. Moses prayed that he would be a descendant of his, and his prayer was granted. There are many similar teachings of our rabbis, of blessed memory, that concern such matters.

In the Book of Kings it is written, "*Thus said YHVH, a son will be born to the House of David, Josiah by name, and he shall slaughter upon you* [*the altar*] *the priests of the high places.*"[24] There was a long time before Josiah was born. Therefore Jereboam and the priests of the high places were compelled, God forbid, to maintain this altar and Josiah was compelled to do this good deed.

Now listen to me and stir your souls. God's knowing is His will, and His will is His knowing. For the will involves what one desires to do and is the root of the entire chain of emanation, from great to small. There is nothing other than it. For "*all that YHVH desires to do, He does.*"[25] This is in itself the knowing, through knowing the essence of His will. He is the will and He is the knowing. He knows everything from the essence of His will. I already wrote at length above that the will contains opposites. All ways are within it. The choice is granted to human beings to arouse whatever power they wish. God created Adam upright and commanded him not to arouse the power of evil. But as a result of his sin, he came to know good and evil. As a result, darkness and punishment were drawn [from the will]. These are not merely arbitrary (*heskemii*). Rather, the reward of a commandment is the root of the commandment, above in its root. And the reward of a transgression is a transgression. All of this is rooted in the will, because the will contains all things and their opposites. Similarly, the Torah, which is drawn from this will, contains forty-nine aspects of impurity and forty-nine aspects of purity, forbidden and permitted, guilty and innocent. And "both of these are words of the Living God." For all are contained in the power of the "*great voice that does not cease.*"[26] According to the arousal below, so is the inclination to bring to realization. No matter what it is, nothing is separate, God forbid. Each is an actualization of one of the ways [contained in the will].

Before a person does something, whether good or evil, these ways were already prepared. There is evidence in the verse in *parashat re'eh*, "*See this day I set before you blessing and curse.*"[27] The verse says, "Look, there are ways before you." Learn from this that the ways precede the action.

Similarly, in *parashat neẓavim* from "*see, I have placed before you this day, life and good . . .* "28 until "*so choose life . . .* "[29] Thus there is a way of the righteous and a way of the wicked and the root of all is the supernal will. It is the knowing of the essence of God's will in the root of the entire chain of emanation. Everything that a person does draws on a supernal power. Only, the righteous person chooses and follows the straight path of the Holy and the wicked person chooses its opposite.

What they cleave to corresponds to their action. Everything depends on the arousal below. If Adam had remained upright and had not aroused the power of evil, then all of his descendants, throughout all of the generations, would have been worthy of being in a different state than they are in now. For the source of goodness would have been opened and it would have extended from stage to stage and from branch to branch. But after he sinned a source of another kind involving good and evil was opened. The Holy One, blessed be He, showed him all of the generations with their expounders, sages, and leaders. According to the sources that were now opened, He showed him how the manifestation and branches upon branches should be. Thus, in actuality, they are not absolutely determined. For whoever so wishes may exert himself and diverge from this manifestation. He can open another of the sources and draw forth [from the divine will] as he wishes. He has the power to assert his will. However, the Holy One, blessed be He, showed Adam how the manifestation should be, according to the source that is presently opened. Certainly, through the power of the human will, myriad things were changed from the way that they should have been according to the present opening of the source. And many things remained as they should be. For example, "[he showed me the book of Adam and written in it was 'Samuel Yarhinaah is called a sage, he is not called rabbi.' "[30] There are thousands of matters like this. If Samuel had desired not to learn Torah at all, God forbid, he could have chosen not to. However, he chose the good way and followed it.

Nevertheless, there are many things that were changed as a result of human choosing. They cleaved to another source. But everything is contained within the divine will, for the source and root of all the ways is located there. Look closely at the language of passage from chapter *ba-meh madliqin*, which we cited above. He said, "That person deserved to fall . . . "[31] There is a difference between "what should come to a person (*ra'uiy*)" and "what is held for him (*muḥzaq*)." As we learn, "The first-born takes a double portion . . . from what is held [by the estate] and not from what should come [to the estate]."[32] I mean that the nature of the opening of the supernal source determines what should occur. But that fate is not yet held for the person until the choice is made. Then the divine knowing is "determined" (*muḥzaq*).

For God knows through the knowledge of the essence of His will and not through knowing something external to itself. In other words, an impression is made above, whether one walks in darkness and damages, arousing the power of judgment, or whether one walks in light and spreads light above. Everything returns from below to the supernal source above. Then the knowing above is knowing of the divine essence and is fixed and absolute. Thus the verse says, "*Now I know that you fear God.*"[33] But the verse says "now" and uses the past tense for "I know (*yada'ti*)." The meaning is "now I know in a confirmed way what I knew before was to be expected of you."

After I wrote the above, God granted me to find some obscure matters in Nahmanides's writings, which incline toward my words. Here is what he wrote in *parashat va-yelekh*:

> And the sense of "*For I knew his* [*evil*] *urge with which he acts today*"[34] [is] like the sense of "[*Now I know*] *that you fear God*,"[35] which refers to the knowing in actuality. For the divine knowledge of the future is potential. Had Israel not sinned in the wilderness and had their [evil] urge not become known in actuality, it would not have been proper for the song to testify and say concerning them, "It is revealed before Me that you will sin, and I call you to witness that many evils and afflictions will find you, such as this and that." But it would have been proper that He simply give them the Torah with its promises. "*If you are willing and will listen, you shall eat the goodness of the Land. And if you refuse and rebel, you shall eat of desolation.*"[36] But now that their evil urge and lusting heart is known also to them, He tells them all that will occur to them. This is like what is said in the verse, "*Because I know how stubborn you are, your neck is like an iron sinew . . . Therefore, I told you long ago, before it would happen, I let you know.*"[37]

From this, one can understand the words of our rabbis, of blessed memory, in tractate *'Avodah Zara*:

> David was not worthy of that deed and Israel were not worthy of that deed. . . . [So why did they do it? To teach you] that if an individual sinned, [one can say "cease" in the case of an individual] and if the community sinned, [one can say "cease" in the case of the community].[38]

The meaning is that from the perspective of how Israel's source was opened, it was not proper for this to have occurred. On the contrary, the opposite should have occurred. For when Israel received the Torah, they opened the supernal source of goodness. Similarly, David was known for his piety. But [divine knowledge] changed to "determined (*muḥzaq*)" through the force of the choice that they made. But, according to [the disposition of the source], they should not have committed this sin.

So they said, "if the community sinned" or "if the individual sinned." The meaning of their words is that, they were not deserving of the sin, but of the good that is drawn forth from the sin. For even, as a result of the strength of their choosing, a way of goodness emerges from those actions, which inclines toward what is proper (*ra'uiy*). In other words, "if an individual sinned" or "if the community sinned"[39]

All the future events that the Holy One, blessed be He, showed Adam and Moses, our rabbi, of blessed memory, were all according to what should occur. That is to say, it was the future that was prepared to happen, according to the opening of the source. This is the aspect of the verse, "*He who announced the generations from the start*."[40] Nevertheless, the power to choose is granted, whether for good or ill. Many things remained the way that they had been prepared, according to what was proper. The power to choose did not overcome them. However, many things were altered by the power of choosing, which opens another source. Nevertheless, everything is in the supernal source, in the root of the will, and the will is the divine knowing. For this knowing is not of what is external to itself.

Thus one may understand a teaching of our rabbis, of blessed memory, which Rashi cited in his commentary to *parashat ve-yera*, on the verse "*where he is*."[41]

> A person is judged according to the deeds that he is doing now and not according to the deeds that he will do in the future. For the ministering angels were protesting and saying, Master of the Uni-

> verse, are You raising up a well for someone whose descendants are going to kill Your children with thirst? He answered them, What is he now, righteous or wicked? They answered, Righteous. He said to them, I judge him according to his present deeds. This is the meaning of "*where he is.*" Where did he kill Israel with thirst? When Nebuchadnezer exiled them. For it is written, "*the in the steppe pronouncement ... meet the thirsty with water.*"[42] When they were leading them near the Arabs, Israel would say to those who arrived, please lead us to our cousin, Ishmael, and he will have mercy on us. As it is written, "*caravans of Dedanites.*"[43] Do not read "*Dedanim* (Dedanites), but *Dodim* (uncles). They met them, bringing them meat and salt fish and swollen waterskins. Israel thought they were full of water. When they put them in their mouths and opened them, the wind entered their bodies and they died.[44]

A question may be raised. If the ministering angels wished to prevent the raising up of a well for Ishmael, then [they must have known that] he would certainly die as a result. Scripture attests to this, "*And she placed the boy* [*under one of the bushes*] ... *for she said let me not see the boy's death.*"[45] How could the ministering angels think that he would die? What would come of the future in which Ishmael would kill Israel with thirst? If Ishmael were to die now, the knowledge of the future would be annulled. However, the explanation is as has been indicated. Divine knowledge of the future is conditional, but is not determined. It is only what is prepared at the present time in accordance with the opening of the source. Then God's foreknowledge through knowing Itself is such. However, it may be changed through the power of human choice. Thus the ministering angels asked the Holy One, blessed be He, to change [the future] from conditional to absolute. But the Holy One, blessed be He, did not wish to and only said, "*where he is.*"[46] [This meant] that free will is granted to him, and if Ishmael wished to assert himself so as not to sin, or if Israel would be entirely righteous in that generation, the future would not be determined according to the way it is conditionally prepared to occur.

All the matters in the Torah are like this. For example, the word "*venoshantem (when you are long established)*" [in Deuteronomy 4:25] alludes to the number of years that the Land of Israel would exist.[47] Had they not sinned, this allusion would never have been realized. If you say, then what purpose would the allusion serve, know that just as the divine will contains all manner of opposites, as I have explained, so the Torah and all of its words and allusions change into many meanings and transformations. All are true, all are contained in the Torah, and one is free to choose. I will provide evidence from the root of all matters. For if Adam had not sinned, this Torah would have been prepared in another way than its present one, as is written in *Pardes*, *Sha'ar ha-Neshamah*, which I transcribed above.

Similarly, if Jereboam ben Nabat had immediately destroyed the altar and repented, this would have been the preparation that would have annulled [the future] in which Josiah would come and destroy it. Another case is Nineveh. There was preparation for a future in which Nineveh should have been destroyed within forty days. It was later changed because of the power of their choice.

Thus divine knowledge has not changed and will not change. For it never involves something outside of itself. Rather, God's knowledge concerns the essence of His will. Both before human action and after it, divine knowledge is sustained, for He knows through knowing His essence. It does not extend beyond Himself. The power to choose is granted to human beings to create an impression above and to open a source in the divine will, according to human desire. For the divine will contains everything and its opposite.

The reason that a person has the power to arouse above, according to his choice and will, is because he is made in the holy likeness and image. He also contains the "other side." This aspect contains supernal and lower powers. Therefore, the key of the sources is in his hand and the advice for him is, "*therefore, choose life*."[48] For the divine will is more pleased with goodness. For [it is the nature] of the truly good will to do good to others. For its good impulse was to bring goodness into existence so that it could be received. Even evil was not essentially created so that evil would exist, but in order to be transformed to good, as I discussed at length above.

Something very similar to what I have written can be found in *Pardes, Sha'ar 'Aẓmut ve-Khelim*, chapter nine. However, it will be clear to a very discerning reader that there is one major difference. If his view is like mine, thank God that I have managed to be in accord with him and thoroughly to explain this matter. For there is no doubt that this is the view of the great Rabbi Nahmanides, of blessed memory, in *parashat va-yelekh*, which I transcribed above. Blessed is the One who grants knowledge.

The Great Gate

Know my sons, may their Rock protect them, that this matter of the keys that are entrusted to human hands has remained a secret concealed by the true kabbalists who enter into the counsel of God. It has been passed on from kabbalist to kabbalist, going back to Moses on Sinai. For both the external and internal keys truly have been given over to human beings. Thus a person does not only worship in order to open [the sources which supply his needs], but the essence of worship is required above (*ẓorekh gavoha*), in order to unite the Great Name with its powers, until *Eyn Sof.* This is accomplished through learning Torah and fulfilling the commandments. Their root is the divine emanation that has been manifested for the human being who is in the supernal image and likeness. By means of fulfilling the Torah and commandments, he arouses supernal power and, so to speak, strengthens it. For I have already alluded above in many places that the basis of the emanation of the structure is *Tif'eret* and *Malkhut*. They are the roots of the worlds and the secret of "*turn from evil and do good*,"[1] in other words, the negative and positive commandments. Thus, since "first in thought, last in deed," through performing a good deed below, force is added to the power above, so to speak, and great love, friendship, and bonding [is increased] between the two lovers, mentioned above. The faces of those two cherubs were turned toward each other, "*like a male and female embracing*."[2] For we, House of Israel, emerged with our souls from the belly of our Mother, that is to say, from the Name *'ADoNay*, the source of Israel. As it is written, "*bless 'Elohim YHVH* [3] *in assemblies,* [*you who are*] *from the source of Israel.*"[4] [We emerge] through the coupling of [*Malkhut* with] *Tif'eret*, whose ejaculator is "*Ẓaddiq the foundation of the world.*"[5] From [this union] the souls fly forth. For the Living God is in our midst.

Therefore, the families of Israel number 65. As it is written, "*For you are ha-me'at (the least)* [*of all the nations*]."[6] Five less than all of the nations.[7]

The nations are 70 and Israel are 65 families, like the numerical value of the Name *'ADoNaY*. When the branches of the attribute *'ADoNay*, which are the roots of Israel, shine, they shine against the countenance of the Great Name. Then the Name is united with its Glory, which is the secret of "*YHVH is One and His Name One*."[8] This causes love and union above. As a result, the *Shekhinah* is with Israel, which is the secret of "*I placed my Sanctuary (miSHKkaNi) in your midst*."[9] But if, God forbid, Israel sins, there is a separation between those who are cleaving and the *Shekhinah* is, so to speak, in exile. And "*the maid servant will supplant her mistress*,"[10] as we shall go on to explain. Then the Name is not complete, God forbid, for *vav* and *heh* are lacking. For it has already been explained above concerning the letters *vav heh*, which is the structure [of the seven lower *sefirot*], that the external princes have access there. Here is what Rabbi Galante wrote:

> In all actions, the thing affected has to be similar to what affects it. Consequently, since the divine essence is beyond limitation, in order to create limited creatures it was necessary for these ten *sefirot* to be emanated from [the divine essence], so that they would be a bit more similar to us, through their gradual descent from cause to effect until the hub of the earth. Thus the thing effected could be somewhat similar to what was affecting it. The beginning of the thought in the world of emanation is for the final action, in other words, to cause the final attribute to be emanated, which affects all of the things that are affected. Therefore all of the modes of governance (*hanhagot*) ascend and descend through this attribute, whether to lovingkindness or compassion, or their opposites.
>
> This is explained in the *Zohar*, *parashat Terumah*: "Even here, '*time to act*'[11] remains without a *tiqqun* and without completion. What is the reason? "*For they have violated Your Torah*"[12]; because Israel has been idle below from [carrying out] the teachings of the Torah; because that 'time' stands or departs or rests, depending on Israel."[13]
>
> For this "time," that is, this final attribute, is not made. In other words, it has not been rectified, but requires to be made, rectified, and adorned, because "they have violated Your Torah." Therefore, she is separated in isolation (*nidah*). But through fulfilling the Torah, she will return to Her existence. This occurrence causes Her to ascend and descend. For it is the root of all of Israel's holy souls, and all of their likenesses are inscribed within

> Her. As explained in the *tiqqunim*, first *tiqqun*, when Israel are concerned with Torah and commandments below, the roots of their souls, which are rooted in Her, sparkle and shine like the splendor of the firmament. Then the arousal of the ones below ascends and reaches her. She appears face to face with the Holy King and shows Her face to Him and says, "See how the son brought Me before You?" which is the secret of female waters. Thus She ascends with Him and does not descend, except because of Israel's sins. For when the guilty increase in the world, they harm those roots, which are rooted within Her. As written in the *tiqqunim*, "It causes that stream from the side of souls to run dry. This is because of the accusations in the surrounding area, beyond His chamber. Then She receives power from the supernal [sources of] severity, which descend, bringing judgments to the world. The world goes up in flames until it is purified from the source of Her judgments. Then She returns to Her house and to the field of holy apples, and is bound together with the three colors of the eyes and eyeball within them, and the world is made fragrant.[14]

The matter has been explained. For when the Great Name is blessed, the one who worships is blessed. He draws forth a blessing through his worship. The prophet, of blessed memory, alluded to this when he said, "*For whoever blesses himself in the land shall bless himself by the true God.*"[15] He said that the cause of one's being blessed in the land is due to the fact that he brought about a prior blessing in the true God. For whoever worships with the proper *kavvanah* unites the Name with its powers. Thus he gives it power and might, which is the secret of "*In 'Elohim we shall make might.*"[16] It is also the secret of "*Give power to 'Elohim.*"[17]

The meaning is that the supernal Wisdom decided to establish the lower image like the supernal image, as the kabbalists taught. The aspects of the human structure are parallel to the aspects of the Chariot. As a result, the human being is prepared so that his structure will be like the structure of the supernal Adam. Therefore this likeness bears a relationship and similarity to the supernal likeness, which is made "*in His image according to His likeness.*" It necessarily follows from this that when this likeness is stirred through its activities, so the supernal likeness will be stirred toward it. And it will hearken and respond to it. Thus it has been demonstrated (*yeẓuyyar*) that through the arousal that is initiated below through our worship, the supernal matters will be aroused above.

For the Torah and commandments, which are intermediate, by their nature contain this power. For they have been emanated and hewn from the source of being and supernal light. Thus they will be the key for opening that source from which they flowed, when it was activated in perfection. They ascend as they have been enacted, according to the likeness below, which is built like the likeness above. For all of the constructions are mutually related, as was explained.

In chapter *ha-Nose'* it is stated that at the time of Rabbi's death, he stretched his ten fingers toward Heaven and said, Master of the Universe, it is revealed and known to You that I labored over the Torah with these ten fingers and I did not derive enjoyment from even my little finger.[18] He made known at the time of his death that all his life he had been a true uniter, elevating all of the branches and uniting them with their roots. He indicated this by extending his ten fingers and admitted that in all his study of Torah and worship, he never requested or intended anything for himself. His only intention was [to fulfill] the need above and no other. Thus he said, "I have labored over the Torah with my ten fingers and did not derive enjoyment from even my little finger." Although he never intended his own benefit at all, from his true uniting wealth and honor were drawn to him beyond that of all of the sages of his generation.

In the *Midrash*, the Holy One, blessed be He, said to Moses, *Go tell Israel that My Name is 'EHYeH asher 'EHYeH (I will be what I will be)*. What is *'EHYeH asher 'EHYeH*? Just as you are with Me, so I am with you.[19] Similarly, David said, "[*YHVH*] *is your shadow at your right hand*."[20] What is the meaning of "*YHVH is your shadow*"? He is like your shadow. If you play with your shadow, it plays with you, and if you weep to it, it weeps back to you, and if you make angry or pleasant faces at it, it does the same to you. So, too, the Holy One, blessed be He, is your shadow. Just as you are now with Him, so He is with you.[21]

This involves what we have explained. The supernal forces are aroused in accordance with the arousal of those below. Thus they compared the relationship of the forces above to those below to that of a shadow and its form, since they are inter-related. Accordingly, the shadow will be aroused in a way that depends on the arousal of the form. Thus depending on the actions that the ones below arouse, the supernal forces will be aroused, either for good or ill. Thus they said, "and if you make angry or pleasant faces at it." And they also said, "just as you are now with Him."

All of this is due to the relationship and similarity between them. Accordingly, the supernal forces will hear and respond to the ones below. This means that the supernal source will open and the *shefa'* of blessing and light will descend. This refers to the future conditions that were recalled by the prophet. For then that relationship and likeness will be preserved in its perfection. Thus he said, "*And on that day, I shall respond, declares YHVH, I shall respond to the heavens and they shall respond to the earth and the earth shall respond with the new grain, wine, and oil, and they shall respond to Jezreel.*"[22] Now the verse was redundant when it said "*and on that day, I shall respond, declares YHVH, I shall respond.*" It was only necessary to say, "*on that day, declares YHVH, I shall respond to the heavens.*" However, the repetition is meant to allude to the fact that the arousal that ascends from the likeness below arouses the supernal and opens the source. Thus the primary supernal forces (*ha-roshim ha-'elyonim*) are blessed. This refers to the will in the first "I shall respond," which indicates that, first, the source of being answers to the arousal that ascends. Then the *shefa'* and light come to the supernal heavens, which is the secret of His Great Name.

They said in *Sefer ha-Bahir*, "How do we know that the heavens are the Holy One, blessed be He? For it is written, "*And You O Heaven shall hear.*"[23,24] Thus the verse said, "*I shall respond to the heavens.*" From there the light is extended and blessing comes to the external earth, the Land of Life, which is the secret of the final *heh* [of the Tetragrammaton]. Thus the verse said, "*And they will respond to the earth.*" First, the Great Name is blessed and united with its powers. Otherwise, there is no place whatsoever for the *shefa'* or blessing. Afterward, the blessing is extended to the ones below. As the verse says, "*And the earth will respond.*" This is the secret of "*And the earth shall yield its produce.*"[25] "*And they shall respond to Jezreel.*" Those who arouse and cause the union are called Jezreel because they sow the seed (*she-zor'im zera'*) of peace above through their good deeds, which are the commandments. [The commandment] is the intermediary that arouses the supernal likeness toward the one below, as we have explained above.

Here is what Rabbi Hayyat wrote in *Sha'ar Merkavah*:

> The ones below arouse the ones above. For the verse says, "*And from my flesh, I see God,*"[26] and it is also written, "*He made a mnemonic (zekher) for His wonders.*"[27] For by means of the things below, we gain insight into the things above. There is a great allusion to this in nature from the stone magnet that attracts iron. For when you take good hold of it and remove all impurities from it, and then break it in two, and place one piece in one corner and the other piece in the other corner, even if they are as far apart as you wish, even a thousand miles, if you place the iron near to one of

> these pieces, you will find that every movement that you make with that piece, the other one also makes at that time. Also, there is a great allusion to this in wine in a cask. For at the time that the vine, which is the mother of the wine in the cask, undergoes a change, through flowering, when a bud appears, the wine in the cask also undergoes a change at that moment, as a result of the change that its mother undergoes, even though that wine is separate and far removed from the vine. This is the allusion in what the sage said, "*And your mouth like new wine, going directly to my beloved, moving the lips of sleepers.*"[28] Our rabbis, of blessed memory, said, "His lips murmur in the grave." The meaning is that when a *halakhah* is mentioned in this world in the name [of a deceased sage], his lips also move in the grave at that moment, which is similar to what the new wine does, as has been explained. Also fruit becomes moldy at the time that the trees produce flowers and bud. From all of these matters there is faithful testimony for the fact that a human being also creates an impression above through all of the steps that one takes below, whether for good or ill. This is because he was created from the supernal ones in the divine image. He was connected to his God, like a chain of iron that hangs in the air. For when you move its lowest link, you also move the highest. The commandments are from the ten *sefirot*. When a person fulfills them below, he, so to speak, bestows power above from *Eyn Sof* in the supernal form, by way of the channels of thought, to that attribute, which is related to this commandment. Then the supernal ones are blessed because of the ones below.[29]

This matter that we have raised concerning "worship for the needs above" is explained in scripture, written in the Torah, repeated in the Prophets, and reiterated in the Writings, Mishnah, Talmud, Midrash, and, the last is beloved, in the *Zohar*.

Written in the Torah: "*And now let my Lord's power be great.*"[30] It is also written, "*riding through the heavens with your help.*"[31] And the opposite, God forbid, is, "*You have forgotten the Rock that gave birth to you.*"[32]

Repeated in the Prophets: "*What will You do for Your Great Name?*"[33]

Reiterated in the Writings: "*And David made a Name.*"[34] The meaning of "*made*" is related to *tiqqun*, as is explained in the *Zohar*, which I shall transcribe later. The meaning of "*David made a Name*" is related to "*You made them.*" "*Them*" is spelled deficiently. All of this will be explained below. Because of this matter, the righteous are called people of action, since through their good actions they establish (*metaqqen*) and make the Glory. This is the secret of the power in "*and now let my Lord's power be great*."

Also reiterated in the Writings, King David, may peace be upon him, said, "*YHVH our Lord, how majestic is Your Name in all of the earth !*"[35] Daniel said, "*Shine Your Countenance upon Your Temple, which is destroyed, for the sake of ADoNaY.*"[36] In other words, build the building so that the queen will not sit in the house of the maidservant. For it is beneath the queen's honor to be outside her palace, and even more so to be under another's authority. Since the Temple is the throne for the supernal Glory, the *Shekhinah*, which is alluded to by this Name, he said "for the sake of '*ADoNaY*." For when the *Shekhinah* dwells in the Temple and rests among Israel, who are Her children, the Great Name is united with Its Glory. And the children's Mother crowns King Solomon and causes light to be emanated upon him from the source. For when the lower *Shekhinah* rests among the ones below, the supernal *Shekhinah* also rests among the supernal ones. Since this is the case, the presence of the *Shekhinah* in Israel is for the need above. This is the reason for the sacrifices (*'avodot*) that were in the Temple, the place of the *Shekhinah*. They were meant to draw Her constantly among those below, so that She would be permanently in the Temple. As a result, the supernal matters would be united from the beginning of thought until its end. That is the union of the Great Name. Therefore, the sacrifices were the cause of the *Shekhinah*'s presence among those below, and Her presence below was [to fulfill] the need above. Daniel, peace be upon him, knowing that this was so, prayed that the Temple, which is the place of the *Shekhinah*, be built so that She would return to Her place. As a result of Her returning below, She would also return above. Then the intention of creation would be complete. For so our rabbis, of blessed memory, said in *Bereishit Rabbah*, "the essence of the *Shekhinah* was among the ones below."[37]

And in the Midrash of Rabbi Simeon bar Yohai is written:

> "*Great is YHVH and much praised.*"[38] When is the Holy One, blessed be He, called very great? When He is with the community of Israel. As it is written, "*be'ir (in the city) of our God.*"[39] In the city of our God, He is great. "*Be'ir (in the city) of our God*" means with the city of our God. Rabbi Yehudah said to him, Why is "*of our God*" required here? He answered, So it is indeed. It is the city of the power of God and praise of Israel. What is the meaning? It means that a king without a lady is not a king and is not great and is not praised.[40]

Therefore, if He is in the city that is "*of our God*" . . . in other words, if He is in a complete union with Her . . . He is great. The cause and reason for this union is the perfection of the soul in the Torah and the commandments. This is the allusion in scripture's saying, "*of our God.*" In other words, we receive His divinity and do His commandments.

In the Mishnah: We learn "and all your deeds shall be for the sake of heaven."[41] In other words, to unite the Name, which is *Malkhut*, as is known, with Heaven, which is *Tif'eret*, as is known. The sages also taught in the language of the *Mishnah*, in chapter *Rabbi Meir 'Omer*, at the end of the chapter, "He said, everything that the Holy One, blessed be He, created in His world He only created for His Glory."[42] This means that one must worship the Name for the Glory of the Name, to increase the power above, to unite the Great Name with its Glory. It is true that the exoteric explanation is that He created it for His Glory. As the *Zohar* wrote, "so that His divinity would be known,"[43] so that there would be creatures who would know and recognize Him. Both of these explanations are true and depend on each other, as will be explained below.

In the Talmud: In the first chapter of *Berakhot*,

> it is taught in a *baraita*, Rabbi Ishmael ben Elisha said, Once I entered the innermost in order to burn incense and I saw *Akatriel YaH YHVH Zevaot* sitting on a high and exalted throne. He said to me, Ishmael, my son, bless me. I said, May it be Your will that Your compassion overcome Your anger, may Your compassion roll over Your attributes, and may You behave toward Your children with compassion, and go beyond the requirements of judgment for them. He nodded in assent to me with His head. So we learn, do not take the blessing of an ordinary person lightly.[44]

At first glance this passage seems very strange, as is the passage that precedes the *baraita* of Rabbi Ishmael.

> Rabbi Yohannon said in the name of Rabbi Jose, How do we know that the Holy One, blessed be He, prays? For it is written, "*And I will bring them to My holy mountain and cause them to rejoice in the House of My Prayer.*"[45] "Their prayer" is not written, but "*My Prayer.*" From this, we learn that the Holy One, blessed be He, prays. What does He pray? Rav Zutra bar Toviah said in the name of Rav, May it be My will that My compassion will overcome My anger, may My compassion roll over My attributes, may I act with

> compassion toward My children, and may I go beyond the requirements of judgment for them.[46]

I shall explain these two passages according to the method I used above in explaining the passage from *Midrash Rabbah* concerning the verse "*and His abode will be in Shalem*."[47] It is also stated there that the Holy One, blessed be He, prayed. The issue is as follows. Just as bringing about the coupling of *Tif'eret* and *Malkhut*, the secret of *vav heh*, the roots of the worlds, depends on the arousal of the ones below, so the coupling of *Ḥokhmah* and *Binah*, which are the roots of the structure, depend on the arousal of *Malkhut*. This is the secret of "May it be My will," which is the arousal of the supernal root. Afterward, He said, "May My compassion overcome My anger." This was to indicate that the structure and its root are all one united unity, only one is concealed and the other revealed.

The intention of the blessing of Rabbi Ishmael, the High Priest, was the same. "May it be your will." [Literally, he said], "May it find favor from before You," and not "may it find favor before You." For He is the supernal root. When the compassion rolls over the attributes, the cherubs are face to face, "*like a male and female embracing*."[48] As a result, *shefa'* descends below, so that the children who are borne in the belly will be treated with compassion.

In tractate *Shabbat*, chapter *Rabbi Akiva*, is written,

> When Moses ascended on high, he found that the Holy One, blessed be He, was binding crowns for the letters. He said to him, Moses, there is no peace in your city. He answered, Is there a servant who gives peace to his master? [The Holy One] said, You should help me. Immediately, he said, "*Now may the power of my Lord increase, as You have said, saying.*[49,50]

Here is what the *'Avodat ha-Qodesh* writes in the introduction:

> They wanted to inform us that this matter is extremely difficult. It cannot be grasped by any intellect. This is because the human intellect cannot imagine that the supernal *tiqqun* is placed in the hands of those below and that worship and prayer are for [the purpose of fulfilling] the need above, were it not that the Holy One, blessed be He, revealed this secret to the Lord of the Prophets, until he wondered at this. Thus they said, "He was binding crowns." This is the binding together and union of the letters,

which is the secret of the powers of the united Name, [in which these powers] are bound together. "Letters (*'otiot*)" comes from the expression "*morning came* (*'ata'*)."[51] For as a result of binding the crowns, light and *shefa'* always come and never cease. Therefore, they called these powers " *'otiot*," since they come to each other and join themselves together. And they are the letters, and the Torah is woven from the letters. Eveything emanates and comes from these powers. Thus they called them *'otiot* to inform us faithfully that the union, which is for the needs above, depends on learning the Torah and fulfilling it, for this is the great cause. Neglect of the Torah causes a cessation of the flow from the source and separation of the union. Thus He said, "There is no peace in your city." In other words, peace departs from the city of our God because of creation's damaging and transgressing against the Torah. Therefore, I am showing you how and what will correct this. It is through binding crowns and uniting them, through improving their deeds, returning to the way of Torah, and fulfilling its commandments. Thus that damage will be corrected. When [Moses] heard this, he was amazed and said, "Is there a servant . . . ?" In other words, "Is it possible that the perfect worshipper should have such power? This is amazing. How can this follow from that?" It was accepted that prayers and worship draw forth compassion, but he raised a question through expressing surprise, so that an answer would come properly from the mouth of God and he would be faithful in receiving it. Then God answered him, "You should have helped me." In other words, He told you, O person, what is good and what *YHVH* requires of you, that is, to help Him in His action. If there is no cause for this, how will there be a result? Won't the lack of aid and agent frustrate the cause?[52] It may be that God revealed His secret, the reason, to His servant, the faithful one of His House, [for] "immediately, He said to him." In other words, when Israel sinned, Moses required that learning and the correct advice. He advised and indicated this to him by way of the *tiqqun* for what they spoiled. Thus [he could] bring near what they had removed from each other, and restore those who had been driven off because of their sin. This secret is explained nicely in the verse, "*Now may the power of my Lord increase*,"[53] and in mentioning those qualities that he mentioned when he prayed for them,[54] and in God's answer to him, when He said, "*I have pardoned, according to your words. Nevertheless, as I live, and as the whole world is filled with the Glory of YHVH . . .*"[55] It is all established and explained, for the sages of the heart. And [Moses] said, "*As You have said, saying.*" For You are the guide for finding and opening for pardon. You taught me the secret of prayer and the supplication that You will answer. Were it not for Your will to pardon and forgive, it would not be sought without asking You.[56]

In the Midrash:

"*And they shall go without strength before the pursuer.*"[57] Rabbi Azariah said in the name of Rabbi Judah bar Simon, When Israel does the will of God, they add power to the strength that is above, as scripture says, "*In God we shall make power.*"[58] When Israel does not do the will of God, they weaken, so to speak, the great power above. As it is written, "*You have forgotten the Rock that gave birth to you.*"[59] Rabbi Judah bar Simon said in the name of Rabbi Levi, the son of Rabbi Tarfon, When Israel does the will of the Holy One, blessed be He, they add power to the strength that is above, as scripture says, "*Now may the power of my Lord increase.*" [60]And when thay do not do the will of the Holy One, blessed be He, they weaken, so to speak, the great power that is above and go themselves without strength before the pursuer.[61]

In the *Zohar:*

"Israel is the perfection of the Holy Name. When Israel below are perfect in their worship, so to speak, the Holy Name is perfect . . . When Israel are not perfect below in their worship and are condemned to exile, so to speak, the Holy Name is not complete above."[62]

It is also written there: "So to speak, the Holy One, blessed be He, said, when Israel are righteous below, My power is increased over everything. When they are not righteous, they weaken, so to speak, My power above."[63]

In *Sifre*: Something similar is found. " '*To You, who sit in Heaven, I raise my eyes,*'[64] were it not for the fact that I am sitting in heaven. Scripture also says, '*who built His chambers in heaven and stablished His vault on the earth.*'[65]"[66]

In the Midrash of Rabbi Nehunia ben Ha-Kanah:

> "And how can [a person] treat his Master with *Ḥesed* (kindness)? Through the study of Torah. For whoever learns Torah for its own sake bestows *Ḥesed* on his Creator. As it is written, '*He rides in the heaven with your help and with His majesty in the skies.*'[67] Thus the meaning is, when a person learns Torah for its own sake, you help Me and I ride in the heavens, then [He is] '*with His majesty in the skies.*' "[68]

In the Midrash of Rabbi Simeon Bar Yohai:

> "Come and see. '*Trust in YHVH and do good.*'[69] What is the meaning of '*and do good*'? Through the action below, an action is caused above. This has been explained. '*And you shall do them.*'[70] You, so to speak, make them.[71] For through that arousal that you make below, there is arousal above. In this sense, it is written, '*do good.*' And '*good*' can only refer to *Ẓaddiq*.[72] Since you are 'making' that one, surely that one will be aroused. Then, '*Abide in the Land and pursue faith.*'[73] It is all one. '*Abide in the Land,*' the supernal Land.[74] For there is nothing in the world that can rest with Her until that '*Good*' is aroused toward Her. Since he aroused [*Yesod*], he, so to speak, makes it. Then, '*populate the Land.*' Dwell with Her, eat Her fruit, and enjoy Her. '*And pursue faith.*' That is the Land, and it is all one. As it is written, '*And Your faithfulness at night.*'[75] '*And pursue faith,*' that is, lead Her in all that you desire."[76,77]

Thus it has been explained that according to the deed below, so there is a corresponding response and arousal above. Through a good deed, "*Ẓaddiq*, the foundation of the World," who is called "good," will be aroused. And He will be united with His companion. The person who causes this through his deeds is the one who, so to speak, makes that matter and union occur above. As it is written, "and do good," for this is the *tiqqun* of the Glory. This person makes peace in the heavenly retinue. He also partakes of its goodness and dwells in that Land. Thus the verse says, "abide in the Land," alluding to the secret of the Land of Life.

It is also explained that as long as a person does not do that good, mentioned here, which is the union of *Ẓaddiq* and *Ẓedeq*,[78] it is impossible to abide in the Land. However, for arousing the Good to come and rest in its place, a person is considered as if he made it and rectified it. Then, "*abide in the Land and pursue faith.*" For then he will lead that "*faith*" in accord with the secret of the verse, "*And all of his deeds are faithful,*"[79] according to his will. For just as he did the supernal will above through his good deeds, so his will will be done. Then, "*You will decree and it shall be fulfilled.*"[80]

Another related matter is also clarified in the *Zohar*.

> "*And you shall do them.*" What is the meaning of "*And you shall do them*"? Since scripture already said, "*You shall follow,*" and "*You shall keep* [*them*]," why does it say, "*And you shall do them*"? Whoever does the Torah's commandments and follows its paths, it is as if he, so to speak, made it above. The Holy One, blessed be He, said, [it is] as if he made Me. They have explained this. Thus scripture said, "*And you shall do them.*" "*And you shall do them,*" is written indeed. For they were aroused because of us, to join together, so that the Holy Name will be as it should be. "*And you shall do them,*" indeed. In a similar vein, Rabbi Simeon said, "*And David made a name.*"[81] Did David make it? Rather, because he followed the ways of the Torah and did the commandments of the Torah and directed the Kingdom properly, he, so to speak, made a name above. There was no king in the world who merited this like David, who arose in the middle of the night. He would praise the Holy One, blessed be He, until the Holy Name ascended the Throne, when the light of day arose. [Then,] he, so to speak, really made a Name, as it is written, "*And the son of the Israelite woman pronounced the Name and cursed It.*"[82] For this reason, "*David made a Name.*" Therefore, it is written, "*And you shall do them.*" If you endeavor to do them, so that the Holy Name will be properly rectified, all of the blessings that are above will be present among you, in their proper form.[83]

From all of this, it is explained that through their worship and good deeds, the righteous add power to the strength above. According to the passage from *Midrash 'Eykha*, above, "When Israel does God's will, they add power to the strength above. As it is written, '*In God, we make power.*' "[84] For in fulfilling the Torah and the commandments, they draw forth light from Eden to the River and from the River to the Garden, which is the secret of *Keneset Yisrael*, which is *'Elohim*. We place power and force in it. Then it becomes stronger through Israel's aid. For Israel is the lower power and draws light and might to it from the "*peak of Amana.*"[85] And they unite

Her with Her lover, which is the secret of the righteous of the world of light who enlighten Her eyes. The *ẓaddiq* below arouses the *ẓaddiq* above. Both are established and make the supernal Glory and increase its strength, one from below and one from above. The *ẓaddiq* who is above becomes strengthened when there are *ẓaddiqim* (righteous ones) below who increase His power, in accordance with the secret of "*give power to 'Elohim.*"[86]

In the *Midrash* of Rabbi Nehuniah ben ha-Qanah, the following is written:

> It is taught: there is one pillar from the earth to the firmament and *ẓaddiq* is his name. [He is named] after the righteous ones. When there are righteous ones in the world, he becomes strong. If not, he weakens. He bears the entire world, as it is written, "*And ẓaddiq is the foundation of the world.*"[87] If he is weak, the world is not able to remain in existence. Accordingly, even if there is only one *ẓaddiq* in the world, he supports the world.[88]

The following was said, concerning this pillar, in tractate *Hagigah*, chapter *'eyn dorshin*. "Rabbi Eleazar ben Shamua says, It stands on one pillar and *ẓaddiq* is its name. As it is written, '*And ẓaddiq is the foundation of the world.*' "[89] It reaches from the earth, which is the secret of the Land of Life, to the firmament, which stands in the middle.[90] Concerning it, it is written, "*For all is in the heaven and on the earth.*"[91] It is He who unites "heaven" and "earth" and joins them so that they are one. He is called *ẓaddiq*, because of the *ẓaddiqim* (righteous ones). When there are righteous ones in the world, they arouse Him through their good deeds, which increase His power. He becomes stronger because they make power within Him and draw light and *shefa'* to Him from the source of all. Then He empties His load in His companion. He bears the entire world, which is the secret of the kingdom (*Malkhut*) of the House of David. If the opposite is the case, the opposite occurs. Everything is aroused by those below.

In Midrash Shoḥer Tov: " '*I speak with righteousness and have the power to save.*'[92] With what '*righteousness*'? With the righteousness that you did when you accepted the Torah. For were it not so, how would My kingdom have existed?"[93]

In the *Mekhilta*, is written: " '*Whom You redeemed for Yourself from Egypt, nations and their Gods.*'[94] Rabbi Akiva says, Were it not that scripture is so written, it would be impossible to say it. Israel, so to speak, said before the Holy One, blessed be He, You redeemed yourself. And so it is in *Sifre*."

Here is what Nahmanides, of blessed memory, the greatest of the later sages in the true wisdom, wrote in his commentary on the verse "*that I might dwell in their midst.*"[95]

> There is a great secret in this matter. For according to the plain meaning, the *Shekhinah* is in Israel for the sake of people (*ẓorekh hedyot*) and not for the need above. However, the matter is related to the verse which says, "*Israel, in you I am glorified.*"[96] And Joshua said, "*What will You do for Your Great Name?*"[97] And there are many verses like this: "*He desired it for his dwelling place,*"[98] "*Here I shall rest, for I desired it.*"[99] And it is written, "*And I shall remember the Land.*"[100]

Here is what Rabbenu Bahya wrote in his commentary on that *parashah*, concerning the verse, "*And they shall know that I am YHVH who brought you out of the Land of Egypt to dwell within your midst.*"[101]

> It says that the exodus was so that "[*I would*] *dwell within your midst.*" For otherwise He would not have brought them out. This indicates that the presence of the *Shekhinah* in Israel is also for the need above, and not for the human need. And in my opinion, this is what the Prophet Hosea said, "*I am YHVH your God from the Land of Egypt, you will not know any other god but Me, and there is no other savior besides Me.*"[102] It says that I only brought you out of the land of Egypt because "*I am YHVH your God.*" So you would accept My divinity upon you. And so that you would know no other god. Thus he mentioned "*the Land of Egypt,*" in the middle. I found a similar explanation in *Midrash Tehillim* on the verse, "*When Israel went out of Egypt.*"[103]
>
> "Rabbi Joshua ben Levi said, Israel was redeemed from Egypt because of the Tabernacle. As it is written, '*And God saw the Children of Israel.*'[104] And it is written, '*And Moses saw all of the work.*'[105] There is another place from which this may be learned, '*who brought them out of the Land of Egypt,*' on condition that '[*I would*] *dwell in their midst.*' "[106]
>
> Thus it is written, "*He desired it for His dwelling place.*"[107] And it is written, "*Here I shall rest, for I desired it,*"[108] and there are many verses that attest to this. I already mentioned this in my remarks on "*and God said . . .*"[109]

And on the verse "*and God said . . . ,*" he wrote as follows:

> From here, you can understand that the *Shekhinah* is in Israel not only for ordinary needs, but for the need above. For since the united Name is proclaimed, through the Glory, the Glory receives additional Holy Spirit. Thus it says, "*May the Glory of YHVH be forever, may YHVH rejoice in His deeds.*"[110] Thus Israel has the power to either weaken or increase the power above, depending on their deeds. For, it is written, "*You have weakened the rock that bore you.*"[111] And it is written, "*We shall make power in God.*"[112]

You have seen how all are agreed that worship is for the need above. For thus a person rectifies the Great Name and the *ẓaddiq* makes the form like its Maker, according to the secret that the lower Adam is made in the image and likeness of the supernal Adam, as has been explained. So when he sanctifies his inner and outer limbs, one limb strengthens another, which is the secret of the limbs of the supernal Chariot. He adds power to them. But if, God forbid, the human likeness changes, I mean if one turns from the side of holiness and cleaves to the side of impurity, he does damage in all of the worlds. The damage also reaches above, as explained in many places in the *Zohar* and *tiqqunim*. Here is a bit from *parashat 'aḥarey mot*:

> Rabbi Judah said, When the righteous multiply in the world, good spirits ascend from *Keneset Israel*, she is blessed by the Holy King, and her face shines. But when the wicked increase in the world, good vapors do not ascend from *Keneset Israel*, so to speak, and she tastes bitterness from the other side. Then it is written, "*He hurled the earth from the heavens.*"[113] And her face darkened. Rabbi Jose said, When the righteous increase in the world, it is written, "*His left hand is under my head and His right hand embraces me.*"[114] But when the wicked increase in the world, it is written, "*He drew back His right hand.*"[115] Rabbi Hezkiah says, From here [we learn], "*A grumbler separates his friend.*"[116] In other words, he separates the King from the Lady. As it is written, "*Do not reveal the nakedness of your father and the nakedness of your mother.*"[117,118]

It is also written there:

> Whenever Israel does the will of the Holy One, blessed be He, the Holy One, blessed be He, makes His dwelling-place with *Keneset Israel*. And whenever Israel does not do the will of the Holy One, blessed be He, the Holy One, blessed be He, does not make His

> dwelling-place with *Keneset Israel.* What is the reason? Because Israel is the firstborn son of the Holy One, blessed be He. As it is written, "*My son, My firstborn, Israel.*"[119] The Mother is *Keneset Israel*, as it is written, "*Do not abandon the Torah of your Mother.*"[120,121]

It is also written there:

> See what is written, "*A wise son will make his father glad.*"[122] As long as he follows the straight path and is wise, he makes his father glad. This is the Holy King above, "*He makes His father glad.*" But if that son encounters trouble on his path, what is written? "*A foolish son is his mother's sorrow.*"[123] "*His mother's sorrow,*" indeed. This is *Keneset Israel.* The secret of the matter is in the verse, "*Your mother was dismissed for your crimes.*"[124,125]

The following is also written in the *Zohar*:

> We have learned, the wicked, so to speak, make flaws above. What are flaws? As it is written, "*Did He destroy? No. The flaw is His children's.*"[126] For all of those *tiqqunin* were not done properly. One verse says, "*He donned righteousness like armor.*"[127] The verse also says, "*He clothed Himself in the garments of vengeance.*"[128] Rabbi Isaac explained, He wore righteousness when Israel was righteous and when they were not righteous, He wore the garments of vengeance. Rabbi Jose asked, What are flaws? As we have learned, the fathers are not adequately blessed from that watering of the stream, and how much more so the sons? As it is written, "*Did He destroy? No. The flaw is His children's.*"[129] Why does it say, "*lo lo,*" twice? Once for above and once for below. This is as Rabbi Simeon said, "Whenever there are many wicked in the world, the Holy Name is not, so to speak, blessed. But whenever there are not many wicked in the world, the Holy Name is blessed. As it is written, "*May sinners perish from the world . . . bless YHVH O my soul, halleluyah.*"[130] Rabbi Abba said, This verse is really as it is written, "*Did He destroy? No. The flaw is His children's.*" Who is it that caused the harm? It is the "*crooked and twisted generation.*"[131] Because these were wicked and the generation was found to be so, after Moses said all of these things and mentioned the Holy Name properly, he said, "*never fails, He is*

> *righteous and upright.*"[132] A matter properly set up. But, "*Did He destroy? No. The flaw is His children's.*" What is the reason? This is because they were "*a crooked and twisted generation.*" Rabbi Judah said, "*lo lo.*" In other words, they did it to themselves. The wicked cause blessings to depart from the world. Rabbi Abba said, "*lo lo.*" We have established it. And so it is. What is written after it? "*Will you requite YHVH like this?*"[133] To thus repay the Holy One, blessed be He, for all the good that He caused for you and did toward you?[134]

There are countless passages like this in the *Zohar* and *Midrashim*. The kabbalists have also expounded in their books on the fact that when *Keneset Israel*, which is below, conducted themselves properly in their pure land, acting in accord with righteousness and the Torah, the *Shekhinah* was among them, as a fine and lovely Holy Spirit, and as a canopy and crown above the Glory. As it is written, "*This is known in all of the Land.*"[135] And it is written, "*YHVH is King, let the Land rejoice.*"[136] The allusion is to the Land of Life. The opposite case is like a bird who strays from her nest, who leaves her home and lodgings. It is like the meaning of the verse "*plunders his father and puts his mother to flight.*"[137] It is also written, "*Why are you like a stranger in the Land and like a guest who stops for the night?*"[138] And as our rabbis, of blessed memory, expounded in *Midrash Tihillim*, concerning the meaning of the *Shekhinah* in exile:

> "*I will rejoice in your salvation.*"[139] Rabbi Abahu said, This is one of the five most difficult places in scripture. For the salvation of Israel is the salvation of the Holy One, blessed be He. "Our salvation" is not written here, but "*your salvation.*" David said, Our salvation is "*your salvation.*"[140] Rabbi Berekhiah the priest said, Why is it written, "*He is a ẓaddiq and saved*"?[141] "A savior" is not written here, but "*saved.*" When they return in the future, the *Shekhinah* will return with them. As it is written, "*And YHVH our God will return.*"[142] "And He will cause to return," is not written here, but "*He will return.*"[143]

They treated this at length, for it is well known throughout the entire range of kabbalistic writings.

However there is a great problem concerning all of the above. Many verses indicate that the commandments and transgressions do not concern it. Eliphaz said: "*Does Shaddai gain if you are righteous? Does He profit if your conduct is blameless?*"[144] Elihu said, "*If you sin what effect do you have on Him? If you are righteous, what do you give to Him?*"[145] There are many verses of this type.

I found that the author of *'Avodat ha-Qodesh* addressed himself to this problem. I will transcribe all that he wrote, because it is a great homily. Afterward, with God's help, I will reveal my own view. Here is what he wrote in the third chapter of *ḥeleq ha-'avodah*:

> I saw among the sayings of our rabbis, of blessed memory, a matter that, on the surface, seems to contradict what has been received and confirmed, without any doubt whatsoever; namely, that worship is for the need above as well. For they said the following in the eighth chapter of *Midrash Yelamdenu*: "And what does it matter to the Holy One, blessed be He, if one ritually slaughters an animal and eats it or if one pierces an animal and eats it? Do you benefit Him? Do you harm Him? Or what does it matter to Him if you eat pure animals or if you eat impure animals? For it is written, '*If you are wise, you are wise for yourself.*'[146] Therefore, the commandments were only given in order to purify people through them. As it is written, '*The saying of YHVH is pure . . .*'[147] Why? In order to protect you, as it is written, '*He is a shield for all who trust in Him.*'[148]"[149]
>
> Upon initial reflection, it seems that it makes no difference to Him if one ritually slaughters and eats or if one kills and eats, or whether one eats pure or impure animals. For nothing of this sort harms or benefits Him, and nothing affects Him at all. This may be seen from the plain meaning of the verses that were mentioned. "*Does Shaddai gain if you are righteous? Does He profit if your conduct is blameless?*"[150] These are the words of Eliphaz to Job. And Elihu said to him, "*If you sin how do you affect Him? . . . If you are righteous, what do you give to Him? . . . Your wickedness affects men like yourself.*"[151] King Solomon, may he rest in peace, said, "*If you are wise, you are wise for yourself.*"[152] From all of this, it appears that human good and evil do not affect what is above at all, but only those who do them. However, the opposite has already been explained. For worship is for the need above. As far as food is concerned, they said the following in the *Midrash* of Rabbi Simeon bar Yohai:
>
> "Come and see. Whoever eats from these forbidden foods cleaves to the other side, and soils his body and soul. An impure

spirit rests over him and grips his bones, which has no portion in the supernal God, and does not come from its side, or cleave to it. If he thus departs from this world, all of these [impure spirits] that cleave to the side of impurity, cleave to him and render him impure. He is judged as a person who is loathsome to his Master. Loathsome in this world and loathsome in the next world. Concerning this, it is written, '*and become impure through them.*'[153] ['*Become impure*'] is spelled without an *'alef* because there is no healing for his loathsomeness and he cannot go out of his impurity forever. Woe to them. Woe to their souls, which will never cleave to the Bundle of Life, for they have become impure. Woe to their bodies. Concerning them is written, '*their worms shall not die and their fire will not be extinguished. They shall be a horror to all flesh.*'[154] What is '*a horror*'? Their stench. What is the cause of this? That side to which they cleaved. Israel comes from the right side, and if they cleave to the left side, they damage that side, they damage their bodies, and they damage their souls. They are damaged in this world and in the next. How much more so, a person who cleaves to the side of impurity, for everything is interconnected. And it is written, '*For you are a Holy people to YHVH your God.*'[155]"[156]

Thus they have made it explicitly clear that those who make themselves impure through eating what the Torah has forbidden, damage "that side." This refers to the right side. For they said, "Israel comes from the right side." It is the side of holiness and purity, the secret of the divine emanation. Therefore, the [eating of] pure and impure animals does affect the upper realm as well. There is much concerning this in the *Midrash* of Rabbi Simeon bar Yohai, especially in the Torah portions on plagues and forbidden sexual relationships. Among them is the following:

"Rabbi Hiyya said in the name of Rabbi Isaac, the greatest diminishment is only found below because it is found above. And it is only found above when it is found below in the sins of the world. For we have learned that everything is interdependent. This depends on that and that on this."[157]

As for their saying "What does it matter to the Holy One, blessed be He . . . " and "The commandments were only given [to purify people . . .]," this does not contradict what we have said. However, from what we have said, it will be clear to the wise of heart that worship is for the need above as well. For when they said, "What does it matter to the Holy One, blessed be He," they meant the unique Lord, the Root of Roots, to whom nothing matters at all. All of the verses cited also have this reference. As for their imagining that a person's righteousness and bitterness do not affect Him at all, but only the perpetrator of good and evil, this is in regard to the the unique Lord. However, there is a total need [to affect] the Glory, which pours *shefa'* over the supernal heads in order to unite the beginning of thought with its end, for such is the pure will and holy desire. All of the commandments and forms of worship came in order to attest to this, to complete the intention, and to indicate that this is so. We were commanded to do them for this purpose. Doing them and dealing with them always completes the intention; namely, the uniting of the Great Name with its Glory, which is "the need above as well." Performing the commandments and carrying out the correct forms of worship with the proper intention, brings a person into *devequt* with the supernal things. This is the secret of "*and you shall cleave to Him*"[158] and "*to cleave to Him.*"[159] This is joining the lower ones with the supernal ones, which they strived to do in this life in order to establish them as they should be. This is the meaning of their saying "The commandments were only given to purify people." This refers to the joining together and *devequt* with the United Name, by means of the commandments. For they are the cord that binds together those who do and fulfill them and the United Name. However, those negative commandments, which we were cautioned against violating, so as not to be rendered impure, also came for the need of the Glory. For the impurity of a person who violates them below also reaches above, to the sanctified Temple. This is the secret of "*He defiled the Temple of YHVH.*"[160] For whoever commits transgressions arouses the external things, the secret of the opposites, which are the side of impurity. They came and imparted pollution in Eve and defiled the Temple. "*Then because of evil the zaddiq is taken.*"[161] And our souls dry up and there is no taste at all. We were commanded not to arouse that side, which is the dross that comes out of silver, but to drive it off so that it will not come within the Holy, so that the silver will be clean and pure, and free of dross. This is the secret of "*if you remove dross from silver . . . if you remove evil from the King's presence.*"[162] For this reason the Torah cautioned us not to transgress the negative commandments. In all cases the meaning is to purify people through them. Implied in the expression *le-ẓaref* (purify) is to bind together all things and also to separate, ward off, and exclude the dross from the silver.[163] Thus scripture said, "*Every saying of God is pure.*"[164] "*The saying of YHVH is pure.*"[165] From all of this it is clear that all human actions, whether good or bad, affect what is above.

Maimonides wrote as follows, in *Moreh Nevukhim*, part three, chapter twenty-six: "I found among the teachings of our rabbis, of blessed memory, in *Bereishit Rabbah*, a teaching that seems to say, when one first thinks about it, that some of the commandments have no reason, but are merely commands [to be obeyed]. No other purpose was intended and they are of no benefit. Thus they said there, 'What does the Holy One, blessed be He, care if one ritually slaughters from the throat [of an animal] or from the back of the neck? We must say, the commandments were only given so that people would be purified through them.' As it is written, '*the word of YHVH is purified.*'[166]"[167] Although this passage is very strange and nothing similar to it can be found among their words, I have an interpretation, which you shall now hear. It is neither inconsistent with their words, nor does it violate a universal principle; namely, that one should seek a beneficial purpose in existence for every commandment. "*For it is no empty matter.*"[168] The verse says, "*I did not say to the seed of Jacob, seek Me for nothing, I YHVH speak righteousness, I declare things that are right.*"[169] I will tell you what every person of sound mind should believe concerning this matter. The commandments, in general, have a necessary cause. He commanded them because of one benefit. However, it may be said that portions of them are merely for the sake of commanding something. The example for this is killing an animal because of the need for good food. The benefit of this is clear, as we shall explain. However, the requirement for ritual slaughter rather than stabbing,[170] and to sever the esophagus and windpipe in a particular place, are meant, like other such commandments, "to purify people." The same thing will be explained from the example of slaughtering from the throat rather than the back of the neck. However, the truth of the matter is that when it became necessary to eat animals, the commandment intended to bring about an easy death in an easy manner. For beheading would only be possible with a sword or something similar, but ritual slaughter is possible with anything. To bring about an easier death, it was required that the knife be sharp.[171]

It is necessary to respond and say that if, in his view, his reason is sufficient for explaining the passage in *Bereishit Rabbah*, "What does it matter to the Holy One, blessed be He, whether one ritually slaughters at the throat or the back of the neck?" it is not adequate for explaining what was said in *Midrash Yelamdenu*, "What does He care if one eats pure or impure animals?" For it appears from their words that they are declaring that some of the commandments in general are only for the sake of commanding something and that no other purpose was intended. This is true of them in general and not merely concerning a portion of them. It appears from their words that they chose an example from which the principle concerning all of the commandments in general can be inferred. It is said in *Va-Yiqra Rabbah, parashat shemini*, " '*This is the Torah of the animal . . .*'[172] As it is written, '*Every saying of God is purified.*'[173] Rav said the commandments were only given to Israel in order to purify people with them. Why? As it is written, '*He is a shield to all who take refuge in Him.*'[174]"

So it appears from the meaning of "*Every saying of God is purified*" that the rabbis spoke concerning the generality of the commandments. Thus they said in *Midrash Shoḥer Tov*, "Rav said the Holy One, blessed be He, only gave the commandments to Israel in order to purify them, as it is written, '*The saying of YHVH is purified.*'[175]" Therefore, their words concern the generality of the commandments and not a portion of them, as the Rav held. Moreover, even the parts of the commandments were intended for the benefit of the soul, which is the ultimate success. Thus they said in *Va-Yiqra Rabbah, parashat shemini*, "Rabbi Berekhiah said in the name of Rabbi Isaac, In the future the Holy One, blessed be He, will make a feast for His servants, the righteous, and whoever has not eaten meat which is not kosher in this world will merit to see it in the world that is coming. As it is written, '*Fat from animals that have died or that have been torn by beasts may be put to any use, but you must not eat it.*'[176] This is so that you can eat it in the future. Accordingly, Moses cautioned Israel and said, '*This is the animal that you may eat.*'[177]"[178]

Thus severing the windpipe and esophagus in the designated place is part of the commandment and it purifies the animal and makes it fit for eating. As a result, the soul derives great benefit.

But slaughtering the animal from the back of the neck renders it unfit, makes the soul impure, and distances it from the ultimate success. Therefore, severing the windpipe and esophagus in the designated place, which is part of the commandment, according to the opinion of the Rav, involves that great intended benefit and is not merely for the sake of commanding something, as he says. Moreover, the kabbalists received teachings concerning the reason for this commandment which are the secret of the world. They were concealed from the Rav.

In *Midrash Shoḥer Tov*, they said, " '*The way of God is perfect.*'[179] If the way of God is perfect, how much more so your way should be perfect. What does it matter to the Holy One, blessed be He, if one slaughters from the windpipe and eats, or from the tail? Rabbi Berekhiah said in the name of Rabbi Jacob, If in this world you did not eat the fat of animals that have died or been torn by beasts, on your life, a great feast is prepared for you in the world to come. As it is written, '*And you shall eat your fill.*'[180]"[181]

In saying "If the way of God is perfect, how much more so your way . . . " they alluded to what was explained above as the secret of "to purify the people through them." This involves supernal and lower perfection and their union. The Holy One, blessed be He, is the unique Lord. What does it matter to Him how one slaughters? . . . For everything is for the need of the Glory, which is the secret that whoever is purified and warned against eating dead and impure animals merits that purification. Therefore the commandments as a whole and in their parts cause that purification, which is the perfection and joining together of the supernal ones and those that are below are included and merit that perfection. Therefore, there is nothing in a commandment or its part in which the purpose and benefit of the soul's success as well as the union of the Great Name with its Glory was not intended. This is well known to those who know the truth. In order to indicate that there is no word or story in the Torah in which this benefit was not intended, and especially in the commandments as a whole and in their parts, the Lord of the prophets said, "*Take to heart all of these words . . . for it is no empty matter for you.*"[182] All of the kinds of perfection and success cleave to these words and are drawn from them. Thus he said, "*They are your life.*"[183] This refers to the life of the world to come. "*And through this word*

> *you will extend your days upon the land.*"[184] In other words, the life of this world is also drawn from them.[185]

Now his response to the problem does not seem to me to be correct. For he explains the verses that declare that actions do not affect God as applying to *Eyn Sof*, but that human actions do affect the world of emanation. If that is the case, why did scripture say, "*If you sin how do you affect Him? . . . if you are righteous what do you give Him?*"[186] For even if one does not affect and give to *Eyn Sof*, one affects and gives to the divine emanation, which is the revelation of *Eyn Sof*, through which everything comes. For the concealment of *Eyn Sof* is rendered complete by means of the divine emanation. Accordingly, *Eyn Sof* is not alluded to in the Torah, neither by word, nor letter, nor any part of a letter. Moreover, the passage from *Midrash Yelamdenu*, "What does it matter to the Holy One, blessed be He, . . . " was interpreted by the Rabbi as applying to *Eyn Sof*. But this is very unlikely, since in the great majority of cases, "the Holy One, blessed be He" refers to the divine emanation and most commonly indicates *Tif'eret* and occasionally, *Malkhut*.

Therefore, my sons, may their Rock protect them, listen to me and enliven your souls. I will teach you the way to understand this matter of worship for the need above.

First, I will cite the views of the later kabbalists concerning the matter of increasing or weakening the power that is above. I will begin with their disagreement and then present what God has granted me. Here is what is written in *Ma'arekhet ha-'Elohut*, *ma'arekhet ha-ta'am*:

> For Thought in creation was in *Tif'eret*, so that the species could exist, as we explained above. But the emergence of Thought from potential to actual took place by means of *'Atarah*, which became the foundation stone. It is the Ruler of the supernal world and is called "firstborn." In other words, it is designated with its power, as in the verse, "*I will appoint him firstborn.*"[187] However, it cannot be said that it is called Ruler of the World in the literal sense, because it rules over the world and watches over it. Rather, it draws from above and bestows below, like the *Midrash*, "He made Compassion and Judgment partners and created the world."[188] It is also similar to the parables of the architect and the agent, which are applied in the *Midrash* on *parashat Noah*, on the verse, "*and His heart was saddened.*"[189] "It may be compared to a king who had a palace built by an architect. He saw it and it did not please him.

With whom should he be angry? Not with the architect." There is another parable in *parashat Noah* concerning a king who transacted business by means of an agent and suffered a loss. With whom should he be angry? Not with the agent. There is another parable in the *Midrash* concerning a wetnurse who was chastised because of the stench of the prince. All of these parables allude to the concealment of the divine countenance which shines at the time of anger. This is the meaning of the verse, "*when I bring clouds over the earth* . . . "[190] This alludes to the earth's becoming dark, when the light of the sun does not shine. The words "architect," "agent," and "wetnurse" allude to the Ruler of the World. The "prince" alludes to *Tif'eret*. Thus the parables alluded to the fact that if the King is pleased with the architect's work, or the agent's trade, or the wetnurse's rearing, he comes and resides in the builder's building or will take part in the agent's trade, or will dwell with his son in his house. And he will proclaim peace for the architect, agent, and wetnurse, and all will be in peace. But if their deeds do not please him, because they have been been swayed by the stubbornness of their heart, then the king's heart will be saddened and he will withdraw from [the house] because of the serpent's contamination in his house. For a person cannot live in the same house with a serpent. For one is lowly and the other is upright. The serpent's contamination would be added to Eve. The nations ascend to greatness through that contamination, because the celestial rulers that are assigned over them are sustained by it. When there is an ascendency to the nations through this contamination, Israel decends through their sins and impurity. They are sent with their mother from their native land [and placed in] subjugation to the nations in a land that is not theirs. They enslave and afflict them, for their power is there. Because of the mother's cleaving to her children, she shares their affliction. As it is written, "*In all of their suffering, He suffers.*"[191] This is the explanation of the chastisement and impurity that they suffer as a result of the contamination. Consider also the *Midrash*, "When they were exiled to Egypt, the *Shekhinah* was with them. When they were exiled to Elam, the *Shekhinah* was with them. What must be understood here is what we explained above. Through the merit of the righteous one who makes the form like its Maker, the *Shekhinah* is present among those below, and She especially rests on the pure form, because like finds like. She is aroused until the female

> surrounds the male and he grows wise in Torah, wisdom, and commandments. For he constantly struggles over them until he prophesies and knows the future. But when a person rebels against the Torah and commandments, which are in the divine likeness, he renders his form impure and is considered like an animal, who is removed from holiness and prophecy, as a result of its actions."[192] And he is not worthy to make use of the King's scepter. This is the secret of the matter. For in every case in which *shefa'* is removed, it is not a matter of the nursemaid's lack in any sense, God forbid. Rather, the destructive children receive the opposite of good *shefa'* because they rebel. When the mother is dismissed, the children are dismissed. As it is written, "*I am about to destroy them with the earth.*"[193] It is concealed here that in destroying the earth, they will also be destroyed. For it will receive a great blow, so that they will return from their way and return with Her from the house of bondage to the house of the king, within. Therefore, the lack is entirely Israel's. It is they who receive the opposite of the good they would have deserved, had they been good.[194]

Here is what is written in Rabbi Hayyat's commentary on "It is not a matter of the wetnurse's lack."

> It does not mean that the essential purpose is to place a lack in her, for she did not sin. Rather, it is to chastise the children. As a result she will be lacking in the Temple. For it is not possible to chastise the children without her being dismissed and driven out with them. I forced myself to interpret the Rabbi's words in this manner, even though I know it is patchwork that the language will not bear. For if this is not his meaning, he is contradicting what he said above, concerning the parable of the wetnurse, agent, and architect. If their work does not please the king, his heart will be sad. And he will depart from the wetnurse, agent, and architect. And this is the meaning of the chastisement which the wetnurse receives because of Israel's iniquity and the impurity that she received because of the contamination of the serpent. The *Shekhinah* goes with them into exile. Thus his words contradict each other. Also in the beginning of this Gate, he said that if the wife will rebel in her work, the husband will also rebel in his and leave his house. He will depart and divorce his wife. If the children refuse [to obey him], he will deliver them to the hand of their sin. The

wife will be divorced from her husband and the compassionate father will be far removed. Near this, he said the opposite. "As has been explained, it is not a matter of there being a reduction of power, holiness, and honor in the *'Atarah* or separation, because of the improper deeds of the ones below, God forbid, as many ignorant ones have thought, due to the weakness of their understanding of the words of our rabbis, of blessed memory, and of the kabbalists . . . " See now, my brother how his words contradict themselves? If his meaning is not as I have interpreted it, it is forbidden to listen to his words, and even more so to believe in them. Whoever pursues this view of his has to be weak-minded in the wisdom of the Kabbalah, which is entirely based on this axis. If it seems incredible to you how the *Shekhinah* receives a flaw through Israel's sins and how Israel causes the departure of the *Eyn Sof* and *'Atarah*, come and see what is written in *Sefer ha-Tiqqunim*: "Elijah said, Master of the Universe, you are known as the cause of everything and the Lord of everything. And each of the *sefirot* has a name by which it is known and angels are called by these names. But You have no known Name, but fill all of the Names. You are the perfection of everything. For when You depart from them, all of those Names remain like a body without a soul."[195] Therefore, according to this they are subject to perfection and deficiency, depending entirely on human action. I wish to clarify this further, so that you may know the meaning of the departure of the *Eyn Sof* from the *sefirot*, as well as the *'Atarah*'s departure to the *Eyn Sof*, and her fall. Surely, you must know that the *'Atarah* is called "vapor (*hevel*) of the mouth" and it is one of the vapors that the sage called "*vapor of vapors*."[196] You will find that there are seven vapors in that verse, which designate the structure [of the seven *sefirot*], which are increased and strengthened by the "vapor of the mouth" that emerges from the mouth of the righteous, whether in Torah or in prayer. As it is written, "*There is a vapor made on the earth*."[197] And the *'Atarah* is also the letter *heh*[198] and is called *lev* (heart). Therefore, it is *hevel* and *hevel* spelled backward is *lahav* (flame), because She is a flame connected to the coal. She is one of the flames referred to in the verse, "*The voice of YHVH kindles flames of fire*."[199] The secret of this matter is based on these two aspects, vapor and flame. For the vapor that emerges from the mouth consists of three things: water that emerges from the brain, fire that emerges from the heart, and air that emerges from the lungs. The letters that are expressed by way of the five parts of the mouth are composed of these three elements. Thus He first created the letters *alef*, *mem*, *shin*. For these three are called "Mothers." They are air, water, and fire. Thus the author of *Sefer Yeẓirah* said, "Twenty-two letters in the eye like wind, he extended them like water, he lit them like fire."[200] These vapors ascend to the light of the attribute that is composed of the three elements, water, air, fire, namely *'Atarah*. They strengthen and add power to Her in a manner that extends above by way of the vapors that ascend from the earth, which become clouds in the air. They pour rain onto the earth. For like finds its like and is aroused. At least, the arousal arises from it. For if there were no vapors ascending from the dry land, no rain would fall to earth. As it is written, "*A vapor ascended from the earth and watered the surface of the land*."[201] No more and no less. This concerns the *'Atarah*. For when She is dry because of the sins of Israel, vapors do not ascend and extend out from Her to *Eyn Sof* in such a way that they will pour out [*shefa'*] upon Her. It is also necessary that concealed vapors descend to Her from *Eyn Sof*. They have an impact upon each other, as in the case of the sense of sight. For the object of sight releases sparks that reach the sense of sight and the sense of sight also sends out sparks to receive them. The two can meet in no other manner, as is known to the students of nature. In the same way, concealed vapors descend from *Eyn Sof* to the world of emanation until they reach *'Atarah*. The two groups of sparks meet and then "*gladness and joy abide there, thanksgiving and the sound of music*."[202] I will give you a nice analogy concerning the matter, involving a magnet. Has not Rabbi Azriel compared the relationship between the divine emanation and the *Eyn Sof* to a magnet which attracts iron? . . . [203]

He also continued as follows: "This matter can also be understood from a flame. For a flame casts light in the three colors that are also found in the rainbow, when the lights above Her, which are the Patriarchs, shine into Her."[204] For She is the "lens that does not shine" and contains the colors. But the lights come from above and the colors within Her ascend toward them. The analogy for this is a lit candle that has been extinguished, yet a smoky vapor remains in it. If this candle is placed below a lit candle, very close to it, the smoky vapor that is in the candle will draw down the flame and it will be lit. Even though it is the nature of fire to rise above, it descends below toward the smoky vapor of the candle. Even though they do not actually meet, there is power in the vapor to draw the flame to it. This is, so to speak, what occurs with the *'Atarah*. She contains something like the smoky vapor in relation to the attributes above her. For She is the lens that does not shine. When the smoky vapor that is within Her ascends, it meets the flame that is in *Eyn Sof* and draws it below. This is true as long is there is nothing to prevent it. For the sins of Israel extinguish the smoky vapor so that it cannot ascend to the flame. Pay attention to this matter. *Guard it more than anything, for it is the source of life.*[205,206]

The author of the *Ma'arekhet ha-'Elohut* also wrote the following in *Ma'arekhet ha-Ta'am*, just above this.

It is also important to contemplate and know that with the ascent of Thought, the *'Atarah* became the "foundation stone," which receives from all, watches over the world below and directs it. This is not a matter of there being a reduction of power, holiness, or honor in Her, or of separation because their deeds were not proper, God forbid. Rather, that Thought was the epitome of perfection in regard to creation, as required for its existence.[207]

Here is what Rabbi Hayyat wrote there:

"It is not a matter of there being a reduction of power, holiness . . . " If the Rabbi means that the *'Atarah* does receive harm as a result of Israel's sins, his honor remains in place. This is a philosophical matter, but not the true opinion of the kabbalists. For what is the chastisement of the wetnurse and the dismissal of the mother? As it is written, "*Because of your crimes your mother was dismissed.*"[208] And it is written, concerning the time of the generation of the flood, "*and the earth became corrupt.*"[209] And what is the meaning of the "cutting" that a person does through his transgressions and the union that he brings about through fulfilling the commandments? All the reasons for the commandments revolve around this axis. We must necessarily declare that our transgressions cause a flaw in Her and also in all of the children. For the mother departs from the children. The *Zohar* interprets the verse, "*Do not take the mother over the children,*"[210] as "Do not take the mother from over the children." The flaw consists in this. The clear light is removed above and does not visit the earth. For the visitation is in order to benefit the ones below who make the form like its Maker. If there is no righteous person to draw down *shefa'* from the supernal *mazal*, the *'Atarah* is also flawed and lacks that *shefa'*. This is the explanation of "*and his heart was sad*,"[211] according to the interpretation of Nahmanides. I will give you an analogy from human breasts. As long as the infant nurses from them, he sucks and draws milk to the breasts from the sources. If there is no one nursing, there will be no milk. The same is true of the waters of a well. As long as the waters are depleted, the waters will increase. If not, not only will the waters not increase, but they will be lacking. The same is true in regard to the world of emanation. I am amazed at the Rabbi. For it seems from his words that there is no difference between the Emanator and the emanation. This was the doubt that caused him to say this. This would be fine, if we were attributing this to the first emanator, the *Eyn Sof*, the Cause of Causes.[212] However, in the world of emanation, the strap is loosed. It has already been explained in *Derush ha-'Aẓilut* that in the beginning the Holy One, blessed be He, had to create the world by means of the divine emanation, which is subject to perfection and deficiency, in order to do harm or good. The author himself said this at the beginning of the book:

"You must know that in my referring to the beginning and end of the *sefirot*, my meaning is not, God forbid, that there is a beginning or end to divinity. For I already explained in *'Avodat ha-'Ahdut* that divinity is not limited. Rather, I was referring to the world of emanation, which has a beginning and end, according to the order of all of creation."

Perhaps we can give him the benefit of the doubt and patch up his language and say that he meant to warn us against making the error of saying that the *'Atarah* was left as a foundation stone, to be the Head of the lowly, because of the reduction of Her holiness, and also so that She could undergo separation from above when the ones below sin. For this was not the intention, God forbid, except for the reason that he stated; namely, that it was necessary to be so in order to maintain the existence of the ones below.[213]

Here is what Rav Paz, who also authored a commentary on *Ma'arekhet ha-'Elohut*, wrote:

"It is not a matter of there being a reduction of power and holiness in Her . . . " Even though it appears that there are words in the written and oral Torahs that indicate that when the ones below do not do God's will, that flaw ascends above, God forbid, it does not cause any deficiency in the Divine Names. However, when Israel does God's will, the blessing is drawn down from above. Then all of those preying lions seek their food from God and the accusers become defenders of Israel, who are called God's children. The blessing is then present in the world. Below, "*Strangers will stand and graze your sheep, foreigners will be your plowmen and vintners*."[214] But if, God forbid, they do not do God's will, the *shefa'*, blessing, and providence ascend from below to above. Divine providence departs from the ones below and also from the powers that operate in the lowly world. Then the "*lions roar for prey*," [215] for there is no divine protector and aid. It is they who prevent the blessing and *shefa'*, until [Israel] returns in repentance. For God does not withhold sustenance. It is human beings, themselves, who cause these withholders, who were only created to carry out true and upright judgment with the permission of their creator. When the *shefa'* is removed from them, because of the ones below, the defenders become accusers. Thus it is explained that there is no deficiency above due to the ones below. You may yet ask how one can explain the verses in the Torah that declare that deficiency does reach above. For example, "*I am with him in suffering*,"[216] "*In all of their suffering, He suffers*,"[217] "*Because of your crimes, your mother was dismissed*,"[218] and the like. The meaning is that although the leader remains in his house and treasury, it is not pleasant for him as long as another authority is set up as ruler. It is as if he did not possess the means to provide what he lacks, except by means of others, as if the leader suffers over this matter. *Because of this the earth trembles*:[219] "*a slave who becomes king . . . a slave-girl who replaces her mistress*."[220] Thus it is explained. One should not deviate to the right or left.[221]

Certainly, the view of the *Ma'arekhet ha-'Elohut* is as explained by Rav Paz. The kabbalist Mattathias Delacrut wrote something very close to Rav Paz's view in his commentary on the Recanati. I will transcribe the Recanati from the beginning of *parashat Noah*.

"*And the earth was corrupt before God and the earth was full of violence*."[222] He said the supernal earth was corrupted, due to the sin of Adam. The term "corruption" is related to "*He is a companion to vandals (ba'al mashḥit)*"[223] and also "*For your people have acted corruptly.*"[224] The meaning is that they separated the Divine Names (*Havayot*). Also "*corrupt children,*"[225] "*do not destroy its trees,*"[226] "*he spoiled it on the ground,*"[227] and "*did He destroy?*"[228] The meaning of "*I am about to destroy them* 'et *the earth*"[229] is "*with the earth.*" As our rabbis, of blessed memory, said in *Bereishit Rabbah*: "Concerning a prince who had a wetnurse. As long as he was disobedient, the wetnurse was chastised."[230] She is called a "wetnurse" because everything nurses from there. As it is written, "*You will eat the good things of the earth.*"[231] And the meaning of "*and the earth was full of violence*"[232] is like the verse, "*You came and defiled My land; you made My possession abhorrent.*"[233] And it is written, "*They caused a delightful land to be turned into a desolation.*"[234] The meaning of "*delightful (ḥemdah)*" is complete (*kelulah*) as in " and God completed (*va-yikhal*) . . . , which the *Targum Yerushalmi* renders "*ve-hamid* . . . " Until She nursed from the forces of impurity instead of the forces of holiness and purity.[235]

And God said to Noah, "The end of all flesh . . . "[236] The attribute of judgment is called "the end of all flesh," as in the matter of receiving authority and taking the soul. It is designated to punish the wicked, etc. Because it does not act without authority, as indicated in the verse, "*If the snake bites without a spell* . . . ,[237] meaning they whisper to it from above, the verse states," *it came before Me*,[238] to receive permission to destroy them for their evil deeds. This is the secret meaning of the verse, "*Thieves are entering and bands rove outside.*"[239] Understand this entire verse well. In *Bereishit Rabbah*, Rabbi Hanina ben Pazi said, No evil thing descends from above.[240] They responded, But it is written, "*Fire and hail, snow and smoke.*"[241] He said to them, "*A stormy wind does His command.*"[242] "*For the earth is full of violence.*"[243] All of this is due to the attribute of judgment's complaint that because of their sin, the earth is full of violence. And She nursed from the forces of impurity, instead of the forces of holiness and purity.[244]

Here is what Rabbi Mattathias Delacrut wrote:

> "And She nursed from the forces of impurity . . . " For when there is no righteous person in the world to arouse Her through the supernal *ẓaddiq*, the forces of impurity, which are the messengers of judgment, are aroused. They hasten to enter and deposit their corruption through their accusation. This is from the power of

> the supernal serpent, strict judgment, which does their work, according to the judgment. Then the moon fulfills its original intention, shining to them, watching over them, to act through them, according to their power. According to the judgment that is decreed, the supernal King of Kings withdraws from dispensing compassion and activating the forces of holiness, which are the emissaries of compassion. This is the meaning of nursing and bestowing *shefa'*, which is so frequently mentioned. For example, "She nurses from them and their *shefa'* is in her." The meaning of "chastisement" and "corruption" is similar. For example, "as if the leader suffered because of this," "for she will long for her first husband," "because of these, the earth will tremble to exact vengeance upon her children," so that they will turn from their wicked ways. I discussed this at length so that there can be no error, making pure out of impure, in arguing that there is a deficiency in the wetnurse, God forbid. Rather, the deficiency is in the "*corrupt children*" as explained at the end of the *Ma'arekhet ha-Ta'am.*[245]

The matter of nursing from the forces of impurity is well explained in the *Pardes*, and also the matter of the serpent's contamination of Eve and menstruation. All of this alludes to the charges of the accusers, which ascend to the highest heights, reaching the True Judge, blessed be He. Then the beneficial *shefa'* is withheld, etc. See *Pardes*, *Sha'ar ha-Ẓinnorot*, chapter four, and *Sha'ar ha-Temorot*, chapter six. I transcribed some of this above.

In truth, one can easily see that there is nothing to the questions that Rav Hayyat raised against the passage in *Ma'arekhet ha-'Elohut,* nor is his evidence convincing. For all of the evidence that he brought concerns the deficiency and perfection of the *'Atarah*. This is not for the sake of the *'Atarah* itself, God forbid, but concerns the form in which *shefa'* is bestowed upon creation. This is also somewhat indicated by the analogy that he brought concerning the milk that the wetnurse receives as long as the infant nurses. It is clear that this milk is not for the benefit of the wetnurse herself, but for the benefit of the infant who nurses. Only, it is a joy and pleasure for her when there is something for the infant to nurse. Similarly, so to speak, there is great pleasure above before Me. For I spoke and My will was done. The True Good desires good.

I will proceed to strengthen this. It is known that although the divine emanation has ten attributes, there is no end to them. It is said explicitly in

Sefer Yeẓirah, "Ten *sefirot belimah*, their measure is ten, which have no end."[246] The *Pardes* explained:

> "Ten *sefirot belimah* . . . " to understand the meaning of this word, it has to be divided in two, "*beli* (without) *mah*." The meaning of *mah* is *mahut* (essence). The intention is to indicate that the ten *sefirot* are without essence, since their essence is beyond our comprehension. Even if we say that this one is Judgment and that one is Compassion, and so on, we can only comprehend this through their actions. However, from the standpoint of their essence, they are inconceivable (*beli mah*). This expression is also related to the word "*blom* (block off)." As it is written, "*his jewelry to block off*."[247] For it is proper for a person to block off his mouth and not to say too much about their essence, because of the limitations of his comprehension and their depth. Or it may be related to the concept of concealment. As in the verse, "*his jewelry to block off*," the reference is to the covering of the jewelry and its concealment. Thus the *sefirot* are called *belimah*, in other words, *sefirot* of concealment, for they are hidden. All three of these interpretations have the same intention, to indicate their concealment and the limits of comprehension, and that it is not proper to say too much about them because of their concealment. The text said "their measure is ten." Because this leads to the inference that they are limited, God forbid, the text continues, "which have no end." Even though the statements that they have a limit and have no limit contradict each other, it has already been explained in the preceding chapters that from the point of view of their relationship to the *Eyn Sof*, they are unlimited. However, from the point of view of their actions, which are extended to us, their actions are limited by our capacity to receive them. For we are limited creatures. It is a mark of the greatness of our Maker that from a state of limitlessness, He limits Himself and contracts Himself for the benefit of those below, who are limited creatures. Concerning this, the intelligent reader should not be confused. For it is not remote. "*For even the heavens and the uppermost heavens cannot contain Him*,"[248] although the Temple can. Nevertheless, because of love of Israel, He contracted Himself between the two boards of the Ark, as our rabbis, of blessed memory, have explained.[249,250]

Therefore, it is not correct to speak of addition or deficiency regarding the [*sefirot* of the] divine emanation, from the point of view of their existing with *Eyn Sof*, who is a soul for them, to which they cleave. However, in regard to the bestowal of *shefa*ʻ to those below, this bestowal is subject to deficiency and increase, depending on the arousal of those below.

In order to understand this well, I will begin with what the *Pardes* wrote in chapter thirteen of *Sha'ar ha-Mahut ve-ha-Hanhagah*: "For the union of the *sefirot* has three modes . . . "[251] Now I will bring two of the ways, and the third way will be mentioned at the end. These two ways will be discussed at length according to the what was added to the discussion by Rabbi Sheftel Segal, of blessed memory, in his work, *Shefa*ʻ *Tal.*

> [My purpose is] to enlighten you concerning the understanding of this secret, when one can speak of *Malkhut* as empty of *shefa*ʻ, God forbid. Is it not the Lord of all, which contains all of the good of the divine emanation? She Herself is the essence of divinity, the essence of the emanation, as is known. So how can emptiness be attributed to divine emanation? It is also a matter of cutting off and separation, God forbid, when She is empty, God forbid, and the rest of the *sefirot* are full. In order to understand this, you need to know that there are three modes of uniting the *sefirot*. Since our subject, the emptiness of *Malkhut*, involves understanding two of these modes, we will not trouble ourselves over the third mode, but will explain the two modes of union. Thereby, the clarification that we seek will be attained. The first mode of union involves their uniting as a result of emanation. In other words, the intention of the *Eyn Sof* was to create finite and limited worlds, and for the Limitless to create limitation, in order to reveal the power of Its divinity to other than Itself. [This other] is finite and limited. Also, [it was intended] to watch over them and all of their needs, involving their sustenance and existence. The world was to continue according to its way, without destruction and annulment, God forbid, for even a moment. However, it is not possible for the Unlimited to create the limited and finite [directly]. However, [it was accomplished] by means of Its emanations, which descended ten degrees, according to the secret of cause and effect. From the ten degrees of emanation, another ten degrees descended, according to the secret of cause and effect. These are the ten [*sefirot*] of the world of creation, which is called the Throne of Glory. From the ten stages of creation, another ten stages descended, according

to the secret of cause and effect. These are the ten [*sefirot*] of the world of formation. From the ten stages of formation, another ten stages descended, which is the secret of the world of making. Finally, the stages descended to the level of actual limitation, until all the worlds were united and connected like the parts of a candelabra. Thus the *Eyn Sof* watches over them from the beginning of their emanation. For He bestows His *shefa'* in them and illuminates them with His light. The *shefa'* of this light causes them to join together in a true and strong union. This *shefa'* is never lacking. They are all equally nourished from the best of this *shefa'*. All of their banks are full and satisfied. Splendor and joy is in its place. From this perfection, they bestow bread, law, and food upon the rest of the worlds, creation, formation, and making. The maintenance of the connection of the worlds and the elements, until the hub of the earth, depends on this *shefa'*. If, God forbid, the thought would arise to withhold this *shefa'* for even a moment, all of the material worlds would come to an end and be lost in a moment. But the spiritual elements would return to their source, as before their emanation. This is the correct intention one should have in mind when reciting the Shema'. One unites all of the worlds from below to above, until the First Cause, blessed be He. For all of them are interconnected and united, each effect with its cause, level after level, until the First Cause. He, through His great and holy *shefa'*, connects, unites, and sustains them, from the first point until the point of the hub, which is the center of the earth. If the lack of His *shefa'* would be imagined for even one moment, all of them would vanish and the spiritual elements would return to their source. However, the intention of union of the recitation of the Shema' is not that the *Eyn Sof* should bestow more *shefa'* on the emanated [*sefirot*] than He did when they were emanated from Him. For the maintenance of the connection of the worlds and elements, which is the basis of the world's proper functioning, depends on [this *shefa'*]. For [if that were the intention], there would be a change in divine emanation itself, God forbid. Sometimes there would be an increase in *shefa'* and sometimes less of an increase, so that *shefa'* would be lacking. Rather, the correct intention in reciting the *Shema'* is that we unite all of the *sefirot*, one with another, and all of them with the Emanator. And we shall make Him king over all creatures, great and small. For He, with His great and holy *shefa'*, [which is bestowed] by means of His emanations, is the cause of their existence. This is our faith, but not to increase *shefa'* beyond what was in effect at the time of their emanation, so that the world could exist. For all creatures were created in the state of their greatest perfection. As our rabbis, of blessed memory, said, "All creatures were created with their [full] character, stature, and mentality (*da'at*)."[252] In other words, [they were created] in their full state of perfection. Therefore, one should not [intend to] add or detract from this. It is also found in the words of Rabbi Simeon bar Yohai that in the union of the recitation of the Shema', one should add *shefa'*. The meaning is that because of Adam's sins and also our sins, the condition of the earth deteriorated and the *shefa'* that was bestowed on all the worlds at the stage of emanation was reduced. It is no longer at the same degree of power and might as it was before Adam's sin. Consequently, we increase *shefa'* through the union of the recitation of the Shema', so that the divine emanation will bestow a great light on the worlds, just as it did before the sin, and the worlds will be strengthened as before. But this does not mean that additional *shefa'* will be created in the very essence of the divine emanation by the Emanator, blessed be He. For the *shefa'* in the essence of the divine emanation will always remain in its full power and strength, as it always has been, in the great light [that they receive] from the Emanator. Therefore, in this union, which is the basis of their existence, there is never a surplus or lack. This is the first union in the divine emanation. The second union in the divine emanation involves their being filled with the *shefa'* of favor and God's blessing, in order to bestow it upon all of the worlds, according to what has been allotted to each of them, at the time of their emanation. Each *sefirah* has its own treasury. For example, *Keter* is the treasury for absolutely pure compassion, without any admixture. *Ḥokhmah* is the treasury of wisdom. *Binah* is the treasury of repentance. *Ḥesed* is the treasury of lovingkindness. *Gevurah* is the treasury of wealth. *Tif'eret* is the treasury of Torah. And so it is for all of them, [*shefa'* is released], depending on the need of human action at a particular time. For sometime, the need is for pardon, forgiveness, and atonement. Then it is necessary to draw down *shefa'* from the supernal whiteness that is *Keter*, which whitens the sins of Israel, by means of *Binah*. For *Binah* is the essence of the return to pardon. By means of *Binah* in union with the Father, which is *Ḥokhmah*, that *shefa'* is released to *Malkhut*.

Binah and *Malkhut* are united by the six *sefirot* between *Binah* and *Malkhut*:*Ḥesed*, *Gevurah*, *Tif'eret*, *Neẓaḥ*, *Hod*, and *Yesod*. This is the secret of the High Priest's count on the Day of Atonement: "One, one and one, one and two, one and three, one and four, and so on until one and seven. He counted one three times to indicate the first three *sefirot*, which are considered as one. He counted up to seven, which is *Malkhut*, and he would count one with each of them to indicate the gradual descent of the *shefa'* and its bestowal. For that is the essence of the worship of the Day of Atonement, to draw down pardon and atonement to *Malkhut*.

There are occasions when *Ḥokhmah* is required, in order to become wise in Torah. Then one draws down the *shefa'* of *Ḥokhmah* by way of *Ḥesed*. This is the meaning of "whoever wishes to be wise should go to the south."[253] For *Ḥesed* is south and from there it continues to *Tif'eret*, which is the Torah, and from there to *Malkhut*, which is called "lower wisdom."

Sometimes wealth is required. Then one draws the *shefa'* of *Binah* to *Gevurah*. Thus the saying, "Whoever wishes to be wealthy should go to the north."[254] In other words, one intends that *Binah* will open her treasury of wealth for him, into *Gevurah*. From there it goes to *Malkhut*. Sometimes might and power are required to take vengeance on their enemies. Then *Binah*, as the root and source of judgment, bestows the *shefa'* of judgment to *Gevurah*, from there it continues to *Hod*, and from there to "*the sword that exacts the vengeance of the covenant*,"[255] with the aid of *Neẓaḥ*, which conquers. Then they prevail over their enemies and defeat them. There are myriad cases of this [bestowal of *shefa'*]. All are initiated in response to human action, through which the *shefa'* that they require is generated. In truth, these bestowals of *shefa'* are not meant to maintain the world's existence and the cohesiveness of the hierarchical stages, from cause to effect, from the first to last point, so that it can remain permanently in existence and not be destroyed. For the world will remain in existence without these bestowals of *shefa'*. Rather these bestowals are according to the activities carried out by human beings. As the lower ones act below, so is the response toward them from above. As the *Zohar* puts it, "Through the arousal of those below, the action above is aroused." Therefore, this *shefa'* is a great benefit and is an addition of *shefa'* in the divine emanation beyond that *shefa'* that was bestowed for the purpose of maintaining the existence of the world and its proper functioning.

Thus there are two unions that occur in the world of emanation. They are two types of bestowal of *shefa'*. The first is for maintaining the world's existence and the second depends on the deeds of those below. Now that you know this secret, the light of the Living God will enlighten your mind concerning the emptiness that is, so to speak, found in *Malkhut*. We may say that in the case of the first union, all of the *sefirot* are equally involved. There is no question of emptiness or separation, God forbid. Rather, divine providence permanently affects each of them equally, from the first *sefirah*, *Keter*, to the last *sefirah*, *Malkhut*. All partake equally of goodness, in glory, joy, and gladness, in spirituality, light, and splendor. Each is overflowing with radiance. There is neither lack nor surplus. For in the category of divinity there is neither deficiency nor excess, as is explained in *Sefer Moreh Nevukhim*.

However, in the case of the second union there is deficiency and excess, which fulfills the needs of human governance, in accordance with the deeds and actions of the ones below. For this *shefa'* is not essentially for maintaining the world's existence and cohesiveness through cause and effect so that it can remain in existence and not vanish for a moment. Nor does it affect the supremely perfect Divine Light, which He requires for Himself. For without it, this *shefa'* remains glorious in its place of might, and in the ultimate state of perfection. It has no need to receive any perfection from another. However, [the second union] is for human needs. It is this *shefa'* that is occasionally lacking, depending on their actions. Here one may speak of the emptiness of *Malkhut*. For example, when Israel has need of wealth, but is not deserving, *Binah* will not bestow wealth to *Malkhut*, by way of *Gevurah*. Thus *Malkhut* is, in a sense, empty of wealth. Not that She, Herself, is empty, God forbid, for there is no good that She lacks. Rather, She is empty in the sense of not having received that wealth that Israel requires. Similarly, when Israel needs to take revenge against their enemies and are not worthy, God forbid, She does not receive power and might of victory to bestow to Israel, so that they can defeat their enemies. The same explanation holds for the rest of the cases: She is empty of the *shefa'*, which She would have received, which Israel requires. But She herself suffers neither emptiness nor deficiency. For in regard to Her essence, She is full of goodness and She has in Her possession all the goodness of the divine emanation that Her divinity requires.[256]

He also wrote there:

When the *shefa'* for administering the lower worlds, which comes from the arousal of those below, is lacking, all [of the *sefirot*], so to speak, dry up from the lack of that additional *shefa'*. For the *shefa'* that is required for the lower worlds is only revealed through the arousal of those below, when they merit it. This is the secret of the *Shekhinah*'s presence among those below for the sake of the need above. When the *Shekhinah* bestows *shefa'*, it is, so to speak, for the need of the *sefirot*. For they also, in a manner of speaking, receive *shefa'* and great benefit. When they have room to bestow, their own *shefa'* also increases. For as long as they are bestowing, their *shefa'* increases. This is the secret of the teaching that the *Shekhinah* pursues the righteous person, so that he will be a chariot for Her, in order that She can bestow *shefa'* through him. For Her *shefa'* also increases as a result of Her bestowal, just like a woman who nurses. As long as she nurses, her milk increases. Even so, as long as the *Shekhinah* bestows, She receives additional *shefa'*. The same is true for the *sefirah* above Her. As long as it brings forth the concealed and reveals it, its *shefa'* also increases, from what is concealed above it. For all the *sefirot*, up to *Binah*, are called the *Shekhinah*, and some say up to *Ḥokhmah*. For *Ḥokhmah* is also called *Shekhinah*. The reason is because *Malkhut* is the *Shekhinah*, the lower Mother who dwells over the lower worlds below Her, and especially over the righteous, who are a chariot for Her, so that She can bestow *shefa'* through them. *Ḥokhmah* dwells over *Binah*, which dwells over the extremities and *Malkhut*, in order to bestow their power. However, when it is said that the *Shekhinah* dwells among those below for the sake of the need above and that the *shefa'* of the *sefirot* themselves increases, do not think, God forbid, that the *shefa'* which increases is for the sake of its essence. For we have already said that the *shefa'* which is required for the union of the essence of the *sefirot* is never lacking or in excess. For they are in a state of ultimate perfection. However, the *shefa'* that increases is for the sake of administering the worlds, so that *shefa'* will increase in the [*sefirot*], and great *shefa'* can be bestowed upon

> the worlds. It is like the milk which increases in the nursing woman. It is not for her own need, but for the sake of the child.
>
> Similarly, the *shefa'* that increases in the *sefirot* is for the sake of the worlds below them. It is meant to be bestowed to them. Why then does the *Shekhinah* pursue the righteous person, when the increase in Her *shefa'* is not for Her own need? It is because "the cow wishes to nurse more than the calf wishes to be nursed."[257] This is because of the secret that it is the nature of one who is perfect and whole to help another to become whole and to bestow some of its perfection on the other. For that reason, the *Shekhinah* pursues the righteous in order to complete the others and to bestow *shefa'* upon them, by means of the righteous. Thus the *Shekhinah* needs to be present among the ones below so that through Her, the *sefirot* can bestow *shefa'*. For due to their perfection, it is their nature to bestow. Thus bestowing is necessary for them, in order to fulfill the nature of their perfection.[258]

Thus his words have explained that "the need above" basically means that it is a pleasure for God, so to speak, when His will to bestow good is done. A saying of the rabbis in chapter *Hayyah Qore'* somewhat inclines to this idea. "Fortunate is the person who grows up in Torah and who labors in Torah, and who is a source of pleasure for his Creator. For His will is done."[259] The meaning is that God does not require human actions for the sake of His perfection and essence, but it is a pleasure for the Creator when His will is done.

Thus the verses and *midrashim* have been explained which indicate that whether a person acts righteously or wickedly, God is not affected. Rather, in a manner of speaking, He receives pleasure when they do His will, and the opposite is the case when they do the opposite, God forbid.

However, in the introduction to *Sefer 'Avodat ha-Qodesh*, he explained this rabbinic saying, "And he is a source of pleasure (*naḥat*) for His creator in the world."

> The meaning is that "*and He descended*"[260] is translated "*u-neḥat*. This is the secret of bringing down divine favor and the holy spirit to the supernal principals. From there, pleasure and will reach the Creator. All of this comes about through fulfilling the Torah and the commandments for their own sake.[261]

It is known that it is the method of the author of *'Avodat ha-Qodesh* throughout his entire work to explain that worship is for the sake of the need that is above in the very essence of the divine emanation. It adds power and rectifies and unites the Divine Name. In the opposite case, the opposite occurs, God forbid. This tends toward the view of Rabbi Hayyat. It is also true that according to their simple meaning, the verses and sayings that allude to the issue of worship for the sake of the need above also tend to mean God's essential need for it. Consider, for example, the *Midrash*, "The Holy One, blessed be He, said to Moses, you should have helped Me." Also, "He said to Rabbi Ishmael, Ishmael, My son, bless Me." And so indicate most of the verses and rabbinic sayings. This is especially the case in regard to the third of the three unions of the *sefirot*, which the *Pardes* wrote about in chapter thirteen of *Sha'ar Mahut ve-ha-Hanhagah*, which I promised to transcribe. This is indeed a matter that affects Him in essence.

Here is what is written in the *Pardes*:

> There is a third union which is specific to four of the *sefirot*, *Ḥokhmah*, *Binah*, *Tif'eret*, and *Malkhut*. This involves coupling, which only applies to these four *sefirot*. This is like the coupling of a man and his wife. This is something that can only be comprehended through comparing the second union to the food that a person bestows upon his wife, if it is occasionally supplied by a trustee, while the third union is the sexual act itself that he performs with her in order to bring out a vessel for his action.[262] This union is so wondrous a matter that it cannot be comprehended, but only made intelligible in this way. We shall broaden the explanation in a separate chapter of this Gate.[263]

He also wrote there:

> The third union, which is the union of coupling, as a result of sin will also cause a deficiency in *Binah*, because Her union depends on the union of *Tif'eret* and *Malkhut*. As long as there is no union of Son and Daughter below, there is no union of Father and Mother above. So Rabbi Simeon bar Yohai explained in the *Tiqqunim*, see there.[264,265]

Clearly this coupling is a matter of divine perfection and God raises it for a great need, the union of His Name. And so in the future the verse will be fulfilled that says, "*And the light of the moon shall become like the light of the sun.*"[266]

According to this approach, the question remains unresolved. Thus it is possible to say that those verses and rabbinic sayings that indicate that whether a person acts righteously or wickedly, God is not affected, refer to the matter of permanent existence, which is the first of the [three] unions of the *sefirot* that I transcribed above. This involves the *shefa'* that is determined at the beginning of divine emanation as required for their existence. This is the acceptance of the yoke of the Kingdom of Heaven, which involves neither deficiency nor surplus. It is a constant matter.

However, human action causes an additional bestowal of *shefa'* in them, which descends from them below. As a result, whatever is blessed in the earth will be blessed in God, amen. For through this additional bestowal of *shefa'*, the Divine Name is blessed and united. However, this is not a constant matter. Rather, it depends on human action. Sins cause this bounty to be withheld and produce a deficiency in this perfection. For the ultimate purpose in creating human beings was "*to serve and guard it*" and to rectify this in order to unite the Divine Name.

It also seems to me that the matter can be explained according to what was clarified above at length in the introduction. A person is only permitted to contemplate his world and structure, which is the structure below. This refers to the seven days of creation, for actions have their source there. This is from *Ḥesed* and below, "*A world of Ḥesed will be built.*"[267] But concerning what exists from a person's world and above, namely the first three *sefirot*, which are considered as one, there it is said, "You have no business with concealed matters." They are not the world of a person, for no actions are drawn from there. Rather, they are the concealed world, the world of God, His Thought, Wisdom, and Understanding. They are much more His very essence than those that were revealed so that actions could be drawn from them, according to the ways of human beings. In God's world, that is, in the first three *sefirot*, if a person is righteous or wicked, what effect will he have? However, in the world of a person, that is the structure from *Ḥesed* and below, it is correct to speak of the power of *Ḥesed* and the complete power, according to the arousal of a human being and his actions. For actions are drawn from them. According to the actions, there is an arousal in them. They then receive great *shefa'*, glory, power, and joy. Also the Name is rendered complete, as I already explained at length above in this introduction. For the main part (*kelal*) of the structure is *Tif'eret* and *Malkhut*. *Malkhut* is the source of Israel, where their souls are rooted. Thus when there are righteous ones in a generation, the roots of their souls shine. *Malkhut* pours out female waters, which is the arousal of the good deeds that shine in the roots of their souls. *Tif'eret* shines male waters toward Her face, which are bestowed upon Him from His holy source. Then the union of the Name is complete. From there, peace and blessings are extended throughout all of the worlds.

If the opposite occurs, God forbid, there is no union above to pour out, so to speak, good, and there is no *shefa'* below. This is [the secret of] menstruation and "*a maid servant supplants her mistress.*" "*An enemy threatens the supernal Jerusalem.*"[268] I have already written above, in the name of the kabbalists, that one should not think that the *qelippot* actually enter within the divine emanation, as many of those who were attracted to Kabbalah in our generation thought. Even though the apparent meaning seems to compel this view, it is necessary to understand and arrange these matters [properly].

The meaning is that the cry of the enemies enters. But they are called "others," because they are outside the *yeshivah* and do not enter to view the Pleasantness of *YHVH*. They cry out the crimes and transgressions of Israel, saying, "These are idol worshippers, these are idol worshippers, these are incestuous, etc." Then the anger and jealousy of *YHVH* begins to smoke. Instead of saying, "They are My people," He says to them, "[You are] not My people," God forbid, and expresses anger. Where great *shefa'* and compassion should have been bestowed to the attributes, the power of judgment is aroused. The "dross of gold" is bestowed upon the external forces and the judgment is sealed. This is what is meant by the entering [of the *qelippot*] into holiness. They themselves do not actually enter, but only their charges and declarations of the crimes of Israel. Their cry enters there to raise anger, to arouse judgment, and to exact vengeance. This is called "entering into holiness." Not only is judgment bestowed, but the faces of compassion depart and fear and judgment prevail. This attribute is damaged until vengeance is taken for that matter or compassion is revealed and illuminates the place of darkness. Then with the increase of water, the fire is extinguished, and the world is placed in judgment. Otherwise, that place is damaged. For it is darkness, when the faces of compassion are concealed from it. It administers judgment.

From the structure and below there is foreign contact. This is the secret of "this world," as explained above in the introduction. But from *Binah* and above, the "wine is reserved." This is the secret of the "world to come." At that level there is no "need above" for the efforts of human beings.

However, it would seem that an objection can be raised. If a human being can cause and prevent the union below, which is the coupling of

Tif'eret and *Malkhut*, he would also have an effect from *Binah* and above. For, as I have explained, there is no coupling of *Ḥokhmah* and *Binah*, that is, of Father and Mother, unless there is a union of the Son and Daughter, who are *Tif'eret* and *Malkhut*. However, this may also be resolved when we explain the nature of the coupling of *Ḥokhmah* and *Binah* after the emanation of the vocalized forms of *YHVH*. At first, the matter is true. When the will to manifest arose, the structure was emanated by means of *Ḥokhmah* and *Binah*. However, afterward, what is the significance of their coupling? This matter is explained in the *Pardes*, chapter seventeen of *Sha'ar ha-Mahut ve-ha-Hanhagah*:

> For the existence of the divine emanation is maintained by the Father and Mother. There are two aspects to the union of a man and his wife. The first is to give birth to a new being and the second is to raise the shoots, that is, to ensure that the offspring will be lively (*mezoraz*), as was explained above in chapter three of the preceding Gate. Similarly, the union of *Binah* and *Ḥokhmah* is not for the purpose of producing a new being, but to establish the vitality of the emanated forms of *YHVH* (*ha-havayyot)*, so that they will function properly (*'omdim be-ẓevyonam*). The meaning is that *Tif'eret* and *Malkhut* must be crowned in order to be united. However, they can only be crowned with those crowns of praise, which enliven and arm the *sefirot*, through the union of *Ḥokhmah* and *Binah*. So Rabbi Simeon bar Yohai explained in the *Zohar*.[269,270]

Therefore, their coupling is not for themselves, but for the needs of the structure. As is known, *Binah* is the root of the structure. From this root, [the structure] extends to the emanated forms of *YHVH* that are below. However, from the essence of *Binah* and above, we have no business in those concealed matters. Not only are they unaffected by human action, but they are beyond the capacity of the human intellect to comprehend. Thus everything has been well explained.

I still have to make known to you that even below in the divine emanation, when one speaks of the exile of the *Shekhinah*, the meaning is a spark of the *Shekhinah* and not the *Shekhinah* Herself. Here is what is written in *Pardes*, chapter four of *Sha'ar 'ABY'A*:

> This angel is called by two names. Sometimes he is called Metatron and sometimes he is called Mitatron, with a *yod*. The meaning is that when the angel is a garment for the *Shekhinah*, She is con-

> cealed within him and displays Her actions through him. Then he is called Mitatron, with a *yod.* [The *yod*] alludes to the *Shekhinah*, who contains ten [*sefirot*]. She descends, concealed within him. But it is not actually the *Shekhinah*, but a spark and light that emanates from the *Shekhinah*. This is a spark and light that consists of ten sparks. This matter is called the "exile of the *Shekhinah*," so to speak, and is explained in the *Tiqqunim*.[271,272]

And the Galante commentary on "*He cast the earth from heaven*,"[273] wrote:

> "You already know from the beginning of the *Ra'aya Mehemna*, that whenever we speak of the secret of exile, we refer to the *Shekhinah* of the world of creation. This means a spark that sparkles from Her into the world of creation. For concerning the *Shekhinah* of the world of emanation, is written, "*I am YHVH. It is My Name and I will not give My Glory to another*."[274,275]

In order to establish this matter, I will transcribe the view contained in the words of the Maggid that spoke through the Great Rabbi who authored the *Beyt Yosef*.[276] We managed to obtain manuscript copies from which I will transcribe what pertains to our subject.

> Surely you know that the God of the world is *YHVH*. You should know that the Holy One, blessed be He, and the entire celestial academy are sending you greetings. They have sent Me to you to make known to you supernal words and the greatest secrets. Thus you will know the greatness of the goodness of the Holy One, blessed be He, and His compassion and lovingkindness. His right hand is outstretched to receive those who return to the holy service. Do you not realize that you have a great problem concerning the holy *sefirot*, in regard to *Malkhut*? She is united with the *sefirot*. However, in a few passages, it appears that this is not so, God forbid. For example, in that passage in *Sefer ha-Bahir* that begins with nine *sefirot* and ends with Her. Many other passages also have that meaning, so that finally the author of *Minḥat Yehudah* found it possible to say that it is like the tool of a ship. . . .[277] May the Master of Compassion absolve them of this view. At least, he should not be punished for what was said, for it was not said to intentionally sin before the Holy One, blessed be He, but is entirely an error. Another problem, in some places we see that She

is the daughter of Abraham. In other places She is called the daughter of *Binah*. In a few places, She is said to be the daughter of *Gevurah*. Another problem. It appears that there is change in the *sefirot*, God forbid. As it is said, "He arises from the throne of judgment and sits on the throne of compassion." This leads to the conclusion that they are not the essence of divinity, God forbid. Another problem. In many places the rabbis said that sin reaches the *Shekhinah* and the *sefirot*, and in a few places they say that human sins do not at all reach the the Holy One, Blessed be He, and His *Shekhinah*. When you saw the holy *Tiqqun*, we let you know the truth of the matter and the secret of secrets. Do you not know that when it arose in the Will of Wills, the Most Ancient *Eyn Sof*, to create worlds, one blow was struck and one light shined, which contains three? As our teachers said, "One point contains three: length, breadth, and depth." That light was one and three were contained within it, namely *Keter*, *Ḥokhmah*, and *Binah*. Afterward, one light was struck from each of these three. One light was struck from *Ḥokhmah*, which contained two, namely, *Ḥesed* and *Neẓaḥ*. With *Ḥokhmah* itself, they make three. One light was also struck from *Binah* which contained two, namely *Gevurah* and *Hod*. With *Binah* itself, they make three. One light was struck from *Keter* which contained three, namely *Tif'eret*, *Yesod*, and *Malkhut*. Because [*Keter*] is closer to *Eyn Sof* and similar to it, since it is more concealed, three are contained in the light that emerged from it, as in the case of *Eyn Sof*. Now, since *Keter*, *Ḥokhmah*, and *Binah* were one light, and *Malkhut* emerged from *Keter*, while Abraham emerged from *Ḥokhmah*, it is as if both came from the same place. As Abraham said of her in the verse, "*And besides, it is indeed so, she is my sister, the daughter of my father, but not of my mother*."[278] In other words, she and I were drawn from supernal *Keter*, for he is the father. For that reason, she is called the daughter of *Binah*. For since *Binah* is included in *Keter* and *Malkhut* emerged from *Keter*, it is as if she emerged from *Binah*. Since *Gevurah* is the attribute of judgment and *Malkhut* is the attribute of light judgment, it is said that she nurses from it. Each one of these supernal *sefirot* contains ten, since all were contained in *Eyn Sof*. For all of them emerged from the primordial light. Ten were contained in that light, just as all of a person's descendants are contained within him. Even so, when each one of the lights that is contained in that light was struck, it brought forth other lights. They were brought forth with all of the lights contained in it. Thus each of the ten contains all ten. And those *sefirot* become a hundred, and from a hundred, they become many thousands, beyond calculation. All ten of these *sefirot* form one union, which is the essence of divinity. For these are to *Eyn Sof* like a flame connected to a coal. This is like the soul and the human body with its limbs. It is all one whole. Similarly, everything forms a complete union without any separation in the world, God forbid. And *Malkhut*, which is the Lady, and the rest of the *sefirot* are all one, in complete union with *Eyn Sof*. The whole was, is, and will be, as Menahem Recanati wrote. This is the world of complete union. From there, the world of separation begins. In other words, all of the worlds depend on the utterance of the Holy One, blessed be He. Nevertheless, they are not His very essence, like these ten. Between the world of complete union and the world of complete separation, there is a world that is somewhat in union. It consists of all ten *sefirot*. But it has an aspect of separation in it and is a receptacle for the ten supernal *sefirot*, like the snail whose shell is part of its body. It is called "*there*,"[279] because concerning it, it is said, "*He stood with him there*."[280] For "*YHVH descended be-'anan (in a cloud)*."[281] This is the secret of *'ab* and the straight *nun* and the bent *nun*, which are *Ḥokhmah*, *Tif'eret*, and *Malkhut*. "*Ve-Ya'AVOR AB RYO (and he passed) over His face*."[282] Not over the face of Moses, but over the face of God. This world that is between the world of union and the world of separation is Metatron, in whom all ten *sefirot* are contained. Elisha, the "other" erred concerning him when he said that there are two powers, God forbid. For he saw that [Metatron] directs the world of separation. The secret of "other gods" applies there, and the governing angels of the nations have access there. For no governing angel is permitted to ascend to the ten supernal *sefirot*. There the serpent contaminated Eve, to separate himself from the world of union. Sins reach there to separate it from the world of complete union. But there is no flaw, God forbid, in the ten supernal *sefirot*. As it is written, "*If you are righteous, what do you give Him?*"[283] "*And if your sins are many, what do you do to Him?*"[284] "*From there*," the world mentioned, "*there is a separation and it becomes four tributaries*."[285] These are the four camps of the *Shekhinah*. Between the world mentioned and the four camps of the *Shekhinah* is the Tree of the Knowledge of Good and Evil, which is mentioned at the end of the holy *Tiqqunim*. It is called the *Teli* whose head is good and whose tail is evil.[286] That is the place of Adam's sin, which mixed good with evil. The ten supernal *sefirot* are the essence of divinity and are complete unity, as I have said. There is no change there at all. Rather, depending on how a person acts, so they respond to him.[287]

Later, the Maggid came to him again and spoke as follows:

God is with you in all that you are doing. I have gone forth to inquire after you and to see you. I will bring you a saying of the most concealed secret of secrets, which I taught you concerning the holy *sefirot*. We saw that you have not understood the matter well. Do you not know that the supernal *sefirot* emerged from the *Eyn Sof* in the manner that I taught you? I told you that between the world of union and the world of separation there is a world that contains an aspect of union and consists of ten *sefirot*. It also contains an aspect of separation. This is the *Shekhinah*, which unites with the ten supernal *sefirot*. She contains seven, corresponding to the supernal seven, according to the secret of seven and the "*seven pipes*."[288] These seven are the seven degrees and the three supernal degrees are also contained in them, in a secret and concealed manner, parallel to the three supernal ones. It all forms one complete union with the supernal *sefirot*. Do not imagine, God forbid, that there is any separation there in any sense whatsoever. Whoever imagines so, God forbid, cuts the shoots; with it there is more cutting, the cutting of the *Shekhinah*, which is that world that I mentioned. Whoever separates Her from the ten supernal *sefirot* has a great punishment. Therefore, you should know that that world, which is the *Shekhinah*, is united with the ten supernal *sefirot* in a complete union, without separation. As for My telling you that there is an aspect of separation, this does not mean that it is separated at all [from the ten supernal *sefirot*]. Rather, the bestowal of *shefa'* through Metatron, which is the world of separation, is small. From there the entire universe is nourished, from the horns of bulls to the eggs of lice. Since *shefa'* is bestowed upon the world of separation and not on the supernal *sefirot*, which bestow to the *Shekhinah*, which is also in a state of union, we say that there is an element of separation. But not that that world is in any way separated. It is in a complete union with the ten supernal *sefirot*. That is the secret of the union, which unites the *Shekhinah* with the Holy One, blessed be He. For I told you that its relationship to the ten supernal *sefirot* is like that snail whose shell is part of itself. It forms one whole without any separation whatsoever.[289]

Afterward, the Maggid came a third time and spoke to him:

We saw that you had a problem with what I taught you concerning the most concealed secret of secrets, will of wills, namely that there are ten supernal *sefirot* and the *Shekhinah* and holy Lady. If so, we should say that there are eleven. But the author of *Sefer Yeẓirah* said explicitly, "ten and not nine . . . and not eleven." You should know that the Holy One, blessed be He, and the entire supernal academy sent Me to you to teach you the secret and truth of the matter. Do you not know that the ten supernal *sefirot* shined from the *Eyn Sof* in the manner that I taught you? The *Eyn Sof* struck and sent forth one light that contained three lights . . . They were completed as ten supernal *sefirot* . . . Afterward, each one of the ten supernal *sefirot* beat and sent forth one light as a receptacle, like that snail . . . , which is in a union with it. All of these ten lights that shine from the ten supernal *sefirot* are contained as a whole. It is the great *Shekhinah*, through which the ten supernal *sefirot* bestow *shefa'* in order to nourish the entire world. She is in a state of perfection with the ten supernal *sefirot*. For She emerged as a result of their striking against each other. Since She came to be, it is possible to think that She should be counted and to say that the *sefirot* are eleven. Thus the author of *Sefer Yeẓirah* taught you that it is not so, for She is not like the supernal *sefirot*. For the *sefirot*, *Keter*, *Ḥokhmah*, and *Binah* emerged from *Eyn Sof*. *Ḥesed* and *Neẓaḥ* emerged from *Ḥokhmah*. *Gevurah* and *Hod* emerged from *Binah*. *Tif'eret*, *Yesod*, and *Malkhut* emerged from *Keter*. But the *Shekhinah* is a vessel for all of them and emerged from all of them. For each one of the supernal *sefirot* sends forth a light and She is made up of all of [those lights]. Thus She is with them in unity, but not in emanation. Her union with all of the ten supernal *sefirot*, so that they shine within Her, is conditioned by the merits and sins. There is the secret of "blessed be the Name of the Glory of His *Malkhut* for ever." And there all of the positive and negative commandments are required for uniting Her with all of the ten *sefirot*. For since She emerged from all of them, one has to unite Her with all of them, and to turn Her ten *sefirot* toward the ten supernal *sefirot*. For when these are turned as one, there is perfection and joy in all of the worlds. This is the secret of the verse, "*And 'Elohim said let us make a person in our image, according to our likeness.*"[290] For that *'Elohim*, which is *Binah*, said to the ten supernal *sefirot*, "Let us make a person." In other words, let each one of us strike and bring forth one light, so that from the totality of the ten lights, a person will be formed, that is to say, the Lady, for a female is also called a person. As it is written, "*The beauty of a person to dwell in a house.*[291] Who is it that dwells in the house? The woman. The person should be "*in our image*," in other words, it should be a receptacle for all of us. And it should be "*in our likeness*," that is, it should be made up of ten *sefirot* like us. The reason that *Binah* spoke here is that the two higher *sefirot* are contained within Her and She decrees and carries out what they say. Do not ask why She said this at this very time and not before. For concerning that question it is said, "Do not ask what is before and after, do not inquire into what is too wondrous for you." From this you can understand the secret of the disagreement concerning whether there were two faces or a tail. For if you argue that they were two faces, you would have to say that the light that each of the ten *sefirot* emitted was contained within it and was not visible, until *Binah* said "*let us make a person*." For at that moment, that light shined and all of those lights were bound together so that a person was made. But if you hold that it was a tail, you have to say that that light was visible in each *sefirah*. Then when *Binah* said "*let us make a person*," those lights were collected together and that person was made, which is like a female that is turned toward all of the limbs of the male when they unite. Thus when the ten *sefirot* of the Lady are united with the ten supernal *sefirot*, they are turned toward each other. This is perfect joy. It is the joy of the entire universe and the secret of the union that we need to constantly unite. This is the meaning of bringing forth the woman from Adam's rib. As it is written, "*For YHVH 'Elohim built the rib.*"[292] For the Lady emerged from the interaction of the ten suernal *sefirot*, which is the world of the male. Come and see how "*from my flesh, I can see God.*"[293] For just as the *Eyn Sof* brought forth ten supernal *sefirot* and the ten supernal *sefirot* brought forth the *Shekhinah*, and they form a union, so the Holy One, blessed be

> He, acted in creating a human being. As it is written, "*And He blew the soul of life into his nostrils.*"[294] The allusion is to the *Eyn Sof.* And from that "*soul of life*" the body of Adam, which is like the ten supernal *sefirot*, was constituted. And from the body of Adam, the female, which alludes to the Lady, was constructed. For She was created from the lights of the ten *sefirot*. As we have said, each *sefirah* shined one light into Her, for She is a receptacle. That receptacle unites Her in a complete union. All of those lights are contained together and made as one. She is the *Shekhinah*, which is like the female who receives and is impregnated from the male. [Seed] descends to her from all of his limbs. Just as she administers the house and distributes food to all, so the Lady receives from all of the supernal *sefirot* and is impregnated by them, and distributes sustenance to the entire world. That is the secret and truth of the matter, which the Holy One, blessed be He, and all of His academy sent Me to make known to you.[295]

Thus he has explained that merits and sins only reach the *Shekhinah*, which is the Lady. Nahmanides alluded to Her in saying, "She is with them in unity, but not in emanation." Many were confused by his words; however the Maggid has made it very clear. For the *Shekhinah*, the Lady, forms a unity with the ten supernal *sefirot*, like "the snail whose shell is part of itself." But She is not with them in emanation, since the ten supernal *sefirot* originate in *Eyn Sof*, like a flame connected to a coal, and the Lady *Shekhinah* is from the ten *sefirot*. As far as the ten supernal *sefirot* are concerned, "*If you are righteous, what do you give Him, if your sins are many, what do you do to Him?*"[296] From what the Maggid says, the meaning is that everything that is said concerning the union of the Name, the coupling of *Tif'eret* and *Malkhut*, and many other related issues, concerns the illumination which shines into their receptacle and their union with it. This is similar to what the *Pardes* wrote in chapter fifteen of *Sha'ar Mahut ve-ha-Hanhagah*. When Ezekiel said, "*I flung myself down on my face*,"[297] he reached *Keter*. But neither he nor any prophet ever perceived the [*sefirot* of the] world of emanation itself. Ezekiel perceived their forms like a seal of wax. He perceived this in the world of formation, as explained in chapter six of *Sha'ar 'ABY'A*.[298] Here is what he wrote in chapter two of *Sha'ar Heykhalot*:

> Now it is worthwhile to know that the prophets do not draw from the *sefirot* themselves. For the *sefirot* are not revealed in any sense whatsoever, not even to Moses, our Rabbi. The difference be-

> tween our Rabbi, Moses, and the rest of the prophets is that Moses prophesied from the Palace of *Raẓon*, which is the sixth palace, which we shall explain, and the rest of the prophets from the Palace of *Nogah*, which is the third. Daniel and his companions, who speak with the Holy Spirit in vision and dream, gazed at the second palace, which we are discussing. Moreover, when Moses, our Rabbi, prophesied from the Palace of *Raẓon*, by means of the connection of *Tif'eret* and *Malkhut*, which are revealed in that palace, his prophecy came through a perfectly clear lens. No intermediary was necessary between Him and the palace in order to see prophetic matters. Thus it was "*plainly and not in riddles*."[299] But the rest of the prophets united these *sefirot* in the third palace, and those who speak with the Holy Spirit united them in the second.[300]

Thus I say that the Maggid's meaning is that all that is said about the union of the Name concerns this receptacle and garment, which is the Lady, *Shekhinah*. She causes Her Glory to shine within the Throne. She is a spark from the ten supernal *sefirot*. The secret of the exile of the *Shekhinah* refers to when this spark is extended to Metatron. The meaning of the saying of our rabbis that "the Name is complete and the Throne is complete" is as follows. The "Name is complete" refers to the secret of this spark, which is called the Lady *Shekhinah*. The Throne is the world of creation, for the Name is the soul of the Throne. More should not be said in this inquiry. May God forgive me for having said as much as I have.

Whatever may have been said up till now, at least it is known with certainty that as a result of a person's freely chosen deeds there is an effect very high above, and worship involves a need that is above. The ultimate purpose of one who worships is to do everything for God's Name, to cause his Creator pleasure. It is not for his own needs and to receive a reward, but for the sake of His Name, in love. Ultimately the Glory will arrive, for through the increase of *shefa'* above, that is caused by the arousal of the one worshipping, it descends below and there is peace in everything.

By means of the Torah and commandments, a person is connected to the Holy One, blessed be He, and the passage in the *Zohar* has been completely explained: "Three are connected: the Holy One, blessed be He, the Torah, and Israel," as begun in the introduction.

The Great House

In the Name of God. This is the book, Generations of Adam. Blessed is God who helped me until this point. Many words were produced, concerning great matters. As a result, human action has been explained regarding both a person's [divine] image and the likeness of his soul and body. Just as his Torah has been explained, so has his formation which involves the garments of light that became garments of skin. Yet in the future his eye will be opened to great light, the light that is concealed. [We have also explained] the true light, God's light that is concealed for the future, according to the secret of "*on that day YeHYeH YHVH will be One.*" This is entirely dependent on the spiritual arousal of human beings, who through their freedom of will have been granted the power to arouse the supernal. [We have also explained] how everything is foreseen, yet permission is granted. Thus is the ultimate purpose of the creation of human beings. Also, the meaning of the "world to come" and its eternity [has been explained]. For the cloud will perish along with the contamination of the serpent, which Adam drew down through his sin. Evil will be transformed to good and then there will be a world that is completely good.

These themes have been explained in this precious introduction, which is called *The Generations of Adam*, because all of the causes and events of human life and its purpose have been mentioned within it. In order to seal this introduction as a *Great House*, I thought it well to bring a *baraita*, which after reflection can be seen to allude to all of these matters mentioned above. It is from tractate *Shabbat, chapter ha-Boneh*:

> "*And you shall write them* [*on the doorposts.*]"[1] so that the writing will be whole, so that *alefs* will not be *ayins*, nor *ayins alefs*, *kafs* will not be *bets*, nor *bets kafs*, *gimmels* will not be *ẓadis*, nor *ẓadis gimmels*, *dalets* will not be *reshs*, nor *reshs dalets*, *hehs* will not be

> *ḥets*, nor *ḥets hehs*, *vavs* will not be *yods*, nor *yods vavs*, *zayins* will not be *nuns*, nor *nuns zayins*, *tets* will not be *pehs*, nor *pehs tets*, bent letters will not be straight, nor straight ones bent, *mems* will not be *samekhs*, nor *samekhs mems*, open *mems* will not be closed *mems*, nor closed *mems* open, a Torah section that is open will not be sealed, nor a sealed one open, if he wrote prose in the form of a song, or a song in the form of prose. If he did not write it with ink, or if he wrote the Divine Name in gold, these are concealed.[2]

Certainly this *baraita*, which involves the form of the entire Torah, contains many allusions, wonderful matters, and great secrets. Therefore, I want to reveal what I am able. My heart tells me that [the *baraita*] alludes to all of the matters that are alluded to in this introduction and speaks of the three that are bound together: the existence of God, the Torah, and the human being with all of his generations. God revealed the existence of His divinity by means of the world that He created, *creatio ex nihilo*, so that His divinity would be known to the human being. As the ultimate purpose of creation, the human being would receive the Torah and fulfill its commandments.

In explaining the secrets of this *baraita*, I will not follow the order of the words of the *baraita*. I will follow the order of the subjects, while the *baraita* arranges the words according to the order of the letters of the alphabet.

This is the meaning of " 'You shall write them' write them whole." By means of the Torah, we, the Israelite Nation, are connected to the Holy One, blessed be He. Thus there are six hundred thousand letters in the Torah, corresponding to six hundred thousand souls. Then, together, all will be complete (*tamim*). Concerning God, it is said, "His deeds are perfect (*tamim*)."[3] He is complete and completes Himself with their completeness. In other words, "The Torah [of *YHVH*] is complete (*temimah*)."[4] And concerning us, the House of Israel, is said, "*Be whole (tamim) with YHVH your God.*"[5]

Concerning God's existence, [the *baraita*] alludes not to write "*dalet*s like *resh*s, nor *resh*s like *dalet*s." This alludes to His unity. For the *dalet*, which is the last letter of "*YHVH our God, YHVH is One ('ehaD)* "[6] is written large. Also the *resh* at the end of "[*Do not bow down to*] *another ('aheR) God* "[7] is written large. God forbid, if a person would change the *dalet* to a *resh* or the *resh* to a *dalet*, he would be a heretic. For concerning such a person is said, "*They are a generation (DoR) of perversities (tahpukhot).*"[8] For they change (*mehapkhin*) *dalet* to *resh* and *resh* to *dalet*. But Judah still rules (*RaD*) with God. They are faithful to God and "*do not bow down to another God*," but only "*YHVH our God YHVH is One*."

"*Vav*s will not be *yod*s, nor *yod*s *vav*s." This alludes to a great secret that I revealed in this introduction, concerning the Name *YHVH*. For there is a difference in level, involving the ascent of *vav* to *yod*. In other words, it was still written as a *vav*, *YHVH*, even during the period of wholeness, when the Temple existed and the Name was complete. But in the future His great concealed light will be most revealed as a *yod*, which is the secret of the Name as *YHYH*. Therefore, in regards to the past, *vav* should not be written as *yod*. But in the future, *yod* will not be written *vav*. The form in which the letters of the Torah are written alludes to the past, present, and future. Therefore, the letter may not be changed from its form (*temunato*).

"*Zayin*s may not be written as *nun*s, nor *nun*s as *zayin*s." This alludes to the creation of the world, which declares God's agency. The introduction has already dealt with the great secret of "the world exists for six thousand years and is destroyed for one." This corresponds to the six days of creation and the Sabbath. So the cycle will repeat itself, according to the secret of the *shemitot* and the Jubilees, until fifty thousand generations, when the Holy One, blessed be He, has ordered the spirit to return above, as has been explained in the introduction. Every seventh thousand year, which is a Sabbath, is marked by additional holiness. However, all the holinesses of the seventh thousand years cannot be compared to the fiftieth thousand year. We can acquire an inclination of this from the case of our Rabbi Moses, who attained all of the Gates of Understanding, except the fiftieth gate. This is alluded to by "*zayin*s should not be *nun*s."[9] During the period of the *zayin*s, do not think of *nun*. As our rabbis, of blessed memory, said in their comment on the verse "*from one end of the heavens to the other* . . . ,"[10] "a person only has his world [to reflect on], and not what is before or after it."[11] The passage is brought above. However, during the period of the *nun*s, it is not like the period of the *zayin*s, because [the state of the world] will undergo a great elevation.

"*Tet*s may not be written as *peh*s, nor *peh*s as *tet*s." To explain this, we have to begin by citing a teaching of our rabbis that concerns the relationship of the letter *tet* to light. We shall also transcribe the words of the Rokeaḥ, which indicate the relationship of the letter *peh* and light. Afterward, I will explain a rabbinic passage in *Baba Kama*, at the end of chapter, *ha-Parah*.

> Rabbi Joshua said, if a person sees a *tet* in his dream, it is a good sign for him. What is the reason? If we say, because it is written, "*tov* (good),"[12] I can say that it is written, "*I will sweep it with a broom (ve-Te'tetiha bi-meTa'Ta') of extermination.*"[13] But we said one *tet*. Then I can say, [because it is written,] "*Her impurity (Tum'atah) clings to her skirts.*"[14] We said *tet* followed by a *bet*. Then I can say, [because it is written,] "*Her gates have sunk (tav'u) in the ground.*"[15] It is rather because scripture first used it favorably. For from "in the beginning," the letter *tet* is not written until "*and God saw that the light was good (Tov).*[16]"[17]

As for the letter *peh*, it is mentioned in the *Rokeaḥ*, in the order of prayers for the Day of Atonement, section 216:

> In every verse of the *Yoẓer* for the Day of Atonement, "Then on the Day of Atonement. . . . " But in the verse that begins with *peh*, light is concealed, "open the gate for us." Therefore, in the verse that precedes the one that begins with *peh*, light is mentioned twice, to complete the one that begins with *peh*. Why was light concealed in the verse that begins with *peh*? Because there are eighty[18] letters from "*in the beginning*," until "*on the face (peney) of the water.*"[19] Afterward is written, "*And God said let there be light.*" Therefore, [it is concealed] in the eighty faces of the first verse, which begins with eighty "*wonders of Your testimony*,"[20] then it continues, "*the beginning of Your words spread light.*"[21] For darkness, which is the first night, preceded the light, [which came with the verse,] "*Let there be light.*" The distance of a day or night is ten parasangs and each parasang equals four miles. Therefore, the distance of a day is forty miles. Since a mile equals two thousand cubits, this equals eighty thousand cubits. Therefore, the night was dark for a measure of the distance of eighty thousand cubits. Afterward, light was created through the first saying. When you began to speak, there was light.[22] Therefore, the light was concealed in the verse that begins with *peh*, because in *Sefer Yeẓirah* it says that "with the letter *peh*, *Nogah* was created in the world." On the fourth day, it is written, "Let there be lights." Why was a light created with *peh*? So that the lights would not take it, in order to be seen, before the beginning of the fourth day. The first, second, and third days plus the night of the fourth equal eighty-four hours. When the morning of the fourth day began to shine, the lights

> were seen. Thus there were eighty-five (*peh*) hours. This is the meaning of "*the beginning of Your words spread light and grant understanding to the simple . . .* [23]"[24]

Know that there are two levels to the concealed light; this is alluded to in the verse, "*How great is Your goodness, which You have hidden away for those who fear You, that You do in the sight of human beings, for those who trust in You.*"[25] The first level is in the world of souls, which is the world to come. It is constant and never ceases. In other words, the righteous who have already died and those who will not die until the time of resurrection enjoy the concealed light. [The second level concerns] the future world to come, which is eternal. This is the the world to come that [will follow the resurrection]. In it, they will enjoy [the light] in body and soul together, eternally, as I explained at length above in this introduction. This will be the world that is entirely good, so the great goodness that is hidden away will be most greatly increased. This is alluded to by "*How great is Your goodness that You have hidden away.*" This is the *tet* of goodness (*tuv*). It will begin with *tet* and increase from *tet*. This is as the *Rokeaḥ* wrote in the passage cited above.

> The Day of Atonement corresponds to the world to come. For it occurs on the tenth and the world to come is also the tenth. For the Torah preceded the world by two thousand years. This world lasts for six thousand years and is destroyed for one thousand. Thus in the tenth thousand, the world to come will begin.[26]

When he says "will begin," he means the great increase [of goodness] will begin. For in the seventh thousand year of destruction, which is the *tet* (ninth) thousand, there will certainly be great spiritual delight for the righteous.

The letter *peh* alludes to the fact that light follows darkness and night. This refers to the world of souls that is presently in effect after death. A person departs from this world, which is called night, to the supernal world, as indicated in tractate *Baba Meẓi'a*, chapter *ha-Po'alim*.

> Rabbi Zera expounded, and some say Rav Joseph taught, Why is it written, "*You bring darkness and it is night, in which all of the beasts of the forest creep*"?[27] "*You bring darkness and it is night*" refers to this world, which is like night. "*In it all of the beasts of the forest creep*" refers to the wicked in it, who are like the beasts

> of the forest. "*When the sun rises, they are gathered up and couch in their dens.*"[28] "*The sun rises*" for the righteous. The wicked "*are gathered up*" in Gehennom "*and couch in their dens.*"[29]

Concerning this, scripture said, "*You acted for those who trust in You.*"[30] It says, "*You acted,*" past tense. However, the light that will come to the world after the resurrection is still hidden away, and it is of a much higher order than that of the world of souls. Thus it is referred to as having been enacted compared to the concealed light, which is most spiritual. Thus we find the aspect of *tet*, "*How great is Your goodness (Tuvkha)*, and the aspect of *peh*, "*You acted (Pa'alta) for those who trusted in You.*" Thus one must not confound *tet* with *peh* or *peh* with *tet*.

"*Bets* may not be written as *kafs*, nor *kafs* as *bets*." This alludes to the Torah and the light that is concealed within it. In *Midrash Rabbah, Bereishit*, is written: "Rabbi Simon said, light is written five times, corresponding to the five books of the Torah."[31] In tractate *Sanhedrin*, chapter *Zeh Borer*, is written, " '*He made me to dwell in darkness like those long dead.*'[32] Rabbi Jeremiah said, This refers to the Babylonian Talmud."[33] On the face of it, this is a strange statement. For the Talmud is light and enlightens us. Also the Torah is our life and the length of our days. Yet he calls them "*the long dead*!" Also the *Midrash* of Rabbi Simon explained the light mentioned at the beginning of Genesis as referring to the five books of the Torah. It is written there, "*And God separated between the light and the darkness,*"[34] for the Holy One, blessed be He, concealed it. How does concealing apply? This would be understandable if the concealment refers to the light that appears to human beings. However, the Torah is one, as it is written, "*One Torah there will be for you.*"[35] And it is two Torahs, a written Torah and an oral Torah. But in truth, it is all one Torah. For the entire oral Torah is alluded to in the written Torah, such as those cases where it is asked, "Where in scripture do we learn this?" and "What is the source of this matter?" There is nothing that is not well alluded to in the Torah. It is only that the intellect has darkened and its light diminished because of Adam's sin. For his garments of light have been concealed and he is clothed in a garment of skin. "*They have eyes, but will not see.*"[36] This is the meaning of "*and God separated.*" The Holy One, blessed be He, saw [the deeds of the wicked] and concealed [the light]. Thus, due to the diminution of the human intellect, the written Torah is only understood after great effort. As our rabbis, of blessed memory, said, "Words of Torah are only fulfilled when one kills himself over them. As it is written, '*This is the Torah of a person when he dies in a tent.*'[37]"[38] For this reason, the written Torah requires a clarification and commentary, in other words, the Talmud. Otherwise it would have been self-explanatory. As we have seen in generation after generation. The earliest authorities had a clear intellect. Thus they understood deep matters without a commentary. Subsequent authorities could not understand without a commentary. Afterward, there were commentaries on commentaries, according to the darkening of the intellect.

Therefore, had Adam not sinned, his intellect would have remained clear. Thus he would have been able to understand the written Torah. Through this understanding, he would have known everything, and the oral Torah would not have been required. However, because of his sin, the light departed, and he brought death upon the world. Thus he had to labor hard and required an oral Torah, which is the commentary, and he had to kill himself over it. Finally, the [oral] Torah had to be written. Thus is explained the *Midrash*, " '*He made me dwell in darkness like the long dead.*'[39] This is the Babylonian Talmud." In other words, the darkness and death that [Adam] brought to the world caused this. If the Temple had continued to exist and the light had gone on to increase, as in the future, then the Torah would be light that delights the heart, rather than darkness over which one must kill oneself. This is the secret of the two lights. It has already been written in *Qol Bokhim*. "*Me'orot* (lights) is spelled with the letters of light (*'OR*) and death (*MaVeT*)." This is the meaning of "*He made me dwell in darkness like the long dead.*" Death (*mavet*) was made from the letters of *me'orot* and the letters *'or* darkened and were not light. It also should have been the case that "*the Torah is light*," one Torah. But now there are two Torahs and in the future, when the clear garments of light will be restored, the written Torah will be made clear to us by the light of the intellect. There will be no need for the clarification of the oral Torah.

As a result of this discussion, it is possible to resolve a difficulty in a passage from chapter, *Ha-Boneh*:

> The rabbis said to Rabbi Joshua ben Levi, Nowadays young students come to the Bet Midrash and say such things that even in the days of Joshua bin Nun, their like was not said: "*alef bet*—teach (*'alef*) understanding (*binah*), *gimmel dalet*—bestow upon the poor (*gemol dalim*), . . . and so on until *heh vav*—this is the Name of the Holy One, *zayin ḥet tet yod kaf lamed*—and if you do so, the Holy One, blessed be He, nourishes you, is gracious to you, does well to you, and gives you an inheritance, and binds a crown for you for the world to come. Simple *mem* closed *mem*—an open

> passage a closed passage, a bent *nun* a simple *nun*—a bent faithful one a simple faithful one, *samekh ayin*, support (*semokh*) the humble (*'aniyim*). He made thirty-one mnemonics in the Torah and acquired it, bent *peh* simple *peh*—an open mouth closed mouth, a bent *ẓadi* a simple *ẓadi*, a bent *ẓaddiq* (righteous one) a simple righteous one, in other words, a bent faithful one a simple faithful one. Scripture added a bent one to its bent one. This indicates that the Torah was given with nods of assent.[40]

This is surprising. They have explained all of the simple letters and also the double letters, *mem*, *nun*, *ẓadi*, *peh*, *kaf*, except for the simple *kaf*. However, according to what we have explained, it can be understood.

I will begin with a rabbinic saying from chapter *Rabbi Akiva*.

> Rabbi Simay expounded, when Israel stated "*we shall do*" before "*we shall hear*," six hundred thousand ministering angels came and bound two crowns for each one of the Israelites. One for "*we shall do*" and one for "*we shall hear*." But when they sinned, a hundred twenty thousand angels of harm descended and dismantled them, as it is written, "*so the Israelites were stripped of their jewels from Mount Horeb*."[41] Rabbi Yohannon said, Moses merited all of them and took them. For the next verse says, "*And Moses will take the tent* . . . "[42] . . . *Resh* Lakish said, In the future, the Holy One, blessed be He, will return them to us, as it is written, "*and the ransomed of YHVH will return, and come with rejoicing, and with everlasting joy on their heads*,"[43] joy that was always above their heads.[44]

The enlightened will understand that "we will do and we will hear" are the written Torah and the oral Torah. They are the two crowns. In the passage cited above from chapter *Ha-Boneh*, in the exposition of the meaning of the letter *kaf* it says, "And binds a crown for you in the world to come." This refers to the simple *kaf*, for it also alludes to a crown, since there are two crowns. Since the meaning of the simple *kaf* is no different from the meaning of the bent *kaf*, there was no need to mention it. In mentioning only the one *kaf*, there was an allusion to the matter that I explained. In the future, the two Torahs, which are two crowns, will be one crown. One crown will contain two crowns, because in the future the garments of light will be restored. This is what was explained in the passage from chapter *Rabbi Akiva*, "Joy that was always above their heads." The reference is to the joy from the beginning of creation. In other words, the light that was concealed will be restored above their heads. In the word *simḥat* (joy), there is an allusion to the oral Torah. For the oral Torah is the arguments, expositions, and disagreements of the sages, which is for the sake of heaven, "[. . . *the Book of the Wars of YHVH speaks of*] *Waheb in Suphah* . . ."[45] This is alluded to in the word *simḥat*, whose initial letters may be rearranged to form an acronym for "the sages increase peace (*talmidey hakhamim marbim shalom*)."

There is no need to raise the question why, when they placed "*we shall do*" before "*we shall hear*," they were given two crowns. After all, contamination of the serpent ceased and they should have had garments of light. This question was already addressed in the course of a discussion of another matter in *Pardes*, *Sha'ar ha-Neshamah*, chapter six.

> This is what must be asked here. Since our rabbis, of blessed memory, explained that when Israel stood at Mount Sinai, their contamination ceased,[46] why were they not brought [immediately] into the lower Garden of Eden? Why was dwelling in this world, and the Land of Israel, and other things still required? God enlightened us with a wonderful exposition that explained the meaning of the garments. After Adam was expelled from Eden, he lost his garment and remained naked. As it is written, "*They knew that they were naked*."[47] For the light had left them and their spirits remained naked and unclothed until the Holy One, blessed be He, clothed them in garments of skin, made from the atmosphere of this world. Thus they remain in this world until, as a result of good deeds and fulfilling the commandments, they are clothed in the Garden of Eden, as I explained. Thus it is true that when Israel stood on Mount Sinai, their contamination ceased. For they greatly purified their matter. However, had they entered the Garden of Eden, they would have done so naked, without a garment, because they had not yet fulfilled the commandments. If one has not fulfilled the commandments, he has nothing to be clothed in, as I explained. Do not say, God forbid, that they should enter there in the garments that they wear in this world, since they have purified their matter. This is the sign that one should not think that because a person has undergone a complete purification, he can then enter the Garden of Eden during his life, with his murky matter, unless he removes that garment and it ceases to exist. He must wear garments that are like that world.[48]

However, in the future, the Holy One, blessed be He, will bind one crown that will be one united Torah. Then they will ascend very high, since this one Torah will be extremely united with the secret of its inner nature, which is entirely Divine Names. For corporeal action will be cancelled and everything will be greatly purified, like the Torah study that was prepared for Adam in the Garden of Eden had he not sinned. This is explained in the chapter of *Pardes*, quoted above.

To return to our subject, it is now impossible to do without two Torahs, a written Torah and an oral Torah. This is the secret of why the Torah begins with the letter *bet*.[49] However, concerning the Ten Commandments, the *Zohar* said, "*One gold kaf (spoon) of ten shekels.*"[50] In other words, the Ten Commandments parallel the Ten Divine Utterances, which became *y v d*, spelled in full, which is *kaf*.[51] [The Ten Commandments] begin with *alef*, " '*anokhi (I am)* [*YHVH your God*]." They alluded to this in saying "do not mix *bet* with *kaf*, or *kaf* with *bet*." Now is the stage of *bet*, the stage of the future is *kaf*. This *kaf* is a crown, as they explained, "He connects a crown for you in the world to come."

"*Alef*s *may not be written as ayin*s, *nor ayin*s *as alef*s." We have already discussed at length the secret of the "garments of *'or* (light)," spelled with an *alef*. Later, Adam was clothed in "*garments of (skin)*," spelled with an *ayin*. In the future, the "garments of *'or*" with an *alef* will be restored at an even higher level. Therefore, the first *alef* may not be mixed with an *ayin*. Afterward, "*light increases from the darkness*,"[52] and there will be an open *ayin* (eye). "*No eye has seen it, O God, but You*."[53] It will be on a higher level than the *alef* of the first "garments of light."

"*Hehs* may not be written as *ḥets*, nor *ḥets* as *hehs*." It is written in tractate *Menaḥot*, chapter *Ha-Qomeẓ Batra*:

> Rav Ashi said, We saw that the careful copyists of Rav's school make a staff on the top of the *ḥet* and they let the leg of the *heh* hang down. "They make a staff on the top of the *ḥet*," in other words, He lives in the heights of the world. "And they let the leg of the *heh* hang" . . . Why was this world created with a *heh*? Because it is like an *exedra*,[54] so that whoever wishes to leave can go out. Why does its leg hang? So that if one turns and repents, they let him in there. But they do not help him to enter through the same opening through which he left.[55]

It is written at the end of chapter *'Eyn 'Omdim* of tractate *Berakhot*:

> Rabbi Hiyya bar Abba said in the name of Rabbi Yohannon, All of the prophets only prophesied to penitents. As for the completely righteous, "*No eye has seen it, O God, but You.*"[56] This disagrees with Rabbi Abbahu. For Rabbi Abbahu said, In the place where penitents stand, the completely righteous do not stand. For it is written, "*Peace, peace for the distant and the near.*"[57] It begins with the distant and then returns to the near. Rabbi Yohannon tells you, What is the meaning of "*distant*?" He was far from a transgression from the beginning. What is the meaning of "*near*?" He was close to a transgression and was distanced from it now.[58]

Know that one is speaking about one matter and the other is speaking about another. They do not disagree. Even though the Talmud says they diverge, the meaning is that they are divided, each speaking about a different matter. As Onkelos translated the verse in *Parashat Mattot* "*and take from the half of the Children of Israel,*"[59] "and from the division of the Children of Israel." We can distinguish between repentance from fear and repentance from love. In other words, a completely righteous person is superior to a penitent who repents from fear. But a penitent who repents from love is superior to a completely righteous person. Thus we can speak by way of the simple meaning. However, there is also a great allusion in these matters. For if Adam had remained in garments of light, as he was created, and not brought upon himself the evil urge, he would have been perfectly righteous. After he was clothed in garments of skin he had no remedy except repentance. This is also true for all of his descendants who followed him in the darkness of matter. This matter is close to a loss and close to a reward. It is close to a loss if he does not purify himself, and close to a reward if he does purify himself. Then he would be good and a bestower of good. He is good to himself, because he purifies himself. He is good to others, because he breaks and subdues the *qelippot* and purifies and sweetens them. Then "*the light increases from the darkness,*" as I have explained above. Therefore, there are advantages and disadvantages. It can be argued that it would have been better if Adam had remained in garments of light. For then he would have been completely righteous and all of the worlds would have been fortunate. But it can also be maintained that, on the contrary, it is better that he become a penitent. For the elite reach a higher level with an additional spiritual enhancement. Compare the disagreement between the School of Hillel and the School of Shammai, concerning whether it is better for a person to have been born or not to have been born.

Now "*ḥet* lives in the heights of the world," because this refers to the completely righteous, which is the secret of the garments of light. Then the *Shekhinah* is present below and we cleave to it. As our rabbis, of blessed memory, explained, "From the moment that the Holy One, blessed be He, began creating the world, it was desired that the *Shekhinah* be present below."[60] For then the world would be in its height, exalted above, pure and clean. And then the Living God, who Lives and Exists, would dwell in the heights of the world. From Him, vitality would be bestowed upon Adam, and he would live forever. However, the *heh* alludes to the penitents, for the world is like an *exedra*.

The *heh* is open below. Here is what is written in *Tomer Devorah*:

> "The world was created with [the letter] *heh*." The Holy One, blessed be He, created the world open to the side of evil. Thus sin is rampant. Matter, the evil urge, and damage are in all directions. Like an *exedra*, it is not closed off. There is a huge opening to the side of evil, which is below. Whoever wishes to leave the world finds how open the way is for him. Wherever he turns, he will encounter sin and iniquity, leading to the external forces. But the *heh* is open above, so that if he wishes to return, the [forces of holiness] will receive him. It was objected, why do they not help him to return through the way he went out? The reason is that it is not enough that a penitent be held in check by the boundaries of the righteous. For the righteous who have never sinned require only the slightest boundary. However, a slight boundary is not sufficient for one who has sinned and then repented. He has to establish several difficult boundaries for himself. For he has already transgressed that slight boundary. If he approaches there, his urge will easily seduce him. He needs to keep himself at a great distance from there. Therefore, he cannot re-enter through the opening of the *exedra*, which can be breached, but must ascend and enter through the narrow (*ẓar*) opening. He must afflict himself (*ve-ya'aseh kamah ẓarot*) and seal the breaches. For this reason, [it was said], "In the place that penitents stand, [the completely righteous do not stand]." For they cannot enter the opening of the righteous in order to be among the righteous. Rather, they must be sorry and ascend to the upper opening, and afflict themselves, and be much further removed from sin than the righteous. Thus

> they ascend and stand on the rung of *heh*,[61] the fifth palace in the Garden of Eden, in other words, the top of the *heh*. The righteous, on the other hand, stand in the opening of the *heh*, the entrance of the *exedra*. Thus when a person repents (*ya'aseh TeSHuVaH)*, *heh* returns to its place (*TaSHuV Heh*).[62]

In the future, when the garments of light will be restored, the levels of the completely righteous will reach their ultimate state of complete goodness. For the dross will go out and no dregs will remain in the wine. This is the secret of the verse, "*No eye has seen, O God, but You.*"[63] It refers to the wine that has no dregs (*yayin meshumar*). I already discussed this above. It was to this that they alluded in saying "*Hehs* may not be written as *ḥets*, nor *ḥets* as *hehs*."

"*Gimmel*s may not be written as *ẓadi*s, nor *ẓadi*s as *gimmel*s." This also alludes to the cancelling of the contamination of the serpent. It is known that the root of all virtues is submission, and it is the root of repentance. The greatest quality of all the virtues is humility. Although our rabbi, Moses, was the greatest of the prophets, the Torah only praises him for his extraordinary humility. Thus, "it is taught that envy, desire, and honor, expel a person from the world." Adam left the world and brought death upon himself and all the generations. This was due to these vices, which came from the serpent, which became jealous when he saw Eve. Thus he incited her to desire, as it is written, "*For it is a desire for the eyes*,"[64] and to honor, as it is written, "*And you shall be as God.*"[65] Adam's sin is the "*root sprouting poison, weed, and wormwood*"[66] of all the sins. For it brought the serpent's contamination and the evil urge to the world. The remedy for this is the virtue of humility. For a person who is very humble and whose soul is like dust is not jealous or desirous and flees from honor. Now it is said in the passage from chapter *Ha-Boneh*, "a bent *nun*, a simple *nun*, a bent faithful one, a simple faithful one . . . a bent *ẓadi* a simple *ẓadi*, a bent righteous one a simple righteous one, in other words, a bent faithful one a simple faithful one. Scripture added a bent one to its bent one. This indicates that the Torah was given with nods of assent."[67]

The issue is explained in the fourth chapter of Maimonides's *Shemonah Peraqim*, which was written as an introduction to tractate *Avot*.

> Good deeds are those that are equally located on the mean between two extremes that are both evil. One is excessive and the other is deficient. Virtuous qualities are states of the soul

> (*tekhunot nafshiot*) and traits (*kinyanim*) that are intermediate between evil states, one of which is excessive and the other deficient. An example is moderation (*zehirut*), which is an intermediate quality between the extreme of desire and the lack of the feeling of pleasure. Thus moderation is one of the good functions and states of the soul that produce moderation are virtuous qualities. But excessive desire is the first extreme, while the total lack of the feeling of pleasure is the other extreme. Both are completely evil. The two states of the soul that necessarily result in excessive desire, which is the excessive state, and the absence of feeling, which is the deficient state, are both moral vices. Similarly, generosity is intermediate between prodigality and stinginess, and bravery is intermediate between rashness and cowardice . . . and dignity is intermediate between haughtiness and abasement.[68]

Notice how in that chapter Maimonides heaped praise on choosing the intermediate way, except in the case of humility, which is between pride and dejection; he advised not remaining in the middle, but inclining toward the latter extreme, and to be of humble spirit. As it is said in the *Mishnah*, at the beginning of chapter *Ben Zoma*, "Be very, very humble in spirit, for a person's hope is worms."[69] He wrote similarly in *Sefer ha-Mada'*, *Hilkhot De'ot*, chapter one. Our rabbis, of blessed memory, spoke at length of this in the first chapter of tractate *Sotah*.

Thus they said, "Be very, very humble in spirit," meaning, do not follow the middle way, but incline to the latter extreme so that you will be very humble in spirit. Similarly, it is written, "*And Moses was very humble.*"[70] [Scripture] added the word "*very.*" Thus they said, " . . . a bent righteous one. Scripture added a bent one to its bent one." Now they said in the first chapter of *Sotah*, "Rav Hiyya bar Abba said in the name of Rav, a sage has to have an eighth of an eighth of pride,"[71] which is his portion. Similarly, Rava said there that "the one that has it deserves excommunication and the one that lacks it deserves excommunication." Rashi explains this latter as "a little pride, for without it the locals will not fear him and he will have no power to rebuke them."[72] Therefore, a sage should not incline completely to the latter extreme, but must retain the slightest bit of pride, for the sake of the Torah's honor, so that he will be able to teach it and to admonish. Otherwise, one should have "none of it at all."[73] The least speck of pride should not be in him. He should follow the latter extreme completely and be humble of spirit.

Now the matter of *gimmel*s and *ẓadi*s can be explained. Rashi explained there, "They are similar in their written form, but one is above [the line] and one is below [the line]. In other words, a bent righteous one is above, alluding to what was said above. Even though a great person who admonishes the multitude adds bending to his bending, he still requires the tiniest bit of pride for the sake of heaven, in order to inspire fear so that they will accept his admonishing. Thus the head remains above, even though he is bent over, the head of the righteous one, [i.e., the *ẓadi*], is above. However, the *gimmel* is the opposite. The head is below, alluding to the ordinary person. Not only must he add bending to his bending, but he must be like one who has no head at all. He is bowed to the earth like one who is truly like the dust of the earth. He should completely follow the latter extreme of a humble spirit. Thus [it was said], "Do not mix *gimmel*s with *ẓadi*s, or *ẓadi*s with *gimmel*s." The reason for the great importance of humility is as I have written. Thus the sin of Adam, which contains all sins, is rectified. In the future when the serpent's contamination and the *qelippot* will come to an end, it is written, "*And I will cause you to walk upright*."[74] *For YHVH will dwell in our midst*.[75] "*YHVH is King, dressed in pride*."[76]

"*Mem*s may not be written as *samekh*s, nor *samekh*s as *mem*s." A closed *mem* has four sides. *Samekh* is similar to it, except that *mem* is square and *samekh* is round. There are great allusions concealed in this matter. It is written, "*I have spread you like the four winds of heaven*."[77] Our rabbis, of blessed memory, explained in the first chapter of *'Avodah Zara*, "Just as the world cannot do without winds, so the world cannot do without Israel."[78] Thus the level of Israel is great, with four flags to the four winds. Know that winds allude to the Torah and purity of action. How so? Repentance, prayer, and charity are well known for purity of action. And study is great. "For study of Torah is equal to all of them." These are contained in the Mishnah, "The world stands on three things: Torah, worship, and acts of loving-kindness." The first is Torah. The second is prayer, which is contained in worship. As our rabbis, of blessed memory, said "What is the worship of the heart? You must say that it is prayer which replaces sacrifices." The third is charity, and they are also included together. Fourth is repentance. These four walls are the four winds, as I shall explain. Two directions remain, above and below. In other words, heaven is above and the earth is below. God is, so to speak, in heaven, in the very most heights. He is the most supreme height. Human beings are on the earth below. The four winds remain, which allude to the matters explained above. By means of them, a person on the earth below can cleave to the supreme height.

To begin, I will recall that east is called front and west is called back. South is right and north is left. It is said concerning the face of the Holy One, blessed be He, that "*in the light of the king's countenance is life.*"[79] For he is lovingkindness and charity. As it is written, "*You bestowed life and lovingkindness on me.*"[80] And it is written, "*Charity will save from death.*"[81] Also, "*Lovingkindness and truth stand before Your countenance.*"[82] And also, "*I will see Your face in righteousness.*"[83] Now the creation of the world came from God's lovingkindness, graciousness, and generosity. As it is written, "*A world of lovingkindness will be built.*"[84] How did creation begin? "*God said let there be light and there was light.*"[85] Thus the east alludes to this, since light reaches the world from there. And it is written, "*A sun of charity with healing in its wings.*"[86] East is called front, because "*in the light of the king's countenance is life.*"[87] And it is written, "*Your righteousness walks before You.*"[88] Therefore, the flag of Judah is toward the east, for the kingdom of the House of David is prepared with charity. As scripture testified concerning David, "*And David executed justice and charity.*"[89] Our rabbis, of blessed memory, said that even in meting out justice, he acted with charity. For he justly ruled in favor of this one and obligated that one. Afterward, he would return [the fine] from his own pocket to the one obligated to pay. Thus he used to pray, "*I have done justice and righteousness, do not abandon me to my oppressors.*"[90] For he was afraid that there were many swindlers who would form a partnership. One would bring the other to trial so that one would be declared guilty and David would return his fine to him. Later, they would divide it. Therefore, he would pray, "Master of the Universe, '*do not abandon me to my oppressors.*' Frustrate their plan." Thus it is explained in *Midrash Shemuel.*

Also in the Book of Chronicles, you will find David's generosity to the Temple. He and his ministers joyously made great donations. And then "*David blessed YHVH before the entire congregation . . .* "[91] as recounted in the Book of Chronicles. Thus the custom which I saw observed in the Land of Israel seems most fitting. When the *Gabbai* collects charitable offerings in the synagogue, he does so after the liturgical passage, "*and David blessed* [*YHVH before the entire congregation*]." They say that this tradition comes from Rabbi Isaac Luria. It may be that the reason is that after his generosity and the generosity of his ministers, "*David blessed . . .* " Thus it is fitting to collect charity at this time, and not as is done in the other countries, where the *Gabbai* makes his collection during the repetition of the standing prayer. As a result people's minds are not on listening to the prayer in order to answer Amen, as is required. Therefore this custom is a very fine one.

Returning to our subject, the eastern wind, from which light reaches the world, is called front. Thus it is said, "*May YHVH shine His countenance upon you.*"[92]

The right hand of the Holy One, blessed be He, is outstretched to receive penitents. The south wind is the right, as it is written, "*North and right (south), You created them.*"[93] Therefore, the flag of Reuben is there. In the *Midrash*, "The Holy One, blessed be He, said to Reuben, you were the first to do repentance. Therefore, on your life, your descendant stands and is [the first prophet] to call for repentance. Who is he? Hosea son of Beeri, as it is written, '*Return Israel to YHVH your God.*'[94]"[95] One may raise an objection to this. How could the *Midrash* say that Reuben was the first to do repentance? Have not our rabbis, of blessed memory, spoken very much of the repentance that Adam did? He spent one hundred and thirty years fasting and entered the waters of Gihon, and so on.[96] Cain also did repentance. The author of *Reishit Ḥokhmah* answered that they did repentance for transgressing prohibitions. However, Reuben was the first to do repentance for not having fulfilled positive commandments. That is to say, honoring one's parents is a positive commandment.[97] This solution seems farfetched, for their honor is compared to the honor of God, as explained in chapter *'Elu Meẓi'ot*.[97] I would humbly suggest this explanation. They did not begin to repent at first on their own, before the Holy One, blessed be He, showed them an allusion of repentance. However, Reuben began to do repentance as a result of his own initiative. He was not stimulated to do so from above. In the case of Adam, the initiative was as described in *Bereishit Rabbah*:

> "*And now, lest he reach out his hand.*"[98] Rabbi Abba bar Kahane said, It teaches that the Holy One, blessed be He, made an opening of repentance for him. As it is written, "*and now.*" "*And now*" is an allusion to repentance, as it is written, "*And now . . . what does YHVH ask of you . . . ?*"[99] Similarly, the Holy One, blessed be He, said to Cain, "*If you do right, there is uplift.*"[100]

But Reuben began to do repentance on his own initiative.

It is also possible to explain the meaning of [Reuben] began (*pataḥ*) as saying that [repentance] was closed and he opened (*pataḥ*) it. In other words, he revealed the concealed. For in the case of Adam and Cain, their sin was well known. So what was revealed when they began to do repentance? However, Reuben's sin was completely concealed. As our rabbis, of blessed memory, said, "Whoever says that Reuben sinned is mistaken, for he defended his mother's honor."[101] On the contrary, as can be seen, he fulfilled a commandment.[102] This was alluded to by our rabbis, of blessed memory,

"One should examine one's deeds." In other words, one should examine and reflect on them to see if perhaps some sin is concealed in them. This is what Reuben did. For he reflected that even though he had acted for the sake of heaven, to honor his mother, perhaps he had acted in a way that dishonored his father. This is the meaning of "opening"; he opened what was locked and examined his deeds.

It is written concerning the back of the Holy One, blessed be He, "*And you shall see My back*."[103] There He taught our rabbi, Moses, the order of prayer with the thirteen attributes. As our rabbis, of blessed memory, explained, The Holy One, blessed be He, wrapped Himself in a prayershawl, like a prayer leader, and said, "When My children act according to this order . . . " The west is called "back." And our rabbis, of blessed memory, said, the *Shekhinah* is in the west. Therefore, we are obligated to direct our prayers to the Holy of Holies, which is in the west. The flag of Ephraim, from whom Joshua is descended, is there. Our rabbis, of blessed memory, said, "It is forbidden for a sage to fall upon his face [in supplication], until he is assured that he will be answered like Joshua."[104]

Therefore, the front, right, and back allude to charity, repentance, and prayer. The *bet* in *bereishit* (in the beginning) alludes to these three directions. And the north remains open.[105] The meaning is that "*evil begins from the north*."[106] For the north is the secret of *Gevurah* and the forces of judgment. The *qelippot*, which are the emissaries of judgment, are emanated and nourished from there. The Torah begins with *bet* to allude to these three walls. But the supreme world of the Torah is not alluded to. Know that the Torah preceded the world by two thousand years. They also said in the *Midrash* that the Torah begins with *bet*, which is a blessing (*berakhah*). All of their words are true, so I shall explain.

Know that were it not for the serpent's contamination and the sins, there would be no need for repentance. Even prayer would hardly have been needed as it is now. For nothing would have been lacking, just as will be the case in the future, according to the secret of the cessation of the serpent's contamination. Our rabbis, of blessed memory, said, "In the future the Land of Israel will bring forth biscuits and woolen garments, and there will be peace and quiet in the Land." It is even more clear that there will be no need for charity. For there will be no paupers among you. And the Torah will only exist in its spiritual qualities, which is the secret that it is entirely Names of God. But the Holy One, blessed be He, foresaw the curse of the serpent in the future. Thus the Torah began with the *bet* of blessing (*berakhah*), which alludes to these three, repentance, prayer, and charity. This rectifies sin that derives from the accursed serpent, and one enters into blessing. Now our rabbis, of blessed memory, said, "The Holy One, blessed be He, created the evil urge, so He created antidotes for it, namely the Torah." In other words, through the power of the Torah, the north, which is open toward evil, can be sealed off. In other words, this is effected through "*turn from evil and do good,*" which alludes to the negative and positive commandments. Then this direction is transformed to good. As our rabbis, of blessed memory, said, "The tradition must be clear as a cold, north-wind day."[107] Therefore the Torah was given from the Mouth of *Gevurah*, which is in the north, as is known. As Rashi explained, concerning the Ten Commandments, " '*and 'Elohim said . . .* '[108] Whenever the term *'Elohim* is used it refers to a judge."[109] For the root of the Torah is *Ḥesed*, as it is written, "*And a Torah of Ḥesed is on her tongue.*"[110] For it is taken from supernal *Ḥokhmah*, which is supernal *Ḥesed*, as is known to the kabbalists. This is alluded to in the verse, "*from His right hand a flaming Law for them.*"[111] Nevertheless, it was given amid lightning and thunder, by means of *Gevurah*, which is on the left. Thus, "*Longevity is in his right hand and wealth and honor in his left.*"[112] Concerning this wealth, our rabbis, of blessed memory, said, "Whoever wishes to become wealthy should go to the north." For there is no poverty, but the poverty of Torah. Concerning this is said, "*Gold will come from the north.*"[113] It says in *Bereishit Rabbah*, " '*The gold of that land is good.*' There is no Torah like the Torah of the Land of Israel."[114] "Whoever wishes to be wise should go to the south." This refers to the enlightened portion of the Torah and its secrets, which our rabbis, of blessed memory, called "a great matter, the work of the Chariot." This does not concern positive and negative commandments. However, from the north is "*turn from evil and do good,*" as I have explained. Thus the righteous transform the attribute of judgment to compassion. Therefore, the north, which is open from the side of judgment, is closed in the Torah. The flag of Dan, whose name derives from *din* (judgment), is located there. As Rachel said, "*YHVH judged me.*"[115] And the secret is "*Dan will be a serpent,*"[116] for the power of the serpent nurses from there. If a criminal harms you, draw him to the court. When the Torah was given, the four sides were complete and became a closed *mem*, which is the closed *mem* in the verse "*in token of abundant authority and unending peace.*"[117]

Now a human being is like a ladder. He is established on the earth and his head is toward the heavens. In other words, the Holy One, blessed be He, took the human body from the earth, from the place of the altar of earth, so that he would be sanctified. But his head, that is, his soul, is from the highest heights. We the Israelite Nation are called human. This is the secret of the six directions. The human is above and below, and the four directions that surround him indicate the sanctification mentioned above. The *Shekhinah* is above his head. I found the following concealed teachings of Rabbi Isaac Luria in *Sefer Kanfey Yonah*:

> East, west, north, and south have the numerical value of the seven Divine Names that may not be erased: *'El*, *'Elohim*, *YHVH*, *'EHYeH*, *Shadday*, *Ẓeva'ot*, *'ADoNaY*. They are the seven clouds of glory that surround Israel from every side. Know that the Name *YaH* is not counted among them, because it is the first two letters of *YHVH* and the last two of *'EHYeH*. But the Name *'El* is not the beginning of the Name *'Elohim*, but a combination of the three *yods* and the *alef* from the Name of 63, which equals *'El* (31). East (*mizraḥ*) equals *nahar* (river).[118] "A river goes forth from Eden to water the garden."[119] West (*ma'arav*) equals twelve permutations of the Name *YHVH*.[120] North (*ẓafon*) equals choosing (*beḥirah*) with one for the word itself.[121] Thus "*and He chose David His servant*."[122] This is the secret of choosing, which is explained in its place, for because of it the power of the sinner is concealed for the righteous. It is all according to justice and righteousness. There are indications of this in the words of our rabbis, of blessed memory. They said, "And your indicator is the candelabra in the south." What was being alluded to here when they specified "your indicator"? Clearly, they meant to specify that this is a good sign, since south (*darom*) equals *ner* (lamp),[123] and a person's wisdom enlightens like the lamp of God. South (*darom*) equals *ner* (lamp): "*The lamp of YHVH is the soul of a human being*."[124] For it is the daughter of a priest, the daughter of Abraham the pious one.[125]

Thus there are a number of secrets concerning the four directions.

Now I will explain the issue of the *samekh* and *mem*. *Samekh* is similar to a closed *mem*. Only, the *mem* is square and the *samekh* is round. There is a very important allusion here. For this World of Making, which contains heaven and earth and all of their hosts, is round. For we see that the heaven is round and the spirituality of the World of Making is the power of heaven, just like the soul in the body. Therefore, it is alluded to by *samekh*. Above it in the World of Formation is the Camp of the *Shekhinah*, Michael, Gabriel, Uriel, and Raphael. The four flags of Israel corresponded to them, as mentioned in *Ba-Midbar Rabbah*, the *Zohar*, and kabbalistic writings.[126] These four Camps of the *Shekhinah* are imagined in our minds as if they formed a square. They are each parallel to the four animals in the world that is above it. These also form a square: the human, bull, eagle, and lion that bear the Throne.

Now I will reveal the secret to you. Our rabbis, of blessed memory, distinguished actions between those that are done out of love and those done out of fear. Similarly, in regard to repentance, there is a distinction between repentance from fear and repentance from love, as is explained in tractate *Yoma*.[127] Those who act out of fear cleave to corporeality; in other words they are motivated by their own fear. Thus the person cleaves to the corporeal world and its roots, which are alluded to by the form of *samekh*. However, when one acts from love, it is the love of the Holy One, blessed be He. He wishes to cleave to Him and to enter into spirituality. Thus is fulfilled in him, "*I will let you move among those that stand*."[128] "Great is repentance that reaches the Throne." In other words, it reaches the square of the animals that is above the square of the Camps, mentioned above. This is the secret of the closed *mem* of the verse "*in token of abundant authority and unending peace*."[129]

Now when you place a circle within a square, just as the World of Making is within spiritual worlds, the square overlaps by four corners. The sprinklings of sacrifice to *YHVH* alluded to these four corners. As the *Mishnah* teaches, "It came to the southeastern corner, the northeastern, northwestern, and southwestern."[130] These corners are alluded to by "*in blazing anger He has cut off all the corners of Israel*."[131] For even though there certainly were penitents and virtuous people (*ba'aley ma'aseh*) among them, they were not on the level of the *mem*, but only the *samekh*. In other words, they acted out of fear. As it is written, "*He drew back His right hand because of the enemy*."[132] For the Holy One, blessed be He, drew back His right hand, which is open to receive penitents, because they were only doing repentance "*because of the enemy*," in other words, because of fear. Then the corners of the square that overlap the circle were cut off. This is the secret of "*and the daughter of Zion is left like a booth in a vineyard*."[133] I have a tradition concerning the word *booth*. As a result of this allusion the laws of the walls of the *sukkah* will be explained. The preferred way to fulfill the commandment is with four sides, but even three fulfill the law before the fact. The *halakhah* is that even two are acceptable and somewhat of a third.[134] The four sides allude to the four walls that I mentioned, repentance, prayer, charity, and Torah. The *samekh* of *sukkah*, which goes around and surrounds all sides, alludes to this. However, there are Israelites that are not proficient in Torah and do not have the capacity to understand. Thus they hold three sides, which are the three walls of repentance, prayer, and charity. Corresponding to this is the *kaf* of *sukkah*, which goes around in three directions. However, sometimes there are those that cannot even hold three. For they are not proficient in Torah and are also too poor to give charity. Thus they hold two sides, which are the two walls of repentance and prayer, which every Israelite can fulfill. There is still "somewhat of a third," in other words to give something small. As our rabbis, of blessed memory, explained, "Even a poor person who receives charity has to give a small amount of charity."[135] The *heh* of the word *sukkah* corresponds to this, for it has two whole sides and somewhat of a third. Thus the *halakhah* is two must be as required and somewhat of a third.

Now a *sukkah* is a temporary residence, for it is alluded to in the verse, "*The needy will never cease to be in your land*."[136] However, "*the bayit (house) will be built with wisdom*."[137] The kabbalists explained that the *bet* of *bereishit* ("in the beginning") alludes to *Ḥokhmah* (wisdom). As the *Targum Yonaton* has it, *bereishit* is translated "with *Ḥokhmah*." This is a permanent house. As I have indicated, the bet of *bereishit* alludes to the square that afterward, when the Torah was given, became a closed *mem*. At the time of redemption, the verse will be fulfilled that says "*in token of abundant authority*."[138] For there is no redemption unless complete repentance is done. Then prayer will be pure, according to the secret of "*I will let them rejoice in My House of Prayer*."[139] This is the secret of *devequt* and connection. "*There shall be no needy among you*."[140] There will be lovingkindness, but not charity. For lovingkindness pertains to both the needy and the rich. The study of Torah will increase. Thus the verse will be fulfilled that says, "*The earth will be full of knowledge* [*of YHVH*]."[141] All of this is the secret of the *bet* that becomes a closed *mem*. Then it will be a faithful house (*bayit*).

However, *sukkah* alludes to the reduction of the walls (*meḥiẓot*), as it is written, "*And the daughter of Zion is left like a booth in a vineyard*."[142] Thus the *bet* of *bereishit* is large and the *heh* in the word "*be-Hibar'am*"[143] is small. Concerning this verse, our rabbis, of blessed memory, said, "Creation was done with a *heh*." For both *bet* and *heh* consist of three lines. The three lines of *bet* allude to "*There shall be no needy among you*."[144] The lines of the *heh* allude to "*The needy will never cease to be in your land*."[145] It all depends on the majority of the deeds and merit. Thus is explained that *mems* should not be written like *samekhs*.

Our rabbis, of blessed memory, said that the *mems* and *samekhs* that were on the tablets remained in place as the result of a miracle. For both of them allude to this great matter, except that the *mem* is above the *samekh*. Nevertheless, the *samekh* is also holy. This is in keeping with the rabbinic saying, "A person should always [be concerned with Torah and commandments], even when it is not for its own sake, so that through acting not for its own sake, he may come to do it for its own sake."[146] However, when the Temple was destroyed, because they did not come to act for its own sake, scripture said, "*has become a mas (slave)*."[147] In other words, the *mem* became a *samekh*, "*for He cut . . . all of its corners*."[148] Do not be perplexed by the fact that the *mem* in the word "*le-mas*" is open and not closed. Know that this is the secret of the "*walls of Jerusalem which are breached (hem peruẓot)*."[149] There is an open *mem* here instead of a closed one. For the breacher ascended and it was opened. Thus it says, "*and became a slave*," for it only came about because of the enemy, that is, from fear. This is a *samekh*, and they did not reach the level of the closed *mem*. For it became open, that is to say, breached and opened without. This is the secret of Moses' mask. For when Israel sinned they could not gaze at Moses' face. As a result of the sin of the calf, the tablets were shattered, and [the effect] continued throughout every generation. As our rabbis, of blessed memory, said, "There is no divine visitation that is not a punishment for the calf"[150] and it continued until the destruction of the Temple. As a result of our many transgressions, the Divine Name is not complete. That is to say, the letters *vav heh* [are not united]. When the tablets were shattered the miracle of the *mem* and *samekh* was cancelled and the *mem* was breached. This is the secret of the *masveh* (mask), which stopped the projection of light from his face, which is open *mem* closed *mem*. It "became *le-MaS*."[151] The *mem* and *samekh* that are in the tablets, with the *vav* and *heh* of the Divine Name spell *masveh* (mask). Thus the verse says, "*How lonely sits the city*."[152] The initial letters form an acronym spelling enmity (*'eyvah*), which is written concerning the serpent. "*And I will place enmity [between you and the woman . . .]*."[153] As the *Zohar* states, "Enmity that the serpent increased until the Temple was destroyed." And the verse ends with "*le-mas*." The allusion of *vav heh* and the serpent has already been explained above at length. For the serpent caused the Name to be incomplete. This is the meaning of *masveh*. In the future it will be rectified and the projection of light will be restored.

After this, it says, "Do not write a *mem* as a *samekh*." This alludes to receiving a reward for learning Torah and correcting one's actions. This is explained in the discussion of the eternal existence of the future in *'Avodat ha-Qodesh, ḥeleq ha-'Avodah*, chapter 43:

> It is written at the end of *Ta'anit*, "Rabbi Helbo said that Ulla said in the name of Rabbi Eliezer, In the future the Holy One, blessed be He, will hold a dance for the righteous, and He will sit among them, and each one of them will point to Him with his finger. As it is written, '*And they shall say on that day, this is our God, we hoped*

> *in Him and He saved us.*'[154]"[155] It says in *Va-Yiqra Rabbah*, chapter eleven, "In the future, the Holy One, blessed be He, will be the chief dancer for the righteous in the future that is coming. As it is written, '*Take note of its heylah.*'[156] '*Le-holah*' (to its dancer) is written. It is as though they were pointing to Him with a finger and saying '*For this is God, our God, forever. He will lead us 'al-mut.*'[157] [It means that He will lead us in the dance] like maidens (*ke-'alemot*), through the urging of the maidens, like those maidens mentioned in scripture, '*among maidens playing drums.*'[158] Onkelos translated [then '*al-mut*'], 'to be lifted up.' [It means] a world that has no death in it.[159] [It can also be read as] ' '*olamot* (worlds),' 'He will lead us in two worlds,' in this world and the world that is coming."[160] Similarly, it is written in the Palestinian Talmud, tractate *Sukkah*, "A round dance and a dancer that has no beginning or end."[161] This is a metaphor for the endless delight [that is coming]. Thus the world to come, after the resurrection of the dead, is called a world that is entirely good, a world that is entirely long. Then the righteous attain their ultimate enlightenment. For the *Shekhinah* is in the center and they surround Her. This is the dance and dancer. To allude to that wondrous enlightenment, they said, "Each one points at [the *Shekhinah*] with his finger."[162]

The circle represents something that constantly returns without end. The meaning is a circle within a square and a square within a circle. The circle is *samekh* and the square is a final *mem*. In this world, the world of action, the square is higher than the circle, thus it encompasses it. But in the future, in the world of the reward, the square is within the circle, for the circle represents eternity. Thus the meaning of "*samekh*s must not be written as *mem*s, nor *mem*s as *samekh*s" has been explained.

"Bent letters must not be written as straight, nor straight letters as bent." This may be explained according to the exposition of the young students: "a faithful bent one and a faithful straight one, an open mouth and a closed mouth, a bent righteous one and a straight righteous one." Thus one must not be made like the other.

"Closed letters should not be written as open ones, nor open ones as closed." This is also explained by the exposition of the young students: "an open saying and a closed saying." Rashi explained, "There are matters that one is permitted to explain and there are others that one is commanded to conceal, for example, the Work of the Chariot."[163] It seems to me that they alluded here to the secret that resolves the difficulty that Rashi mentioned. "How does the *mem* allude to *ma'amar* (saying)? We can find thousands of other words that begin with *mem*." We can accept "a bent faithful one . . . , an open mouth . . . , a bent righteous one," because the form of the letter alludes to this.

I will begin with a matter explained in the *Pardes*. Four letters allude to the union of the Name *YHVH*, their testimony overlaps, as a seal within a seal. They are *alef*, *lamed*, *mem*, and final *mem*. *Alef*: there is a *yod* above and a *yod* below, and a *vav* in the middle. This totals twenty-six. *Lamed*: it has the form of a *kaf* with a *vav* standing above it. Thus it equals *kaf* plus *vav* (26). *Mem* has the form of a *kaf* with a *vav* at its side. Final *mem*: it is the same, except that it is closed, because the *vav* seals it. And the testimony is a seal within a seal. In other words, *alef* points to *lamed*, because when *alef* is spelled, the letter after *alef* is *lamed*. *Lamed* points to *mem*, because when spelled, *mem* follows *lamed*. *Mem* points to a final *mem*, because it is spelled *mem* final *mem*.

Now I will explain the matter. *Alef* and *lamed* indicate the essence of the divine emanation. *Mem* and final *mem* allude to what is revealed in the emanation from our point of view. How so? *Alef* alludes to the Name *YHVH* that contains the emanation that is revealed. *Lamed* alludes to the emanation when it is concealed, for example in *Binah*. For it has already been made known that *lamed* is a tower that flies in the air, which is *Binah*, as the kabbalists have explained. Thus *alef* and *lamed* allude to the Emanation, when concealed and revealed. This is represented by *'EL 'eḥad* (one God).

The *mem* final *mem* alludes to our point of view. It is the secret of the will and knowledge, which I discussed in detail above. For divine knowledge precedes human choice. It is knowledge of His Essence, which is open, in accordance with the way that the source and root are opened. However, it is closed in terms of what has been registered there. Human beings have the power to choose. Then the knowledge is registered, according to the source that opens. No knowledge is projected from God, God forbid. Rather, He knows through knowing His essence. This is the Name *YHVH* that is alluded to by "open and closed." All is a manifestation of His power and no other. For His mode of knowing is His will, as I explained at length above. This is the secret of "an open saying and a closed saying." The meaning of "saying" is will, as Nahmanides explained in his commentary on Genesis. "Every time it is written '*and He said*,' in the [creative] utterances, it means will and desire."

"An open section should not be closed, nor a closed section left open." This can be explained according to what Rabbi Hayyat wrote in *Ma'arekhet ha-Shemot*:

> A house requires windows for light. But it also has to have its breaches and weak places sealed, so that thieves will not break in. For a breach calls out to a thief. In the same way, a Torah scroll has open sections and closed sections. If what must be open is sealed or if what must be sealed is open, the scroll is rejected. For light comes to us from the open sections, which are windows. Concerning them, the sage said, "*This one stands behind our walls, looking through the windows, peeping through the lattice.*"[164] The closed sections are necessary so that Satan will not enter through them. For there are places of chastisement in the Torah. If Satan finds a way and crack to enter there, he will inject his contamination and poison, and draw a bow against us. And he will make accusations against us. Sealing in the Torah below indicates sealing above in the Torah that contains everything. For it is complete wisdom, so that an uncircumcised and impure person will not come there. Nevertheless, it is necessary to open its windows in order to receive its light. It shines for us in a manner that Satan cannot discern, so that he will not make accusation against us. Thus the verse says, "*peeps through the lattice*," like one who secretly peeps at the object of his desire. This is so that Samael and his party will not discern this. The letters *mem*, *nun*, *ẓadi*, *peh*, and *kaf*, which have a second form that is always used at the end of a word, have another secret in addition to what I said above. For these letters indicate great judgment. They are like a weapon and always come at the end of a word, just as one places weapons and catapults around a house and tower, in order to defend it.[165]

"If he wrote prose in the form of a song, or a song in the form of prose." Our rabbis, of blessed memory, distinguished between *shirah* and *shir*.[166] Now it is *shirah*, the feminine form. However, in the future there will be a *shir ḥadash* (a new song), the masculine form. Our rabbis, of blessed memory, said, "All of the Torah was said in the masculine gender."[167] This alludes to the future. However, the *shirah* that was already said, concerning what was in the past, was in the female form. As it is written, "*This shirah, saying*."[168] The same is true for all of the other cases in which it is said "*shirah*"; it refers to the past.

"Or if he did not write it with ink." In chapter *Ba-meh behemah* is written,

> The Holy One, blessed be He, said to Gabriel, go and write a *tav* in ink on the forehead of the righteous, so that the angels of harm will not prevail over them, and a *tav* in blood on the foreheads of the wicked, so that the angels of destruction will prevail over them. The attribute of judgment said before the Holy One, blessed be He, Master of the Universe, how are these different from those? He answered, these are completely righteous and those are completely wicked. So they said to Him, Master of the Universe, they could have rubbed it off and did not. He answered, it is clearly known to Me that if they rub it out, it will not be accepted. They said to Him, Master of the Universe, if it is clear to You, how is it clear to them? Thus it is written, "*Kill the old, youth and maiden, women and children; but do not touch any person who bears the tav. Start at My Sanctuary. And they began with the old men that were before the building.*"[169] Rav Joseph taught, do not read "*My sanctuary,*" but "My sanctified ones." These are the people who fulfilled the entire Torah from *alef* to *tav*. Immediately, "*And six men entered by the way of the upper gate that faces north, each had a club in his hand; among them was another, dressed in linen with a writing case at his waist. They went and stood next to the altar of bronze.*"[170] The "*altar of bronze*?" What did the Holy One, blessed be He, say to them? "Begin from the place where they say the *shirah* before Me. Who were the six men? Rabbi Hisda said, '*qeẓef*, '*af*, *ḥemah*,' *mashḥit*, *meshaber*, and *mekhaleh*."[171] What is the difference? The *tav*. Rav said, the *tav* gives life and the *tav* kills.[172]

This matter alludes to the inquiry into why the Torah does not explicitly mention the rewards of the soul as well as the rewards of the body. I have discussed this at length above. The view of the *'Avodat ha-Qodesh* is that it is because eternity applies to both body and soul. For [the body] will live forever. This in itself is the promise that comes in the Torah, as explained above. Thus he said, "The *tav* gives life." This is all by means of the Torah. Therefore, it has to be written in ink.[173] According to my approach, which I presented above, on the contrary, the words of the Torah essentially refer to spiritual entities; they are only applied by analogy to material things. The passage in the Palestinian Talmud, tractate *Sheqalim*, alludes to this:

> Rabbi Phineas said in the name of Resh Lakish, The Torah that the Holy One, blessed be He, gave to Moses was given to him in white fire inscribed in black fire. It alludes to the revealed teachings, which are emanated from the concealed teachings, according to the secret of the verse, "*I am black but comely.*"[174]

For materiality has a root above and there are levels upon levels. Therefore, we have to write with ink, which is black, on the white parchment.

"If he wrote the Divine Name in gold." The serpent's contamination that Adam brought upon the world should have been rectified in the giving of the Torah. Thus scripture says, "*Now if you will hearken to My voice and keep My covenant, you shall be My treasured possession from all of the peoples. For the entire world is Mine, but you shall be to Me a kingdom of priests and a holy nation.*"[175] The verse intended to admonish them not to hold to the way of their first ancestor, who abandoned his own mind and followed the way of the serpent's mind. He was told, "*since you listened to the voice of your wife.*"[176] Now that the intention was to rectify the world and to renew it through giving the Torah, they were told that they should listen to His voice, to accept the obligation of doing all of His commandments. This is His voice and not the voice of Satan, which is the serpent, the evil urge. Adam listened to the latter and brought death upon the world and all of his descendants. "*And you shall keep My covenant.*" Not like Adam who transgressed the covenant and broke the law.

It is written in chapter, *'Eḥad Diney Mamonot*:

> Rabbi Isaac said, he was one who disguised his circumcision. Here it is written, "*But they, like Adam, transgressed the covenant.*"[177] There it is written, "[*And if any male who is uncircumcised fails to circumcise the flesh of his foreskin* ...] *he has broken My covenant.*"[178] Rav Nahman said, He was a heretic. Here it is written, "*But they, like Adam* ... " and there it is written, "*Because they abandoned the covenant of YHVH.*"[179,180]

The words of both of them are true. For he drew uncircumcision and impurity into the world. He covered over and sealed up the holy covenant. This is heresy and idol worship. Thus [the Torah] came to correct what Adam had distorted. For he did not listen to the voice of God, but to the voice of his wife. He did not keep the covenant, but brought death upon himself and all of his descendants. He was punished by having to labor for his food. So when Israel accepted the Torah, they restored the crown to its rightful place. The world was made fragrant and the contamination ceased. This is found in chapter *'Eyn Ma'amidin.*[181]

And in the *Midrash*, [it says]:

> "*Behold I am sending an angel before you.*"[182] As it is written, "*I said you are 'Elohim.*"[183] If Israel had waited for Moses and not done that deed, neither the exiles nor the angel of death would have prevailed over them. . . . Thus scripture says, "*ḥarut on the tablets.*"[184] What is the meaning of "*ḥarut*"? Rabbi Judah and Rabbi Nehemiah explained it. Rabbi Judah said, freedom (*ḥerut*) from the exiles. Rabbi Nehemiah said, freedom from the angel of death.[185]

They were alluding to all kinds of benefit and happiness which would result from accepting the Torah. For in saying "freedom from exiles," they meant that they would be a kingdom of priests. In saying "freedom from the angel of death," the meaning is eternal existence, which is alluded to in "*and you shall be My treasured possession and a holy nation.*" As our rabbis, of blessed memory, said, " '*All who remain . . . in Jerusalem will be called Holy.*'[186] [Concerning all who are inscribed for life in Jerusalem], just as the Holy exists forever, so they exist forever."[187]

But they regressed when Satan danced among them around the golden calf, which they made. And they said, "*This is your God, O Israel.*"[188] Thus they wrote the Divine Name in gold.

"These are concealed." For the light remains concealed until the future. [Then] "*a new light will shine in Zion,*"[189] and the verse will be fulfilled for us that says, "*Arise and shine because your light has come.*"[190]

Blessed is *YHVH* forever, amen and amen.

Notes to Text

Introduction

[1] Proverbs 6:23.
[2] Psalms 19:9.
[3] Ecclesiastes 2:14.
[4] Literally, "a single lamp (*ner*)."
[5] B.T., *Kiddushin*, 40b.
[6] I.e., the lamp and light are united.
[7] B.T., *Avot*, 2:5.
[8] B.T., *Avot*, 3:9.
[9] Psalms 50:16.
[10] Literally, "against his face."
[11] *Nigleh* and *nistar*. These two technical terms may also be understood as referring to exoteric and esoteric aspects of Torah.
[12] I.e., the Tetragrammaton, *YHVH*.
[13] Psalms 91:14.
[14] Deuteronomy 4:4.
[15] See n. 7.
[16] Psalms 27:4.
[17] Job 28:28.
[18] See n. 8.
[19] See *Mishnah Hagigah* 2:1. Only such a person is permitted to learn the secrets of *ma'aseh merkavah*.
[20] I.e., the author of Proverbs, according to tradition, King Solomon.
[21] See n. 1.
[22] Prayer Book, blessing before the *Shema'*.
[23] Exodus 18:20.
[24] Proverbs 8:33.

[25] Leviticus 19:17.

[26] B.T., *Shabbat*, chapter 16, 119b.

[27] Lamentations 1:6.

[28] See n. 26.

[29] B.T., *Shabbat*, chapter 5.

[30] According to the medieval commentator Rashi, this refers to a king who failed to forewarn the entire nation of Israel. See the commentary of Rashi, ad loc.

[31] B.T., *Shabbat*, 54b.

[32] Ibid., 55a.

[33] Ezekiel 9:4.

[34] Ezekiel 9:6.

[35] B.T., *Shabbat*, 55a, Rashi.

[36] Ezekiel 9:6.

[37] I.e., *MeQuDaSHaY* instead of *MiQeDaSHY*.

[38] B.T., *Shabbat*, 55a.

[39] I.e., Maimonides.

[40] If one knows that an admonition will not be heeded, it is better to be silent. A blatant transgression is worse than one committed without forewarning.

[41] Leviticus 19:17.

[42] Proverbs 9:8.

[43] *Mishneh Torah*, *Hilkhot De'ot*, 6:7, *Hagahot Maymuniot*, ad loc.

[44] B.T., *'Arakhin*, 16b.

[45] Isaiah 50:6.

[46] See n. 43. The *Hagahot Maimuniot* cites *Tanḥuma*, *tazri'a*, as the midrashic source.

[47] This is the view cited in the name of Rabbi Moses of Coucy.

[48] Proverbs 9:8.

[49] B.T., *Yevamot*, 65b.

[50] *Mishneh Torah*, *Hilkhot Shevitat Asor*, 1:7. The text is a direct quotation from the *Mishneh Torah* and not the *Hagahot Maimuniot*.

[51] One of the most important early German halakhic authorities, Rabbi Asher wrote commentaries that are included in all standard editions of the Talmud. Born c. 1250 in Germany, Rabbi Asher died in 1327 in Toledo, where he had served as rabbi for the last twenty years of his life.

[52] Rabbi Isaac ben Abba Mari of Provence (c.1122–c.1193).

[53] Leviticus 19:17.

[54] Proverbs 9:8.

[55] B.T., *Sanhedrin*, 101b.

[56] B.T., *Ketubbot*, 105b.
[57] Leviticus 27:37.
[58] B.T., *Sanhedrin*, 27b.
[59] Proverbs 24:25.
[60] B.T., *Tamid*, 28a.
[61] Proverbs 9:8.
[62] B.T., *'Arakhin*, 16b.
[63] Deuteronomy 31:12.
[64] Deuteronomy 1:1.
[65] Ibid.
[66] 1 Samuel 8:1.
[67] Song of Songs 1:8.
[68] 2 Kings 2:12.
[69] B.T., *Moed Katan*, 26a.
[70] Proverbs 6:23.
[71] Psalms 119:1.
[72] B.T., *Berakhot*, 31a.
[73] The blessing that precedes the recitation of *Shema'* (Hear, O Israel) (Deuteronomy 6:4).
[74] Psalms 37:31.
[75] B.T., *Megillah*, 15a; *Ḥullin*, 104b.
[76] Song of Songs 7:10.
[77] See B.T., *Bekhorot*, 31b.
[78] Proverbs 6:23.
[79] J.T., *Pesaḥim*, chapter 10, *Halakhah* 5.
[80] B.T., *Yoma*, 86b.
[81] B.T., *Baba Batra*, 165a.
[82] Rabbi Eleazar Rokeaḥ of Worms (c.1160–c.1238).
[83] Leviticus 18:5.
[84] For a discussion of the term *kavvanah* in Kabbalah see Scḥolem, *Kabbalah*, pp. 176–182.
[85] Psalms 91:15.
[86] See *Pesiqta Rabbati* 22:7 and *Midrash Tehillim* 91:8.
[87] Psalms 119:18.
[88] A Spanish-Turkish kabbalist (1480/81–after 1543), author of *'Avodat ha-Qodesh*, *Tola'at Ya'aqov*, and *Derekh 'Emunah*. See Elliot K. Gisburg, *Sod ha-Shabbat* (*The Mystery of the Sabbath*): From the *Tola'at Ya'aqov* of R. Meir ibn Gabbai, SUNY: 1989.
[89] Kabbalist of Safed (1522–1570), author of *Pardes Rimmonim*, *'Elimah Rabbati*, *Tomer Devorah*, *'Or Yaqar*, and other works. For a discussion of his

thought see J. Ben-Shlomo, *The Mystical Theology of Rabbi Moses Cordovero* (Hebrew) (Mosad Bialik: 1965); and the articles of Brakha Sack mentioned in the Introduction.

[90] Safed kabbalist (1534–1572). On Luria see the Introduction to this volume.

[91] Literally, "sons."

[92] Job 11:6.

[93] Proverbs 6:23.

[94] B.T., *Rosh Ha-Shanah*, 27a.

[95] B.T., *Rosh Ha-Shanah*, 32a.

[96] Genesis 49:10.

[97] Psalms 72:17. The meaning of the word *yinnon* in the verse is uncertain. It may be from a root meaning "to awaken." Thus the verse would mean "may his name awaken." However, the new JPS translation reads: "May his name endure."

[98] B.T., *Sanhedrin*, 98b.

[99] B.T., *Horayot*, 14a. The meaning is that Rav Joseph was an erudite scholar, while Rabbah was more ingenious in disputation.

[100] See B.T., *Baba Meẓi'a*, 84a.

[101] Ibid.

[102] The origin of these three aspects of love seems to be Genesis Rabbah 80:7. In the literature that popularized the Kabbalah of Safed they became associated with levels of mystical cleaving to God. They are especially common in De Vidas' *Reishit Ḥokhmah*. See Pacter's Hebrew article in the Tishby Jubilee volume.

[103] On these two primary affective aspects of cleaving to God, see Tishby, *Wisdom of the Zohar*, pp. 974–998.

[104] Genesis 37:2.

[105] Deuteronomy 32:9.

[106] Psalms 58:11.

[107] Genesis 4:26, 5:1. A note on this verse reads: "Nahmanides wrote in the name of R. Sharira Gaon that the knowledge of physiognomy and the secret of chiromancy was transmitted orally. Some of these are contained in the order of the verse that follows, 'male and female He created them.' Secrets and mysteries of Torah are only transmitted to one in whom one sees the signs that he is worthy of them. These are the words of the Gaon. But we did not merit them [the knowledge of physiognomy and chiromancy]."

[108] Genesis 5:2.

[109] Ezekiel 1:26.

[110] Job 19:26.

[111] Deuteronomy 4:35.
[112] Deuteronomy 4:4.
[113] Deuteronomy 7:11.
[114] B.T., *Eruvin*, 21a. The talmudic interpretation is based on Deuteronomy 7:11.
[115] *Avot*, 4:2.
[116] Deuternomy 29:17.
[117] Deuteronomy 30:19.
[118] Psalms 16:5.
[119] Rashi on Deuteronomy 30:19.
[120] Isaiah 45:7.
[121] B.T., *Pesaḥim*, 50b.
[122] B.T., *Shabbat*, 31b.
[123] Ecclesiastes 3:14.
[124] Psalms 9:17.
[125] Rabbi Joseph Albo, fifteenth-century Spanish philosopher.
[126] Genesis 4:26, 5:1.
[127] I.e., the Kabbalah.
[128] B.T., *Kiddushin*, 2b.
[129] *Zeh* equals twelve (7 + 5 = 12). *Zo't* equals twelve (7 + 1 + 4 = 12) when the *tav*, which is usually valued at 400, is reduced to 4.
[130] Numbers 15:29.
[131] Genesis 37:2.
[132] Rashi, ad loc.
[133] Genesis 5:1.
[134] Job 19:26.
[135] Genesis 1:28 (see Rashi).
[136] Genesis 5:2.
[137] Isaiah 14:14.
[138] Ezekiel 1:26.
[139] Cf. Ecclesiastes 3:20.
[140] Paraphrase of Proverbs 24:4.
[141] Psalms 147:19.
[142] *Zohar*, vol. 3, 73a.
[143] See *Zohar*, vol. 3, 81b.

The House of YHVH [I]

[1] *Zohar*, vol. 3, *'aḥarey mot*, 73a. This is the passage mentioned at the end of the introduction. See above.
[2] The *Zohar* passage connects God, Torah, and Israel.

NOTES TO TEXT

[3] Ecclesiastes 12:13.

[4] Proverbs 25:11. An alternative translation: "Words properly spoken are like apples of gold in silver settings."

[5] See the Targum to Genesis 26:8. In other words, the unusual word for filigree, *maSKiyyot*, is related to an Aramaic root meaning "to see."

[6] Maimonides, *Guide of the Perplexed*, 6b–7a.

[7] The *Pardes Rimmonim* (Jerusalem, 1962) reads "we speak."

[8] *Pardes* has "so that we will be able to speak to Him."

[9] *Pardes* lacks the example of Abraham and Isaac. The text reads: "For their names are arbitrary, but the name does not declare anything at all about the person's character. And his name declares nothing concerning his essence."

[10] *Pardes* adds "and His existence."

[11] Prayer Book.

[12] I.e., the Kabbalah.

[13] Reads: "which teaches some of His hiddenness and concealment."

[14] *Pardes Rimmonim*, Gate 19: *Gate of the Tetragrammaton*, chapter 1, 87b.

[15] I.e., Moses Cordovero in the passage previously cited.

[16] *Pelaḥ ha-Rimmon* (Jerusalem, 1962), Gate 4: *Essence and Vessels*, chapter 1, 12a.

[17] Ecclesiastes 5:7.

[18] Literally, "sages of truth."

[19] *Zohar*, vol. 2, 42b.

[20] Isaiah 40:25.

[21] Deuteronomy 4:15.

[22] Isaiah 6:3.

[23] *Ma'arekhet ha-Elohut*, chapter 3, commentary of Judah Hayyat.

[24] *Pirqey de-Rabbi Eliezer*, chapter 3.

[25] Deuteronomy 4:4.

[26] Psalms 34:15, 37:27.

[27] Isaiah 59:2. The verse is slightly misquoted.

[28] Psalms 34:15, 37:27.

[29] B.T., *Shabbat*, 104a.

[30] Literally, "the true wisdom."

[31] Morning prayers.

[32] Rabbi Meir Ibn Gabbai.

[33] For a discussion of this Medieval mystical term, see Idel, *Kabbalah: New Perspectives*. A possible translation would be "spiritual energy."

[34] The indwelling divine presence.

[35] See *Tanḥuma, ve-yaqhel*, 7.

[36] *Vav* alludes to *Tif'eret* and the five *sefirot* located around it, viz. *Ḥesed, Gevurah, Neẓaḥ, Hod, Yesod.*

[37] See introduction to *Tiqquney Zohar.*

[38] I.e., consisting of the four letters of the Tetragrammaton, alone.

[39] See above, n. 15.

[40] See above, n. 17.

[41] Exodus 3:15. Literally, the verse means "This is My Name forever."

[42] Deuteronomy 32:3.

[43] Another name for *Ḥesed.*

[44] Deuteronomy 32:4.

[45] Ibid.

[46] Ibid.

[47] Ibid.

[48] Ibid.

[49] Ibid.

[50] Another name for *Malkhut.*

[51] Deuteronomy 32:4.

[52] *Zohar*, vol. 3, 297a. I have translated from the Margoliot edition of the *Zohar.* The version cited in the *SHeLaH* is inaccurate.

[53] The initial letters of *hu' u-shemo 'ehad* spell *hu'* (He).

[54] *Shemo* (*His Name*) = 300 + 40 + 6 = 346; *razon* = 200 + 90 + 6 + 50 = 346.

[55] *Zohar*, vol. 2, 239a.

[56] I.e., Rabbi Moses Cordovero.

[57] *Ke-dimyon.* Literally, "through the likeness." The divine emanation, or world of the *sefirot* is the likeness or image through which concealed divinity is grasped.

[58] The first emanation, the will, or *Keter*, is so close to the *Eyn Sof* as to be virtually identical to it. Some earlier kabbalists, notably Joseph Gikatilla, did argue that the two were identical. Cordovero tries to clarify this problem.

[59] *Pardes Rimmonim*, Gate 11: *Sha'ar ha-Ẓaḥẓaḥot*, chapter 5, 63c.

[60] Proverbs 3:20.

[61] *Pardes Rimmonim*, Gate 4: *Sha'ar 'Aẓmut ve-Khelim*, chapter 9, 22a.

[62] I.e., the will, *Keter.*

[63] I.e., Rabbi Moses ben Maimon, Maimonides.

[64] I.e., the eternal things, the *sefirot.*

[65] *Pelaḥ ha-Rimmon*, Gate 4: *'Aẓmut ve-Khelim*, chapter 3, 12d.

[66] Ecclesiastes 5:7.

[67] Psalms 33:9 conflated with 148:5.

[68] I.e., Rabbi Moses ben Nahman. See RaMBaN on Genesis 1:3. Also see Chavel's notes, which mention Maimonides, *Guide of the Perplexed*, part 1, chapter 65.

[69] The name *YHVH* is derived from the verb "to be."

[70] This verb may also be translated as "and although they discard." It is, in fact, the same verb used by Cordovero in describing the process of transformation that wool undergoes when made into a garment. Nevertheless, since the verb is conventionally used in kabbalistic literature to indicate the process of emanation, I have translated it here accordingly.

[71] *Pardes Rimmonim*, Gate 14: *Sha'ar ha-Meẓi'ut*, chapter 1, 72d–73a.

[72] Ibid., 73a.

[73] I.e., regarding the subtle root that is concealed within *Eyn Sof.*

[74] I.e., Rabbi Isaac Luria.

[75] This is called the Name of 72 (*'AB*) because the sum of the numerical value of its letters is 72.

[76] This is the Name of 63 (*SaG*) because its sum is 63.

[77] This is the Name of 45 (*MaH*) because its sum is 45.

[78] This is the Name of 52 (*BeN*) because its sum is 52.

[79] Genesis 1:3.

[80] See above. 72 + 63 + 45 + 52 = 232.

[81] *Zohar*, *hashmatot*, 263a.

[82] I.e., the third person singular imperfect of the verb "to be."

[83] This sentence seems intended to be taken as a direct quote from *Ginat Egoz*. However, it does not appear as such. Since it is at best a paraphrase which conflates concepts drawn from scattered sentences found in the first part of *Ginat Egoz*, I have chosen to separate it from the direct quote.

[84] This Name contains the same letters as the Name *YHVH*.

[85] I.e., the Tetragrammaton, sometimes translated as the complete name of God.

[86] Joseph Gikatilla, *Ginat Egoz* (Jerusalem, 1989), Part 1, *Sha'ar ha-Havayah*, p. 23. I have translated the entire passage from this corrected text. The versions in the printed editions of the SHeLaH are greatly abridged.

[87] See pp. 66f.

[88] Ecclesiastes 5:7.

[89] Psalms 104:24.

[90] Ibid.

[91] Proverbs 24:3.

[92] This is the way the Sullam interprets the passage.

[93] Another name for *Malkhut*.

[94] Ecclesiastes 1:7.

[95] Literally, "in their being created."

[96] Genesis 2:4.

[97] I.e., with "the earth," *Malkhut*, represented by the second *heh* in the Name *YHVH*.

[98] *Zohar*, vol. 3, 43a.

[99] Another name for *Ḥesed*.

[100] Cf. Genesis 2:10.

[101] Genesis 1:11.

[102] *Pardes Rimmonim*, Gate 5: *Sha'ar Seder ha-'Aẓilut*, chapter 5, 26a-b.

[103] Psalms 104:24.

[104] See p. 76.

[105] Genesis 2:8.

[106] The nine times that God said "*let there be*" in the first chapter of Genesis, plus "*in the beginning*" which the rabbis counted in order to form ten divine creative utterances.

[107] Literally, "countenances," the term takes in the meaning of structures based on a particular *sefirah* that are composed of all ten *sefirot*.

[108] Exodus 20:11.

[109] Job 19:26.

[110] Psalms 11:4.

[111] I.e., *Malkhut*.

[112] Deuteronomy 4:32.

[113] B.T., *Hagigah*, chapter 1, 11b.

[114] Job 19:26.

[115] The letters that spell *Binah* can be arranged to spell BeN YaH, son of *yod* and *heh*. In other words, *Binah* reveals *Tif'eret*, the son of *Ḥokhmah* and *Binah*, which are identified with the letters *yod* and *heh* of the Name *YHVH*.

[116] The act of creation, more specifically the section in Genesis that describes the stages of creation.

[117] Genesis 1:3.

[118] Genesis 1:2.

[119] The four material elements are represented by the four archangels in the world of *Yeẓirah*.

[120] See Ezekiel, chapter 1.

[121] *Yod* has the numerical value of ten.

[122] Job 28:12. Literally, the verse means "from where (*me'ayin*) may wisdom (*ve-ha-Ḥokhmah*) be found (*timaẓe'*)."

[123] This is a pun. The word for two, *du*, is formed by the two letters *dalet* and *vav*.

[124] Zechariah 1:16.
[125] The letter *dalet* has the numerical value of 4. The other three legs are *Ḥesed*, *Gevurah*, and *Tif'eret*.
[126] Psalms 118:20.
[127] Ecclesiastes 7:24.
[128] *Sefer Yeẓirah*, chapter 1, *Mishnah* 5.
[129] Compare Genesis 1:27.
[130] These *sefirot* are arranged according to the three lines of lovingkindness, judgment, and compassion.
[131] *'Avodot*. Another possible translation: "sacrifices."
[132] Exodus 12:42.
[133] *Zohar*, vol. 2, 38b.
[134] *Be-sod hoẓa'atan le-fo'al.*
[135] *Be-gufo*. Perhaps the text should read "*ke-gufo*."
[136] B.T., *Menahot*, 93b.
[137] Obscure, possibly, a reference to Psalms 91:14.
[138] Numbers 6:23.
[139] Numbers 6:27.
[140] B.T., *Sotah*, 38a.
[141] Rabbi Asher ben Yehiel (c. 1250–1327).
[142] Meir Ibn Gabbai, *'Avodat ha-Qodesh*, 33a.
[143] Rabbi Todros Abulafia (1234–c. 1300), author of *'Ozar ha-Kavod ha-Shalem*, on the *agadot* of the Talmud.
[144] I.e., the Name consists of a passive rather than an active participle.
[145] The name Torah is derived from a root meaning "to teach."
[146] Rabbi Simeon bar Yohai. A reference to the *Zohar*.
[147] Ezekiel 17:13.
[148] Psalms 36:7.
[149] B.T., *Berakhot*, 96.
[150] Psalms 36:7.
[151] Exodus 7:1.
[152] Exodus 22:27.
[153] Psalms 50:11.
[154] Song of Songs 1:13.
[155] Exodus 12:41.
[156] Genesis 18:3.
[157] Song of Songs 1:7.
[158] Isaiah 3:7.
[159] Ecclesiastes 11:3.
[160] Exodus 20:24.

[161] Although the printed texts do not identify this section as a citation, it is found in *Pardes Rimmonim*, Gate 19: *Sha'ar Shem Ben Dalet*, chapter 1, 87a.

[162] Rabbi Joseph Gikatilla.

[163] *Sha'arey 'Orah* (Ben-Shlomo, ed., Jerusalem, 1981), p. 48.

[164] Job 36:2.

[165] Both equal 65. The letters *YHVH* are pronounced as *Adonay*, which has the same numerical value as *heykhal* (chamber) which indicates *Malkhut*. Although this is indicated as a direct quote, its source is not specified. It seems likely that the source is *Pardes Rimmonim*; however, I have not located it.

[166] I.e., 21.

[167] Proverbs 8:30.

[168] I.e., 1 + 2 + 3 + 4 = 10.

[169] Thus the secret of *ve-'EHYH* (*vav 'EHYH*) is that the sum of the letters of the alphabet up to and including *vav* equal *'EHYH*.

[170] I.e., 26 + 4 + 1 = 31.

[171] When *YHVH* is spelled this way, its numerical value is 63.

[172] I.e., 10 + 10 + 10 + 1 = 31, the sum of *'El*.

[173] Deuteronomy 4:35, 39.

[174] Isaiah 44:6.

[175] Exodus 3:15.

[176] Exodus 6:3.

[177] I.e., 26 + 314 = 340.

[178] B.T., *Hagigah*, 12a.

[179] Because *YHVH* is pronounced *Adonay*.

[180] Habakkuk 2:20.

[181] Exodus 3:15.

[182] Usually pronounced "KUZO."

[183] Isaiah 42:24.

[184] I.e., 26 + 39 = 65.

[185] Exodus 23:21.

[186] See p. 83.

[187] I.e., when one considers the *alef* as formed by two *yod*s and a *vav*.

[188] Song of Songs 6:3.

[189] I.e., the final *heh*, representing *Malkhut*, is interpreted as *dalet yod*.

[190] Deuteronomy 4:35.

[191] This is the first line of the *Qaddish*.

[192] I.e., when spelled *yod vav dalet heh alef vav alef vav heh alef*.

NOTES TO TEXT

The House of Wisdom [I]

[1] Psalms 19:8.

[2] Deuteronomy 4:36.

[3] Actually, *'esrim ve-shishah* and *Keter Torah* each equal 1231. However, *'aseret ha-dibrot* equals 1587! Text should read *ha-devarim*.

[4] *Avot*, 1:1.

[5] Sabbath morning *'Amidah*.

[6] *Pardes Rimmonim,* Gate 1, chapter 2.

[7] *Tiqquney Zohar*, *Tiqqun* 13, 29a; *Tiqqun* 69, 101a.

[8] *Midrash Rabbah*; Genesis, 17:5.

[9] Psalms 89:3.

[10] I.e., the oral Torah originated in *Binah*. Nevertheless, it is only a portion of what is contained in *Binah*, since Moses only attained forty-nine of its fifty Gates.

[11] Represented in Hebrew by the letters *lamed bet*.

[12] These two letters are pronouns which are declined by adding the letters of the Divine Name.

[13] I.e., *alef* is formed by a *yod* above, a *vav* in the middle, and a *dalet* below.

[14] See, for example, Rabbenu Bahya, *Kad ha-Qemaḥ*.

[15] Exodus 20:2.

[16] Job 11:9.

[17] Psalms 119:96.

[18] Ecclesiastes 7:24.

The House of Israel [I]

[1] Psalms 34:15, 37:27.

[2] I.e., creation began on the 25th of *Elul*, but the Adam was created on the sixth day, the first of *Tishrei*. Thus *Rosh Ha-Shanah* is celebrated on the anniversary of the creation of Adam.

[3] Psalms 66:3.

[4] Genesis 1:26.

[5] *Bereishit Rabbah*, 5:3.

[6] The reference is to *Tif'eret* and *Malkhut*.

[7] I.e., to the *sefirot Ḥesed*, *Gevurah*, *Tif'eret*, *Hod*, *Neẓaḥ*, and *Yesod*.

[8] I.e., in the *Zohar*.

[9] Exodus 31:17.

[10] *Zohar*, vol. 1, 30a.

[11] B.T., *Baba Qama,* 104b. In the talmudic passage the word *deyoqeni* means "signatory," i.e. one who carries the seal of the person who designated him to be his agent.

[12] Genesis 9:6.

[13] B.T., *Baba Batra*, 58a.

[14] B.T., *Moed Qatan*, 15a.

[15] *'Avodat ha-Qodesh.*

[16] *Zohar*, vol. 3, 71b.

[17] *Zohar*, vol. 3, 21a.

[18] *Pardes Rimmonim*, *Sha'ar ha-Neshamot.*

[19] Genesis 2:7.

[20] I.e., not from the angels.

[21] Proverbs 2:6.

[22] The source for this mystical idea may be in *Sefer ha-Bahir.*

[23] Job 32:8.

[24] This may mean that the soul originates in *Binah* and descends through *Tif'eret* (truth) and *Malkhut* (faith). See the *Levush* to Recanati's commentary, 9:2. Another possibility is that it simply means "according to the Kabbalah."

[25] 2 Kings 4:30.

[26] *Sifre*, *Mattot.*

[27] I.e, *Sefer ha-Bahir.*

[28] Exodus 31:17.

[29] *Sefer ha-Bahir*, 57.

[30] Ecclesiastes 8:2.

[31] Nahmanides, *Commentary on the Torah* (Chavel, ed.), p. 33.

[32] Leviticus 22:12.

[33] *Zohar*, vol. 3, 7a.

[34] Song of Songs 2:3.

[35] Such a person has been brought into a state of wholeness which involves the union of male and female.

[36] Hosea 14:9.

[37] I.e., the souls are the fruit of the coupling of *Tif'eret* and *Malkhut.*

[38] *Zohar*, vol. 1, 85b.

[39] Literally, "embryo."

[40] *Pardes Rimmonim*, Gate 5: *Sha'ar ha-Mahut ve-ha-Hanhagah*, chapter 22, 53a.

[41] Proverbs 20:27.

[42] I.e., the word *ner* (lamp) can be understood as an acronym for *nefesh ruaḥ*, two aspects of the divine soul.

[43] I.e., they are the emanations of *Malkhut* and *Tif'eret*.
[44] *Tiqquney Zohar*, *Tiqqun* 21, 49b; *Tiqqun* 18, 34a.
[45] *Pardes Rimmonim*, *Sha'ar ha-Mahut ve-ha-Hanhagah*, chapter 22.
[46] Genesis 2:7. See above, n. 35.
[47] Job 32:8. See above.
[48] The letter *nun* equals 50. *Dara'* means court or courtyard in Aramaic.
[49] Genesis 2:7.
[50] I.e., after *Tif'eret* and *Malkhut* had emerged from their root in *Binah* and taken their assigned places in the structure of the divine emanation as the seven lower *sefirot*.
[51] This is discussed in "House of YHVH."
[52] I could not find the source of the midrash as cited. However, compare *Mekhilta, be-Shalaḥ*, chapter 9. Also see *Mekhilta*, *Bo*, chapter twelve. Some of the midrashim say six children in one belly and some say 600,000. Compare *Tanḥuma* (Warsaw), *Shemot*, *Piqudey*, chapter nine.
[53] Numbers 11:21.
[54] Literally, "all of them are in his power."
[55] Job 23:3,4.
[56] Job 38:4.
[57] *Midrash Rabbah*, *Shemot*, 40.
[58] Psalms 89:3.
[59] Genesis 2:7.
[60] New souls are the result of the coupling of *Tif'eret* and *Malkhut* in their place. The souls, which were included in the soul of Adam and Eve, come from *Tif'eret* and *Malkhut* when they were contained within *Binah*. Then they are represented by the letters *dalet* and *vav*. As such, they can mean two and also together form the letter *heh*, the first *heh* in the Name *YHVH*, which represents *Binah*.
[61] See B.T., *Menaḥot*, 29b.
[62] Genesis 2:4.
[63] Ecclesiastes 7:12.
[64] Isaiah 64:3.
[65] Leviticus 1:13.
[66] B.T., *Berakhot*, 57b.
[67] B.T., *Berakhot*, 61a.
[68] Genesis 2:7.
[69] Genesis 3:20.
[70] Aspects of *Binah*, drawn from its upper portion, *ḥayyah*, which is also a *yod*, i.e., related to *Ḥokhmah*.
[71] Genesis 2:15.

[72] I.e., the seven lower *sefirot* from *Ḥesed* to *Malkhut.*

[73] Genesis 3:22.

[74] Rashi on Genesis 3:22.

[75] Cf. Ecclesiastes 7:12.

[76] Genesis 1:26.

[77] The word *lev* (heart) is formed by the two letters *lamed* and *bet.*

[78] The letters *lamed bet* also equal 32. These "32 Paths of Wisdom" are mentioned in the beginning of *Sefer Yeẓirah.*

[79] See, e.g., *Pardes Rimmonim*, Gate 23: *Sha'ar 'Erkhey ha-Kinnuyyim*, chapter 11, p. 22g.

[80] Ibid., chapter 12, p. 24a.

[81] I.e., Rabbi Eliezer the Great and Rabbi Ami.

[82] *Zohar*, vol. 3, 277b.

[83] Genesis 1:27.

[84] The word for human being, *adam*, and the Name *YHVH*, when its spelling is completed by the letter *alef*, equal 45. These are the forty-five lights mentioned in the passage.

[85] Genesis 1:27. It has already been explained that the letters of the Tetragrammaton represent Father and Mother, Son and Daughter, i.e., *Ḥokhmah* and *Binah*, *Tif'eret* and *Malkhut.*

[86] Genesis 2:7.

[87] I.e., when the spelling of the letters is completed by the letter *alef.*

[88] *Zohar Hadash*, *Midrash Ruth*, *Ma'amar Ruaḥ ve-Nishamah.*

[89] According to this system, the integers of numbers larger than nine are added together to form a "small number." In this case, Adam equals 1 + 4 + 40 = 1 + 4 + 4 = 9.

[90] Ecclesiastes 7:28.

[91] *'Emet* is 1 + 40 + 400 + 1 + 4 + 4 = 9.

[92] Genesis 1:27.

[93] Genesis 2:7.

[94] Genesis 1:31.

[95] Genesis 2:3.

[96] Micah 7:20.

[97] Deuteronomy 32:9.

[98] The literal meaning of *ḥevel* in this verse is "portion." However, the word can also mean "rope." Here, the latter meaning is enlisted to indicate that the human soul is emanated from the divine realm.

[99] Genesis 1:26.

[100] $(10 \times 5) + (5 \times 10) = 100$.

[101] $(6 \times 5) + (5 \times 6) = 60$.

[102] I.e., 70 + 90 = 160.
[103] Numbers 13:20.
[104] Deuteronomy 11:12.
[105] Numbers 14:10.
[106] 90 + 30 + 40 = 160.
[107] Proverbs 3:18.
[108] Genesis 1:26.
[109] *Zohar Hadash, Midrash Ruth, Ma'amar Ruaḥ ve-Nishamah.*
[110] Job 10:11.
[111] Ezekiel 34:31.
[112] Job 10:11.
[113] *Zohar*, vol. 1, 20b.
[114] Hosea 14:9.
[115] Song of Songs 2:3.
[116] Ibid., 3:10.
[117] *Mishnah, Shabbat,* 16:1.
[118] Literally, "I was looking into." The verb here seems to connote meditative speculation.
[119] Genesis 1:26.
[120] *Zohar*, vol. 1, 34b.
[121] *Oẓar Midrashim* de-R. Eliezer ben Hyrkenus, 32, beginning "*be-shishi.*"
[122] Genesis 2:7.
[123] Exodus 20:24.
[124] *Midrash Rabbah*, *Bereishit*, 14:8.
[125] *Zohar*, vol. 2, 24b.
[126] A name for *Ḥesed*.
[127] Genesis 9:6.
[128] Genesis 1:27.
[129] Genesis 2:24.
[130] *Sefer ha-Bahir*, section 172.
[131] This is a pun. The term for anger is *ḥaron 'af*, which incorporates the word for nose.
[132] *Raḥamim* (compassion) is the attribute associated with *Tif'eret*, which is represented by the Name *YHVH*. When the eyes are lowered the two eyes, which correspond to two *yods*, are united with the nose, corresponding to *vav*. Thus 26, the sum of *YHVH*, is formed and compassion is manifested. When the eyes "wander," only the nose, representing anger, remains.
[133] In *a"t b"sh*, the first letter of the alphabet, *alef*, becomes the last letter,

tav, the second letter, *bet*, becomes the next to the last letter, *shin*, and so on. Thus *YHVH* becomes *mzpz*.

[134] Morning blessings.

[135] The letter *heh* is spelled out with only two letters, *heh alef*. Each of the other letters requires three letters to complete its spelling.

[136] The word *yad* has the numerical value of 10 + 4 = 14.

[137] Lamentations 1:6.

[138] I.e., the tip of a circumcised penis.

[139] Their bodies form the *shin* and the *dalet*, but not the *yod*.

[140] I.e., the numerical value of *YHVH*.

[141] Deuteronomy 30:12.

[142] I.e., the *neshamah* resides in the brain, the *ruaḥ* in the heart, and the *nefesh* in the liver.

[143] The letters that form the word *Melekh* are an acronym for *moah* (brain), *lev* (heart), and *kaved* (liver).

[144] Ezekiel 1:12.

[145] Genesis 1:26.

[146] I.e., *Malkhut*.

[147] Isaiah 26:9.

[148] I.e., *Tif'eret*.

[149] Isaiah 26:9.

[150] I.e., *Binah*.

[151] Psalms 150:6.

[152] Genesis 1:26.

[153] Psalms 39:7.

[154] *Zohar*, vol. 3, 104a–104b.

[155] Genesis 2:7.

[156] Exodus 20:24.

[157] *Midrash Rabbah*, *Bereishit*, 14:8.

[158] Exodus 14:19–21.

[159] Each of the three verses contains seventy-two letters. The seventy-two three-letter Names are formed by taking the first letter from Exodus 14:19, the last letter from Exodus 14:20, and the first letter from Exodus 14:21, and so on. The first letter in each verse corresponds to *Ḥesed*, the middle letter to *Gevurah*, and the third to *Tif'eret*.

[160] *'Avodat ha-Qodesh*, *Ḥeleq Ha-Yiḥud*, chapter 18.

[161] See, e.g., *Zohar*, vol. 1, 103b. Also see Daniel Chanan Matt's note in *Zohar: The Book of Enlightenment* (New York, 1983), p. 222.

[162] Ezekiel 1:26.

[163] Obscure: "*mevinah ha-na'ot mi-beli na'ot*."

[164] Exodus 24:10. Literally, "a pavement of sapphire."
[165] *U-kemo she-ha-davar ha-sefirii yitra'u vo ha-Ẓurot.*
[166] Text reads: *'Eyn.*
[167] I.e., 20+400+200=620.
[168] Exodus 14:19–21.
[169] Literally, "fear," another name for *Gevurah.*
[170] Genesis 1:2 begins: "And the earth was waste and void (*va-vohu*)." The second letter in "*va-vohu*," a *bet*, is the forty-second letter of Genesis.
[171] *Tif'eret* includes *Ḥesed* and *Gevurah*, which are likened to white and red, and also the two *parẓufim*, which will become *Tif'eret* and *Malkhut*. The "two" plus the seventy branches of the tree equal 72.
[172] Prayer Book.
[173] Mattathias Delacrut, Introduction to his *Commentary on Sha'arey 'Orah*
[174] Ezekiel 1:26.
[175] Genesis 1:26.
[176] *Midrash Rabbah*, *Bereishit*, 82:7.

The Faithful House [I]

[1] *Pardes Rimmonim*, Gate 22, *Sha'ar ha-Kinnuyim*, chapter one, 105a. This passage is not identified as a quotation in the printed editions of the SHeLaH.
[2] A hymn that appears at the beginning of the Morning Service. Its author is Daniel ben Judah (c. 1300).
[3] Genesis 44:4.
[4] Exodus 36:8.
[5] Compare Psalms 7:14.
[6] Exodus 15:17.
[7] Deuteronomy 29:19.
[8] Exodus 22:23. I.e., "I will become angry."
[9] 1 Samuel 20:4.
[10] Genesis 1:3.
[11] Isaiah 47:8; Zephaniah 2:15.
[12] Genesis 24:51.
[13] Ecclesiastes 1:16.
[14] Psalms 42:8.
[15] Isaiah 6:3.
[16] B.T., *Berakhot*, 6a.
[17] Song of Songs 1:2.

[18] *Midrash Rabbah*, Song of Songs, 1:5.
[19] The root for kiss, *NSHQ*, can also mean weapon.
[20] B.T., *Kiddushin*, 30b.
[21] Job 20:24.
[22] Another possible translation is "from the sickness of harmful ways of thinking."
[23] *Midrash Rabbah*, Song of Songs 1:5. I.e., the impure pond is made pure.
[24] Deuteronomy 4:4.
[25] Esther 3:1.
[26] Genesis 1:26.
[27] *Midrash Rabbah*, Genesis 64:7.
[28] Genesis 26:13. The *Midrash* means that the Torah does not mention jealousy toward Isaac until Genesis 26:14. That verse also speaks of Isaac's wealth in livestock. However, the extent of his wealth was already emphasized in the previous verse. When people became jealous of Isaac's wealth they talked about his livestock, which made him greater than Abimelech with his silver and gold.
[29] Isaiah 54:15. Many interpretations for this obscure verse exist.
[30] Isaiah 54:17.
[31] Genesis 22:1.
[32] Genesis 22:12.
[33] Psalms 34:4.
[34] Ibid.
[35] Deuteronomy 32:51.
[36] Deuteronomy 8:10.
[37] Isaiah 24:15.
[38] Exodus 31:13.
[39] B.T., *Baba Meẓi'a*, 59b. Literally, "My sons prevailed over Me."
[40] The root NẒḤ can also mean eternal.
[41] Obscure. Last three words are from Exodus 23:2.
[42] Jeremiah 13:17.
[43] According to sources cited in *Qehillat Ya'aqov*, *mistarin* (secrets) refers to *Tif'eret*.
[44] Nehemiah 4:15.
[45] Exodus 11:4.
[46] Exodus 19:11.
[47] Isaiah 6:3.
[48] Genesis 18:21.
[49] Genesis 18:33.
[50] Genesis 28:13.

[51] Genesis 35:13.
[52] Isaiah 33:10. Also Psalms 12:6.
[53] B.T., *Sanhedrin*, 38b.
[54] *'Arugat ha-Bosem*. I was unable to locate this source.
[55] Proverbs 1:5.
[56] From the blessings said before the Shema'.
[57] Isaiah 40:25.
[58] I.e., the limbs of the human body symbolically represent the *sefirot*, although there is no actual physical resemblance between them.
[59] *Midrash Rabbah*, *Bereishit*, 47:8.
[60] Genesis 12:9. Since the *sefirot* are considered to be facing east, the south is on the right side, the place of *Ḥesed.*
[61] Genesis 31:53.
[62] I.e., *Tif'eret*.
[63] Genesis 25:27.
[64] Joseph Gikatilla, *Sha'arey 'Orah*, introduction (Ben-Shlomo ed.), pp. 49–50.
[65] Genesis 17:19.
[66] Job 19:26. In other words, the choice of verb seems to allude to the capacity for a divine erection and the *sefirah*, *Yesod.*
[67] Song of Songs 2:6, 8:3.
[68] Ibid., 1:2.
[69] I.e., Hebrew, the language of the Torah.
[70] *Pardes Rimmonim*, Gate 22, *Sha'ar ha-Kinnuyim*, chapter 1, 105a.
[71] Psalms 94:9.
[72] Job 34:2.
[73] Proverbs 27:19.
[74] Zechariah 4:2.
[75] 1 Samuel 9:9.
[76] The note in *Pardes* says that this story is told in *Zohar*, vol. 3, 304. I did not find it there.
[77] Ecclesiastes 5:7.
[78] The question at issue in the talmudic discussion is whether a bill of divorce has to explicitly identify itself as such. A document that affirms that the bearer is free to marry, but which does not explicitly identify the woman for whom it is intended, is called here "an indication (or 'hand') that is not beyond doubt."
[79] See B.T., *Gittin*, 85b.
[80] Exodus 21:24.
[81] Leviticus 24:18.

[82] Zechariah 4:10.
[83] Ecclesiastes 5:7.
[84] Micah 6:4.
[85] Numbers 10:31.
[86] Song of Songs 3:11.
[87] Job 19:26.
[88] *Pardes Rimmonim*, Gate 22: *Sha'ar ha-Kinnuyim*, chapter 1, 105a-d.

The Temple

[1] See B.T., *Sotah*, 35a.
[2] Exodus 20:2.
[3] Exodus 20:3.
[4] Isaiah 40:26.
[5] Psalms 16:3.
[6] I.e., Maimonides.
[7] Deuteronomy 28:30. "You will betrothe a woman and another man *yishgalenah*." The verse is read "*yishkavenah* (will lie with her)."
[8] 2 Kings 18:27.
[9] Literally, "clean language."
[10] B.T., *Sanhedrin*, 68b.
[11] Genesis 39:6.
[12] See *Midrash Rabbah*, Genesis 86:7. The meaning is that Joseph was using a euphemism to refer to Potiphar's wife.
[13] Nahmanides, *Commentary on the Torah*, Exodus 30:13, p. 492.

The Ultimate House

[1] A paraphrase of Ecclesiastes 4:12.
[2] Maimonides, *Mishneh Torah*, *Hilkhot Teshuvah*, 9:1.
[3] The Hebrew word used here is "*toledot*."
[4] Nahmanides, *Commentary on the Torah*, Exodus 6:2, (Chavel, ed.), pp. 303–304.
[5] Nahmanides, *Commentary on the Torah*, Leviticus 26:11 (Chavel, ed.), pp. 184–185.
[6] Deuteronomy 30:15,19.
[7] Joseph Albo, *'Iqqarim*, *Ma'amar* 4, chapter 19.

[8] This follows logically according to an argument that says if a lesser premise is true, a greater one must certainly be true.

[9] I.e., when the world is renewed, both the body and the soul will be immortal as was originally intended.

[10] Joseph Ibn Shem Tov, *'Eyn ha-Qore'*.

[11] See Friedberg, *Beyt 'Eqed Sefarim*, v. 1, p. 257, no. 1363.

[12] The text in the SHeLaH adds: "since they did not inherit the truth, they were not able, etc."

[13] Nissim Gerondi, *Derashat Bereishit.*

[14] Joseph Ibn Shem Tov, *'Eyn ha-Qore'*.

[15] Exodus 20:2.

[16] Abraham ben Shem Tov Bibago, *Derekh 'Emunah* (Constantinople, 1522). See Friedberg, v. 1, p. 246, no. 1097.

[17] Ezekiel 29:3.

[18] *Shemot Rabbah*, 5, 14; *Tanḥuma* (Warsaw), *va-era*, 15.

[19] I.e., the body.

[20] Exodus 20:2,3.

[21] Meir Ibn Gabbai, *'Avodat ha-Qodesh, Ḥeleq ha-'Avodah*, chapter 17, pp. 36c–37c.

[22] Ecclesiastes 4:12.

The Faithful House [II]

[1] The letter *vav* was pronounced like a w.

[2] I was not able to identify this source.

[3] B.T., *Berakhot*, 8a, b.

[4] Numbers 32:3.

[5] See *Zohar*, vol. 3, 152.

[6] *Pardes Rimmonim*, Gate 27: *Sha'ar ha-'Otiot*, chapter 1, 59a.

[7] Paraphrase of Psalms 69:32.

[8] Psalms 1:2.

[9] B.T., *Avot*, 1:13.

[10] Two *midrashim* seem to be conflated here. See *Tana de-Bei Eliahu Zuta*, 4, 7 and *Tanḥuma* (Warsaw), *ki tisa*, chapter 30.

[11] P.T., *Ta'anit*, 23:1.

[12] Song of Songs: 2:4.

[13] *Midrash Rabbah*, Numbers, 2:3.

[14] Jeremiah 36:27.

[15] B.T., *Mo'ed Qatan*, 26a.

[16] I.e., when held in thought.
[17] *Pardes Rimmonim*, Gate 27: *Sha'ar ha-'Otiot*, chapter 2, 59c–59d.
[18] Cf. Exodus 21:24.
[19] Isaiah 40:18.
[20] I.e., the divine creative speech.
[21] B.T., *Berakhot*, 31b.
[22] B.T., *Sanhedrin*, 9b, 10a.
[23] Psalms 48:2, 145:3.
[24] I.e., within the *sefirot*.
[25] See, for example, B.T., *Sanhedrin*, 9b and 10a. This talmudic ruling literally should be rendered "A person is considered as his own relative." This means that a person cannot incriminate himself through his own testimony. However, the words *qarov le-'azmo* can mean either "his own relative" or "close to himself." The mystical reading exploits the latter possibility.
[26] Leviticus 26:4.
[27] Hosea 2:23.

The House of Israel [II]

[1] Genesis 1:26.
[2] Job 19:26.
[3] Ezekiel 1:27.
[4] The higher entities correspond to the forms in this world. Cf. Ecclesiastes 5:7.
[5] "Primordial Man."
[6] Isaiah 44:13.
[7] The totality of *Tif'eret* includes the *sefirot* from *Ḥesed* to *Yesod*.
[8] This is a pun. The letters that complete the spelling are called *millu'im*, "fillings."
[9] These are the *milluy* of *YHVH*.
[10] $6 + 4 + 1 + 1 + 6 + 1 = 19$. *HaVaH* (Eve) is $8 + 6 + 5 = 19$.
[11] *Pirqey de-Rabbi Eliezer*, chapter 11.
[12] Genesis 1:21.
[13] *Midrash Rabbah*, *Bereishit*, 8:10.
[14] Isaiah 4:3.
[15] B.T., *Baba Batra*, 75b.
[16] I.e., from *Binah*.
[17] These are the letters that spell *yod*.

[18] I.e., the head above, the legs below, and the four sides of the trunk, front, back, left, and right.

[19] I.e., Adam.

[20] Deuteronomy 4:4.

[21] Numbers 11:16.

[22] Numbers 6:27.

[23] Yisrael is 10 + 300 + 200 + 1 + 30 = 541. 541 + 72 = 613.

[24] I.e., 31, which is equal to three *yod*s and an *alef.*

[25] I.e., *llvv* equals 30 + 30 + 6 + 6 = 72.

[26] I.e., 26.

[27] I.e., three *alef*s and one *yod* equals 13. *'Ehad* equals 1 + 8 + 4 = 13.

[28] 1 Samuel 12:22.

[29] Literally, "When they are joined one to one, they become two ones."

[30] I.e., *'ahavah* equals 1 + 5 + 2 + 5 = 13.

[31] God repeatedly addresses Ezekiel in this way. See, for example, Ezekiel, chapter 2. *Ben adam*, here translated as "human being," literally means "son of man."

[32] Exodus 32:7.

[33] B.T., *Berakhot*, 32a.

[34] Ben He He is a Tanna quoted in *Avot*, 5:23. Also see B.T., *Hagigah*, 9b. There the *Tosafot* bring a tradition that Ben He He and another unusually named Tanna, Ben Bag Bag, were converts. See Benzion Dinur's commentary to *Massekhet Avot*, p. 135. According to the *Tosafot*, Ben He He's name was formed from the letters *heh* that were added to the names of Abram and Sari, when they became Abraham and Sarah, the parents of converts.

[35] Genesis 17:4,5.

[36] Genesis 18:19.

[37] See Rashi, ad loc.

[38] Therefore converts are "the secret of the Name of 52," since they are considered children of Abraham. Abraham is identified with *adam*, the Name of 45. His offspring, the convert, is thus the "son (*ben*) of *adam*." *Ben* has the value of 52.

[39] I.e., *yod* is always spelled *yvd. Vd* equals 6 + 4 = 10, the value of *yod.*

[40] See n. 34 above.

[41] I.e., the Name of 52 is spelled *hh vv hh.*

[42] The Name Bag is here understood as meaning twice (*bet*) *gimmel* which is worth 3, total 6, the value of *vav.*

[43] Literally, "Grandfather Israel." Here the term implies *Tif'eret. Yisrael Sabba* is contrasted with *Keneset Yisrael*, which represents *Malkhut.*

[44] Isaiah 44:13.

[45] Psalms 11:4.

[46] Perhaps the text should be emended to read: "Before it is the Name *YHVH*, which dwells within the Name *ADoNaY*."

[47] Deuteronomy 7:7.

[48] *Ha-me'at* can be read as "five less." Rashi's comment appears in his commentary to Numbers 26:36.

[49] Genesis 2:4. This is one of a number of cases where a letter of the Torah is written small or larger than normal.

[50] *Mispar qatan* reduces all values to a single digit. For example, the letter *lamed*, which equals 30, becomes 3 + 0 = 3. According to this method, *'ELoHeY* equals 1 + 3 + 5 + 1 = 10.

[51] I.e., 1 + 3 + 2 + 1 + 3 = 10.

[52] Cf. B.T., *Sanhedrin*, 39b.

[53] I.e., 20 + 8 + 2 + 3 + 3 + 400 + 50 + 5 + 10 + 40 = 541. *Yisrael* equals 10 + 300 + 200 + 1 + 30 = 541.

[54] Micah 2:13.

[55] *R'osham* equals 200 + 1 + 300 + 40 = 541.

[56] Psalms 40:6.

[57] Literally, "the crown of a good name."

[58] Menahem Azariah da Fano, *Pelaḥ ha-Rimmon*.

[59] Maimonides, *Mishneh Torah, Hilkhot Terumot*, 3:1. Although the *Mishnah*, *Terumot*, chapter 4, discusses various proportions of produce that should be offered as *terumah*, Maimonides states that there is no specific measure specified in the Torah. Also compare B.T., *Ḥullin*, 137b.

[60] The six *sefirot*, from *Ḥesed* to *Yesod*, emerge from *Binah*, their "King."

[61] I.e., *Malkhut*.

[62] *Avot*, 5:23. This is the teaching said in the name of Ben He He.

[63] Exodus 6:2.

[64] Leviticus 19:12.

[65] Leviticus 22:31.

[66] Rashi, Exodus 6:2.

[67] Jeremiah 16:21.

[68] Rashi, Exodus 6:9.

[69] Deuteronomy 4:35,39.

[70] Exodus 6:2.

[71] Exodus 5:23.

[72] Deuteronomy 8:5.

[73] Ezekiel 38:23.

[74] *Sefer ha-Yashar*, attributed to Rabbenu Tam (Jerusalem, 1978), p. 8.

NOTES TO TEXT

The House of Wisdom (II)

[1] Deuteronomy 33:4.
[2] Exodus 20:2,3.
[3] B.T., *Makkot*, 23b–24a.
[4] Literally, "in the world of deed."
[5] B.T., *Eruvin*, 22a.
[6] *Avot*, 4:2.
[7] *Avot*, 2:1.
[8] Leviticus 26:3.
[9] Proverbs 12:11; 28:19.
[10] Proverbs 31:12.
[11] Menahem Recanati, *Commentary on the Torah* in *Levushey 'Or Yeqarot* (Jerusalem, 1961), p. 69c.
[12] On the *ẓaddiq* as foundation of the world and as establisher and maintainer of cosmic order, see Yehuda Liebes, "The Messiah of the Zohar," in *Studies in the Zohar* (Albany: SUNY Press, 1993); and Green, "*Ẓaddiq* as *Axis Mundi* in later Judaism," in Fine, ed., *Essential Papers in Kabbalah.*
[13] Psalms 119:126.
[14] The verb *la-'asot* can also mean "to make."
[15] Numbers 19:20.
[16] B.T., *Berakhot*, 7a.
[17] Ibid.
[18] Ibid.
[19] Deuteronomy 10:20.
[20] Ezekiel 1:26.
[21] Or, "a limb holds a limb."
[22] Genesis 1:1.
[23] Deuteronomy 34:12.
[24] I.e., *Malkhut.*
[25] Isaiah 49:3.
[26] Isaiah 29:23.
[27] Leviticus 11:44,45.
[28] Recanati, *Commentary on the Torah*, p. 51c,d.
[29] Exodus 15:2.
[30] I was not able to find this *Zohar* passage.
[31] Psalms 145:18.
[32] Micah 7:20.
[33] 2 Samuel 7:23.
[34] The *Zohar* text says: "He must intend heart and will."

[35] *Zohar*, vol. 2, 57a.
[36] *Zohar*, vol. 2, 60a.
[37] Psalms 19:8.
[38] Literally, "selected from all service [or worship]."
[39] Cf. Deuteronomy 5:19.
[40] *Zohar*, vol. 2, 83b.
[41] Psalms 133:2.
[42] Psalms 133:2.
[43] Numbers 4:27.
[44] Proverbs 27:9.
[45] *Zohar*, vol. 3, 7b–8a.
[46] Genesis 8:21.
[47] Psalms 145:15.
[48] I.e., *Malkhut*.
[49] *Zohar*, vol. 3, 58a.
[50] *Sefer ha-Bahir*, section 97.
[51] Leviticus 26:3.
[52] Leviticus 26:4.
[53] Genesis 18:19.
[54] *'Oseh* can mean either "does" or "makes."
[55] *Zohar*, vol. 3, 113b.
[56] *Sha'arey 'Orah*, chapter 8, pp. 52–53.
[57] Proverbs 28:19.
[58] Song of Songs 4:12.
[59] Isaiah 5:7.
[60] Isaiah 5:2.
[61] *Zohar*, vol. 2, 4a.
[62] Leviticus 26:3,4.
[63] Genesis 37:24.
[64] Isaiah 45:8.
[65] 2 Chronicles 6:27.
[66] B.T., *Hagigah*, 12b. The word for heavens, *sheḥaqim*, comes from a root which can mean "grinding."
[67] I.e., *Yesod* and *Malkhut*.
[68] Isaiah 54:13.
[69] See 2 Chronicles 3:17.
[70] Song of Songs 2:15.
[71] Deuteronomy 6:25.
[72] I.e., Moses.
[73] Deuteronomy 33:26.

[74] Genesis 33:20. The verse literally should be read, "And he (i.e., Jacob) called Him 'El, the God of Israel."

[75] Psalms 68:35.

[76] *'Avodat ha-Qodesh, Ḥeleq ha-'Avodah*, chapter 18, pp. 37c–38c.

[77] I.e., it would not have had a corporeal effect.

[78] Isaiah 11:9.

[79] N.B. This is an important *Midrash* that is often found in Hasidic texts.

[80] 1 Samuel 16:7.

[81] Genesis 2:9.

[82] Genesis 2:15.

[83] *Batey Midrashot* B, chapter 1, 5. See MaHaRal, *Derush al ha-Torah*, 11b.

[84] The idea of fulfilling commandments in a more spiritual way had great meaning for the early Hasidic masters. See Arthur Green, *Devotion and Commandment* (Hebrew Union College Press, 1989).

[85] 2 Samuel 7:19.

[86] B.T., *Yoma*, 39a.

[87] Isaiah 64:3.

[88] Proverbs 25:11.

[89] B.T., *Sukkah*, 28a.

[90] See Jacob ibn Habib, *'Eyn Ya'aqov, Sukkot*.

[91] Leviticus 18:5.

[92] B.T., *Eruvin*, 22a.

[93] B.T., *Yoma*, 39a.

[94] Genesis 1:16.

[95] Proverbs 6:23.

[96] *Midrash Rabbah, Bereishit*, 2:5.

[97] Lamentations 3:6.

[98] B.T., *Sanhedrin*, 24a.

[99] Genesis 1:4.

[100] *Midrash Rabbah, Bereishit*, 2:5. Also see B.T., *Hagigah*, 12a.

[101] Originally Adam was created with garments of light which became garments of skin after he sinned. The concept of garments of light goes back to *Bereishit Rabbah*, 20:12 and appears in the *Zohar*, vol. 1, 36b and vol. 2, 229b.

[102] Genesis 2:15.

[103] The words for skin and blind are spelled with the same letters, *ayin, vav, resh*.

[104] Proverbs 25:11.

[105] Literally "orchard."

[106] The "material" commandments allude to the spiritual entities which are their name in Holy Language above.
[107] Isaiah 11:9.
[108] Numbers 19:14.
[109] B.T., *Berakhot*, 63b.
[110] Lamentations 3:6.
[111] B.T., *Sanhedrin*, 24a.
[112] Proverbs 6:23.
[113] Genesis 1:16.
[114] Lamentations 3:6.
[115] B.T., *Gittin*, 60b.
[116] B.T., *Shabbat*, 104a.
[117] Job 11:9.
[118] Exodus 3:4.
[119] After Exodus 34:29. The verse speaks of the "skin of his face." "Skin" and "light" are homonyms in Hebrew.
[120] B.T., *Baba Batra*, 75a.
[121] Proverbs 6:23.
[122] Exodus 31:18.
[123] *Midrash Rabbah*, *Shemot*, 41:6.
[124] See Numbers 12:1.
[125] Exodus 34:27.
[126] Numbers 12:7.
[127] *Midrash Rabbah*, *Shemot*, 47:9.
[128] Numbers 19:14.
[129] Deuteronomy 4:44.
[130] B.T., *Berakhot*, 8a.
[131] Lamentations 3:6.
[132] B.T., *Ketubbot*, 75a.
[133] Genesis 40:10.
[134] B.T., *Hulin*, 92a.
[135] I.e., the intellectual darkness alluded to by Lamentations 3:6.
[136] Numbers 19:14.
[137] Zechariah 11:7.
[138] Zechariah 4:15.
[139] Zechariah 4:11.
[140] B.T., *Sanhedrin*, 24a.
[141] *Midrash Shoher Tov*, *Mishley* 10.
[142] This does not seem to be a passage in the *Zohar*, but rather a list of *Zohar*ic categories gleaned from various passages.

[143] B.T., *Pesaḥim*, 64a.

[144] Genesis 2:1.

[145] Genesis 2:3. A better translation would be, "which God made, by way of creating." I have supplied a strictly literal translation so that the English version of the verse will better serve Isaiah Horowitz's homiletic interests.

[146] Exodus 35:2.

[147] Genesis 2:2.

[148] See Rashi on Genesis 2:2.

[149] Psalms 84:8.

[150] B.T., *Berakhot*, 64a. Isaiah Horowitz slightly misquoted the saying, substituting *Ẓaddiqim* for scholars.

[151] B.T., *Sanhedrin*, 90a.

[152] Literally, "a person of the land" or ignoramus. Here the term has the specific connotation of a person who does not keep the customs of levitical cleanliness.

[153] Those that separate themselves from an *'am ha-arez*. These are the people who ate their ordinary meals in a state of levitical purity which is incumbent on priests.

[154] I.e., the priests and their household.

[155] *Mishnah*, *Hagigah*, 2:7.

[156] Psalms 84:8.

[157] Exodus 3:15.

[158] *Avot*, 3:9.

[159] Isaiah 66:16.

[160] Leviticus 5:12.

[161] B.T., *Berakhot*, 28a. It would seem that the vowel, *qamaẓ*, which usually represents *Keter*, here represents *Ḥesed*, identified with the priest and the right side. Thus one ascends from *Gevurah*, represented by *sheva*, to *Ḥesed*.

[162] Exodus 3:15.

[163] *Tiqquney Zohar*, *Haqdamah*, 5a (*Margoliot*).

[164] Psalms 34:15; 37:27.

[165] Exodus 3:15.

[166] Genesis 1:1.

[167] Psalms 96:11. These words begin with the letters *YH (Yismaḥu Ha-shamayim)*.

[168] Ibid. These words begin with VH (Ve-tagel Ha-arez).

[169] *Tiqquney Zohar*, *Tiqqun* 51, p. 86b (*Margoliot*). Cordovero's text differs slightly.

[170] *Pardes Rimmonim*, Gate 20, *Sh'ar ha-Shemot*, chapter 1, p. 89a-b.

[171] Therefore, "day," the written Torah, is expressed with the attribute of "night," the *heh* which represents *Malkhut*, and "night" is expressed by the attribute for "day," *vav*, which represents *Tif'eret*.

[172] According to Jewish mystical tradition, a very powerful Name, formed from three verses in Exodus, each of which has seventy-two letters. The Name is composed of seventy-two groups of three letters. Each one is made as follows. The first letter is taken from the first verse, the second letter follows reverse order of the second verse, and the third letter follows the consecutive order of the third verse. The verses are Exodus 14:19–21.

[173] See *Sefer Yeẓirah*.

[174] I.e., the 216 letters of the Name of 72 plus the 32 paths of wisdom equal 248 limbs.

[175] White is associated with *Ḥesed* and red with *Gevurah*.

[176] I.e., (1 + 30 + 80) + (30 + 40 + 4) + (5 + 10) + (10 + 6 + 4) + (40 + 40) = 300.

[177] When the letters *YHVH* are exchanged according to the system of ATBaSH, they become MZPZ. This Name equals 300 (40 + 90 + 80 + 90), which is also the sum of *be-raḥamim* (2 + 200 + 8 + 40 + 10 + 40), "with compassion."

[178] See Moses Cordovero, *Pardes Rimmonim, Sha'ar ha-She'arim*, chapter 2.

[179] Ezekiel 40:1.

[180] Exodus 23:13.

[181] Rashi, ad loc.

[182] Deuteronomy 32:46.

[183] Exodus 20:8.

[184] Deuteronomy 5:12.

[185] Deuteronomy 6:13; 10:20.

[186] Deuteronomy 13:11.

[187] B.T., *Kiddushin*, 39b.

[188] Psalms 119:3.

[189] Ecclesiastes 12:13.

[190] *'Avodat ha-Qodesh, Ḥeleq ha-Yiḥud*, chapter 25, p. 23a.

[191] Deuteronomy 6:5.

[192] B.T., *Berakhot*, 54a.

[193] I.e., he must then not only do what is commanded, but also not do what the "evil urge" advocates. This makes the positive commandment an opportunity to observe a negative commandment at the same time.

[194] *Sifra*, *Qedoshim*, chapter 11, 93d (A. H. Weiss edition). It is there

attributed to Rabbi Eliezer ben Azariah. See Piekarz, *Bi-Yemey Ẓemiḥat ha-Hasidut*, p. 210, n. 11.

[195] B.T., *Makkot*, 23b.

[196] Psalms 119:3.

[197] In other words, the person does not merely refrain from committing a transgression. The desire to transgress is aroused and then actively overcome. Thus observing the negative commandment acquires an active element, which is understood as the positive commandment within the negative.

[198] Song of Songs 5:2.

[199] From the liturgical poem, *Lekha, Dodi*, of Solomon Alkabez, which is part of the *Qabbalat Shabbat* service.

[200] Ecclesiastes 7:14.

[201] B.T., *Eruvin*, 13b.

[202] Genesis 22:7.

[203] *Pardes Rimmonim*, Gate 8: *Sha'ar ha-Makhri'in*, chapter 2, 56d–57a.

[204] Ecclesiastes 7:14.

[205] Exodus 34:6.

[206] The letters that spell *ve-ya'avor* are *ayin bet*, which equal 72, and *resh yod vav*, which equal 216.

[207] Numbers 28:3.

[208] Song of Songs 5:10.

[209] Job 31:2.

[210] Job 10:11.

[211] Job 31:2.

[212] Ezekiel 1:27.

[213] I.e., 45.

[214] *Zohar*, vol. 1, 88a.

[215] Job 31:2.

[216] *Mekhilta, be-Shalaḥ*, 15,1.

[217] "Our teacher, Moses" in Hebrew is *MoSHeH RaBbeYNU*. This equals (40 + 300 + 5) + (200 + 2 + 10 + 50 + 6) = 613.

[218] *YHVH 'ELoHeY Yisrael* is (10 + 5 + 6 + 5) + (1 + 30 + 5 + 10) + (10 + 300 + 200 + 1 + 30) = 613.

[219] *Israel* is *YiSRAeL*, i.e., 10 + 300 + 200 + 1 + 30 = 541 + 72 = 613.

The House of Israel [III]

[1] B.T., *Berakhot*, 33b.

[2] I.e., the coupling occurs below *Binah*, in the place that *Tif'eret* and *Malkhut* occupy after emerging from *Binah*.

[3] Genesis 3:22.
[4] Genesis 19:13.
[5] *Midrash Rabbah, Bereishit*, 50:9.
[6] Job 24:13.
[7] 1 Chronicles 4:23.
[8] 1 Chronicles 4:22.
[9] Genesis 36:31.
[10] Genesis 1:2.
[11] On the walnut (*'egoz*) as a mystical symbol, see Liebes, *Peraqim*. Also see Dan, "*Hokhmat ha-Egoz*—Its Origin and Development," *JJS* 17 (1966), pp. 73–82; and Altmann, "Elazar of Worms' *Hokhmat ha-Egoz*," *JJS* 11 (1960), pp. 101–113.
[12] *Zohar*, vol. 1, *Hashmatot, siman* 29, p. 263a.
[13] See *Midrash Rabbah, Bereishit*, 9:2.
[14] Isaiah 25:8.
[15] Isaiah 45:18.
[16] Job 10:11.
[17] Psalms 12:9.
[18] Genesis 3:1. The literal meaning of the verse is "the snake was wisest (*'arum*)." It is here being read as "*'erom* (naked)."
[19] Ezekiel 16:22.
[20] Genesis 3:6.
[21] Proverbs 5:5.
[22] Genesis 3:6.
[23] Genesis 2:9.
[24] Ecclesiastes 7:29.
[25] Genesis 2:9.
[26] Proverbs 5:5.
[27] Ecclesiastes 7:26.
[28] Genesis 3:24.
[29] Genesis 2:17.
[30] Isaiah 65:22.
[31] I.e., the Tree of Life.
[32] Isaiah 25:8.
[33] *Zohar*, vol. 3, p. 107a-b. Compare *Zohar*, vol. 1, p. 221a-b.
[34] Genesis 3:22.
[35] Judah Hayyat, *Commentary on Sefer Ma'arekhet ha-'Elohut*, chapter 9, *Sha'ar ha-Harisah*, pp. 115b–116b.
[36] Ramban on Genesis 2:17.
[37] Job 23:13.

[38] Literally, "He is in one . . . "
[39] Job 23:14.
[40] Genesis 1:10.
[41] Genesis 1:11.
[42] *Zohar*, vol. 1, p. 12a.
[43] I was unable to locate the source.
[44] B.T., *Avodah Zarah*, 54a.
[45] B.T., *Eruvin*, 13b.
[46] Ecclesiastes 12:11.
[47] Exodus 20:1.
[48] B.T., *Hagigah*, 3b.
[49] See *Genesis Rabbah*, chapter 20, 12 on Genesis 3:21. The verse speaks of "garments of skin" (*kutenot 'or*). In Rabbi Meir's Torah, the *ayin* in the word, *'or* was replaced by an *alef*, producing the word *'or* (light).
[50] Psalms 104:4.
[51] Genesis 3:21.
[52] Exodus 39:1.
[53] Psalms 27:4.
[54] Psalms 140:14.
[55] *Zohar*, vol. 2, p. 229b.
[56] Isaiah 11:9.
[57] This concept was very influential on Hasidism.
[58] Job 10:11.
[59] 1 Samuel 16:7.
[60] Genesis 3:6.
[61] Genesis 6:6.
[62] Genesis 25:26.
[63] B.T., *Megillah*, 16a.
[64] Ecclesiastes 7:14.
[65] Ezekiel 1:26.
[66] Job 14:4.
[67] If it were obvious that something polluted would be constituted from the sperm, it would not be permitted to develop.
[68] *Pardes Rimmonim, Sha'ar ha-Temurot*.
[69] Ibid. See Joseph Dan, "No Evil Descends from Heaven," in Cooperman, ed., *Jewish Thought in the Sixteenth Century* (Cambridge, Mass., 1983), pp. 89–105.
[70] B.T., *Shabbat*, 151b.
[71] Genesis 2:7.
[72] *Nefesh ḥayyah* can mean either "living soul" or "soul of a beast."

[73] Isaiah 58:11.

[74] Genesis 6:13.

[75] *'Avodat ha-Qodesh, Ḥeleq ha-Yiḥud*, chapter 18, p. 18b-c.

[76] Literally, "good stones."

[77] B.T., *Sanhedrin*, 59b. This passage is explained in the "House of David," below.

[78] B.T., *Shabbat*, 119a.

[79] Isaiah 11:6–9.

[80] Genesis 4:9.

[81] B.T., *Hagigah*, 15b.

[82] Genesis 2:9.

[83] Ecclesiastes 7:12.

[84] Genesis 4:1.

[85] B.T., *Hagigah*, 12b.

[86] Proverbs 10:25.

[87] Isaiah 55:1.

[88] I was unable to locate the source.

[89] *Sefer Ta'amey Miẓvot*, attributed to Ibn Farhi. Alexander Altmann refuted the theory of Farhi's authorship in "On the Question of Authorship of *Sefer Ta'amey Miẓvot* Which Is Attributed to R. Isaac Ibn Farhi" (Hebrew) *Kiryat Sefer* 40 (1965), pp. 256–276, 405–412.

[90] Job 19:26.

[91] Job 38:13.

[92] This entire section of the *Pardes*, the anonymous Aramaic text, is not cited in the *Shelah*.

[93] I.e., to *Yesod.*

[94] Psalms 133:3.

[95] See Proverbs 2:16; 7:5.

[96] As, for example, Exodus 20:3 and Deuteronomy 5:7.

[97] This seems to be the same anonymous text quoted above. This time it is included in the *Shelah*, but not in full.

[98] *Pardes Rimmonim*, Gate 7: *Sha'ar Seder ha-Ẓinnorot*, chapter 4, p. 34a-b. The translation that follows is not a continuation of the *Pardes* chapter.

[99] Psalms 5:5.

[100] Proverbs 5:5.

[101] Psalms 12:9.

[102] Or, perhaps, "in the best parts of the Land," referring to non-Jewish hegemony in the Land of Israel.

[103] Malachi 3:6.

[104] Lamentations 2:7.

[105] Isaiah 62:6.
[106] *Zohar*, vol. 1, 40a.
[107] Genesis 18:25.
[108] Lamentations 2:7.
[109] *Meqanna*, possibly, "that mourns."
[110] Lamentations 2:7.
[111] Abraham Galante, *Qol Bokhim*, pp. 27b–28a.
[112] Genesis 1:26.
[113] Genesis 3:1.
[114] Genesis 3:2.
[115] Psalms 36:12.
[116] Genesis 3:7.
[117] *Sefer ha-Bahir*, section 200.
[118] Psalms 49:13.
[119] Ecclesiastes 12:13.
[120] B.T., *Berakhot*, 6a.
[121] *Sefer ha-Yashar*, attributed to Rabbenu Tam.
[122] B.T., *Sanhedrin*, 59b.
[123] Psalms 12:9.

The House of David [I]

[1] I have been unable to locate the source.
[2] Jeremiah 1:14. "North" is associated with the left side.
[3] Translating *'avanim tovot* literally. This expression conventionally means "precious stones." This is from the passage cited in "House of Israel III," B.T., *Sanhedrin*, 59b.
[4] *Sefer Yeẓirah*, 4:16.
[5] Cf. *Sefer Yeẓirah*, 4:3.
[6] *Sefer Yeẓirah*, 2:4.
[7] B.T., *Sanhedrin*, 59b.
[8] I.e., it presides over everything in the worlds of creation, formation, and making.
[9] Proverbs 5:5.
[10] Exodus 4:4.
[11] See n. 7 above.
[12] Isaiah 60:21.
[13] Ecclesiastes 10:8.
[14] Ezekiel 36:34,35.

[15] Lamentations 4:21.
[16] Isaiah 11:8.
[17] The text says, "*Me'urat* can be spelled defectively without the *vav*." Thus spelled, the word means "cursed" rather than "den."
[18] Ezekiel 36:26.
[19] Ibid.
[20] *Zohar*, vol. 3, 254a.
[21] Ecclesiastes 7:14.
[22] Isaiah 41:27.
[23] Isaiah 25:8.
[24] B.T., *Baba Meẓi'a*, 84b. The snake held its tail in its mouth and was blocking the entrance to the cave.
[25] B.T., *Sanhedrin*, 59b.
[26] Genesis 2:15.
[27] Galante, *Qol Bokhim*, Lamentations 11:8.
[28] *Sefer ha-Bahir*, section 200.
[29] B.T., *Baba Batra*, 21a.
[30] Deuteronomy 30:15.
[31] Deuteronomy 4:4.
[32] Compare B.T., *Sotah*, 14a. Several sources seem to be conflated here.
[33] Genesis 3:19.
[34] Genesis 1:31.
[35] Nahmanides, *Commentary on the Torah*, *Bereishit*, 2:17.
[36] Song of Songs 6:4.
[37] Deuteronomy 4:4.
[38] *Midrash Rabbah*, Song of Songs, 6:1. Cf. *Midrash Rabbah*, *Ba-Midbar*, *Naso*, 12:18.
[39] Psalms 101:1.
[40] Psalms 101:8. "Each morning (*liveqarim*)" can also mean "for the cattle."
[41] *Midrash Tehillim*, 101:4.
[42] Exodus 26:15.
[43] B.T., *Yoma*, 72a.
[44] *Mishnah*, *Shabbat*, 16:1.
[45] Proverbs 13:20.
[46] *Tanḥuma* (Buber), *Bereishit*, chapter 21.
[47] Psalms 33:1.
[48] Lamentations 2:9.
[49] B.T., *Sotah*, 9a.
[50] *Tanḥuma* (Warsaw), *va-yiqra*, *aḥarey mot*, chapter 2.

[51] Ecclesiastes 7:1.
[52] Hosea 2:23.
[53] I was unable to locate the source.
[54] See *Sefer Yeẓirah*, 1:5.
[55] Psalms 5:5.
[56] Or, perhaps, "byproducts."
[57] Psalms 49:13.
[58] Proverbs 16:28. I.e., he separates his friend from holiness.
[59] Ibid.
[60] Genesis 3:4.
[61] *Midrash Rabbah*, *Bereishit*, 20:2.
[62] Psalms 143:3.
[63] Genesis 1:31.
[64] The last letters of the first three words of this verse spell *'emet*. The word *me'od* has the same letters as Adam.
[65] Job 28:27,28.
[66] Genesis 3:1.
[67] Genesis 3:6. This verse begins with the word, "*ve-ter'a* (and she saw)." The first two letters are *vav* and *tav*.
[68] Genesis 3:6,7.
[69] Jeremiah 9:20.
[70] Psalms 89:49.
[71] *Zohar Hadash*, *Midrash ha-Ne'elam al Midrash 'Eykhah*, 91d.
[72] Jeremiah 9:20.
[73] Genesis 3:6.
[74] Genesis 1:31.
[75] *Midrash Rabbah*, *Bereishit*, 9:12.
[76] Ibid., 9:8.
[77] B.T., *Eruvin*, 13b.
[78] Ecclesiastes 4:2,3.
[79] Ecclesiastes 4:3.
[80] *Beyt ha-Midrash*, Jellinek, 5, 126.
[81] I was unable to locate the source.
[82] Ecclesiastes 4:3.
[83] B.T., *Hagigah*, 13b; *Kohelet Rabbah*, 1:15.
[84] I was unable to locate the source.
[85] Jeremiah 23:19.
[86] Job 22:16.
[87] The verb *qumtu* can mean either "were rushed forward" or "shriveled up."

[88] B.T., *Hagigah*, 13b–14a.
[89] Genesis 1:31.
[90] Although Isaac Luria is not cited explicitly and the characteristic components of his system are not utilized, Isaiah Horowitz seems to be presenting a point of view here that may have been strongly influenced by the Lurianic outlook.
[91] Ecclesiastes 2:13.
[92] See B.T., *Shabbat*, 144b, 145a. However, there, it is Adam who squeezes the grapes.
[93] Literally, "preserved."
[94] This section on spiritual transformation, rather than suppression of evil, is one of the most influential teachings of our author. See the Introduction to this work.
[95] Psalms 139:22.
[96] Genesis 1:31.
[97] Isaiah 52:8. The meaning of the verse is "every eye will behold . . . "
[98] Isaiah 64:3.
[99] B.T., *Berakhot*, 34b; *Sanhedrin*, 99a.
[100] Exodus 17:16.
[101] Text reads "*vav heh*."
[102] Genesis 3:1.
[103] Proverbs 16:28.
[104] *'Avodat ha-Qodesh*. I was unable to locate the passage.
[105] B.T., *Shabbat*, 12a.
[106] *'Avodat ha-Qodesh*.
[107] B.T., *Sukkah*, 45b; *Sanhedrin*, 97b.
[108] Or, "that will cause the light to be stronger than darkness."
[109] Hosea 14:10.
[110] Ecclesiastes 4:3.
[111] Ecclesiastes 4:2.
[112] Psalms 116:15.
[113] 1 Chronicles 16:15.
[114] Rashi on *Hagigah*, 14a.
[115] 1 Chronicles 16:15.
[116] Ecclesiastes 7:14.
[117] I have not been able to identify this text and consequently cannot determine precisely where the citation ends.
[118] Ecclesiastes 4:3.
[119] It is not clear where the citation ends.
[120] Psalms 104:31.

[121] Leviticus 26:4.
[122] B.T., *Shabbat*, 30b.
[123] See Leviticus 26:3–12.
[124] Text conflates Isaiah 11:9 with Habakkuk 2:14.
[125] Jeremiah 23:29.
[126] Rashi, *Commentary on the Torah*, Genesis 33:20. Compare B.T., *Shabbat*, 88b.
[127] I.e., Leviticus 26:3–12.
[128] Leviticus 26:11.
[129] Psalms 49:13.
[130] Genesis 3:22.
[131] Leviticus 26:12.
[132] Numbers 23:23.
[133] Leviticus 18:5.
[134] B.T., *Berakhot*, 17a. Maimonides abridged the citation.
[135] Song of Songs 3:11.
[136] Isaiah 51:11.
[137] Maimonides, *Mishneh Torah, Hilkhot Teshuvah*, chapter 8, 2.
[138] Cf. Isaiah 65:17 and Jeremiah 31:21.
[139] B.T., *Ketubbot*, 111b.
[140] B.T., *Shabbat*, 114a.
[141] B.T., *Sanhedrin*, 92a.
[142] Ibid., 91b.
[143] *Hasagat ha-RABaD, Mishneh Torah, Hilkhot Teshuvah*, chapter 8,2.
[144] *'Avodat ha-Qodesh, Ḥeleq ha-'Avodah*, chapter 41, 55b–55c.
[145] Joseph Albo, *'Iqqarim, Ma'amar Revi'i*, chapter 31. Quoted in *'Avodat ha-Qodesh, Ḥeleq ha-'Avodah*, chapter 41, 55d–56a.
[146] Isaiah 60:21.
[147] *Mishnah*, *Sanhedrin*, 10:1.
[148] Deuteronomy 5:16.
[149] Deuteronomy 22:7.
[150] B.T., *Kiddushin*, 39b.
[151] Proverbs 31:25.
[152] *Midrash Rabbah*, *Shemot*, 52:3.
[153] Isaiah 60:21.
[154] Psalms 104:16.
[155] Exodus 24:11.
[156] B.T., *Berakhot*,17a.
[157] Proverbs 16:15.
[158] Isaiah 35:10

[159] Isaiah 43:7.
[160] B.T., *Baba Batra*, 75b.
[161] Proverbs 10:25. I.e., the *sefirah*, *Yesod.*
[162] 1 Chronicles 29:11.
[163] Isaiah 4:3.
[164] B.T., *Baba Batra*, 75b.
[165] Isaiah 4:3.
[166] Isaiah 2:11.
[167] I.e., If the world will be destroyed during this period, where will the righteous be?
[168] Psalms 46:3.
[169] Isaiah 41:31.
[170] B.T., *Sanhedrin*, 92a–92b.
[171] Deuteronomy 8:3.
[172] Exodus 16:4.
[173] B.T., *Sanhedrin*, 92a.
[174] Isaiah 60:21.
[175] Ibid.
[176] I.e., Nahmanides.
[177] See the passage above from *Sanhedrin*, 92a–92b.
[178] *'Avodat ha-Qodesh*, *Ḥeleq ha-'Avodah*, chapter 42, 56a–56c.
[179] Ibid., chapter 41, 56a.
[180] B.T., *Rosh Ha-Shanah*, 31a.
[181] B.T., *Sanhedrin*, 97a.
[182] I was not able to locate this *Zohar* passage.
[183] Isaiah 64:3.
[184] Deuteronomy 15:11.
[185] B.T., *Berakhot*, 34b.
[186] *Mishneh Torah*, *Hilkhot Melakhim u-Milḥamotehem*, chapter 12, 1.
[187] Genesis 3:22.
[188] B.T., *Hagigah*, 12a; *Sanhedrin*, 38b.
[189] Genesis 3:17,18.
[190] Zechariah 8:12.
[191] Isaiah 44:23.
[192] See Genesis 1:16.
[193] Isaiah 44:23.
[194] Ibid.
[195] Isaiah 44:22.
[196] I.e., B.T., *Berakhot*, 34b.
[197] *'Avodat ha-Qodesh*, *Ḥeleq ha-'Avodah*, chapter 38, 53c–53d.

[198] Deuteronomy 19:8,9.
[199] *Midrash Tehillim*, chapter 100, *pisqa* 4. Not quoted exactly.
[200] *Offerings*, or *qorbanot*, come from the root *qrb*, which means "to bring near."
[201] Psalms 107:8.
[202] *Tola'at Ya'aqov, Sitrey Ḥag ha-Shavuot*, 33b–33c.
[203] Psalms 100:4.
[204] Psalms 56:13.
[205] Jeremiah 7:34.
[206] Ibid.
[207] *Midrash Tehillim*, 100, 4.
[208] Zechariah 14:9.
[209] *'Avodat ha-Qodesh, Ḥeleq ha-'Avodah*, chapter 43, 58a–58b.
[210] Deuteronomy 19:9.
[211] Genesis 15:19.
[212] Cf. *Midrash Rabbah, Bereishit*, 44:23. Check *Yerushalmi, Kiddushin*, chapter 1:8, 19a, and *Yalqut Shimoni*, part 1, *remez* 78, 884 and part 2, 986.
[213] Psalms 72:8.
[214] I.e., those mentioned explicitly in Genesis 15:19–21.
[215] P.T., *Ma'aser Sheniy*, 29b.
[216] I could not find the source for this apparent quotation.
[217] See Ezekiel 44:25.
[218] Isaiah 25:8.
[219] Deuteronomy 19:8,9.
[220] Isaiah 2:4.
[221] Exodus 21:13.
[222] Genesis 4:9.
[223] Genesis 4:10.
[224] Moses is the reincarnation of the good portion of Abel's soul and Balaam is the *qelippah*. See *Sha'ar ha-Pesuqim, Balaq*, 37c.
[225] 2 Samuel 3:33.
[226] B.T., *Sanhedrin*, 98a.
[227] Deuteronomy 19:8,9.
[228] Ibid.
[229] Zechariah 13:2.
[230] *Sefer ha-Liqqutim, Devarim, siman* 19, 59b–59c.
[231] Leviticus 26:11.
[232] The order follows the promises in section *be-ḥuqqotay*, Leviticus 26.
[233] B.T., *Shabbat*, 30b.
[234] Leviticus 26:6.

[235] Leviticus 26:9.
[236] See Rashi on Leviticus 26:9. Another possible translation: "with a proud carriage."
[237] Leviticus 26:11,12.
[238] Psalms 49:13.
[239] Psalms 104:31.
[240] Ecclesiastes 2:13. Literally, "[as] light is superior to darkness."
[241] Numbers 23:23.
[242] See B.T., *Berakhot*, 52b.
[243] Isaiah 45:7.
[244] Amos 4:13.
[245] Isaiah 42:5.

The House of *YHVH* [II]

[1] B.T., *Berakhot*, 52b.
[2] Ibid.
[3] Deuteronomy 4:24.
[4] See B.T., *Yoma*, 21b.
[5] Deuteronomy 4:24.
[6] Deuteronomy 4:4.
[7] *Zohar*, vol. 1, 50b–51a.
[8] Psalms 133:3.
[9] See B.T., *Berakhot*, 8a.
[10] I was unable to identify this source.

The House of David [II]

[1] Isaiah 64:3.
[2] Ecclesiastes 2:13.

The House of Wisdom [III]

[1] Deuteronomy 5:19.
[2] Or, "He did not continue to be seen in that solemnity."
[3] Exodus 20:1.
[4] Deuteronomy 29:14.

[5] Malachi 1:1.
[6] Isaiah 48:16.
[7] Isaiah 48:16.
[8] Deuteronomy 5:19.
[9] *Midrash Rabbah*, *Shemot*, 28:6.
[10] Deuteronomy 17:11.
[11] Deuteronomy 17:12.
[12] P.T., *Peah*, 2:6.
[13] Leviticus 20:26.
[14] Exodus 20:4.
[15] Ecclesiastes 5:5.
[16] Ibid.
[17] Exodus 20:5; Deuteronomy 5:9.
[18] See Scḥolem "The Meaning of the Torah in Jewish Mysticism," in *On the Kabbalah and Its Symbolism* (New York, 1965), pp. 32–86. Margoliot brings as a possible talmudic source, B.T., *Berakhot*, 21a.
[19] Exodus 20:4.
[20] Exodus 34:1.
[21] Exodus 20:5.
[22] *Zohar*, vol. 2, 87a–87b.
[23] *'Avodat ha-Qodesh*, *Ḥeleq ha-Takhlit*, chapter 20, 82b–82c.
[24] Psalms 147:5.
[25] Ecclesiastes 10:8.
[26] B.T., *Moed Qatan*, 5a on Leviticus 18:30.
[27] B.T., *Baba Batra*, 16a.
[28] B.T., *Eruvin*, 13b.
[29] *Hiddushey ha-RYTVA*, *Eruvin*, 13b.
[30] B.T., *Gittin*, 6b. The story of the concubine is told in Judges 19.
[31] In either case, the concubine was guilty of infidelity.
[32] Ecclesiastes 12:11.
[33] Ibid.
[34] Exodus 20:1.
[35] B.T., *Hagigah*, 3b.
[36] Ecclesiastes 1:7.
[37] Ecclesiastes 3:20.
[38] *Zohar*, vol. 3, 6b.
[39] Ecclesiastes 12:11.
[40] B.T., *Hagigah*, 3b.
[41] Ibid.
[42] Ecclesiastes 7:24.

[43] *'Avodat ha-Qodesh, Ḥeleq ha-Takhlit*, chapter 23, 86a.

[44] I.e., it does not strengthen the *qelippot* and condemn one of the parties to Gehinnom.

[45] B.T., *Eruvin*, 13b. The text says "they were at ease and submissive."

[46] B.T., *Megillah*, 13a.

[47] Genesis 22:7.

[48] *Pardes Rimmonim*, Gate 8: *Sha'ar ha-Makhri'in*, chapter 2, 56d–57a.

[49] *Mishnah, Parah*, 1:1. These definitions are important for two *halakhot*, the "red heifer" (see Numbers 19:1–14) and the calf whose neck is broken (see Deuteronomy 21:3ff.). In order to fulfill these laws, the rabbis had to determine how old an animal was meant by these terms.

[50] Exodus 18:4.

[51] *Midrash Rabbah, ba-midbar*, 19:6; *Tanḥuma* (Warsaw), *huqat*, 8.

[52] Deuteronomy 30:12.

[53] See B.T., *Baba Mezi'a*, 59b. Rabbi Joshua cites Deuteronomy 30:12 against Rabbi Eliezer, in order to prove that a heavenly voice cannot decide the *halakhah*.

[54] Literally, "a son is his father's leg." See B.T., *Eruvin*, 70b.

[55] Deuteronomy 5:19.

The House of YHVH [III]/The House of David [III]

[1] Psalms 136:7.

[2] This is one of two blessings that precedes the Shema' in the morning service.

[3] Isaiah 60:3.

[4] See *Tur*, *'Oraḥ Ḥayyim*, *siman* 51.

[5] Psalms 136:8,9.

[6] Isaiah 26:4. Literally, the verse likens God to "an everlasting rock."

[7] I.e., the emanated seven lower *sefirot*.

[8] This is Horowitz's kabbalistic reading of the verse.

[9] According to rabbinic exegesis, *'olam* refers to the Jubilee year. See B.T., *Kiddushin* 15a.

[10] The meaning seems to be that each of the lower *sefirot* is a kind of sphere that contains the entire structure formed by the seven lower *sefirot* within it. Each of the seven contains seven, corresponding to the seven *shemitot* that lead to the Jubilee.

[11] Genesis 2:15.

[12] Zechariah 14:9.

[13] Ibid.
[14] From "on that day (*ba-yom ha-hu'*)."
[15] Psalms 132:13. *Hu'* and *'ivah* have the same letters.
[16] Micah 7:8.
[17] Isaiah 60:1.
[18] Genesis 1:3.
[19] Ecclesiastes 11:3.
[20] The letter *vav* represents the number 6.
[21] See Nahmanides on the Torah, *Be-shalaḥ*, 16:6.
[22] Ecclesiastes 1:9.
[23] Ecclesiastes 2:22. Literally, "What does a man get [for all the toil and worrying he does under the sun]?"
[24] The numerical value of these various combinations of letters is 45.
[25] Ecclesiastes 11:3.
[26] Ecclesiastes 1:9.
[27] This may be translated "what was, is, will be."
[28] Ezra 7:26.
[29] Zechariah 14:9.
[30] Genesis 3:20.
[31] Ecclesiastes 2:22.
[32] An allusion to Ecclesiastes 7:12.
[33] *Midrash Rabbah*, Song of Songs, 1:36.
[34] 1 Chronicles 16:31.
[35] *Yismaḥu Ha-shamayim Ve-tagel Ha-'areẓ.*
[36] Genesis 22:14.
[37] Genesis 14:18.
[38] Psalms 76:3.
[39] Genesis 22:14.
[40] Exodus 23:17.
[41] Genesis 22:14.
[42] Lamentations 5:18.
[43] This is the continuation of Exodus 23:17.
[44] Psalms 102:17.
[45] *Midrash Rabbah*, Genesis, chapter 56,10, 115a.
[46] Deuteronomy 11:12.
[47] Psalms 25:14.
[48] B.T., *Baba Batra*, 75b.
[49] Hosea 11:9.
[50] B.T., *Ta'anit*, 5a.
[51] Habakkuk 2:20.

[52] *Zohar Ḥadash*, Song of Songs, *ma'amar* 5.
[53] Genesis 12:1.
[54] Genesis 2:4.
[55] *Midrash Rabbah*, *Bereishit*, 12, 9.
[56] Micah 7:20.
[57] Psalms 89:3.
[58] Genesis 12:1,2.
[59] Genesis 18:18.
[60] Ecclesiastes 11:3.
[61] Genesis 18:4.
[62] *YHVH*, when spelled *yod vav dalet heh yod vav yod vav heh yod*, equals 72. *Ḥesed* also equals 72.
[63] This is the Name of 72 that is formed from the letters of the three verses, Exodus 14:19–21. Each verse contains 72 letters. Thus the entire Name contains 216 letters.
[64] Genesis 12:6.
[65] Of the four animals mentioned in Ezekiel's vision, the lion is associated with *Ḥesed*.
[66] Deuteronomy 16:16.
[67] Therefore, it is associated with *Ḥesed* and Abraham.
[68] Proverbs 24:3.
[69] Psalms 76:3.
[70] Isaiah 26:7.
[71] Deuteronomy 32:9.
[72] *Ḥevel* may mean either "inheritance" or "rope."
[73] Ecclesiastes 7:14.
[74] B.T., *Shabbat*, 104a.

The House of the Walled City

[1] Deuteronomy 7:4, 11:17.
[2] The text says "the will of the body."
[3] B.T., *Ta'anit*, 4a.
[4] This entire paragraph is designated "a gloss."
[5] Deuteronomy 5:19.

The House of Choosing

[1] I.e., predestination.
[2] Maimonides, *Mishneh Torah*, *Sefer ha-Mada'*, *Hilkhot Teshuvah*, chapter 5, *halakhah* 5.

NOTES TO TEXT

[3] The unity of God's essence and knowledge is treated in the sequel to the passage quoted above and in *Mishneh Torah*, *Sefer ha-Mada'*, *Hilkhot Yesodey ha-Torah*, chapter two, *halakhah* 10.

[4] 1 Samuel 14:6.

[5] Proverbs 8:7.

[6] *Mishneh Torah*, *Sefer ha-Mad'a*, *Hilkhot Yesodey Torah*, chapter 2, *halakhah* 10.

[7] *Tola'at Ya'aqov*, *Sitrey Rosh Ha-Shanah*.

[8] Deuteronomy 4:39.

[9] Deuteronomy 6:4.

[10] Nehemiah 9:6.

[11] Deuteronomy 22:8.

[12] B.T., *Shabbat*, chapter 2, 32a.

[13] Isaiah 41:4.

[14] Rashi's commentary on B.T., *Shabbat*, 32a.

[15] Deuteronomy 34:1.

[16] Ibid.

[17] Judges 18:30.

[18] Deuteronomy 34:2.

[19] Ibid.

[20] Ibid.

[21] Ibid.

[22] Deuteronomy 34:3.

[23] 1 Kings 7:46; 2 Chronicles 4:17.

[24] 1 Kings 13:2.

[25] Paraphrase of Psalms 135:6.

[26] Deuteronomy 5:19.

[27] Deuteronomy 11:26.

[28] Deuteronomy 30:15.

[29] Deuteronomy 30:19.

[30] B.T., *Baba Mezi'a*, 85b–86a.

[31] B.T., *Shabbat*, 32a.

[32] *Mishnah*, *Bekhorot*, chapter 8, *mishnah* 9.

[33] Genesis 22:12.

[34] Deuteronomy 31:21.

[35] Genesis 22:12.

[36] Isaiah 1:19,20.

[37] Isaiah 48:4,5.

[38] B.T., *Avodah Zara*, 4b–5a.

[39] Rashi understands the *Gemara* to mean that these actions were only

committed so that there would be a pretext for repentance. The good way that emerges from the sin is the possibility of repentance.

[40] Isaiah 41:4.

[41] Genesis 21:17.

[42] Isaiah 21:13,14.

[43] Ibid.

[44] Rashi on Genesis 21:17.

[45] Genesis 21:15,16.

[46] Genesis 21:17.

[47] See Rashi's commentary to Deuteronomy 4:25. *Ve-noshantem* equals 852, implying that the Israelites would be exiled after 852 years.

[48] Deuteronomy 30:19.

The Great Gate

[1] Psalms 34:15.

[2] 1 Kings 7:36. The literal meaning is probably, "according to the exposed region." However, the rabbis explained it as I have translated. See B.T., *Yoma*, 54a-b, and see Rashi's comment there on the verse.

[3] Pronounced *ADoNaY*.

[4] Psalms 68:28.

[5] Proverbs 10:25.

[6] Deuteronomy 7:7.

[7] *Ha-me'at* can be read as "five fewer."

[8] Zechariah 14:9.

[9] Leviticus 26:11.

[10] Paraphrase of Proverbs 30:23.

[11] Psalms 119:126.

[12] Ibid.

[13] *Zohar*, vol. 2, 155b.

[14] Galante, *Qol Bokhim*.

[15] Isaiah 65:16.

[16] Psalms 61:14. The literal meaning is "with God we shall triumph."

[17] Psalms 68:35.

[18] B.T., *Ketubot*, 104a.

[19] B.T., *Berakhot*, 9b.

[20] Psalms 121:5.

[21] Although this section seems to be quoted from the *Midrash*, I could not locate the source.

[22] Hosea 2:23,24.
[23] 1 Kings 8:32,34,36,39.
[24] *Sefer ha-Bahir*, section 100.
[25] Leviticus 26:4.
[26] Job 19:26.
[27] Psalms 111:4.
[28] Song of Songs 7:10.
[29] *Ma'arekhet ha-'Elohut*, *Perush ha-Hayyat*, chapter 11, *Sha'ar ha-Merkavah ha-'Elyonah*, pp. 161b–162a.
[30] Numbers 14:17.
[31] Deuteronomy 33:26. The verse is usually understood as "riding through the heavens in order to help you."
[32] Deuteronomy 32:18.
[33] Joshua 7:9.
[34] 2 Samuel 8:13.
[35] Psalms 8:2,10.
[36] Daniel 9:17.
[37] *Midrash Rabbah*, *Bereishit*, 19:13.
[38] Psalms 48:2.
[39] Ibid.
[40] *Zohar*, vol. 3, 5a.
[41] *Avot*, 2:12.
[42] *Avot*, 6:11.
[43] *Tiqquney Zohar*, Introduction 2.
[44] B.T., *Berakhot*, 7a.
[45] Isaiah 56:7.
[46] B.T., *Berakhot*, 7a.
[47] Psalms 76:3.
[48] 1 Kings 7:36.
[49] Numbers 14:17.
[50] B.T., *Shabbat*, 89a.
[51] Isaiah 21:12.
[52] The text here is very awkward and cannot be translated literally.
[53] Numbers 14:17.
[54] See Numbers 14:18.
[55] Numbers 14:20,21.
[56] *'Avodat ha-Qodesh*, Introduction, pp. 3d–4a.
[57] Lamentations 1:6.
[58] Psalms 60:14. Literally, "With God we shall triumph."
[59] Deuteronomy 32:18.

[60] Numbers 14:17.
[61] *Midrash Rabbah*, *Eikha*, 1,33.
[62] *Zohar*, vol. 3, 4b.
[63] *Zohar*, vol. 2, 65b.
[64] Psalms 123:1.
[65] Amos 9:6.
[66] *Sifre*, *Brakhah*, *pisqa* 5.
[67] Deuteronomy 33:26.
[68] *Sefer ha-Bahir*, section 185.
[69] Psalms 37:3.
[70] Leviticus 22:31, et al.
[71] Compare *Midrash Rabbah*, *va-yiqra*, chapter 35. The verb, *'aseh* can mean both "do" and "make."
[72] I.e., the *sefirah*, *Yesod*.
[73] Psalms 37:3.
[74] I.e., *Malkhut*.
[75] Psalms 92:2.
[76] The word for "pursue," *re'eh*, is related by the author of the *Zohar* to the Aramaic root that means "desire."
[77] *Zohar*, vol. 3, 110b.
[78] I.e., the union of *Yesod* and *Malkhut*, who are called "Righteous One (*Ẓaddiq*) and Righteousness (*Ẓedeq*)."
[79] Psalms 33:4.
[80] Job 22:28.
[81] 2 Samuel 8:13.
[82] Leviticus 24:11.
[83] *Zohar*, vol. 3, 113a-b.
[84] Psalms 60:14.
[85] Song of Songs 4:8.
[86] Psalms 68:35.
[87] Proverbs 10:25.
[88] *Sefer ha-Bahir*, section 102.
[89] B.T., *Hagigah*, 12b.
[90] I.e., it extends from *Malkhut* to *Tif'eret*.
[91] 1 Chronicles 29:11.
[92] Isaiah 63:1.
[93] *Midrash Tehillim*, 20:3 (abbreviated).
[94] 2 Samuel 7:23.
[95] Exodus 29:46.
[96] Isaiah 49:3.

[97] Joshua 7:9.
[98] Psalms 132:13.
[99] Psalms 132:14.
[100] Leviticus 26:42.
[101] Exodus 29:46.
[102] Hosea 13:4.
[103] Psalms 114:1.
[104] Exodus 2:25.
[105] Exodus 39:43.
[106] *Midrash Tehillim* on Psalm 114:1.
[107] Psalms 132:13.
[108] Psalms 132:14.
[109] Exodus 20:1.
[110] Psalms 104:11.
[111] Deuteronomy 32:18. Literally, the verse means "you have forgotten . . ." However, here the verb *teshi* is related to the root *tashash*, which means "weaken."
[112] Psalms 60:14.
[113] Lamentations 2:1.
[114] Song of Songs 2:6.
[115] Lamentations 2:3.
[116] Proverbs 16:28.
[117] Leviticus 18:7.
[118] *Zohar*, vol. 3, 74a.
[119] Exodus 4:22.
[120] Proverbs 1:8.
[121] *Zohar*, vol. 3, 74a.
[122] Proverbs 10:1.
[123] Ibid.
[124] Isaiah 50:1.
[125] *Zohar*, vol. 3, 74b.
[126] Deuteronomy 32:5.
[127] Isaiah 59:17.
[128] Ibid.
[129] Deuteronomy 32:5.
[130] Psalms 104:35.
[131] Deuteronomy 32:5.
[132] Deuteronomy 32:4.
[133] Deuteronomy 32:6.
[134] *Zohar*, vol. 3, 297a-b.

[135] Isaiah 12:5.
[136] Psalms 97:1.
[137] Proverbs 19:26.
[138] Jeremiah 14:8.
[139] Psalms 9:15.
[140] *Midrash Tehillim*, 13, 14.
[141] Zechariah 9:9.
[142] Deuteronomy 30:3.
[143] Compare *Tanḥuma* (Warsaw), *aḥarey mot*, 12.
[144] Job 22:3.
[145] Job 35:6,7.
[146] Proverbs 9:12.
[147] Psalms 18:31.
[148] Ibid.
[149] *Tanḥuma* (Warsaw), *Shemini*, 8.
[150] Job 22:3.
[151] Job 35:6, 8.
[152] Proverbs 9:12.
[153] Leviticus 11:43.
[154] Isaiah 66:24.
[155] Deuteronomy 14:3.
[156] *Zohar*, vol. 3, 41b.
[157] *Zohar*, vol. 3, 47a.
[158] Deuteronomy 10:20.
[159] Deuteronomy 11:22; 30:20; Joshua 22:5.
[160] Numbers 19:13,20.
[161] Isaiah 57:1.
[162] Proverbs 25:4.
[163] The root *ẒRoF* has both senses in Hebrew, "to join together" and "to eliminate dross."
[164] Proverbs 30:5.
[165] Psalms 18:31.
[166] Ibid.
[167] *Midrash Rabbah*, *Bereishit*, 44.
[168] Deuteronomy 32:47.
[169] Isaiah 45:19.
[170] In other words, the upper rather than the lower part of the throat must be cut.
[171] Maimonides, *Moreh Nevukhim*, part 3, chapter 26, 58b–59a. *The Guide*

of the Perplexed, vol. 2, trans. Shlomo Pines (Chicago: University of Chicago Press, 1963), 508–509.

[172] Leviticus 11:46.

[173] Proverbs 30:5.

[174] Ibid.

[175] Psalms 18:31.

[176] Leviticus 7:24.

[177] Leviticus 11:2.

[178] *Midrash Rabbah, va-Yiqra, Shemini*, 13,3.

[179] Psalms 18:31.

[180] Joel 2:26.

[181] *Midrash Shoḥer Tov*, 18.

[182] Deuteronomy 32:46,47.

[183] Deuteronomy 32:47.

[184] Ibid.

[185] *Sefer 'Avodat ha-Qodesh, Ḥeleq ha-'Avodah*, chapter 3, pp. 26c–27c.

[186] Job 35:6,7.

[187] Psalms 89:28.

[188] *Pesiqta Rabbati*, 40:3.

[189] Genesis 6:7. See *Midrash Rabbah, berakhot*, 8:3.

[190] Genesis 9:14.

[191] Isaiah 63:9.

[192] Text here is difficult.

[193] Genesis 6:14.

[194] *Ma'arekhet ha-'Elohut, Ma'arekhet ha-Ta'am.*

[195] *Tiqquney Zohar*, introduction.

[196] Ecclesiastes 1:2. Literally, "vanity of vanities."

[197] Ecclesiastes 7:6.

[198] The *'Atarah* or *Malkhut* is identified with the final *heh* in the Tetragrammaton.

[199] Psalms 29:7.

[200] *Sefer Yeẓirah*. See chapter 2.

[201] Genesis 2:6.

[202] Isaiah 51:3.

[203] *Ma'arekhet ha-'Elohut*. I was unable to locate this passage.

[204] I.e., when the lights of *Ḥesed*, *Gevurah*, and *Tif'eret*, which are called the Patriarchs, shine into *Malkhut*.

[205] Paraphrase of Proverbs 4:23.

[206] Judah Hayyat, Commentary on *Ma'arekhet ha-'Elohut, Ma'arekhet ha-Ta'am*.

[207] *Ma'arekhet ha-'Elohut, Ma'arekhet ha-Ta'am.*
[208] Isaiah 50:1.
[209] Genesis 6:11.
[210] Deuteronomy 22:6.
[211] Genesis 6:6.
[212] I.e., if we maintain that it is not impaired by human sin.
[213] Judah Hayyat, Commentary on *Ma'arekhet ha-'Elohut.*
[214] Isaiah 61:5.
[215] Psalms 104:21.
[216] Psalms 91:15.
[217] Isaiah 63:9.
[218] Isaiah 50:1.
[219] Paraphrase of Proverbs 30:21.
[220] Proverbs 30:23.
[221] Commentary of Rav Paz on *Ma'arekhet ha-'Elohut.*
[222] Genesis 6:11.
[223] Proverbs 28:24.
[224] Exodus 32:7.
[225] Isaiah 1:4.
[226] Deuteronomy 20:19.
[227] Genesis 38:9.
[228] Deuteronomy 32:5.
[229] Genesis 6:13.
[230] *Midrash Rabbah*, *Bereishit*, 31–7.
[231] Isaiah 1:19.
[232] Genesis 6:11.
[233] Jeremiah 2:7.
[234] Zechariah 7:7.
[235] Recanati, *Commentary on the Torah*, Genesis, Noah, 19a–b.
[236] Genesis 7:13.
[237] Ecclesiastes 10:11.
[238] Genesis 7:13.
[239] Hosea 7:1.
[240] See Moshe Halamish, "A Gnomic Collection," *Sinai* 80 (1977), p. 278.
[241] Psalms 149:8.
[242] Ibid.
[243] Genesis 6:13.
[244] Recanati, *Commentary on the Torah*, Genesis, Noah, 19a–b.

[245] Mattathias Delacrut, *Be'or ha-Levush, 'Even Yeqarah*, on Recanati's Commentary, Genesis, Noah, 19b.

[246] *Sefer Yeẓirah*, 1:5.

[247] Psalms 32:9.

[248] 2 Chronicles 2:5.

[249] *Tanḥuma, va-yakhel*, 7, *Bereishit Rabbah* 4:4.

[250] *Pardes Rimmonim*. I did not locate the source.

[251] *Pardes Rimmonim*, Gate 5: *Sha'ar ha-Mahut ve-ha-Hanhagah*, chapter 13, 45b.

[252] B.T., *Rosh Ha-Shanah*, 11a.

[253] B.T., *Baba Batra*, 25b.

[254] Ibid.

[255] Leviticus 26:25. This verse refers to *Malkhut*.

[256] *Shefa' Tal*. I was unable to locate the passage.

[257] B.T., *Pesaḥim*, 112a.

[258] *Shefa' Tal*.

[259] B.T., *Berakhot*, 17a.

[260] Genesis 12:10.

[261] *'Avodat ha-Qodesh*, introduction.

[262] The commentary *'Asis Rimmonim* explains this as a reference to the "holy souls and all spiritual entities" that are the result of this union. See *'Asis Rimmonim*, 24b.

[263] *Pardes Rimmonim*, Gate 8: *Sha'ar Mahit ve-Hanhagah*, chapter 13, pp. 45b–45c.

[264] See *Tiqquney Zohar*, *Tiqqun* 69, p. 103.

[265] *Pardes Rimmonim*, Gate 8: *Sha'ar ha-Mahut ve-ha-Hanhagah*, chapter 13, p. 45c.

[266] Isaiah 30:26.

[267] Psalms 89:3.

[268] Paraphrase of Lamentations 4:12.

[269] See *Zohar*, vol. 3, 61b.

[270] *Pardes Rimmonim*, Gate 8: *Sha'ar ha-Mahut ve-ha-Hanhagah*, chapter 17, 48d.

[271] See *Tiqquney Zohar*, *Tiqqun* 21, p. 59.

[272] *Pardes Rimmonim*, Gate 16: *Sha'ar 'ABY'A*, chapter 4, 79a.

[273] Lamentations 2:1.

[274] Isaiah 42:8.

[275] *Qol Bokhim*.

[276] The reference is to Joseph Karo. Over the course of several decades Karo received teachings from a heavenly mentor, the spirit of the *Mishnah*,

which spoke through him. See Werblowsky, *Joseph Karo: Lawyer and Mystic* (Philadelphia, 1977). Also see Lawrence Fine, "Maggidic Revelation in the Teaching of Isaac Luria," in Reinharz and Swetschinski, eds., *Mystics, Philosophers, and Politicians: Essays in Jewish Intellectual History in Honor of Alexander Altmann* (Durham, 1982), pp. 141–157.

[277] I was unable to locate the source.

[278] Genesis 20:12.

[279] Some texts read: "*ha-Shem* (the Name)."

[280] Exodus 34:5.

[281] Ibid.

[282] Exodus 34:6.

[283] Job 35:7.

[284] Job 35:6.

[285] Genesis 2:10.

[286] The Teli, which is perhaps a dragon, is mentioned in *Sefer Yeẓirah*, 6:1.

[287] Yehiel Abraham Barlev, ed., *Maggid Mesharim* (Petah Tikva, 1990), pp. 200–203. This section concludes the entry that has been assigned to Shemot.

[288] Zechariah 4:2.

[289] *Maggid Mesharim*. I was unable to locate the passage.

[290] Genesis 1:26.

[291] Isaiah 44:13.

[292] Genesis 2:22.

[293] Job 19:26.

[294] Genesis 2:7.

[295] *Maggid Mesharim*.

[296] Job 35:7,6.

[297] Ezekiel 1:28.

[298] See *Pardes Rimmonim*, Gate 8: *Sha'ar Mehut ve-Hanhagah*, chapter 15, p. 46a.

[299] Numbers 12:8.

[300] *Pardes Rimmonim*, Gate 24: *Sha'ar Heykhalot*, chapter 2, p. 46c.

The Great House

[1] Deuteronomy 6:11.

[2] B.T., *Shabbat*, 103b.

[3] Deuteronomy 32:4.

[4] Psalms 19:8.
[5] Deuteronomy 18:13.
[6] Deuteronomy 6:4.
[7] Exodus 34:14.
[8] Deuteronomy 33:20.
[9] *Zayin* = 7 and *nun* = 50.
[10] Deuteronomy 4:32.
[11] Cf. B.T., *Hagigah*, 11b.
[12] Genesis 1:4.
[13] Isaiah 14:23.
[14] Lamentations 1:9.
[15] Lamentations 2:9.
[16] Genesis 1:4.
[17] B.T., *Baba Kama*, 55a.
[18] *Peh*=80.
[19] Genesis 1:1.
[20] Psalms 119:129.
[21] Psalms 119:130.
[22] The Aramaic text here is difficult to render literally.
[23] Psalms 119:130.
[24] *Sefer ha-Rokeaḥ* on the *siddur*.
[25] Psalms 31:20.
[26] *Sefer ha-Rokeaḥ*.
[27] Psalms 104:20.
[28] Psalms 104:22.
[29] B.T., *Baba Mezi'a'*, 83b.
[30] Psalms 31:20.
[31] *Midrash Rabbah*, *Bereishit*, 3:4.
[32] Lamentations 3:6.
[33] B.T., *Sanhedrin*, 24a.
[34] Genesis 1:4.
[35] Numbers 15:29.
[36] Psalms 115:5.
[37] Numbers 19:14.
[38] B.T., *Shabbat*, 43b.
[39] Lamentations 3:6.
[40] B.T., *Shabbat*, 104a.
[41] Exodus 33:6.
[42] Exodus 33:7.
[43] Isaiah 35:10.

[44] B.T., *Shabbat*, 88a.
[45] Numbers 21:14.
[46] See B.T., *Shabbat*, 146a.
[47] Genesis 3:7.
[48] *Pardes Rimmonim*, Gate 30: *Sha'ar ha-Neshamah*, chapter 6, 75a-b.
[49] The letter *bet* = 2.
[50] Numbers 7:14.
[51] *Yod* = 10. When the letter *yod* is spelled out as *yod* (10) *vav* (6) *dalet* (4), its value is 20, represented by the letter *kaf*.
[52] Ecclesiastes 2:13.
[53] Isaiah 64:3.
[54] It is open on one side, the bottom.
[55] B.T., *Menaḥot*, 29b.
[56] Ecclesiastes 2:13.
[57] Isaiah 57:19.
[58] B.T., *Berakhot*, 34b.
[59] Numbers 31:30.
[60] *Midrash Rabbah*, *Bereishit*, 3:9.
[61] That is, the fifth rung.
[62] Cf. *The Palm Tree of Deborah*, trans. Louis Jacobs (New York, 1960), p. 58.
[63] Isaiah 64:3.
[64] Genesis 3:6.
[65] Genesis 3:5.
[66] Deuteronomy 29:17.
[67] B.T., *Shabbat*, 104a.
[68] *Shemonah Peraqim*, chapter 4.
[69] *Avot*, 4:4.
[70] Numbers 12:3.
[71] B.T., *Sotah*, 5a.
[72] Rashi, ad loc.
[73] B.T., *Sotah*, 5a.
[74] Leviticus 26:13.
[75] Compare Joshua 22:19.
[76] Psalms 93:1.
[77] Zechariah 2:10.
[78] B.T., *'Avodah Zara*, 10b.
[79] Proverbs 16:15.
[80] Job 10:12.
[81] Proverbs 10:2.

[82] Psalms 89:15.
[83] Psalms 17:15.
[84] Psalms 89:3.
[85] Genesis 1:3.
[86] Malachi 3:20.
[87] Proverbs 16:15.
[88] Isaiah 58:8.
[89] 2 Samuel 8:15.
[90] Psalms 119:121.
[91] 1 Chronicles 29:10.
[92] Numbers 6:25.
[93] Psalms 89:13.
[94] Hosea 14:2.
[95] Cf. *Pesiqta Rabbati*, 3:5.
[96] B.T., *Eruvin* 18b, *Bereishit Rabbah*, 20:11.
[97] B.T., *Baba Mezi'a*, 32a, *Bereishit Rabbah* 21:6.
[98] Genesis 3:22.
[99] Deuteronomy 10:12.
[100] Genesis 4:7. *Midrash Rabbah*, *Bereishit*, 21:6.
[101] Cf. B.T., *Shabbat*, 55b.
[102] I.e., he honored his mother.
[103] Exodus 33:23.
[104] B.T., Ta'anit, 12b.
[105] The letter *bet* is open on the left, which represents north.
[106] Jeremiah 1:14.
[107] B.T., *Eruvin*, 65a.
[108] Exodus 20:1.
[109] Rashi, *Commentary on the Torah*, ad loc.
[110] Proverbs 31:26.
[111] Deuteronomy 33:2.
[112] Proverbs 3:16.
[113] Job 37:22.
[114] *Midrash Rabbah*, *Bereishit*, 16:4.
[115] Genesis 30:6.
[116] Genesis 49:17.
[117] Isaiah 9:6. The *mem* in the word here translated as abundant, *le-marbeh*, is written with a closed or final *mem* instead of the form used when *mem* is not the final letter of a word.
[118] MiZRaḤ = 40 + 7 + 200 + 8 = 255. NaHaR = 50 + 5 + 200 = 255.
[119] Genesis 2:10.

[120] Ma'ARaV = 40 + 70 + 200 + 2 = 312. Twelve permutations of *YHVH* = 12 × 26 = 312.
[121] ẒaFON = 90 + 80 + 6 + 50 = 226. BeḤYRaH = 2 + 8 + 10 + 200 + 5 = 225, plus one for the word itself = 226.
[122] Psalms 78:70.
[123] Darom = 4 + 200 + 6 + 40 = 250. NeR = 50 + 200.
[124] Proverbs 20:27.
[125] *Sefer Kanfey Yonah.*
[126] *Ba-Midbar Rabbah* 2:8; *Zohar*, vol. 3, 118b.
[127] B.T., *Yoma*, 86a.
[128] Zechariah 3:7.
[129] Isaiah 9:6.
[130] *Mishnah Tamid*, 33b.
[131] Lamentations 2:3.
[132] Ibid.
[133] Isaiah 1:8.
[134] See Maimonides, *Mishneh Torah*, *Hilkhot Sukkah*, chapter 4:2.
[135] I have not located the source.
[136] Deuteronomy 15:11.
[137] Proverbs 24:3.
[138] Isaiah 9:6.
[139] Isaiah 56:7.
[140] Deuteronomy 15:4.
[141] Isaiah 11:9.
[142] Isaiah 1:8.
[143] Genesis 2:3.
[144] Deuteronomy 15:4.
[145] Deuteronomy 15:11.
[146] B.T., *Sotah*, 47a.
[147] Lamentations 1:1.
[148] Lamentations 2:3.
[149] Nehemiah 2:13.
[150] B.T., *Sanhedrin*, 102a.
[151] Lamentations 1:1.
[152] Ibid.
[153] Genesis 3:15.
[154] Isaiah 25:9.
[155] B.T., *Ta'anit*, 31a.
[156] Psalms 48:14. The word *ḥeylah* probably means "wall."
[157] Psalms 48:15. *'Al-mut* probably means "beyond danger."

[158] Psalms 68:26.
[159] *'Al-mut* can be read as "beyond death."
[160] *Midrash Rabbah*, *va-Yiqra*, 11:9.
[161] P.T., *Megillah*, chapter 3, *Halakhah* 4.
[162] *'Avodat ha-Qodesh*, *Ḥeleq ha-'Avodah*, chapter 43, p. 57c.
[163] Rashi on B.T., *Shabbat*, 104a.
[164] Song of Songs 2:9.
[165] *Ma'arekhet ha-'Elohut*, Hayyat commentary, *Ma'erekhet ha-Shemot*.
[166] These are two forms meaning "song." The first is feminine, the second masculine.
[167] See *Midrash Rabbah*, *Shir ha-Shirim*, chapter 1, 36.
[168] Exodus 15:1.
[169] Ezekiel 9:6,7.
[170] Ezekiel 9:2.
[171] These are all terms meaning anger and destruction.
[172] B.T., *Shabbat*, 55a.
[173] I.e., because according to the account in Ezekiel, chapter nine, the *tav* that is written in ink gives life.
[174] Song of Songs 1:5.
[175] Exodus 19:5,6.
[176] Genesis 3:17.
[177] Hosea 6:7. Literally, "But they, to a man, have . . ."
[178] Genesis 17:14.
[179] Deuteronomy 29:24.
[180] B.T., *Sanhedrin*, 38b.
[181] B.T., *Avodah Zarah*, 22b.
[182] Exodus 23:20.
[183] Psalms 82:6.
[184] Exodus 32:16. Literally, "inscribed on the tablets."
[185] *Midrash Rabbah*, *Shemot*, 32, 1.
[186] Isaiah 4:3.
[187] B.T., *Sanhedrin*, 92a.
[188] Exodus 32:4.
[189] Morning blessing before the Shema'.
[190] Isaiah 60:1.

Bibliography

Altmann, Alexander, "Free Will and Predestination in Saadia, Bahya, and Maimonides," *Essays in Jewish Intellectual History* (Hanover, 1981).

Avivi, Joseph, "Lurianic Manuscripts in Italy until the Year 1620" (Hebrew), in *Aley Sefer 11* (1984).

Ben-Sasson, H. H., "Isaiah ben Abraham Ha-Levi Horowitz," in *Encyclopedia Judaica* (Jerusalem, 1972), vol. 8, 990-994.

Cohen, Seymour J., *The Holy Letter: A Study in Jewish Sexual Morality* (Northvale, N.J., 1993).

Dan, Joseph, *Hebrew Ethical and Homiletical Literature* (Hebrew) (Jerusalem, 1975).

———, "No Evil Descends from Heaven," in Bernard Cooperman, ed., *Jewish Thought in the Sixteenth Century* (Cambridge, Mass., 1983).

Elbaum, Jacob, *Openness and Insularity: Late Sixteenth Century Jewish Literature in Poland and Ashkenaz* (Hebrew) (Jerusalem, 1990).

———, *Repentance and Self-Flagellation in the Writings of the Sages of Germany and Poland 1348-1648* (Hebrew) (Jerusalem, 1992).

Faierstein, Morris, *All Is in the Hands of Heaven: The Teachings of Rabbi Mordecai Joseph Leiner of Izbica* (New York, 1989).

Fine, Lawrence, "Kabbalistic Texts," in Barry W. Holtz, ed., *Back to the Sources* (New York, 1984).

———, *Safed Spirituality* (New York, 1984).

Foxbrunner, Roman A., *HaBaD: The Hasidism of R. Shneur Zalman of Lyady* (Tuscaloosa, 1992).

Ginsburg, Elliot K., *Sod ha-Shabbat* (The Mystery of the Sabbath) from the Tola'at Ya'aqov of R. Meir ibn Gabbai (Albany, 1989).

Horowitz, Isaiah, *Sha'ar ha-Shamayim* (Jerusalem, 1985).

BIBLIOGRAPHY

Idel, Moshe, "Sexual Metaphor and Praxis in the Kabbalah," in David Kraemer, ed., *The Jewish Family* (New York, 1989).

Jacobs, Louis "The Communications of the Heavenly Mentor to Rabbi Joseph Karo," in *Jewish Mystical Testimonies* (New York, 1977).

Krassen, Miles, "Visiting Graves," in *Kabbalah: A Newsletter (Current Research in Jewish Mysticism)*, vol. 3, no. 1 (1988).

———, *Devequt and Faith in Zaddiqim: The Religious Tracts of Meshullam Feibush Heller of Zbarazh* (University of Pennsylvania, 1990).

Loewenthal, Naftali, *Communicating the Infinite: The Emergence of the Habad School* (Chicago, 1990).

Matt, Daniel, *The Zohar: Book of Enlightenment* (New York, 1983).

Newman, Eugene, *Life and Teachings of Isaiah Horowitz* (London, 1972).

Pachter, Mordecai, "Elijah de Vidas' *Beginning of Wisdom* and Its Abbreviated Versions" (Hebrew), *Qiryat Sefer* 47 (1972), pp. 686-710.

Piekarz, Mendel, *The Beginning of Hasidism: Ideological Trends in Derush and Musar Literature* (Hebrew) (Jerusalem, 1978).

Sack, Bracha, "Cordovero's Influence on Hasidism" (Hebrew), in *Eshel Be'er Sheva* 3 (1986), pp. 229-246.

———, "The Influence of Cordovero on Seventeenth-Century Jewish Thought," in Isadore Twersky and Bernard Septimus, eds., *Jewish Thought in the Seventeenth Century* (Cambridge, 1987), pp. 365-372.

Safran, Bezalel, "MaHaRaL and Early Hasidism," in *Hasidism: Continuity or Innovation* (Cambridge, 1988).

Schecter, Solomon, "Safed in the Sixteenth Century—A City of Legists and Mystics," in *Studies in Judaism, Second Series*.

Scholem, Gershom, "Devekut, or Communion with God," *The Messianic Idea in Judaism* (New York, 1971).

———, "Tselem: The Concept of the Astral Body," *On the Mystical Shape of the Godhead* (New York, 1991).

Sherwin, Byron, *Mystical Theology and Social Dissent* (London, 1982).

Wolfson, Elliot, "The Influence of Luria on the Shelah" (Hebrew), in *Jerusalem Studies in Jewish Thought*, vol. 10, *Lurianic Kabbalah* (Jerusalem, 1992).

Werblowsky, *Joseph Karo: Lawyer and Mystic* (Philadelphia, 1977).

Index

INDEX

INDEX

INDEX

INDEX